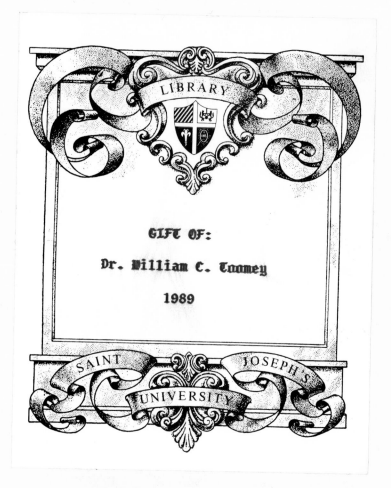

THE CRIMINOLOGIST: CRIME AND THE CRIMINAL

THE CRIMINOLOGIST: CRIME AND THE CRIMINAL

CHARLES E. REASONS
UNIVERSITY OF NEBRASKA, LINCOLN

GOODYEAR PUBLISHING COMPANY, INC.
PACIFIC PALISADES, CALIFORNIA

Copyright © 1974 by Goodyear Publishing Company, Inc.

All rights reserved. No part of this book may be reproduced in any form or by any means without permission in writing from the publisher.

Library of Congress Card Catalog Number: 73-86435

ISBN: 0-87620-168-0
Y-1680-1

Current printing (last digit): 10 9 8 7 6 5 4 3 2 1

Printed in the United States of America

Library of Congress Cataloging in Publication Data

Reasons, Charles E   comp.
    The Criminologist.

    1. Crime and criminals—Addresses, essays, lectures.
2. Police—Addresses, essays, lectures. 3. Corrections—
Addresses, essays, lectures.   I.   Title
HV6028.R4   364'.08   73-86435
ISBN 0-87620-168-0

*Dedicated to Tad,
in hopes his generation
will evidence a more just justice.*

CONTENTS

PREFACE

A cursory examination of books of readings in criminology will reveal that they are largely a reflection of the writing in criminology texts. In fact, they usually consist of articles footnoted in texts which are thought to be essential for further illumination upon a specific topic. The relative uniformity and singularity of such books of readings raises an interesting question in the sociology of knowledge concerning the structure of criminological thought.

In an era of increasing conflict and divisiveness between rich and poor, white and nonwhite, and old and young, a number of issues arise which increasingly confront the criminologist. Why has the criminologist emphasized certain types of crimes and criminals while neglecting others? What is the significance of interest groups in formulating, enforcing and administrating laws? How is the criminologist to confront the nature and extent of political crime, corporate crime, state lawlessness, and the politicization of prisoners? While I hardly claim to answer these questions, this book will address itself to these and other topics which will hopefully serve as a catalyst for further inquiry.

While the traditional topics of criminological concern are recognized as appropriate areas of investigation, it is felt by the author that the above topics should be incorporated into criminological focus! The following selection of articles is believed to be a much needed complement to the traditional approach, rather than its repetition.

I would like to acknowledge the initial stimulation into this area provided by Professor David Sternberg during my graduate training. Furthermore, I appreciate the encouragement provided by Dave Grady of Goodyear in pursuing this topic and the helpful criticism provided by Professors Hugh Whitt, Donald Gibbons, and Jerome Rabow. Finally, the support of Arna and Tad is greatly acknowledged.

PART ONE:

SOCIAL THOUGHT AND SOCIAL STRUCTURE: THE CRIMINOLOGIST, CRIME AND THE CRIMINAL

It appears that an era of radical writings has descended upon academia—particularly within the social sciences,[1] and increasingly so in sociology. As Kuhn has noted,[2] the route to "normal sciences" can be quite trying for a young discipline attempting to establish its creed. He presents his own assessment of the state of social sciences in a discussion of his year retreat with a group of social scientists:

> Particularly, I was struck by the number and extent of the overt disagreements between social scientists about the nature of legitimate scientific problems and methods. Both history and acquaintance made me doubt that practitioners of the natural sciences possess firmer or more permanent answers to such questions than their colleagues in the social sciences. Yet, somehow, the practice of astronomy, physics, chemistry, or biology normally fails to evoke the controversies over fundamentals that today often seem endemic among, say, psychologists or sociologists. Attempting to discover the source of that difference led me to recognize the role in scientific research of what I have since called "paradigms." These I take to be universally recognized scientific achievements that for a time provide model problems and solutions to a community of practitioners.[3]

Thus, the recent emergence of radical writing could be interpreted as an attempt to view the world through a new paradigm. While discrediting traditional, status-quo paradigms, new paradigm entrepreneurs attempt to erect their own as *the* paradigm. The importance of scientific revolutions and paradigm change is that "data which were formerly thought important are now regarded as inconsequential, problems which were recognized as unexplained but relatively unimportant now became critical. A new set of ways of conceptualizing, of relating data to each other, of ways of defining problems, of research techniques, usually accompanies such scientific revolution."[4] Both the nature and scope of radical sociology are still in a stage of becoming, with the concept "radical" remaining somewhat elusive.

1

According to Webster, the meaning of *radical* includes (1) of or from the root or roots, going to the foundation, or source of something; fundamental, basic; and (2) favoring fundamental or extreme change, specifically, favoring such change of social structure; very leftist.[5] Radical sociological literature appears to combine these two aspects in its definitions. According to John Howard, radical sociology is concerned with the analysis of social problems from the point of view emphasizing the social structure as an important independent variable in both the cause and maintenance of specific social problems:

Radical sociology generates its own definition of social problems partly by asking questions about system defects and about the possible role of social structure in perpetuating problems and defeating the intentions of meliorative policy.[6]

Another, more comprehensive perspective is offered by Albert Szymanski:

The goal of radical sociologists should be above all the formulation and propagation of a sociology relevant to the practical problems facing man. We must conceive of our contribution to the building of a decent society in terms of (1) the development of an understanding of the organizations and dynamics of our society, (2) the development of an understanding of how that society can be changed and a humane social organization substituted, and (3) the dissemination of these understandings to our fellow social scientists, our students, and to men in general.[7]

Therefore, both the substance of radical sociology and the role of the radical sociologist are important.

The rise of radical sociology must be understood in the context of the rapid demystification of American society during the 1960s and the subsequent radicalization of other academic disciplines, Blacks, students, priests, poor people, and so on. Many graduate students during the 1960s were active in and/ or sympathetic with the New Left and became disappointed and somewhat disillusioned with the brand of "professionalism" imparted by most graduate schools.[8] Social scientists in general and sociologists in particular have been increasingly viewed by some as "part of the problem," rather than "part of the solution." As Becker and Horowitz note:

Whenever someone is oppressed, an "establishment" sociologist seems to lurk in the background, providing the facts which make oppression more efficient and the theory which makes it legitimate to a larger constituency.[9]

So radical sociology *is* concerned with "whose side we are on." According to Becker and Horowitz, radical sociology is isomorphic with good sociology, that is, sociological work producing meaningful descriptions of organizations and events, valid explanations of how they come about and persist, and realistic proposals for their improvement or removal. Radical sociology demystifies privilege and domination through sociological exposés, without concern for group or self-interest.[10] The political commitment of the sociologist is revealed by the kinds of "causes" included in his analysis, for the way blame is assigned will determine the political alternatives for change. Thus, "structural" blame suggests radical change of the institutional structure producing the problems; "individual deficiency" blame suggests changing individuals.[11]

CRIMINOLOGY

The substantive area of criminology has increasingly become politicized with "new" paradigms arising to challenge the "traditional" perspectives. Ideology has been very important in the rise and subsequent changing focus in the study of crime. In a well-presented socio-historical analysis, Radzinowicz[12] describes the rise of the liberal position in criminology as a concomitant of the enlightenment, with growing scientism, emphasis upon reason, and revolt against unquestioning acceptance of tradition and authority. The system of criminal justice was subject to a great deal of attack. Montesquieu, Voltaire, and Beccaria, among others, condemned the legal institutions of the time for their arbitrariness, secrecy, and cruel and oppressive nature. This "classical school" of criminology arose as a reaction to the abuses of the time and its leaders called for reform.[13] Of major importance was Beccaria's *Of Crimes and Punishments* (1764) which suggested major reforms in existing legal institutions based upon a belief in human reason and the perfectibility of social institutions. Such an enlightened perspective would be forwarded by Bentham and Blackstone in their own work.

The scientific revolution in the seventeenth century changed man's attitude toward custom and tradition profoundly. As Von Baumer states: "The Age of Science made the intoxicating discovery that melioration depends not upon change from within (St. Paul's birth of the new man), but upon change from without (scientific and social mechanics)."[14] The classical school's emphasis upon free will and the rational man was to become increasingly eroded in the nineteenth century. With further understanding of the role played by motives and other internal factors in human action, finer distinctions could be made regarding criminal responsibility. In fact, Mannheim[15] views the history of criminal law as a history to exculpate offenders because of their general incapacity to act with a guilty mind, for example children and the insane. During the enlightenment, the aim of reformers was to set the individual free by restricting the law to maintain public order, not control morals.

RISE OF POSITIVISM

The upheaval in economic, social, political, and cultural life accompanying the Industrial Revolution gave impetus to a humanitarian movement, which aided in the rise of the social sciences.[16] The French Revolution and Industrial Revolution had created rival classes and nations. The principles of individualism, science, and progress were espoused by John Stuart Mill as a means of reforming European society. Agnosticism, science, and social service were the new Holy Trinity.[17] The positivistic philosophy of Comte was to be used in making a better social order. Social reform and sociology were very much interrelated.[18] The methods of inquiry of the natural scientists were extended to man and society. This signified the growing secularization of Western thought and culture. Human nature was believed to be rational and social, with man viewed as pursuing his own self-interest. Nature was a closed system with universal rules and, thus, man could predict and understand what it would do. Faith in reason, science, and the future largely replaced faith in revealed religion.[19]

The rise of positivism was to greatly influence the structure of criminological thought. The major characteristics of positive thought[20] are that it (1) denies free will, (2) divorces science and law from morals, (3) proclaims the priority of science and believes in the existence of invariable social laws, (4) emphasizes the unity of the scientific method for social and natural sciences, (5) emphasizes the criminal, (6) emphasizes quantitative research, not qualitative, and (7) holds causality and determinism as paramount concerns to be pursued through observation. Unlike the classical school, the positive school became committed to the thesis that any measure necessary to protect society (the accused and, of course, the convicted person are automatically excluded therefrom) is justifiable.[21] The belief in the ability to use techniques of social control (e.g., law) to make a better society produced much legislation for the purpose of guiding man's morals. Thus, scientism and positivism as a panacea for man's ills led to increasing "overcriminalization" and the belief in the perfectibility of "deviants" through the uses of the social sciences and the law. Begun in the work of Quetelet and Guerry, positivism emerged as the legitimate criminological perspective with Lombroso and the Italian school.[22] Positivism established new trends in the study of crime, including (1) a focus upon the individual criminal, (2) stimulating scientific studies of crime, (3) studies showing the priority of social influences in crime causation, (4) the establishment of international bodies and congresses, and (5) influencing penal codes.

Early criminological positivism was immersed in the inherent pathologies of the criminal using a medical model, with emphasis upon diagnosis, prognosis, and treatment. Therefore, the emphasis was upon changing the nature of the criminal. The search for the causes of criminal behavior became the "cause célèbre" of criminological inquiry.

Criminology (consisting of the sociology of law, etiology of criminal behavior, and penology) has historically been imbued with the positivist spirit and paradigm[23] and many criminologists continue to focus upon the "causes of criminal behavior." This had led from the measuring of skulls to psychic conflict, self-concept, and anomie, with essentially the same results—no answer to the question of cause.[24] Such analyses have been made principally within the context of the legalistic definition of the subject matter of criminology, that is, behavior violating criminal law. As Glaser notes,[25] "Crime is any unlawful act punishable by the state. Criminology, the study of crime, is therefore a discipline whose boundaries are determined by government." The criminologist is the person whose "professional training, occupation role, and fiduciary reward are concentrated toward a scientific approach, study, and analysis of the phenomena of crime and criminal behavior."[26]

Further verification of the positivist bent of criminology may be found in contemporary texts. Gibbons suggests[27] that "discovery of the causes of crime (and juvenile delinquency) is the principal business of the criminologist-sociologist." Although most texts recognize the three major areas of emphasis in criminology previously mentioned (sociology of law, etiology of criminal behavior, and penology), they deal almost exclusively with the etiology of criminal behavior and penology. The law is a given which has not normally been something to be scrutinized, either in its formulation, enforcement, or administration. The increasing divisiveness of recent times magnifies the fact that different perceptions of criminality were vying for public attention. For example, Ralph Nader is leading a consumer movement that could bring about increasing criminalization of manufacturers and corporate executives. The ecology movement is bringing into focus the need for more stringent controls upon those destroying our environment. The consciousness of the younger generation may be producing a shift in perspective of societal wrongdoing.[28] Certain segments of society view the brutal destruction wrought upon Indochina as a crime of unimaginable magnitude, the fraudulent dealing of large manufacturers and corporations suggest they are "ideal delinquents," the prosecution and persecution of political criminals (e.g., war protesters) is viewed as criminal, and the lawlessness of the law (riots, 1967; Chicago, 1968; Kent State, Jackson State, Southern University, etc.) and of political leaders and their accomplices (ITT, Watergate, bugging, surveillance of political "deviants," etc.) is an increasing problem of "law and order." As Reich notes:

> The cry of police lawlessness misses the point. In a large city the bureaucracies are also lawless, the building inspectors make threats and collect bribes; the liquor licensing authority is both arbitrary and corrupt; the zoning system is tyrannical and subject to influence.[29]

In recent years there has been an increasing erosion of the legitimacy of the state due to (1) a belief that the law and legal institutions are not only unresponsive but illegitimate, (2) a condemnation of the bureaucratic delays, judicial indifference, and overt racism of most courts, (3) a rejection of, and in many instances a contempt for, establishment officials—police, judges, and lawyers, and (4) an affirmation of individual rights and an identification with group, class, racial, and sexual liberation.[30]

The evident divisiveness and conflict has brought about changing perspectives on crime and society among segments of the general public. Subsequently, there is a growing realization among some criminologists of the importance of interest groups in determining what crime is and which type of crime will be of major concern to law enforcement and administration of justice personnel, and thus to the criminologist.[31] This book is an effort to support these attempts at "demystifying" the law and redirecting criminological attention from its traditionally myopic perspective.

I would suggest that this book is radically different from other readers in criminology in many ways. It brings a number of areas into criminological focus which have not been traditionally covered in criminology classes. Also, the topics are viewed from the perspective that criminology deals with an inherently political phenomenon which should be viewed in the context of power, conflict, and interest groups in our society. Finally, this book fails to contain the usual plethora of articles dealing with the causes of criminal behavior. In fact, some of the areas covered are not "normal crimes" for the criminologist. If this nontraditional content might be somewhat perplexing for the criminologist, it is even more perplexing to some members of society why criminologists only relate to some crimes. Therefore, an important aspect of this book is an analysis of criminological thought and some of its "focal concerns" and emphases.

AMERICAN CRIMINOLOGICAL THOUGHT

The first section concerns itself with the structure of American criminological thought. In the first article, Miller provides an analysis of ideological underpinnings of criminological thought and policy. As previously noted, the fact that the sociocultural milieu impinges upon and influences thought patterns in science is hardly startling.[32] Nonetheless, it is easy to immerse oneself in doing criminology without understanding the influence of the historical and contemporary milieu upon one's perspective. Therefore, one might study offenders all his life without questioning how the specific behavioral acts became criminalized or the subsequent processing of such actors in the criminal justice system. In fact, this has been a major oversight of criminologists. While going to great ends to scrutinize, characterize, count, and describe the criminal, little effort has been given to the other areas of criminological import.

Although Jeffery's article on the structure of American criminological thought was published in 1956, it still reflects the major thrust of criminologists.[33] Jerome Halls's comment is still applicable: "The most serious criticism of twentieth-century criminology is that it has gone whole hog positivistic."[34] Although there are some recent excellent analyses of sociolegal development, these are quite the exception rather than the rule.[35] Most textbooks on criminology still place their emphasis upon "kinds of people" analysis of criminals arrested and confined. Great emphasis remains upon "focal concerns," "opportunity structures," "self-concept," "drift," "techniques of neutralization," "typologies," "labeling," and so on, with relatively little emphasis upon the fact that law is created, enforced, and administered in a politically organized society characterized by conflict, differential power, and influence. In an intensive and extensive critical assessment of criminological theory, Dessaur points out that:

> Where the penal law is used to secure the norms of a debatable ideology, the only thing we can hope to detect by empirical research is what kind of conduct and/or what kind of people the adherents of this ideology should like to eradicate. We are getting information about the (ideological) interests the penal law is serving, not about the "psychological causes of crime. . . . The logical and the empirical objection to dogmatic labelling of criminals (etiological criminology) imply that in traditional criminology (carefully jotting down all sorts of sociographic and psychological variables about criminals without even looking critically at their raison d'etre), we shall either draw from the hat what we put into it, or draw nothing at all. By this I mean the following: It is the penal law, its scope, its subdivisions, the selection of deviant behavior that is made by it, and the selective enforcement of it that determines whether the criminals tend to be rebels, psychopaths, or rational profit-seekers.[36]

The major issue still remains one of studying crime versus studying the criminal. However, these are not mutually exclusive and can, in fact should, be integrated into a comprehensive theory.[37] American criminology was born in an era of reformism and rapidly gained a reputable status envied by criminologists in other societies.[38] It was this reformist bent that brought attention to the criminal, who was to be rehabilitated. Thus, "applied" criminology has been the major thrust of the work in our society. One trained in criminology is expected to be well equipped to "solve" the crime problem in our never-ending "war on crime," but only within the proper ideological context of those currently in political power. Therefore, institutional changes are usually less favored than changes in the individual. It is much easier for those in power, and wed to current crime control techniques, to accept an "individual deficiency" assessment of the crime problem and its subsequent implications for change than an indictment of the laws and/or agencies of the criminal justice system as major areas in need of change. Public administrators are reluctant to apply the results of criminological research because of (1) the status-quo nature of existing civil servants, (2) limited practical contribution of research, (3) reformist ideas among researchers which conflict with authorities, (4) public opinion, and (5) the attitude of those government officials which reflects the interests of the administration and trends in public opinion.[39] The politicization of the criminologist is evident in his research.

When the researcher comes forward with certain ideas about man and society, and methods to approach those ideals, he leaves his sanctuary to confront politically opposing positions. Under these circumstances how can one hope that those responsible for administration will not look upon these researchers as a political pressure group whose weapon in the social struggle is called "scientific research"? . . . We may conclude then that researchers, by becoming spokesmen for reform, are regarded by administration as representatives of a pressure group who use scientific research as a tool to disguise plans for a test of strength designed towards the exercise of power.[40]

Given the inherently political nature of crime and the politics of its enforcement and administration, it should be fairly evident that threats to the established definitions of crime or to the practices of those who enforce or administer these laws will bring about a swift response. Although recent years have seen a tremendous growth in money for the war on crime, it appears to have gone principally for weapons of a lethal nature, rather than the scientific study of the war games. The funds will undoubtedly increase because of (1) the increasing attention of the public and politicans to the rising crime and its new forms, (2) rising costs of the administration of justice, (3) the new prominence of justice as a part of social policy, ranking side by side with education, health, and welfare, and (4) the action-orientation of the "new breed" of academicians.[41] However, what if one does not want to study the offender? What if one wants to study the criminogenic nature of the FBI, Justice Department, Congress, Bureau of Narcotics, or local police? The obvious implication is that in order to obtain research funding one must research proper, acceptable topics according to recognized, acceptable methods. One who becomes a "grantsman" is normally held to the granting agency's perspective of meaningful research. Therefore, in order to break with traditional perspectives and topics one must usually venture out on his own without the support of government agencies.

Wolfgang has recently suggested a change in criminological concern. "We have focused long enough on the offender and his weaknesses. It is time we look to ourselves—to this chaotic, decaying, degrading system and indict it for its failures."[42] By calling for us to demystify the police department, district attorney's office, courts, probation, parole, and prison and make them accountable to various publics, he presents a potential powder keg to the student of crime. Such emphasis is necessary in order to revolutionize the criminal justice system. However, such analyses will not be easy given the traditional secrecy and paranoia of such agencies. Professor Wolfgang has taken an activist, potentially humanistic perspective of the criminologists' role. Such inquiry may not elicit large grants, but it is necessary; for "making the criminal justice system accountable means making it more responsible and more humane."[43]

In the second article of this section, Gibbons and Garabedian review trends in criminological thought from "conservative" to "liberal" to "radical" criminology. In describing conservative criminology they emphasize the uncritical acceptance by these criminologists of societal definitions of "bad guys," their faith in the perfectability of the criminal justice system, and their wedding to establishment institutions and funding. The authors fail to emphasize the point, however, that conservative criminology focused upon the criminal and his deficiencies and pathologies rather than the law or criminal justice system.

The "good guy" and "bad guy" dichotomy is important because it still pervades criminological thought. As Poveda has noted: "The image of the criminal in any given historical era emerges from those positions in the social structure which constitute a threat to the established power systems."[44] As social, political, and economic circumstances have changed so has the image of the criminal. The perpetuation of the imagery of the "dangerous classes" is apparent in the consistent and persistent attention given to the lower-class criminal. This emphasis upon "common crime" and the "common criminal" helps to maintain our stereotypes of crime and the criminal.[45]

The social sciences accept the stereotype of the criminal as a given, for to challenge it would involve heavy penalties. The penalties are to be isolated from the main stream of professional activity, to be denied resources for research, and to be denied official patronage with its rewards in material and status.[46]

If a researcher becomes reliant upon grantsmanship for his research, it is safe to stay within acceptable boundaries in research areas and subsequent modes of inquiry. Furthermore, "the precarious sources of financial backing for university research force the researcher to become somewhat of an opportunist: he must seize the opportunity when it arrives and exploit it with the greatest economy of means."[47] Recent revelations indicate the "pork barrel" nature of LEAA funds and the wastage and frivolous spending for hardware appear to have reached the magnitude of a "crime wave."[48]

The liberal-cynical perspective arose with the greater theoretical and methodological sophistication of criminologists. It recognizes that crime is a function of the values and institutions of a society—that is, societies have the criminals they deserve. This functional approach tends to demystify the "bad guy" imagery that crime is some sort of pathological disease of society, and bolster the image that the "pathological is normal," as observed by Durkheim. The authors note that etiological (causal) analysis necessitates more sophistication. They continue their discussion of "causes of criminal behavior" in their review of a recent article by Gresham Sykes. "New" forms of criminality are discussed, including "hedonistic" crime and delinquency as sport or play, political crime, symbolic/alienated crime, and pragmatic-amoral crime.[49] Crime and delinquency as sport and play is hardly new, however the form it is taking is potentially more devastating. Our increasing reliance on technology (e.g., computerized data systems) is easily vulnerable to tampering. Sykes also mentions changing card sections at football games as a new form of this "crime"! Might this new crime be related to the increasing dehumanization and objectification of man by technology? To a large extent, technology has become the "opiate of the intellectual"[50] in a society where we are all data on cards—one should not be too surprised when the "data" bites back!

Political crime is one of the oldest forms of criminal behavior. However, recent events have thrust the political criminal to the forefront of public attention. Sykes emphasizes the violent nature of such crime and suggests it is spreading to new groups marked by diversity of age, sex, race, class, and ideological commitment. By emphasizing the destruction of draft records, dynamiting, and so on, he maintains the establishment perspective of political crime and violence. But what of the Watergate affair, ITT, increasing pervasive observation of political dissidents, assassinations of village leaders in Indochina, massive violence and the millionfold effect of bombing in Indochina,[51] and the "violence" of continual hunger, impoverishment, and poor housing in the United States?

All available evidence indicates that crime in America will not effectively be reduced until we make basic changes in the structure and quality of American life. Respect for law and order will not be restored until respect for the nature of our society is restored. Our confrontation with crime cannot be successful if we persist in viewing it as a battle with some alien force. Since America's crime problems are largely of our own creation, we have it well within our power to modify them and to bring them within reasonable control.[52]

I am not attempting in any way to excuse or condone the kinds of violent political crimes Sykes mentions. However, by taking the establishment's definition of the phenomena he unwittingly perpetrates a singular stereotype. I believe a recent article in a popular magazine catches the import of this "crime wave" by noting:

No longer is it only governments and ruling classes that possess the power to inflict fear on large segments of humanity. Today it is the common man—acting singly or in groups—who is making terror a common event in common places: a downtown street, an athletic contest, an airliner high above the earth.[53]

While the state maintains legitimate control of violence, citizens are increasingly exhibiting violence of their own.

In his discussion of "pragmatic-amoral" crime, Sykes cites divorce and the fact that the concept of the wrongfulness of divorce is being eroded. He notes further:

And I am arguing that there are a number of areas of criminal behavior for which this same sort of "slipping out from morality" may be occurring for a significant number of people.[54]

Traditional conceptions of morality regarding divorce, premarital and extramarital sex, drug use, and so on, are being challenged and are changing among certain segments of society, but it hardly strikes me as a major crime wave, unless one is wed to the traditional moral order.

Finally, Sykes strikes a note of 1984 and social engineering in a discussion of the increased efforts to prevent crimes by keeping better records of actual and potential criminals. He asks:

Is this the ultimate police state bearing down on us? Or is this the beginning of a more rational, enlightened way of dealing with the crime problem?
There is, of course, no sure answer available to the social sciences, because a
major part of the answer depends on precisely how such techniques might be
employed and that lies in the realm of prophecy.[55]

The fact that such decisions are and will be made in the area of politics, not
prophecy, suggests that criminologists have a responsibility to recognize the
political nature and possible ramifications of their activity. It is interesting to
note that although Sykes mentions at the end of his article that the area of
civil liberties, particularly privacy and freedom, should be of increasing concern, such infringements of our freedoms (e.g., wiretapping and surveillance
of politically dissident citizens) do not gain recognition as part of the "new
crime waves."

The more extreme liberal perspective that Gibbons and Garabedian discuss
is characterized by its emphasis upon the law and its formulation rather than the
causes of criminal behavior. This segmented thinking by the authors fails to acknowledge the interrelationship between law formulation, enforcement, and administration. Gibbons has exhibited such thinking elsewhere:

This discussion starts from the view that continued study of crime causation is desirable and is a proper topic for sociologists. While we agree that the
sociology of criminal law and sociological analysis of correctional organizations
ought to be encouraged, we believe that crime causation continues to be an important topic for sociological study.[56]

The authors correctly recognize the varying degrees of consensus in the
formulation of laws, but more important for Quinney's theory of the "social
reality of crime" is the operation of interests at all stages of the criminal justice
system. For example, all "decent citizens" abhor forcible rape, but are there
differences in prosecutions, convictions, and sentencing which might reflect
interest group activities? The most obvious example is that of interracial rape
and the differential administration of justice.[57] Nonetheless, there are obvious
variations in support for say marihuana laws versus forcible rape. Although we
may all abhor theft in the abstract, what are the differences in types of theft
(e.g., corporate price fixing versus grand larceny) and the penalties and procedures attached to these crimes? What does this tell us about interests, power,
and politics? Gibbons and Garabedian point out that the social conflict perspective fits nicely with the liberal approach by not questioning the health of
institutions. However, the prospects of amelioration of criminality are dim,
with cynicism replacing faith in the perfectability of the legal-correctional
machinery. Since the structure of social control agencies contributes to the
crime problem, change is less easily made. Decriminalization, diverting offenders
from official processing, and reducing prison populations are possible alternatives
that will reduce the magnitude of the problem.

TOWARD A RADICAL CRIMINOLOGY?

The radical criminology discussed by Gibbons and Garabedian consists of
a fairly unsophisticated extraction of the radical press's discussion of the legal
system. Their basic revelation is the political nature of law which is already
heavily evident in the writings of Quinney and Chambliss and Seidman. The

authors fail to note that radical sociology is gaining legitimacy as a competing paradigm. The "allegation" of racism in the law, its enforcement and administration, is not difficult to establish in recent years.[58] Gibbons and Garabedian suggest a number of areas of inquiry which criminologists should investigate, such as political repression and white-collar crime. Unfortunately, they fail to see the importance of such concepts as oppression, conflict, and persecution for criminology. Are they any more difficult to operationalize than focal concerns, anomie or differential association? The authors provide a critical assessment of Quinney's analysis that law is the instrument of the powerful oppressing the powerless, correctly noting that decentralization of law (e.g., community control) has a potential tyrannical nature.[59] Nonetheless, the importance of interest groups in the making and taking of crime and criminals remains an area of major importance for criminological analysis.[60]

The conception that crime is a product of the social system is an increasingly widespread perspective in criminological circles. It appears in the nature of "kinds of environment" theories emphasizing differential opportunity structures, poverty, racism, and so on, as important causal factors. However, this particular approach usually fails to lead to an explicit indictment of specific system policies, practices, and conditions. Although it is suggested that various indices of "social pathology" are a product of structural variables, such structural realities are not identified as specific products of specific actions and policies of individuals and groups with interests to protect. These harmful conditions are treated in antiseptic, apolitical terms that obscure the reality of the situation. Only a few criminologists have explicitly recognized the import of power, politics, and people in creating, sustaining, and shaping those conditions conducive to criminality—inequality, racism, differential opportunities, inadequate housing, and so on.[61] One might run into the sticky question of antecedent conditions in traditional neo-positivist criminological analysis. For example, the finding that poverty is associated with an increased preponderance of certain kinds of criminality and victimization might provoke the analyst to ask why such large inequities in the distribution of goods exist in a "society of plenty," and this might lead to a critical analysis of economic policy rather than of criminal characteristics.[62]

The economic analysis of crime has a long tradition in criminological thought and it has been given much impetus recently in the United States.[63] An important aspect of this approach is the classical "rational man" assumption regarding criminal behavior. Promoting cost-benefit analysis, systems analysis, and program budgeting, economists are swarming into the field of criminology to bring rationality to the issue of crime and punishment. Gordon, an economist, reveals in the third article of this section that both conservative and liberal analyses of crime assume the irrationality of the criminal. Although the economists' injection of rationality and free will into criminological analysis is in keeping with the emergence of soft-determinism, their assumptions regarding the effects of remedial actions are tenuous.

Gordon presents a radical analysis of crime and the state which assumes the rationality of criminal behavior within the basic structure of social and economic institutions. In discussing ghetto crime, organized crime, and corporate crime, he notes their common rationality in terms of a capitalistic society. Little hope of reform is anticipated unless fundamental changes in our institutions are made; given the vested interests in operation, such change is unlikely. In closing, Gordon suggests that we reform the community, not the criminal, with the criminal as an active agent of change.

Taylor has been critical of the relationship between the criminologist and the criminal.[64] He strikes an academic nerve end in his assessment of the nature of graduate education: "The best student being he who regards society as being so complex, and accounts of its nature so diffuse, that his mind fairly races with ideas and his will to action completely deserts him." An important insight concerning the sociology of social problems is touched upon. Social problems are created in a politically organized society by certain interest groups having the power to get their "problem" to the forefront of societal concern.[65] Therefore, crime as a social problem is a product of enterprise. The increasing amount of crime helps ensure the criminologist a "comfortable future."

He notes that criminologists are inherently tied to the state since the basis of crime is the state's definition of harm. Although the political nature of crime is hardly contestable, this allegation neglects the fact that certain kinds of behavior subject to criminal sanction reflect other interests, such as antitrust, consumer protection, fraud, and pollution. Laws reflect other interest groups that are in continual flux. For example, the "crimes without victims" movement potentially could eliminate approximately 50 percent of the crime in the United States—including vagrancy, prostitution, drunkenness, and drug use—thus reflecting new interests in operation.

The labeling school of deviant behavior is lauded by Taylor for its recognition of the symbiotic relationship between the deviant and the normal society. Thus, as Marx acutely observed:

> The criminal produces not only crime but also the criminal law, he produces the professor who delivers lectures on this criminal law, and even the inevitable textbook in which the professor presents his lectures as a commodity for sale in the market. . . . Further, the criminal produces the whole apparatus of the police and criminal justice, detectives, judges, executioners, juries, etc. . . . The criminal therefore appears as one of those national "equilibrating forces" which establish a just balance and open up a whole perspective of "useful" occupations.[66]

This basically functional position is part of the increasing recognition among students of deviant behavior that a perspective based upon appreciation rather than correction might be more appropriate.[67]

The politicization of criminals is something that appears to be occurring quite rapidly in our penal system. The suggestion by Taylor that we should redirect the energies of the criminal into political channels is very appropriate within the context of "kinds of environment" theories. However, the approach is quite the contrary to the legal system's reliance on "individual responsibility" and "culpability" and the "repentant" function of corrections. If the state and specific practices of the state are identified as important causal factors, the essence of crime is threatened. The conservative, status-quo nature of the legal system is not predisposed toward such analysis. Such politicization is potentially quite threatening to the very viability of present definitions of crime and criminality.

Finally, Taylor points out the communicative function of crime. The need to view crime from the eyes of the criminal is nothing new. However, interpreting the "boy's own story" appears to be different within a sociopolitical perspective.

In the last article, Reasons critically reviews the history of the racial variable in criminological thought. A historical analysis of criminological concern with race reveals its importance in indicting the immigrant. The prominence of genetic interpretations of crime reflected an era of social Darwinism, imperialism, and racist ideology; the need to protect racial purity from the degeneracy of "alien" races was prominent in criminological writing in the early twentieth century.[68] Concern with the immigrant "races" turned attention to the "racial enemy from within"—that is, Blacks—and earlier "kinds of people" theories as reflected above, changed to a "kinds of environment" approach emphasizing the causal importance of external forces upon the criminal.

The political nature of crime has only recently emerged as a concern among criminologists, whereas the history of the law in relation to nonwhites provides a clear example of the influence economic and political power have upon the scales of justice. Although explicit racism has been eliminated from the law in recent years, institutionalized racism is still evident and the racial variable will remain of major concern to criminologists, as it will to the other social scientists. However, a politically oriented power/conflict approach will increasingly be applied to such analysis. The politicization of crime and criminological study may be disheartening to many criminologists, but it portends the rise of new paradigms that will challenge older, apolitical, antiseptic, value-free perspectives.

NOTES

[1] Charles Hampden-Turner, *Radical Man* (Cambridge: Schenkman Publishing, 1970).

[2] Thomas S. Kuhn, *The Structure of Scientific Revolutions,* 2nd ed. (Chicago: University of Chicago Press, 1970).

[3] Ibid., p. viii.

[4] *See* Roland L. Warren, "The Sociology of Knowledge and the Problems of the Inner City," *Social Science Quarterly* 52 (December 1971):470.

[5] *Webster's New World Dictionary of the American Language* (Cleveland: World Publishing Company, 1962), p. 1199.

[6] John Howard, "Notes on the Radical Perspective in Sociology," in *Where It's At: Radical Perspectives in Sociology,* ed. Steven E. Deutsch and John Howard (New York: Harper and Row, 1970), pp. 1-9. The emphasis upon social structure as a cause of social problems is not really that new; however, the interpretation given to such a finding and the role of the sociologist vis-à-vis the "problem" has changed, as will be evident in the following discussion.

[7] Albert Szymanski, "Toward a Radical Sociology," *The Human Factor* 8 (November 1968).

[8] *See* J. David Colfax and Jack L. Roach, *Radical Sociology* (New York: Basic Books, 1971).

[9] Howard S. Becker and Irving Louis Horowitz, "Radical Politics and Sociological Research: Observations on Methodology and Ideology," *American Journal of Sociology* 78 (July 1972):48.

[10] This is not necessarily true, as Colfax and Roach note: "So far there is little evidence that the present generation of academic radicals is more sincere or more highly motivated in its commitment to radical change than the generation of the '30s. It is entirely possible that, like previous generations of academic radicals, the current generation will become similarly disillusioned, frightened, and hypocritical, and that self-interest, advancing age, declining ideals, and social and institutional repression will take their toll." Colfax and Roach, *Radical Sociology*, p. 13.

[11] *See* Warren, "Sociology of Knowledge," for a discussion of this approach. Also of importance is John Horton, "Order and Conflict Theories of Social Problems," *American Journal of Sociology* 71 (May 1966):701-713. Although there are important distinctions in the nominal definitions of cause and blame, within the context of this discussion the author is suggesting that by focusing upon certain phenomena as causal and thus not focusing upon others, one suggests that responsibility for an outcome—crime—lies in these causes. Fault is specific, personalized, and condemning and is readily applicable to the legal principle of individual responsibility. This leads to the personification of such inanimate objects as poverty and housing, but it is important to understanding the ramifications of such demystification for "remedies" to the problem.

[12] Leon Radzinowicz, *Ideology and Crime* (New York: Columbia University Press, 1966).

[13] *See* George B. Vold, *Theoretical Criminology* (New York: Oxford University Press, 1958), pp. 14-26.

[14] Franklin Le Von Baumer, *Main Currents of Western Thought* (New York: Alfred A. Knopf, 1964), pp. 249-250.

[15] Herman Mannheim, *Comparative Criminology* (New York: Houghton Mifflin, 1965).

[16] *See* Howard E. Becker and Harry Elmer Barnes, *Social Thought from Lore to Science,* vol. 2 (New York: Dover Publications, 1961).

[17] *See* Von Baumer, *Main Currents.*

[18] *See* Becker and Barnes, *Social Thought,* pp. 670-671.

[19] *See* Von Baumer, *Main Currents,* pp. 357-365.

[20] *See* Herman Mannheim, *Pioneers in Criminology* (Chicago: Quadrangle Books, 1960). For an excellent discussion of positivism in criminology, *see* David Matza, *Delinquency and Drift,* chap. 1 "The Positive Delinquent." (New York: John Wiley, 1964). While noting that all social science is deterministic, Matza distinguishes between "hard" and "soft" determinism. The former has long been the major thrust of American criminological analysis and rigidly adheres to the characteristics of positivism noted above; soft determinism allows for the incorporation of a degree of free will or choice in human behavior. In a later discussion of deviance, Matza, *Becoming Deviant* (Englewood Cliffs: Prentice-Hall, 1969) notes that the positive school of criminology separated the study of crime from the workings and theory of the state and he suggests we take a naturalist perspective of deviance, including crime. Traditional positivist criminology views man as object, the naturalist perspective sees man as subject. Much of positivistic criminology has been devoid of naturalist content.

[21] *See* C. R. Jeffery, "The Historical Development of Criminology," *Journal of Criminal Law, Criminology and Police Science* 50 (May-June 1959): 3-19.

[22] *See* Radzinowicz, *Ideology,* pp. 29-59.

[23] Edwin H. Sutherland and Donald R. Cressey, *Criminology* (Philadelphia: J. B. Lippincott, 1970), p. 3.

[24] *See* Leslie T. Wilkins, "The Concept of Cause in Criminology," *Issues in Criminology* 3 (Spring 1968):147-165. Of course, determinism and free will are not mutually exclusive but a matter of degree, i.e., some are more free than others. *See* Arthur Pap, *An Introduction to the Philosophy of Science,* chap. 17, "Determinism and Indeterminism" (New York: The Free Press, 1962). For a good discussion of the problems of the concept of cause, *see* Gideon Sjoberg and Roger Nett, *A Methodology for Social Research* (New York: Harper and Row, 1968), pp. 293-298.

[25] Daniel Glaser, "Criminology and Public Policy," *The American Sociologist* 6 (June 1971):30.

[26] *See* Marvin E. Wolfgang, "Criminology and the Criminologist," *Journal of Criminal Law, Criminology and Police Science* 54 (June 1963):160.

[27] Don C. Gibbons, *Society, Crime and Criminal Careers* (Englewood Cliffs: Prentice-Hall, 1968), p. 7.

[28] *See* Charles A. Reich, *The Greening of America* (New York: Random House, 1970).

[29] *See* Reich, *Greening,* p. 135.

[30] Robert Lefcourt, ed., *Law Against the People: Essays to Demystify Law, Order and the Court* (New York: Random House, 1971), p. 11.

[31] *See* Richard Quinney, *The Social Reality of Crime* (Boston: Little, Brown, 1970) and William J. Chambliss and Robert B. Seidman, *Law, Order and Power* (Reading, Mass.: Addison-Wesley Publishing, 1971). For an excellent discussion of the definition of crime and the criminologist's role, *see* Herman and Julia Schwendenger, "Defenders of Order or Guardians of Human Rights?" *Issues in Criminology* 5 (Summer 1970):123-157 and the subsequent exchange: Clayton A. Hartjen, "Legalism and Humanism: A Reply to the Schwendengers," and Herman and Julia Schwendenger, "The Continuing Debate on the Legalistic Approach to the Definition of Crime," in *Issues In Criminology* 7 (Winter 1972): 59-81.

[32] For example, *see* C. Bend and M. Vogelfanger, "A New Look at Mills's Critique," in *Mass Society in Crisis,* ed. Bernard Rosenberg, Israel Gerver, and F. Williams Howton (New York: Macmillan, 1971), pp. 271-281; I. L. Horowitz, *Professing Sociology: Studies in the Life Cycle of Social Science* (Chicago: Aldine Publishing, 1968); and Alvin Gouldner, *The Coming Crisis of Western Sociology* (New York: Basic Books, 1970).

[33] Clarence R. Jeffery, "The Structure of American Criminological Thinking," *The Journal of Criminal Law, Criminology and Police Science* 46 (January-February 1956):658-672.

[34] Ibid.

[35] It is recognized by the author that attention has increasingly been given to the criminal justice system and its problems, but much of this discussion provides technological and/or manpower remedies for the problems of the system, which must be better coordinated to meet the needs of the "clients." Such "solutions" are very much tied to a specific causal model of the criminal, without giving much attention to the lawmaking process.

[36] C. I. Dessaur, *Foundations of Theory-Formation in Criminology* (The Hague: Moutan and Co., 1971), pp. 17-18.

[37]*See* Quinney, *Social Reality*, for the best representation of such a comprehensive theory of the "social reality of crime."

[38]For a discussion of the development of American criminology see Leon Radzinowicz, *In Search of Criminology*, chap. 7, "A Vast Laboratory (Cambridge: Harvard University Press, 1962). The subsequent dominance of the United States in criminological research is explained by a number of factors, including (1) the prominence of social sciences, (2) the fact that criminology is not wed to faculties of law and their juristic view, (3) the prevalence of crime, which has received much public attention, and (4) the availability of money for research and study.

[39]*See* Dennis Szaba, Marc Libbanc, and Andre Normandeau, "Applied Criminology and Government Policy: Future Perspectives and Conditions of Collaboration," *Issues in Criminology* 6 (Winter 1971):55-83. The authors argue for the concept of criminology as an applied science. However, it remains to be resolved as to whom it is applied, by whom, for what purposes, and with what results!

[40]Ibid., p. 68. Given the politicization of traditionally powerless groups, e.g., nonwhites and poor, when the criminologist assigns "blame" (causes) for crime he increasingly must be accountable to nonestablishment groups. He cannot please all the people all of the time!

[41]Ibid. The action-orientation of the "new breed" will undoubtedly be tempered by the reaction of establishment institutions and actors.

[42]Marvin E. Wolfgang, "Making the Criminal Justice System Accountable," *Crime and Delinquency* 18 (January 1972):15-22. Such an appeal is even more striking given the "kinds of people" focus of much of Professor Wolfgang's work.

[43]Ibid., p. 22.

[44]Tony G. Poveda, "The Image of the Criminal: A Critique of Crime and Delinquency Theories," *Issues in Criminology* 5 (Winter 1970):61.

[45]This is not to suggest that lower class "criminality" is not more prevalent in arrest, processing, and institutionalized statistics. A casual observation of drunk court will verify such "criminality." (Drunkenness makes up over 25 percent of our crime.) However, the question is why are only poor people processed for drunkenness, vagrancy, addiction, etc.? More analyses of statute formulation and differential processing are needed.

[46]David Chapman, *Sociology and the Stereotype of the Criminal* (London: Tavistock Publications, 1968), p. 23. "A theme in this essay is that of the contribution made by the sociologist and criminologist to the creation and maintenance of the stereotype of crime and the criminal. This stereotype asserts that crime is a distinctive kind of behavior and that criminals are created by special physical, psychic, social, or environmental factors. Such theories are maintained and diffused by researchers that are based on socially determined groups, generally chosen without controls, often by critera that prejudge the issue." Ibid., p. 244.

[47]Szaba et al., *Applied Criminology*, p. 59.

[48]"Study: Anti-Crime Program has no Substantial Impact," *Lincoln Evening Journal* (November 3, 1972):1.

[49]Gresham M. Sykes, "The Future of Criminality," *American Behavioral Scientist* 15 (January-February 1972):403-419.

[50]John McDermott, "Technology: The Opiate of the Intellectual," *New York Review of Books* (July 31, 1969).

[51] Sykes's definition of political crime is quite appropriate for our activities in Indochina: "Illegal acts that have as their objective the destruction of the society's system of power, changes of policy by means of violence, or the forceful removal of those exercising power in the system." (Sykes, "Criminality," p. 413.)

[52] Edwin M. Schur, *Our Criminal Society: The Social and Legal Sources of Crime in America* (Englewood Cliffs: Prentice-Hall, 1969), p. 237. For a recent indictment of delinquency policy *see* Edwin M. Schur, *Radical Non-Intervention: Rethinking the Delinquency Problem* (Englewood Cliffs: Prentice-Hall, 1973).

[53] "Behind the Rise in Crime and Terror," *U.S. News and World Report* (November 13, 1972):41-49. The article goes on to identify the "New Left" as the purveyor of violence, including student revolutionaries inciting riots around the country. The increasing armament of terrorists and criminals reflects the Garrison Society, the siege of the big cities, etc. Why? Emotional instability and derangement: "Vanishing is the stability anchored to a fixed hierarchy of values and authority in this world and the next. What is emerging in the West is a free-form attitude toward human relationships and responsibilities. . . . This shift, decades in the making, blossomed during the 1960s when youthful rebels promised an Aquarian age of harmony and understanding as restraints loosened." (It fails to mention the civil rights movement in the late 1950s and early 1960s!) "To a remarkable extent, crime and terrorism are becoming the 'theater of the streets,' promised by young radicals." Along with a desensitization to violence is an undercurrent of hostility toward authority, even among the law-abiding. They note terrorist folk heroes, e.g., D. B. Cooper and "The Battle Hymn of Lieutenant Calley," and excuses provided by some intellectuals ("lumpen intelligentsia") who talk of a theology of violence. The shift of guilt from the aggressor to society is also noted, and the need to return to traditional "sensibility" and "perspectives" is urged.

[54] Sykes, "Criminality," p. 417.

[55] Ibid., p. 417.

[56] *See* Don Gibbons, "Observations on the Study of Crime Causation," *American Journal of Sociology* 77 (September 1971):263. The author fails to distinguish between "crime causation" and the "causes" of criminal behavior. Quinney, *Social Reality,* presents the best systematic attempt at presenting a complete theory of crime "causation."

[57] *See* Marvin Wolfgang and Bernard Cohen, *Race and Crime: Conceptions and Misconceptions* (New York: Human Relations Press, 1970).

[58] *See* Charles E. Reasons and Jack L. Kuykendall, *Race, Crime and Justice* (Pacific Palisades: Goodyear Publishing, 1972).

[59] For some interesting insights into the manner by which Quinney arrived at his "world view," *see* "Dialogue with Richard Quinney," *Issues In Criminology* 6 (Summer 1971):41-54. *Also see* Richard Quinney, "The Ideology of Law: Notes for a Radical Alternative to Legal Oppression," *Issues In Criminology* 7 (Winter 1972):1-35.

[60] For an excellent delineation of power/conflict propositions, *see* Austin T. Turk, "Conflict and Criminality," *American Sociological Review* 31 (June 1966):338-352. *Also see* R. Serge Denisoff and Charles H. McCaghy, *Deviance, Conflict and Criminality* (New York: Rand McNally, 1973).

[61] *See* Schur, *Criminal Society;* Quinney, *Social Reality;* Chambliss and Seidman, *Law, Order and Power.*

[62] For example, Ferdinand Lundberg, *The Rich and the Super-Rich* (New York: Bantam Books, 1968); Suzanne Keller, *Beyond the Ruling Class* (New York: Random House, 1968).

[63] For an excellent overview and bibliography, see Richard F. Sullivan, "The Economics of Crime: Introduction to the Literature," *Crime and Delinquency* 19 (April 1973):138-149.

[64] *See* Laurie Taylor, "The Criminologist and the Criminal," *Catalyst* No. 6 (Summer 1970):45-54.

[65] For a recent discussion of this perspective, see Robert Ross and Graham L. Staines, "The Politics of Analyzing Social Problems," *Social Problems* 20 (Summer 1972):18-40.

[66] B. Boltomore, *Karl Marx: Selected Writings in Sociology and Social Philosophy* (New York: McGraw-Hill, 1964).

[67] *See* David Matza, *Becoming Deviant* (Englewood Cliffs: Prentice-Hall, 1969).

[68] For a representative perspective of the time, see David A. Orebough, *Crime, Degeneracy and Immigration* (Boston: The Gorman Press, 1929). Mr. Orebrough, a Chicago attorney, argues that the final outcome of the battle with crime depends on race quality—heredity, education, and tradition as factors in the development of "racial soul." Genuine reform necessitates eugenics education and the elimination of the degenerate and inferior non-Nordic races.

IDEOLOGY AND CRIMINAL JUSTICE POLICY: SOME CURRENT ISSUES

WALTER B. MILLER

There is currently in the United States a widespread impression that our country is experiencing a major transitional phase—a period in which long-established social arrangements and the moral and conceptual notions that undergird them are undergoing substantial change. Optimists see this process as a transition from one relatively effective social order to another; pessimists see it as a one-way passage to catastrophe.

It is hard to judge the validity of these conceptions. Few generations have been free from the conviction that the nation was in the throes of "the crisis of our times," and such perceptions have not always corresponded with judgments of later historians.[1]

Since criminal behavior, ways of thinking about crime, and methods of dealing with crime make up an intrinsic component of any social order, the notion of a transitional phase also affects the perceptions and actions of both criminals and criminal justice system personnel. As soon as one considers crime as one facet of a larger set of social and historical shifts, however, a paradox emerges. One gets an impression both of striking and substantial change, and striking and substantial stability.

This paradox seems to apply equally to crime and to societal response to crime. On the one hand, patterns of contemporary criminal behavior reflect substantial shifts—*e.g.*, a massive increase in drug use and drug-related crimes, a new dimension of political motivation affecting many adult prisoners. On the other hand, an impression of changelessness and stability is evident in the relatively unchanging nature of youth crime and periodic attention to youth gang violence.[2]

A similar paradox affects those responsible for making and implementing criminal justice policy. On the one hand, we seem to be in the midst of a radical shift in conceptualizing and coping with crime, indicated by a host of current slogans such as decentralization, decriminalization, deinstitutionalization, victimology and others. On the other hand, there is a surprising sameness in the basic issues which these slogans reflect—issues such as free will versus determinism, individual rights versus state's rights, concentration versus diffusion of power. Do these concerns represent progressive movement or merely contemporary replays of ancient dramas?

Intriguing as it might be to explore these issues with respect to the behavior of both those who engage in crime and those who attempt to deal with it, I shall treat only the latter. The terms "criminologist" or "criminal justice per-

Walter B. Miller, "Ideology and Criminal Justice Policy: Some Current Issues" *The Journal of Criminal Law and Criminology*. 64 (June 1973) pp. 141-162. Reprinted by permission of the journal and the author.

sonnel" will be used here to refer to those persons who maintain some consistent responsibility for dealing with criminals and their behavior.

One may seek to escape this paradox by employing the concept of "ideology." Ideology is also a central element in the complex patterns of change and stability, and a key to their understanding. A useful point of departure may be found in a quotation from Myrdal's *An American Dilemma:*

> The place of the individual scientist along the scale of radicalism-conservatism has always had strong influences on both the selection of research problems and the conclusions drawn from research. In a sense, it is the master scale of biases in social science.[3]

It is this master scale, and its influence on the field of criminal justice, which will be my major concern here.

The term "ideology" may be used in many ways.[4] It will be used here only to refer to a set of general and abstract beliefs or assumptions about the correct or proper state of things, particularly with respect to the moral order and political arrangements, which serve to shape one's positions on specific issues. Several aspects of ideology as used in this sense should be noted. First, ideological assumptions are generally pre-conscious rather than explicit, and serve, under most circumstances, as unexamined presumptions underlying positions taken openly. Second, ideological assumptions bear a strong emotional charge. This charge is not always evident, but it can readily be activated by appropriate stimuli, in particular by direct challenge. During the process of formation, ideological premises for particular individuals are influenced by a variety of informational inputs, but once established they become relatively impervious to change, since they serve to receive or reject new evidence in terms of a self-contained and self-reinforcing system.

The major contention of this presentation is that ideology and its consequences exert a powerful influence on the policies and procedures of those who conduct the enterprise of criminal justice, and that the degree and kinds of influence go largely unrecognized. Ideology is the permanent hidden agenda of criminal justice.

The discussion has two major aims. First, assuming that the generally implicit ideological basis of criminal justice commands strong, emotional, partisan allegiance, I shall attempt to state explicitly the major assumptions of relevant divergent ideological positions in as neutral or as nonpartisan a fashion as possible. Second, some of the consequences of such ideologies for the processes of planning, program, and policy in criminal justice will be examined.

I shall use a simple conceptual device for indicating ideological positions—a one-dimensional scale that runs from five on the right to zero in the middle to five on the left. Various ideological positions under consideration will be referred to this scale, using the terms "left" and "right" in an attempt to achieve neutrality. Although not all eleven possible distinctions will be made in every analysis, five scale distinctions on each side seem to be the minimum needed for present purposes. Later discussions will in some instances attribute considerable importance to differences as small as one scale degree.

The substance of ideologically divergent positions with respect to selected issues of current concern will be presented in three ways. Positions will be formulated first as "crusading issues"—shorthand catchwords or rallying cries that furnish the basic impetus for action or change in the criminal justice field. Such catch phrases are derived from a deeper and more abstract set of propositions as to desired states or outcomes. These will be designated "general assumptions." Third, differentiated positions will be delineated for all points along the full range of the scale—extreme right to extreme left—for three major policy issues.[5]

IDEOLOGICAL POSITIONS

Right: Crusading Issues

Crusading issues of the right differ somewhat from those of the left; they generally do not carry as explicit a message of movement toward new forms, but imply instead that things should be reconstituted or restored. However, the component of the message that says, "Things should be different from the way they are now," comes through just as clearly as in the crusading issues of the left. Current crusading issues of the right with respect to crime and how to deal with it include the following:

1. *Excessive leniency toward lawbreakers.* This is a traditional complaint of the right, accentuated at present by the publicity given to reform programs in corrections and policing, as well as to judicial activity at various levels.
2. *Favoring the welfare and rights of lawbreakers over the welfare and rights of their victims, of law enforcement officials, and the law abiding citizen.* This persisting concern is currently activated by attention to prisoners' rights, rehabilitation programs, attacks on police officers by militants, and in particular by a series of well-publicized Supreme Court decisions aimed to enhance the application of due process.
3. *Erosion of discipline and of respect for constituted authority.* This ancient concern is currently manifested in connection with the general behavior of youth, educational policies, treatment of student dissidents by college officials, attitudes and behavior toward law-enforcement, particularly the police.
4. *The cost of crime.* Less likely to arouse the degree of passion evoked by other crusading issues, resentment over what is seen as the enormous and increasing cost of crime and dealing with criminals—a cost borne directly by the hard working and law abiding citizen—nevertheless remains active and persistent.
5. *Excessive permissiveness.* Related to excessive leniency, erosion of discipline, and the abdication of responsibility by authorities, this trend is seen as a fundamental defect in the contemporary social order, affecting many diverse areas such as sexual morality, discipline in the schools, educational philosophies, child-rearing, judicial handling of offenders, and media presentation of sexual materials.

Right: General Assumptions

These crusading issues, along with others of similar import, are not merely ritualized slogans, but reflect instead a more abstract set of assumptions about the nature of criminal behavior, the causes of criminality, responsibility for crime, appropriate ameliorative measures, and, on a broader level, the nature of man and of a proper kind of society. These general assumptions provide the basic charter for the ideological stance of the right as a whole, and a basis for distinguishing among the several subtypes along the points of the ideological scale. Major general assumptions of the right might be phrased as follows:

1. The individual is directly responsible for his own behavior. He is not a passive pawn of external forces, but possesses the capacity to make choices between right and wrong—choices which he makes with an awareness of their consequences.
2. A central requirement of a healthy and well functioning society is a strong moral order which is explicit, well-defined, and widely adhered to. Preferably the tenets of this system of morality should be derived from and grounded in the basic precepts of a major religious tradition. Threats to this moral order are threats to the very existence of the society. Within the moral order, two clusters are of particular importance:
   a. Tenets which sustain the family unit involve morally-derived restrictions on sexual behavior, and obligations of parents to maintain consistent responsibility to their children and to one another.
   b. Tenets which pertain to valued personal qualities include: taking personal responsibility for one's behavior and its consequences; conducting one's affairs with the maximum degree of self-reliance and independence, and the minimum of dependency and reliance on others, particularly public agencies; loyalty, particularly to one's country; achieving one's ends through hard work, responsibility to others, and self-discipline.
3. Of paramount importance is the security of the major arenas of one's customary activity—particularly those locations where the conduct of family life occurs. A fundamental personal and family right is safety from crime, violence, and attack, including the right of citizens to take necessary measures to secure their own safety, and the right to bear arms, particularly in cases where official agencies may appear ineffective in doing so.
4. Adherence to the legitimate directives of constituted authority is a primary means for achieving the goals of morality, correct individual behavior, security, and other valued life conditions. Authority in the service of social and institutional rules should be exercised fairly but firmly, and failure or refusal to accept or respect legitimate authority should be dealt with decisively and unequivocally.
5. A·major device for ordering human relations in a large and heterogeneous society is that of maintaining distinctions among major categories of persons on the basis of differences in age, sex, and so on, with differences in religion, national background, race, and social position of particular importance. While individuals in each of the general categories should be granted the rights and privileges appropriate thereto, social order in many circumstances is greatly facilitated by maintaining both conceptual and spatial separation among the categories.

Left: Crusading Issues

Crusading issues of the left generally reflect marked dissatisfaction with characteristics of the current social order, and carry an insistent message about the desired nature and direction of social reform. Current issues of relevance to criminal justice include:

1. *Overcriminalization.* This reflects a conviction that a substantial number of offenses delineated under current law are wrongly or inappropriately included, and applies particularly to offenses such as gambling, prostitution, drug use, abortion, pornography, and homosexuality.
2. *Labelling and Stigmatization.* This issue is based on a conception that problems of crime are aggravated or even created by the ways in which actual or potential offenders are regarded and treated by persons in authority. To the degree a person is labelled as "criminal," "delinquent," or "deviant," will he be likely to so act.
3. *Overinstitutionalization.* This reflects a dissatisfaction over prevalent methods of dealing with suspected or convicted offenders whereby they are physically confined in large institutional facilities. Castigated as "warehousing," this practice is seen as having a wide range of detrimental consequences, many of which are implied by the ancient phrase "schools for crime." Signalled by a renewed interest in "incarceration," prison reform has become a major social cause of the left.
4. *Overcentralization.* This issue reflects dissatisfaction with the degree of centralized authority existing in organizations which deal with crime—including police departments, correctional systems, and crime-related services at all government levels. Terms which carry the thrust of the proposed remedy are local control, decentralization, community control, a new populism, and citizen power.
5. *Discriminatory Bias.* A particularly blameworthy feature of the present system lies in the widespread practice of conceiving and reacting to large categories of persons under class labels based on characteristics such as racial background, age, sex, income level, sexual practices, and involvement in criminality. Key terms here are racism, sexism, minority oppression and brutality.

Left: General Assumptions

As in the case of the rightist positions, these crusading issues are surface manifestations of a set of more basic and general assumptions, which might be stated as follows:

1. Primary responsibility for criminal behavior lies in conditions of the social order rather than in the character of the individual. Crime is to a greater extent a product of external social pressures than of internally generated individual motives, and is more appropriately regarded as a symptom of social dysfunction than as a phenomenon in its own right. The correct objective of ameliorative efforts, therefore, lies in the attempt to alter the social conditions that engender crime rather than to rehabilitate the individual.
2. The system of behavioral regulation maintained in America is based on a type of social and political order that is deficient in meeting the fundamental needs of the majority of its citizens. This social order, and the official system of behavioral regulation that it includes, incorporates an

obsolete morality not applicable to the conditions of a rapidly changing technological society, and disproportionately geared to sustain the special interests of restricted groups, but which still commands strong support among working class and lower middle class sectors of the population.

3. A fundamental defect in the political and social organization of the United States and in those components of the criminal justice enterprise that are part of this system is an inequitable and unjust distribution of power, privilege, and resources—particularly of power. This inequity pervades the entire system, but appears in its more pronounced forms in the excessive centralization of governmental functions and consequent powerlessness of the governed, the military-like, hierarchical authority systems found in police and correctional organization, and policies of systematic exclusion from positions of power and privilege for those who lack certain preferred social characteristics. The prime objective of reform must be to redistribute the decision-making power of the criminal justice enterprise rather than to alter the behavior of actual or potential offenders.

4. A further defect of the official system is its propensity to make distinctions among individuals based on major categories or classes within society such as age, sex, race, social class, criminal or non-criminal. Healthy societal adaptation for both the offender and the ordinary citizen depends on maintaining the minimum separation—conceptually and physically—between the community at large and those designated as "different" or "deviant." Reform efforts must be directed to bring this about.

5. Consistent with the capacity of external societal forces to engender crime, personnel of official agencies play a predominantly active role, and offenders a predominantly reactive role, in situations where the two come in contact. Official agents of behavioral regulation possess the capacity to induce or enhance criminal behavior by the manner in which they deal with those who have or may have engaged in crime. These agents may define offenders as basically criminal, expose them to stigmatization, degrade them on the basis of social characteristics, and subject them to rigid and arbitrary control.

6. The sector of the total range of human behavior currently included under the system of criminal sanctions is excessively broad, including many forms of behavior (for example, marijuana use, gambling, homosexuality) which do not violate the new morality and forms which would be more effectively and humanely dealt with outside the official system of criminal processing. Legal codes should be redrafted to remove many of the behavioral forms now proscribed, and to limit the discretionary prerogatives of local authorities over apprehension and disposition of violators.

AN IDEOLOGICAL SPECTRUM: DIFFERENTIATED POSITIONS OF LEFT AND RIGHT

The foregoing ideologically-relevant propositions are formulated as general assumptions common to all those designated as "left" or "right." The present section will expand and differentiate these generalized propositions by distributing them along the ideological scale proposed earlier. Charts I, II, and III (See

Appendix) present thirty differentiated positions with respect to three major issues of relevance to criminal justice policy. Statements concerning each issue are assigned ten positions along scales running from right five through left five. The three issues are: conceptions as to the causes of crime and the locus of responsibility for criminality; conceptions of proper methods of dealing with offenders; conceptions of proper operating policies of criminal justice agencies. Not included in these tables is a theoretically possible "centrist" position.

Several features of the charts in the appendix should be noted. Statements representing ideologically-influenced positions on the scale are formulated in a highly condensed and simplified manner, lacking the subtleties, qualifications, and supporting arguments which characterize the actual stances of most people. The basic model is that of an "ideal type" analysis which presents a series of simplified propositions formulated to bear a logical relationship to one another and to underlying abstract principles, rather than to reflect accurately the actual positions of real people.[6] Few readers will feel entirely comfortable with any of the statements exactly as phrased here; most will feel instead that given statements might reflect the general gist of their position, but with important qualifications, or that one can subscribe to selected parts of statements at several different points along the scale. On the other hand, few readers will fail to find some statements with which they disagree completely; it is most unlikely, for example, that one could support with equal enthusiasm the major tenets attributed here to positions at left four and right four.

In "placing" oneself with respect to the scaled positions outlined here, one should look for those statements with which one feels least uncomfortable rather than expecting to find formulations which correspond in all respects to his viewpoint. The process of ascertaining discrepancies between actual positions and those represented here as "pure" examples of rightist or leftist ideology serves one of the purposes of ideal-typical analysis; few are ideological purists, but this type of analysis makes it possible to identify positions which correspond more or less closely to ideological orthodoxy. Those whose positions are closer to the extremes will feel least comfortable with statements attributed to the opposing side of the spectrum; those closer to "centrist" positions will tend to find orientations congenial to their own at a larger number of scale positions, possibly including positions on both sides of the spectrum.

To say that the statements show some logical relationship to one another and to underlying principles is not to say that they are logically consistent; in fact, several obvious inconsistencies appear in the charts. For example, right five maintains that criminals are unwitting puppets of a radical conspiracy and, at the same time, holds that they are responsible for their own behavior. Left four calls for maximum access to information concerning the inner workings of criminal justice agencies and, at the same time, advocates minimum access by employers, personnel departments and others to criminal records of individuals. If one fails to find in internal consistency the "logical" basis for these propositions, where do the logical relationships lie?

Although some degree of logical inconsistency is likely in almost any developed set of propositions about human behavior, the consistency in the above propositions lies largely in the degree to which the interests of particular classes of persons are supported, defended, and justified. The inconsistencies often lie either in the means advocated to achieve such ends or in the rationales used to defend or exculpate favored interests and condemn opposing ones. In the above examples, if one assumes that a basic interest of left four is maximum protection of and support for actual or putative offenders, then these ends are served in the one instance by maximum access to information which might reveal errors, inequities or violations in their treatment by criminal justice officials, and in the other by denying to potential employers and others access to information that might jeopardize their welfare. Similarly, in attempting to reconcile the apparent contradiction in assertions that offenders are pawns of a radical conspiracy and also that they are directly responsible for their behavior, a rightist could argue that offenders are indeed responsible for their behavior, and that they make a deliberate personal choice to follow the crime-engendering appeals of the radicals.

While statements at different scale positions frequently present differing orientations to the same sub-issue (*e.g.*, scope of criminal law, appropriate degree of restraint of offenders, extent to which "rehabilitation" should be an objective), not all of the statements on each major issue treat all of the included sub-issues. The positioned statements are defective with respect to "dimensionality," the possibility of full scalability across all issues. Each of the included sub-issues represents an independently scalable dimension. The "cause" issue incorporates approximately 14 distinguishable dimensions or sub-issues, the "offender" issue 15, and the "agencies" issue 18. To include a separate statement for each dimension at each scale position for all three issues would require a minimum of 470 statements—an impractical number for a presentation at this level. Selection of sub-issues and their assignment to given positions was guided by an attempt both to produce internally-coherent statements and to cover a fairly broad range of sub-issues.

One often finds convergences at the extremes of a distribution of ideological positions. Several instances can be found in the charts; for example, both right five and left five attribute criminality to deliberate or systematic efforts or policies of highly-organized interest groups, although of differing identities (radicals, the ruling class). If quantifiable weights can be assigned to the scalable dimensions of the chart, two major types of distribution are included—"opposition" and "convergence" distributions. "Opposition" distributions occur where the maximum weight or magnitude is found at one extreme of the scale and the minimum at the other, with intermediate positions showing intermediate values. Examples may be found in the sub-issues "degree of coercive power to be exercised by official agencies"; (left five espouses the minimum degree, right five the maximum, with others occupying intermediate positions), and "degree of personal culpability of offenders" (right five maximum, left five minimum, others in between). Policy disputes involving this type of distribution tend to be most difficult to resolve.

In "convergence" distributions similarities or partial similarities are found in the positions of those at opposing ends of the spectrum. One instance is found in attitudes toward rehabilitation of offenders—an objective strongly opposed by partisans at both left four and right four, although for different reasons. A rather complex but crucial instance is found in the statements concerning "localized" versus "centralized" authority. Both left four and right four call for increased local autonomy, whereas the more "moderate" of both left and right favor continued or increased federal authority and support for criminal justice programs and operations. The apparent convergence of the extremes is, however, complicated by a number of factors. One relates to which branch of government exercises authority; another relates to the particular policy area at issue. Those at left four are not adverse to strong federal initiatives to improve social-service delivery capacity of local welfare agencies. Those at right four, while decrying the iron grip of federal bureaucrats over local affairs, are not adverse to strong federal initiatives to improve technological capacity of local police forces. The more extreme leftists seek greatly increased local autonomy for citizen control over police and correctional operations, but welcome strong federal power in formulating and enforcing uniform civil rights measures. The more extreme rightists adamantly oppose the use of centralized power to enforce "mixing" of racial and other social categories or to compel uniform operations of local police, courts and corrections, but welcome strong federal power in the development and maintenance of military forces, or a strong federal investigatory branch with the power to probe corruption and collusion in local programs, particularly those of left-oriented agencies.

The unifying principle behind these apparent contradictions is the same as that noted for intraposition inconsistencies; ideologically-derived objectives are supported despite possible discrepancies involving the means to achieve them or the identity of sources of support. An additional dimension of considerable importance is also involved—that of time. Ideological positions of left and right are delineated on the basis of a given point in time earlier designated as "current." But specific stances of the left and right can change rapidly in response to changing circumstances, or they can even reverse themselves. Moreover, some of the "crusading issues" currently fashionable will become passé in the near future.

The "decentralization" issue again provides a good example. Whether one favors more or less power for "centralized" or federal agencies depends on the current ideological complexion of the several federal departments or branches. Viewed very broadly, in the early 1930's the left looked to the executive branch as a prime source of support for policies they favored, and the right to the judicial and legislative; in the 1960's the left viewed both the executive and judicial as allies, the legislature as a potential source of opposition, and sought more power for the High Court and the Presidency. At present the right views the executive as supportive, and the left looks to the legislature as an ally in an attempt to curb the power of the presidency. Reflecting these shifts have been changes in attitudes of the left and right toward "local control." While traditionally a crusading issue of the right (state's rights), the banner for community control was taken up in the 1960's by the left as an effective method of bypassing entrenched political power at the local level—primarily with respect to civil rights. Recently the trend has begun to reverse because of a resurgence of the right's traditional "anti-big-government" stance and an increasing resort to local control by community groups pursuing rightist causes (*e.g.,* exclusion of blacks from white schools).

Further detailed analyses of convergences and divergences, consistencies and contradictions, past, present and future fashions of both these issues and others could be developed. It might be useful at this point, however, to briefly consider a more fundamental level—the basic philosophical underpinnings of the two sides—and to compress the variety and complexity of their varied positions into a single and simple governing principle.

For the right, the paramount value is order—an ordered society based on a pervasive and binding morality—and the paramount danger is disorder—social, moral and political. For the left, the paramount value is justice—a just society based on a fair and equitable distribution of power, wealth, prestige, and privilege—and the paramount evil is injustice—the concentration of valued social resources in the hands of a privileged minority.

Few Americans would quarrel with either of these values since both are intrinsic aspects of our national ideals. Stripped of the passion of ideological conflict, the issue between the two sides could be viewed as a disagreement over the relative priority of two valuable conditions: whether *order with justice*, or *justice with order* should be the guiding principle of the criminal justice enterprise.

These are ancient philosophical issues, and their many aspects have been argued in detail for centuries. Can both order and justice be maximized in a large, heterogeneous, pluralistic society? Can either objective be granted priority under all circumstances? If not, under what circumstances should which objective be seen as paramount? It might appear that these issues are today just as susceptible to rational discussion as they have been in the past; but this is not so, because the climate militates against such discussion. Why this is so will be considered shortly—after a brief discussion of the ideologies of the formal agencies of criminal justice.

IDEOLOGICAL COMPLEXION OF CRIMINAL JUSTICE AGENCIES

The ideological positions of four major professional fields will be discussed —academic criminology, the police, the judiciary, and corrections. Rather than complex analysis or careful delineation, tentative impressions will be offered. Each system will be characterized on a very gross level, but it is important to bear in mind the possibility that there is as much ideological variability within each of the several systems as there is among them. Of particular importance within these systems are differences in age level, social class and educational level, and rank.

Academic Criminologists: This group is included not out of any presumption about the importance of the role they play, but rather because academic criminology provides the platform from which the present analysis is presented. Probably the most important point to make here is that the day-to-day ideological environment of the average academic criminologist, viewed within the context of the total society, is highly artificial; it reflects the perspectives of a deviant and unrepresentative minority. Academic criminology, reflecting academic social science in general, is substantially oriented toward the left, while the bulk of American people are oriented toward the right.[7] Furthermore, the members of the large liberal academic majority do proportionately more writing and speechmaking than those of the small conservative minority, so that their impact on the ideological climate exceeds even their large numbers. If the proportion of right-oriented persons in academic criminology comes close to being just the reverse of that in the general population, then this marked ideological divergence certainly has implications for those situations in which academicians come in contact with the public, particularly where they interact with representatives of other criminal justice branches. It also has an important impact on their own perceptions of the ideological positions of the public and other criminal justice professionals.

Police: The bulk of police officers have working-class backgrounds, and the contemporary working class is substantially rightist. Archie Bunker is a caricature, but the reality he exaggerates is a significant one. Rightist ideology in one of its purest versions may be found in the solemn speeches of Officer Joe Friday to temporarily discouraged young police officers or disgruntled citizens. Among police departments, differences in ideological complexion are found in different regions (for example, West Coast departments generally have higher proportions of college-trained personnel), different sized communities, and departments with different personnel policies. Within departments, age differences may be important (some younger officers are less rightist), as well as differences in rank and function (some departments have more liberally-oriented chiefs or research and planning personnel). The majority of working police professionals, however, subscribe to the ideological premises here designated as "rightist."

Judiciary: The legal and judicial field is probably characterized by greater ideological diversity than either the police or corrections. One reason is that leftist positions are more common among those with college degrees than among those with less education. Since college education is a prerequisite to formal legal training, lawyers are more likely to have been exposed to the leftward orientation characteristic of most academic faculties, particularly those of the larger and more prestigious universities.[8] Judges show enormous variation in ideological predilections, probably covering the full range from right five to left four. Variation is related to factors such as the law school attended, size of jurisdiction, social status of jurists and their clientele, region, level of the court. While public attention is often directed to the actions of highly moralistic, hard line judges at right four and five positions, such jurists are probably becoming less common.

Ideological orientations of the legal profession have recently been subject to public attention, particularly in connection with two developments. First, the Supreme Court has in the recent past been associated with a series of decisions that reflect basic tenets of the left. Included have been such issues as increased protection for the rights of suspected and accused persons, inadmissibility of illegally-obtained evidence, minimization of distinctions based on race, reduction of discretionary powers of law-enforcement personnel, and reduction of judicial discretion in juvenile proceedings.[9] These decisions and others were perceived by the right as posing a critical threat to an established balance of power and prerogatives between law-enforcement personnel and offenders, seriously endangering the law-enforcement process and the security of the public.

The second development is the emergence during the past ten years of a group of young left-oriented lawyers whose influence is probably disproportionate to their small numbers. Able, dedicated, active on a variety of fronts, many representing low-income or black clients, their activities became best known in connection with Federal Anti-Poverty programs. Many of these lawyers have assumed positions along the ideological scale as far left as the left three and left four positions.

Despite these well-publicized manifestations of leftward orientations in some sectors of the legal profession, it is unlikely that a substantial proportion of the profession consistently espouses the tenets of the left, particularly those of left three and beyond. The more liberal judges are generally found in federal and higher-level state courts, but conservative views are still common among jurists of the lower level courts, where the great bulk of day-to-day legal business is transacted. Moreover, as part of the ideological shifts noted earlier, the Burger court is regarded by the right with considerably less antipathy than the Warren court.[10]

Corrections: Corrections, the current hot spot of the criminal justice field, probably contains a mixture of ideological positions, with the bulk of correctional personnel ranged along the right. The average lower-echelon corrections employee has a working-class background similar to that of the average patrolman, and thus manifests the rightist orientation characteristic of that class. As in the case of police, age may be an important basis for differentiation, with older officials more likely to assume right-oriented positions. Among other bases are size of the institution and age level of the bulk of inmates. Juvenile corrections tends to have a higher likelihood of left-oriented staff, both at administrative and lower-echelon levels.

Prison reform is currently one of the most intense crusading issues of the left. While most reform efforts are exerted by persons not officially part of the correctional system, there has been some influx of left three and four persons into the official system itself, particularly among younger staff in juvenile correction facilities.

CONSEQUENCES OF IDEOLOGY

If, as is here contended, many of those involved in the tasks of planning and executing the major policies and procedures of our criminal justice system are subject to the influence of pervasive ideological assumptions about the nature of crime and methods of dealing with it—assumptions which are largely implicit and unexamined—the question then arises: what are the consequences of this phenomenon?

While both the crusading issues and graded ideological positions presented earlier were phrased to convey the tone of urgent imperatives, the assumptions from which they arise were phrased in relatively neutral terms as a set of general propositions about the nature, causes, and processes of coping with crime. So phrased and so regarded, these assumptions are susceptible to rational consideration. Their strengths and weaknesses can be debated, evidence can be employed to test the degree of validity each may possess, contradictions among them can be considered, and attempts made to explain or reconcile differences among them. Formulated and used in this manner, the question arises: why are they characterized here as "ideological"?

The scale of ideology presented comprises a single major parameter—substantive variation along a left-right scale with respect to a set of issues germane to crime and the criminal justice process. But there is an additional important parameter which must also be considered: that of intensity—the degree of emotional charge which attaches to the assumptions. It is the capacity of these positions to evoke the most passionate kinds of reactions and to become infused with deeply felt, quasi-religious significance that constitutes the crucial element in the difference between testable assumptions and ideological tenets. This dimension has the power to transform plausibility into ironclad certainty, conditional belief into ardent conviction, the reasoned advocate into the implacable zealot. Rather than being looked upon as useful and conditional hypotheses, these assumptions, for many, take the form of the sacred and inviolable dogma of the one true faith, the questioning of which is heresy, and the opposing of which is profoundly evil.

This phenomenon—ideological intensification—appears increasingly to exert a powerful impact on the entire field. Leslie Wilkins has recorded his opinion that the criminal justice enterprise is becoming progressively more scientific and secularized;[11] an opposite, or at least concurrent, trend is here suggested—that it is becoming progressively more ideologized. The consequences are many. Seven will be discussed briefly: Polarization, Reverse Projection, Ideologized Selectivity, Informational Constriction, Catastrophism, and Distortion of Opposing Positions.

Polarization. Polarization is perhaps the most obvious consequence of ideological intensification. The more heavily a belief takes on the character of sacred dogma, the more necessary it becomes to view the proponents of opposing positions as devils and scoundrels, and their views as dangerous and immoral. Cast in this framework of the sacred and the profane, of virtuous heroes and despicable villians, the degree of accommodation and compromise that seems essential to the complex enterprise of criminal justice planning becomes, at best, enormously complicated, and at worst, quite impossible.

Reverse Projection. This is a process whereby a person who occupies a position at a given point along the ideological scale perceives those who occupy any point closer to the center than his own as being on the opposite side of the scale. Three aspects of this phenomenon, which appears in its most pronounced form at the extremes of the scale, should be noted. First, if one grants the logical possibility that there can exist a "centrist" position—not a position which maintains no assumptions, but one whose assumptions are "mixed," "balanced," or not readily characterizable—then this position is perceived as "rightist" by those on the left, and "leftist" by those on the right.

A second aspect concerns the intensity of antagonism often shown by those occupying immediately adjacent positions along the ideological scale. Perhaps the most familiar current manifestation of this is found in the bitter mutual denunciations of those classified here as occupying the positions of left four and left five. Those at left four are often taken by those at left five as far more dangerous and evil than those seen as patent facists at right four and five. Left fours stand accused as dupes of the right, selling out to or being coopted by the establishment, and blunting the thrust of social activism by cowardly vaccilation and compromise.

A third aspect of reverse projection is that one tends to make the most sensitive intrascale distinctions closest to the point that one occupies. Thus, someone at right four might be extremely sensitive to differences between his position and that of an absolute dictatorship advocate at right five, and at the same time cast left four and five into an undifferentiated class of commies, communist dupes and radicals, quite oblivious to the distinctions that loom so large to those who occupy these positions.

Ideologized Selectivity. The range of issues, problems, areas of endeavor, and arenas of activity relevant to the criminal justice enterprise is enormous. Given the vastness of the field relative to the availability of resources, decisions must be made as to task priorities and resource allocation. Ideology plays a paramount but largely unrecognized role in this process, to the detriment of other ways of determining priorities. Ideologized selectivity exerts a constant influence in determining which problem areas are granted greatest significance, which projects are supported, what kinds of information are gathered and how research results are analyzed and interpreted. Divergent resource allocation policies of major federal agencies can be viewed as directly related to the dominant ideological orientation of the agency.

Only one example of ideologized selectivity will be cited here. The increasing use of drugs, soft and hard, and an attendant range of drug-related crime problems is certainly a major contemporary development. The importance of this problem is reflected in the attention devoted to it by academic criminologists. One major reason for this intensive attention is that explanations for the spread of drug use fit the ideological assumptions shared by most academicians (drug use is an understandable product of alienation resulting from the failure of the system to provide adequate meaning and quality to life). Also one major ameliorative proposal, the liberalization of drug laws, accords directly with a crusading issue of the left—decriminalization.

Another contemporary phenomenon, quite possibly of similar magnitude, centers on the apparent disproportionate numbers of low-status urban blacks arrested for violent and predatory crimes, brought to court and sent to prison. While not entirely ignored by academic criminologists, the relatively low amount of attention devoted to this phenomenon stands in sharp contrast to the intensive efforts evident in the field of drugs. Important aspects of the problem of black crime do not fit the ideological assumptions of the majority of academic criminologists. Insofar as the issue is studied, the problem is generally stated in terms of oppressive, unjust and discriminatory behavior by society and its law-enforcement agents—a formulation that accords with that tenet of the left which assumes the capacity of officials to engender crime by their actions, and the parallel assumption that major responsibility for crime lies in conditions of the social order. Approaches to the problem that involve the careful collection of information relative to such characteristics of the population itself as racial and social status run counter to ideological tenets that call for the minimization of such distinctions both conceptually and in practice, and thus are left largely unattended.

Informational Constriction. An attitude which is quite prevalent in many quarters of the criminal justice enterprise today involves a depreciation of the value of research in general, and research on causes of crime in particular. Several reasons are commonly given, including the notion that money spent on research has a low payoff relative to that spent for action, that past research has yielded little of real value for present problems, and that research on causes of crime in particular is of little value since the low degree of consensus among various competing schools and theorists provides little in the way of unified conclusions or concrete guidance. Quite independent of the validity of such reasons, the anti-research stance can be seen as a logical consequence of ideological intensification.

For the ideologically committed at both ends of the scale, new information appears both useless and dangerous. It is useless because the basic answers, particularly with respect to causes, are already given, in their true and final form, by the ideology; it is dangerous because evidence provided by new research has the potential of calling into question ideologically established truths.

In line with this orientation, the present enterprise, that of examining the influence of ideology on criminal justice policy and programs, must be regarded with distaste by the ideologically intense—not only because it represents information of relevance to ideological doctrine, but also because the very nature of the analysis implies that ideological truth is relative.

Catastrophism. Ideological partisans at both extremes of the scale are intensely committed to particular programs or policies they wish to see effected, and recurrently issue dire warnings of terrible catastrophes that will certainly ensue unless their proposals are adopted (Right: Unless the police are promptly given full power to curb criminality and unless rampant permissiveness toward criminals is halted, the country will surely be faced with an unprecedented wave of crime and violence; Left: Unless society promptly decides to provide the resources necessary to eliminate poverty, discrimination, injustice and exploitation, the country will surely be faced with a holocaust of violence worse than ever before). Such predictions are used as tactics in a general strategy for enlisting support for partisan causes: "Unless you turn to us and our program. . . ." That the great bulk of catastrophes so ominously predicted do not materialize does not deter catastrophism, since partisans can generally claim that it was the response to their warnings that forestalled the catastrophe. Catastrophism can thus serve to inhibit adaptation to real crises by casting into question the credibility of accurate prophets along with the inaccurate.

Magnification of Prevalence. Ideological intensification produces a characteristic effect on perceptions of the empirical prevalence of phenomena related to areas of ideological concern. In general, targets of ideological condemnation are represented as far more prevalent than carefully collected evidence would indicate. Examples are estimates by rightists of the numbers of black militants, radical conspirators, and welfare cheaters, and by leftists of the numbers of brutal policemen, sadistic prison personnel, and totally legitimate welfare recipients.

Distortion of the Opposition. To facilitate a demonstration of the invalidity of tenets on the opposite side of the ideological scale it is necessary for partisans to formulate the actual positions of the opposition in such a way as to make them most susceptible to refutation. Opposition positions are phrased to appear maximally illogical, irrational, unsupportable, simplistic, internally contradictory, and, if possible, contemptible or ludicrous. Such distortion impedes the capacity to adequately comprehend and represent positions or points of view which may be complex and extensively developed—a capacity that can be of great value when confronting policy differences based on ideological divergencies.

IMPLICATIONS

What are the implications of this analysis for those who face the demanding tasks of criminal justice action and planning? It might first appear that the prescription would follow simply and directly from the diagnosis. If the processes of formulating and implementing policy with respect to crime problems are heavily infused with ideological doctrine, and if this produces a variety of disadvantageous consequences, the moral would appear to be clear: work to reverse the trend of increased ideological intensification, bring out into the open the hidden ideological agenda of the criminal justice enterprise, and make it possible to release the energy now consumed in partisan conflict for a more direct and effective engagement with the problem field itself.

But such a prescription is both overly optimistic and overly simple. It cannot be doubted that the United States in the latter 20th century is faced with the necessity of confronting and adapting to a set of substantially modified circumstances, rooted primarily in technological developments with complex and ramified sociological consequences. It does not appear too far-fetched to propose the major kinds of necessary social adaptation in the United States can occur only through the medium of ardently ideological social movements—and that the costs of such a process must be borne in order to achieve the benefits it ultimately will confer. If this conception is correct, then ideological intensification, with all its dangers and drawbacks, must be seen as a necessary component of effective social adaptation, and the ideologists must be seen as playing a necessary role in the process of social change.

Even if one grants, however, that ideology will remain an inherent element of the policy-making process, and that while enhancing drive, dedication and commitment it also engenders rigidity, intolerance and distortion—one might still ask whether it is possible to limit the detrimental consequences of ideology without impairing its strengths. Such an objective is not easy, but steps can be taken in this direction. One such step entails an effort to increase ones' capacity to discriminate between those types of information which are more heavily invested with ideological content and those which are less so. This involves the traditional distinction between "fact" and "value" statements.[12] The present delineation of selected ideological stances of the left and right provides one basis for estimating the degree to which statements forwarded as established conclusions are based on ideological doctrine rather than empirically supportable evidence. When assertions are made about what measures best serve the purposes of securing order, justice and the public welfare, one should ask "How do we know this?" If statements appear to reflect in greater or lesser degree the interrelated patterns of premises, assumptions and prescriptions here characterized as "ideological," one should accommodate one's reactions accordingly.

Another step is to attempt to grant the appropriate degree of validity to positions on the other side of the scale from one's own. If ideological commitment plays an important part in the process of developing effective policy, one must bear in mind that both left and right have important parts to play. The left provides the cutting edge of innovation, the capacity to isolate and identify those aspects of existing systems which are least adaptive, and the imagination and vision to devise new modes and new instrumentalities for accommodating emergent conditions. The right has the capacity to sense those elements of the established order that have strength, value, or continuing usefulness, to serve as a brake on over-rapid alteration of existing modes of adaptation, and to use what is valid in the past as a guide to the future. Through the dynamic clash between the two forces, new and valid adaptations may emerge.

None of us can free himself from the influence of ideological predilections, nor are we certain that it would be desirable to do so. But the purposes of effective policy and practice are not served when we are unable to recognize in opposing positions the degree of legitimacy, validity, and humane intent they may possess. It does not seem unreasonable to ask of those engaged in the demanding task of formulating and implementing criminal justice policy that they accord to differing positions that measure of respect and consideration that the true idealogue can never grant.

APPENDIX

Chart I

Sources of Crime: Locus of Responsibility

Left

5. Behavior designated as "crime" by the ruling classes is an inevitable product of a fundamentally corrupt and unjust society. True crime is the behavior of those who perpetuate, control, and profit from an exploitative and brutalizing system. The behavior of those commonly regarded as "criminals" by establishment circles in fact represents heroic defiance and rebellion against the arbitrary and self-serving rules of an immoral social order. These persons thus bear no responsibility for what the state defines as crime; they are forced into such actions as justifiable responses to deliberate policies of oppression, discrimination, and exploitation.

4. Those who engage in the more common forms of theft and other forms of "street crime" are essentially forced into such behavior by a destructive set of social conditions caused by a grossly inequitable distribution of wealth, power, and privilege. These people are actually victims, rather than perpetrators of criminality; they are victimized by discrimination, segregation, denial of opportunity, denial of justice and equal rights. Their behavior is thus a perfectly understandable and justified reac-

Right

5. Crime and violence are a direct product of a massive conspiracy by highly-organized and well-financed radical forces seeking deliberately to overthrow the society. Their basic method is an intensive and unrelenting attack on the fundamental moral values of the society, and their vehicle is that sector of the populace sufficiently low in intelligence, moral virtue, self-control, and judgment as to serve readily as their puppets by constantly engaging in those violent and predatory crimes best calculated to destroy the social order. Instigators of the conspiracy are most often members of racial or ethnic groups that owe allegiance to and are supported by hostile foreign powers.

4. The bulk of serious crime is committed by members of certain ethnic and social class categories characterized by defective self-control, self-indulgence, limited time-horizons, and undeveloped moral conscience. The criminal propensities of these classes, which appear repeatedly in successive generations, are nurtured and encouraged by the enormous reluctance of authorities to apply the degree of firm, swift, and decisive punishment which could serve effectively to curb crime.

Chart I—Continued

Left   *Right*

tion to the malign social forces that bring it about. Forms of crime perpetrated by the wealthy and powerful—extensive corruption, taking of massive profits through illicit collusion, outright fraud and embezzlement—along with a pervasive pattern of marginally legal exploitative practices—have far graver social consequences than the relatively minor offenses of the so-called "common" criminal. Yet these forms of crime are virtually ignored and their perpetrators excused or assigned mild penalties, while the great bulk of law-enforcement effort and attention is directed to the hapless victims of the system.

Since criminality is so basic to such persons, social service programs can scarcely hope to affect their behavior, but their low capacity for discrimination makes them unusually susceptible to the appeals of leftists who goad them to commit crimes in order to undermine the society.

3. Public officials and agencies with responsibility for crime and criminals must share with damaging social conditions major blame for criminality. By allocating pitifully inadequate resources to criminal justice agencies the government virtually assures that they will be manned by poorly qualified, punitive, moralistic personnel who are granted vast amounts of arbitrary coercive power. These persons use this power to stigmatize, degrade and brutalize those who come under their jurisdiction, thus permitting them few options other than continued criminality. Society also manifests enormous reluctance to allocate the resources necessary to ameliorate the root social causes of crime—poverty, urban deterioration, blocked educational and job opportunities—and further enhances crime by maintaining widespread systems of segregation—separating race from race, the poor from the affluent, the deviant from the conventional and the criminal from the law-abiding.

3. The root cause of crime is a massive erosion of the fundamental moral values which traditionally have served to deter criminality, and a concomitant flouting of the established authority which has traditionally served to constrain it. The most extreme manifestations of this phenomenon are found among the most crime-prone sectors of the society—the young, minorities, and the poor. Among these groups and elsewhere there have arisen special sets of alternative values or "countercultures" which actually provide direct support for the violation of the legal and moral norms of law-abiding society. A major role in the alarming increase in crime and violence is played by certain elitist groups of left-oriented media writers, educators, jurists, lawyers, and others who contribute directly to criminality by publicizing, disseminating, and supporting these crime-engendering values.

Chart I—Continued

Left

Right

2. Although the root causes of crime lie in the disabling consequences of social, economic, and educational deprivation concentrated primarily among the disadvantaged in low-income communities, criminal behavior is in fact widely prevalent among all sectors of the society, with many affluent people committing crimes such as shoplifting, drunkenness, forgery, embezzlement, and the like. The fact that most of those subject to arrest and imprisonment have low-income or minority backgrounds is a direct consequence of an inequitable and discriminatory application of the criminal justice process—whereby the offenses of the more affluent are ignored, suppressed, or treated outside of a criminal framework, while those of the poor are actively prosecuted. A very substantial portion of the crime dealt with by officials must in fact be attributed to the nature of the criminal statutes themselves. A wide range of commonly pursued forms of behavior such as use of drugs, gambling, sexual deviance—are defined and handled as "crime," when in fact they should be seen as "victimless" and subject to private discretion. Further, a substantial portion of these and other forms of illegal behavior actually reflect illness—physical or emotional disturbance rather than criminality.

2. A climate of growing permissiveness and stress on immediate personal gratification are progressively undermining the basic deterrents to criminal behavior—self-discipline, responsibility, and a well-developed moral conscience. The prevalent tendency by liberals to attribute blame for criminality to "the system" and its inequities serves directly to aggravate criminality by providing the criminal with a fallacious rationalization which enables him to excuse his criminal behavior, further eroding self-discipline and moral conscience.

1. Crime is largely a product of social ills such as poverty, unemployment, poor quality education, and unequal opportunities. While those who commit crimes out of financial need or frustration with their life conditions deserve understanding and compassion, those who continue to commit crimes in the absence of adequate justification should in some de-

1. The behavior of persons who habitually violate the law is caused by defective upbringing in the home, parental neglect, inadequate religious and moral training, poor neighborhood environment, and lack of adequate role-models. These conditions result in a lack of proper respect for the law and insufficient attention to the basic moral principles which deter

Chart I—Continued

Left

gree be held accountable for their behavior; very often they are sick or disturbed persons who need help rather than punishment. Officials dealing with crime are often well-meaning, but they sometimes act unjustly or repressively out of an excessively narrow focus on specific objectives of law-enforcement. Such behavior in turn reflects frustration with the failure of society to provide them adequate resources to perform their tasks for which they are responsible, as it also fails to provide the resources needed to ameliorate the community conditions which breed crime.

Right

criminality. The federal government also contributes by failing to provide local agencies of prevention and law-enforcement with sufficient resources to perform adequately the many tasks required to reduce or control crime.

Chart II

Modes of Dealing With Crime: Policies With Respect to Offenders

Left

5. Since the bulk of acts defined as "crime" by the ruling classes simply represent behavior which threatens an invalid and immoral social system, those who engage in such acts can in no sense be regarded as culpable, or "criminal." There is thus no legitimate basis for any claim of official jurisdiction over, let alone any right to restrain, so-called offenders. Persons engaging in acts which help to hasten the inevitable collapse of a decadent system should have full and unrestrained freedom to continue such acts, and to be provided the maximum support and backing of all progressive elements. The vast bulk of those now incarcerated must be considered as political prisoners, unjustly deprived of freedom by a corrupt regime, and freed at once.

Right

5. Habitual criminals, criminal types, and those who incite them should bear the full brunt of social retribution, and be prevented by the most forceful means possible from further endangering society. Murderers, rapists, arsonists, armed robbers, subversives and the like should be promptly and expeditiously put to death. The more vicious and unregenerate of these criminals should be publicly executed as an example to others. To prevent future crimes, those classes of persons who persistently manifest a high propensity for criminality should be prevented from reproducing, through sterilization or other means. Those who persist in crimes calculated to undermine the social order should be completely and permanently removed from the society, preferably by deportation.

Chart II—Continued

Left

4. All but a very small proportion of those who come under the jurisdiction of criminal justice agencies pose no real danger to society, and are entitled to full and unconditional freedom in the community at all stages of the criminal justice process. The state must insure that those accused of crimes, incarcerated, or in any way under legal jurisdiction be granted their full civil rights as citizens, and should make available to them at little or no cost the full range of legal and other resources necessary to protect them against the arbitrary exercise of coercive power. Criminal justice processing as currently conducted is essentially brutalizing—particularly institutional incarceration, which seriously aggravates criminality, and which should be entirely abolished. "Rehabilitation" under institutional auspices is a complete illusion; it has not worked, never will work, and must be abandoned as a policy objective. Accused persons, prisoners, and members of the general public subject to the arbitrary and punitive policies of police and other officials must be provided full rights and resources to protect their interests—including citizen control of police operations, full access to legal resources, fully developed grievance mechanisms, and the like.

3. Since contacts with criminal justice officials—particularly police and corrections personnel—increase the likelihood that persons will engage in crime, a major objective must be to divert the maximum number of persons away from criminal justice agencies and into service programs in the com-

Right

4. Dangerous or habitual criminals should be subject to genuine punishment of maximum severity, including capital punishment where called for, and extended prison terms (including life imprisonment) with airtight guarantees that these be fully served. Probation and parole defeat the purposes of public protection and should be eliminated. Potential and less-habituated criminals might well be deterred from future crime by highly visible public punishment such as flogging, the stocks, and possibly physical marking or mutilation. To speak of "rights" of persons who have chosen deliberately to forfeit them by engaging in crime is a travesty, and malefactors should receive the punishment they deserve without interference by leftists working to obstruct the processes of justice. "Rehabilitation" as a policy objective is simply a weakly disguised method of pampering criminals, and has no place whatever in a proper system of criminal justice. Fully adequate facilities for detection, apprehension, and effective restraint of criminals should be granted those police and other criminal justice personnel who realize that their principal mission is swift and unequivocal retribution against wrongdoers and their permanent removal from society to secure the full protection of the law-abiding.

3. Rampant permissiveness and widespread coddling of criminals defeat the purposes of crime control and must be stopped. Those who persist in the commission of serious crime and whose behavior endangers the public safety should be dealt with firmly, decisively and forcefully. A policy of strict pun-

Chart II—Continued

Left

Right

munity—the proper arena for helping offenders. There should be
maximum use of probation as an
alternative to incarceration, and
parole as an alternative to extended incarceration. However,
both services must be drastically
overhauled, and transformed from
ineffective watchdog operations
manned by low-quality personnel
to genuine and effective human
services. Institutionalization
should be the alternative of last
resort, and used only for those
proven to be highly dangerous, or
for whom services cannot be provided outside of an institutional
context. Those confined must be
afforded the same civil rights as
all citizens, including full access to
legal resources and to officially-
compiled information, fully-oper-
ational grievance mechanisms,
right of petition and appeal from
official decisions. Every attempt
must be made to minimize the
separation between institution and
community by providing frequent
leaves, work-release furloughs, full
visitation rights, full access to citizen's groups. Full rights and the
guarantee of due process must be
provided for all those accused of
crimes—particularly juveniles,
minorities, and the underprivileged.

ishment is necessary not only because it is deserved by offenders
but also because it serves effectively to deter potential criminals
among the general public. A major
effort must be directed toward increasing the rights and resources of
officials who cope with crime, and
decreasing the rights and resources
—legal, statutory, and financial—of
those who use them to evade or
avoid deserved punishment. Prede-
tention measures such as bail, suspended sentences and probation
should be used only when it is certain that giving freedom to actual
or putative criminals will not jeopardize public safety, and parole
should be employed sparingly and
with great caution only in those
cases where true rehabilitation
seems assured. The major objective
both of incarceration and rehabilitation efforts must be the protection of law-abiding society, not
the welfare of the offender.

2. Since the behavior of most of
those who commit crimes is symptomatic of social or psychological
forces over which they have little
control, ameliorative efforts must
be conducted within the framework of a comprehensive strategy
of services which combines indi-
vidually-oriented clinical services
and beneficial social programs.
Such services should be offered in
whatever context they can most
effectively be rendered, although

2. Lawbreakers should be subject to
fair but firm penalties based primarily on the protection of society, but taking into account as
well the future of the offender.
Successful rehabilitation is an important objective since a reformed
criminal no longer presents a
threat to society. Rehabilitation
should center on the moral re-
education of the offender, and instill in him the respect for authority and basic moral values which

Chart II—Continued

Left

the community is generally preferable to the institution. However, institutional programs organized around the concept of the therapeutic community can be most effective in helping certain kinds of persons, such as drug users, for whom external constraints can be a useful part of the rehabilitative process. Rehabilitation rather than punishment must be the major objective in dealing with offenders. Treatment in the community—in group homes, halfway houses, court clinics, on probation or parole—must incorporate the maximum range of services, including vocational training and placement, psychological testing and counseling, and other services which presently are either unavailable or woefully inadequate in most communities. Where imprisonment is indicated, sentences should be as short as possible, and inmates should be accorded the rights and respect due all human beings.

1. Effective methods for dealing with actual or putative offenders require well-developed and sophisticated methods for discriminating among varying categories of persons, and gearing treatment to the differential needs of the several types thus discriminated. A major goal is to insure that those most likely to benefit from psychological counseling and other therapeutic methods will receive the kinds of treatment they need, rather than wasting therapeutic resources on that relatively small group of offenders whose behavior is essentially beyond reform, and are poor candidates for rehabilitation. All those under the jurisdiction of criminal justice agencies should be treated equitably and

Right

are the best safeguards against continued crime. These aims can be furthered by prison programs which demand hard work and strict discipline, for these serve to promote good work habits and strengthen moral fiber. Sentences should be sufficiently long as to both adequately penalize the offender and insure sufficient time for effective rehabilitation. Probation and parole should not be granted indiscriminately, but reserved for carefully selected offenders, both to protect society and because it is difficult to achieve the degree of close and careful supervision necessary to successful rehabilitation outside the confines of the institution.

1. An essential component of any effective method for dealing with violators is a capability for making careful and sensitive discriminations among various categories of offenders, and tailoring appropriate dispositional measures to different types of offenders. In particular, the capacity to differentiate between those with a good potential for reform and those with a poor potential will insure that the more dangerous kinds of criminals are effectively restrained. Probationers and parolees should be subject to close and careful supervision both to make sure that their activities contribute to their rehabilitation and that the community is protected from repeat violations by

Chart II Continued

Left

humanely. Police in particular
should treat their clients with
fairness and respect—especially
members of minority groups and
the disadvantaged. Careful consideration should be given before
sentencing offenders to extended
prison terms to make sure that
other alternatives are not possible.
Similarly, probation and parole
should be used in those cases
where these statutes appear likely
to facilitate rehabilitation without endangering public safety.
Prisoners should not be denied
contact with the outside world,
but should have rights to correspondence, visiting privileges, and
access to printed and electronic
media. They should also be provided with facilities for constructive use of leisure time, and program activities aimed to enhance
the likelihood of rehabilitation.

Right

those under official jurisdiction.
Time spent in prison should be
used to teach inmates useful skills
so that they may re-enter society
as well-trained and productive
individuals.

Chart III

Modes of Dealing with Crime:
Policies with Respect to Criminal Justice Agencies

Left

5. The whole apparatus of so-called
"law-enforcement" is in fact
simply the domestic military apparatus used by the ruling classes
to maintain themselves in power,
and to inflict harassment, confinement, injury or death on those
who protest injustice by challenging the arbitrary regulations devised by the militarists and mon-
opolists to protect their interests.
To talk of "reforming" such a
system is farcical; the only con-
ceivable method of eliminating
the intolerable injustices inherent
in this kind of society is the total
and forceful overthrow of the entire system, including its so-called

Right

5. Maximum possible resources
must be provided those law-
enforcement officials who
realize that their basic mission is
the protection of society and
maintenance of security for the
law-abiding citizen. In addition to
substantial increases in manpower,
law-enforcement personnel must
be provided with the most modern,
efficient and lethal weaponry
available, and the technological
capacity (communications, com-
puterization, electronic surveillance, aerial pursuit capability) to
deliver maximum force and facilities possible to points of need—the
detection, pursuit, and arrest of

Chart III—Continued

Left

"law-enforcement" arm. All acts which serve this end, including elimination of members of the oppressor police force, serve to hasten the inevitable collapse of the system and the victory of progressive forces.

4. The entire American system of criminal justice must be radically reformed. Unless there is a drastic reduction in the amount of power now at the disposal of official agencies—particularly the police and corrections, a police state is inevitable. In particular, unchecked power currently possessed by poorly qualified, politically reactionary officials to deal with accused and suspected persons as they see fit must be curtailed; their behavior brutalizes and radicalizes the clients of the system. To these officials, "dangerous" usually means "politically unacceptable." Increasing concentration of power in entrenched bureaucracies must be checked, and the people given maximum rights to local control of their own lives, including the right to self-protection through associations such as citizens councils and security patrols to counter police harassment and brutality and to monitor the operations of local prisons. Means must be found to eliminate the extensive corruption which pervades the system—exemplified by venal criminality within police departments and the unholy alliance between organized crime, corrupt politicians, and those who are supposedly enforcing the laws. Most of the criminal offenses now on the books should be eliminated, retaining only a few truly dangerous crimes such as forceful rape, since most of the offenses which consume law-enforcement

Right

criminals, and in particular the control of terrorism and violence conducted or incited by radical forces.

4. The critical crime situation requires massive increases in the size of police forces and their technological capacity to curb crime—particularly in the use of force against criminals and radical elements. It is imperative that police command full freedom to use all available resources, legal and technical, without interference from leftist elements seeking to tie their hands and render them impotent. The power of the courts to undermine the basis of police operations by denying them fundamental legal powers must be curbed. The nation's capacity for incarcerating criminals—particularly through maximum security facilties—must be greatly expanded, and prison security strengthened. The "prison reform" movement rests on a mindless focus on the welfare of convicted felons and a blind disregard for the welfare of law-abiding citizens. Particularly pernicious is the movement now underway to unload thousands of dangerous criminals directly into our communities under the guise of "community corrections" (halfway houses, group homes, etc.). The local citizenry must unite and forcefully block this effort to flood our homes and playgrounds with criminals, dope addicts, and subversives. Increasing concentration of power in the hands of centralized government must be stopped, and basic rights returned to the local community—including

Chart III—Continued

Left

Right

energies have no real victims, and should be left to private conscience. However, statutes related to illegality by business interests, bureaucrats, corporations and the like should be expanded, and enforcement efforts greatly increased. Virtually all prisons should be closed at once, and the few persons requiring institutional restraint should be accommodated in small facilities in local communities.

the right to exclude dangerous and undesirable elements, and the right to bear arms freely in defense of home and family. Strict curbs must be imposed on the freedom of the media to disseminate materials aimed to undermine morality and encourage crime.

3. The more efficiency gained by law enforcement agenices through improvements in technology, communications, management, and so on, the greater the likelihood of harassment, intimidation, and discrimination directed against the poor and minorities. Improvements in police services can be achieved only through fundamental and extensive changes in the character of personnel, not through more hardware and technology. This should be achieved by abandoning antiquated selection and recruitment policies which are designed to obtain secure employment for low-quality personnel and which systematically discriminate against the minorities and culturally disadvantaged. Lateral entry, culture-free qualification tests, and other means must be used to loosen the iron grip of civil-service selection and tenure systems. The outmoded military model with its rigid hierarchical distinctions found among the police and other agencies should be eliminated, and a democratic organizational model put in its place. The police must see their proper function as service to the community rather than in narrow terms of law-enforcement. As part of their community re-

3. Law enforcement agencies must be provided all the resources necessary to deal promptly and decisively with crime and violence. Failure to so act encourages further law breaking both by those who are subject to permissive and inefficient handling and by those who become aware thereby how little risk they run of being caught and penalized for serious crimes. The rights of the police to stringently and effectively enforce the law must be protected from misguided legalistic interference— particularly the constant practice of many judges of granting freedom to genuine criminals laboriously apprehended by the police, often on the basis of picayune procedural details related to "due process" or other legalistic devices for impeding justice. The scope of the criminal law must be expanded rather than reduced; there is no such thing as "victimless" crime; the welfare of all law-abiding people and the moral basis of society iself are victimized by crimes such as pornography, prostitution, homosexuality and drug use, and offenders must be vigorously pursued, prosecuted, and penalized. Attempts to prevent crime by pouring massive amounts of tax dollars into slum communi-

Chart III—Continued

Left

sponsibility, law enforcement agencies should stringently limit access to information concerning offenders, especially younger ones, and much of such information should be destroyed. There must be maximum public access to the inner operations of police, courts and prisons by insuring full flow of information to the media, full accountability to and visitation rights by citizens and citizen groups, and full public disclosure of operational policies and operations. The major burden of corrections should be removed from the institutions, which are crime-breeding and dehumanizing, and placed directly in the communities, to which all offenders must at some point return.

ties are worse than useless, since such people can absorb limitless welfare "benefits" with no appreciable effect on their criminal propensities. Communities must resist attempts to open up their streets and homes to hardened criminals through halfway houses and other forms of "community corrections."

2. A basic need of the criminal justice system is an extensive upgrading of the quality of personnel. This must be done by recruiting better qualified people—preferably with college training, in all branches and at all levels, and by mounting effective in-service training programs. Higher quality and better trained personnel are of particular importance in the case of the police, and training must place more stress on human relations studies such as psychology and sociology, and relatively less stress on purely technical aspects of police work. Quality must be maintained by the development and application of performance standards against which all personnel must be periodically measured, and which should provide the basis for promotion. Sentencing procedures must be standardized, rationalized, and geared to specific and explicit rehabilitative objectives rather than being left to the often arbitrary and capri-

2. There should be substantial increases in the numbers and visibility of police, particularly in and around schools, places of business, and areas of family activity. Although a few bad apples may appear from time to time, the bulk of our police are conscientious and upstanding men who deserve the continued respect and support of the community, and who should be granted ample resources to do the job to which they are assigned. Some of the proposed prison reforms may be commendable, but the burden to the taxpayer must never be lost sight of: most of the reforms suggested or already in practice are of dubious benefit or yield benefits clearly not commensurate with their costs. More effort should be directed to prevention of crime; in particular, programs of moral re-education in the schools and communities, and the institution of safeguards against the influence of those in the schools, media and elsewhere

Chart III–Continued

Left

cious whims of particular judges.
Corrections as well as other criminal justice agencies must be
made more humane and equitable, and the rights of prisoners
as individuals should be respected.
Attempts should be made to reduce the degree of separation of
prison inmates from the outside
world. Changes in both legislation
and law enforcement policies
must be directed to reducing the
disparities in arrest rates between
richer and poorer offenders, so
that commensurately fewer of
the poor and underprivileged and
more of the better off, are sought
out, convicted, and imprisoned.
Promising programs of humane
reform must not be abandoned
simply because they fail to show
immediate measurable results, but
should receive continued or increased federal support.

1. There must be better coordination of existing criminal justice
   facilities and functions so as to
   better focus available services on
   the whole individual, rather than
   treating him through disparate and
   compartmentalized efforts. This
   must entail better liaison between
   police, courts and corrections and
   greatly improved lines of communication, to the end of enabling
   each to attain better appreciation,
   understanding and knowledge of
   the operational problems of the
   others. Coordination and liaison
   must also increase between the
   criminal justice agencies and the
   general welfare services of the
   community, which have much to
   contribute both in the way of prevention of crime and rehabilitation of criminals. Local politicians
   often frustrate the purposes of
   reform by consuming resources in
   patronage, graft, and the financial

Right

who promote criminality by
challenging and rejecting the
established moral values which
serve to forestall illegal and immoral conduct.

1. The operations of the police
   should be made more efficient, in
   part through increased use of
   modern managerial principles and
   information processing techniques.
   Police protection should focus
   more directly on the local community, and efforts should be
   made to restore the degree of personal moral integrity and intimate
   knowledge of the local community which many older policemen
   had but many younger ones lack.
   Prison reform is important, but
   innovations should be instituted
   gradually and with great caution,
   and the old should not be dis-
   carded until the new is fully
   proven to be adequate. There
   should be much better coordination among law enforcement
   agencies, to reduce inefficiency,
   wasteful overlap, and duplication
   of services. The federal government must assume a major role in

Chart III—Continued

Left

support of entrenched local interests, so the federal government must take the lead in financing and overseeing criminal justice reform efforts. Federal resources and standards should be utilized to substantially increase the level and quality of social service resources available to criminal justice enterprises, promulgate standardized and rationalized modes of operation in local communities, and bring administrative coherence to the host of uncoordinated efforts now in progress.

providing the leadership and financial resources necessary to effective law-enforcement and crime control.

NOTES

[1]A few examples of perceptions that "our times" are witnessing radical or unprecedented changes are found in selected excerpts from statements published in 1874, 1930, and 1939, respectively.

> Society has grave charges to answer in regard to its influence on the present and rising generation.... The social conditions of the present age are such as to favor the development of insanity. The habits inculcated by ... growing wealth ... among individuals of one class and the stinging poverty ... of another ... nurture dispositions which might ... under more equitable distributions ... have died out. Have we not seen [youth] emerging from the restraints of school, scoffing at the opinions of the world, flouting everything but their own conceit ...?

Dickson, *The Science and Practice of Medicine in Relation to Mind, and the Jurisprudence of Insanity* (1874), quoted in M. Altschule, "Roots of Modern Psychiatry" 122, 133 (1957).

> In our nineteenth century polity, the home was a chief reliance ... discipline was recognized as a reality ... the pressure of the neighborhood ... was strong ... in the urban industrial society of today there is a radical change.... This complete change in the background of social control involves much that may be easily attributed to the ineffectiveness of criminal justice....

Pound, *Criminal Justice in America* (1930), quoted in F. Tannenbaum, "Crime and the Community" 29 (1938).

> Men's ways of ordering their common lives have broken down so disastrously as to make hope precarious. So headlong and pervasive is change today that ... historical parallels are decreasingly relevant ... because so many of the variables in the situation have altered radically.... Professor James T. Shotwell recently characterized "the anarchy we are living in today" as "the most dangerous since the fall of Rome."

R. Lynd, "Knowledge for What" 2, 11 (1939).

[2]An analysis involving long-term trends in youth gang violence and periodically recurrent representations of such violence as a new phenomenon engendered by contemporary conditions is included in Miller, *American Youth Gangs: Past and Present,* in A. Blumberg, "Issues in Criminology" (in preparation).

[3]G. Myrdal, "An American Dilemma: The Negro Problem and Modern Democracy, 1038 (1944). Myrdal's citation of the "radicalism-conservatism" scale is part of an extended discussion of sources of bias in works on race-relations, appearing as Appendix 2, "A Methodological Note on Facts and Valuations in Social Science," at 1035-64. His entire discussion is germane to issues treated in this article.

[4]A classic treatment of ideology is K. Mannheim, "Ideology and Utopia" (1936). *See* ch. II.1 "Definition of Concepts." *See also* G. Myrdal, *supra* note 3, at 1035-64. There is an extensive literature, much of it sociological, dealing with ideology as it relates to a wide range of political and social phenomena, but the specific relation between ideology and criminal justice has received relatively little direct attention. Among more recent general discussions are E. Shils, "The Intellectuals and the Powers" (1972); Orlans, *The Political Uses of Social Research*, 393 "Annals Am. Acad. Polit. & Soc. Sci." 29 (1971); Kelman, *I.Q., Race, and Public Debate*, 2 Hastings Center Rep. 8 (1972). Treatments more specific to crime and criminal justice appear in L. Radzinowicz, "Ideology and Crime" (1966); Andanaes, *Punishment and the Problem of General Prevention*, 8 "Int'l. Annals Criminology" 285 (1969); Blumberg, *The Adversary System*, in C. Bersani, "Crime & Delinq." 435 (1970); Glaser, *Criminology and Public Policy*, 6 "Am. Sociologist" 30 (1971).

[5]The substance of ideologically-relevant statements formulated here as crusading issues, general assumptions, or differentiated positions was derived from examination and analysis of a wide range of materials appearing in diverse forms in diverse sources. Materials were selected primarily on the basis of two criteria: that they bear on issues of current relevance to criminal justice policy, and that they represent one possible stance with respect to issues characterized by markedly divergent stances. With few exceptions, the statements as formulated here do not represent direct quotes, but have been generalized, abstracted or paraphrased from one or more sets of statements by one or more representatives of positions along the ideological scale. A substantial portion of the statements thus derived were taken from books, articles, speeches, and media reporting of statements by the following: Robert Welch, writer; John Schmitz, legislator; Gerald L. K. Smith, writer; Meyer Kahane, clergyman; Edward Banfield, political scientist; William Loeb, publisher; George Wallace, government; Julius Hoffman, jurist; L. Patrick Gray III, lawyer; William Rehnquist, jurist; William Buckley, writer; Spiro Agnew, government; Robert M. McKiernan, police; Howard J. Phillips, government; Lewis F. Powell Jr., jurist; Andrew Hacker, political scientist; Kevin Phillips, writer; Victor Reisel, labor; Albert Shanker, educator; Fred P. Graham, lawyer/ writer; Warren Burger, jurist; James Q. Wilson, political scientist; Hubert H. Humphrey, legislator; James Reston, writer; Jacob Javits, legislator; Ramsey Clark, lawyer; Tom Wicker, writer; Earl Warren, jurist; James F. Ahearn, police; Henry Steele Commager, historian; Alan Dershowitz, lawyer; Julian Bond, legislator; Herbert J. Gans, sociologist; Ross K. Baker, political scientist; Russell Baker, writer; William Kunstler, lawyer; Benjamin Spock, physician; Noam Chomsky, anthropologist; Richard Cloward, sociologist; Herman Schwartz, lawyer; Richard Korn, sociologist; Michael Harrington, writer; Richard Quinney, sociologist; Frank Reissman, sociologist; Tom Hayden, writer; Eldridge Cleaver, writer; H. Bruce Franklin, professor; Abbie Hoffman, writer; Phillip Berrigan, clergyman; Jerry Rubin, writer. Among a range of non-academic reports, pamphlets, and periodicals which served as sources for statements by these and other persons were: John Birch Society Reprint Series; Ergo: The Rational Voice of Libertarianism; New Solidarity: National Caucus of Labor Committees; The Hastings Center Report; S.D.S. New Left Notes; Guardian; Ramparts; National Review; The Nation; The New Republic; The New York Review; Commentary; Fortune; Time; Life; Newsweek; New York Times; New York Times Magazine; The Washington Post; The Manchester Union Leader. It should be noted that the substance of materials appearing in published sources represents the publicly-taken positions of the individuals involved. The relation between public positions and "actual" or private positions can be very complex, ranging from "close" to "distant" along a "degree of correspondence" axis, and with variation involving changes over time, differences according to the subissue involved, nature of audience addressed, and other factors.

[6]The classic application of ideal-type method is that of Max Weber. *See, e.g.,* the discussion of Weber's method and typology of authority and coordination in A. Henderson & T. Parsons, Max Weber: "The Theory of Social and Economic Organization" 98, 329 (1947). In the field of criminology, MacIver applies ideal-type analysis to discussions of social causality in general and crime causality in particular. R. MacIver, "Social Causation," 174 *passim* (1942). Neither of these applications directly parallels present usage, but underlying principles are similar.

[7]Several recent studies provide indirect evidence of differences between academics

and the general public in the likelihood that one will characterize his ideological position as "right" or "left." Of 60,000 professors surveyed by the Carnegie Commission, approximately 70% characterized themselves as "left" or "liberal," and fewer than 25% as "conservative" or "middle-of-the-road." A survey of social science professors by Everett Ladd and Seymour Lipset showed that approximately 70% voted against the "conservative" presidential candidate in 1972, compared with approximately 75% against four years before. These studies were reported in Hacker, *On Original Sin and Conservatives*, N.Y. Times, Feb. 25, 1973, § 6 (Magazine) at 13. Henry Turner and Carl Hetrick's survey of a systematic sample of members of the American Political Science Association showed that approximately 75% characterized themselves as Democrats (among academics "Democratic" almost invariably means "liberal," whereas it generally means "conservative" in blue collar populations), a percentage which has remained stable for ten years. Those designating themselves as "Republicans" had declined to about 10% at the time of the survey. Turner and Hetrick's survey also showed that the Democratic majority was significantly more active in publication and political activity than the non-Democratic minority. H. Turner & C. Hetrick, "Political Activities and Party Affiliations of American Political Scientists," (paper delivered at the 1971 Meetings of the American Political Science Association).

By comparison, a Gallup survey conducted in 1972 found that 71% of a systematically-selected sample of voters designated themselves as "conservative" (41%) or "middle-of-the road" (30%), with 24% characterizing themselves as "liberal." A survey by Daniel Yankelovich during the same period found that 75% of the voters surveyed viewed themselves as "conservative" (37%) or "moderate" (38%), and 17% as "liberal" (15%) or "radical" (2%). *See* Rosenthal, *McGovern is Radical or Liberal to Many in Polls*, N.Y. Times, Aug. 27, 1972, at 34, col. 3. An earlier poll by Yankelovich of American college students, seen by many as among the most liberal of large population categories, showed that approximately 70% reported themselves as holding "mainstream" positions, and that among the remainder, conservatives outnumbered left-wing radicals by two-to-one. D. Yankelovich, "The Changing Values on Campus: Political and Personal Attitudes of Today's College Students" (1972).

[8]Hacker states that ". . . the higher one climbs on the prestige ladder [of American colleges and universities] the less likely are conservatives to be found on the faculty." Hacker, *supra* note 7, at 71.

[9]Issues involved here fall into two general clusters: those affecting the rights and resources available to law-enforcement officials relative to those available to persons suspected, accused, or convicted of crimes; those relating to the conceptual or physical separation or combining of major population categories. Stands of the right and left with respect to the first cluster have been delineated in several places (right crusading issue 2; left general assumptions 3, 5; right policies respecting offenders 3, 4, respecting agencies 3, 4; left policies respecting offenders 3, 4, respecting agencies 3, 4). Major decisions of the United States Supreme Court during the 1960's which appear to accord with ideological stances of the left and to run counter to those of the right include: Mapp v. Ohio, 367 U.S. 643 (1961), which reduced resources available to law-enforcement officials and increased resources available to the accused by extending limitations on the admissibility of illegally-obtained evidence; Escobedo v. Illinois, 378 U.S. 478 (1964), and Miranda v. Arizona, 384 U.S. 436 (1966), which reduced the power of law-enforcement officials to proceed with criminal processing without providing suspects with knowledge of and recourse to legal rights and resources; *In re* Gault, 387 U.S. 1 (1967), which reduced the power of judges to make dispositions in juvenile proceedings and increased the legal rights and resources of defendants; Katz v. United States, 389 U.S. 347 (1967), which reduced prerogatives of law-enforcement officials with respect to the gathering of evidence by increasing protection of suspects against intrusions of privacy; Gilbert v. California, 388 U.S. 263 (1967), and United States v. Wade, 388 U.S. 218 (1967), which decreased the freedom of law enforcement officials to seek identification of suspects, and increased the legal rights and resources available to suspects.

With respect to the second cluster, separation of population categories, stands of the right are delineated under general assumption 5, sources of crime 4, policies respecting criminal justice agencies 4, and of the left under crusading issue 5 and general assumption 4. The landmark decision here was Brown v. Board of Education, 347 U.S. 483 (1954), which held that racially segregated public education was *per se* discriminatory. While preceding the above-cited decisions by about a decade, *Brown* set a precedent for later court actions which provided support for the diminution of categorical segregation, as favored by the left, and reduced support for the maintenance of such separation, as espoused by the right.

[10]It has been widely held that the Burger Court, reflecting the influence of right-oriented Nixon appointees such as Justices Rehnquist and Powell, would evince marked support for rightist ideological premises, stopping or reversing many of the initiatives of the Warren Court in areas such as equal protection and due process. This viewpoint is articulated by Fred P. Graham, who writes, "Mr. Nixon's two new justices are strikingly like his first two appointments in conservative judicial outlook, and . . . this cohesion is likely to produce a marked swing to the right–particularly on criminal law issues. . . ." Graham, *Profile of the "Nixon Court" Now Discernible*, N.Y. Times, May 24, 1972, at 28, col. 3. *See also* Graham, *Supreme Court, in Recent Term, Began Swing to Right That Was Sought by Nixon*, N.Y. Times, July 2, 1972, at 18, col. 1; *Nixon Appointees May Shift Court on Obscenity and Business*, N.Y. Times, October 2, 1972, at 16, col. 4. However, Gerald Gunther, in a careful review of the 1971 term of the Burger court, characterizes the court essentially as holding the line rather than moving to reverse the directions of the Warren Court or moving in new directions of its own. Gunther writes "There was no drastic rush to the right. The changes were marginal. . . . The new Court . . . has shown no inclination to overturn clear, carefully explained precedent." Gunther, *The Supreme Court 1971 Term, Foreword: In Search of Evolving Doctrine on a Changing Court: A Model for Newer Equal Protection*, 86 Harv. L. Rev., 1, 2-3 (1972). *Cf.* Goldberg, *Supreme Court Review 1972, Foreword–The Burger Court 1971 Term: One Step Forward, Two Steps Backward?*, 63 J. Crim. L.C. & P.S. 463 (1972). Although the court has shown an inclination to limit and specify some of the broader decisions of the Warren Court (*e.g.*, limiting rights to counsel at line-ups as dealt with in *Gilbert* and *Wade, see* Graham, July 2, 1972, *supra*), there does not appear at the time of writing any pronounced tendency to reverse major thrusts of Warren Court decisions relevant to presently-considered ideological issues, but rather to curb or limit momentum in these directions.

[11]Wilkins, *Crime in the World of 1990,* 4 Futures 203 (1970).

[12]The classic formulations of the distinction between "factual" and "evaluative" content of statements about human behavior are those of Max Weber. *See, e.g.,* A. Henderson & T. Parsons, *supra* note 6, at 8 *passim. See also* G. Myrdal, *supra* note 3.

CONSERVATIVE, LIBERAL AND RADICAL CRIMINOLOGY: SOME TRENDS AND OBSERVATIONS

DON C. GIBBONS AND PETER GARABEDIAN

INTRODUCTION

There are a good many critical observations which could be made about the current state of criminology, some dealing with the lack of conceptual and logical rigor in this field, others centering about substantive theoretical short-comings. Regarding the first point, Lachenmeyer's commentary about the language problems of sociology applies with equal force to criminological writing.[1] We still have a long way to go before our conceptual language is precise enough that it can truly be said that we know exactly what we are talking about, both in sociology generally and in criminology specifically. Sociological writing continues to resemble evocative poetry at least as much as it parallels crisp, lucid scientific prose.

However, it seems safe to assume that criminologists share enough of a general perspective or point of view and a language of discourse that we can address substantive issues with some measure of common understanding. The task of this brief paper is to suggest that even as criminological analysis has changed over the decades from a conservative posture to a dominant liberal-cynical one, some further shifting in the direction of radical criminology is now discernible. Further, some of the implications of a radically oriented criminology are explored in this essay.

Let us point out that these labels, conservative, liberal-cynical, and radical, do not quite capture the essence of the theoretical postures we wish to describe, but we cannot think of terms that do a better job. More importantly, let us indicate that although our remarks imply that we are identifying distinct schools of thought, we actually wish to draw attention to some points along a continuum of theoretical orientations. Thus it should be noted that "liberal-cynical" is a summary term for a bunch of viewpoints that differ somewhat in specifics. We shall elaborate upon these differences in the remarks to follow. Finally, it is probably also the case that because of the requirement of brevity, we have exaggerated the nature of criminological viewpoints in the characterizations below.

Don C. Gibbons and Peter G. Garabedian, "Conservative, Liberal and Radical Criminology: Some Trends and Observations" Original paper presented to the Rocky Mountain Social Association (April 1972). Reprinted with permission of the authors.

CONSERVATIVE CRIMINOLOGY

By conservative criminology, we mean the kind of endeavor represented in the writings and activities of such persons as Faris,[2] Barnes and Teeters,[3] and a host of other writers in the period up to the 1950s. That brand of criminology was characterized, first, by a relatively *low level of conceptualization.* A "good guy" and "bad guy" image of criminality was often put forward, in which offenders were viewed as persons who were "out of step" in a basically sound society. Take the contents of the widely-used text by Barnes and Teeters. These authors exhibited some degree of anger about organized crime and white-collar criminality, but the overall theme of this work was that criminal offenders are societal misfits produced by deleterious social conditions. A low level of conceptualization was also revealed in the fact that "multiple-factor" theory was often advocated, in which it was asserted that criminality was the result of some stew or admixture of negative social factors.

Some sense of the theoretical posture of Barnes and Teeters can be gained from their comments about vagrants, in which they declare that: "Most vagrants are socially inadequate, whether the offense for which they are arrested is loitering, disorderly conduct, or drunkenness."[4] Or, consider their observations about homosexuality. They tell us:

Certain homosexuals, through biological factors such as inborn glandular anomalies and defects, may be irresistibly impelled to behave as they do. Others are led into this behavior through mistakes and exaggerations in family relations, faulty sex education, accidental sex experiences, the denial of normal sex experiences, and the like. There appears to be no physical foundation for their homosexual trends, but they cannot help being as they are. Homosexuals, then, have been conditioned by their physical make-up, or by peculiar types of environment or experiences.[5]

Conservative criminology often involved some critical observations about the police for the use of the "third degree" and the like, along with some concern about prison conditions and the lack of resources for correctional treatment. However, there was no hint of the modern theme that the police are "pigs," that is, lackeys of an oppressive power structure, or even much recognition of the structural problems of modern police agenices. In general, old-time criminology tended toward *a faith in the ultimate perfectibility of the police and criminal justice machinery.* In this view, if we "throw out the rascals" who currently manage these operations and replace them with "professionals," high-caliber police work and effective correctional therapy would be within our grasp. Also, it is worth noting that a number of the representatives of conservative criminology could be found from time to time acting as consultants to the correctional bureaucracies, serving on parole boards, or participating in other ways in the operations of the criminal justice machinery.

LIBERAL-CYNICAL CRIMINOLOGY

Quite probably, many would agree that the movement toward a sociologically sophisticated brand of criminology became accelerated in the writings of Sutherland, particularly as summarized in his *Principles of Criminology.*[6] We have termed this version of criminological thought "liberal-cynical criminology," for reasons elaborated below.

In most versions of modern criminological analysis, the social order or societal structure is still seen as relatively viable, with little in the way of any suggestion that American society is headed on any course toward total dissolution. However, liberal-cynical criminology acknowledges that the criminogenic influences which produce criminality are exceedingly pervasive and intimately bound up with the core institutions of modern society. In liberal criminology, the task of uncovering etiological influences in lawbreaking requires that we engage in a penetrating examination of many central features of American society. One must now be a first-rate sociologist if he is to be a competent criminologist. Indeed, the theoretical and empirical work that has been produced by criminologists such as Cloward and Ohlin, Cohen, Short, Schrag, Cressey, Hirschi, and a host of others in the past two decades represents modern sociological analysis at its best. The older notion of criminology as some kind of half-baked sociological stepchild has pretty well disappeared with the rise of this liberal brand of criminological inquiry.[7]

Sykes has recently summarized the main directions of modern sociological theorizing about criminality.[8] He claims that three perspectives stand out, including the view that lawbreaking is the result of ordinary learning processes occurring within a criminogenic culture. The paired formulations of Sutherland and Cressey about differential social organization and differential association are the most prominent examples of this argument. A second causal orientation is the social control one, holding that criminality breaks out when personal and social controls become attenuated. Hirschi's study serves as illustrative of this approach.[9] The third argument is the *anomie* one, asserting that criminality is a "normal," innovative response to a situation of cultural discontinuity between ends and means. Sykes also observes:

> When we look at the sociological theories of crime causation that are sketched-in so hurriedly above, they evidently share something of a common viewpoint. They all are inclined to assume that the criminal or the delinquent wants very much of the same thing that everyone wants, and what everyone wants is often said to be money, prestige, and personal aggrandizement, in a kind of bastardized version of the American Dream—for the delinquent, the goals are legitimate but the means used to reach them are deviant. When the criminal behavior is expressive rather than instrumental, as in the case of enraged assault, we are inclined to relegate the offender, as I pointed out before, to the analyst's couch or to the mental hospital.[10]

Several variants of liberal-cynical thought are apparent in contemporary criminology. As one case in point, one of us has recently argued that situational elements need to be given more emphasis in formulations about crime causation, along with more attention to various kinds of relatively mundane "folk crime" in modern societies.[11] This shift in orientation would reduce the emphasis now given to motivational factors thought to distinguish offenders from the rest of us. These notions are consistent with those of the "labeling" school of deviance analysis, in which it is argued that deviant behavior of various kinds arises out of value-pluralism in contemporary society, that initial acts of nonconformity represent cases of "risk-taking" behavior, and that societal responses to the deviant play a major role in determining the subsequent course pursued by him. It would be relatively easy to identify a good number of other recent criminological statements that run parallel to these views.

In a somewhat similar vein, Sykes has recently argued that new forms of criminality are coming to light in the United States and that some fundamental changes in American lawbreaking are now occurring.[12] First, he suggests that crime and delinquency are beginning to emerge as a species of sport or play, in which these activities are engaged in for hedonistic rather than instrumental ends. Automobile theft-joyriding, vandalism, and students defrauding the telephone company by means of elaborate electronic gimmicks come to mind as examples of this kind of criminal mischief.

A second and more ominous form of "new crime," according to Sykes, consists of various kinds of political crime, including assassinations, destruction of draft records, dynamiting of transmission towers, and so forth. Sykes defines political crime as "illegal acts that have as their objective the destruction of the society's system of power, changes of policy by means of violence, or the forceful removal of those exercising power in the system."[13] Crimes of this sort have occurred in the past in this country, of course, but Sykes maintains that crime as a form of political expression bids fair to become much more frequent in the decades ahead.

Rather closely allied to political crime is a third form of "new lawbreaking," revolving around alienation from societal values, in which "breaking the law" becomes an important symbolic gesture, not simply a rationally selected means or act of retaliation directed against a specific person, but a deliberate affront to society as a whole.[14] Trashing, "ripping off" department stores, destruction of property, and other acts of this sort arise out of broad rejection of American values in their entirety, rather than constituting a more limited response to disillusionment with the conventional political processes.

A fourth form of new crime identified by Sykes centers about the violation of laws that most people do not regard as having moral force. Here he draws attention to behavior that is illegal but about which the person feels no sense of right or wrong, so that the decision to engage in it becomes a pragmatic one, that is, the risk of getting caught is the main contingency in the decision. Sykes offers the example of premarital sexual behavior, which is prohibited by law.

Impressionistic indications of political crime and lawbreaking arising out of alienation are around in some quantity. One bit of evidence is found in an essay by Kelly Hancock, dealing with bombing incidents in the United States over the past decade.[15] His data indicate that bombing episodes have become quite common in the past ten years, but it also ought to be noted that his material shows that bombing activities arise out of myriad circumstances, so that only a portion of them can be said to be expressions of political discontent.

These are plausible hypotheses about trends in crime which Sykes offers. In our view, criminological analysis needs to shift attention to these facets of contemporary criminality, away from conventional criminological wisdom which holds that most offenders share common American values and are only engaging in innovative illegality as a means to these ends.

A more extreme departure from earlier liberal modes of criminological argument is represented by the work of Turk[16] and Quinney,[17] among others. These theorists would have us pay less attention to criminal persons and queries like "Why do they do it?" and more attention to criminality and criminal law-making processes. Scholars of this social conflict persuasion tell us that crime is a reflection of social power struggles. Some groups manage to get their norms and values embodied in criminal law, with deviations from these standards being defined as crimes. Persons who get labeled as criminals are drawn from the ranks of those who lack social power, such as blacks, lower-class individuals, transients, and youths.

Two things can be said about these newer social conflict formulations about criminality. First, these arguments are still not completely spelled out or conceptually mature. Take one of Quinney's propositions: "Definitions of crime are composed of behaviors that conflict with the interests of those segments of society that have the power to shape public policy."[18] There is more than a kernel of truth to that claim, but are we to take it as applying to all criminal laws? If so, what special interest group is behind laws against homicide, forcible rape, arson, incest, or even many kinds of theft? Would it not be more accurate (although somewhat fuzzy) to claim that these laws arise out of the interests of the whole society?[19] In short, the conflict views that have emerged to date are oversimplified.

The second observation about social conflict perspectives on criminality is that most of them are not, in any fundamental way, major departures from liberal criminology. Although these theories contend that lawbreaking is often the outcome of struggles between the powerful and the powerless, they do not offer any basic challenge to the assumption that American society and its insti-tutions are in a relatively healthy state. Also, these views do not challenge the claim that persons who get labeled as criminals usually have engaged in law-breaking behavior.

To this point, we have not explicitly indicated why we have adopted the label "cynical" to characterize modern criminological thought. Regarding theories of causation, perhaps "pessimistic" would be a more appropriate ad-jective, in that the growing awareness that crime causation is an exceedingly complex phenomenon tends to make the criminologist chary about his ability to completely account for it. Then too, contemporary criminologists who are armed with an appreciation of the complex interweaving of factors in law-breaking are not likely to be very sanguine about the prospects for amelioration of criminality.

The cynical posture of the modern criminologist emerges more strikingly in his observations about the criminal justice system and correctional organiza-tions. The sociologist brings to the analysis of these structures the inside dope-ster's awareness that social organizations are often "screwed up." That is, he knows about all kinds of complex organizations that operate in ways quite different from those sketched in organizational charts or manuals of procedure. This growing sophistication of criminological analysis has been paralleled by a marked decline in the criminologist's faith in the perfectibility of the legal-correctional machinery.

Take the burgeoning literature on the social organization of the police. Wilson has observed a number of police departments in detail, reporting that these structures depart in many ways from the idealized version of professional police departments.[20] Nowhere in his work does he suggest that the police can be changed simply by throwing the sadists and morons out of the department, replacing them with college graduates. Chevigny[21] and Albert Reiss,[22] among others, have provided a number of details regarding police abuse of citizens, all of which suggest that abuse of police power is a complex problem that is not amenable to simple solutions. Then too, there is a growing body of studies of the impact upon police practices of Supreme Court rulings such as *Miranda,* all showing that contrary to popular opinion, these due process standards have not "handcuffed" the police. Instead, the police have managed to find ways to circumvent these strictures.[23]

Along this same line, we have a growing body of studies of the court system, all indicating that a great gulf exists between the justice system in theory and in actual operation. For example, Blumberg claims that the criminal court organization of prosecutors, defense attorneys, judges, and kindred persons is a people-processing "con game," in which the interests of the accused are given short shrift.[24]

The criminological cynic also notes that correctional treatment is often nonexistent; that which does exist is usually little more than crude, intuitive tinkering with offenders. We have seen that nearly all those experimental attempts to remake prisons or training schools into social communities or therapeutic environments have foundered, because of bureaucratic demands for regularity, order, and conformity within correctional institutions and other factors as well. There are few contemporary criminologists who still retain much optimism about the prospects of doing correctional treatment, in institutions or on the outside.[25] Instead, observers such as Irwin have argued that the inadvertent by-product of the prison experience is often to drive the felon further into a career of deviance.[26]

Contemporary criminologists who project a spirit of pessimism and cynicism tend to agree, first, that we ought to strive to reduce criminality by expunging many laws from the books, thereby "decriminalizing" the prohibited behavior. That argument is reflected in books such as those by Packer[27] and Schur.[28] Second, most would agree that Youth Service Bureaus and other devices should be developed in order that many offenders can be diverted away from the regular correctional apparatus. Then too, there is a growing consensus that prison populations should be drastically reduced, prison sentences should be shortened, and more concern for due process and the rights of prisoners ought to be stressed. Finally, most contemporary criminologists would be loath to suggest that "the crime problem" is going to be drastically altered by any of the correctional and preventive efforts now under way.

The thing that makes all of these arguments and analyses cases of liberal-cynical criminology is that they all tend to assume the continued viability of American society as we presently know it. Although it is acknowledged that crime will continue to plague us, it is assumed that criminality will continue pretty much in its present form. Also, it may be possible to make some dent in criminality if we manage to divert some of the money now spent on the Viet Nam war to a "war on crime." Similarly, although there is a good deal of skepticism about the perfectibility of the criminal justice and correctional machinery, the liberal-cynical criminologist tends to assume that this apparatus will continue to creak along, doing at least a minimally acceptable job of containing criminality. If we patch up the system here and there, it will continue to function well enough.

RADICAL CLAIMS AND CONVENTIONAL CRIMINOLOGY

Let us concede that some of the criminological works cited above have a faintly radical tone to them, as when Quinney or Turk speak of interest groups imposing their standards upon the relatively powerless. Nonetheless, there is little similarity between that relatively feeble version of radical thought and the angry prose to be found in such places as the underground press. A body of forcefully stated radical criminological thought can be seen in the pages of the *Berkeley Barb* and other media sources of that kind which is quite unlike the writings of academicians.

The major premises of radical criminological thought are fairly apparent. First, it is alleged that a relatively small bunch of corporation officials, government leaders, and military men comprise a close-knit power structure bent upon exploiting "the people," both in the United States and in formerly colonialized nations elsewhere. Laws have been created as devices for compelling the masses to remain docile. The police are "pigs" who are the mercenaries of oppression, serving as the hired lackeys of powerful interests. Exploitation is most severe in the case of blacks, Chicanos, and other ethnic minorities. Black convicts are political prisoners being held captive as innocent victims of a corrupt, capitalistic, exploitative society. Finally, the police are involved in deliberate policies of genocide, in which they have embarked upon systematic attempts to murder those Black Panthers and others who have dared to fight against the exploitative system.

These views represent a challenge to conventional criminology. At the very least, these divergent representations of reality demand adjudication through evidence.

What of the radical view that black and some other ethnic minority offenders are political prisoners, that is, the innocent victims of a corrupt society? Most contemporary versions of academic or liberal criminology tend to treat these claims as emotion-laden metaphors which represent a shorthand statement about the indirect effects of racial discrimination in producing lawbreaking. Blacks are said to be disproportionately represented in the offender population because of economic stress, unstable or disorganized family life owing to ghetto conditions, and so forth. In short, there are more blacks in the official population of offenders because blacks are more frequently driven to crime than are other persons, so the argument goes. However, the radical contentions about political prisoners emphasize the argument that the police are engaged in differential law enforcement and repression of blacks, so that crime rates very frequently are indicators of *direct* discrimination too. By contrast, the liberal-cynical perspective on criminality tends to play down these direct manifestations of racial discrimination, as when Skolnick claims that the Oakland police do not usually put their racial prejudices into practice in law enforcement.[29] Similarly, although Reiss indicates that the police do engage in violence against citizens, he implies that this kind of conduct is not too common.[30]

There is a fairly extensive literature involving studies of police handling of juveniles showing that black youths are more often reported to the juvenile courts than are white youths.[31] Most of those investigations suggest that black juveniles are disproportionately reported to court because they engage in more serious offenses, not because of racial discrimination. The major study of police handling of juveniles which suggests anything to the contrary is by Ferdinand and Luchterhand, in which these investigators reported that racial discrimination did enter into police decisions.[32]

Our guess is that there is more discriminatory law enforcement and police illegality occurring in the United States than contemporary criminology acknowledges. In addition, even if one were to demonstrate that discriminatory law enforcement is not too widespread in routine police work, we still need to contend with a number of dramatic cases of police abuse of blacks on which much of the "political prisoner" theme is based. We refer here to a series of incidents several years ago in Los Angeles, Detroit, and elsewhere, in which law enforcement agents stormed Black Muslim mosques or other buildings and shot a number of blacks. More recently, there have been a number of cases, such as the killing of Fred Hampton by the Chicago police and other police raids of Black Panther headquarters on phony charges, lending considerable credence to Black Panther claims that the police are engaged in genocide. On the same point, anyone familiar with San Quentin prison and who reads the newspapers must have experienced a good deal of disquiet and disbelief in the case of the alleged prison break by George Jackson.

The radical press expressions of outrage regarding the "pigs" doubtless exaggerate these cases of blatant police discrimination while failing to acknowledge various necessary and positive social roles played by the police. But on the other hand, sociological criminology may be presenting a distorted picture too, in only acknowledging that the police sometimes behave rather badly during the course of bona fide law enforcement work, failing to give citizens proper *Miranda* warnings or subjecting them to various kinds of gratuitous abuse. We may be witnessing some new forms of police criminality, in which law enforcement agencies have begun to engage in proactive repression of some of their "enemies."

The same general observations could be made about criminological silence concerning the radical claims that the federal government and the courts are moving into political repression of citizens through wiretapping, preparation of dossiers on citizens, advocacy of preventive detention, and the like. In particular, we ought to have more to say about the trials of the Chicago Seven, the Seattle Seven, the Catonsville Nine, and the Harrisburg Seven. Is it possible that American society is beginning to show profound rents and tears, as many radicals allege? Is it possible that the police and the courts are beginning to move away from the processing of conventional offenders and into some forms of the "police state"? For example, perhaps the "hassling" of hippie hitchhikers represents a seemingly innocuous sign of more ominous developments in the future.

Take another point of contrast between the criminology in the pages of the radical press and that found in sociology textbooks—white-collar crime. Sutherland certainly did not characterize the 70 corporations that he studied as "exploiters of the people"; instead, he stopped far short of that sort of condemnation.[33] Also, Sutherland and other students of white-collar crime rarely argued that direct, sustained collusion between the government and corporate interests was the major explanation for corporate lawbreaking. Although regulatory agencies were seen as having relatively positive attitudes toward the corporations they are designed to police, there is not much hint of conspiratorial claims about capitalistic exploiters and governmental oppressors in the scholarly literature of criminology.[34]

In this instance too, contemporary criminology may not be sufficient to the task at hand. The recent revelations about ITT, Dita Beard, involvement of the Boeing Company in the political campaign of Senator Jackson, and so on, along with a good many previous reports of close interconnections between American corporations, the federal government, the CIA, and the military, do lend some credence to the picture of the world appearing in the underground press.

SOME SOCIOLOGICAL RESPONSES TO THE RADICAL CHALLENGE

This paper has called for more attention to claims about criminality contained in the radical press, in other words, for a brand of criminology which would examine, sort out, and make sense of various radical claims that are currently given little attention in conventional criminological writings. Those contentions that pass the test of evidence would then be incorporated into the body of contemporary criminological knowledge.

One recent example of sociological writing which shows a marked radical influence is Liazos's critique of contemporary theories of deviance.[35] He argues quite convincingly that deviance analysis continues to center upon garden-variety deviants who are relatively powerless. He contends:

> As a result of the fascination with "nuts, sluts, and preverts," and their identities and subcultures, little attention has been paid to the unethical, illegal, and destructive actions of powerful individuals, groups, and institutions in our society.[36]

Along this same line, Liazos argues that sociological discussions of violence in American society are defective, for they portray violence as restricted to slum dwellers, certain minority groups, street gangs, and "motorcycle beasts." He maintains that the proper study of violence would focus upon *covert institutional violence* in the form of oppression, consumer exploitation through the sale of defective and dangerous products, mass destruction of people and the landscape in Viet Nam, and various other kinds of violence and exploitation which are central to the political and social order.[37]

Liazos would have us banish the concept of "deviance" from the sociological lexicon in favor of the phenomena of oppression, persecution, and suffering. In his view, by failing to do so "we neglect conditions of inequality, powerlessness, institutional violence, and so on, which lie at the basis of our tortured society."[38]

We have no quarrel with Liazos concerning his general thesis that sociological analysis has tended toward undue attention to "nuts, sluts, and preverts." But, the problem is that his presentation is relatively visceral and bombastic and lacking in clear implications for renovations in criminological thought. That is, after we have acknowledged the existence of "covert institutional violence," where do we go from there? Certainly we need to do more than to enter into competition with Ralph Nader, Senator Magnuson[39] or various peace groups opposed to the Viet Nam war by vying with them in condemnation of the ills of modern society. Should we redefine the substantive concerns of criminology, and if so, in what ways? It does not appear to us that oppression, conflict, persecution, and suffering will do as basic units for criminological study. What new kinds of testable theory do we need to generate? What kinds of new research investigations are called for? Answers to these questions are not clear in Liazos's polemical statement.

A beginning version of radical criminology has recently been offered in the scholarly literature by Richard Quinney.[40] In that essay, he rails against the criminal law in contemporary society, claiming that it is the instrument through which the dominant class maintains its power over the weak. Quinney would do away with monolithic criminal law as we presently know it, replacing it with decentralized law. This kind of law would be consistent with "natural law," which endeavors to maximize the individual's efforts to develop his own human potentialities. In the kind of society envisioned by Quinney, "communities would then be free to develop their own systems of regulation, if such systems are at all necessary."[41]

Quinney's case against repressive modern criminal law is based on such evidence as the attacks upon Black Panthers. He notes:

> Over 400 Panthers were arrested in the first year of Nixon's administration. Since the Black Panther party was founded, nearly 30 members have been killed by the police. Offices of the party have been raided by the police in Chicago, Des Moines, Oakland, Los Angeles, and in several other cities. Most of the Panther leaders have been either killed, jailed, or forced into exile. . . . The Panthers held in jails across America today are no different from prisoners held in Santo Domingo, Saigon, or any other center of the American empire.
>
> And there are the continual political trials: Captain Levy, the Presidio mutiny case, the Oakland Seven, the Baltimore Four, the Boston Five, the Chicago Seven, and the Catonsville Nine to name only a few of the most publicized cases.[42]

The kind of analysis found in Quinney's essay will not do. Although his commentary is liberally sprinkled with quotes and comments from such authorities as Fuller, Pound, and Hart, his essay is bombastic and polemical in character. While we have argued above that criminologists and sociologists need to pay more attention to the cases of "repression" that Quinney enumerates in his essay, we do not agree that these stand as convincing proof that modern law in its entirety is a tool by which a handful of powerful persons manage to oppress the rest of us. Claims of that kind tossed off by Quinney slur over the existence of that portion of the criminal law which protects all of us from rapists, murderers, and various predators and which most of us support, the weak and the powerful alike. Then too, many would find unconvincing Quinney's contention that bodies of general law are not really required in complex societies in order to maintain a degree of social order which at the same time promotes individual freedom. Instead, many would continue to agree with Roscoe Pound, who regarded law as a necessary form of social control which constrains persons to contribute to social order and the common good. Finally, Quinney's alternative of decentralized law is poorly thought out. He fails to show that this is a viable alternative to the existing system of laws and legal machinery. Assuming that his proposal is practical or realistic, who is to say that there would be any less tyranny under a decentralized system of laws determined by "the people"?

In our view, Chambliss and Seidman have produced the best sociological statement to date on criminality, laws, and the legal machinery, reflecting some of the concerns of the radical left.[43] They view lawmaking and the implementation of criminal laws by the criminal justice system as reflecting power struggles in modern society. Hence, they assert:

It is our contention that, far from being primarily a value-neutral framework within which conflict can be peacefully resolved, the power of the state is itself the principal prize in the perpetual conflict that is society. The legal order—the rules which the various lawmaking institutions in the bureaucracy that is the state lay down for the governance of officials and citizens, the tribunals, official and unofficial, and the bureaucratic agencies which enforce the law—is in fact a self-serving system to maintain power and privilege. In a society sharply divided into haves and have nots, poor and rich, blacks and whites, powerful and weak, shot with a myriad of special interest groups, not only is the myth false because of imperfections in the normative system: It is *inevitable* that it be so.[44]

The Chambliss and Seidman volume represents a beginning venture in the direction of a propositional inventory about power relations and their impact upon lawmaking and law-implementation in complex societies, reflecting the central theme highlighted in the passage above. The reader will find discussion in the pages of this book of at least some of the forms of "oppression" about which radical press is concerned. Thus Chambliss and Seidman take note of recent instances of police lawlessness and rioting, including attacks upon Black Panthers and the flagrant abuses of citizens' rights by the police at the Democratic National Convention in 1968.[45] On balance, they take a harsher view of the police than contained in most versions of liberal-cynical criminology which we examined earlier.

Mention also ought to be made of Chambliss's report on vice in "Rainfall West," which appears to be a thin disguise for Seattle.[46] This study stands as an example of the sort of research endeavor that is implied by a power and conflict version of criminological analysis. In it, Chambliss reports that a "cabal" of politicians, businessmen, law enforcement agents, and organized criminals are joined together in the management of vice in "Rainfall West." The characterization that emerges from his report is rather different from many contemporary portrayals of organized crime that put forth a portrait of the world as sharply divided into the "bad guys" from the Mafia or Cosa Nostra pitted against the "good guys."[47]

CONCLUDING REMARKS

It is not yet clear what the final form of the criminological response to radical allegations about oppression, repression, and the like will take. Our remarks have been designed to draw attention to the need for new directions in criminological theory, without much effort to explicate the details of that sort of theory or to specify programmatic suggestions for new research. Clearly, those tasks are large ones which cannot be managed in a brief essay such as this one.

We identified the work of Chambliss and Seidman as an initial stab in the direction of a criminology which reflects some of the angry contentions of the radical left. If we begin to pursue the theoretical and research leads suggested by that volume, we are likely to find ourselves spending much more time on the activities of the rich and powerful in our society and less upon garden-variety criminals in prisons and other social warehouses. Then too, the perspective sketched out by Chambliss and Seidman would have us devote more attention than has been customary in the past to the workings of legislatures and the interest groups that endeavor to exert influence upon them, so that detailed study of lawmaking processes is in order.

We might conclude this essay by pointing out that although a conflict and social power perspective on criminality and lawmaking has begun to emerge as an alternative to liberal-cynical versions of criminological thought, the truly radical solutions to problems of crime which the former invites have yet to be more than hinted at in the criminological literature.

Who among modern criminologists has much faith in current responses to crime problems in American society? It is doubtful that many informed students of criminality can be found who are sanguine about contemporary approaches to curtailing lawbreaking. In particular, it appears that most of the expenditures of the federal government on a "War on Crime" through the Law Enforcement Assistance Administration (L.E.A.A.) have had no effect upon the crime problem. For one thing, much of that money has been spent by police agencies for tanks, large armaments, and other gadgetry of that kind. Police agencies are now equipped with the tools to annihilate criminals instead of to "cure" them. Then too, the money that has been pumped into correctional programs has been expended on the same tired old endeavors, which have not worked in the past. We might do as well or better to seek out the run-of-the-mill recidivist property offenders and other conventional criminals who now clog our jails and prisons and give them L.E.A.A. stipends as bribes to stay out of trouble, if we wish to combat crime.[48]

Even more to the point, a radically oriented response to the crime problem would be one that concentrates very heavily upon curtailing the harmful machinations of the powerful who are now involved in the exploitation of the powerless. We do not believe that proposals such as those by Quinney, dealing with decentralized law, speak to the complexities of modern society. But, if those suggestions are not useful ones, the sociological imagination will need to produce viable alternatives to them.

In summary, the radical challenge to criminology is one that cannot be ignored. This paper has attempted to identify some of the issues in this challenge and response. Let us hope that criminological answers will eventually be evolved for these difficult questions.

NOTES

[1]Charles W. Lachenmeyer, *The Language of Sociology* (New York: Columbia University Press, 1971).

[2] Robert E. L. Faris, *Social Disorganization,* 2nd ed. (New York: The Ronald Press, 1955).

[3] Harry Elmer Barnes and Negley K. Teeters, *New Horizons in Criminology,* 3rd ed. (Englewood Cliffs, N. J.: Prentice-Hall, 1959).

[4] Ibid., p. 83.

[5] Ibid., p. 96.

[6] Edwin H. Sutherland and Donald R. Cressey, *Principles of Criminology,* 8th ed. (Philadelphia: J. B. Lippincott, 1970). It ought to be acknowledged that Donald R. Cressey made a number of important substantive changes and revisions in the 5th, 6th, 7th, and 8th editions of this book, which he prepared following Sutherland's death.

[7] Summaries of much of the modern criminological work can be found in Don C. Gibbons, *Society, Crime, and Criminal Careers,* 2nd ed. (Englewood Cliffs, N. J.: Prentice-Hall, 1973); Gibbons, *Delinquent Behavior* (Englewood Cliffs, N. J.: Prentice-Hall, 1970).

[8] Gresham M. Sykes, "The Future of Criminality," *American Behavioral Scientist* 15 (February 1972): 409-19. Among other things, Sykes claims that liberals, both of the sociological kind and of other varieties too, tend to minimize the seriousness of the "crime wave" which is now alleged to be engulfing the United States. Those of a liberal persuasion tend to argue that "crime in the streets" is a slogan or code word for bigotry, that the alleged crime rise is mainly an artifact of improved reporting procedures, and that the police are lawless. However, Sykes agrees with those who maintain that much of the crime wave is real and that it demands vigorous crime control measures. He then goes on to claim that the face of crime is changing in America, calling for new responses to it.

[9] Travis Hirschi, *Causes of Delinquency* (Berkeley: University of California Press, 1969).

[10] Sykes, "Criminality," p. 411.

[11] Don C. Gibbons, "Observations on the Study of Crime Causation," *American Journal of Sociology* 77 (September 1971): 262-78; Gibbons, "Crime in the Hinterland," *Criminology* 10 (August 1972): 177-91.

[12] Sykes, "Criminality," pp. 411-15.

[13] Ibid., p. 413.

[14] Ibid., p. 414.

[15] Kelly Hancock, "Dynamite and Firebombs—Reflections on Contemporary America," Portland State University, mimeographed, n.d. *See also* Philip A. Karber, "Urban Terrorism: Baseline Data and a Conceptual Framework," *Social Science Quarterly* 52 (December 1971): 521-33.

[16] Austin T. Turk, *Criminality and Legal Order* (Chicago: Rand McNally, 1969).

[17] Richard Quinney, *The Social Reality of Crime* (Boston: Little, Brown, 1970); Quinney, "The Social Reality of Crime," in *Crime and Justice in American Society,* ed. Jack D. Douglas (New York: Bobbs-Merrill, 1971), pp. 119-146.

[18] Quinney, "Social Reality," p. 135.

[19] Not everyone agrees that such laws as those against rape or incest arise out of societal consensus. For example, Chambliss and Seidman argue that many citizens would be loath to condemn the person who kills an intruder in his home or who is sexually aggressive toward a female who behaved seductively toward him. *See* William J. Chambliss and Robert D. Seidman, *Law, Order, and Power* (Reading, Mass.: Addison-Wesley, 1971), pp. 61-74. Although this point has merit, it is still possible to argue that few persons can be found who would approve of many actual cases of premeditated homicide, markedly aggressive rape-mutilation, and the like.

[20]James Q. Wilson, *Varieties of Police Behavior* (Cambridge: Harvard University Press, 1968).

[21]Paul Chevigny, *Police Power* (New York: Vintage Books, 1969).

[22]Albert J. Reiss, Jr., *The Police and the Public* (New Haven: Yale University Press, 1971).

[23]These studies are summarized in Gibbons, *Society, Crime,* pp. 54-59.

[24]Abraham S. Blumberg, "Criminal Justice in America," in Douglas, *Crime and Justice,* pp. 45-78; Blumberg, *Criminal Justice* (Chicago: Quadrangle Books, 1967).

[25]A generous share of the literature on correctional projects and experiments is reviewed in Gibbons, *Delinquent Behavior,* pp. 247-61; Gibbons, *Society, Crime,* pp. 501-43; Gibbons, "Punishment, Treatment, and Rehabilitation: Problems and Prospects," in *Introduction to Criminology,* ed. Abraham S. Blumberg (New York: Random House, forthcoming). Comparison of these essays with Gibbons, *Changing the Lawbreaker* (Englewood Cliffs, N. J.: Prentice-Hall, 1965) would show them to be markedly more pessimistic in tone than the 1965 volume.

[26]John Irwin, *The Felon* (Englewood Cliffs, N. J.: Prentice-Hall, 1970).

[27]Herbert L. Packer, *The Limits of the Criminal Sanction* (Stanford: Stanford University Press, 1968).

[28]Edwin M. Schur, *Crimes Without Victims* (Englewood Cliffs, N. J.: Prentice-Hall, 1965).

[29]Jerome H. Skolnick, *Justice Without Trial* (New York: John Wiley & Sons, 1966), pp. 80-90.

[30]Reiss, *Police and Public.*

[31]These studies are reviewed in Gibbons, *Delinquent Behavior,* pp. 36-46.

[32]Theodore N. Ferdinand and Elmer G. Luchterhand, "Inner-City Youth, the Police, the Juvenile Court, and Justice," *Social Problems* 17 (Spring 1970): 510-27.

[33]Edwin H. Sutherland, *White Collar Crime* (New York: The Dryden Press, 1949).

[34]Indeed, much attention continues to focus upon those who commit crimes *against* large-scale organizations and corporations, rather than upon crimes perpetrated by these structures against common citizens. For example, *see* Erwin O. Smigel and H. Laurence Ross, eds., *Crimes Against Bureaucracy* (New York: Van Nostrand-Reinhold, 1970).

[35]Alexander Liazos, "The Poverty of the Sociology of Deviance: Nuts, Sluts, and Preverts," *Social Problems* 20 (Summer 1972): 103-20.

[36]Ibid., p. 111.

[37]Ibid.

[38]Ibid., p. 119.

[39]Senator Warren G. Magnuson and Jean Carper, *The Dark Side of the Marketplace* (Englewood Cliffs, N. J.: Prentice-Hall, 1968).

[40]Richard Quinney, "The Ideology of Law: Notes for a Radical Alternative to Legal Repression," *Issues in Criminology* 7 (Winter 1972): 1-35.

[41]Ibid., p. 26.

[42]Ibid., pp. 29-30.

[43]Chambliss and Seidman, *Law, Order,* pp. 2-74.

[44]Ibid., p. 4.

[45]Ibid., pp. 274-286; *also see* Rodney Stark, *Police Riots* (Belmont, Calif.: Wadsworth Publishing, 1972).

[46]William J. Chambliss, "Vice, Corruption, Bureaucracy, and Power," *Wisconsin Law Review* 4 (1971): 1150-1173.

[47]Perhaps we should anticipate new problems for the individual researcher, as well as increased resistance to criminological endeavors, as our attention turns to sociological probing into the behavior of corporations, legislatures, and local governments. On this point, Chamblis (ibid.) reports harassment by the police of a university professor who was snooping into the affairs of the crime cabal in "Rainfall West." Then too, we may find that as we go about publishing research reports on crime syndicates or corporate misbehavior, we may encounter the risk of civil suits directed at us by the "deviants" identified in our reports. In the case of Chambliss's essay on "Rainfall West," it seems likely that an interested person would have little difficulty penetrating the disguise provided by Chambliss for some of the public figures he discusses, such as "Sheriff McAllister." We may find that these powerful deviants will not suffer the kind of treatment at our hands that powerless Skid Road alcoholics or other "nuts, sluts, and preverts" have endured in the past. A more detailed discussion of this point can be found in Don C. Gibbons and Joseph F. Jones, *The Study of Deviance* (New York: Basic Books, forthcoming).

[48]We ought to acknowledge that the "War on Crime" actually serves an important latent function. Crime is a business in modern society, in the sense that large numbers of persons who might otherwise be unemployed are being subsidized by federal funds to work on crime control.

CAPITALISM, CLASS AND CRIME IN AMERICA

DAVID M. GORDON

Like a brush fire, crime in the United States has seemed recently to be raging out of control. The public, the government, and the experts have all raced to cool the blaze. In one way or another, we have all been drawn into the fight. With slogans and occasional compassion, with weapons, courts, prisons, and patrols, especially with perplexity and confusion, we have probably served in the end to frustrate our own good intentions, to fan the flames rather than douse them. We seem to have as much trouble understanding the problem of crime as we do effecting its solution.

Meanwhile, amidst the confusion, orthodox economists have been striding elegantly to our rescue. Cool, fearless, the perfect picture of professionalism, they have been promising to guide us toward "optimal" crime prevention and control. Off with our silliness! Off with our psychological muddle-headedness! Gary Becker, a sort of guru among them, explains how easily we can understand it all:

> A useful theory of criminal behavior can dispense with special theories of anomie, psychological inadequacies, or inheritance of special traits and simply extend the economist's usual analysis of choice.[1]

As I have read and thought recently about the problem of crime in the United States, I've found myself returning over and over to the same conclusions —that the public's understanding of the problem is mistaken, that the government's policy responses are misguided, and that the recent orthodox economic analyses have been misleading. This paper attempts to amplify those impressions. I have not tried to present a detailed brief against the conventional wisdom and the orthodox economic view. Instead, I intend to articulate my differences with those positions by formulating an alternative, radical analysis of criminal behavior and by evoking an alternative normative view of an appropriate social response to crime.

The paper has five sections. The first offers a brief descriptive summary of the nature and extent of crime in the United States. The second surveys some conventional public perspectives on the problem of crime, while the third outlines recent orthodox economic approaches to the problem. In the fourth section, I sketch the framework of a radical economic analysis of crime in the

David M. Gordon, "Capitalism, Class and Crime in America" *Crime and Delinquency* (April 1973) pp. 163-186. Reprinted with permission of the National Council on Crime and Delinquency, from *Crime and Delinquency*, April 1973, pp. 163-186.

United States. In the final section, I amplify an alternative normative view of the appropriate social response to criminal behavior.[2]

1. CRIME IN AMERICA

To compare analytic approaches to the problem of crime, one must first clarify its empirical dimensions. Several useful summaries of the nature and extent of American crime are easily available, especially in the summary report by the President's Crime Commission and in Ramsey Clark's recent book.[3] Relying primarily on the basic facts documented in those sources, I have tried in the following paragraphs to outline the most important questions about the problem of crime which any analysis must try to resolve.

It seems important to emphasize, first of all, that crime is ubiquitous in the United States. Our laws are so pervasive that one must virtually retire to a hermitage in order to avoid committing a crime. According to a national survey conducted in 1965 by the President's Crime Commission, 91 percent of all adult Americans "admitted that they had committed acts for which they might have received jail or prison sentences."[4] The Crime Commission also found that in 1965 "more than two million Americans were received in prisons or juvenile training schools, or placed on probation"—well over 2 percent of the labor force. Criminal behavior, it appears, is clearly a norm and not an aberration.[5]

Given that ubiquity, it seems equally important to emphasize our extraordinary selectivity in our attention to the problem of crime. We focus all our nearly paranoid fears about "law 'n' order" and "safe streets" on a limited number of crimes while we altogether ignore many other kinds of crime, equally serious and of much greater economic importance.

One can sketch the dimensions of this selectivity quite easily. The crimes on which the public *does* concentrate its fears and cannons are often lumped together as "urban" or "violent" crimes. These crimes can be usefully summarized by those for which the FBI accumulates a general statistical index. Seven "Index Crimes" are traced in the Bureau's periodic Crime Report: willful homicide, forcible rape, aggravated assault, robbery, burglary, larceny (of more than $50), and motor vehicle theft. Together, these seven crimes encompass the raging fire in fear of which we hide inside our homes.

Some basic facts about these seven fearsome crimes are well known. The measured incidence of the Index Crimes has been increasing rapidly in the United States in the past 10 to 15 years.[6] The Index Crimes occur twice as frequently in large cities as they do on the average throughout the country. Within large cities, they occur most frequently in ghetto areas. The threat and tragedy of violent crime notwithstanding, almost all of these crimes are economically motivated; as Clark notes quite simply, "their main purpose is to obtain money or property."[7] Seven-eighths of them are crimes against property; only one-eighth are crimes against the person, and many of the relatively few "violent" crimes actually occur inadvertently in the process of committing crimes against property.

A large part of the crime against property is committed by youth. Clark concludes from the scattered statistics that half of all property crime is committed by persons under 21.[8] Certainly more important in considering the evolution of public attitudes, blacks commit disproportionate numbers of these seven Index Crimes (and are also disproportionately the victims of the same crimes). Although arrest rates bear an obviously spurious relationship to the actual incidence of crime, some of the figures seem quite astonishing.[9] In 1968, for instance, official statistics indicate that 61 percent of those arrested for robbery were black and nearly half of those arrested for aggravated assault were black, despite the fact that blacks constitute only 12 percent of the population. As astonishing as those figures sometimes seem, however, the public exaggerates them further; public attitudes often appear to presume that *all* of the Index Crimes are committed by blacks and that every black male is on the verge of committing a crime.

The crimes to which the public and the media choose to pay almost no attention seem just as obvious. Many kinds of relatively hidden profitable crimes, most of them called "white-collar" crimes, occur with startling frequency. Tax evasion, price fixing, embezzlement, swindling, and consumer fraud capture billions of dollars every year.

Illicit gains from white-collar crime far exceed those of all other crime combined. . . . One corporate price-fixing conspiracy criminally converted more money each year it continued than all of the hundreds of thousands of burglaries, larcenies, or thefts in the entire nation during those same years. Reported bank embezzlements cost ten times more than bank robberies each year.[10]

The selectivity of public opinion is matched, moreover, by the biases of our governmental system for the enforcement and administration of justice, which prosecutes and punishes some crimes and criminals heavily while leaving others alone. Some defenders of the system occasionally argue that it concentrates most heavily on those crimes of the greatest magnitude and importance, but the data do not support this view: the Index Crimes on which the system focuses account for small proportions of the total personal harm and property loss resulting from crime in the United States. For example, deaths resulting from "willful homicide" are one-fifth as frequent as deaths from motor vehicle accidents; although many experts ascribe nearly half of motor vehicle accidents to mechanical failure, the system rarely pays attention to those liable for that failure. The economic loss attributable to Index Crimes against property—robbery, burglary, and so on—are one-fifth the losses attributable to embezzlement, fraud, and unreported commercial theft, and yet the system concentrates almost exclusively on the former.

One can much more reasonably argue, as many have in other contexts, that the selectivity of our police, courts, and prisons corresponds most closely to the relative *class status* of those who perpetrate different crimes. We seem to have a dual system of justice in this country, as both the Crime Commission and Goldfarb have most clearly shown.[11] The public system concentrates on crimes committed by the poor, while crimes by the more affluent are left to private auspices. Our prisons function, as Goldfarb notes, like a "national poorhouse," swallowing the poor, chewing them up, and occasionally spitting them back at the larger society. When the more affluent get in trouble, in contrast, private psychiatric and counseling assistance supplant prosecution: "In the classes of offenses committed by rich and poor *equally,* it is rarely the rich who end up behind bars."[12]

Finally, none of the system's selectivity works as intended. The public seems to think that concentration on a few crimes will at least improve the effectiveness of the system in controlling those few crimes—leading to greater prevention and deterrence and perhaps to greater rehabilitation. Buoyed by that hope, the various governments in the United States spent roughly $4.2 billion on police, prisons, and the courts in 1965, while private individuals and corporations spent an additional $1.9 billion on prevention and insurance. And yet, despite those billions, our systems of enforcement and administration of justice appear considerably to exacerbate the criminality they seek selectively to control. The prisons in particular, as Clark notes, are veritable "factories of crime": "Jails and prisons in the United States today are more often than not manufacturers of crime. Of those who come to jail undecided, capable either of criminal conduct or of lives free of crime, most are turned to crime."[13] More generally, very few of those who get started in crime ever actually leave it as a result of the system's deterrent or rehabilitative effects. According to Clark's statistical summaries, roughly half of those released from prison eventually return, and fully 80 percent of serious crime is committed by "repeaters"—by those who have been convicted of crime before.[14]

These very brief descriptive observations clearly suggest the questions an economic analysis must seek to answer about the problem of crime: *Why* is there so much crime? Why do the public and government concentrate so selectively on such a small part of the criminal activity in this country? And why do all our billions of dollars fail so miserably in curbing even that small part of the total problem?

2. CONVENTIONAL PUBLIC ANALYSES

Conventional public analyses of crime divide roughly into two views—conservative and liberal—the specific features of which correspond to more general "conservative" and "liberal" perspectives on social problems. The two perspectives begin from some relatively common general views of society and its governments, diverging more and more widely as they debate the specifics of crime prevention and control.[15]

The conservative perspective on crime has an appealing simplicity.[16] Since conservatives believe that the social "order" is ultimately rational and is adequately reflected in the laws of our governments, they also believe that those who violate it can be regarded as irrational citizens and social misfits. As such, criminals should be punished regardless of the social forces that may well have produced their criminality; they represent a threat to the safety and property of those who act with civility and reason, and they should be isolated until society can be sure of their good behavior. The more violent the crimes, the more seriously we must regard their consequences.

Since criminals (and especially violent ones) act irrationally, we can deter and prevent their actions only by responding to them with comparably irrational actions—principally by the threat or application of raw force. Toward that end, conservatives engage in two kinds of policy calculations. First, they discuss the potential deterrence of a variety of crime-prevention techniques: if only enough deterrent force could be mustered, they assume, crime could be stopped; typically, they urge more police and more equipment to prevent crime. Second, they tend to favor preventive detention as a necessary means of protecting the social order from the threat of probable criminality; they make their argument, normally, on relatively pragmatic grounds.[17]

Liberals tend to agree with conservatives, ultimately, that the social order tends toward rationality. They are more likely to pay attention to imperfections in the social order, however, and are therefore more likely to favor government action to correct those imperfections. As a justification for government action, they usually rely on what has been called the "pluralistic" view of democratic governments—that those governments generally act in everyone's interests because they are constantly checked and balanced by the competition of many different interest groups for the favors of government action.[18]

Given those general predilections, liberals tend to regard the problem of criminal activity as a much more complicated dilemma than do their conservative counterparts.[19] Since the social order can be viewed as an ultimately rational state, those who violate it can indeed be regarded as "irrational." At the same time, however, liberals regard the interactions of individuals with society as extremely complex processes, fraught with imperfections in the allocation and distribution of social rewards. Through those imperfections, some individuals are much more likely than others to be *pushed* toward the irrationality of criminal behavior. Criminality should be regarded as irrationality, but we should nonetheless try to avoid *blaming* criminals for their irrational acts. And since different individuals are pushed in very different ways by different social circumstances, there is a wide variety of behavior among criminals. As the Crime Commission concludes: "No single formula, no single theory, no single generalization can explain the vast range of behavior called crime."[20]

Some of these heterogeneous crimes are more serious than others, liberals continue, because they are more violent and therefore more threatening. Liberals tend to agree with conservatives and the FBI that the FBI Crime Index adequately encompasses the potentially most violent crimes. But liberals tend to disagree with conservatives in arguing that these kinds of relatively violent crimes cannot simply be prevented by force, that they cannot ultimately be curbed until the social imperfections which underlie them are eliminated. The prevalence of "violent" crime among youth, blacks, and ghetto residents derives from the diseases of poverty and racism in American society, most liberals have finally concluded. Given those basic social imperfections, as the Crime Commission argues, "it is probable that crime will continue to increase . . . unless there are drastic changes in general social and economic conditions."[21]

Can we do nothing about crime until we eliminate the sores of poverty and racism? Liberals respond on two different levels. On the one hand, they argue that we can marginally improve our prevention of crime and our treatment of criminals if we can at least marginally rationalize our system of enforcement and administration of justice. We need more research, more analysis, more technology, more money, better administration, and more numerous and professional personnel.[22] And since liberals place considerable faith in the dispassionate beneficence of the government, they expect that the government's responses to crime can be improved simply by urging the government to make those improvements.

On another level, liberals argue strongly—and in relatively sharp opposition to many conservatives—that we should not tolerate abridgments of civil liberties while we wait for our ultimate solutions to the problems of crime. Though a bit confused and rarely articulated with any real coherence, the liberals' defense of civil liberties appears to derive from the high priorities they conventionally place on social equality and justice, while conservatives seem to be more swayed by their own concern for social order and the preservation of the integrity of private property. However confused its sources, this debate between liberals and conservatives cannot easily be ignored. "A coincidence of events has heightened the traditional tensions between the forces of enforcement and of justice, and has greatly increased the likelihood of a constitutional crisis somewhere down the line."[23]

In short, the conventional liberal and conservative analyses of crime pose fairly simple answers to the most important questions about crime. They argue that criminals are essentially irrational, with liberals adding that such irrationality sometimes seems, in one sense or another, partially justified. They agree that we should concentrate most heavily on trying to prevent the most violent crimes, and they both conclude that the admitted selectivity of public opinion and governmental response roughly corresponds to the degree of violence latent or manifest in different kinds of crime. Conservatives suspect that we have not been willing to apply enough force to deter and punish those kinds of criminals. Liberals suspect that we have failed because poverty and racism are deeply rooted in our society but that we can at least marginally improve our enforcement and administration of justice in the short run through more rational public policies and that we can ultimately curb crime through public action to eliminate the basic social causes of crime.

3. ORTHODOX ECONOMIC ANALYSIS

In the past few years, redressing a historic neglect, several orthodox economists have tried to clarify our analysis of criminal behavior and our evaluation of alternative public policies to combat it.[24] Although a few nineteenth-century classical economists like Jeremy Bentham had originally applied economics to the analysis of the problem of crime, economists since then have generally left the problem to sociologists and psychologists. Recent advances in neoclassical micro-economic theory permit us, we are now told, to "extend the economist's usual analysis of choice" to an analysis of criminal behavior and its "optimal" prevention and punishment. Since each of the recent applications of orthodox economics outlines the mode of analysis rather clearly and since the approach so directly reflects the more general predispositions of orthodox micro-economics, a few brief observations about its underlying assumptions are sufficient in order to clarify its differences from both the "public perspectives" outlined above and the radical analysis developed below.

The central and most important thrust of the orthodox analysis is that criminal behavior, like any other economic activity, is eminently rational; in this important respect, the economists differ fundamentally with conventional liberal and conservative public analyses. Becker formulates this central contention quite simply:

> A person commits an offense if the expected utility to him exceeds the utility he could get by using his time and other resources at other activities. Some persons become "criminals," therefore, not because their basic motivation differs from that of other persons, but because their benefits and costs differ.[25]

More specifically, individuals are assumed to calculate the returns to and the risks of "legitimate" employment and "criminal" activity and base their choices between those two modes of activity on their cost/benefit calculations. Stigler adds: "The details of occupational choice in illegal activity are not different from those encountered in the legitimate occupations."[26]

Given those assumptions of rationality, orthodox economists argue that we can construct some "optimal" social policies to combat crime. They assume, first of all, that there is a social calculus through which the costs and benefits of criminal offenses to each member of society can be translated into a common metric—the calculus is conveniently expressed in terms of a "social welfare function." Society (through its several governments) should then try to minimize the "social loss" from criminal offenses as measured by the social welfare function. In their formulation of the parameters of these calculations, they hypothesize that criminals respond quite sensitively in their own decision making to variations in the level and probability of punishment. They also assume that, as Becker puts it, "the more that is spent on policemen, court personnel, and specialized equipment, the easier it is to discover offenses and convict offenders."[27] They then proceed to the final argument: we can choose (through our governments) some combination of punishment levels and social expenditures—with expenditures determining the probability of capture and conviction—which will minimize our social losses from crime subject to the revenue constraints in our public and private budgets.

Behind the orthodox economic analysis lie two fundamental assumptions. First, although the assumption is rarely made explicit, the economists obviously assume that, in a democratic society, everyone's preferences have an equal chance of influencing the final outcome and that public policy formulations can adequately reflect the costs and benefits of criminal offenses to all individuals in society. Without that assumption, the basis for minimization of social "losses" through a social welfare function is undercut.[28]

Second, the orthodox economists assume some simple and identifiable relationships among the amount of money we actually spend on prevention and enforcement, the amount of prevention and enforcement we would *like to achieve,* and the amount of prevention and enforcement we can *actually achieve.* This involves the assumption, noted above, that larger expenditures automatically increase the probability of apprehension and conviction. It also involves another, related assumption—that the level of government expenditures on prevention and punishment accurately reflects society's desired level of prevention and enforcement instead of, for example, the influence of vested interests in maximizing expenditures. If a state or locality spends more on its police, courts, and prisons, *ceteris paribus,* orthodox economists assume that they do so because they seek to deter crime more effectively through the expected increase in the probability of arrest and punishment.

4. A RADICAL ANALYSIS

This section outlines the structure of a radical analysis of crime in the United States. Many points in the argument will seem quite obvious, simple elaborations of common sense. Other points will bear some important similarities to one or another of the views described in the preceding sections. Taken all together, however, the arguments in the following analysis seem to me to provide a more useful, coherent, and realistic interpretation than the more conventional models. In the analysis, I have tried as simply as possible to apply some general hypotheses of radical economic analysis to a discussion of the specific problem of crime in this country. My intention, quite clearly, is to argue that we cannot realistically expect to "solve" the problem of crime in the United States without first effecting a fundamental redistribution of power in our society.

I have divided the analysis into five separate parts. The first sketches the major hypotheses of the general radical framework through which I have tried to view the problem of crime. The second tries to explain a basic behavioral *similarity* among all the major kinds of crime in the United States. Given that fundamental similarity, the third part seeks to explain the most important dimensions of *difference* among various crimes in this country. Given a delineation of the sources of difference among crimes, the fourth part attempts a historical explanation of the origins of those sources of difference—an analysis, as it were, of the underlying causes of some immediate causes of difference. The fifth part argues that we cannot easily reverse history, cannot easily alter the fundamental social structures and trends that have produced the problem of crime today. A final paragraph provides a brief summary of the central hypotheses of the entire argument.

Some General Assumptions

The radical analysis of crime outlined in this section applies several basic radical assumptions or hypotheses.[29] It presumes, first of all, that the basic structure of social and economic institutions in any society fundamentally shapes the behavior of individuals in that society and, therefore, that one cannot in fact understand the behavior of individuals in a society like the United States without first understanding the structures and biases of the basic "system-defining" institutions in this country. It argues, furthermore, that the "social relations of production" in capitalist societies help define an economic class structure and that one cannot therefore adequately understand the behavior of individuals unless one first examines the structure of institutionally determined opportunities to which members of the respective economic classes are more or less confined.[30] The analysis depends, at another level, on the radical theory of the State, according to which radicals hypothesize that the activities of the State in capitalist societies serve primarily to benefit members of the capitalist class— either directly, by bestowing disproportionate benefits upon them, or indirectly, by helping preserve and solidify the structure of class inequalities upon which capitalists so thoroughly depend.[31] The radical analysis expects, finally, that various social problems in capitalist societies, although they may not have been created by capitalists, cannot easily be solved within the context of capitalist institutions because their solution would tend to disrupt the functioning of the capitalist machine. If the disruptive potential of solutions to such problems therefore inclines the State to postpone solution, one can expect to solve those problems only by changing the power relationships in society so that the State is forced to serve other interests than those of the capitalist class.[32]

Each of these general hypotheses underlies all of the more specific hypotheses about crime which follow.

Competitive Capitalism and Rational Crime

Capitalist societies depend, as radicals often argue, on basically competitive forms of social and economic interaction and upon substantial inequalities in the allocation of social resources. Without inequalities, it would be much more difficult to induce workers to work in alienating environments. Without competition and a competitive ideology, workers might not be inclined to struggle to improve their relative income and status in society by working harder. Finally, although rights of property are protected, capitalist societies do not guarantee economic security to most of its individual members. Individuals must fend for themselves, finding the best available opportunities to provide for themselves and their families. At the same time, history bequeaths a corpus of laws and statutes to any social epoch which may or may not correspond to the social morality of that epoch. Inevitably, at any point in time, many of the "best" opportunities for economic survival open to different citizens will violate some of those historically determined laws. Driven by the fear of economic insecurity and by a competitive desire to gain some of the goods unequally distributed throughout the society, many individuals will eventually become "criminals." As Adam Smith himself admitted, "Where there is no property, . . . civil government is not so necessary."[33]

In that respect, therefore, radicals argue that nearly all crimes in capitalist societies represent perfectly *rational* responses to the structure of institutions upon which capitalist societies are based. Crimes of many different varieties constitute functionally similar responses to the organization of capitalist institutions, for those crimes help provide a means of survival in a society within which survival is never assured. Three different kinds of crime in the United States provide the most important examples of this functionally similar rationality among different kinds of crime: ghetto crime, organized crime, and corporate (or "white-collar") crime.[34]

It seems especially clear, first of all, that ghetto crime is committed by people responding quite reasonably to the structure of economic opportunities available to them. Only rarely, it appears, can ghetto criminals be regarded as raving, irrational, antisocial lunatics.[35] The "legitimate" jobs open to many ghetto residents, especially to young black males, typically pay low wages, offer relatively demeaning assignments, and carry the constant risk of layoff. In contrast, many kinds of crime "available" in the ghetto often bring higher monetary return, offer even higher social status, and—at least in some cases like numbers running—sometimes carry relatively low risk of arrest and punishment.[36] Given those alternative opportunities, the choice between "legitimate" and "illegitimate" activities is often quite simple. As Arthur Dunmeyer, a black hustler from Harlem, has put it:

> In some cases this is the way you get your drug dealers and prostitutes and your numbers runners. . . . They see that these things are the only way that they can compete in society, to get some sort of status. They realize that there aren't any real doors open to them, and so, to commit crime was the only thing to do; they can't go back.[37]

The fact that these activities are often "illegal" sometimes doesn't really matter;

since life out of jail often seems as bad as life inside prison, the deterrent effect
of punishment is negligible. Dunmeyer expresses this point clearly as well:

> It is not a matter of a guy saying, "I want to go to jail [or] I am afraid of
> jail." Jail is on the street just like it is on the inside. The same as, like when you
> are in jail, they tell you, "Look, if you do something wrong you are going to be
> put in the hole." You are still in jail, in the hole or out of the hole. You are in jail
> in the street or behind bars. It is the same thing.[38]

In much the same way, organized crime represents a perfectly rational kind
of economic activity.[39] Activities like gambling and prostitution are illegal for
varieties of historical reasons, but there is a demand for those activities nonetheless. As Donald Cressey writes: "The American confederation of criminals thrives
because a large minority of citizens demands the illicit goods and services it has
for sale."[40] Clark makes the same point, arguing that organized crimes are essentially "consensual crimes . . . , desired by the consuming public."[41] The simple
fact that they are both illegal and in great demand provides a simple explanation
for the secrecy, relative efficiency, and occasional violence of those who provide
them. In nearly every sense the organization of the heroin industry, for example,
bears as rational and reasonable a relationship to the nature of the product as the
structures of the tobacco and alcoholic beverages industries bear to the nature of
their own products.[42]

Finally, briefly to amplify the third example, corporate crime also represents a quite rational response to life in capitalist societies. Corporations exist to
protect and augment the capital of their owners. If it becomes difficult to perform that function one way, corporate officials will quite inevitably try to do it
another. When Westinghouse and General Electric conspired to fix prices, for instance, they were resorting to one of many possible devices for limiting the potential threat of competition to their price structures. Similarly, when Ford and
General Motors proliferate new car model after new car model, each differing
only slightly from its siblings, they are choosing to protect their price structures
by what economists call "product differentiation." In one case, the corporations
were using oligopolistic power quite directly; in the other, they rely on the
power of advertising to generate demand for the differentiated products. In the
context of the perpetual and highly competitive race among corporations for
profits and capital accumulation, each response seems quite reasonable. Sutherland made the same points about corporate crime and linked the behavior of
corporations to lower-class criminality:

> I have attempted to demonstrate that businessmen violate the law with
> great frequency. . . . If these conclusions are correct, it is very clear that the
> criminal behavior of businessmen cannot be explained by poverty, in the usual
> sense, or by bad housing or lack of recreational facilities or feeblemindedness or
> emotional instability. Business leaders are capable, emotionally balanced, and in
> no sense pathological. . . . The assumption that an offender must have some such
> pathological distortion of the intellect or the emotions seems to me absurd, and
> if it is absurd regarding the crimes of businessmen, it is equally absurd regarding
> the crimes of persons in the lower economic class.[43]

Class Institutions and
Differences Among Crimes

If most crime in the United States in one way or another reflects the same kind of rational response to the insecurity and inequality of capitalist institutions, what explains the manifold differences among different kinds of crimes? Some crimes are much more violent than others, some are much more heavily prosecuted, and some are much more profitable. Why?

As a first step in explaining differences among crimes, I would apply the general radical perspective in a relatively straightforward manner and argue quite simply that many of the most important differences among different kinds of crime in this country are determined by the *structure of class institutions* in our society and by the *class biases* of the State. That argument has two separate components.

First, I would argue that many of the important differences among crimes in this society derive quite directly from the different socioeconomic classes to which individuals belong. Relatively affluent citizens have access to jobs in large corporations, to institutions involved in complicated paper transactions involving lots of money, and to avenues of relatively unobtrusive communication. Members of those classes who decide to break the law have, as Clark puts it, "an easier, less offensive, less visible way of doing wrong."[44] Those raised in poverty, on the other hand, do not have such easy access to money. If they are to obtain it criminally, they must impinge on those who already have it or direct its flow. As Robert Morgenthau, a former federal attorney, has written, those growing up in the ghetto "will probably never have the opportunity to embezzle funds from a bank or to promote a multimillion dollar stock fraud scheme. The criminal ways which we encourage [them] to choose will be those closest at hand—from vandalism to mugging to armed robbery."[45]

Second, I would argue that the biases of our police, courts, and prisons *explain* the relative violence of many crimes—that many of the differences in the degree of violence among different kinds of crime do not cause the selectivity of public concern about those crimes but *are* in fact *caused by* that selectivity. For a variety of historical reasons, as I noted above, we have a dual system of justice in this country; the police, courts, and prisons pay careful attention to only a few crimes. It is only natural, as a result, that those who run the highest risks of arrest and conviction may have to rely on the threat or commission of violence in order to protect themselves. Many kinds of ghetto crimes generate violence, for instance, because the participants are severely prosecuted for their crimes and must try to protect themselves however they can. Other kinds of ghetto crimes, like the numbers racket, are openly tolerated by the police, and those crimes rarely involve violence. It may be true, as Clark argues, that "violent crime springs from a violent environment,"[46] but violent environments like the ghetto do not always produce violent crimes. Those crimes to which the police pay attention usually involve violence, while those which the police tend to ignore quite normally do not. In similar ways, organized crime has become violent historically, as Cressey especially argues,[47] principally because its participants are often prosecuted. As long as that remains true, the suppliers of illegal goods require secrecy, organization, and a bit of violence to protect their livelihood. Completely in contrast, corporate crime does not require violence because it is ignored by the police; corporate criminals can safely assume they do not face the threat of jail and do not therefore have to cover their tracks with the threat of harming those who betray them. When Lockheed Aircraft accountants and executives falsified their public reports in order to disguise cost overruns on the C-5A airplane in 1967 and 1968, for instance, they did not have to force Defense Department officials at knifepoint to play along with their falsifications. As Robert Sherrill reports in his investigation of the Lockheed affair, the Defense Department officials were entirely willing to cooperate.[48] "This sympathy," he writes, "was reflected in orders from top Air Force officials to withhold information regarding Lockheed's dilemma from all reports that would be widely circulated." If only local police were equally sympathetic to the "dilemmas" of street-corner junkies, the violent patterns of drug-related crimes might be considerably transformed.[49]

In short, it seems important to view some of the most important differences among crimes—differences in their violence, their style, and their impact—as fundamental outgrowths of the class structure of society and the class biases of our major institutions, including the State and its system of enforcement and administration of justice. Given that argument, it places a special burden on attempts to explain the historical sources of the duality of the public system of justice in this country, for that duality, coupled with the class biases of other institutions, plays an important role in determining the patterns of American crime.

The Sources of Duality

One can explain the duality of our public system of justice quite easily, it seems to me, if one is willing to view the State through the radical perspective. The analysis involves answers to two separate questions. First, one must ask why the State ignores certain kinds of crimes, especially white-collar crimes and corporate crimes. Second, given that most crimes among the poor claim the poor as their victims, one must ask why the State bothers to worry so incessantly about those crimes.

The answer to the first question draws directly from the radical theory of the State. According to the radical theory, the government in a capitalist society like the United States exists primarily to preserve the stability of the system which provides, preserves, and protects returns to the owners of capital. As long as crimes among the corporate class tend in general to harm members of other classes, like those in the "consuming" class, the State will not spontaneously move to prevent those crimes from taking place. On the other hand, as Paul Sweezy has especially argued,[50] the State may be pressured to prosecute the wealthy if their criminal practices become so egregiously offensive that their victims may move to overthrow the system itself. In those cases, the State may punish individual members of the class in order to protect the interests of the entire class. Latent opposition to the practices of corporations may be forestalled, to pick several examples, by token public efforts to enact and enforce antitrust, truth-in-lending, antipollution, industrial safety, and auto safety legislation. As James Ridgeway has most clearly shown in the case of pollution,[51] however, the gap between the enactment of the statutes and their effective enforcement seems quite cavernous.[52]

The answer to the second question seems slightly more complicated historically. Public responses to crime among the poor have changed periodically throughout American history, varying according to changes in the patterns of the crimes themselves and to changes in public morality. The subtlety of that historical process would be difficult to trace in this kind of discussion. But some patterns do seem clear.

Earlier in American history, as Clark has pointed out,[53] we intended to ignore many crimes among the poor because those crimes rarely impinged upon the lives of the more affluent. Gambling, prostitution, dope, and robbery seemed to flourish in the slums of the early twentieth century, and the police rarely moved to intervene. More recently, however, some of the traditional patterns of crime have changed. Two dimensions of change seem most important. On the one hand, much of the crime has moved out of the slums: "Our concern arose when social dynamics and population movements brought crime and addiction out of the slums and inflicted it on or threatened the powerful and well-to-do."[54] On the other hand, the styles in which ghetto criminals have fulfilled their criminal intent may have grown more hostile since World War II, flowing through what I have elsewhere called the "promised land effect."[55] As Claude Brown points out, second-generation Northern blacks—the slum-born sons and daughters of Southern migrants—have relatively little reason to hope that their lives will improve. Their parents migrated in search of better times, but some of those born in the North probably believe that their avenues for escape from poverty have disappeared.

The children of these disillusioned colored pioneers inherited the total lot of their parents—the disappointments, the anger. To add to their misery, they had little hope of deliverance. For where does one run to when he's already in the promised land?[56]

Out of frustration, some of the crime among younger ghetto-born blacks may be more vengeful now, more concerned with sticking it to whitey. Coupled with the spread of ghetto crime into other parts of the city, this symbolic expression of vengefulness undoubtedly heightens the fear that many affluent citizens feel about ghetto crime. Given their influence with the government, they quite naturally have moved toward increasing public attention to the prevention and punishment of crimes among the poor.

Once the patterns of public duality have been established, of course, they acquire a momentum and dynamic all their own. To begin with, vested interests develop, deriving their livelihood and status from the system. The prison system, like the defense industry, becomes a power of its own, with access to public bureaucracies, with workers to support, and with power to defend. Eldridge Cleaver has made special note of this feature of our public system:

The only conclusion one can draw is that the parole system is a procedure devised primarily for the purpose of running people in and out of jail—most of them black—in order to create and maintain a lot of jobs for the white prison system. In California, which I know best—and I'm sure it's the same in other states—there are thousands and thousands of people who draw their living directly or indirectly from the prison system; all the clerks, all the guards, all the bailiffs, all the people who sell goods to the prisons. They regard the inmates as a sort of product from which they all draw their livelihood, and the part of the crop they keep exploiting most are the black inmates.[57]

In much the same way, the police become an interest and a power of their own.[58] They are used and manipulated by the larger society to enforce the law selectively: "We send police to maintain order, to arrest, to jail—and to ignore vital laws also intended to protect life and to prevent deaths."[59] As agents of selective social control, the police also inevitably become the focus of increasing animosity among those they are asked selectively to control. Manipulated by the larger society, hated by those at the bottom, the police tend to develop the men- tality of a "garrison."[60] They eventually seek to serve neither the interests of the larger society nor the interests of the law but the interests of the garrison. One reaches the point, finally, where police interests interject an intermediate membrane screening the priorities of the state and society on the one hand and the interests of their victims on the other. "When enforcement of the law con- flicts with the ends of the police, the law is not enforced. When it supports the ends of the police, they are fully behind it. When it bears no relation to the ends of the police, they enforce it as a matter of routine."[61]

The Implausibility of Reform

One needs to ask, finally, whether these patterns can be changed and the trends reversed. Can we simultaneously eradicate the causes of crime and reform our dual system of justice? At the heart of that question lies the question posed at the beginning of this essay, for it simultaneously raises the necessity of ex- plaining the failures of our present system to prevent the crime it seeks most systematically to control.

I would argue, quite simply, that reform is implausible unless we change the basic institutions upon which capitalism in the United States depends. We cannot legitimately expect to eradicate the initial causes of crime for two rea- sons. First, capitalism depends quite substantially on the preservation of the conditions of competition and inequality. Those conditions, as I argue above, will tend to lead quite inevitably to relatively pervasive criminal behavior; with- out those conditions, the capitalist system would scarcely work at all. Second, as many have argued, the general presence of racism in this country, though capi- talists may not in fact have created it, tends to support and maintain the power of the capitalists as a class by providing cheap labor and dividing the working class. Given the substantial control of capitalists over the policies and priorities of the State, we cannot easily expect to prod the State to eliminate the funda- mental causes of racism in this country. In that respect, it seems likely that the particular inequalities facing blacks and their consequent attraction to the op- portunities available in crime seem likely to continue.

Given expectations that crime will continue, it seems equally unlikely that we shall be able to reform our systems of prosecution and punishment in order to mitigate their harmful effects on criminals and to equalize their treatment of different kinds of crime. First and superficially, as I noted above, several im- portant and powerful vested interests have acquired a stake in the current system and seem likely to resist efforts to change it. Second and more fundamentally, the cumulative effect of the patterns of crime, violence, prosecution, and punish- ment in this country plays an important role in helping legitimize and stabilize the capitalist system. Although capitalists as a class may not have created the current patterns of crime and punishment, those patterns currently serve their interests in several different ways. We should expect that the capitalists as a class will hardly be able to push reform of the system. Given their relative reluctance to reform the system, we should expect to be able to push reform only in the event that we can substantially change the structure of power to which the State responds.

The current patterns of crime and punishment support the capitalist system in three different ways.

First, the pervasive patterns of selective enforcement seem to reinforce a prevalent ideology in this society that individuals, rather than institutions, are to blame for social problems. Individuals are criminally prosecuted for motor accidents because of negligent or drunken driving, for instance, but auto manufacturers are never criminally prosecuted for the negligent construction of unsafe cars or for their roles in increasing the likelihood of death through air pollution. Individual citizens are often prosecuted and punished for violence and for resisting arrest, equally, but those agents of institutions, like police and prison guards, or institutions themselves, like Dow Chemical, are never prosecuted for inflicting unwarranted violence on others. These patterns of selectivity reinforce our pervasive preconceptions of the invulnerability of institutions, leading us to blame ourselves for social failure; this pattern of individual blame, as Edwards and MacEwan have especially argued,[62] plays an important role in legitimizing the basic institutions of this kind of capitalist society.

Second, and critically important, the patterns of crime and punishment manage "legitimately" to neutralize the potential opposition to the system of many of our most oppressed citizens. In particular, the system serves ultimately to keep thousands of men out of the job market or trapped in the secondary labor market by perpetuating a set of institutions which serves functionally to feed large numbers of blacks (and poor whites) through the cycle of crime, imprisonment, parole, and recidivism. The system has this same ultimate effect in many different ways. It locks up many for life, first of all, guaranteeing that those potentially disaffected souls keep "out of trouble." As for those whom it occasionally releases, it tends to drive them deeper into criminality, intensifying their criminal and violent behavior, filling their heads with paranoia and hatred, keeping them perpetually on the run and unable, ultimately, to organize with others to change the institutions which pursue them. Finally, it blots their records with the stigma of criminality and, by denying them many decent employment opportunities, effectively precludes the reform of even those who vow to escape the system and to go "straight."[63]

The importance of this neutralization should not be underestimated. If all young black men in this country do not eventually become criminals, most of them are conscious of the trap into which they might fall. The late George Jackson wrote from prison: "Blackmen born in the U.S. and fortunate enough to live past the age of eighteen are conditioned to accept the inevitability of prison. For most of us, it simply looms as the next phase in a sequence of humiliations."[64] And once they are trapped, the cycle continues almost regardless of the will of those involved. Prison, parole, and the eventual return to prison become standard points on the itinerary. Cleaver has written:

I noticed that every time I went back to jail, the same guys who were in Juvenile Hall with me were also there again. They arrived there soon after I got there, or a little bit before I left. They always seemed to make the scene. In the

California prison system, they carry you from Juvenile Hall to the old folks' colony, down in San Luis Obispo, and wait for you to die. Then they bury you there. . . . I noticed these waves, these generations . . . graduating classes moving up from Juvenile Hall, all the way up.[65]

And those who succeed finally in understanding the trap and in pulling themselves out of it, like Malcolm X, Claude Brown, Eldridge Cleaver, and George Jackson, seem to succeed precisely because they understood how debilitating the cycle becomes, how totally dehumanizing it will remain. Another black ex-con has perfectly expressed the sudden insight which allowed him to pull out of the trap:

> It didn't take me any time to decide I wasn't going back to commit crimes. Because it's stupid, it's a trap, it only makes it easier for them to neutralize you. It's hard to explain, because you can't say it's a question of right and wrong, but of being free or [being] trapped.[66]

If the system did not effect this neutralization, if so many of the poor were not trapped in the debilitating system of crime and punishment, they might gather the strength to oppose the system that reinforces their misery. Like many other institutions in this country, the system of crime and punishment serves an important function for the capitalist class by dividing and weakening those who might potentially seek to overthrow the capitalist system. Although the capitalists have not created the system, in any direct sense, they would doubtlessly hate to have to do without it.[67]

The third and perhaps most important functionally supportive role of the current patterns of crime and punishment is that those patterns allow us to ignore some basic issues about the relationships in our society between institutions and individuals. By treating criminals as animals and misfits, as enemies of the state, we are permitted to continue avoiding some basic questions about the dehumanizing effects of our social institutions. We keep our criminals out of sight, so we are never forced to recognize and deal with the psychic punishment we inflict on them. Like the schools and the welfare system, the legal system turns out, upon close inspection, to be robbing most of its "clients" of the last vestiges of their personal dignity. Each one of those institutions, in its own way, helps us forget about the responsibilities we might alternatively assume for providing the best possible environment within which all of us could grow and develop as individuals. Cleaver sees this "role" of the system quite clearly:

> Those who are now in prison could be put through a process of real rehabilitation before their release. . . . By rehabilitation I mean they would be trained for jobs that would not be an insult to their dignity, that would give them some sense of security, that would allow them to achieve some brotherly connection with their fellow man. But for this kind of rehabilitation to happen on a large scale would entail the complete reorganization of society, not to mention the prison system. It would call for the teaching of a new set of ethics, based on the principle of cooperation, as opposed to the presently dominating principle of competition. It would require the transformation of the entire moral fabric.[68]

By keeping its victims so thoroughly hidden and rendering them so apparently inhuman, our system of crime and punishment allows us to forget how sweeping a "transformation" of our social ideology we would require in order to begin solving the problem of crime. The more we forget, the more protected the capitalists remain from a thorough re-examination of the ideological basis of the institutions upon which they depend.

It seems useful to summarize briefly the analysis outlined in this section, in order both to emphasize the connections among its arguments and to clarify its differences with other "models" of crime and punishment. Most crimes in this country share a single important similarity—they represent rational responses to the competitiveness and inequality of life in capitalist societies. (In this emphasis on the rationality of crime, the analysis differs with the "conventional public analyses" of crime and resembles the orthodox economic approach.) Many crimes seem very different at the same time, but many of their differences—in character and degree of violence—can usefully be explained by the structure of class institutions in this country and the duality of the public system of the enforcement and administration of justice. (In this central deployment of the radical concepts of class and the class-biased State, the analysis differs fundamentally with both the "public" and the orthodox economic perspectives.) That duality, in turn, can fruitfully be explained by a dynamic view of the class-biased role of public institutions and the vested interests which evolve out of the State's activities. For many reasons, finally, it seems unlikely that we can change the patterns of crime and punishment, for the kinds of changes we would need would appear substantially to threaten the stability of the capitalist system. If we managed somehow to eliminate ghetto crime, for instance, the competitiveness, inequalities, and racism of our institutions would tend to reproduce it. And if, by chance, the pattern of ghetto crime was not reproduced, the capitalists might simply have to invent some other way of neutralizing the potential opposition of so many black men, against which they might once again be forced to rebel with "criminal acts." It is in that sense of fundamental causality that we must somehow change the entire structure of institutions in this country in order to eliminate the causes of crime.

5. A NORMATIVE VIEW OF CRIME

Strangely enough, I find it easiest to evoke an alternative normative view of crime and to compare it with our current social responses to the problem by drawing on a recent exchange in the legal literature.

In a widely heralded article written in 1964, Herbert Packer, a leading American legal expert on criminal process, argued that most legal discussion of criminal procedure involves a conflict (or dialogue) between two different models of the criminal process. He called one of these the "Crime Control Model" and the other the "Due Process Model." The emphases embodied in each model closely resemble the difference in emphasis between the general conservative and liberal views of crime, respectively, as described in the second section of this article. The Crime Control Model, according to Packer, "is based on the proposition that the repression of criminal conduct is by far the most important function to be performed by the criminal process." The Due Process Model, on the other hand, derives from the "concept of the primacy of the individual and the complementary concept of limitation on official power."[69]

In reply to Packer's article, John Griffiths argued that Packer's two models represent qualitatively similar views of the relationship between the criminal and society, deriving from some common ideological assumptions about the law.[70] Griffiths calls this set of shared assumptions the "Battle Model of the Criminal Process." He argues that both the conservative and liberal views derive from a common vision of conflict and hostility between the aberrant, deviant individual on the one hand and the social "order" on the other. To illustrate the communality of the two models proposed by Packer, Griffiths suggests a third model which closely resembles what I presume to be the radical vision of how society should respond to its "criminals." He calls this the "Family Model of the Criminal Process," suggesting that society's treatment of criminals could easily be patterned after the treatment by families of those family members who betray the family trust. The Family Model begins from an assumption, Griffiths writes, of "reconcilable—even mutually supportive—interests, a state of love."[71] In contrast to the Battle Model, the Family Model would propose that "we can make plain that while the criminal has transgressed, we do not therefore cut him off from us; our concern and dedication to his well-being continue. We have punished him and drawn him back in among us; we have not cast him out to fend for himself against our systematic enmity." As in the best families, society would work actively, supportively, and lovingly to restore the state of trust and mutual respect upon which the family and society should both be based. Rather than forcing the criminal to admit his failure and reform himself, we would all admit our mutual failures and seek to reform the total community—in which effort the criminal would play an important, constructive, and educative role.

The Battle Model, as Griffiths describes it, obviously reflects not only liberal and conservative views of crime but the manifest reality of our social treatment of criminals in this country; it is reflected exactly in a psychiatrist's recent description of the ideology underlying the California prisons:

> The people who run these places . . . believe that the way to get a man's behavior to change is to impose very strict controls and take away everything he values and make him work to get it back. But that doesn't make him change. It just generates more and more rage and hostility.[72]

The Family Model, in contrast, illustrates the fundamentally different priorities which might motivate institutional responses to criminal behavior in a radically different kind of society, one in which human needs were served and developed by social institutions rather than sacrificed to the interests of a single dominant class. That vision of social response may seem like a very distant dream in this country, but it seems like a dream worthy of all our most determined pursuit.

NOTES

[1]Gary Becker, "Crime and Punishment: An Economic Approach," *Journal of Political Economy* (March-April 1968):170

[2]I am not an expert on crime and I have not pursued extensive research about the problem. The thoughts in this paper draw mainly on some limited elementary reading; as a layman in the field, I offer these thoughts with considerable hesitation, which has especially affected by style of argument. Since I do not speak with authority, I have tried wherever possible to include quotes from respected and respectable "authorities" to support my arguments.

[3]President's Commission on Law Enforcement and Administration of Justice, *The Challenge of Crime in a Free Society* (Washington, D.C.: U.S. Government Printing Office, 1967); Ramsey Clark, *Crime in America* (New York: Simon and Schuster, 1970). For some useful summaries of the basic data, see the first two reading selections in the chapter on crime in *Problems in Political Economy: An Urban Perspective,* ed. David M. Gordon (Lexington, Mass.: D. C. Heath, 1971). Another useful summary of information about "urban crime" can be found in Marvin E. Wolfgang, "Urban Crime," in *The Metropolitan Enigma,* ed. James. Q. Wilson (Cambridge, Mass.: Harvard University Press, 1968). For much more detailed information, see the appendices to President's Commission. *Corrections* (1967), *The Courts* (1967), and *Crime and Its Impact—An Assessment* (1967). For some interesting comments on the Crime Commission Report, *see* James Q. Wilson, "Crime in the Streets," *The Public Interest,* No. 5, Fall 1966.

[4]President's Commission, *Challenge of Crime,* p. v.

[5]One should add, of course, that these figures refer only to those harmful acts which actually violate some law. Many other tangibly harmful acts, like faulty manufacture of automobiles or certain kinds of pollution, have not yet been declared illegal.

[6]Clark also notes, in *Crime in America,* that the increase may be misleading, simply because many kinds of crime are much more likely to be reported these days than were comparable crimes, say, 30 years ago.

[7]Ibid., p. 38.

[8]Ibid., p. 54. Violent crimes, on the other hand, are more frequently committed by adults. As Clark explains it (p. 55), "It takes longer to harden the young to violence."

[9]The reason that the arrest rates may be spurious is that, as Clark and Ronald Goldfarb ("Prison: The National Poorhouse," *The New Republic,* November 1969) have especially noted, blacks are much more likely than whites to be arrested whether they have committed a crime or not. Despite that immeasurable bias in the arrest statistics, it is nonetheless assumed that blacks commit a larger percentage of most crimes than their share of urban populations.

[10]Clark, *Crime in America,* p. 38.

[11]President's Commission and Goldfarb, "Prison."

[12]Goldfarb, "Prison," p. 312 (emphasis in the original). It is one thing to cite this "duality" as fact, of course, and quite another thing to explain it. I cite it now as a phenomenon requiring explanation and shall try to explain it later.

[13]Clark, p. 313.

[14]Ibid., p. 55.

[15]For an easy reference to the differences between the general "liberal" and "conservative" views, *see* "General Perspectives—Radical, Liberal, Conservative," chap. 1 in Gordon, *Political Economy.* For a good example of traditional discussion of the problem, *see* Edwin H. Sutherland, *Principle of Criminology,* 6th ed. (Philadelphia: Lippincott, 1960).

[16]For the clearest exposition of the conservative view on crime, *see* the chapter on crime in Edward C. Banfield, *The Unheavenly City* (Boston: Little, Brown, 1970).

[17]Banfield (ibid., p. 184) has clearly formulated the conservative equation: "In any event, if abridging the freedom of persons who have not committed crimes is incompatible with the principles of free society, so, also, is the presence in such society of persons who, if their freedom is not abridged, would use it to inflict serious injuries on others. There is, therefore, a painful dilemma. If some people's freedom is not abridged by law-enforcement agencies, that of others will be abridged by lawbreakers. The question, therefore, is not whether abridging the freedom of those who may commit serious crimes is an evil—it is—but whether it is a lesser or a greater one than the alternative."
For the increasing tendency of the Nixon administration to apply the conservative perspective in its policies toward crime, *see* Richard Harris, *Justice* (New York: Dutton,

1970). For a superb analysis of the legal aspects of the major Nixon crime legislation, *see* Herbert Packer, "Nixon's Crime Program and What It Means," *New York Review of Books* (Oct. 22, 1970).

[18]For a summary of the general liberal perspective, *see* chap. 1 in Gordon. For a good statement of the pluralist argument, *see* Arnold Rose, *The Power Structure: Political Process in America* (New York: Oxford University Press, 1968).

[19]The clearest expressions of the liberal view of crime are contained in three reports of Presidential commissions published in the late 1960s: President's Commission, *The Challenge of Crime;* National Advisory Commission on Civil Disorders, *Report* (New York: Bantam Books, 1968); National Commission on the Causes and Prevention of Violence, *To Establish Justice, To Insure Domestic Tranquility* (New York: Bantam Books, 1970).

[20]President's Commission, p. v.

[21]Ibid., p. 5.

[22]Wolfgang writes ("Urban Crime," p. 275), "Urban crime might be reduced by significant proportions if more talent, time, and funds were put into public use to produce the kind of research findings necessary to make more rational informed decisions." The Commission on Violence concluded (*To Establish Justice,* p. 40), "We reiterate our previous recommendations that we double our national investment in the criminal justice process."

[23]Fred P. Graham, "Black Crime: The Lawless Image," *Harper's* (September 1970), p. 68. This debate, indeed, has some fascinating historical roots, for both the liberal and conservative positions have borrowed in very different ways from classic nineteenth-century liberalism, especially from the work of John Stuart Mill. For one of the clearest comparisons of the two perspectives and their common legacies, *see* Robert Paul Wolff, *The Poverty of Liberalism* (Boston: Beacon Press, 1968).

[24]For the most notable pieces of the recent literature, *see* Becker, "Crime and Punishment"; George Stigler, "The Optimum Enforcement of Laws," *Journal of Political Economy* (May-June 1970); Lester C. Thurow, "Equity and Efficiency in Justice," *Public Policy* (Summer 1970); and Gordon Tullock, *General Standards: The Logic of Law and Ethics,* Virginia Polytechnic Institute, 1968, unpublished manuscript; and "An Economic Approach to Crime," *Social Science Quarterly* (June 1969). Some attempts have been made to apply the orthodox analysis empirically; for one such attempt, still unpublished at the time of writing, *see* William Landes, "An Economic Analysis of the Courts," National Bureau of Economic Research, 1970, unpublished manuscript.

[25]Becker, p. 176.

[26]Stigler, "Optimum Enforcement," p. 530.

[27]Becker, p. 174.

[28]Becker admits (p. 209) that the analysis is hampered by "the absence of a reliable theory of political decision-making." Tullock is the only one who makes the underlying political assumption precise and explicit. He writes (*General Standards,* p. II-2): "My first general assumption, then, is that the reader is not in a position to assure himself of special treatment in any legal system. That is, if I argue that the reader should favor a law against theft, one of the basic assumptions will be that he does not have a real opportunity to get a law enacted which prohibits theft by everyone else but leaves him free to steal himself." He adds that this assumption "will . . . underlie all of the specific proposals" he makes in his manuscript.

[29]For a summary of those basic perspectives in richer detail, see my introduction to chap. 1 in Gordon and the selection by Edwards and MacEwan in Richard Edwards, Arthur MacEwan, and others, "A Radical Approach to Economics," *American Economic Review* (May 1970), reprinted in Gordon.

[30]For an amplification of these contentions, *see* Gordon and especially Edwards and MacEwan, "Radical Approach." There is some confusion, admittedly, about the proper

definition of the concept of class in the radical literature, in part because Marx himself used the term in several different meanings. For a useful discussion of the different kinds of meaning of the concept, *see* Stanislaw Ossowski, *Class Structure in the Social Consciousness* trans. Sheila Patterson (New York: Free Press, 1963). For a clear description, however short, of the analytic link in the Marxist analysis between the "social relations of production" and the definition and determination of "economic class," *see* Robert Tucker, *The Marxian Revolutionary Idea* (New York: W. W. Norton, 1969).

[31]For a useful discussion of the radical theory of the state, *see* Paul Sweezy, "The State," chap. 13 of *The Theory of Capitalist Development* (New York: Monthly Review Press, 1968), partially reprinted in Gordon; and Ralph Milliband, *The State in Capitalist Society* (New York: Basic Books, 1969).

[32]The argument is best illustrated by the "problems" of racism and sexism in capitalist societies. Capitalists did not create the problems but the phenomena of racism and sexism serve useful functions in the United States through their pervasiveness. They help forge large pools of cheap labor and help divide the labor force into highly stratified competitive groups of workers, among whom united worker opposition to capitalists becomes relatively more difficult to develop. If one somehow erased the phenomena of racism and sexism by creating a perfect equality of opportunities among the races and sexes, the process through which capitalists are able to accrue their profits and keep the working class divided would be substantially threatened. In that respect, one can hardly expect capitalists to favor the eradication of racism and sexism spontaneously, although they might be forced to move toward their eradication if the costs of not doing so become too high. For more on this kind of reasoning, see the chapters on employment, education, and poverty in Gordon.

[33]Adam Smith, *The Wealth of Nations* (New York: Modern Library, 1937), p. 670.

[34]This is not meant to imply, obviously, that there would be no crime in a communist society in which perfectly secure equal support was provided for all. It suggests, quite simply, that one would have to analyze crime in such a society with reference to a different set of ideas and a different set of institutions.

[35]Our knowledge of ghetto crime draws primarily from the testimony of several ex-ghetto criminals, as in Claude Brown, *Manchild in the Promised Land* (New York: Macmillan, 1965); Eldridge Cleaver, *Post-Prison Writings and Speeches* (New York: A Ramparts Book by Random House, 1969); George Jackson, *Soledad Brother* (New York: Bantam Books, 1970); and Malcolm X, *Autobiography* (New York: Grove Press, 1964). For more analytic studies, *see* Clifford Shaw and Henry McKay, *Juvenile Delinquency and Urban Areas* (Chicago: University of Chicago Press, 1969); and Marvin E. Wolfgang and Franco Ferracuti, *The Subculture of Violence* (New York: Barnes and Noble, 1967). For interesting evidence on the different attitudes toward crime of poor and middle-class youth, *see* Leonard Goodwin, "Work Orientations of the Underemployed Poor," *Journal of Human Resources* (Fall 1969). For a bit of "analytic" evidence on the critical interaction between job prospects and rates of recidivism, *see* Robert Evans, Jr., "The Labor Market and Parole Success," *Journal of Human Resources* (Spring 1968).

[36]For more on the structure of jobs available, see chap. 2 in Gordon. One often finds informal support for such contentions. A Manhattan prostitute once said about her crimes, "What is there to say. We've got a living to earn. There wouldn't be any prostitution if there weren't a demand for it." Quoted in the *New York Times,* May 29, 1970. A black high school graduate discussed the problem at greater length with an interviewer in Herb Goro, *The Block* (New York: Random House, 1970), p. 146: "That's why a lot of brothers are out on the street now, stinging, robbing people, mugging, 'cause when they get a job, man, they be doing their best, and the white man get jealous 'cause he feel this man could do better than he doing. 'I got to get rid of him!' So they fire him, so a man, he lose his pride. . . . They give you something, and then they take it away from you. . . . And people tell you jobs are open for everybody on the street. There's no reason for you to be stealing. That's a lie! If you're a thief, I'd advise you to be a good thief. 'Cause you working, Jim, you ain't going to succeed unless you got some kind of influence."

[37]Claude Brown and Arthur Dunmeyer, "A Way of Life in the Ghetto," in Gordon, p. 292.

[38]Ibid., p. 293. A friend of Claude Brown's made a similar point about the ineffectiveness of the threat of jail (Brown, *Manchild,* p. 412): "When I go to jail now, Sonny, I live, man. I'm right at home. . . . When I go back to the joint, anywhere I go, I know some people. If I go to any of the jails in New York, or if I go to a slam in Jersey, even, I still run into a lot of cats I know. It's almost like a family."

[39]For two of the best available analyses of organized crime, *see* Donald Cressey, *Theft of the Nation: The Structure and Operations of Organized Crime* (New York: Harper & Row, 1969); and Norval Morris and Gordon Hawkins, *The Honest Politician's Guide to Crime Control* (Chicago: University of Chicago Press, 1969).

[40]Cressey, *Theft,* p. 294.

[41]Clark, *Crime in America,* p. 68.

[42]As Cressey *(Theft)* points out, for instance, it makes a great deal of sense in the heroin industry for the supplier to seek a monopoly on the source of the heroin but to permit many individual sellers of heroin at its final destination, usually without organization backing, because the risks occur primarily at the consumers' end.

[43]Edwin H. Sutherland, "The Crime of Corporations," in Gordon, p. 310.

[44]Clark, p. 38.

[45]Robert Morgenthau, "Equal Justice and the Problem of White Collar Crime," *The Conference Board Record* (August 1969), p. 20

[46]Clark, p. 39.

[47]Cressey, *Theft.*

[48]Robert Sherrill, "The Convenience of Being Lockheed," *Scanlan's Monthly* (August 1970), p. 43.

[49]It is possible to argue, as this point suggests, that heroin addicts would not be prone either to violence or to crime if heroin were legal and free. The fact that it is illegal and that the police go after its consumers means that a cycle of crime and violence is established from which it becomes increasingly difficult to escape.

[50]Sweezy, "The State."

[51]James Ridgeway, *The Politics of Ecology* (New York: Dutton, 1970).

[52]This rests on an assumption, of course, that one learns much more about the priorities of the State by looking at its patterns of enforcement than by noting the nature of its statutes. This seems quite reasonable. The statutory process is often cumbersome, whereas the patterns of enforcement can sometimes be changed quite easily. (Stigler, "Optimum Enforcement," makes the same point.) Furthermore, as many radicals would argue, the State in democratic societies can often support the capitalist class most effectively by selective enforcement of the laws rather than by selective legislation. For varieties of relatively complicated historical reasons, selective enforcement of the law seems to arouse less fear for the erosion of democratic tradition than selective legislation itself. As long as we have statutes which nominally outlaw racial inequality, for instance, inadequate enforcement of those laws seems to cause relatively little furor; before we had such laws in this country, protests against the selective statutes could ultimately be mounted.

[53]Clark, pp. 55-56.

[54]Ibid., p. 55.

[55]Gordon.

[56]Brown, *Manchild,* p. 8.

[57]Cleaver, *Writings,* p. 185.

[58]For some useful references on the police, *see* Paul Chevigny, *Police Power* (New York) Pantheon, 1969); William Westley, *Violence and Police* (Cambridge, Mass.: M.I.T. Press, 1970); and James Q. Wilson, *Varieties of Police Behavior* (New York: Basic Books, 1969). For a review of that literature, with some very interesting comments about the police, *see* Murray Kempton, "Cops," *New York Review of Books,* Nov. 5, 1970. For one discussion of the first hints of evidence that there may not, in fact, be any kind of identifiable relationship between the number of police we have and their effectiveness, *see* Richard Reeves, "Police: Maybe They Should Be Doing Something Different," *New York Times,* Jan. 24, 1971.

[59]Clark, p. 137.

[60]Westley, *Violence and Police.*

[61]Ibid.

[62]*Supra* note 29.

[63]For the most devastating story about how the neutralization occurs to even the most innocent of ghetto blacks, *see* Eliot Asinof, *People vs. Blutcher* (New York: Viking, 1970).

[64]Jackson, *Soledad.*

[65]Cleaver, *Writings,* pp. 154-55.

[66]Bell Gale Chevigny, "After the Death of Jail," *Village Voice,* July 10, 1969; partially reprinted in Gordon.

[67]One should not underestimate the importance of this effect for quantitative as well as qualitative reasons. In July 1968, for instance, an estimated 140,000 blacks were serving time in penal institutions at federal, state, and local levels. If the percentage of black males in prison had been as low as the proportions of white men (by age groups), there would have been only 25,000 blacks in jail. If those extra 115,000 black men were not in prison, they would likely be unemployed or intermittently employed. In addition, official labor force figures radically undercount the number of blacks in the census because many black males are simply missed by the census-taker. In July 1968, almost one million black males were "missed" in that way. On the conservative assumption that one-fifth of those "missing males" were in one way or another evading the law, involved in hustling, or otherwise trapped in the legal system, a total of 315,000 black men who might be unemployed were it not for the effects of the law were not counted in "measured" unemployment statistics. Total "measured" black male unemployment in July 1968 was 317,000, so that the total black unemployment problem might be nearly twice as large as we "think" it is were it not for the selective effects of our police, courts, and prisons on black men.

[68]Cleaver, *Writings,* pp. 179, 182.

[69]Herbert Packer, "Two Models of the Criminal Process," *University of Pennsylvania Law Review* (November 1964).

[70]John Griffiths, "Ideology in Criminal Procedure, or a Third 'Model' of the Criminal Process," *Yale Law Journal* (January 1970).

[71]Ibid., p. 371.

[72]Quoted in the *New York Times,* Feb. 7, 1971, p. 64.

RACE, CRIME AND THE CRIMINOLOGIST

CHARLES E. REASONS

The relationship between race and crime has long been a subject of concern among criminologists (Bonger, 1943; Wolfgang and Cohen, 1970; Reasons and Kuykendall, 1972)—in examining some of the contemporary textbooks in criminology one usually will find a section devoted specifically to this subject (Barnes and Teeters, 1959:163-76; England and Taft, 1964:103-19; Sutherland and Cressey, 1970:132-51; Johnson, 1964:81-89). Whereas several inquiries into the treatment of racial minorities in the judicial process have been conducted (Sellin, 1928, 1935; Johnson, 1941; Lemert and Roseberg, 1948; Hindelang, 1969) most of the research has been concerned with identifying and interpreting differential arrest rates by race (Brinton, 1932; Beach, 1932; Haynes, 1942; Von Hentig, 1945; Moses, 1936, 1947; Stewart, 1964; Rice, 1966; Forslund, 1970; Green, 1970; Reasons, 1972).

RACE, SCIENCE, AND EXPLANATION

Why has there been so much attention given to the racial variable in criminological writing? The most obvious answer appears to be that this variable is related to crime, and since an important task of the criminologist as a scientist is to empirically ascertain such relationships, the racial variable must be considered. But what do we mean when we say that this variable is *related* to crime? This relationship usually denotes the finding that the two variables of race and crime are associated with one another in a seemingly significant manner. The description of this relationship, or our doing sociography (Seeley, 1963), is the essence of much criminological research.

The fact that these two variables are related may leave us seeking an answer to the question of *why* they are related—thus we move to doing sociology, that is, explaining. After identifying the relationship between race and crime, criminology texts attempt to explain that relationship, for, according to Sutherland and Cressey (1970:132), "any general theory of criminal behavior should explain all the ratios, e.g., sex, age, race and also the variations in the ratios." By explanation we usually mean concern with the explanation of events, not with reasons or evidences one might cite in favor of propositions (Hospers, 1960).

Is an explanation of why arrest rates vary by race a statement of causation? It would seem that this is implied in most of the research, although not always explicitly stated. Although the concept of "cause" is tactfully avoided in

Charles E. Reasons, *Race, Crime and the Criminologist*. Prepared especially for this volume.

much empirical work, sociology in general and criminology specifically have largely operated from a deterministic model of sorts (Wilkins, 1968). Criminological investigation has remained very immersed in a positivistic, deterministic approach (Matza, 1964:1-32).Even though the nature of the causes of crime has changed from a genetic to a sociologistic frame of reference, they remain based on a deterministic model.

A historical analysis of criminological writing concerning the racial variable provides an excellent example of the influence of the social milieu upon criminological thinking. It may be that such an analysis may tell us as much, or more, about criminologists as it does about criminals (Mills, 1943; Horowitz, 1968). The Dutch criminologist, William Adrian Bonger, traces the beginning of genetic analysis to the Italian school of criminology at the end of the nineteenth century (Bonger, 1943). The belief in innate differences in potentiality for criminal behavior reflected an era of social Darwinism, imperialism, and racist ideology (Gossett, 1963). American interest in the criminogenic effect of "race" arose with the great concern about the immigrant and his supected high rate of crime (Ferracuti, 1968). The president of the California State Law Enforcement League epitomized the public concern in a 1925 article (Grant, 1925) in which he said:

> It is the law-breaking foreigners who we are talking about now. Schooled in low standards of morality, they seek to impose their European customs upon their new-found Land of Liberty. . . . Foreigners are predominant in all the big movements of lawlessness and these movements aim at anarchy.

Concern with ethnicity and nativity turned to concern with race as the urbanization of racial minorities increased. As the attention to nativity and crime diminished, race and crime came to the forefront of public concern in the 1960s. In a survey for the President's Commission, crime was found to be second only to race as the public's greatest domestic concern (President's Commission, 1967). The shift from the earlier "kinds of people" approach epitomized by Hooton (1939) has been to a "kinds of environment" approach which is cogently summarized by Wolfgang and Cohen (1970:34) in their explanation of differential crime rates:

> None of these figures demonstrates that Negroes as a race are more prone to crime. They do demonstrate that the average black citizen is more likely than the average white citizen to be exposed to a plethora of conditions that result in his being arrested, convicted, and imprisoned. *Most of these conditions are inherent in the social structure and are not subject to control by the individuals* (italics added).

Therefore, although a deterministic model is still evident, external forces in the social milieu, rather than personal failings, are identified as the principal explanatory variable. In fact, this seems to be a logical outcome of Mertonian theory of deviance, which when taken to its deterministic end indicates the need for change in the social structure (Merton, 1968). Although much literature emphasizes such structural defects, most ameliorative plans emphasize changing potential or actual criminals, rather than major social institutions and structures. The increasing politicization of marginal people—such as blacks, Chicanos, poor

—is largely due to their increasing realization of the need for structural change.[1] As a number of minorities have attempted to change their life situation through collective action, they have increasingly recognized that the scales of justice are almost inevitably weighted against them. This realization is nothing more than the basic fact that the law is largely an instrument of those who have power. According to a noted criminologist (Short, Jr., 1970, 2):

> In the making of law, in their ability to secure protection under the law, and in advantages accruing from discretion of its enforcement, those with the greatest political and economic power benefit the most. *Thus, the young and the economically and politically impotent have been the primary focus of attention, not only of laws but of criminologists* (italics added).

THE POLITICS OF CRIME

The basically political nature of crime is fairly obvious, but attention to this essential feature has only recently emerged as an important aspect of criminological writing[2] (Quinney, 1970; "Crime, Law, and the State," 1970; Chambliss and Seidman, 1971). The criminologist as "moral alchemist," like other students of deviant behavior, has often failed to make such fundamental distinctions. An important facet of the political approach to crime is the analysis of the emergence of crime, through the establishment of laws. Such analyses have dealt with drugs (Becker, 1963; Dickson, 1968; Gusfield, 1966; Reasons, 1972), prostitution (Reasons, 1970), theft (Hall, 1952), vagrancy (Chambliss, 1964), sexual statutes (Sutherland, 1950), and juvenile delinquency (Platt, 1971). These have provided insight into the political nature of crime and the varying interest groups that are influential in lawmaking.

The history of the American legal structure in relationship to nonwhites in our society provides a clear example of the influence economic and political power have upon the scales of justice.[3] One of the biggest obstacles to a frank national confrontation of the problems of race relations in our society is the reluctance of most Americans to admit that the original Constitution and both common law and statutory law thereafter provided for inequality along racial lines (Miller, 1966; Vann Woodward, 1969; Stampp, 1970; Willhelm, 1969; Cohen and Mause, 1968). Only within the last few decades has the American legal structure rid itself of the remaining explicit manifestations of racism in the law (Crockett, Jr., 1969).

Nonetheless, legal definitions of race remain important concerning a number of facets of life ("Legal Definitions of Race," 1958). This has been partly due to the attempts by blacks, Native-Americans, and Chicanos to change their political and economic situation through collective action. Their use of the legal structure in an attempt to correct long-standing inequities is a relatively new phenomenon which is becoming more widespread (Greenberg, 1959; Brown, Jr., 1970). In fact, one judge has proposed that we recognize a new field of law—the law of race relations (Larson, 1969). Of course one must realize that the elimination of explicit racism in the law does not signal the end to discrimination along racial lines. Institutional racism in the law is still apparent (Knowles and Prewitt, 1969). Proclaiming equality before the law does not change substantially the economic and political situation of nonwhites. The combination of being nonwhite, economically disadvantaged (Wald, 1970; Tenbroek, 1966), and culturally different (Swett, 1969) makes "equality before the law" a myth of enormous proportions.

Now that marginal people are entering into the political arena in increasing numbers, the political nature of crime becomes more apparent (Horowitz and Liebowitz, 1967). With a number of groups vying to legitimize their definitions of rightness over others, conflict is exacerbated and a conflict approach to crime may be appropriate (Turk, 1966). Although Mertonian anomie theory is recognized as important in the explanation of crime, it is not usually connected with culture conflict; nonetheless they are not contradictory and may be quite complementary to one another (Schafer, 1968). The increasing divisiveness in our society is reflected in the growing split in sociology concerning the place of the academician vis-à-vis contemporary issues. This debate is particularly acute in the area of deviance in general (Becker, 1967; Gouldner, 1968) and one would anticipate its more complete emergence in criminology in the near future.

SO WHAT?

What do all these "revelations" concerning crime, race, and the criminologist suggest? One might contend that the continued concern of sociologists with the racial variable is merely a manifestation of a peculiar kind of racism (Schuman, 1969) or a reflection of a general societal obsession (Miller, 1966). Of course scientific racism has a long history (Comas, 1961), and such accusations are in part true. Since the racial variable has been found to be of less import than others in the analysis of arrest rates (Green, 1970) should we then eliminate the racial variable from criminological analysis?

Geis (1965) concludes that criminal statistics concerning race are misleading and readily subject to misinterpretation, and that their elimination would do little harm. Although his argument is compelling,[4] the elimination of such classification will hardly eliminate the public concern with the issue and may have some unintended consequences. For example, the author attempted to analyze the impact of the racial variable in court processing in a large urban area. It was discovered that such statistics were no longer kept because of prior concern with discrimination. Needless to say, a defendant's race may still be important in the court setting regardless of whether it is officially recorded or not.[5]

Inevitably, this paper raises many more questions than it answers. Nonetheless, a few concluding observations may be made concerning the topic at hand. It seems that the racial variable will remain important in criminological writing, as it will in more general sociological work and popular literature.

Although the racial variable will remain one of the "focal concerns" of criminologists, the traditional, antiseptic "kinds of environment" approach will yield to a more politically oriented conflict approach, in keeping with the contemporary milieu. Such a shift in focus portends an increasing divisiveness between practitioners of the traditional approach and those of the new perspective. Of course, this reflects the growing schism between young academicians and their professional elders in a number of disciplines. Many young criminologists today were active in or identified with the "youth movement" of the 1960s and operate under somewhat different assumptions concerning the nature of our society than do their professional elders.

The growing awareness of and concern with the political nature of crime
y be quite discomforting to the criminologist, particularly with reference to
underclass in general and racial minorities in particular. The "realization"
t the causes of minority crime largely transcend individual responsibility[6]
gests that the focus of criminological writing, and consequently of criminoists, will undergo further change. If a "plethora of conditions" are translated
o a number of political issues, what then? Criminologists will increasingly be
afronted with this question for which their professional socialization has
gely failed to prepare them. It may be that many are very "fit in an unfit fits" for the demands of contemporary society. As is true of the scientific enterse, many of the "significant others" of criminology today will become the
insignificant mothers"[7] of tomorrow as the social milieu and ideological orienions shift in the future.

OTES

[1]In Mills' terms (1959), problems previously conceived of in terms of "personal
ubles" are being viewed as "public issues of the milieu." Such a change in interpretation
reases the perception of such people as "enemy" deviants, rather than "sick" or "repent" deviants by those in power. *See* Gusfield, 1968.

[2]Much of the following is elaborated upon in Reasons and Kuykendall, 1972.

[3]For an excellent discussion of crimes perpetrated against blacks by whites, *see*
arin, 1967. He rhetorically poses a question concerning such racist atrocities, "Is white
ne, crime?"

[4]For an inciting, though hardly insightful, discussion of how differential rates indie the moral degeneracy of society, *see* Charles E. Rice, "The Negro Crime Rate: Its
uses and Cure," *Modern Age* 10 (Fall 1966):343-358.

[5]For an interesting discussion of the unintended consequences of liberal (usually
ite) thinking, *see* Lewis Coser, "Unanticipated Conservative Consequences of Liberal
eorizing," *Social Problems* 16 (Winter 1969):263-272.

[6]The author is not referring to legal culpability, strictly defined, but to the causal
ationships posited by criminologists, among others. It appears that there is growing conn among young lawyers with this broader "indictment."

[7]I would like to thank Bill Yoels for contributing the concept "insignificant
thers" as a contemporary complement to "significant others."

EFERENCES

nes, Harry Elmer, and Negley K. Teeters
    1959 *New Horizons in Criminology.* Englewood Cliffs: Prentice-Hall.

ach, Walter C.
    1932 *Oriental Crime in California.* Palo Alto: Stanford University Press.

cker, Howard S.
    1963 *Outsiders: Studies in the Sociology of Deviance.* New York: The Free Press.
    1967 "Whose Side are We On?" *Social Problems* 14 (Winter):239-247.

nger, William Adrian
    1943 *Race and Crime.* New York: Morningside Heights.

nton, Hugh P.
    1932 "Negroes Who Run Afoul of the Law." *Social Forces* 2 (October):96-101.

Brown, Jr., Allison W.
    1970 "A New Legal Weapon for Blacks." *Trans-Action* 7 (June):4-5.

Chambliss, William J.
    1964 "A Sociological Analysis of the Law of Vagrancy." *Social Problems* 12 (Summer):67-77.
    1970 "Crime, Law and the State." *Catalyst* (Summer).

Chambliss, William J., and Robert B. Seidman
    1971 *Law, Order and Power.* Reading, Mass.: Addison-Wesley.

Cohen, Warren H., and Phillip J. Mause
    1968 "The Indian: The Forgotten American." *Harvard Law Review* 81 (June):1818-1858.

Comas, Juan
    1961 "Scientific Racism Again?" *Current Anthropology* 2 (October): 303-340.

Crockett, Jr., George W.
    1969 "Racism in the Law." *Science and Society* (Spring):223-230.

Dickson, Donald
    1968 "Bureaucracy and Morality: An Organizational Perspective on a Moral Crusade." *Social Problems* 16 (Fall):143-156.

England, Ralph W., and Donald R. Taft
    1964 *Criminology.* New York: Macmillan Company.

Ferracuti, Franco
    1968 "European Migration and Crime." In *Crime and Culture: Essays in Honor of Thorsten Sellin,* ed. Marvin E. Wolfgang. New York: John Wiley, pp. 189-220.

Forslund, Morris A.
    1970 "A Comparison of Negro and White Crime Rates." *Journal of Criminal Law, Criminology and Police Science* 61 (June):214-217.

Geis, Gilbert
    1965 "Statistics Concerning Race and Crime." *Crime and Delinquency* 11 (April): 142-150.

Gossett, Thomas
    1963 *Race: The History of an Idea.* Dallas: Southern Methodist University Press.

Gouldner, Alvin W.
    1968 "The Sociologist as Partisan: Sociology and the Welfare State." *The American Sociologist* 3 (May):103-116.

Grant, Edwin
    1925 "Scum from the Melting Pot." *American Journal of Sociology* 30 (May): 641-651.

Green, Edward
    1970 "Race, Social Status, and Criminal Arrest." *American Sociological Review* 35 (June):476-490.

Greenberg, Jack
    1959 *Race Relations and American Law.* New York: Columbia University Press.

Gusfield, Joseph
    1968 *Symbolic Crusade: Status Politics and the American Temperance Movement.* Urbana: University of Illinois Press.

Hall, Jerome
    1952 *Theft, Law and Society.* Indianapolis: Bobbs-Merrill Company.

Haynes, Norman S.
      1942   "Variability in the Criminal Behavior of American Indians." *American Journal of Sociology* 47 (January):602-613.

Hindelong, Michael J.
      1969   "Equality Under the Law," *Journal of Criminal Law, Criminology and Police Science,* 60 (September).

Hooton, Earnest Albert
      1939   *Crime and the Man.* Cambridge: Harvard University Press.

Horowitz, Irving
      1968   "The Sociology of Social Problems: A Study of the Americanization of Ideas." In *Professing Sociology: Studies in the Life Cycle of Social Science.* Chicago: Aldine Publishing Company, pp. 80-100.

Horowitz, Irving, and Martin Liebowitz
      1967   "Social Deviance and Political Marginality: Toward a Redefinition of the Relation Between Sociology and Politics." *Social Problems* (Winter):118-129.

Hospers, John
      1960   "What is Explanation?" In *Essays in Conceptual Analysis,* ed. H. Brotman et al. London: Macmillan, pp. 94-119.

Johnson, Elmer Hubert
      1964   *Crime, Correction and Society.* Homewood: The Dorsey Press.

Knowles, Louis L., and Kenneth Prewitt
      1969   *Institutional Racism in America.* Englewood Cliffs: Prentice-Hall.

Larson, Arthur
      1958   "Legal Definition of Race." *Race Relations Law Reporter* 3 (June):571-588.
      1969   "The New Law of Race Relations." *Wisconsin Law Review* 2:470-524.

Lemert, Edwin M. and Judy Roseberg
      1948   *The Administration of Justice to Minority Groups in Los Angeles County.* Berkeley: University of California Press.

Matza, David
      1964   *Delinquency and Drift.* New York: John Wiley.

Merton, Robert K. (ed.)
      1968   "Social Structure and Anomie." In *Social Theory and Social Structure.* New York: The Free Press, pp. 185-248.

Miller, Loren
      1966a "Race, Poverty and the Law." In *The Law of the Poor,* ed. Jacobus Tenbroek (San Francisco: Chandler Publishing), pp. 62-82.
      1966b *The Petitioners: The Story of the Supreme Court of the United States and the Negro.* Cleveland: World Publishing.

Mills, C. Wright
      1943   "The Professional Ideology of Social Pathologists." *American Journal of Sociology* 49 (September):165-180.

Moses, Earl R.
      1936   "Community Factors in Negro Delinquency." *Journal of Negro Education* 5 (April):220-227.
      1947   "Differentials in Crime Rates Between Negroes and Whites on Comparisons of Four Socio-Economically Equated Areas." *American Sociological Review* 12 (August):411-420.

Platt, Anthony
      1971   *The Childsavers: The Invention of Delinquency.* Chicago: The University of Chicago Press.

President's Commission on Law Enforcement and the Administration of Justice
    1967   *The Challenge of Crime in a Free Society.* Washington D.C.: Government
           Printing Office.

Quinney, Richard
    1970   *The Social Reality of Crime.* Boston: Little, Brown.

Reasons, Charles E.
    1970   "A Developmental Model for the Analysis of Social Problems: Prostitution and
           Moral Reform in Twentieth Century America." Presented at the Pacific
           Sociological Association Meetings, Anaheim, California, "Deviant Section."
           15 pp.
    1972a "An Inquiry in the Sociology of Social Problems: The Drug Problem in
           Twentieth-Century America." Unpublished Dissertation, Washington State
           University.
    1972b "Crime and American Indian." In *Native Americans Today: Sociological Per-*
           spectives, ed. Howard Bahr, Bruce Chadwick, and Robert Day. New York:
           Harper and Row.

Reasons, Charles E., and Jack L. Kuykendal, eds.
    1972   *Race, Crime and Justice.* Pacific Palisades: Goodyear Publishing.

Sagarin, Edward
    1967   "Race and Crime: A Revisit to an Old Concept." Paper presented to the joint
           meeting of the American Orthopsychiatric Association and the American
           Society of Criminology, March 1967, Washington, D.C.

Schafer, Stephen
    1968   "Anomie, Culture Conflict, and Crime in Disorganized and Overorganized
           Societies." In *Crime and Culture: Essays in Honor of Thorsten Sellin,* ed.
           Marvin E. Wolfgang. New York: John Wiley, pp. 83-92.

Schuman, Howard
    1969   "Sociological Racism." *Trans-Action* 7 (December):44-48.

Seeley, John R.
    1963   "Social Science? Some Probative Problems." In *Sociology on Trial,* ed.
           Maurice Stein and Arthur Vidic. Englewood Cliffs: Prentice-Hall, pp.
           57-650.

Sellin, Thorsten
    1928   "The Negro Criminal: A Statistical Note." *Annals of the American Academy*
           of Political and Social Science 140 (November): 52-64.
    1935   "Race Prejudice in the Administration of Justice." *American Journal of*
           Sociology 41 (September): 213-217.

Short, Jr., James
    1970   *Modern Criminals.* Chicago: Aldine Publishing.

Stampp, Kenneth M.
    1970   *The Civil Rights Record: Black Americans and the Law, 1849-1970.* New
           York: Thomas Y. Crowell.

Stewart, Omer
    1964   "Questions Regarding American Indian Criminality." *Human Organization* 24
           (Fall):250-253.

Sutherland, Edwin, and Donald R. Cressey
    1950   "The Diffusion of Sexual Psychopath Laws." *American Journal of Sociology*
           56 (September):142-148.
    Sutherland, Edwin, and Donald R. Cressey
    1970   *Principles of Criminology.* New York: J.B. Lippincott.

Swett, Daniel
    1969 "Cultural Bias in the American Legal System." *Law and Society Review* 5 (August):79-110.

Tenbroek, Jacobus
    1966 *The Law of the Poor.* San Francisco: Chandler Publishing.

Turk, Austin
    1966 "Conflict and Criminality." *American Sociological Review* 31 (June):338-352.

Vann Woodward, C.
    1969 "Our Racist History." *The New York Review of Books* 12 (February 27): 338-352.

Von Hentig, Hans
    1945 "The Delinquency of the American Indian." *The Journal of Criminal Law* 36 (July-August):75-84.

Wald, Patricia
    1970 "Poverty and Criminal Justice." In *The Sociology of Punishment and Correction,* ed. Norman Johnson, Leonard Savitz, and Marvin E. Wolfgang. New York: John Wiley, pp. 271-296.

Wilkins, Leslie T.
    1968 "The Concept of Cause in Criminology." *Issues in Criminology* 3 (Spring): 147-165.

Willhelm, Sidney M.
    1969 "Black Man, Red Man, and White American: The Constitutional Approach to Genocide." *Catalyst* (Spring):1-62.

Wolfgang, Marvin, and Bernard Cohen
    1970 *Crime and Race: Conceptions and Misconceptions.* New York: Institute of Human Relations Press.

PART TWO:

LAW AND THE MAKING OF CRIMINALS

The study of crime has largely been the study of criminals—as Jeffery points out in his article regarding American criminological thought, little attention has been given to the study of law. A cursory review of criminology texts points out that such a focus is the exception, rather than the rule. Nonetheless, the sociology of law is often acknowledged as a facet of criminological study.

Criminology consists of three principal divisions, as follows: (a) the sociology of law, which is an attempt at systematic analysis of the conditions under which criminal laws develop and which is seldom included in general books on criminology, (b) criminal etiology, which is an attempt at scientific analysis of the causes of crime, and (c) penology.[1]

A broader conception of the content of the sociology of law is generally recognized to include the creation of laws, their enforcement, and their administration. The neglect of the sociological study of law is evident when one notes that nearly all empirical studies in the sociology of law in America have occurred since 1950; since then a number of studies have been done principally dealing with the enforcement and administration of justice.[2] Few studies have dealt with the emergence of criminal laws within a sociohistorical context.[3]

The relative neglect of sociological analysis of the law is related to a number of factors. The lack of legal studies as part of liberal arts education has hampered such inquiry. There is a mystique and sacredness attached to the law and legal bodies which is in part due to the general public's lack of knowledge concerning the law. This was not always the case, however: Blackstone's Commentaries were lectures given at Oxford University to liberal arts students and American colonists acquired legal education in order to establish control systems in their new land. Edmund Burke's comments on the influence of Blackstone reflect this interest:

In no country perhaps in this world is the law so general a study. The profession itself is numerous and powerful, and in most provinces it takes the lead.

The greater number of deputies sent to the congress were lawyers. . . . I have been told by an eminent bookseller, that in no branch of his business, after tracts of popular devotion, were so many books as those on the law exported to the plantations.[4]

This reflects the basic fact that law and legal education is powerful and has been principally in the hands of those making policy. With the professionalization of law and its institutionalization in the form of law schools, a professional monopoly was established concerning the diffusion of legal education.

As our society has grown more urbanized and our law ways more complex, young men have had progressively fewer opportunities to learn about the workings of our legal system; at the same time the United States has become probably the most law-run and lawyer-run country in the history of mankind.[5]

This professional monopoly has concentrated a great deal of power in the hands of the legal profession. Ours is a government of laws, made and interpreted by man. The equating of legal knowledge and power is verified by the estimate that since the Civil War well over 50 percent of all elected or government officials have been lawyers.[6] The law is, of course, too important to be left to lawyers.[7]

Another major impediment to the sociological study of the law has been the barrier of discipline and training. Both sociologists and lawyers have created a professional jargon and way of looking at things which have only inhibited joint efforts. Furthermore, the neopositivist thrust of American sociology kept many from investigating law and its "speculative" nature rather than following European scholars.

Finally, although American criminologists have long been concerned with the control of human behavior, questioning of normative practices, that is, laws, was not of major importance. The laws were a given and the focus of attention was upon those who violated the law.[8] It was a perspective based on puritanical pragmaticism and natural-science positivism. The emergence of some new schools of jurisprudence in the twentieth century greatly influenced the study of law as a social phenomenon.

Historically, varying schools of jurisprudence have presented their interpretations of the original nature of the legal order. A number of schools of jurisprudence have denied that lawmakers have value-choices in the creation of laws,[9] including natural, cultural, and historical schools.[10] These schools suggest that the law and its agents (e.g., enforcers and administrators) stand above and apart from society, comprising a neutral framework within which social struggle and conflict takes place. This consensus perspective views the state as a value-neutral organ for the resolution of conflict. Therefore, although the adversary proceedings put the state against the accused, it occurs within the "neutral" framework of the court. The judge epitomizes the evenhanded, nonbiased, neutral arbitrator of institutionalized conflict. This perspective is still largely held among many segments of our society. Such beliefs are central to our democratic ideals of the "blind" nature of justice and the equity of our political and legal system. The presumed nonpolitical and unbiased nature of the judicial system has obscured the basically political nature of crime. In order to understand the law, its enforcement and administration, we must demystify the conceptions of the nature and functions of law and place it in the context of power, politics, and people.[11]

This brings us to those schools of jurisprudence which suggest that law is a legitimizing weapon of the highest order and those making, enforcing, and administering laws are merely attempting to perpetuate the existing state. These schools, including the utilitarian, sociological, and realist, have demystified the nature of laws by suggesting that they are man-made and state given, and not found in some natural state of things beyond the influence and control of man. Rather than the state and its legal actors being value-free, these perspectives invest participants in the legal system with values, feelings, and bias—all the trappings of human beings.

Roscoe Pound, an important leader of sociological jurisprudence, greatly aided in the demystification of the law by emphasizing the crucial distinction between "law in the books" and "law in action." The "ought" which is defined by the law is not necessarily the "is" of law. Therefore, Pound continuously exhorted the need for investigating the law in operation, rather than merely looking at the law in the books. Legal realists view law as created by the judge, for according to Holmes:

The life of the law has not been logic, it has been experience. The felt necessities of the time, the prevalent moral order and political theories, institutions of public policy, avowed or unconscious, even the prejudices which the judges share with their fellowmen have had a good deal more to do than the syllogism in determining the rules by which men should be governed.[12]

Quinney's theory[13] regarding the "social reality of crime" puts the value-choice approach within a conflict perspective of society, emphasizing that the differing values existing within society and law are the realization of one group's victory over other groups. Rather than being a neutral framework for the collective interests of society, law is an instrument of those in power used to maintain their position and privilege.

Increasing awareness regarding the political nature of crime has arisen with heightened conflict between traditionally powerless groups, such as students and youth, the poor, and the nonwhite, and those in power.[14] The basically political nature of crime has largely been neglected by criminologists. Traditionally submerged in a consensus perspective of society, viewing the state as neutral, the increasing questioning of the legitimacy of specific laws and ultimately of the authority of the state by certain segments of society has caused some change in criminological focus. Some criminologists have begun to critically investigate the origin, enforcement, and administration of laws within the context of interests, power, and conflict.

In this section the basically political nature of crime as a phenomenon created and shaped by the powerful within the state is emphasized. The first article, by Mark Kennedy, provides an excellent analysis of the emergence of crime and the political body called the state and how definitions of "crime" and "punishment" are inherently political. By showing how penal sanctions are behaviorally no different then crimes, Kennedy vividly illustrates the basically political nature of their definitions. This negates the traditional antiseptic, value-free, politically neutral perspective towards the legal order. Of particular importance are his suggested areas for criminological study. For example, he notes that crime and crime rates are manufactured by the state. He then provides an illuminating account of how crime emerged as a political phenomenon with the rise of the state.

Viewing the state as the independent variable in crime production makes sense both legally and sociologically. In commenting upon this product of the state Marx notes:

Now, if crimes observed on a great scale thus show, in their amount and their classification, the regularity of physical phenomena . . . is there not necessity for deeply reflecting upon an alteration of the system that breeds these crimes, instead of glorifying the hangman who executes a lot of criminals to make room only for the supply of new ones?[15]

Marx actually took a functional perspective regarding crime and the state. Therefore, while the state produces the criminal,

the criminal produces not only crime but also the criminal law; he produces the professor who delivers lectures on this criminal law, and even the inevitable textbook in which the professor presents his lectures as a commodity for sale in the market. . . . Furthermore, the criminal produces the whole apparatus of the police and criminal justice, detectives, judges, executioners, juries, etc. . . . The criminal therefore appears as one of those "equilibrating forces" which establish a just balance and open up a whole perspective of "useful occupations."[16]

The viewing of law as an instrument of interests has become a growing area of concern among some American criminologists. Quinney articulately presents what many dissident leaders of the 1960s suggested, that criminal law is made, enforced, and administered by interest groups for their own gains. A conflict perspective has become a paradigm of increased usefulness in criminological study.[17]

Quinney's article provides an essentially Marxist analysis of crime. The basically self-serving nature of the law for those in power is hardly contestable, but can this be eliminated? Societies with other ideologies seem to evidence the same extent of self-serving use of the law. In addressing the fact that the state controls the means of violence, he merely is pointing out a fact of all states, not just those which call themselves capitalists. As previously noted in the rise of crime with the rise of the state, it seems inevitable that the law will predominantly serve some interests more than others. As Chambliss and Seidman note:

It is our contention that, far from being primarily a value-neutral framework within which conflict can be peacefully resolved, the power of the state is itself the principal prize in the perpetual conflict that is society. The legal order —the rules which the various lawmaking institutions in the bureaucracy that is the State lay down for the governance of officials and citizens, the tribunals, official and unofficial, and the bureaucratic agencies which enforce the law—is in fact a self-serving system to maintain power and privilege. In a society sharply divided into haves and have nots, poor and rich, blacks and whites, powerful and weak, shot with a myriad of special interest groups, not only is the myth false because of imperfections in the normative system: *It is inevitable that it be so* (italics added).[18]

The inevitability of the above does not negate the fact that differentials in power and privilege are subject to change. Therefore, those who desire a more just distribution of social, economic, and political power and privilege need not despair. It is obvious we do not have to concern ourselves immediately with a nirvana of complete equality given the disparities evident in our society.

Although Quinney's demystification of the law in capitalist society is provocative, he fails to address the nature of the socialist society (state?). The establishment of a socialist state necessitates the need for law and subsequently interest group input. As he has previously asked: "Can a law be created apart from private interests which assures individual fulfillment within a good society?"[19] His own answer in that text, plus other evidence, suggests not.

In his concluding remarks, he becomes more "academic" and identifies the research and theoretical implications of his work. His suggestion of a "reflexive" and "critical" criminology fits appropriately into the ramifications of paradigm challenge and change.

The temporal and cultural relativity of criminal definitions should immediately alert the student of crime that there is nothing inherent in the behavior which makes it criminal. Criminality of certain behavior is a status conferred upon that specific behavior by the state's political apparatus. Where political movements agitating for change are successful, this fundamental fact is often quite evident. Therefore, crime may be viewed as phenomena created by individuals in concerted action to have their definitions of rightness win out and become legitimated in public policy—that is, laws and regulations.[20]

In the area of "crimes without victims" the nebulous nature of harm provides an excellent example of the fact that what is to be considered crime is principally a political judgment.[21] This problem of "overcriminalization" is excellently reviewed by Dobrovir in an article for the President's Commission on Violence.[22] By suggesting that the returns for criminalizing "victimless" crime are outweighed by the negative consequences of such statutes, the basically political nature of such definitions are emphasized. Since we are a pluralistic society with varying values in different segments of the population, these manifestations of the imposing of one segment's values upon other segments magnifies conflict. In their creation, enforcement, and administration such statutes vividly portray the influence of power and interest groups in the area of criminal justice. A movement to eliminate and/or change such statutes is underway nationally and will provide an excellent example of the politics of crime.

The drug problem epitomizes the relevancy of conflict to the study of crime. In no other area of "criminal" activity is there as much controversy and rigidity as in the area of drug-taking. Reasons's paper attempts to illuminate the fact that agencies invested with the control of a criminal activity have a vested interest in maintaining their control over definition of the nature of the problem and subsequent efforts to deal with the problem. Rather than merely being a reactive participant to the emerging drug problem, the Federal Bureau of Narcotics has been an important actor in shaping legal and social definitions of the problem and maintaining the "criminal approach" in spite of periodic opposition. This has been carried out through conscious, planned political action to maintain the viability of the bureau and its definition of the problem.[23]

By analyzing organizations invested with "eradicating" a problem we may become aware of their impact upon the problem. The importance of analyzing the law and its agents as independent variables in the creation and maintenance of criminal behavior is succinctly stated in the dissenting view of three members of the President's Task Force on Narcotics and Drug Abuse:[24]

Many persons concerned with the problem have for years been questioning whether the criminalization of narcotics and marihuana distribution has not served to defeat the object of controlling and perhaps eliminating drug abuse and the crime associated with it. The gnawing question to which there has never been a satisfactory answer is whether the policy of criminalization does in fact make the drug user a proselytizer of others in order that he may obtain the funds to acquire his own drugs. . . . In this important area the Commission has been unable to face the fundamental questions. Instead, for reasons that are quite understandable but in our view not justifiable, it assumes that the laws and the traditional methods of enforcement which have obtained for over 50 years are the only proper way in which to meet the problem. . . . *The time will come when we will have to determine causal relationships and consider the possibility that traditional methods of law enforcement produce more rather than less crime, particularly of a collateral character* (italics added).[25]

Therefore, organizations invested with dealing with the crime problem should be viewed as important facets of the problem.

NOTES

[1]Edward H. Sutherland and Donald R. Cressey, *Criminology,* 8th ed. (New York: J. B. Lippincott, 1970), p. 3. This "bible" in criminology recognizes the importance of studying the emergence of law and its change, but only four pages are given to that subject, pp. 8-12. Undoubtedly the next edition will have a more expanded section concerning the emergence of law and sociolegal change. It should be kept in mind that this text is a standard bearer in the positivist tradition in criminology.

[2]For an extensive discussion *see* Jerome H. Skolnick, "The Sociology of Law in America: Overview and Trends," *Social Problems* ("Law and Society," supplement to Summer 1965 issue):1-39. More recent studies may be found in the annual bibliography in each May issue of *Law and Society Review.*

[3]Notable exceptions are summarized in Richard Quinney, *The Social Reality of Crime* (Boston: Little, Brown, 1970), pp. 43-97.

[4]Quoted in Harold J. Berman and William R. Greiner, *The Nature and Functions of Law* (Brooklyn: The Foundation Press, 1966), p. 1.

[5]Ibid., p. 4.

[6]*See* Robert Leftcourt, *Laws Against the People: Essays to Demystify Law, Order and the Courts* (New York: Random House, 1971), especially the introduction, pp. 3-17.

[7]Likewise, criminology is too important to be left entirely to the professional criminologist.

[8]For some excellent discussions of this emphasis *see* C. Wright Mills, "The Professional Ideology of the Social Pathologists," *American Journal of Sociology* 49 (September 1943):165-80; Jack D. Douglas "Deviance and Order in a Pluralistic Society," in *Theoretical Sociology,* ed. John C. McKinney and Edward A. Tiryakian (New York: Appleton-Century Crofts, 1970), pp. 367-401.

[9]For a more elaborate discussion of value-choices and models of the law *see* William J. Chambliss and Robert B. Seidman, *Law, Order and Power* (Reading, Mass.: Addison-Wesley, 1971).

[10]*See* Edwin M. Schur, *Law and Society* (New York: Random House, 1968), pp. 17-67, for a good summary of the major schools of jurisprudence.

[11]Chambliss and Seidman, *Law, Order,* p. 3, suggest the perpetration of such "myths" is a normal occurrence in law schools, political science courses on law and criminology, and high school courses dealing with the law. This "Sunday school perspective" of the legal order appears to be an important aspect of socialization.

[12]Ibid., p. 49.

[13]*See* Quinney, *Social Reality.*

[14]For example, *see* Leftcourt, *Laws;* Charles E. Reasons and Jack L. Kuykendall, *Race, Crime and Justice* (Pacific Palisades: Goodyear Publishing, 1972); Jacobus Tenbroek, *The Law of the Poor* (San Francisco: Chandler Publishing, 1966); Jerome Skolnick, *The Politics of Protest* (New York: Ballantine Books, 1969); James S. Campbell et al., *Law and Order Reconsidered* (New York: Bantam Books, 1970); Stuart L. Hills, *Crime, Power and Morality* (Scranton: Chandler Publishing, 1971); George F. Cole, *Criminal Justice: Law and Politics* (Belmont: Duxbury Press, 1972).

[15]T. B. Bottomore, *Karl Marx: Selected Writings in Sociology and Social Philosophy* (New York: McGraw-Hill, 1956), pp. 229-30. See the entire section pp. 215-30 for some of Marx's reflections on the state and law.

[16]Ibid., pp. 158-59.

[17]For a comprehensive discussion of this perspective *see* George B. Vold, *Theoretical Criminology* (New York: Oxford University Press, 1958); Austin T. Turk, "Conflict and Criminality," *American Sociological Review* 31 (June, 1966):338-52; and Richard Quinney, *Social Reality,* especially pp. 29-97.

[18]Chambliss and Seidman, p. 4.

[19]Quinney, p. 42.

[20]For some examples of this perspective *see* Charles E. Reasons, "An Inquiry in the Sociology of Social Problems; the Drug Problem in Twentieth-Century America," unpublished dissertation, Washington State University, 1972; K. T. Erickson, *Wayward Puritans: A Study in the Sociology of Deviance* (New York: John Wiley, 1966); Louis Filler, *Crusaders for American Liberalism* (Yellow Springs: The Antioch Press, 1950); Howard S. Becker, *The Outsiders* (New York: The Free Press, 1963); Joseph Gusfield, *Symbolic Crusade: Status Politics and the American Temperance Movement* (Urbana: University of Illinois Press, 1966); Anthony M. Platt, *The Child Savers: The Invention of Delinquency* (Chicago: University of Chicago Press, 1969).

[21]*See* Edwin Schur, *Crimes Without Victims* (Englewood Cliffs: Prentice-Hall, 1965); Norval Morris and Gordon Hawkins, *The Honest Politician's Guide to Crime Control* (Chicago: University of Chicago Press, 1969), pp. 3-28.

[22]*See* William A. Dobrovir, "The Problems of Overcriminalization," in *Law and Order Reconsidered,* Report of the Task Force on Law and Law Enforcement to the National Commission on the Causes and Prevention of Violence (New York: Bantam Books, 1970), pp. 600-621.

[23]This is not to villify the bureau, but merely to point out the important symbiotic relationship between "keepers of deviants" and their "clientele."

[24]President's Commission on Law Enforcement and the Administration of Justice, *Task Force Report: Narcotics and Drug Abuse* (Washington D. C.: Government Printing Office, 1967), pp. 302-303.

[25]The "war" on drugs instituted by the Department of Defense appears to have produced such an unintended consequence. A six-volume report on Drug Abuse Control Activities Affecting Military Personnel in the Department of Defense conducted by the General Accounting Office suggests that "the military crackdown on drugs has not been effective and may have driven servicemen from marihuana to heroin and other narcotics." *Lincoln Evening Journal,* August 15, 1972, Lincoln, Nebraska.

BEYOND INCRIMINATION

MARK C. KENNEDY

If crime and punishment are injurious to life, then each belongs to the same class of conduct and should not be viewed as two independent species of harms. Yet, what appears more certain, more part of daily experience than the assumption that "each" is independent of the other?[1] The very manner in which officious persons make dutiful their daily rounds—impersonally making decisions, soberly passing judgements, patiently accepting contrition, exacting punishments, and excusing us our misdeeds—puts us in a position to do little but accept our own conduct as culpable, theirs as beyond incrimination.

This assumption is especially difficult for professionalists to deny. What is more characteristic than treating "crime" and "punishment" as independent species—without reference either to their sameness or to how continuity of both depends on the character of dominating institutions?[2] To deny this assumption, and voice the idea that crime and penal sanctions are the same implies certain risks. But to accept it uncritically promises certain rewards which accrue from university services to commerce, and to local and federal governments. This includes sociological services to police, prison systems, corrections departments for developing programs of rehabilitation for probationers and parolees. Some may lack for desire, others perhaps wit, still others the courage either to deny the scientific value of this assumption or to discuss the institutional foundations on which it rests.

For to teach that penal sanctions are behaviorally no different from crimes might slur officialdom, offend the State, profane its sources of power, challenge the legitimacy of its monopoly over the power to pardon and punish the disobedient, jeopardize the transactions between university administrations and their off-campus supporters, and risk loss of one's own tenure and career—and this, quite apart from whether the sameness of crime and punishment is valid on scientific grounds.[3] For it is the State—as a community of ruling officials[4]— which both creates and sustains this dichotomy between crime and punishment. Ironically, it is the State which may also destroy it.

With penal sanction, law, and the State set over in one universe, and with crime and poverty in another, professionalists seek immediate causes of crime in ghettoes, slums, broken homes, and in "multiple dwellings" where "undersocialization" is said to spawn "predelinquents" and "hard-to-reach youth." Ultimate causes are sought in impersonal conditions issuing from population density: social distance, anonymity, social isolation, social mobility—in short, social dis-

Mark C. Kennedy, "Beyond Incrimination" *Catalyst* No. 6 (Summer 1970) pp. 1-37. Reprinted by permission of the journal.

organization. In "the other universe" separated from this "causal" picture are differentially enforced laws, differential justice, differential punishments and privileges—all the conditions which, though ignored, account for slums, ghettoes, broken homes. Thus, when solutions are advanced, they never include major changes in criminal law, penal codes, institutional reconstruction, or any revamping of the power structure. These are assumed to be immutable "givens," and instead of changing them, some call for greater police powers and more law enforcement while others call for more work release programs (of some value to industrialists on the make for cheap labor), more psychiatric services and social workers (to "resocialize" predelinquents), more qualified probation and parole officers, and more community resources at their disposal.

What all this submerges are scientifically valid questions: (1) Are crimes and crime rates manufactured by the State? Does fixing penal sanctions to once-legal behavior accomplish this? (2) Are old crimes abolished by removal of law enforcements and penal sanctions? When a punishable act passes under civil law by removal of penal sanction, who gains and who loses? (3) What is the relation between successful political movements and revision of criminal laws? What acts, specifically described and proscribed under old criminal laws, become fully legitimate with the deposition of an old State and when it is replaced by a revolutionary regime? What effects would this have on the nature of crime and crime rates? (4) When a new State ascends and an old one collapses, do former executioners become murderers and do former murderers become executioners? At what point in revolution do punishments become crimes? (5) In countries undergoing transformation to collective ownership of instruments of production, what does private ownership mean with reference to them? If, under law, the fruits of labor are to be equally shared, what does theft mean? Under capitalism, is crime a form of entrepreneurship; under socialism, is entrepreneurship a form of crime?

Though vital to any sociology of crime and punishment, these questions are pushed aside because of the predominance of theory, research, and programs of amelioration which rest squarely upon the falsifiable assumption that crime and punishment repose in separate universes as independent species of conduct. What then is the status of this assumption? What is the nature of crime and punishment? How are they the same? What are their sustained differences?

Answers to these questions are not set forth as exhaustive or final. The problem is to explore the implications of recasting conceptions of crime and punishment into a new framework, to see what becomes explicit when these behaviors are conceived as belonging to the same class, originally separated and subsequently reified by the State as independent species. Of equal concern are implications of these sustained differences. This calls for answering two different orders of questions.

First order questions: Are we dealing with phenomena universal to all cultures, or with culturally specific phenomena limited to a period of history? If the latter, what sociocultural conditions account for such cultural and historical specificity? What institutions explain the emergence of crime and punishment as a unit class? Answers, though brief, must reveal how crime and punishment, as defined, depend for their origin and continuity upon the origin and continuity of certain institutions, and where the latter are absent, the former do not exist.

Thus, it must be shown that crime comprises but one of several kinds of all norm violations, that penal sanction is but one of many kinds of reprisals against such violations. This does not mean that crime and penal sanction are behavioral ly different but establishes that both emerge and continue together as manifesta- tions of singular institutional facts.

A second order of questions is relevant to showing that there are no behavioral attributes intrinsic to harms of crime and punishment which warrant the assumption that they belong to behaviorally independent classes. This calls for more than establishing crime and punishment as a single class of harms, for it must be shown (1) that the criteria for separating them refer to phenomena ex- ternal to actual behaviors classed by legal procedure as crime versus punishment, (2) that even within the criminal law itself, the criteria by which crime is identified procedurally apply with equal validity to punishment. Relevant ques- tions are:

1. What behavioral attributes common to both crime and punishment are shared, and not shared, by other classes of harms? Do these attributes justify separating these harms into different classes? If not, what criteria external to these behaviors warrant their separation into different classes?
2. Do legal criteria for identifying crime also identify punishment and/or penal sanction?

These questions will be seen to establish that the attributes by which the dif- ferent legal categories of behavior (civil, criminal) are established are but criteria external to the interactions legally categorized. It will be seen that behaviors called crime and punishment not only belong to the same class but that the very differentiae of crime apply with equal validity to punishment.

THE NATURE OF CRIME AND PUNISHMENT

Crime is here defined as a violation, by act or omission, of any criminal law. According to that law, it is also a specific conduct leading to a harm and is an act construed as a harm against a State. It follows that deviation from norms which are not criminal laws are not crimes. It also follows that in any society where such laws are absent there is no crime. Crime, then, is unique behavior. To understand this calls for some knowledge of the characteristics of criminal law as unique law.

Punishment is an intended harm imposed by one or more parties upon an individual over whom those who impose that harm have assumed or have been granted jurisdiction as a right—a right contingent upon superior coercive power or upon collectively given power to exempt an offender from any reprisal for his offense. Penal sanction is a special case of punishment, and both are special cases of intended harms generally. They differ from acts of war, for example, only in- sofar as reciprocal acts of war assume political equality between contenders.

Crime and Criminal Law in Relation to the State

Under criminal law no act is crime until it violates a norm having the followin; characteristics: uniformity, specificity, politicality, and penal sanction. Procedural ly, these characteristics become *criteria* for legal classification of any act as crime versus not-crime. In legal procedure, uniformity is more an assumption than a work ing criterion, thus we are concerned only with the latter three characteristics. Any law failing to detail the conduct proscribed lacks specificity, and violating it is not a crime. Any law neither created nor recognized by the State as a bona fide part of its legal order and which fails to define the proscribed act as a harm against the State lacks politicality, its violation is not a crime. Any law in which a punishment is not prescribed lacks penal sanction, and its violation is not a crime.[5]

It follows that any society having no laws like this has no crime, and that crime is a unique class among all violations of conduct norms. Since politicality and penal sanction (the decisive characteristics of criminal law) presuppose a State, there can be no crime in any society which has no State.[6] The latter are still abundant in parts of the world yet untouched by Western political and economic institutions.[7]

While Stateless societies have emerged apart from Western influence, they are rare, and societies having what Weber described as "formally rational States" are either Western or have come by such political communities through Western influence. Since the formally rational State is, roughly, a post-fifteenth-century development of Western culture,[8] it follows that crime in its present character did not exist before that period and at the advent of feudal States—apart from Roman law—crime as such did not exist. The same is true of penal sanction. Both are linked to the formal laws of the State and to civil institutions supported by it. Both types of law are managed by the State as a monopoly.

But while both are unique in contrast with those norm violations and punishments common to societies without States, neither seems behaviorally different from the other—in part because both crime and punishment are intended harms, and in part because both emerged historically with and are now founded upon individualism as a common ideology or value system which has as its basic premise the belief that each individual (and not social institutions) is fully responsible for his own conduct and its consequences.[9] While the era of individualism is now at an end in the West, its hold is still very evident in the State, in citizenship, in criminal law and legal procedures, and in the dominance of penal sanctions over the use of the power to pardon.

Historical Conditions of the Advent of Crime and Penal Sanction

It is an oversimplification to say that these two classes of harms arose together in post-fifteenth-century Europe as a function of the advent of formally rational States, but what finally took place, beginning with the thirteenth century, amounts to that. What was fundamental to the birth of crime and penal sanction was fundamental to political, economic, religious, and familistic transformation generally, and essential to the transformations of these institutions was the transformation of the ethic of shared responsibility for individual conduct (the cooperative ethic) to the ethic of individual responsibility.

In part as the legacy of the collapse of feudalism and in part as a consequence of the rise of institutions of capitalism which this collapse afforded, individualism as a generalized social movement emerged from a fact of institutional chaos to a social philosophy and a normative order and transformed, as it grew, the whole of Western society and its culture. Early or late, it came eventually to find social expression in religion as Protestantism; in philosophy as empiricism and idealism, in scholastic inquiry as deductive and inductive methods of natural science, in economy as new institutions of private property, the market, entrepreneurship, rational accounting, and the redivision of labor along new social lines.

It found social expression politically with the birth of formally rational States, citizenship, the theory of social contract, and the rise and diffusion of two interlinked bodies of calculable law (civil and criminal). Just as egoism came to play a major part in psychological inquiry. All the while, kinship was being nucleated and dispossessed, and religion was atomized and made impotent as a social control. On every side, with each new expression of individualism, the society based earlier on the ethic of shared responsibility for individual conduct vanished from the scene. When fealty was for sale, altruism was dead.[10]

The emergence of individualism, in transforming all social institutions, transformed the relation of individuals to each other, of each individual to society, and created a new relation between each person and the emergent State. In all these relations, the legal fiction that each citizen is alone responsible for his own conduct and its consequences, good or bad, became reified both at the level of self or personality and at the level of law and judicial practice. Individualism as an attitude of self is basic to guilt, and as a premise of both civil and criminal law it is elemental to the whole legal practice of incrimination. What we witness in the advent of crime and penal sanction is but one facet of the total transformation of institutional life. Remembering this, we now must look at crime and punishment in a more singular and comparative way.

Feudal Institutions in Relation to Harms and Their Disposal

Between the period of the last invasion of Moslems, Hungarians, and Scandinavians, and the middle of the eleventh century, Europe developed what came to be called the institutions of feudalism. This period, in Bloch's astute analysis, was the first feudal age—the second feudal age extending from the middle of that century roughly to the thirteenth.[11] In the present analysis, the first feudal age is important because its normative order and institutional systems were founded on the ethic of shared responsibility for individual conduct. Criminal law and penal sanctions had not emerged, and no territorial power had been able successfully to obtain from local social worlds the power to pardon an offender his harms; citizenship and the formally rational State were absent, and so were the institutions of capitalism. Customary law and the oral tradition prevailed and were imbedded in the religious mentality, the epic, and the folk memory.[12] Kinship and vassalage were knit by companionage—so greatly that fealty was meaningful in a double sense. Vassalage and kinship were unthinkable without friendship or companionage. Public authority had not emerged, and while vassalage meant subjection, subjection was personal and of a quasi-family character. Feudal society differed as much from those based wholly on kinship as it differs from societies dominated by the State.[13]

The second feudal age is important because in it the ethic of shared responsibility began to give way, and its normative order and institutions began to transform. A vernacular literature emerged and the oral tradition and customary law began to wane. Calculable law began to emerge, along with a host of other changes which account for the rise of citizenship, the formally rational State, and the increasing scope of the institutions of capitalism. Profound changes in economic institutions took place as the ethic of individual responsibility began to find reality in one's relation to himself, to others, and to society and State.

The thesis which will be supported historically and cross-culturally is simply that crime and penal sanction are twin products of the origin and continuity of the State and citizenship, that these institutions, founded on emergent civil and criminal law, emerged as a cluster of new institutions (entrepreneurship, private property, and the market system) all of which were originally the social manifestations of the ethic of individual responsibility for individual behavior. Thus, it follows that in absence of the State, in the absence of its laws, crime and penal sanction do not exist, and in the absence of the institutions of capitalism, their special features cannot exist.

During the first feudal age, the legal system was the rule of custom and oral tradition. It rested on the belief that whatever has been has the right to be.[14] Precedent, not innovation, ruled. It was the normative foundation of feudal society—finding its expression not in hierarchy as we know that word today but in the mutually binding obligations of mutually given oaths all the way up the feudal scale. Land, the only real capital, was tied up solidly by customary obligations and could not for that reason become a commodity for sale in any market. Labor had the same provisions. The whole notion of exclusive proprietary rights was repugnant to people generally. As Bloch put it:

> For nearly all land and a great many human beings were burdened at this time with a multiplicity of obligations differing in nature, but all apparently of equal importance. None implied that fixed proprietary exclusiveness which belonged to the conception of ownership in Roman law. The tenant who—from father to son, as a rule—ploughs the land and gathers in the crop; his immediate lord, to whom he pays dues and who, in certain circumstances, can resume possession of the land; the lord of the lord, and so on right up the feudal scale—how many persons there are who can say, each with [equal] justification . . . "That is my field!"[15]

While landed wealth was differentially though mutually shared, its usufruct did not pass from hand to hand in any important way through any market system. Just as private property was absent, so was trade—except in a marginal and irregular way. While buying and selling was not unknown, no one lived by it unless they were the few who were generally scorned as banished persons or pariahs. Even barter was peripheral, for the chief means for the distribution of goods and services—as demanded by customary law—was "aid" or tallage, and the corvée or boon work in return for protection. In such a system wages were meaningless. "The corvée furnished more laborers than hire."[16] Customary law possessed no norms which bore any similarity to civil and criminal laws of post-fifteenth-century Europe, and certainly it possessed none having the decisive characteristics of criminal law—politicality and penal sanction. Both State and citizen were absent as continuous elements of society. These presume an ethic not present in the first feudal age—that of individual responsibility for one's conduct.

Just as the ethic of shared responsibility found institutional expression in vassalage, feudal land tenure, and the feudal system for the distribution of goods and services, so was it the basis for kinship solidarity and the restoration of peaceful relations between offenders and the wronged. What linked vassalage to the kinship system was companionage or friendship, but friendship which carried a profounder meaning by far than it carries today. People united by blood were not necessarily friends, but friendship did not exist unless people were united by blood. Moreover, friendship obligations were weakened by the fact of differential status between friends of blood. If anything, this gave them strength. Any harm falling upon one fell upon all. Any avengement suffered by one was suffered by all members of the companionage.[17] *Treue* and fealty have their meaning here.

Even when infrequently a man was brought before a court, the ethic of shared responsibility found expression in *compurgation* or oath-helping. A collective oath was enough to clear a man accused or to confirm a complaint brought against the accused. If compurgation should result in a draw, the dispute could be settled either by trial by battle or by voluntary compensation. A defeated champion in trial by battle might be either the accused or the plaintiff, but his defeat was also the defeat of the companionage who "stood surety" for him. *Punishment was an act of war and was collective.* Those of a companionage who were not killed in battle were often hanged upon defeat. Guilt was never established until defeat was received as the verdict of God. This did not mean, however, that guilt was not felt or feared. It meant only that the "structure" of guilt was different then than now. Guilt was the fear of bringing shame upon one's kindred, not shame for having killed (for example) a member of another kindred. It had nothing to do with conscience but everything to do with honor. And the dishonor of one was the dishonor of all.[18]

Perhaps nothing better exemplifies the cooperative ethic more than the extrajudicial and quasi-judicial vendetta or *faida.* Kinship vengeance neatly balanced kinship protection of the accused from vengeance.[19] In any feud it was impossible to distinguish acts of punishment from acts of war; it was also impossible to distinguish acts of crime from acts of war. Crime and punishment were never known until after the battle was over, and when over, the guilty had already been punished. Feudal justice did not require the death of the individual who had done the killing. It did not require the death of one or more of his kinsmen who protected him. Guilt was more of a projection than a feeling on the part of the killer, unless the killer had slain one of his own. In that case, punishment was self-imposed if imposed at all.

Feuds might be forestalled or terminated by arbitration and compensation, but in a social climate where "the very corpse cried out for vengeance . . . and hung withering in the house till the day when vengeance was accomplished" arbitration and compensation were ordinarily futile gestures—at least in the early stages of the feud. But a rotten corpse or even one whose bones are white may be ample inducement later on for accepting compensation. As the will for avenging the dead waned, the desire for reconciliation with indemnity heightened, and the adage "buy off the spear or feel it in your breast" had practical results.[20]

Judicial procedures, Bloch observes, were little more than "regularized vendettas" and were used only when relatives preferred that means to the feud or compensation.[21] The role of public "authority" in all matters of harms and counterharms and their settlements was negligible. No territorial authority could intervene to impose punishment on an individual without becoming, under custom, the object of a collective vendetta. Penal sanction was absent because it asumes something that did not exist—that the individual and not the kindred of he individual is responsible for the conduct of the individual. In the first feudal ge, any "law" having politicality and penal sanction would have been scorned as n attempt by outsiders to profane the bonds of kinship and companionage. But even well into the second feudal age these customs persisted as did the thic on which they rested. In the thirteenth century, courts still recognized that ny act done by one individual involved all his kindred. In Paris, Parlement still ecognized the right of a man to take his vengeance on any relative of his assail- nt. In cases where such a victim took action in court on the grounds that he had ot been involved, those grounds would not have been recognized. The assailant vould have been freed.[22] The idea that each man is a citizen of the State and is lone responsible for his own conduct and its consequences was not to be found ither in court procedure, in the characteristics of custom, or in judicial deci- ions. The State could not lodge and process complaints. That was a prerogative f the relatives alone.[23]

The power to pardon a man for any offense whatever rested not in the State or in any public authority. Forgiveness was fully a matter to be settled or granted or arranged with indemnity between disputant clans. In Flanders as in Normandy, even down to the thirteenth century, a murderer could not receive is pardon either from the King or the judges until he had first been reconciled with the kindred of the slain.[24] It is easy to pass over the significance of the power to pardon, but doing so would be a major error. For whoever has the power to pardon or to forgive also holds the power to mete out penal sanctions or to punish, and prior to the emergence of formally rational States and citizen- ship, the power to forgive without punishment resided among the kindreds—and punishment without forgiveness was an act of war in interclan disputes. It fol- lows that neither crime nor penal sanctions can have any meaning until the power to pardon becomes the clear monopoly of the State—until the ethic of ndividual responsibility and citizenship become sociocultural facts.

Rusche and Kirchheimer observe that even to the mid-sixteenth-century the power to pardon still reposed with the offended party and not with the State. In cases punishable by law the offender could keep his harm out of court by compensating the offended party. Even a man sentenced to punishment by the State could avoid punishment by compensating the victim.[25] The power to pardon shifts ever so slowly to a territorial power when custom and the coopera- tive ethic is strong. In this connection, Weber observed that in ancient India and China, the "State" was devoted to making verses, literary masterpieces and was without power to punish or to pardon offenders, due to the deeply imbedded customs of strong peasant clans. The same applied in Europe until Roman law broke the power of similar kindreds.[26]

In the second feudal age down to 1250, repopulation and the makings of an economic revolution took shape. Given the persistence of customary law the commercial principle or what Weber called the "alien ethic"[27] grew not internal- ly but externally and toward the East. Cloth centers emerged nearly everywhere —Flanders, Picardy, Bourges, Languedoc, Lombardy—but from the end of the eleventh century, with the creation of artisans and merchants on a vastly larger scale, in urban places, internal trade came into its own. With it came the institu- tionalization of private property, citizen-entrepreneurship, and the market system. Men of commerce began to compete with each other with the same un-abashed ruthlessness as had characterized international trade prior to the intern-alization of this ethic.[28] Under the market ethos, since society could not share one's risks and costs, it could not share one's opportunities and gains. Each man as an entrepreneur was responsible for himself, his conduct, and its consequences good or bad. This ethic came eventually to expression in civil and criminal law and in the rational State. But in judicial processes, especially in criminal law pro-cedures, this ethic held little significance because States had not yet developed a clear monopoly over the power to pardon, and few of the ruthless practices com-mon to the newly developing world of commerce had come to be proscribed under any legal order. Whether acts of war or of punishment and crime, the only intended harms proscribed were for the most part "blood harms" and had little to do with violations of private property, breaches of market contracts, and en-titlement to allodial (private) property.[29]

Which acts of intended violence, in feuds or war or in trials by combat, are crimes and which are punishments? In the absence of any singular, dominant State capable of continually reducing feuds to crime and penal sanction, crime and penal sanction disappear, and where kinship solidarity between kindreds is strong, war disappears. Interclan marriages may have preserved solidarity in the first feudal age. Certainly no State functioned to do this. In the twelfth century, crime was held not to exist during an interregnum—not even when destruction of royal palaces was involved. In any such power vacuum, people, as usual, relied on customary means of terminating disputes. The rationale was stated simply enough: "We served our emperor while he lived; when he died, we no longer had a sovereign."[30]

Collective reprisals against feudal principalities in the second feudal period were commonplace. In 1127, for example, the Duke of Brittany confessed inabil-ity to protect his monasteries from assaults by his own vassals. Evidently the expansion of feudalism by subinfeudation reduced certain marriages up and down the feudal scale, and with this, fealty and companionage were reduced to meaninglessness. Incentives for settling feuds by indemnity had thus vanished, and the feud along with other acts of feudal justice ceased to restore solidarity. In the absence of fealty the strength of authority collapsed and no principality could muster sufficient military force, eventually, to fill the void.[31]

Throughout both feudal ages there emerged no clear distinction between a personal leader or champion and the abstract idea of power. Not even kings were able to rise above family sentiments.[32] Against the force of custom and shared responsibility for individual conduct, States of the first feudal age were weak. With the force of custom and shared responsibility, they were strong. As bonds of fealty waned with the expansion of feudal estates—from top to bottom of the feudal scale—the ethic of shared responsibility for conduct collapsed. Feuds, wars, petty violence increased in frequency and savagery. The forms of tradition remained *as forms,* but interpersonal sentiments favoring peace gave them no meaning. What gave them meaning was the temper of violence and irreparably wounded honor. In all this, traditional authority, stripped of fealty and com-panionage, was powerless. Toward the close of the second feudal age, feudalism of old had collapsed, and feudal authority in the midst of chaos was on the threshold of transformation. Under the ethic of shared responsibility, crime and penal sanction did not exist. Without it, and before the development of citizenship and the formally rational State—toward the end of feudalism—only reprisals and counterreprisals existed. In neither situation was there either criminal law or a force strong enough to impose it on each individual as an individual. Individualism without ethic and without institutions to regularize it was born of the collapse of feudal institutions.

Rational Institutions and Their Relation to Crime and Penal Sanction

The institutional chaos of the latter Middle Ages—extending well into the fourteenth century—and the steady decline of the ethic of shared responsibility left feudal authority impoverished and impotent to arrest the increasing savagery of interminable feuds, wars, petty violence and brigandage. The vassalage, tied to landed interests, could no longer rely on fealty and tallage from lesser ranks for their political and economic support. Nor could perpetuity of landed wealth be relied upon from the fourteenth century on. Royal revenues and power were drying up as fealty declined, and of necessity royal authority sought revenues elsewhere, if only to raise armies to put down recalcitrants in the realm.

Not all was chaos. Petty merchants throughout Europe, once objects of scorn, had already begun to develop, with their artisans, the institutions of private property, exchange of titles to property in markets growing steadily in the second feudal age, and a labor force freed from feudal ties. Even by the thirteenth century, these merchants had become dedicated to the business of creating opportunities for continued, renewable gains—calling for stern rejection of sentiment and sympathy for any who might lose heavily in trade relations. It called for monklike pursuit of gain. Initially banished, outside the feudal city, these pariahs grew with every decline of feudal institutions, and with them grew the ethic of individual responsibility. In the midst of feudal anomie, this ethic—expressed institutionally in market contracts—finally supplanted the cooperative ethic. It did so with the eventual alliance between European monarchs and the rising merchant class.

The alliance created the formally rational State and citizenship and had direct bearing upon the advent of crime and penal sanction. Petty merchants throughout Europe gained fantastic wealth and with it power directly in consequence to the wars and feuds of the landed nobility. Such wars, in absence of fealty and tallage, had to be financed from outside the system. War loans, using land as collateral, were made to such nobles by merchants. Lands once held by nobles in perpetuity under laws of primogeniture and entail were regularly mortgaged by both parties in conflict. Every war meant that the land of one of the parties in conflict would fall to the merchant making the loan and not to the winner of the battle. Dobb observed that from the Wars of the Roses onward, the landed wealth of Europe fell in this manner into the hands of merchants like fish into their nets.[33] As most wealth had been landed wealth held out of the market by laws of primogeniture and entail, this transfer of land to the merchant class made land a commodity for buying and selling *as private property* in the interest of profit. Any labor attached to such land under serfdom was freed from feudal ties to that land, and so were the nobles themselves. Human relations underwent profound transformation.

The plight of monarchs in raising revenues became more acute since revenues had come previously from landed nobles all the way up the feudal scale. Now in the hands of merchants, changing hands with every sale, land came to resemble mobile capital. It became clear that the destiny of monarchs was at once the prosperity of merchants. In this way the State cut its bond with family relations. The kinship aspects of the feudal State vanished. Tied to the interests of an entrepreneurial world, authority and power became abstract. In aligning itself with capital and the interests of capital, the State came to guarantee as law both the ethic and the practices which had emerged among merchants prior to the alliance.

The annuity bond arising from personal debts and war loans, the stock certificate, the bill of exchange, the commercial company, the mortgage, trust deeds, and the power of attorney—all were practices of merchants which grew with the collapse of feudal institutions and which became guaranteed in law with the alliance between monarchs and the entrepreneurial class.[34] With this alliance the remnants of shared responsibility for gains and losses were bypassed along with the social control value of customary law, kinship as a restraint upon power, and the sentiments of fealty and companionage. Local feudal worlds such as kindreds and medieval cities lost all autonomy and authority as the nation-state emerged. Everywhere cities in Europe came under the power of competing national States as a condition, Weber observed, of perpetual struggle for power in peace and war:

This competitive struggle created the largest opportunities for modern capitalism. The separate States had to compete for mobile capital, which dictated to them the conditions under which it would assist them to power. Out of this alliance of the state with capital, dictated by necessity, arose the national citizen class, the bourgeoisie in the modern sense of the word. Hence, it is the closed national State which afforded to capitalism its chance for development—and as long as the national state does not give place to a world empire capitalism also will endure.[35]

Just as the national State came to recognize and guarantee, as well as create, civil laws relating to market relations, private property, labor, imports, exports, tariffs, it likewise came to have full power to create and impose criminal laws which related to the same institutions of capitalism. Under the ethic of individual responsibility, any citizen, even one forgiven by his kin or community, could be penally sanctioned as an individual by an abstract State and without much probability of reprisal against the State on the part of those who had forgiven him. With the advent of the formally rational State, punishment was no longer an act of war. And any violation of criminal law—defined by the State—came to be seen as a harm against the State.

With authority behind the institutions of capitalism, and as the commercial principle became intense and diffused through the commercial and industrial revolutions, criminal law proscribed far more behaviors as crimes than had ever existed even in the second feudal age. In addition to the short list of blood harms, fornication, and adultery which had been dealt with on the shared responsibility basis, the State created new crimes and punishments directly as the institutions of capitalism advanced. Moreover, the older blood harms—including he older forms of justice—became criminal in that the State now specifically roscribed them and fixed to them penal sanctions. Thus the State obtained a monopoly over the processing of acts of violence.

Apart from the older harms criminal laws were established primarily for he protection and development of the institutions of capitalism. The reference here is not simply to penal sanctions levied against robbery, theft, burglary, or other violations of private property. It is to penal sanctions which directly controlled the manner in which social structure would develop in cities. It is to penal sanctions which had direct bearing on determining the organization of the division of labor in society and consequently upon the class structure of commercial settlements.

Criminal laws strangled the ability of lower classes (those alienated from landed feudal ties who had migrated to cities as "free labor") to possess tools or capital goods, raw materials, and also, on pain of heavy penal sanction, forbade association with guild masters.[36] In short, upward mobility became a crime unless guild masters themselves chose to elevate the status of an artisan. Thus penal sanctions guaranteed by the State guaranteed a continuous labor force (whether employed or not) and created two classes of citizens—one bound by criminal laws and penal sanctions, and another bound only by nonpunitive civil laws. The situation is hardly different today in this respect.[37] Under the formally rational State, second-class citizens are never in a position to be governed only by civil laws—they are never, therefore, beyond incrimination.

Cross-Cultural Parallels

These historical observations have significant cross-cultural parallels. Wherever we witness a "third-world" country adopting political and economic systems roughly similar to those under the formally rational State, we find the ethic of shared responsibility for individual conduct giving way to the ethic of individual responsibility for individual conduct. Whenever we see any Western national State engaged in active warfare with any country governed by the ethic of shared responsibility, we see a State engaged in the savage business of reducing this ethic to that of individual responsibility, and in the transformation of customary institutions to "rational" institutions founded upon calculable law. This is done either directly, or indirectly through the establishment of puppet regimes on foreign soils. Submission of every individual in a territory—as an individual—to a single power reduces a war of political equals to submission of individuals as individuals and reduces a great many practices of the vanquished to the status of crimes.

The power to pardon under the formally rational State also played an increasing role in the determination of crime and penal sanction as well as a most significant role in the determination of two forms of "justice" which up to the present time measures the difference between the privileged and the nonprivileged in relation to crime and its prosecution. The State acquired the power to pardon because the power to forgive-without-punishment became meaningless in the last days of feudalism and because a few still stable forms of feudalism yielded that power to emergent States. Thus, replacing a diffused, collective act of forgiveness was the impersonal, concentrated power to pardon invested in a separated political community as an enforceable monopoly. This empowered the State to levy penal sanctions.

It was observed that the power to pardon relative to the rendering of penal sanctions is rarely used, and that penal sanctions coupled with the meaningless-ness of forgiveness locally, undermines the restorative power of society. The reference here was to the use of full pardon. There are, however, partial or quali-tative pardons which are implicit in the reduction of corporal punishments to fines, and in some cases eventually to the abolition of fines. This amounts to the gradual abolition of punishment by means of partial pardon. It also means the abolition of crime to which penal sanction was fixed.

Just as the State can manufacture crimes by proscribing specific acts and fixing to them penal sanctions, so can the State abolish a crime by removal of these sanctions. But partial abolition of crime stems from reduction of a given penal sanction from capital or corporal punishments to fines.

As Rusche and Kirchheimer have already observed, this reduction partially legitimates the behavior to which the fine becomes attached.[38] In effect, the fine means the State's willingness to withhold punishment provided that the violator is willing and able to pay the price. It goes without saying that if the fine is a negligible amount in relation to the profit made by violating the law, under capitalism, then it will continue to be violated at no expense to the State. For those who are unable to pay such fines, the prison walls loom large indeed. It is in this sense that the State partially pardons the wealthy their harms against others in society but fails to pardon the poor for the same crimes. It is thus no mere play on words to say that crime is what poor men are in jail for.

Then what is partly legitimate for upper classes becomes totally "immoral" for lower classes. In either case the State cannot lose. Revenues from wealthy lawbreakers are more than sufficient to offset fiscal costs associated with operat-ing and maintaining prisons—especially when one views what sink holes most prisons are. If such revenues prove inadequate, then the rest is made up by the public tax dollar. If prison maintenance comes wholly through taxes and bond issues, then revenues from fines make up a clear profit for the treasury of the State.

But there is more to this partial pardon, because of a basic ambiguity re-garding how to conceive the fine. Is it actually a penal sanction? Is it, to the contrary, a tax levied for the privilege of violating criminal law? Or, is it a price charged by the State for the right or license to violate laws for which only the poor would be imprisoned? In any case, the State either becomes an entrepre-neurship which exchanges the right to violate criminal law for a price called a fine—or else it becomes an agency in which the fine is standard fiscal policy very like a tax on the rich and less rich to pay for punishing the poor for having vio-lated criminal laws the State itself created! There is a subtle mechanism here, in that the State is always in a position to proscribe as criminal only those acts which are bound to maximize revenues—if the price is right—and to maximize (or minimize) imprisonment if the price is not right or if it is beyond the ability of people to pay it.

Through manipulations such as these, the State can increase or decrease crime rates at will just as it can create whole new categories of crimes for partial legitimation when revenues are wanting. The central irony—in view of the active role of the State in the manufacture of crime—is that every civil and criminal law created by the State assumes that only the individual citizen is responsible for the act he performed and for its consequences. Through this legal fiction the

State exempts itself from any responsibility for crimes and crime rates and at once exonerates itself from any guilt for having punished any man for a crime the State invented.

This ethic of individual responsibility is a legal fiction and is both socially and psychologically insupportable. It is the central myth of both citizen and State. Yet, despite the State's causal role in crime, the myth lives on as an eternal verity among most of the very people the State has punished and "rehabilitated," and among those whose lives and fortunes are governed by legally imposed conditions over which such people have little or no control. As long as consensus over the verity of this myth is high, good citizens will continue to ascribe to criminal laws a moral significance, and to this extent the position of the State is strong and secure against any serious threat of a general uprising from among those it governs.

But consensus changes. The moral value of such laws and sanctions then falls suspect. The fictional character of the theory of individual responsibility becomes clear as noonday, for the very laws thought to have had great moral significance come to be recognized not as a grass roots manifestation of Durkheimian society but as the product of the class-bound State, bound to its narrowed interests in "peace" and war—demanding submission from second-class citizens to laws and judicial practices which serve only the interests of a few.

The illusion that the State represents the interests of all citizens then passes away, and even fools could see the vast differences between society and the political community exploiting society in the name of society and public welfare. Since fools could see it, so could most criminologists who now pander to the interests of the State in the name of science. And in the interest of saving their skins, they would "discover" and reveal what people had come to know already—that there are no scientific grounds for defining crime as an act against society and every reason to define criminal laws and penal sanctions as subdued warfare waged by one powerful segment of civil society against an individuated segment of citizens. Short of any general recognition of this, the professionalist's sinecure, begotten of service to the State and its institutions (in the name of science) is not at risk, and because of sinecure the role of the State in the manufacture of crimes is scarcely noted.

Stateless Societies in Relation to Harms and Their Disposal

The Nuer, the Bantu of Kavirondo, and the Tallensi are without States in that no one of them possesses a separated, continuous political community having any judicial, lawmaking, or executive capacity either to govern the members of society as citizens or to be solely in charge of relations with outside tribes in peace or war.[39] Calculable law as it has come to exist in the West—in either of its civil or criminal forms—is absent. Thus, in these societies there are no norms characterized by politicality and penal sanction. Citizenship and entrepreneurship as these appear in formally and substantively rational States are absent. And the only occasion in which a person may come under the ethic of individual responsibility for his conduct is the rare instance when collective punishment is levied in the forms of physical pain, death, and banishment. Even here, where the punished is regarded as a victim of evil spirits and is believed to be practicing witchcraft, it cannot be certain whether it is the individual or the spirit assumed to possess him who is believed to be the victim of punishment. This means that the idea of individual responsibility does not exist as an ethic. All that is known is that magical ceremonies repeatedly failed to terminate harms.

In none of these societies do crime and penal sanction exist. What is observable are harms and counter harms, their settlement by arbitration and compensation (between clans), as well as harms within clans and their settlement magically. Only as a last resort is anything like punishment rendered. It must be emphasized here that punishment is not necessarily a penal sanction. While penal sanction is a punishment, not all punishments are penal sanctions.

Penal sanction is a State-specified punishment *fixed* in law to a conduct *specifically* proscribed by any law which has *politicality*, and crime is the specific conduct to which a penal sanction is fixed. Both imply a State. While punishments may take place in absence of a State, no punishment is a penal sanction unless a State is present. While crime does not exist where penal sanctions are absent, no intended harm can be a crime unless penal sanctions are present. Punishment alone does not signify a crime has taken place, but penal sanction does. In absence of penal sanction, a punishment signifies only that either an intended or unintended harm took place or was believed to have taken place. Punishment without penal sanction is a rule of custom. Penal sanction is a rule of State law.

In further clarification, civil law, as it emerged in Western culture, also implies a State—as well as citizenship and the ethic of individual responsibility for conduct. While it has politicality, it lacks penal sanction. Violations of it, when pressed by an injured party, require only that the party be compensated his loss. Nothing is paid to the State by way of fine or other punishment. But compensation without punishment is not what determines whether a law is a civil one. This is a common error. What makes a law a civil one is the fact that it has *politicality* without penal sanction and is guaranteed by the State—since failure to comply with a civil court order becomes a violation of criminal law and subject to penal sanction. Thus, civil law, either created or recognized by the State as part of its legal order, is calculable and is the epitome of formally rational law.

Some students of culture neglect this point and often violate their own rules of method in doing so by assuming that what is the product of Western culture must apply to all other cultures. Thus Wagner, for example, observed how impossible it is to distinguish criminal from civil law among the Bantu of Kavirondo—as if there were a distinction to be made.[40] That society, without a State, has neither. Custom lacks politicality, guaranteed law, as well as penal sanction. This point is respected, however, by Evans-Pritchard who observed that among the Nuer (a Stateless society also) there is no law in the strict sense because there is no one among the Nuer with legislative or judicial functions.[41]

Without any significant distortion of the situations which we find in these three societies, the following applies. One who kills another from a different clan receives the protection of his own clan since each is jointly responsible for the conduct of any one member. Feuds following such an incident may be avoided by ceremony and mediation conducted by elders or diviners who arrange satisfactory settlement by agreed upon compensation which the clan of the killer days. Punishment does not take place. Feuds may be terminated either by this same method or by the death of any member of the clan of the killer. It is not essential that the killer be the one to die by avengement. In this situation neither crime nor punishment take place. Killings take place and they are acts of warfare. Each clan engaged in a feud operates on the principle of collective responsibility. Even in cases where a killing takes place within a clan, individual responsibility does not appear except in extreme cases of often repeated harms. Among the Bantu of Kavirondo, clan solidarity is so strong that when one kills another the immediate recourse is to sacrifice an animal to propitiate the spirits and to hold purification ceremonies to make it safe for the killer's kinsmen to resume relations with him.[42]

When punishment occurs in these Stateless societies, the most serious forms are banishment and death. Either may take place—but only for intraclan harms—after ceremonies have repeatedly failed to make the offender stop his offenses. Ceremonies of restoration and punishment are collective. Restorations amount to collective forgiveness without punishment and are quite different from formal pardons conducted by a State. Moreover, formal pardons take place most infrequently and penal sanctions are commonplace in societies having States, whereas in Stateless society forgiveness without punishment is commonplace while punishments are rare.

Perhaps the most threatening form of punishment is banishment, and the implications of banishment are both interesting and significant. Only when a man is banished does the principle of individual responsibility apply to him. Only then, out from under the protection of the ethic of shared responsibility for his conduct, does he experience the full meaning of being fully responsible for his livelihood, and for any encounters he may have with others. Deprived of everything which once had meaning for him, he may be set upon by anyone either in his own or from another clan for any reason whatever. The responsibility for the consequences of any act he may perform is his alone to bear.

Like the citizen the banished man is removed from the protection of his kindred and the sentiment attached thereto. Unlike the citizen the banished has no institutional life outside kinship bonds short of migration, perhaps, to cities dominated by Western institutions. Pariahlike, between two worlds, at anyone's mercy, his fate is only his own to ponder. There are no market relations to be established with others like himself, no State to guarantee them under civil laws or to bring market behavior and private property under control of criminal law and penal sanctions. But neither the banished nor the citizen may find either protection or restoration to good standing through traditional institutions of kinship and religion as founded on the ethic of shared responsibility. Therein is their sameness.

While the above historical and cross-cultural observations support answers to first order questions posed initially, and while they support the thesis of this work, drawing them together is reserved until the presentation of the second part of this study which deals with the sameness of crime and penal sanctions. It is sufficient here only to note that crimes and penal sanctions are not universal but are unique forms of intended harms limited to specific countries and to a definite period of Western history. They emerged, roughly, as a post-fifteenth-century phenomenon and as an integral part of a cluster of new institutions expressing individualism as an ethic—viz., formally rational States, citizenship, the institutions of capitalism, and calculable laws composed of two related legal orders (guaranteed civil or commercial laws, and criminal codes which both comprise the legal basis of the citizen role). While general features of crime (blood harms, feuds) are determined by the State and citizenship, special features are determined by the emergence and development of the institutions of capitalism in which innovated criminal laws were instrumental in the creation and early solidification of the division of labor of capitalism, in expropriation of both the tools and materials of work from artisans, and in creating a permanent split between occupational types (entrepreneurs-laborers). Thus these laws solidified for masters only, the role and class of citizen-entrepreneur. With power fully behind this class, any act could become criminal simply by fixing a penal sanction to it and processing it through a growing judicial machinery. When the ethic of shared responsibility collapsed, and when anomie created the ethic and the institutions of individualism, no penal sanction could then be interpreted as an act of war subject to collective reprisal. Then, the formally rational State could stand immune to intended harms lodged against it from outraged clans, for kinship based on the traditional ethic was utterly smashed. Henceforth, any violence by the State against any family member was given and accepted as penal sanctioning of a citizen. Forgiveness without punishment was meaningless, and many forms of communal punishments had become crimes.

CRIME AND PENAL SANCTION AS A SINGLE BEHAVIORAL CLASS

Establishing crime and penal sanction as a single class involves more than observing that each is injurious, for innumerable acts of chance daily result in injury to others. Such acts are neither crimes nor punishments. Moreover, even though crimes and punishments are both intended, the fact of intent does not by itself establish that crimes and penal sanctions are the only harms which intent subsumes. Since there are other intended harms outside the crime-penal sanction complex, crime and penal sanction comprise but one part of the total behavioral class of intended harms.[43]

Even so, it is valid to state that no harm can be either crime or penal sanction without intent, when "intent" is a deliberate functioning to reach a goal. It was established in the first part of this work that feuds, wars, trials by combat, and communally given punishments have, when rational States appear, become crimes and that crimes do not exist prior to the advent of such States. Thus, these acts fall outside the crime-penal sanction complex. Even communally given punishments do not fall within the State-given class of punishments called penal sanctions. Thus, formal punishment in the modern political sense refers only to penal sanctions.

Apart from these "pre-State" harms which do not fall under the crime-penal sanction complex, there are other intended harms which, under modern States, fall outside this complex but are condoned by such States as non-criminal harms. Yet, any one of them can be made a crime by the State, first by defining it as a harm against the State, and second by attaching to it a penal sanction. This method of creating crime—or of abolishing it by removal of penal sanctions—is as characteristic today in the treatment of psychotic and civil harms as it was when, historically, traditional forms of justice (collective reprisals, feuds, trials by combat, and communal punishments) were outlawed as crimes. What then are the other intended harms which fall today outside the crime-penal sanction complex; what attributes characterize them which do not characterize crime and penal sanction? The following may be observed:

1. Harms not proscribed as crime which fall under civil or guaranteed law:[44] violations of civil contract agreements, disputed claims involving legal interpretation of liabilities and obligations under contractual agreements, inability to meet contracted obligations, losses due to another's profit, losses in recovery of bad debts, bankruptcy losses, and innumerable other harms in commercial transactions covered by civil laws and regulated by civil courts and commissions.

2. Harms against the general public by private commercial corporations: fraud, deceptive packaging, mislabeling, distribution of toxic foods, drugs, and cosmetics.[45]

3. Harms "excusable" upon legal proof of nonresponsibility of the offender at the time of his proscribed performance: juvenile harms in certain States, cases of "legal insanity"—as governed by statute, judicial procedure or both.

4. Excused harms involving direct violation of criminal laws but which are formally ignored at law enforcement level, or which are handled extralegally in civil courts or within private professional associations such as the American Medical Association: medical malpractices, fee-splitting among doctors, violations of a variety of criminal laws by corporation executives, violations of rights of minorities by police and military personnel, violations of blue laws. (Interestingly, long unenforced laws come daily to be used by police in violating civil rights of minorities—arresting a man for violating old "syndicalist laws" would fall here.)

Harms listed above share with crimes and penal sanctions the attribute of intent, and they tell us something indirectly about crime and penal sanction as a single behavioral class. A few observations may be made in this connection:

1. With one exception, the above harms are either not punishable or are excusable. Intended harms falling under civil law call only for restitution, not repression.[46]

2. There is nothing intrinsic to any of the above harms, nothing to be observed in behaviors themselves, which could warrant their being outside the crime-penal sanction class of harms. Depending upon whether the State proscribes and penally sanctions any of these harms, any of them could fall under the classification of crime—just as any crime could become a civil harm with the removal of its penal sanction and its definition as a harm against the State. Indeed, this has been much of the history of the making and the abolition of crimes by the State. Debt ceased being a crime in this manner and became a civil matter. Early, traditional action's based upon customs—as seen—became crimes by State manipulation of penal sanctions and politicality. Examples are so numerous as to observe an inte-

gral relation, an interflow through time, between civil and criminal acts. *Either can become the other.*

3. The only criteria which determine whether any behavior is civil or criminal are not behavioral criteria (as many psychologists, ministers, philosophers, and "sociologists" suppose) but are external criteria applied by the State—chiefly, politicality and penal sanction.

4. Whatever determines the civil or criminal status of any specific conduct are the purely external manipulations of law, law enforcement, and penal sanctions; and any group whatever its value system, upon achieving control of political machinery, can make anything criminal (at least for a while) and can prevent condemnation of anything insofar as it can maintain itself securely against collective reprisal.

5. Punishability of an act is determined by the power of the State. Ultimately this power rests upon the intensity and spread of the myth that each individual is responsible for his own conduct and that the State is not. At the same time, this power is determined by who holds command over the means of political violence—the instruments of penal sanction.

What may be inferred from these observations of civil and other harms which bears upon the singular character of crime and penal sanction?

All intended harms of the crime-penal sanction complex are punishable. That is, if crime and penal sanction are essentially the same things, then as a class they *both* must differ from the above-listed harms in being punishable and not excusable. Certainly anything the State defines as criminal is punishable and is not excusable except as the State exercises its power of pardon. Interestingly, in civil harms where the power to pardon rests not with the State but with citizen associations, the State has no power to punish. Only when this power to pardon civil harms is usurped by the State does the State have the power to punish. In any such instance, the usurpation is accomplished by a statute proscribing a civil harm as criminal and pardonable, and fixing to it a penal sanction in lieu of pardon by the State.

The Punishability of Penal Sanctions and the Rebirth of Crime

Anything legally proscribed as criminal is punishable, but is penal sanction itself punishable? If crime and penal sanction are both punishable, then by these external criteria they belong to the same class, and it is only by these external criteria that they differ fundamentally from all other intended harms. Indeed it is vain to look for any State-supported rationale under which penal sanctions performed by the State are punishable as crimes. But one need not search far back in history, or look in vain cross-culturally, for cases where punishments have transmuted into crimes through social movements and revolutions which transform the institutional structure of society. It is exactly in such transformations where the true relation between crimes and penal sanctions is most clearly seen.

With the decay of consensus over the legitimacy of dominating social institutions and laws supporting them, further penal sanctions imposed by the State for violations of such laws have come to be viewed collectively as themselves criminal (in the nontechnical sense). But the technical fact of criminality is not established until the threat of collective reprisal against the State is made good by the deposition of the State, or else is terminated by the collapse of the movement against the State. In the latter case few changes take place in the criminal law and the characteristics of crime remain relatively unchanged. But where political movements succeed where State-supported institutions are transformed, many of the old proscriptions under criminal law disappear—giving place to new proscriptions subject to pardon and penal sanction. Crime is thus reborn but with a different face.

With the rise of a new political community to full power and with full or partial transformation of once dominant institutions, what once was criminal becomes legal, immune to reprisal by the State. If economic institutions are transformed, a host of activities covered only by civil laws and guaranteed restitutions are proscribed as criminal and penally sanctioned. Just as the new State makes legal much of what once was criminal, so it also makes criminal much of what once was legal, as both civil and criminal laws are transformed. Moreover, what once were meted out as punishments by the old State are punished as crimes by the new one.

The Reduction of Crimes and Penal Sanctions to Reprisals

On the eve of successful revolutionary movements, when one State totters and a new one ascends, the dichotomy between crime and penal sanction blurs and vanishes with the decline of the power of the descending State to keep this dichotomy alive and credible in the minds of citizens now risen in open revolt. Citizenship, as a role defined in civil and criminal law, itself disappears as hour by hour the descending State loses ability to secure itself against those reprisals which blindly it insists are crimes. Crime and penal sanctions then reduce merely to intended harms and counterharms—to reprisals and counterreprisals between two separate, warring States.

Until the issue of power is settled in this trial by combat, no harm is either crime or penal sanction, simply because neither the ascending nor the descending State can create and apply to the other any laws having politicality and penal sanction. In this power vacuum, penal sanctions become acts of war; crimes are the same. The object of each State is to transmute the other's harms to the status of crimes, and to force acceptance of its own harms as penal sanctions. This is the primary objective in all warfare involving States locked in a power struggle with other States; it makes no difference whether one State emerged from among those governed by an older State or whether two nation-States are at war. The objective is the same. Wars differ sharply from feuds in this regard. In feuds, political submission is not an objective; avengement is. When feuds end, each party goes back home with its equality intact. When wars end, equality of the parties at war is unthinkable. The vanquished are never at home.

Until this objective is reached, neither the ascending nor the descending State has the power to pardon the other, and forgiveness is impossible. Murders and executions are indistinguishable—having become killings, the casualties of war, they have little meaning until long buried and come to be remembered as heroic sacrifices in the struggle for justice and law. They then become part of the State's community of memories, officially approved by "educated" men. But in the struggle, what is moral and what is not are totally inaccessible to reason, because reason, like God, is anyone's slave until the issue of power is settled. Whatever becomes moral in the long run depends upon how the war is terminated and upon whose values become institutionalized in everyday society as meaningful law, not merely as enforceable statutes.

The above inference that all harms in the crime-penal sanction complex are punishable is supported by every case of institutional transformation in the history of any society undergoing them. Except in social upheaval, penal sanctions are not *immediately* punishable as crimes, but because institutional transformations may be expected to take place at any future time, the following principle is valid:

Any harm punishable by the State as crime stands ultimately in the same status as any harm imposed by that State as punishment.

Penal sanctions are punishable as crimes whenever institutional transformations take place, and the illusion that crime and penal sanction comprise two independent species of behavior is sustained as if factual only when a given State and its institutions are either supported by consensus or else when (by coercion) that State can otherwise keep itself immune to successful reprisals from any source.

The Excusability of Intended Harms in Relation to Crime and Penal Sanction

In the list of intended harms outside the crime-penal sanction complex, it was seen that such harms were either excused or were excusable—that they were not immediately punishable by the State. Neither excusability nor punishability have anything to do with the nature of the actual conduct which is excused or punished. Thus there is nothing intrinsic to behavior itself which determines either its punishability or its excusability. Moreover, any harm in the civil category can—either by revolution or by the State's manipulation of law—become punishable or subject to penal sanction. Also, any harm in the criminal category can become a wholly civil matter by removal of penal sanction. It is the State, therefore, which determines at any given time what specific acts are excusable or punishable.

Even within the crime category, certain harms are excusable or at least are condoned or ignored by the State, inasmuch as scores of violations of various criminal laws, applicable only to professions and executives, are processed as if merely civil matters in courts where no penal sanctions can be meted out. Thus, the more command one has of central institutions, the greater his immunity to punishment, the less his probability of arrest and incrimination in criminal court. This observation means only that differential excusability and punishability is a social fact of differential proximity to political power. It is scarcely headline material—except for sociologists whose slum theory of crime is still prevalent in the classroom. By and large, just as civil laws applied only to the old guild masters, and criminal laws only to artisans, so does the same situation prevail today.

The closer one is to power, the less the risk of incrimination, and the more "civil" are one's harms against others.

Nonpunishability of civil harms today attests only to the positive interest of the State to maintain certain institutions such as semiprivate national and multinational corporations, national and transnational markets, and militarism as part of this complex. Differential excusability will continue to exist insofar as this interest is continuous. The important fact is not that these institutions are "economic" but that business is a system of power,[47] and that these institutions are the means of international power politics and are part of the total arsenal for making war at home and abroad—of reducing behaviors globally to the status of crimes.

Victimization as a Common Feature of Crime and Penal Sanction

There being no behavioral attributes among civil harms to warrant the separation of civil harms from those of the crime-penal sanction complex, it is necessary to see if distinguishing attributes might be found among crimes and penal sanctions which are not common to civil harms. Here, victimization appears as such an attribute, but again under control of the State as will be seen.

Both crime and penal sanction presuppose a victim, i.e., a personal or abstract object upon whom an intended harm is imposed. In both, the victim is clear-cut. For crime, the victim is by definition the State, the political community which defines crime as an intended harm against itself. For penal sanction, the victim is a citizen reduced to the status of convict. Intended harms of civil law jurisdiction presuppose no clear-cut victim, and if the term "victim" has any meaning in market relations, its meaning refers only to nonpunishable torts, unless a clear violation of criminal law is involved and is prosecuted as such. In market relations, if victimization exists without violation of criminal law, the "victim" is indefinite, usually not known personally to the injuring party. "Victims" are diffuse.

Who is the victim when a man deliberately, under capitalism, initiates bankruptcy procedures? Who is the victim in contracts where one man who agreed to hold the other harmless against certain losses incurred those losses even when the second party caused them? Who is the victim when California orange growers corner the market and cause Florida growers heavy losses? Unambiguous answers to such questions are impossible. In most cases, the intent was to make profit by any legal means, not to make victims. Nothing about victimization here is as clear-cut as when a man murders another or when an executioner electrocutes him for having done it. But civil harms do pass under the jurisdiction of criminal law and become crimes. It is just here where the meaning of victim and victimization becomes clear.

When a civil harm passes under criminal law, the absence of a clear-cut victim continues to hold. But since that act is now defined as a harm against the State, the "victim" becomes the State. There are at least three types of "crimes" in which this is seen: (1) acts involving personal indulgence either for pleasure or for inflicting injury or death on oneself, (2) acts involving personal and collective protest, and (3) acts which are outlawed forms of entrepreneurship, or illegal enterprises of capitalism.

The first type includes, for example, "pot smoking," taking LSD, shooting hard narcotics. While other people may be harmed in these acts of self-indulgence, the idea of intended victim is unclear—except by definition when the State intervened to declare itself the victim. *The second type* includes, for example, certain peaceful demonstrations, "sedition," obstructing "justice," alleged treason, failures to comply with draft requirements, active aid to persons to avoid the draft, public speeches against the draft which encourage resistance to the draft or to the other State-supported policies. *The third type* includes, for example, prostitution, shilling, buying and selling hard narcotics, certain forms of gambling, making and selling bootleg whiskey, operating a wire service, playing the numbers game, and a host of other enterprises outlawed by the State as harmful to itself.

The only clear-cut "victim" in any of the above cases is the political community which defined these acts as harms against itself. Nothing seems more clear than that crime, legally construed, refers not to any person as victim but only to the State. When civil harms pass under criminal law, whether a real, personal victim was intended or not is not really an important question in deciding the criminality of the act.

Like civil harms, direct victims are not clearly visible in the above actions. Penal sanctions are fixed to these actions not because they may be harmful to others, for that is incidental, but because the State has proscribed them as harmful to its own interests. In short, crime has nothing to do with the fact that one person may intentionally harm another but everything to do with the manipulation of law, with the application of criteria *external* to the acts of harm themselves. Victimization stands with excusability and punishability as externally imposed characteristics which all too often are regarded as intrinsic to the behavior in question. One of the principle ironies of this is the great lengths that are taken in criminal court procedures to prove that "intent," even if subject to proof, were actually important.

There are indeed other harms proscribed by the State in which a direct victim is clearly visible: theft, burglary, robbery, sexual assault, fraud, embezzlement, confidence games, fee-splitting in medicine, industrial espionage, price-rigging among a multitude of corporation executives in bidding for government contracts, kidnapping. These intended harms cut across the whole scale of social classes. But here an important question arises: *are these harms crimes because the offender had in mind an intended victim, or are they crimes because in each case the State had defined itself as victim?* If there were no difference between the interests of the State and the welfare of all people it governs, then any offense by one person against another would at once be a harm against the State. But the State takes only token action in high crimes, and presses hard on low ones. Apparently, the State is less a victim of high crimes than of low ones like rape, robbery, and embezzlement. In each of the above cases, the fact that an offender may have had in mind an intended victim as object of harm is incidental. A crime, by State definition, is a harm against the State. On a few occasions do murderers have the State in mind as the intended victim; yet it is the State-as-victim for which the man is punished. This must be true, unless the State is willing to say that crime is not a harm against the State.

As in all previous cases, attributes of behavior are not responsible for any legal class of behavior. What is responsible for civil harms and what is responsible for those deemed criminal are criteria external to the social behavior in question. By manipulation of proscription, politicality, and the power to punish and pardon, the State can make itself the symbolic victim of any act whatever—whether actually harmful or not—by defining it as such and by prosecution on the assumption that it is true.

The whole process from arrest through imprisonment to post-confinement adjustment is a process of victimization not of the State but of the person who was judged to have made the State a victim. This process holds the full meaning of incrimination. It constitutes a life-long stigmatization of the "criminal"—a source of wealth for psychiatrists, ministers, police, judges, lawyers, clerks, politicians, social workers, and writers of novels. It is a State-created opportunity for continued renewable gains by a whole hierarchy of occupational types whose lifestyle is utterly dependent upon the continuation, not the termination, of this process. Nothing would harm the State more than to have no crime at all. It is this process which involves identification of the whole person by one act, and ultimately either making that person accept that narrowed self or to accept "rehabilitation" as based on the assumption that the narrowed self was the whole self. Is it not strange that when tried executives serve suspended sentences, they are denied the "benefits" of rehabilitation?

In legal procedure the personal victim of crime, though incidental, is often hard to identify, but the victim of punishment never is. Arrested, mugged, fingerprinted, numbered, tried, punished, released to officials, his identity is externally never uncertain. Punishment is an unambiguous consequence of a symbolic harm, but is only one part of the total process of victimization or incrimination, and unless the incriminated come to see themselves as criminals (either with pride or guilt), there are no behavioral characteristics by which the person of a criminal and the person of a punitive agent are separable as distinctly different species. The attributes which separate crime from penal sanction are external criteria—external to the social interaction to which these criteria are applied. Thus far it has only been shown that crime and penal sanction do not belong to behaviorally independent classes. What remains is to show that they are essentially the same. This recalls the question: do legal criteria for identifying crime also identify punishments meted out by the State?

The Sameness of Crime and Penal Sanction

Establishing that crime and penal sanction are the same may proceed by taking the criteria which the State uses for determining whether an act is criminal, and then testing to see if these same criteria apply with equal validity to penal sanctions. If they do, then even within the criminal law there is no way to differentiate crime from penal sanction on behavioral grounds, because the State's differentiae would establish merely that any penal sanction may also be regarded as criminal.

The differentiae of crime in relation to penal sanction derive from the characteristics of criminal law (uniformity, politicality, specificity, and penal sanction), and of these only specificity refers to the actual conduct in question or on trial. These characteristics are construed legally as criteria by which to determine whether a given performance is a crime, not whether the performer is criminal. Thus, proof of a crime is not itself taken as proof of criminality. Yet, the differentiae of crime, *derived* from the characteristics of criminal law, are used procedurally in court to determine criminality.

The present objective is not to test the scientific value of using these criteria as proofs but to see if they apply also to formal punishment. To demonstrate this, the same procedure used by Sutherland and Cressey will be followed, but with one difference. Instead of providing a case involving a crime to demonstrate the applicability of a given criterion, a case involving a penal sanction will be used (as in table 1). This is sufficient to the kind of proof required here, because if these differentiae are only the differentiae of *crime*, then no one of them could possibly be illustrated with a case of penal sanction—unless, of course, there *is* a real difference behaviorally between crime and penal sanction.[48]

Table 1. The Behavioral Differentiae of Both Crime and Penal Sanction

Rule	Case and Result
1. There must be an external consequence or harm. Mere intention, without harm, is insufficient.	A man is dead, having been executed by the State.
2. There must be a conduct leading to the harm.	In line of command, an authorized person closed the switch and caused a man, condemned in court, to die by electrocution.
3. Intent or *mens rea* (a deliberate functioning to reach a goal) must have been present.	Upon conviction in criminal court, after deliberated verdict of guilty, a man was sentenced to die by electrocution at an appointed time and place. In custody, that man was electrocuted as specified at that time and place.
4. Fusion or concurrence between intent and conduct must have existed.	*Case where fusion is absent:* a prison warden caused the wrong man to be electrocuted but deliberately (in error) acted to execute the condemned one. Penal sanction did not take place.
5. A "causal relation" between the harmful conduct and the harm must have been present.	*Case showing absence of causal relation:* While executing a condemned man, the latter died from food poisoning contracted earlier from the kitchen. This took full effect an instant before the switch was thrown. Penal sanction did not occur because causal relation was absent.

In the above five differentiae, what identifies crime and criminality also identifies penal sanction and punitive agents. In fact, it is far less complicated a task to identify penal sanction by the differentiae of crime than it is to identify crime—owing to the fact that proofs of existence of conduct, external harm, intent, fusion, and causal relation are all authentically recorded in State offices.

The above differentiae refer to behavior and its related attributes having to do with interaction, intent, and causal relations involved with social interaction. They apply as well to penal sanction as to crime. The remaining two differentiae, presented below, are external to actual conduct and its attributes. And they are the only differentiae by which any possible distinction can be made between crime and penal sanction.

Table 2. External Differentiae of Crime

A. The harm must be legally forbidden, i.e., proscribed in penal law.   (Politicality)

B. There must be legally prescribed punishment.   (Penal Sanction)

It is quite obvious that these two differentiae of crime cannot be also the differentiae of punishment by the State. It follows that these externally applied measures are the only measures by which the State not only identifies crime, but they are at once the measures by which the State can manufacture crime at will. There is nothing in the first five differentiae to prevent them from applying with equal validity to penal sanctions. In terms of these few criteria, crime and formal punishment are one and the same forms of conduct. What the additional two differentiae reveal is that the only criteria by which these intended harms are made into distinct and independent classes reduce in the last analysis to power and who holds it. It is power alone which creates and sustains the illusion that crime and punishment are independent, mutually exclusive species of conduct. This illusion is basic to nearly all teachings of modern criminologists, armchair philosophers, psychiatrists, and psychologists—all of whom claim validity for their positions on purely scientific grounds. Ironically, however, no position is less certain than theirs because this dichotomy, created and reified by the State and founded upon the fiction that only the governed are responsible—each for his own harms—is justifiable only on political and ideological grounds. To accept that only individuals *as individuals* are responsible for crime is at once to accept that the State is in no way a determinative factor in its advent and continuation—and this in the face of the fact that by manipulation of these external criteria whole categories of crime, either gradually or by revolutionary means, can be and have been abolished and replaced with others.

SUMMARY

Within the initial definitions, first and second order questions may now be answered on the basis of historical, cross-cultural, and legalistic observations made in the foregoing sections. Crime and penal sanction in being limited to specific countries and to a period of Western history are not universal but are a function of the emergence of formally rational States, of citizenship under such states, and of the transfer of the power of pardon from communities based upon the ethic of shared responsibility to a political or territorial community founded upon the fiction of individual responsibility. With these institutions developed two related legal orders. State guaranteed commercial and/o civil codes, and criminal laws—both of which define the general role expectations of citizenship at any given point in the history of formally rational States and the institutions supporting them.

While general characteristics of crime are determined by the emergence and continuation of the State and citizenship, special characteristics—with reference to what specific acts are proscribed—are determined by the kinds of institutions—socialist, capitalist, etc.—which the State supports. In the present study, these special features are determined by the emergence of the institutions of capitalism and by guaranteed commercial codes corresponding to emergent criminal laws which are meaningful only within a context where the market system, private property, and private laws of contract predominate.

The chief business of the State is to reduce the institutions founded upon the ethic of shared responsibility for individual conduct to those founded upon the fiction of individual responsibility while at the same time avoiding the probability of successful reprisals against itself. Obtaining a clear monopoly over the power to pardon is fundamental to this end. Any weakening of the solidarity of kinship and religious institutions, any weakening of social movements of citizens bent upon reconstruction of institutions supported by the State is instrumental to this end. The power of the State is enhanced accordingly. This principle holds regardless of whether one State, through war, reduces the acts of another to the status of crimes or whether a new State emerges within the corpus of society ruled by the State which is challenged.

With the power to pardon solidified, politicality and penal sanction as chief characteristics of the criminal law uncontestably emerge. It is only then that crime—as defined by the State itself—becomes possible. It is only then that the continuity of crime in some form becomes fundamental to the very existence of the State. And this form is determined by what the State chooses to sanction penally.

That the dichotomy between crime and penal sanction is sustained only by those who command the sources of political power is attested to whenever full or partial institutional transformations take place within societies already governed by a State. With the emergence of strong political movements, this dichotomy disappears as an enforceable entity, as all intended harms by either the ascendent or the descendent State reduce to counting the wounded and the dead—to reprisals and counterreprisals—in short, to war. And until the issue of power is settled, in this trial by combat, crime and penal sanction are meaningless except as war. When the issue of power is settled, the dichotomy is again reified, and if, later, consensus stands behind it crime and penal sanction will again be seen, erroneously, as mutually exclusive species of human conduct. The "morality" of the victorious will have become imposed; murders and executions will have risen again from their status of mere killings, and crimes and penal sanctions will have been reborn. The most crucial condition in keeping this dichotomy credible among the governed is the ability of the State to secure itself against collective reprisal from any source whatever.

Under the characteristics of the criminal law, and under the differentiae of crime, there are no criteria intrinsic to the behaviors called crime which can warrant separating crime and punishment as two mutually exclusive classes of conduct. Any harm punishable by the State as crime stands ultimately in the same status as any harm imposed by that State as a penal sanction. Moreover, of all the differentiae said to identify crime and criminality, the bulk of them apply with equal validity to penal sanctions. The two which clearly distinguish crime from penal sanctions are, again, the external criteria of politicality and penal sanction. And these are the chief measures by which the State can manufacture or abolish crime according to its own interests and, until the advent of institutional transformation, can remain beyond recrimination.

NOTES

[1]This assumption is reified daily by mass media's hue and cry about 'the crime problem,' 'crime waves,' the 'need for more law and order,' 'more law enforcement' in 'society's war on crime,' more (but reformed) prisons, more rehabilitation (for the poor), more psychiatry and social services for 'multiproblem families,' more urban renewal.

[2]Textbooks typically discuss 'crime' under Part I, and 'punishment' under Part II, without discussing their common features or how punishments become crimes and vice versa. They agree that crime is relative but fail to state that the same is so of punishment. Even Rusche and Kirchheimer see punishment in a separate orbit—transforming its methods only when mutations occur in the economic system. *See Punishment and Social Structure* (New York: Columbia University Press, 1939).

[3]These risks and rewards for professional services to off-campus supporters probably mean that any science of crime and punishment will not take place in academia.

[4]Max Weber, *On Law in Economy and Society,* trans. by E. Shils and M. Rheinstein (New York: Simon and Schuster, 1967), pp. 48, 162, 338 ff. The term 'State' is used here in the sense of a coercive political community as defined by Weber. It may be seen as an ascendent political movement or 'community of destiny' in Weber's terms.

[5]E. H. Sutherland and D. R. Cressey, *Principles of Criminology,* 7th ed. (New York: J. B. Lippincott, 1966), pp. 10-13.

[6]This point was first made by C. R. Jeffery in his Ph.D. dissertaion, "An Institutional Approach to a Theory of Crime," Indiana University, 1954, ch. I.

[7]E. E. Evans-Pritchard and M. Fortes, *African Political Systems* (London: Oxford University Press, 1958). See introduction and last three chapters.

[8]Max Weber, *General Economic History,* trans. by Frank Knight (New York: Collier, 1961), pp. 232-258. 'Roughly' is used here because the foundations of Weber's formally rational state appeared incipiently in the twelfth century but did not appear in full until the time Weber specified.

[9]Ibid., p. 232. See references to 'citizenship' and to the internalization of the 'alien ethic' or commercial principle into each European country—as sharply contrasting with co-operative values—making each individual citizen, apart from his clan, responsible for his own conduct in market behavior.

[10]Marc Bloch, *Feudal Society,* trans. by L. A. Manyon, vol. 1 (Chicago: University of Chicago Press, 1964), pp. 208-210.

[11]Ibid., vol. 1, parts I and II.

[12]Ibid., pp. 72-103

[13]Ibid., vol. 2, pp. 443-444.

[14]Ibid., vol. 1, pp. 109-116 ff.

[15]Ibid., p. 116.

[16]Ibid., p. 67.

[17]Ibid., pp. 123-125.

[18]Ibid., p. 125.

[19]Ibid., p. 126. See Bloch's distinction between active and passive solidarity.

[20]Ibid., p. 129.

[21]Ibid., p. 128.

[22]Ibid., pp. 128-129.

[23]Ibid.

[24]Ibid., p. 129.

[25]Rusche and Kirchheimer, *Punishment,* p. 213.

[26]Weber, *General Economic History,* pp. 250 ff.

[27]Ibid., p. 232.

[28]Ibid.

[29]Bloch, vol. 2, pp. 365 ff.

[30]Ibid., p. 409 ff. Acts like this were regular in this period, because principalities were weak—no longer holding consensus and strong military forces. Under weak principalities 'crime' meant only the clash of armies. Upholding custom in feuds led inadvertently (with other causes) to individuation of society through loss of fealty, meaningful epics, and the obsoleteness of the folk memory.

[31]Ibid., Chapter 30, pp. 408-421.

[32]Ibid., p. 10 ff.

[33]Maurice Dobb, *Studies in the Development of Capitalism,* chap. 5, rev. ed. (New York: International Publishers, 1963), especially pp. 186-198.

[34]Weber, *General Economic History,* pp. 247-253 ff.

[35]Ibid., p. 249.

[36]Rusche and Kirchheimer, chap. 2. See reference made to R. H. Tawney and to the latter's support of the above statement (note 19) where the State is described as a class State whose criminal laws protected only the interests of large capitalistic guild masters and held labor captive.

[37]E. H. Sutherland, *White Collar Crime* (New York: Holt, Rinehart, Winston, 1949).

[38]Rusche and Kirchheimer, *Punishment and Social Structure.*

[39]Evans-Pritchard and Fortes, *African Systems.* These observations also applied to other Bantu offshoots—Kikuyu, Meru, Embu—prior to imposition of British rule on these societies. *See* D. H. Rawcliffe, *Struggle for Kenya* (London: Victor Gollancz, 1954), and Jomo Kenyatta's treatment of Kikuyu political institutions in *Facing Mount Kenya* (London: Secker and Warburg, 1938).

[40]Gunter Wagner, "The Political Organization of the Bantu of Kavirondo," in Evans-Pritchard and Meyer Fortes, *African Systems,* pp. 217-218.

[41]E. E. Evans-Pritchard, "The Nuer of the Southern Sudan," in Evans-Pritchard and Meyer Fortes, pp. 293-294.

[42]Wagner, "Bantu," p. 202 ff.

[43]Sutherland and Cressey, pp. 12-13. Jerome Hall's differentiae of crime are reduced by these men to seven criteria. Both Hall and these men fail to indicate that their differentiae of crime apply with equal force to penal sanction. *See* Hall's *Principles of Criminal Law*, 2nd ed. (Indianapolis: Bobbs-Merrill, 1960), pp. 14-26. See definition of intent as differing from motive.

[44]Weber, *On Law*, pp. 12, 49-59; for discussion of State versus extra-State law, see pp. 16-17.

[45]Fred Cook, "The Corrupt Society," *The Nation* (June 1-8, 1963, special issue) *passim*.

[46]Emile Durkheim, *The Division of Labor in Society* (Glencoe, Ill.: Free Press, 1960), pp. 70-133; discussion of repressive and restitutive sanctions.

[47]Robert Brady, *Business as a System of Power* (New York: Columbia University Press, 1943).

[48]Sutherland and Cressey, pp. 12-13.

CRIME CONTROL IN CAPITALIST SOCIETY

RICHARD QUINNEY

The state, contrary to conventional wisdom, is the instrument of the ruling class. Moreover, law is the coercive weapon used by the state to maintain the existing social and economic order. Criminal law, in particular, is established and enforced for the purpose of securing domestic order. Thus, we understand crime in contemporary society in terms of the political reality of the capitalist state and its ruling class.

In the development of a critical-Marxian theory of crime control in capitalist society we must consider the following topics: (1) crime and the ruling class, (2) crime control in the capitalist state, and (3) demystification of criminal law. The objective is a critical understanding of the modern legal order.

CRIME AND THE RULING CLASS

According to liberal intelligence, the state exists to maintain stability in civil society. Law is regarded, accordingly, as a body of rules established through consensus by those who are governed, or rather by the "representatives" of the governed. Such a notion of the state and its law presents a false reality, but one that serves those who benefit from such a conception—those who rule.

An alternative position gets to the deeper meaning of the existence of the state and the legal order. Contrary to the dominant view, the state is created by that class of society that has the power to enforce its will on the rest of society. The state is thus a real, but artificial, political organization created out of force and coercion. The state is established by those who desire to protect their material basis and have the power (because of material means) to maintain the state. The law in capitalist society gives political recognition to powerful private interests.

Moreover, the legal system is an apparatus that is created to secure the interests of the dominant class. Contrary to conventional belief, law is a tool of the ruling class. The legal system provides the mechanism for the forceful and violent control of the rest of the population. In the course of battle, the agents of the law (police, prosecutors, judges, and so on) serve as the military force for the protection of domestic order. Hence, the state and its accompanying legal system reflect and serve the needs of the ruling class. Legal order benefits the ruling class in the course of dominating the classes that are ruled. And it may be added that the legal system prevents the dominated classes from becoming powerful. The rates of crime in any state are an indication of the extent to which the ruling class, through its machinery or criminal law, must coerce the rest of the population, thereby preventing any threats to its ability to rule and possess. Criminal law as a coercive means in establishing domestic order for the ruling class thus becomes a basic assumption in a radical critique of crime.

That American society can best be understood in terms of its class structure violates conventional knowledge. It still comes as a surprise to many citizens that 1 percent of the population owns 40 percent of the nation's wealth, indicating that the liberal perspective dominates, as does the ruling class which profits from the prevailing view. Yet the evidence now overwhelmingly supports the radical critique of American society.[1] The liberal assumption of a pluralistic American economy—with corporations as just one kind of interest group among many others—is negated, however, by the fact that the major portion of the wealth and nearly all the power in American society are concentrated in the hands of a few large corporations. Furthermore, those who benefit from this economy make up a small cohesive group of persons related to one another in their power, wealth, and corporate connections. In addition, the pluralistic conception ignores all the manifestations of the alliance between business and government. From the evidence of radical scholarship, government and business are inseparable.

A critique of the American political economy thus begins with the now examined assumption that life in the United States is determined by the capitalist mode of production. And as a capitalist society, a class division exists between those who rule and those who are ruled. As Miliband writes, in reference to the class structure of capitalist societies:

> The economic and political life of capitalist societies is *primarily* determined by the relationship, born of the capitalist mode of production, between these two classes—the class which on the one hand owns and controls, and the working class on the other. Here are still the social forces whose confrontation most powerfully shapes the social climate and the political system of advanced capitalism. In fact, the political process in these societies is mainly *about* the confrontation of these forces, and is intended to sanction the terms of the relationship between them.[2]

There are other classes, such as professionals, small businessmen, office workers, and cultural workmen, some of these either within or cutting across the two major classes, but it is the division between the ruling class and the subordinate class that establishes the nature of political, economic, and social life in capitalist society.

The ruling class, therefore, in capitalist society is "that class which owns and controls the means of production and which is able, by virtue of the economic power thus conferred upon it, to use the state as its instrument for the domination of society."[3] The existence of this class in America, rooted mainly in the corporations and financial institutions of monopoly capitalism, is well documented.[4] This is the class that makes the decisions that affect the lives of those who are subordinate to this class.

It is according to the interests of the ruling class that American society

is governed. Although pluralists may suggest that there are diverse and conflicting interests among groups in the upper class, what is ignored is the fact
that members of the ruling class work within a common framework in the
formulation of public policy. Superficially, groups within the ruling class may
differ on some issues. But in general they share common interests, and they
can exclude members of the other classes from the political process entirely.

If powerful economic groups are geographically diffuse and often in competition for particular favors from the state, superficially appearing as interest
groups rather than as a unified class, what is critical is not who wins or loses
but what kind of socioeconomic framework they *all* wish to compete within,
and the relationship between themselves and the rest of the society in a manner that defines their vital function as a class. It is this class that controls the
major policy options and the manner in which the state applies its power.
That they disagree on the options is less consequential than that they circumscribe the political universe.[5]

In contrast to pluralist theory, radical theory notes that the basic interests, in
spite of concrete differences, place the elite into a distinct ruling class.

In a radical critique of American society we are able, in addition, to get
at the objective interests that are external to the consciousness of the individuals who compose them. We are able to suggest, furthermore, normative
evaluations of these interests. Pluralists, on the other hand, are bound by the
subjective interests of individuals.[6] The critical perspective allows us to understand the actual and potential interests of classes, of the ruling class as well as
those who are ruled. What this means for a critique of legal order is that we
can break with the official, dominant ideology which suggests the diversity of
interests among numerous competing groups. We are able to determine the
interests of those who make and use law for their own advantage.

The primary interest of the ruling class is to preserve the existing capitalist order. In so doing, the ruling class can protect its existential and material
base. This is accomplished ultimately by means of the legal system. Any
threats to the established order can be dealt with by invoking the final weapon of the ruling class, its legal system. Threats to American economic security abroad are dealt with militarily; an arsenal of weapons manned by armed
forces is ready to attack any foe that attempts (as in a revolution) to upset
the foreign markets of American capitalism.[7] American imperialism fosters and
perpetuates the colonial status of foreign countries, securing American hegemony throughout as much of the world as possible. This has been the history
of American foreign relations, dominated by the corporate interests of the
ruling class.[8]

Similarly, the criminal law is used at home by the ruling class to maintain domestic order. Ruling class interests are secured by preventing any challenge to the moral and economic structure of the ruling class. In other words,
the military abroad and law enforcement at home are two sides of the same
phenomenon: the preservation of the interests of the ruling class. The weapons
of crime control, as well as the idea and practice of law itself, are dominated
by the ruling class. A stable order is in the interest of the ruling class.

From this critical perspective, then, crime is worthy of the greatest consideration. To understand crime radically is to understand the makings and workings of the American empire.

CRIME CONTROL IN THE CAPITALIST STATE

That the legal system does not serve society as a whole, but serves the interests of the ruling class is the beginning of a critical understanding of criminal law in capitalist society. The ruling class through its use of the legal system is able to preserve a domestic order that allows the dominant economic interests to be maintained and promoted. The ruling class, however, is not in direct control of the legal system, but must operate through the mechanisms of the state. Thus it is to the state that we must turn in further understanding of the nature and operation of the legal order. For the role of the state in capitalist society is to defend the interests of the ruling class. Crime control becomes a major device of the state in its promotion of a capitalist society.

Criminologists and legal scholars generally neglect the state as a focus of inquiry. In failing to distinguish between civil society and the political organization of that society, they ignore the major fact that civil society is secured politically by the state and that a dominant economic class is able by means of the state to advance its own interests. Or when the state is admitted into a criminological or legal analysis, it is usually conceived as an impartial agency devoted to balancing and reconciling the diverse interests of competing groups in the society. This view, I am arguing, not only obscures the underlying reality of advanced capitalist society, but is basically wrong in reference to the legal order. In a critical analysis of the legal order we realize that the capitalist state is a coercive instrument that serves a particular class, the dominant economic class.

Several basic observations must be made in a critical analysis of crime control in the capitalist state. First, there is the question of the nature of the state, that is, the complexity of that which we call the state. Second, is the problem of how the dominant economic class relates to the state, that is, how that class becomes a ruling class and how the state governs in relation to the ruling class. Third, we must observe the development of the state in reference to capitalist economy.

"The state," as Miliband notes, is not a thing that exists as such. "What 'the state' stands for is a number of particular institutions which, together, constitute its reality, and which interact as parts of what may be called the state system."[9] Miliband goes on to observe that the state, or state system, is made up of various elements: (1) the government, (2) the administration, (3) the military and the police, (4) the judiciary, and (5) the units of subcentral government.[10] The administration of the state is composed of a large variety of bureaucratic bodies and departments concerned with the management of the economic, cultural, and other activities in which the state is involved. The directly coercive forces of the state, at home and abroad, are handled by the police and the military. They form that branch of the state which is concerned with the "management of violence." The judiciary is an integral part of the state, supposedly independent of the government, which affects the exercise of the state power. Finally, the various units of subcentral government constitute the extension of the central government. They are the administrative devices for centralized power, although some units may exercise power on their own over the lives of the populations they govern.

It is in these institutions that state power lies, and it is in these institutions that power is wielded by the persons who occupy the leading positions within each institution. Most important, these are the people who constitute the *state elite,* as distinct from those who wield power outside of state institutions.[11] Some holders of state power, members of the state elite, may also be the agents of private economic power. But when members of private economic power are not members of the state elite, how are they able to rule the state? Somehow the interests of the dominant economic class must be translated into the governing process, in order for that class to be a true ruling class.

Miliband has observed the essential relation between the dominant economic class and the process of governing.

What the evidence conclusively suggests is that in terms of social origin, education, and class situation, the men who have manned *all* command positions in the state system have largely, and in many cases overwhelmingly, been drawn from the world of business and property, or from the professional middle classes. Here as in every other field, men and women born into the subordinate classes, which form of course the vast majority of the population, have fared very poorly—and not only, it must be stressed, in those parts of the state system, such as administration, the military, and the judiciary, which depend on appointment, but also in those parts of it which are exposed or which appear to be exposed to the vagaries of universal suffrage and the fortunes of competitive politics. In an epoch when so much is made of democracy, equality, social mobility, classlessness, and the rest, it has remained a basic fact of life in advanced capitalist countries that the vast majority of men and women in these countries have been governed, represented, administered, judged, and commanded in war by people drawn from other, economically and socially superior and relatively distant classes.[12]

The dominant economic class is thus the ruling class in capitalist societies.

Viewed historically, the capitalist state is the natural product of a society divided by economic classes. Only with the emergence of a division of labor based on the exploitation of one class by another, and with the breakup of communal society, was there a need for the state. The new ruling class created the state as a means for coercing the rest of the population into economic and political submission. That the American state was termed "democratic" does not lessen its actual purpose.

Hence, the state, as Engles observed in his study of its origins, has not existed in all societies. There have been societies which have had no notion of state power. Only with a particular kind of economic development with economic divisions did the state become necessary. The new stage of development, Engles observes, called for the creation of the state.

Only one thing was wanting: an institution which not only secured the newly acquired riches of individuals against the communistic traditions of the gentile order, which not only sanctified the private property formerly so little valued, and declared this sanctification to be the highest purpose of all human society;

but an institution which set the seal of general social recognition on each new method of acquiring property and thus amassing wealth at continually increasing speed; an institution which perpetuated, not only this growing cleavage of society into classes, but also the right of the possessing class to exploit the nonpossessing, and the rule of the former over the latter.

And this institution came. The *state* was invented.[13]

And the state, rather than appearing as a third party in the conflict between classes, arose to protect and promote the interests of the dominant economic class, the class that owns and controls the means of production. The state continues as a device for holding down the exploited class, the class that labors, for the benefit of the dominant class. Modern civilization, as epitomized by capitalist societies, is thus founded on the exploitation of one class by another. The state secures this arrangement, since the state is in the hands of the dominant economic, ruling class.

And law became the ultimate means by which the state secures the interests of the ruling class. Laws institutionalize and legitimize the existing property relations. A legal system, a public force, is established: "This public force exists in every state; it consists not merely of armed men, but also of material appendages, prisons and coercive institutions of all kinds, of which gentile society knew nothing. It may be very insignificant, practically negligible, in societies with still undeveloped class antagonisms and living in remote areas, as at times and in places in the United States of America. But it becomes stronger in proportion as the class antagonisms within the state become sharper and as adjoining states grow larger and more populous."[14]

It is through the legal system, then, that the state explicitly and forcefully protects the interests of the capitalist ruling class. Crime control becomes the coercive means of checking threats to the existing economic arrangements. The state defines its welfare in terms of the general well-being of the capitalist economy. Crime control in the capitalist state is the concrete means for protecting the interests of the capitalist economy.

DEMYSTIFICATION OF CRIMINAL LAW

The purpose of a critical understanding of crime control is to expose the meaning of criminal law in capitalist society. The false reality by which we live, the one that serves the established system, must be understood. To demystify law in America is the goal of a critical theory of criminal law.

The above critical discussion of criminal law can be summarized in the following assertions:

1. *American society is based on an advanced capitalist economy.*
2. *The state is organized to serve the interests of the dominant economic class, the capitalist ruling class.*
3. *Criminal law is an instrument of the state and ruling class to maintain and perpetuate the existing social and economic order.*
4. *Crime control in capitalist society is accomplished through a variety of institutions and agencies established and administered by a governmental elite, representing ruling class interests, for the purpose of establishing domestic order.*

5. *The contradictions of advanced capitalism—the disjunction between existence and essence—require that the subordinate classes remain oppressed by whatever means necessary, especially through the coercion and violence of the legal system.*
6. *Only with the collapse of capitalist society and the creation of a new society, based on socialist principles, will there be a solution to the crime problem.*

Thus criminal law in America can be critically understood in terms of the preservation of the existing social and economic order. Criminal law is used by the state and the ruling class to secure the survival of the capitalist system. And as capitalist society is further threatened by its own contradictions, criminal law is increasingly used in the attempt to maintain domestic order. The underclass, the class that must remain oppressed for the triumph of the dominant economic class, will continue to be the object of criminal law as long as the dominant class seeks to perpetuate itself. To remove the oppression, to eliminate the need for further revolt, would necessarily mean the end of the ruling class and its capitalist economy.

Criminal law continues to secure the colonial status of the oppressed in the social and economic order of the United States. The events of the last few years relating to crime, including both "disruption" and repression, can be understood only in terms of the crisis of the American system. Moreover, the oppression within the United States cannot be separated from American imperialism abroad. The crisis of the American empire is complete. The war waged against people abroad is part of the same war waged against the oppressed at home. The ruling class, through its control of the state, must resort to a worldwide counterrevolution. A counterinsurgency program is carried out —through the CIA abroad and the FBI, LEAA, and local police at home. A military war is being fought in Asia, while a war on crime with its own weaponry is being fought within the United States. All of this to avoid changing the capitalist order, indeed to protect it and to promote its continuation.

The consequences are revolutionary. Crime and the criminal law can be understood only within the context of this crisis.

By posing on the national level the central issues of the international conflict, by linking the international struggle for self-determination with the internal quest for social equality and social control, the crisis of democracy increasingly presents itself as the revolutionary crisis of the epoch. The movement for the sovereignty of the people within the imperial nation coincides with the struggle for self-determination in the international sphere. Just as domestically the demand for domestic power is a demand to overthrow the corporate ruling class and to make the productive apparatus responsive to social needs, so internationally the precondition of democratic sovereignty and interstate coexistence is the dissolution of the government of the international corporations and financial institutions which have expropriated the sovereignty of nations in order to appropriate the wealth of the world.[15]

Never before has our understanding of legal order been so crucial. Never before has our understanding been so related to the way we must live our lives. To think critically and radically today is to be revolutionary. To do otherwise is to side with oppression. Our understanding of the legal order and our actions in relation to it must be to remove that oppression, to be a force in liberation.

CONCLUSION

The theoretical and research implications of a critical theory of law for the sociologist are far-reaching. The meaning of the above discussion is that everything we have done in criminology and the sociology of law has to be redone. A critical examination of law means uncovering all the orthodox assumptions we have held about law and crime control. Thus, both theoretically and empirically, we must reconsider everything that has preceded us. But more important, a whole new range of problems is now open to us. In the course of developing a critical imagination, we are thinking about things that never appeared to us under previous wisdom. To the question of where a critical theory of legal order will lead, we answer that it will take us to places no one has been before. In thought and in action, we are entering new realms of life, imagination, and human possibility.

NOTES

[1] *See* Richard C. Edwards, Michael Reich, and Thomas E. Weisskopf, *The Capitalist System: A Radical Analysis of American Society* (Englewood Cliffs, N.J.: Prentice-Hall, 1972); Tom Christoffel, David Finkelhor, and Dan Gilbarg, eds., *Up Against the American Myth* (New York: Holt, Rinehart and Winston, 1970).

[2] Ralph Miliband, *The State in Capitalist Society* (New York: Basic Books, 1969), p. 16.

[3] Ibid., p. 23.

[4] Gabriel Kolko, *Wealth and Power in America* (New York: Frederick A. Preager, 1962); G. William Domhoff, *Who Rules America?* (Englewood Cliffs, N.J.: Prentice-Hall, 1967); G. William Domhoff, *The Higher Circles: The Governing Class in America* (New York: Random House, 1970).

[5] Gabriel Kolko, *The Roots of American Foreign Policy* (Boston: Beacon Press, 1969), pp. 6-7.

[6] Isaac D. Balbus, "The Concept of Interest in Pluralist and Marxian Analysis," *Politics and Society* 1 (February 1971): 151-177.

[7] David Horowitz, *Empire and Revolution: A Radical Interpretation of Contemporary History* (New York: Random House, 1969).

[8] William Appleman William, *The Roots of the Modern American Empire* (New York: Random House, 1969).

[9] Miliband, *The State in Capitalist Society*, p. 49.

[10] Ibid., pp. 49-55.

[11] Ibid., p. 54.

[12] Ibid., pp. 66-67.

[13] Frederick Engles, *The Origin of the Family, Private Property, and the State* (New York: International Publishers, 1942), p. 97.

[14] Ibid., p. 156.

[15] Horowitz, *Empire and Revolution*, pp. 257-258.

THE "DOPE" ON THE BUREAU OF NARCOTICS IN MAINTAINING THE CRIMINAL APPROACH TO THE DRUG PROBLEM

CHARLES E. REASONS

The Narcotics Division of the Treasury Department was influential in having its definition of the drug problem institutionalized in the early 1900s; that is, "the criminal approach." Although the "medical approach" was partially vindicated in *Linder* vs. *United States* in 1925,[1] the Narcotics Division and other law enforcement officials did not consider it in their policy, and few reputable doctors cared to challenge existing enforcement practices since many doctors were being convicted and jailed for such practice. Because of propaganda, enforcement policies, and public opinion, lower federal courts would not follow the implications of *Linder*. By persecution through prosecution the medical profession largely acquiesced to the criminal approach, often being literally "handcuffed" in their efforts. Although there remained a group of vociferous critics of the treatment of the problem,[2] the American Medical Association and most of its members came around to the bureau's "way of thinking" and ceased to deal with addicts altogether. Therefore, although the medical approach would still be commented upon in both professional and lay circles, the criminal approach, propagated by the Narcotics Division, would reign through both propaganda and intimidation. The image of the addict and subsequently of addiction was shaped and would determine policy for quite some time. Reflecting upon this change in imagery, Samuel Adams, of late muckraking fame, points out (Adams, 1924):

Legislation dealing with narcotic drugs is one long tragedy of errors, and, for the addict, of terrors. Projected laws, as a rule mysterious, unscientific, and even sinister in origin, regard the addict as a self-indulgent pander to his own evil appetites instead of as a gravely sick man. On this erroneous theory they seek to take narcotic drug addiction, which is a definite and determinable disease, out of the hands of medical experts and give it over to police control.

This is, of course, precisely what happened.

The Narcotics Division, placed within the Bureau of Prohibition from 1920 to 1930, successfully had its definition of the "drug problem" institutionalized into national policy, in spite of opposition. The success of the

Charles E. Reasons, "The 'Dope' on the Bureau of Narcotics in Maintaining the Criminal Approach to the Drug Problem" Revised version of this paper presented to the Pacific Sociological Association (April 1972).

Narcotics Division's efforts is to be found in both increased arrests for federal narcotics violations[3] and increased budgetary appropriation.[4] Thus, as an ongoing bureaucracy attempting to maintain and extend its domain and power, the Narcotics Division was quite successful during this period.

A NEW BUREAU IS FORMED

In August 1930, a separate Bureau of Narcotics was formed, no longer associated with the Bureau of Prohibition. Although its creation was largely an outcome of scandals in the Bureau of Prohibition,[5] it also appears to be related to the colossal failure of the attempt to prohibit alcohol. The prohibition of alcohol was increasingly becoming recognized as both a moral and bureaucratic failure, but the elimination of narcotics would remain a national concern and partially fill the moral void created by the repeal of the Volstead Act. Harry J. Anslinger, Assistant Commissioner of the Bureau of Prohibition, was named the head of the new Bureau of Narcotics. Imbued with the "missionary zeal" of a Bishop Brent and the hard-sell pragmaticism of a Hamilton Wright,[6] Anslinger was to have an enormous impact upon national drug policy for the next 32 years, presiding as the bureau's head. In fact, it may be said that subsequent to 1930 the Federal Bureau of Narcotics would be a personification of the "Anslinger philosophy." An essential ingredient in this philosophy is that the addict is an "immoral, vicious, social leper," who cannot escape responsibility for his actions, who must feel the force of swift, impartial punishment (Meisler, 1960:159). Thus, the criminal approach was the cornerstone of the "Anslinger philosophy." In fact, Anslinger would play a major role in subsequent policies that would further enhance the criminal approach to the "drug problem."[7]

MARIHUANA: A NEW ENEMY

During the 1930s the bureau became aware of a new drug problem—marihuana. Initially, the bureau discounted it as a national threat requiring federal action, nothing that the "publicity tends to magnify the extent of the evil and lends color to an inference that there is an alarming spread of the improper use of the drug, whereas, the actual increase in such use may not have been inordinately large" (U.S. Bureau of Narcotics, 1932:51).[8] At that time the bureau suggested state legislation as a remedy. Coincidentally, the bureau was sending out special representatives to campaign for a uniform state narcotic law, which included control of marihuana (U.S. Bureau of Narcotics, 1933:69). In its report covering 1933, it notes (U.S. Bureau of Narcotics, 1934:36): "A disconcerting development in quite a number of states is found in the apparently increasing use of marihuana by the younger element in the larger cities." Nonetheless, state control was still felt to be adequate.

An increase in newspaper and magazine "revelations" concerning the negative effects of marihuana and its spreading to the youth of the nation aroused the public. According to Schaller (1970:62):

Middle-class white America of the 1930s had almost no contact with marihuana. Instead, it was subjected to a vicarious familiarity through the medium of hysteria-provoking stories that marihuana was a "killer drug" which inspired crimes of violence, acts of sexual excess, impotency, insanity, and moral degeneracy. Special attention was given to its supposed effects on school children, lured by insidious pushers to try the drug in the shadow of the school building.

Thus, marihuana's demonology was being shaped.[9]

The Federal Bureau of Narcotics was to be one of the primary sources in shaping and sustaining such demonology. In its report covering 1936, the bureau first begins its continuous presentation of the "violent addict" myth.[10] In a section entitled "Marihuana Crimes" (U.S. Bureau of Narcotics, 1937: 65-67), brutal murders and other violent attacks are lucidly presented which purportedly illustrate the homicidal tendencies and the general debasing effects arising from marihuana use.

Largely because of public concern, primarily induced by the Bureau of Narcotics, the Marihuana Tax Act was passed in 1937 placing a prohibitively high tax on marihuana and creating a whole new class of criminals. Undoubtedly the bureau shared major responsibility for its enactment. As Dickson notes (1968: 152): "It seems clear from examining periodicals, newspapers, and the Congressional Record that the bureau was primarily responsible for the passage of the act." Anslinger personally provided information for two articles that appeared in *Hygeia,* published by the American Medical Association. He describes the history of marihuana use as a record of "crime, bestiality, and insanity" and notes that its users are all "degenerates" (Schaller, 1970: 68).[11] Many articles appeared in professional and policy journals which can be traced back to the Federal Bureau of Narcotics.

The Marihuana Tax Act was approved by Congress on June 14, 1937, and signed by the president on August 2, 1937. A whole new group of outsiders had been created and would provide much activity for the Bureau of Narcotics agents.[12] Schaller (1970: 74) provides a cogent summary of the preceding events and their subsequent effect:

In law, the Federal Bureau of Narcotics had completely routed the forces of evil. It had shaped a law to its liking and had even triumphed over the scientific method which presumed to question the moral truths of the bureau. The atmosphere was so clouded that serious investigations into marihuana remained stifled for almost 20 years. The dedicated entrepreneurs within the bureau had sold their beliefs not only to Congress and the public, but to a large part of the scientific establishment as well.

Marihuana became the new peril in America. For, while addiction to opiates purportedly was subsiding in the 1930s, according to the bureau's reports, a new enemy arose. Anslinger notes (U.S. Bureau of Narcotics, 1939: 51):

In the fight against narcotics, each victory leads to a new field of battle. Our most recent enemy is marihuana, the use of which as a narcotic drug was virtually unknown in the United States a decade ago. It is a new peril—in some ways the worst we have met and it concerns us all. . . . I believe that informed public opinion is the most powerful weapon with which to fight this dangerous public enemy.

Indeed, through public appearances and publications, the Anslinger philosophy would continue to "inform" the public.

Postwar attention to the drug problem evidenced a tremendous increase in the early 1950s. Prior to this time, relatively little attention was given to this problem in the media; however, this changed greatly. In 1951 the Kefauver Committee on Crime turned its attention to narcotics and marihuana, causing a flurry of public apprehension. It was alleged through numerous publications[13] that drug addiction was on the increase and had captured school children and teenagers. Anslinger provided much of the information concerning the rise of this evil, being at the forefront of such concern. In his statement before the committee in 1950, he had noted that although there had been a historical decrease in addiction, a recent reversal in this trend was manifest, with rising addiction among "young hoodlums." He recommended stiffer penalties and increased personnel for the bureau (U.S. Bureau of Narcotics, 1951: 7-10). In this wave of public attention, dozens of "tough" measures were introduced in the Eighty-first Congress by lawmakers vying for public recognition as saviors in the face of this menace. Both the addict and the pusher were identified as "enemy deviants." In fact, in this era of McCarthyism the drug problem became associated with the major evil of the time—communism. Narcotics were characterized as a means of subversion and corruption and those associated with the illicit drugs were suspect.[14]

Two major pieces of "get tough" legislation were passed in the 1950s. The "Boggs Amendment" of 1951 attached mandatory minimum sentences to narcotic violations, with no probation or suspension for repeaters. The 1956 Narcotics Control Act extended this "get tough" approach with more severe and inflexible penalties (Lindesmith, 1965: 25-33). The Federal Bureau of Narcotics and other law enforcement agencies were instrumental in pushing such legislation through. In response to the "Boggs Amendment" the bureau stated (U.S. Bureau of Narctoics, 1952: 5): "While it is too early to appraise the effectiveness of this legislation, an improvement in narcotic conditions has been noted, and there were definite indications at the end of the year that the increase in teenage addiction has been halted."

Although the bureau cited the positive effects of such legislation (U.S. Bureau of Narcotics, 1955: 5-6; 1956: 7), additional punishment was forthcoming in the Narcotic Control Act of 1956. This further entrenched the tough approach, which subsequently was instituted in state statutes (Eldridge, 1967: 177-231).[15] During this period of heightened fears concerning the drug problem, addiction per se was made a crime.[16] The addict was characterized as a violent, degenerate, un-American social leper who was an enemy to society. Therefore, the addict as an "enemy deviant" and the criminal approach were reaffirmed through congressional and state action.[17]

BUREAU UNDER ATTACK

While the bureau continued to emphasize the positive effect of the tough approach,[18] increasing criticism of the bureau's policy and the law manifested itself during the late 1950s.[19] Increased critical discussion of the medical approach as an alternative to the criminal approach was apparent. Probably the most controversial material to come out at this time was the joint American Bar Association-American Medical Association Report on drug addiction. In 1955-1956 the ABA and AMA appointed a joint committee to explore the problem. In 1958 the joint committee presented an interim report, with a final report in 1959. Both the interim and final reports were published in 1961 by the Indiana University Press and entitled *Drug Addiction: Crime or Disease?*

The interim report illicited a swift and vehement response from the Bureau of Narcotics. The most frightening aspects to the bureau were the suggestion by the joint committee that outpatient experimental clinics be tried for the treatment of drug addicts and the conclusion that law enforcement was not the answer to the problem.[20] This was a direct threat to the bureau's policy and domain and could not be tolerated. Therefore, in response, Anslinger appointed an advisory committee composed of "distinguished experts" in the field of narcotics (e.g. Hale Boggs) to respond to the ABA-AMA report.[21] The report (Advisory Committee to the Federal Bureau of Narcotics, 1959) was largely a personal attack upon those who served on the ABA-AMA committee and the sources cited. It consisted of an eclectic gathering of vehement, emotional responses to this "un-American" approach. In fact, the publication was halted because of its irrational attack upon the Supreme Court (Lindesmith, 1965: 248).

Such was the response of Anslinger, whose views and philosophy had dominated the drug problem for nearly 30 years. Through both moral outrage and bureaucratic needs he responded to this threat to the vitality of his domain. Although few copies of the ABA-AMA report were initially available, the Advisory Committee report was printed in bulk and widely distributed. When the Indiana University Press was to publish the report in 1961, a Federal Bureau of Narcotics agent was sent to the campus to "investigate" its publication (Lindesmith, 1965: 246-248). Thus, the bureau was continuing its efforts to intimidate those whose views were contrary to its own. Nonetheless, mounting criticism was being made of the criminal approach.

In August 1962, Anslinger retired from the bureau and Henry L. Giordano was appointed the new head. He was a less vehement and vociferous critic of opposing perspectives, but the criminal approach was still "the" approach.[22]

A NEW CHALLENGE: KIDS AND DOPE

It appears that public attention to the drug problem greatly increased in the second half of the 1960s. Much of this concern has been with the increased use of drugs, primarily nonopiates, among the youth of the nation. This concern is particularly acute regarding marihuana, as evidenced in the 1966 Annual Report of the Bureau of Narcotics (1967: 2):

The dangerous rise in illicit marihuana traffic and the increased use of marihuana and narcotic drugs by college age persons of middle and upper economic status became more evident at the close of 1966. These facts present a new challenge which must and will be met for the welfare of the country.

This threat was to pose an increasingly more difficult problem for the bureau, for besides being "enemy deviants," many users were "nonconformists" who openly attacked the laws as unjust and corrupt, and even proselytized the use of such drugs.

In response to those asserting that marihuana is no more harmful than alcohol and tobacco, the bureau began to plan a program of counterattack in 1966 (U.S. Bureau of Narcotics, 1967: 25) "to refute this misinformation and to convince or reaffirm the knowledge that marihuana is, indeed, a harmful and dangerous drug." A "Marihuana Task Force" of four agents specially trained in the abuse and dangers of marihuana was assigned to areas where more vocal promarihuana groups and individuals were located. Through speeches, conventions, seminars, symposiums, conferences, and resolutions they began to get the message across to the American public. The bureau had a new and more insidious "enemy" to combat, the open and unabashedly flagrant proselytizer of drugs.

THE ENLIGHTENMENT?

In 1968 there was a reorganization of the agencies responsible for control of narcotics and other dangerous drugs. Under the reorganization plan the drug enforcement agencies of the Department of Health, Education, and Welfare and the Treasury Department (except those involved with customs) were merged and transferred to the Department of Justice as the Bureau of Narcotics and Dangerous Drugs. This move was designed to consolidate agencies for more efficient and effective law enforcement. Indeed, it seems befitting that the drug problem should be invested to the Department of Justice, given the criminal approach that has been emphasized. The annual report— Traffic in Opium and Other Dangerous Drugs—no longer was printed, with a new Bureau of Narcotics and Dangerous Drugs Bulletin appearing. A new director, John E. Ingersoll, took over the bureau and instituted a more enlightened, academic approach to the drug problem. Social scientists have been increasingly relied upon to present evidence and conduct studies concerning drugs, and the perpetration of the classical "dope fiend" mythology is not apparent in the bulletin. Thus, a new "era of enlightenment" seems to have been instituted within the department—however, the criminal approach remains the paramount method of handling the drug problem in the United States. This became apparent in the most recent federal legislation concerning drugs.

On October 27, 1970, President Nixon signed into law the Comprehensive Drug Abuse Prevention and Control Act, which can be said to be the most major drug legislation since the Harrison Act. The bill removes the tax base of control and eliminates the Harrison Act, Opium Smoking Act, Marihuana Tax Act, Narcotics Control Act, and others as the basis for dealing with drugs. Although penalties are generally reduced, reflecting a more enlightened perspective, it still maintains essentially a criminal approach to the problem. Senator Harold Hughes proposed a bill that would create a new federal agency to coordinate prevention of drug abuse, treatment, and rehabilitation. Although the bill had the support of doctors and health experts outside of the government, it was attacked by administration supporters. Ingersoll said "the Justice Department strongly opposed the bill, with particular reference to a generalized finding that drug dependence is 'an illness or a disease' rather than a crime. This broad finding goes far beyond existing court decisions and might be a serious impediment to criminal prosecution" (from Packer, 1970).

Hughes's bill was not adopted, and the medical and scientific interests attacked certain provisions of the administration's bill, particularly those putting control of drug classification, of research funds, and of research in the drug abuse area and medical practice under the purview of the attorney general. This concern was evident when the Committee for Effective Drug Abuse Legislation testified before the House Ways and Means Committee.[23] Dr. Roger Meyer, lecturer at Boston University School of Medicine and former chief of the Center for Studies of Narcotic and Drug Abuse at the National Institute of Mental Health, states such opposition

was not from some fringe group of hippies' allies advocating the overthrow of traditional American values and the "turning on" of our young people. This was the health establishment, with views ranging from liberal to conservative, urging that mistakes of the past be avoided and that Congress legislate a public health approach to the drug problem consistent with several presidential commissions and consistent with the intent of Congress in involving the medical community in the drug abuse and alcoholism areas (U.S. Congress, 1970, p. 398).

Nonetheless, the criminal approach was maintained through the passage of the bill.

Of particular significance throughout the hearings was the great emphasis upon youth and drugs. This was particularly a major point made by administration supporters. John N. Mitchell, attorney general, relies heavily upon this threat to our youth:

In a few weeks the young people of the nation will be returning to school—an event which American parents once looked upon with a smile and a sigh of relief. Today, it is a sad fact that parents view the opening of school with trepidation and concern since the drug traffic in narcotics and pills has penetrated the schoolrooms and schoolyards of America at virtually every level. It is no exaggeration to say that the drug danger threatens the moral and physical health of an entire generation (U.S. Congress, p. 398).

This emphasis on youth and drugs brings out an important symbolic function of the act. The significant moral forces behind such action, particularly in the scheduling of drugs, evidences more than medical and scientific criteria.[24] As is cogently pointed out by Mr. Ingersoll in discussing the attorney general's power to designate drugs for control,[25] "An affirmative decision to control involves more than medical and scientific determinations. It has important policy, legal, and enforcement implications as well." Such phenomena as permissiveness, immorality, irreverence, and self-indulgence were assailed in the congressional hearings as both cause and effect of drug use among youth. Particularly with reference to marihuana, this bill represents the victory of traditional WASP values over the "hippie youth culture." In fact, marihuana has become a symbol of the youth culture and identified with the hang-loose ethic (Roszak, 1968).[26] Discussion of marihuana often evokes visions of illicit sex, long hair, poor personal hygiene, and radicalism in politics to those of the dominant moral order. As Erich Goode notes (1969: 182):

The problem is one of hegemony, of legitimating one distinctive view of the world, and discrediting competing views. The basic problem is subjective evaluations of "objective" consequences. At its basis is a conflict of values and lifestyle.

In conclusion, it appears that the criminal approach will remain the dominant method of handling the drug problem[27]—the Bureau of Narcotics and law enforcement personnel will be kept busy attempting to contain and reduce it in the next decade. For, although emphasis upon treatment and rehabilitation appears more evident today than previously[28] (Sanders, 1970), the drug problem is largely shaped by law enforcement personnel and societal conceptions of the user.[29] Increasing public attention to, and action against, the drug problem in the early 1970s suggests that it will remain a major area of concern for public officials.

NOTES

[1]In a unanimous opinion the Supreme Court rejected the government case for conviction of Dr. Linder for prescribing a small dosage to a patient who was a government informer. It warned the Narcotics Division that "Federal power is delegated, and its prescribed limits must not be transcended even though the ends seem desirable. The unfortunate condition of the recipient certainly created no reasonable probability that she would sell or otherwise dispose of the few tablets entrusted to her and cannot say that by so dispensing them the doctor necessarily transcended the limits of that professional conduct with which Congress never intended to interfere" (Dickson, 1968: 151).

[2]A renowned physician and firm believer in a "medical approach" toward the addict, Dr. E. H. Williams consistently attacked the "criminalization" of the addict. A prominent author, *Who's Who* celebrity, and former associate editor of the Encyclopedia Britannica, he was convicted of narcotics law violations in 1939 for administering to addicts in a Los Angeles narcotics clinic. He had been asked by the Los Angeles Medical Association to treat addicts. The "stool pigeon" who testified in court against him admitted that he was under the influence of drugs supplied to him by the government agents (Lindesmith, 1965: 14-15)! His brother, Dr. Henry Smith Williams, was also a vigorous attacker of the Bureau of Narcotics policy. In his book, *Drug Addicts are Human Beings: The Story of Our Billion Dollar Drug Racket,* 1939, Dr. Williams presents an incisive attack upon those he feels are responsible for this horrendous drug policy. In his preface he states (xxiv): "The active coadjutors of the dope rings, as we shall see, include authorities of the Bureau of Narcotics (upheld by the secretary of treasury); U.S. district attorneys (upheld by the attorney general); and federal district judges (upheld by circuit judges). . . . The essential thing is that the billion dollar racket, and all of its ramifications, is the direct outgrowth of illegal activities of government officials whose supposed function is to sustain the law." In his chapter entitled "The American Inquisition," he describes a number of cases of persecuted doctors, noting that from 1918 to 1938 about 25,000 registered physicians were arraigned for criminal violation of federal laws. The complicity of the Supreme Court is noted because it has not heard the appeal of a convicted physician since 1926, and Dr. Williams concludes that "justice is flouted by fanaticism in the political bureau known as the Department of Justice." The author cannot readily confirm the number of arrests cited by Dr. Williams, but a cursory examination of the Annual Report will find physicians and pharmacists as major targets of arrest, with conviction rates running 90+ percent!

[3]In 1918 there were 888 arrests for federal narcotics violations; in 1925 there were 10,297 (Duster, 1970: 19).

[4]Appropriations soared from $292,000 in 1915 to $1,329,440 in 1925 (Dickson, 1968: 154).

[5]The padding of arrest records by narcotics agents and their collusion with illegal sellers was revealed by a federal grand jury early in 1930, and the Bureau of Prohibition underwent immediate reorganization (Meisler, 1960: 160).

[6]Both Brent and Wright were major figures in the early international and United States movement against narcotics. *See* both Lowes (1966) and Taylor (1969).

[7]Some have offered a "moral entrepreneur" interpretation of Anslinger's role in shaping the drug problem (Becker, 1963); others view Anslinger's actions largely in terms of bureaucratic contingencies (Dickson, 1968). The author is inclined to view the shaping of narcotics policy as largely a combination of these two approaches. For, although Anslinger was a "moral entrepreneur" of strong conviction, he conducted his campaign under the auspices of a large federal bureaucracy. The "public entrepreneur" operating from a governmental position has many benefits over the "private entrepreneur" (Dickson, 1968).

[8]The report also mentions that use is primarily among the Mexicans in the southwest. The racist implication is that we should not worry too much unless it spreads to whites.

[9]For an excellent discussion of drugs and demonology *see* Blum (1969).

[10]*See* Lindesmith (1940) for a presentation of such myths. For an empirical assessment of myths regarding "dope fiends" *see* Reasons (1972).

[11]*See* Mandal (1966) for a discussion of historical misinterpretations.

[12]The bureau reaped the benefits of its efforts when in 1938 one-quarter of all federal drug and narcotics convictions were for marihuana. Furthermore, a decline in budgetary appropriations was halted by this action (Dickson, 1968: 154-155).

[13]Some examples of the popular coverage are "New York Wakes up to Find 15,000 Teenage Dope Addicts," *Newsweek* 37, January 29, 1951, pp. 23-24; "Children in Peril," *Life* 30, June 11, 1951, pp. 116-121; "Facts about Our Teenage Drug Addicts," by Harry J. Anslinger, *Reader's Digest* 59, October 1951, pp. 137-140; "Save Them in Advance: Teenage Drug Addiction," *Colliers* 128, August 4, 1951, p. 744; "Heroin and Adolescents," *Newsweek* 38, August 13, 1951, pp. 504.

[14]*See* U.S. Congress, Senate (1955) for an account of the subversion in the drug traffic.

[15]Under the leadership of the Bureau of Narcotics most states enacted a Uniform Narcotic Law. It supplements federal law and controls small-time traffic. Because state court rules of evidence are less strict, many cooperative cases are processed through state courts (Maurer and Vogel, 1967).

[16]Anslinger personally sent a congratulatory letter to the chairman of the Board of Supervisors of the City of San Diego after it had passed an ordinance prohibiting addiction "per se." He notes that this is the first ordinance of its kind enacted in the United States, and that his office had tried for years to get such legislation passed (U.S. Bureau of Narcotics, 1955: 3-4).

[17]Further evidence of the criminalization of the "drug problem" is the rise in percentage of federal prisoners serving time for narcotics violations noted by the bureau. It increased from 10 percent in 1950 to over 16 percent in 1956 (U.S. Bureau of Narcotics, 1951: 10; 1957: 64).

[18]In the 1959 report the bureau notes (U.S. Bureau of Narcotics, 1960: 13): "Both federal and state severe mandatory penalties for unlawful sale of narcotic drugs and compulsory commitment of addicts are considered important factors in reducing the number of addicts coming to the attention of the bureau each succeeding year."

[19]For example, *see* R. H. Berg, "Dope Addict, Criminal or Patient?" *Look* 21, October 15, 1957, pp. 40-46; Alfred R. Lindesmith, "Dope: Congress Encourages the Traffic," *Nation* 184, March 16, 1957, pp. 228-231; Alfred R. Lindesmith, "Our Immoral Drug Laws," *Nation* 186, June 21, 1958, pp. 558-562; L. Koib, "Let's Stop This Narcotics Hysteria!" *Saturday Evening Post* 229, July 28, 1956, pp. 19 ff; "Should We Legalize Narcotics?" *Coronet* 38, June 1955, pp. 30-35; Alfred R. Lindesmith, "Traffic in Dope, Medical Problem," *Nation* 182, April 21, 1956, pp. 337-339.

[20]The Report notes (Joint Committee of the ABA and AMA on Narcotic Drugs, *961: 162): "While zealous law-enforcement efforts have unquestionably played a part in educing drug addiction—and will indisputably continue to be required in curbing the illicit traffic—experience has not demonstrated that the laws and enforcement policies urged y the United States Narcotics Bureau provide the full answer to the problem."

[21]Anslinger's response to the report was (Advisory Committee to the Federal ureau of Narcotics, 1959): "As for my comment, after reading this report I find it incredible that so many glaring inaccuracies, manifest inconsistencies, apparent ambiguities, important omissions, and even false statements could be found in a report on the narcotic roblem. My suggestion is that the person (unquestionably prejudiced) who prepared this eport should sit down with our people and make necessary corrections." When asked for more specifics the committee was formed.

[22]Giordano states in the 1962 report (U.S. Bureau of Narcotics, 1963: 19) that the Federal Bureau of Narcotics subscribes completely to the view that the federal law oes not consider drug addiction a crime." The same issue notes that 17.7 percent of federal prisoners are there for narcotic law violations (49).

[23]The following, unless otherwise cited, is from U.S. Congress, House (1970).

[24]The scheduling is based primarily upon potential for abuse, medical benefits, and harmful effects. In the "most dangerous" class I, marihuana is to be found. Regarding the olitics of amphetamines, *see* Graham (1972).

[25]The fact that the attorney general has the sole power to classify new drugs as problematic, and change classifications, would suggest that other than medical and scientific considerations are paramount. This power suggests that the "criminal approach" will be with us for some time.

[26]Explicit racism has not manifested itself during the recent concern with the "drug problem." However, implicit in the continual reference to the fact that the narcotic problem used to be a ghetto problem is the idea that such goings on properly belong with "them" but not in the suburbs with the "white kids."

[27]In Ingersoll's message in the bulletin after the passage of the bill he states (Ingersoll, 1971): "As always there is a minority, but vocal, group of dissenters who continue to allege that law enforcement cannot be a vital force in coping with the complex problems our society faces today, including drug abuse. But the podium from which they speak is far removed from the scene. They cannot see the changing, revitalized policeman that is evolving and who regards high education, advanced training, and crime prevention as necessary tools to get the job done. They cannot see the job to be done through their self-induced smog of distortion. The pity is that many others are deceived by these short-sighted views."

[28]For an interesting discussion of the social control functions of a "treatment approach" *see* Hyman (1972). Regarding the larger issue of rehabilitation and totalitarianism *ee* Szasz (1968).

[29]An interesting fact relating to "culture conflict" concerning the youth population is that whereas between 1960 and 1969 total arrests for those under 18 years old increased 105.4 percent, during the same period narcotic drug violations increased 2,453.2 percent (males increased 2,281.1 percent and females 3,468.0 percent). In 1965, 35 percent of the arrests for narcotic law violations were for heroin or cocaine, while in 1969 it dropped to 29 percent. However, in the same period drug law arrests for marihuana rose from 30 percent to 41 percent (Bureau of Narcotics and Dangerous Drugs, 1970: 12).

REFERENCES

Adams, Samuel H.
    1906 *The Great American Fraud.* New York: Collier's Weekly.
    1924 "How to stop the dope peddler." *Collier's* 73 (March 8): 13.

Advisory Committee to the Federal Bureau of Narcotics
    1959 *Comments on Narcotic Drugs: Interim Report of the Joint Committee of the American Bar Association and the American Medical Association.* Washington, D.C.: Government Printing Office.

Becker, Howard S.
    1963 *Outsiders: Studies in the Sociology of Deviance.* New York: The Free Press.

Blum, Richard
    1969 *Society and Drugs.* San Francisco: Jossey-Bass.

Dickson, D.
    1968 "Bureaucracy and Morality: An Organizational Perspective on a Moral Crusade." *Social Problems* 16 (Fall): 143-156.

Duster, Troy
    1970 *The Legislation of Morality.* New York: The Free Press.

Eldridge, William B.
    1967 *Narcotics and the Law.* Chicago: American Bar Foundation.

Goode, E.
    1969 "Marijuana and the Politics of Reality." *Journal of Health and Social Behavior* 10 (June): 83-94.

Graham, James M.
    1972 "Amphetamine Politics on Capitol Hill." *Trans-Action* 9 (January): 14ff.

Hyman, Florence
    1972 "Methodone Maintenance as Law and Order." *Trans-Action* 9 (June): 15-25.

Joint Committee of the American Bar Association and the American Medical Association on Narcotic Drugs
    1961 *Drug Addiction: Crime or Disease?* Bloomington: Indiana University Press.

Lindesmith, Alfred R.
    1940 "Dope Fiend Mythology," *Journal of Criminal Law, Criminology and Police Science* 31 (July-August): 199-208.
    1965 *The Addict and the Law.* Bloomington: Indiana University Press.

Lowes, Peter D.
    1966 *The Genesis of International Narcotics Control.* Geneva, Switzerland: Librairie Draz.

Mandal, J.
    1966 "Hashish, Assassins, and the Love of God." *Issues in Criminology* 2 (Fall): 149-156.

Maurer, David W., and Victor Vogel
    1967 *Narcotics and Narcotic Addiction.* Springfield, Illinois: Charles C. Thomas.

Meisler, S.
    1960 "Federal Narcotics Czar." *Nation* 190 (February 20): 159-162.

Packer, H.
    1970 "A Guide to Nixon's New Crime Control." *New York Review of Books* 15 (October 22): 26-37.

Reasons, Charles E.
    1972 "Dope, Fiends and Myths." A paper presented to the Annual American Sociological Convention, August, 1972, New Orleans, criminology section.

Roszak, T.
    1968 "Capsules of Salvation." *Nation* 206 (April 8): 466-471.

Sanders, M.
   1970   "Addicts and Zealots." *Harper's Magazine* 240 (June): 71-80.

Schaller, M.
   1970   "The Federal Prohibition of Marihuana." *Journal of Social History* 4 (Fall): 61-74.

Szasz, Thomas S.
   1968   "Toward the Therapeutic State." In *The Triple Revolution: Social Problems in Depth,* edited by R. Perrucci and M. Pilisuk, pp. 325-330. Boston: Little, Brown.

Taylor, Arnold H.
   1969   *American Diplomacy and the Narcotics Traffic, 1900-1939: A Study in International Humanitarian Reform.* Durham: Duke University.

U.S. Bureau of Narcotics
   1931-1968   *Traffic in Opium and Other Dangerous Drugs for the Years 1930-1967.* Washington, D.C.: Government Printing Office.

U.S. Bureau of Narcotics and Dangerous Drugs
   1970   *Bureau of Narcotics and Dangerous Drugs Bulletin* 2 (November-December): 12-13.

U.S. Congress, House of Representatives
   1909   Report No. 1878. "To Prohibit the Importation of Opium for other than Medicinal Purposes." Sixtieth Congress, Second Session.
   1970   "Controlled Dangerous Substances, Narcotics and Drug Control Laws." Hearings before the Committee on Ways and Means. Ninety-first Congress, Second Session.

U.S. Congress, Senate
   1955   "Communist China and Illicit Narcotics Traffic." Hearings before the Subcommittee to Investigate the Administration of the Internal Security Laws of the Committee on the Judiciary. Eighty-fourth Congress, First Session.

Williams, Henry Smith
   1938   *Drug Addicts are Human Beings: The Story of Our Billion Dollar Drug Racket.* Washington, D.C.: Shaw Publishing Company.

PART THREE:

POLITICAL CRIME: CRIMINAL POLITICS

It has been observed that political crime is the oldest and most recurring criminal phenomenon in history.[1] Nonetheless, criminologists have in large part failed to investigate this area of criminal activity; as noted in the introductory section to this book, students of crime have largely studied "normal crimes" and subsequently "normal criminals." Although much writing has been done concerning political crime by social critics, journalists, lawyers, political advocates, and others, a number of inhibiting factors may be noted among criminologists. The most obvious factor is that criminologists are generally part of the dominant political order and their focus may connote political problems rather than criminal ones. To suggest that political crimes should be recognized as an area of criminological focus portends the analysis of political trials and the influence of politics upon the legal order; to acknowledge that political trials exist is unsettling to those steeped in the belief that the law is above politics. As one student of political justice notes:

> To say that the thing exists and often entails consequences of importance is, in the eyes of such men of Law Immaculate, equivalent to questioning the integrity of the courts, the morals of the legal profession. These standard-bearers of innocence are apt to contend that where there is respect for law, only those who have committed offenses with punishment under existing statutes are prosecuted; that alleged offenders are tried under specific rules determining how to tell truth from falsehood in the charges preferred; and that intercession of political motivation or aspiration is ruled out by time-honored and generally recognized trial standards, which guide administration of justice among civilized or, to use a now more popular term, free nations.[2]

Such beliefs have been an important part of the mystique and mythology surrounding the law in our society. Based upon a consensus model of society and a bias-free system of law enforcement and administration of justice, the idea that we somehow are immune from political justice is a hallowed concept in our official ideology.

Although a great deal of information exists about political crime and criminals, it is often of a "soft" variety, not easily quantifiable by the empirical, positivistic criminologist. Much rhetoric and speculation surrounds the topic and these are hardly the stock of "scientists." Mills correctly characterized this problem when he suggested that the objection to sociohistorical inquiry based upon the lack of methodological rigor is a version of the "methodological inhibition, and often a feature of the 'know nothing' ideology of the politically quiescent."[3] Of course, this reflects the professional socialization, ideology, and subsequent "intellectual reflexes" of criminologists.[4] An important aspect of such study has been an emphasis largely upon ahistorical, apolitical, empirical analysis of criminals and the criminal justice system.

With the "demystification" of the law through recent events and writings, some criminologists have taken stock of their relationship vis-à-vis political crime. This assessment includes delineating specifically how political crime might be defined and analyzed. All crime is basically political, but political crime has been designated as a special type of criminal definition. According to Quinney, political crime refers to laws created to protect the political order of the state.[5] This strictly legalistic definition identifies such offenses against the state to include conduct threatening the existence of government—treason, insurrection, rebellion, sedition, criminal anarchy, criminal syndicalism—and conduct interfering with government functions—perjury, bribery, corruption, criminal libel by publication.[6] The greater proportion of writing and societal attention has been upon the first category of offenses, those "threatening the very existence of the state." In contemporary American society this "threat" has included Black Panthers, Students for a Democratic Society, antiwar demonstrators, communists, anarchists, and other "deviants."

The history of attempts to outlaw certain groups and ideas that are felt to threaten the viability of the state is the history of the use of the law to protect the state. All nations have such laws and use them at various times to prevent attempts to change the distribution of power in society. These laws are by their very nature repressive of free communication and have been the product of times of national crisis. American examples of such efforts include the Sedition Act of 1798, criminal anarchy laws and criminal syndicalism laws enacted in the early twentieth century, the Smith Act of 1940, the McCarren Act of 1950, and the "Rap Brown" portion of the 1968 Omnibus Bill.

These criminals are characterized as being quite different from conventional criminals in that they announce their intentions publicly, challenge the very legitimacy of laws or their application in specific situations, aim to change the norms they are denying, do not have personal gain as a goal, and appeal to a higher morality by pointing out the void between professed beliefs and actual practices.[7]

Given the above distinctions, the "political criminal"—draft resister, sit-in demonstrator or conspirator—may be difficult to explain according to traditional criminological theories. Social scientists, including criminologists, have already begun to study these "new deviants" and undoubtedly will attempt to explain their behavior according to modifications of traditional paradigms. Although this type of political crime and political criminal is the focus of most writing and popular concern in the area, I will leave such analysis to those funded by LEAA, NIMH, the U.S. Army, and so on. The study of this "new criminal" is obviously of concern to those in power because they are "enemy deviants" who represent a threat to those in political power.[8]

My concern is primarily with another type of political crime which is often overlooked in such analysis. This is "conduct derived from unlawful state power" and is characterized by the criminal behavior of the state through its representatives—police, judges, legislatures. The behavior of officials of the state (police brutality, denial of free speech, restriction of free assembly) which violates specific laws should be analyzed as political crime.[9] Thus, the innumerable blatant examples of official lawlessness in the South's efforts to maintain white supremacy are prime examples of such illegal behavior. This is consistent with the legalistic approach to criminology in the emphasis upon violation of laws by specific officials of the state to suppress political beliefs and actions.

However, when one suggests that specific laws are unjust and state enforcement of them is political crime, the legalistic approach is no longer applicable. Martin Luther King suggested that some laws are "just" and some are "unjust" based upon religious precepts and basic standards of humanity, but the criminologist is adverse to such distinctions because of their "nebulous" nature.[10] The criminologist holds to the view that the state is beyond incrimination and automatically aligns himself with the state. While describing the crimes perpetrated upon blacks in the south by government officials, Mouledous suggests:

> What is central is that the behaviors which we are encouraging or discouraging should not be determined by existing social norms nor by administrative judgment. Sociologists cannot abdicate the responsibility of judgment and accept the state's criteria of crime. A superior referent must be sought.[11]

Thus, the study of political crime may entail a change in our conception of man, including ourselves as criminologists.[12] Rather than merely analyzing those behaviors that are officially prohibited by state laws, we might look at behaviors that violate norms that transcend the political state, such as basic concepts of humanity and justice. Therefore, the criminologist, instead of just reflecting his society and its official definitions of illegal behavior, becomes an advocate of more humane laws and "more just justice." The studies in the sociology of law pointing out the difference between the "law in the books" and the "law in action" suggest areas of change. By systematically assessing the bias and inequities in the creation, enforcement, and administration of laws, criminologists also suggest the need for change given these "ideals." This "advocacy" is seemingly inherent in such studies.

Using a traditional legalistic definition of political crime, Ingraham and Tokoro have done an excellent analysis of the approaches of the United States and Japan to threats to their political viability.[13] The official recognition of political crime in domestic criminal law and the differential treatment of such criminals has been characteristic of Japan but not of the United States. Their approach relates to conceptions of the nature of the state and its claims to legitimacy. By ignoring differences in population ideologies and values, American criminal law attempts to maintain a consensus model of laws and an apolitical conception of their enforcement and administration.[14] By recognizing such a class of laws and criminals and treating them differently, the state acknowledges it does not represent all citizenry. Although we continually emphasize the right to dissent, this does not include violation of the law. The law is heralded as representative of all our values and is to be obeyed until that time that one can bring about its change through "legal" methods.

Dissent and law violation has a long tradition in our society, which is usually not acknowledged.[15] Much of the dissent today portends change and such conflict has many beneficial functions. The "creative extremists" of today may be the forerunners of the "normal society" of tomorrow.[16] Therefore, some view contemporary efforts to change society, including certain law violations, as positive.

The dissent we witness is a reaffirmation of faith in man; it is protest against living under rules and prejudices and attitudes that produce the extremes of wealth and poverty and that make us dedicated to the destruction of people through arms, bombs, and gases, and that prepare us to think alike and be submissive objects for the regime of the computer. . . . The dissent we witness is a protest against the belittling of man, against his debasement, against a society that makes "lawful" the exploitation of humans. This period of belief based on belief in man will indeed be our great renaissance.[17]

In the first article in this section, Clements discusses the nature of repression and suggests areas of investigation. The absence of serious scientific investigation of repression is due to a variety of factors, including the possibility that "to identify repression may be to invite it." Through various methods of control the state attempts to maintain dominance and continuance of its rule. The ability to control threats to those in power is aided to the extent that the deviant can be identified as a small fringe cadre of outsiders insidiously threatening the viability of the majority of citizenry. The villification of such individuals and groups is an important facet of the social reality of the problem as created by the dominant political order.

Kirchheimer notes that in times of political turmoil the resort to judicial action often ensues because of a number of factors, including the state's formal restriction of freedom for successful police and security operations. Control measures become manifestly coercive and victims seek formal adjudication; the regime decides on either total repression or wearing the opposition down by restricting their political availability through continuous proceedings against them or carefully choosing segments of the deviant political activity to scrutinize, in order to dramatize the struggle with foes and rally public support.[18] He also points out[19] that legal repression of political organizations occurs by minority fiat—South African, colonial rule—and by majority rule—American communist and New Left "purges." Repression by majority rule has a much greater aura of justification than by minority rule.

A major method of pursuing repression has been through conspiracy laws. "Throughout various periods of xenophobia, chauvinism, and collective paranoia in American history, conspiracy law has been one of the primary governmental tools employed to deter individuals from joining controversial political causes and groups."[20] The criminal element of conspiracy is not the illegal activity contemplated by the agreement, but the agreement itself. Therefore, a major element of crime is missing, the harm. Although Justice Fortas[21] observed that "the state may defend its existence and its functions, not against words or arguments or criticism, however vigorous or ill-advised, but against action," the repression of dissent through such laws has a long history in our society.

As the "red menace" fades from immediate judicial concern, attention is turned to "organizations or groups, whether of foreign or domestic origin . . . which invite or employ acts of force, violence, terrorism, or any unlawful means, to obstruct or oppose the lawful authority of the Government of the United States."[22] Such charges have not yielded a large number of convictions, but they have put many dissidents "on ice" and have provided a "chilling effect" upon dissent by threatening potential dissidents.

This brings us to the political trial.[23] Three categories of political trials are: (1) a trial involving a common crime[24] (e.g., murder, theft) committed for political purposes with the trial conducted with the view to political benefits accruing from successful prosecution, (2) the classic political trial, a regime's attempt to incriminate its foe's public behavior to evict him from the political scene, and (3) a derivative political trial, where the weapons of defamation, perjury, and contempt are manipulated in an effort to bring discredit upon a political foe.[25] As previously noted, many jurists don't wish to recognize political trials, much less political crimes. As Sternberg forcefully illuminates in the second article, criminal trials of radicals have more recently turned to radical criminal trials. Historically, political radicals have acted according to the rules of courtroom demeanor, but contemporary examples suggest a change in courtroom activities. The changing roles of the participants portend increasing politicization of such "apolitical" events and a repressive response by the state.

The use of enforcement agents in the repression of political threats is discussed in Karmen's article on "agents provocateurs." The time-honored use of undercover agents, discussed in relationship to recent sociopolitical conflict in the United States, appears to be a universal phenomenon of state officialdom who attempt to counter political threats to those in power. Karmen suggests many areas of further research concerning agent recruitment, role types, and infiltration practices as a sequential process. Although this type of investigation could be dangerous to criminologists and "other living things," it would greatly aid in our understanding of the political nature of crime and crime control.

NOTES

[1]*See* Stephen Schafer, "The Concept of the Political Criminal," *Journal of Criminal Law, Criminology and Police Science* 62 (September 1971):380-387, and Otto Kirchheimer, *Political Justice: The Use of the Legal Procedure for Political Ends* (Princeton: Princeton University Press, 1961).

[2]Kirchheimer, ibid., p. 47.

[3]C. Wright Mills, *The Sociological Imagination* (New York: Oxford University Press, 1959), p. 146. *Also see* C. Wright Mills, "The Professional Ideology of Social Pathologists," *American Journal of Sociology* 49 (September 1943):165-180.

[4]An example of such "professional reflexes" was the response of a noted criminologist upon being asked about the importance of politics for the study of crime. He suggested that criminologists should not concern themselves with such things as political philosophies and ideologies, but should concentrate upon studying crime. Such a response reflects the content of traditional criminological concerns and the artificial distinction regarding matters of focus.

[5]*See* Richard Quinney, "Crime in a Political Perspective," *American Behavioral Scientist* 8 (December 1964):19-22, and *The Social Reality of Crime* (Boston: Little, Brown 1970), pp. 56-60. *Also see* Irving Louis Horowitz and Martin Liebowitz, "Social Deviance and Political Marginality: Toward a Redefinition of the Relation Between Sociology and Politics," *Social Problems* 5 (Winter 1967):280-296.

[6]*See* Herbert L. Packer, "Offenses Against the State," *Annals* 339 (January 1962): 77-89.

[7]This classic distinction between "aberrant" and "nonconforming" behavior appears in Robert K. Merton and Robert Nisbet, *Contemporary Social Problems*, 3rd ed. (New York Harcourt, Brace, Jovanovich, 1971), pp. 829-832. Schafer, "Political Criminal," suggests that criminologists distinguish between the "true" political criminal (convictional) and those who are political criminals in appearance but not substance (pseudoconvictional). Although it would seem that such a distinction could be useful, he fails to give examples and/or criteria for making such distinctions. A problem here might be that apologists for the dominant order will label all such criminals as pseudoconvictional.

[8]For the distinction between repentant, dominated, and enemy deviant behavior *see* Joseph R. Gusfield, *Symbolic Crusade: Status Politics and the American Temperance Movement* (Urbana: University of Illinois Press, 1966), pp. 66-68.

[9]For a good anthology *see* Theodore L. Becker and Vernon G. Murray, *Government Lawlessness In America* (New York: Oxford University Press, 1971).

[10]Martin Luther King, Jr., "Letter from Birmingham Jail," in *The Triple Revolution: Social Problems in Depth*, ed. Robert Perrucci and Mark Pilisuk (Boston: Little, Brown, 1968), pp. 612-626.

[11]Joseph C. Mouledous, "Political Crime and Negro Revolution," in *Criminal Behavior Systems: A Typology*, ed. Marshall B. Clinard and Richard Quinney (New York: Holt, Rinehart and Winston, 1967), pp. 217-231, at 229. *See also* Herman and Julia Schwendinger "Defenders of Order or Guardians of Human Rights?" *Issues in Criminology* 5 (Summer 1970):123-157.

[12]Quinney (1970) has noted that we should view the criminal as more of a reasoning, autonomous, creative person rather than the victim of his environment and socialization—an oversocialized conception of man. Therefore, man is an actor, creator, changer, and not merely an "atom" being bounced around in the world by "forces beyond his influence."

[13]*See* B. L. Ingraham and K. Tokoro, "Political Crime in the United States and Japan: A Comparative Study," in *Issues in Criminology* 4 (Fall 1969):145-170.

[14]Our failure to officially recognize such crime has been noted by political criminals. *See* Virginia Engquist and Frances Coles, "Political Criminals in America: O'Hare (1923), Contine and Rainer (1950)," *Issues in Criminology* 5 (Summer 1970):209-220.

[15]For example, *see* Ted Gurr and Hugh Davis Graham, *Violence in America* (New York: Bantam Books, 1969).

[16]*See* Lewis A. Coser, *The Functions of Social Conflict* (New York: The Free Press, 1956).

[17]William O. Douglas, *Points of Rebellion* (New York: Random House, 1970), p. 33.

[18]Kirchheimer, *Political Justice.*

[19]Ibid., pp. 119-172. The revelations regarding executive suite crime, i.e., Watergate, notes that such repression has greatly escalated in recent years.

[20]William E. Brown, "Criminal Conspiracy and Political Dissent," *Tulane Law Review* 44 (1970):587-594. The author notes four major problems of conspiracy law: (1) remoteness from the social harm and proximity to the First Amendment undermine the very criminality of conspiracy, (2) its vagueness permits overboard application, (3) Sixth Amendment venue provisions may be improperly circumvented, and (4) the essential requirement of an agreement might be dispensed with because of relaxed proof standards for this agreement.

[21]Abe Fortas, *Concerning Dissent and Civil Disobedience* (New York: The New American Library, 1968), p. 48.

[22]Nathaniel L. Nathanson, "Freedom of Association and the Quest for Internal Security: Conspiracy from Dennis to Dr. Spock," *Northwestern University Law Review* 65 (May-June 1970):187.

[23]Kirchheimer, pp. 46-118.

[24]Examples would be the "Watergate affair" and the history of assassinations. *See* James F. Kirkham, *Assassination and Political Violence* (New York: Bantam Books, 1970).

[25]The history of conspiracy trials and special inquisitions, e.g., House Internal Security Committee proceedings, are examples of these latter types.

REPRESSION: BEYOND THE RHETORIC

JOYCE M. CLEMENTS

"Repression" is typically an emotionally charged word implying political persuasion and accusation. Definitionally, "to repress" means to restrain, subdue, suppress, or quell; connotatively, "to repress" involves a complex of facts and ideas encapsulating contests of interest and power. Because of the relativism this suggests, repression has found itself almost exclusively the concern of rhetorical debate. Rhetoric is not, of course, without substance, necessarily or even usually; and it is no accident that practitioners of rhetoric are concerned with various themes. Whatever expression of reality rhetoric makes, however, is potentially subject to discredit because of its provocative nature.

The present study proposes to go beyond the rhetoric that couches "repression" to see if it is or might be possible to analyze the structural components of repression. From the viewpoint of a behavioral scientist certainly it is desirable to agree on definitions and constructions so that some systematic description and analysis of repression may be anticipated. How is the word "repression" used and in what contexts? Who uses the word and why? What are the various perceptions of the activity that "repression" connotes? Is "repression" an active political resource, and when and where is it likely to be invoked? Are there certain structural arrangements that will "always" provoke repression?

The utility of trying to answer such questions as these is currently self-evident and compelling from many perspectives. As a matter of fact, the present "appeal" of such a study is so great one wonders that it has not attracted the interest of scholars. But it has not. "Repression" per se has not been a subject of scrutiny for social science, including criminology. From this, are we to gather that the meaning of the word is either obvious or trivial or both? It is far more likely that the dearth of scholarship in this area can be attributed to several social and historical factors.

The first of these is that repression has simply not been compatible with the most dominant model of society, and so has been somehow dismissed as aberrant. Coser (1969) observes that social science has not paid much attention to the types of phenomena associated with repression (violence and conflict, for instance) because of its persistence in viewing society as harmonious,

Joyce M. Clements, "Repression: Beyond the Rhetoric," published in *Issues in Criminology,* Volume 6, Number 1 (Winter 1971) pp. 1-31, by the graduate students of the School of Criminology at the University of California, Berkeley.

orderly, and adaptive. Dahrendorf is explicit about the roots of the "order" model:

> when Talcott Parsons in 1937 [Structure of Social Action] established a certain convergence in the sociological theories of Alfred Marshall, Emile Durkheim, Vilfredo Pareto, and Max Weber, he no longer had in mind an analysis of social conflict; his was an attempt to solve the problem of integration of so-called "social systems" by an organon of interrelated categories. The new question was now "What holds societies together?"—no longer "What drives them on?" The influence of the Parsonian posing of the question on the more recent sociology (and by no means only on American sociology) can be hardly overrated. (1958:170)

A second factor in the failure of social science to study "repression" is perhaps an extension of the former, but has enough distinction to be mentioned separately. The connotations of "power," "violence," "conflict," and "repression" are incongruous with the scholar's commitment to rationality and enlightenment. Gamson (1968:1) suggests the paradox inherent in the study of power when he observes "because power evokes potential without direction, we can be simultaneously excited by its possibilities for creation and alarmed by its possibilities for injury." Social scientists, he suggests, have reacted to the curiosity of power by trying conceptually to tame and harness its potential, thus attempting to curb its wildness and remove its threatening aspects. "Power as an instrument for the achievement of personal goals becomes muted, a theme secondary to the use of power to achieve collective goals" (Gamson, 1968:1). The more "unattractive" aspects of power, its nakedness and bruteness, because of their odium have been tenaciously relegated to the "outs" of research theory.

The prevalence of violent incidents marking virtually every turning place of our history, both domestic and international, has been ascribed to evil ideologies, unenlightened political systems, and power-hungry, violent men. The social sciences have clung to a blind tranquility that has not fostered understanding of the power of events to shatter or dismay (Nieburg, 1969:5).

Irving Louis Horowitz (1964) and other writers of *The New Sociology* would level a series of accusations that we shall consider together as a third explanation. Sociology has failed to involve itself in and with social problems for the following reasons:

1. Concern with macro- or microscopic theories has obscured the middle ground of social reality. The latter deals in "trivialities" and the former shuffles about in "cloudy obscurantism," and neither "contribute to the emergence of a coherent picture of some aspect of the world" (Rapoport:98).
2. Scientism, and bureaucracy have removed the scientist from involvement and commitment. Upholding the myth of scientific objectivity, the social scientist has deemed himself "value-free," and hence has been repelled by subjects that suggest or demand a fusion of reason and emotion. The "new sociologists" insist that values permeate all of social science,

and indeed, that "events or phenomena become meaningful facts at the moment when they enter the realm of values" (Blum:164).
3. Its "sponsors" neither want or allow sociology to concern itself with such things. Research foundations, the Federal Government and other grantors of research monies compel allegiance—responsibility to the client causes reaction, not origination (Winetrout:158), and evokes adaptation to and defense of the American Establishment (Rousseas and Farganis:280). The consequence of alignment with the "folklore of capitalism" (Casanova:69) is that social scientists devote themselves to a confirmation and celebration of social order with its temporary imbalances and rapid return to equilibrium (Horowitz:15).

Another and less pejorative reason why repression has not been the focal point of research is tied to a series of historical observations. During, and in an important sense provoking, the ascendency of sociology as a discipline, the United States was involved in combatting what were perceived as the forces of international evil. From the mid-'30s through the 1950s, the intellectual community was fairly consistent in its support of the United States government. Skolnick (1969) explains the congruence of historical experience that accounts for the "end-of-ideology" and lack of political analysis that characterized the period:

One should take into account the very considerable influence that the Second World War had on the legitimacy of the government . . . there was never much ambivalence on the part of the American People regarding the Second World War. . . . And to a degree that has never been fully appreciated, the critical faculties of the intellectual community were co-opted during [it], so that intellectuals gave themselves wholeheartedly to an "effort." And whenever intellectuals give themselves wholeheartedly to an effort, they leave a vacuum because there's nobody who's being critical of that effort. . . . In the Fifties, there was some skepticism about the role of the United States in Korea, but not too much, partly because the war had the OK of the United Nations, and partly because the Soviet Union at that time, under Stalin, was highly repressive and seemingly regressive. (p. 112)

[The U.S.S.R.] was the new force for evil, and they kept proving it in various ways. For example, the Hungarian Revolution was one illustration of the Soviet Union's capacity for a new form of imperialism. . . . Given the dismal state of the Soviet-dominated countries there was little criticism of America or American society during the Fifties. (pp. 112-113)

The McCarthy period was able to flourish in part because the liberal community was thoroughly disenchanted with the totalitarian tendencies in communism. (p. 111)

The period of U.S. history prior to the country's involvement in the Vietnam War, then, was characterized by relatively unquestioning support for the U.S. government and by finger-pointing at foreign governments.
At this particular time, however, it is baffling to observe the mounting tide of public criticism of governmental policy and the continuing lack of "critical faculty" on the part of sociology. From the mid-'60s, as political polemics have become increasingly more vocal and eventually inundated with arguments and accusations of governmental miscalculations, misconstructions,

mistellings, and mistreatments in both domestic and foreign affairs, the behavioral science community has not set for itself the task of extricating what may be fact from fantasy in the rhetoric of political exchange.

This task has been left to political scientists, historians, and journalists, whose professional roles are apparently more resilient in the face of hortatory meanings and interpretations. "Power," "revolution," "repression," "violence" —these are words somehow more appropriate and acceptable to the description of occurrences and events than to processes and structures. There is and has been great hesitancy to identify "untoward" actions as intimately bound to the behavioral complexes we want so to analyze, predict, and control.

Yet in their attention to occurrences and events, political scientists and historians have increasingly threatened the veracity and tenacity of the order-deviation fetish of the behavioral sciences. The limits of model credibility seem to have been constantly challenged by events, and the locus and focus of evaluation seem to have been shifted. "Vietnamization," My Lai, the invasion of Cambodia, and the Kent and Jackson State tragedies have raised threats to conventional definitions. Who are the "authorities"? Who are "the people"? What are the relations of power and interest that inhere in these roles? Who says who are criminals—can crime have a generic meaning or are the only criminals those who statistically populate the FBI Index and newspaper citations of arrests and convictions?

These are the kinds of questions writ large by recent history. Where are the answers, and who are the men and women to supply them? It seems that these people are figuratively and literally where "gadflies" always have been—on HEW blacklists and internal security files,[1] in academic quagmires,[2] in pragmatic subservience to "the man."[3] Ironically, though most of their societal models deny it, the social scientists' positions describe and confirm the structural relations of power: to identify repression may be to invite it.

This assessment is not attenuated by the formidable difficulties inherent in the subject matter. What Roszak (1969:xi) has said of the "counter-culture" might well be said of "repression": "As a subject of study, [it] possesses all the liabilities which a decent sense of intellectual caution would persuade one to avoid like the plague." Despite the likelihood of analytical "trouble," however, the portentous insistence of rhetoric demands that some attempt be made to identify repression.

SOME BASIC CONCEPTS

When someone says an act is repressive, we usually assume two things: he is speaking of an action by the government and he is speaking from a particular ideological standpoint. The relativity suggested by the latter assumption forces us to ask if there can ever be any generally acceptable "identifying" of repression. Perhaps what is repressive always depends on who, what, when, and where one is in a particular political and social situation.

Undoubtedly there is a great deal of truth to such an observation. What one person holds to be the quashing of an inalienable right, another may deem to be the proper control of behavior subject to state regulation. What is more, an act that is repressive at one time and place may be more or less so at another.

These qualifications do not obviate the fruitfulness of our inquiry, however. We shall not attempt to define repression categorically, but rather hope to locate its theoretical domain within the structure of democratic government. By looking to the values formalized within any particular polity, we shall be able to see the potential place for repression that a system itself carves.

Whatever values are formalized, the political organization that results will account for variances in evaluation like those suggested above. In doing so, its creation will attest to the reality of fundamental differences in interest and differentials in influence among the people to be governed. Whether the government to be formed will represent the decision to conciliate, amalgamate, resolve, or coerce holders of divergent interests, its existence symbolizes recognition of the conflict inherent in social relationship. Accounting for, and contending with, conflict will be one of the polity's major tasks. Essentially, accounting for conflict means that government will aim to create and sustain social unity. Contending with conflict means that the government must establish and maintain social order.

Originally, the people of each political entity define for themselves what order means. However, whatever the definition of order, it will include two elements: the serving of some interests and the controlling of others. Determining the types of interests (originally, the values) that will predominate and why they will predominate is problematic, and the proclivity for choosing and establishing priorities rests with the political philosophy accepted and structured. That these kinds of decisions will be made is not problematic, for all interests cannot conceivably be served at all times. Some "standards" must be assented to by the people whose interests are involved.

Ideally, once the people have assented to some values and established a political and economic system that they think will manifest the values deemed important, the order function has been thoretically defined. If the people support the value definitions that the government represents, then they will "cooperate."

This basis for this cooperation or voluntary control is to be found in an attitude characterized (Gamson, 1968:45) as trust:

Political trust . . . is a kind of "diffuse support" which "forms a reservoir of favorable attitudes or good will that helps members to accept or tolerate outputs to which they are opposed or the effect of which they see as damaging to their wants" (Easton, 1965:373).

Trust represents the sharing of four basic beliefs. For people to "agree"[4] to be governed they must submit to the possibility and advisibility and preferability of a political entity; they must acknowledge or submit to some mutual social and personal objectives; they must be willing to create and to see created a system of relations and institutions that will be designed to serve their mutual interest; and, they must believe that people exist who have the capacity to occupy the role relations specified or suggested by the system of relations created (*see* Gamson, 1968:51). A mandate to govern, then, carries with it these assumptions, and general accord by people is manifest in the *authority* to organize and operate around themselves.

Authority is a specific delegation of the right to establish order by making determinations, by judging, by commanding, by exacting obedience, and by enforcing. Authority issues pragmatically in formalized expectations that take the form of documents, rules, and laws, criteria of trust which are guarantees of both the limits and the freedoms for the governing as well as the governed.

Trust is not necessarily the "prerogative" of all persons who live within its authoritative bounds. The designation of "the people" differs in nearly every polity. "The people" are holders of the trust, are the givers of authority, are the subjects of their own rule. "The people" may include everyone who lives within the territorial boundaries of the state or may be comprised of only one such person. In other words, "the people" are those who determine the philosophical doctrine, the values, and structural arrangements for their system, its potential elite or leaders, and the subjects of its rule.

These "people" are the politically franchised. The population that is "left-over" constitute the remainder of the governed; but they have no political voice, and they are politically oppressed. Almost every political entity has within its rule those whose "rights" are specifically limited in some or all ways. From the creation of the system, these people are distinctly categorized as such. In the United States, for example, the original holders of trust determined that women, blacks, convicted felons, and children, among others, were not entitled to full rights as "the people." Politically, these groups of people were or are oppressed. We are well aware of the groups in Nazi Germany selected for political disfranchisement. In other times and places, oppressions have been defined according to birth in a particular class, economic status, and so on. Just as the numerical range of the people is theoretically limited only by the population of a polity, so too is the range of the oppression conceivably as expansive as the population, minus one.

Regardless of the numbers of people and oppressed, the state amasses and utilizes power to assure and enable its authority. Power is the capacity or ability to act or perform, to make decisions, and/or to exercise force or might. It is used to persuade, induce, or constrain (Gamson, 1968:116-117). Power is inherent in the structure of authority systems, but it is not the same as authority. Power itself does not have qualitative dimensions; it is characterized quantitatively, and its measurement is relative to other power resources in terms of *effectiveness* to control (*see* Gamson, 1968:26). The exercise of power may have qualitative dimensions. Its use may be legal, illegal, extralegal, and is deemed legitimate or illegitimate.

If an act is legal, it conforms to authority, to the written or implied laws and doctrines of the polity. In terms of the exercise of power, illegality is implied when the government uses its control resources to perform an action not specified by the mandate of the people, to "order" when or where it was not intended, or to refrain from doing so when or where it was intended. Obviously, not all government action falls within the legality-illegality jurisdiction. Action not qualified as legal or illegal is said to be discretionary, to be open to interpretation. Uses of control resources (or power) in such cases are extralegal and are relatively unaccountable. "Legality" is essentially the province of the state; it lies within its authority of judging and command to determine what is legal, and within its power to make the determination enforceable. Extralegal implies that authority can be extended by its holder rather than its giver.

What makes the use of power legitimate or illegitimate? Legitimacy "belongs" to the governed (*see also* Nieburg, 1970:53-56). If behavior is seen as legitimate, it conforms with the "oughts" or desires of the population. If it is seen as illegitimate, the government action violates expectations. Legitimacy and trust have the same origins in that they are both political attitudes and they both represent consent. However, legitimacy and trust are not necessarily coincidental. Trust is a formalization of attitude underlying the existence of a particular political entity. Trust represents a set of abstract values operationalized into structure. As such, trust does not "change" over time. Alterations of trust are not at all subtle: when trust agreements and criteria change, the political system changes, and the mandate of the people changes.

Legitimacy may change and its changes are usually quite subtle. Legitimacy can be likened to an historical state of mind; evaluations are made in relation to other social and political (and personal) events. Legitimacy is a sentiment, a transitory attitude about what is permissible and not, what is necessary and not, what is "good" and "bad." If trust and legitimacy were aligned, only legal acts could be described as legitimate. But holding trust constant, we can imagine legal acts that are illegitimate and illegal acts that are legitimate.

A person (or group of persons) evaluates the social order and government action as legitimate if he perceives that his interests are being served. On the other hand, if a person (or group) assesses the probability and reality of his interests being served and meets with disappointment, he is not pleased with the social order and *may* evaluate governmental action as illegitimate. Gamson (1968) categorizes three types of "solidary groups"[5] according to their evaluation of government interest-serving: confident (who perceive the authorities as their group's agent), neutral (who perceive the government, its leaders, and institutions as moderately effective in their functions), and alienated (who perceive that there is little or no likelihood of their interests being served).

Credence for the three types of legitimacy orientations is found in the play-out of conflict anticipated by social interaction. In other words, according to the concepts of unity and order discussed earlier, we would expect some sort of stratification of interest-meeting and "satisfaction." There will be persons or groups, then, whose interests (or some of them) more or less fail to correspond with the original values underlying the governmental base. At the same time, there are people who will believe in the values originally conceived as trust, but who would contend that the government improperly interprets these values in its structure and/or policy. People with either of these value positions can be expected to have neutral or alienated orientations toward the government.

A second kind of evaluation characteristic of neutral or alienated groups does not directly question the values of the system or its interpretation of them, but disputes the way power is distributed and institutionalizes or entrenches itself. In other words, the definition of "effectiveness" and the apparent tendency toward accumulation of "effective power" are questioned. Complaints about power-holding center on "too much government power" (control) and "too much partisan power" (influences). If the government is seen to control excessively, then it will probably be argued that the range of governmental activity is far too expansive or that its operation is too rigid. If some partisans are deemed to have concentrated influence, then it is probably believed that channels for having different interests represented are narrowed or blocked. The influence or power legally available to partisans flows from the following kinds of resources (Gamson, 1968:101-105): ability to hire, fire, and promote; possibility of allocation of money to civic projects; authority to make decisions on a variety of issues; ability to influence large numbers of "the people"; ability to enhance or damage reputations through control of some communication medium; possession of generalized reputation for wisdom on public affairs. Differentials in access to these forms of influence, the ability and opportunity to utilize them, and the subsequent possibility for success in having interests served account for varying legitimacy assessments.

We would expect a legitimacy orientation to change over time in accord with the evaluator's perception of and attachment to his own interests (and changing interests) and in relation to his understanding of social and political reality. Obviously, the range and intensity of dissatisfaction with government action is enormous. But it seems reasonable to suggest that most of the people will feel that governmental action is legitimate if various interests seem to be considered and served with some respect for the heritage of social order. Dissatisfaction and alienation result when unsatisfactory outcomes grow and become generalized (Gamson, 1968:51). In other words, when political value definitions or actions seem to exclude a person's or group's interest, discontent generalizes and one or more objects of legitimacy are questioned.

Needless to say, any government finds it maximally comfortable and efficient to operate when its legitimacy is not extensively questioned. It is optimal for the authorities, therefore, to be supported by a majority of the people, to be surrounded by confident and neutral solidary groups—a condition of social order which would, if attained, embody the ideal of social unity. The predictable harmony that would result from such a concord of ideals and action can be achieved by satisfying as many interests as possible and controlling the rest.

RESOURCES FOR AUTHORITATIVE CONTROL

The existence of a state, then, is a frank recognition of the need to deal with disparate interests and the need for the power to effect unity. The state is given resources to try to bring about the ideal concord manifested in support. As mentioned earlier, the use of these resources has the effect of constraining, persuading, or inducing (*see* Gamson, 1968, chap. 6, "The Management of Discontent": 111-143).

Constraining "undesirable" or "disorderly" behavior is the most blatant domestic use of state power. It is within this area of negative sanction that the systems of law enforcement and the administration of justice fall. By legislative command, certain behaviors are "lawful" and others are "outlawed": expectations of what can be done are generalized and expectations of what "must" be done are not specified. Breaches of these expectations result in the use of power to control offenders, to suppress or quell their illegal behavior.

By the nature of law as a constraint, it is clear that some types of persons will be favored and others will be disadvantaged. "Anatole France made the point succinctly when, in *Battle of the Angels,* he saluted 'the majestic equality of the law' which 'punishes rich and poor alike for sleeping under bridges or stealing loaves of bread'" (Nieburg, 1970:67). Theoretically, insofar as the rule of law is consistent with the trust mandate of the polity, this inevitable situation does not abort the intention of authority. (Of course it may be oppressive.)

As Skolnick (1967:7) points out, however, "when law is *used* as the instrument of social order, it necessarily poses a dilemma" (italics added). The intention of authority in law (theory) and in control (practice) is not necessarily the same, and indeed may be something incompatible. Skolnick addresses this problem in *Justice Without Trial* (p. 6):

The police in democratic society are required to maintain order and to do so under the rule of law. As functionaries charged with maintaining order, they are part of the bureaucracy. The ideology of democratic bureaucracy emphasizes initiative rather than disciplined adherence to rules and regulations. By contrast, the rule of law emphasizes the rights of individual citizens and constraints upon the initiative of legal officials. This tension between the operational consequences of ideas of order, efficiency, and initiative, on the one hand, and legality on the other, constitutes the principal problem of police as a democratic legal organization.

Skolnick poses here a problem that may be generalized to most, if not all, administrative services. The goal of professional and agency efficiency, what with budgets and records, and so on (*see* Goffman, *Asylums*), is not always, or even often, congruent with adamantine pursuits of the *rights* of "clients." The enormous area of discretion open to administrators of law enables them to make interpretations with vigor and pursue zealously the goals they favor.

Police work constitutes the most secluded part of an already secluded system and therefore offers the greatest opportunity for arbitrary behavior. As invokers of the criminal law, the police frequently act in practice as its chief interpreter. Thus, they are necessarily called upon to test the limits of their legal authority. In so doing, they also define the operative legality of the system of administering criminal law (Skolnick, 1967:14).

Thus it is that administrators are able to act in a large area of extralegality as well as within the rule of law. Discretionary behavior may be arbitrary and/or routinized, but regardless of the predictability of occurrence it is as far from accountable as any official behavior can be. When citizens encounter administrative action that seems to abridge or circumvent their rights, they are essentially subjected to unresponsible control. They experience an act that seems to be an abuse of governmental authority. This is the type of situation usually described by a person as repressive, and indeed, this label seems essentially accurate.

Persuasion is a second control method available to the state (*see* Gamson, 1968:125-135). Basically, persuasion consists of reminding people of the original trust investment and convincing them that the government is making good use of its authority. Gamson suggests four techniques of persuasion:

1. The selective withholding of information.

2. The purposeful aggrandizement of leaders.
   Surrounding authorities with trappings of omniscience is another control technique. If the authorities are viewed as distant, awe-inspiring figures, possessed of tremendous intelligence and prescience plus access to privileged information that is essential for forming judgments, then the potential partisan may hesitate to challenge a decision even when he feels adversely affected by it. (p. 126)
3. The humanization of leadership.
   There is . . . a contrasting technique which *minimizes* social distances between potential partisans and authorities. By personal contact and the "humanization" of authorities, potential partisans may be encouraged to identify with them; this identification, in turn, produces trust which makes influence appear less necessary. If the people making the decisions are just like me, then I need not bother to influence them; they may be trusted to carry out my wishes in the absence of influence. (p. 127)
4. The admonishment to "do one's duty."
   The activation of commitments still depends both on the acceptance of a general obligation and on reminders of what that duty is in specific situations. The connections between the top political leaders in a society and the members of a solidary group may be remote and may pass through many links before they reach a person's boss or neighbor or colleague or whoever else happens to be reminding. Nevertheless, at the last link in this chain between authorities and potential partisans, the desire to avoid the embarrassment of being derelict under surveillance is a powerful persuader. (p. 134)

A third method of control is "participation and cooptation." This method involves a certain inducement for involvement in the system. It usually involves some compromise on the part of authorities for a corresponding loss of influence on the part of the discontented.

When the three types of power or control resources outlined here are used "effectively," the state is successful in maintaining the order necessary for the established society's perpetuation. Behavior that cannot be accommodated to the prevailing political system is suppressed (relatively legally, if not completely so) and other potential expressions of discontent are transformed. While conflict is not eliminated, it is controlled, and taunts to the legitimacy of the polity are seen to be manageable or absorbable. The majority of the people are seen to be neutrally oriented toward the state.

LOSS AND RESTORATION OF EFFECTIVENESS

If the use of resources for authoritative control is not successful in rallying neutral and solidary groups to support action of the state, then the government's power, by definition, has lost some of its effectiveness. From the earlier discussion of concepts, we understand that the basis for social control lies in cooperation or voluntary compliance with the state. If, despite coercion, persuasion, and inducement, persons or groups do not hold governmental action to be legitimate, their "cooperativeness" diminishes. If noticeable numbers of people are alienated from the government, the connotation of order changes. Too many people feel that their interests are not being served, and pressure for adjusting satisfactions is heaped upon the state. Discontent, uncontrollable by authoritative techniques, demonstrates that the basis of citizen support is tenuous; consequently, discontent hinders the governmental interest-serving function as it has developed. There are basically two options in this kind of politically discordant situation. The first is for the state to respond to the pressures for adjustment by reassessing interest-serving, to examine operational priorities for their congruence with the underlying values of the political community. Assuming that some realignment of policy, administration or structure is deemed necessary, the appropriate governmental action is theoretically to make changes and compromises to serve more or different interests. If changes and compromises can be brought about, the support of many or most of the alienated should be increased and their legitimacy orientations changed.

There are obvious advantages to the successful use of this option: the effectiveness of power resources can be recouped. In light of analysis of the model presented here, however, the feasibility of this option is questionable. Unless the types of changes to be made are clearly to the advantage of the competing major interests (whose service is established), altering priorities would only serve to transfer support; it would not serve to broaden the base of support. Hypothetically the alienated would become supportive and vice versa.

Major outcome modifications are not likely to be made for very pragmatic reasons. The most obvious explanation is that interests which have established themselves have in doing so, acquired enormous influence resources —money, personal and social influence over large numbers of people (employees, business relations, officials, etc.), long-standing reputations, and so on. Changes that might cause these interest holders to suffer cannot be made by the state because, as the social order has been perpetuated, changes would disable the established system.

The more hopeful projection for this option is that "concessions" can be made that are not extensively unsettling for established interests, yet that will mollify the discontented. The effectiveness of this action would seem to depend on both the artfulness of the authorities and the degree of confirmation and commitment of the alienated. By making conciliatory gestures and concessions, the state should at least be able to placate some of the alienated. Prospects are probably not very good, however, for transforming the discontent of a large segment of people who have experienced "patterns" of disappointment. The alienation of this group is likely to be entrenched beyond the excavation power of new cooptation. By experience they have come to expect little mitigation from expedient measures and temporary compromises.

The first option for restoring effectiveness, re-ordering or adjusting interest serving, then, realistically involves the state's altering in the least disruptive way its operationalizing of some values. For its efforts, the state could expect to increase its support and re-establish authoritative control by transforming the orientation of some of the discontented. The option will be seen to be successful if the numbers of the alienated are no longer noticeable. In other words, the state would not hope to "bring over" all of the disconented; it would, instead, hope to reduce their numbers so that the remaining illegitimacy taunts could essentially be ignored.

The second alternative to try to restore effectiveness of power is to reassess the order function in terms of control, rather than of interest serving. The quiddity of this option is to implement new uses of power to control those discontents who do not respond to authoritative control techniques. This option would be taken if the state decides it cannot or does not want to try to satisfy by granting concessions. Since "normal" constraint, persuasion, and inducement did not change the perception of these people in regard to their interest and state action, an increase in control turns on the continued use and exploitation of these techniques in conjunction with the use of techniques that are "illegal." The latter use of power is clearly an abortion of authority. The former use of power relies on the manipulation of discretionary areas and is clearly an extension of authority. The range of action available by this redefinition of order circumscribes the area of repressive control. Theoretically, the state has the option to use power repressively at any time. It is obvious, however, that this potential need not be explored when authoritative control techniques are adequate to the ordering task. The utilization of excessive extralegal tactics and "illegal" ones is only necessary when threats to the legitimacy of the state are seen to be beyond the tolerance of order.

Control efforts that repress do not base their rationale for application on the legally substantive nature of behavior. (This, of course, does not deny that behavior that is repressed could not also be illegal behavior, but it is by no means necessarily so.) Rather, the expression of discontent that behavior makes defines it as the concern of the new control. The recipients of repressive control are victims or targets rather than "offenders." They are subject to *fate control:* whenever they interact with the control system, the latter may and can affect their outcome, regardless of what they do (*see* Thibaut and Kelley, 1965).

This extension of power sounds both devious and pernicious. Repression is an obtrusive reclamation of effectiveness by the state. It is a marked effort for self-preservation. One would think that such a blatant misuse of the political trust would result in electoral disaster in a democracy. Conjecturely, the people would be credibly agog at the misuse of their mandate. At least, their support for the elite should be shaken and questioned. Such a supposition, however, fails to account for the total range of control in the hands of the state. The use of repressive fate control to "order" the discontented does not abrogate the use of authoritative behavior control in relation to the neutral or solidary citizens. If the governing are perspicacious in evaluating the political attitude of the governed, they can simultaneously increase legitimacy judgments and quash illegitimacy judgments.

LEGITIMATION OF REPRESSION

To simultaneously increase legitimacy judgments, on the one hand, and suppress illegitimacy judgments, on the other, the state must polarize the population into majority (confident) supportive and minority (alienated) repressable groups. The success of polarization will rest upon the state's ability to obfuscate the differences between fate and behavioral control in the eyes of the potentially confident. More simply, polarization will be effected if the majority of the people favor the government's redefinition of order (despite its "unauthorized" nature).

The "strategy" of polarization relies on assuring that the confident and neutral do not experience abridgement of justice themselves so that interpretations of justice made by the state will have credibility. Killing of the discontented must always be in "self-defense"; defamation must always be the insight of expertise; detentions and extravagant bail setting must always be to protect the community from dangerous assault; systematic elimination or incarceration of a certain "criminal element" must always be the objective and professional pursuit of the rule of law; trying of defendants for conspiracy (a felony in most states) to commit misdemeanors must always be represented as the system proving itself; and so on. It is a major benefit to the state that the techniques for order have the same *appearance* regardless of the purpose they are put to. The onus to prove that the intended *use* of control mechanisms is different for behavior and fate control belongs to the pursued.

Assuring that the already confident respect the interpretations of the government is not particularly problematic. The objective sought with this grouping of people is to *keep* their support high. Thus, it is necessary only to continue to *persuade* them that their interests are being served in the best possible way, "under the circumstances." For these people, it will be enough to *remind* them (a control technique elaborated earlier) of their duties as citizens.

Seeing that the neutral come to respect government is crucial and far more problematic to the state's legitimacy drive. This group is large and is capable of exercising a wide range of influence. If this group can be converted from neutrality to *confidence,* a legitimacy base of some magnitude will be available to support governmental action.

To effect this desired situation, the government will attempt to induce support without giving up the major interests it has come to serve (in other words, without making major changes). This is not a simple task, of course, since the group to be induced is not characterized by a high degree of faith that their interests will be served. One viable source of inducement in a turbulent situation is to promise tranquility, to promise security in exchange for renewed and/or continued support.

If the government, in the midst of widespread discontent and uneasiness, can describe the sources of the turmoil and elucidate clear and easily understood methods of "getting at" the sources, and then offer evidence that its methods are working, admiration and confidence (and hence legitimacy) can be built. More simply, if the government can bring about a redefinition of interest and demonstrate how it is serving these newly defined interests, it cannot help attracting allegiance.

How can the majority's interest be redefined? In his Presidential Address to the 64th Annual Meeting of the American Sociological Association (1969), Ralph H. Turner suggests (wittingly or unwittingly) a source of interest mobilization in speaking to the topic of "The Public Perception of Protest."

The nature of the public definition [of protest] undoubtedly has consequences for the course and recurrence of the disturbance, and for short- and long-term suppression or facilitation of reform. One of the most important consequences is probably that a protest definition spurs efforts to make legitimate and nonviolent methods for promoting reform more available than they have been previously, while other definitions are followed by even more restricted access to legitimate means for promoting change (Turner and Killian, 1957:327-328) (Turner, 1969:817).

Public definitions of disturbances are affected by two major perceptions. The first of these is whether or not the disturbance seems "credible" as a protest. According to Turner (1969:818), to be credible as protestors, those involved in a disturbance must seem a definite part of a visible group "whose grievances are already well documented," who appear powerless to effect change in the desired direction, and who show some signs of moral virtue that render them "deserving."

Secondly, "an optimal combination of threat and appeal is necessary for the probability of seeing disturbance as protest." (p. 821) The variability in perceiving appeal or threat is related both to the personal involvement and proximity of the perceiver, and also to his ability to determine the limits and patterns of disorder realistically (p. 821). In relation to this second factor in protest definition, Turner makes the following observations (p. 822):

1. . . . escalation of violence is likely to preclude protest definition because of preoccupation with the threat.
2. Repeated unescalated disturbances are likely to be accompanied by decreasing degrees of interpretation of protest, replaced by increasing tendencies to see the events as deviance.
3. Crime and rebellion are in an important sense easier interpretations to make since they can be inferred from the most conspicuous and superficial aspects of behavior, without a search for the motives and grievances behind the violence and disruption.

The advantages of attending to Turner's observations are fairly obvious for the government. By publicly denying the numbers of the discontented, by repeatedly contradicting their plea of noble intent, and by decrying the uniqueness of their cause, the government can try to discredit the dissatisfied as individuals and as a group and make the "disturbances" they create lack "credibility" as protests. At the same time, the government can emphasize the threat created by the disturbers, can insist that the discontented are tearing at the very fabric of society.

This ploy is not to be underestimated. Undoubtedly, among the alienated solidary groups there will be dissimilar as well as congruent interests represented. Accordingly, there will be varying threats to the legitimacy of the government. Some will have disrespect for the authorities: they will see the incumbents as unresponsive to their needs and will deem the current governmental interpretation of political values illegitimate. Some of the discontented will question the legitimacy of the institutions of government as they originally were created or have come to be. This form of discontent will be characterized by the belief in a reform, revitalization, or restructuring of institutions. A third kind of discontent will question the entire philosophical base of the state and will doubt the legitimacy of a system that could so fail to serve the interests and values deemed important. A more radical form of discontent will question the legitimacy of an entire system or any system. In order to corral and shape citizen support, it is definitely to the advantage of the government to capitalize publicly on the most severe forms of criticism —hence to exaggerate the size and kind of threat to the country. By focusing attention on forms of discontent that most citizens would find excessively intimidating, the government can exonerate itself and draw the uninvolved into a partnership of political consciousness: "the threat is to values we all hold." The *realism* of a governmental definition of this sort has the weight of historical trust and legitimacy to back it up.

Once "protest" definitions are discredited, events can be pointed to as confirmation of the governing's good judgment. Should violence erupt, it is proof of the intent of the disrupters; should government and/or protestors persist in relatively pacifistic demonstrations, the public will be shown the folly and destructiveness in criticism without action or suggestion and be led to believe the behavior deviant. Essentially, if concessions are not made by the government, and if it has fostered tenacious perceptions, the government stands to win admiration no matter what action it takes over time.

The task of discrediting noisy discontent (discontent that makes itself heard) is facilitated by a considerable tradition of abhorrence for collective behavior. From Gustave Le Bon, Ortega y Gasset to contemporary behavioral scientists such as Smelser, Kornhauser, Lipsit, and others, crowds, masses (or whatever groups of dis- or malcontents have come to be known) are seen as somehow demonic, atavistic, irrational, and so on.

Skolnick depicts the perception of the order tradition in *The Politics of Protest*:

"Collective behavior" is thus conceived as nonconforming and even "deviant" group behavior. Under this conception, the routine processes of any given society are seen as stable, orderly, and predictable, operating under the normative constraints and cumulative rationality of tradition. The instability, disorder, and irrationality of collective behavior, therefore, are characteristic of those groups that are experiencing "social strain"—for example, "the unemployed, the recent migrant, the adolescent." [Smelser, Theory of Collective Behavior, 1962:74]. As such, "collective behavior" is characteristically the behavior of outsiders, the disadvantaged and disaffected. (p. 332)

Related to this conception of collective behavior as irrational is an implicit notion that collective behavior is—particularly in its more "explosive" forms—inappropriate behavior. . . . To define collective behavior as immoderate, and its underlying beliefs as exaggerated, strongly implies that "established" behavior may be conceived to the contrary. Needless to say, such an approach has important political implications, which ultimately render much of collective behavior theory an ideological rather than an analytical exercise. (p. 333)

A major shaping of majority interest is possible, then, if the government is able to associate the psychological odium for "collective behavior," the existence of a vociferous group of discontented, and an increasing threat to the security of public and private social relationships. By identifying an "enemy within," the source of turbulence can be made to seem the discontent itself: "the problem is the threat to our established order." The government's inducement for legitimacy, hence support, thus becomes definable in terms of the source of "our" problem.

The problem, "disturbance," is still a rather abstract source, however. The social condition represented by disturbance needs to be pinned down, that is, the people who pose the threat need to be identified and identifiable.

Faced with this challenge to the basic order of our society, free people must protect themselves, their institutions, and the very freedom they cherish. If they do not, this nation, as we know and love it, will perish. Public officials, civic organizations, and individual citizens must become aware of the threat posed by those who plan, or who simply further rebellion, anarchy, and the overthrow of our democratic institutions. We must protect our nations from revolutionary action, whether this be through subtle thrust of invidious propaganda or through the dramatic action of mob violence.

But how? Frequently the dedicated revolutionist hides his purpose and objectives behind an ostensibly righteous cause. Often his very presence remains unnoticed as he works through individuals and groups that he is able to manipulate and use for his own purposes. The aims and methods of his attack upon society are obscured even from the more knowledgeable citizens —so that often revolution is disguised as dissent. Therefore, a thorough knowledge of the nature of the rebel and his techniques is the initial step to prepare for building a strategy to safeguard democracy.

It is essential that we recognize the threat we face, understand the techniques of those who champion revolution and appreciate the deviousness and duplicity of those who assail our democratic society. (Ronald Reagan in Momboisse, 1970:vii).

The state's task, then, is to locate the carriers of "the threat." They can be identified as those who betray cherished values and who seem to deprecate the national way of life. When these people are found, they can be isolated to curtail their heinous influence. They can be labeled, as it were, so that there is no mistake about who they are. It is within the government's power to mold the confines of the category, by publicly reiterating the characteristics of those who seem appropriate as leaders, complicitors, or dupes. Klapp (1959) describes the social process of "villification," and his notations are so appropriate to this point that they justify being quoted at length:

Most, if not all, societies have a concept of an ideally evil kind of person who is thought to be responsible for serious troubles. . . . Each historical period seems to have its own characteristic villains, though many of them seem to be mere variants of more universal patterns.

Villification is a kind of symbol-making that groups engage in under certain conditions in order to repair and defend the social structure and to build consensus and morale for certain kinds of social actions. While to the individual it may be destructive, it is basically a process of mores-conservation and status-definition. The villain himself is a perfected symbol of aggression, the kind of person that people will fight hardest and with the greatest unanimity. The group creates such symbols as part of its defense mechanism—to defend mores and the institutional structure and to maintain normative integration. The more close-knit the group and the higher the we-feeling, we may presume the less will be the tolerance for villains and the greater tendency to define them, to resent encroachments from strangers, to be suspicious of isolates and outsiders, and to feel deviations and antisocial acts as a kind of treason or heresy (Durkheim: repressive law). (p. 71)

Villification is a consensual process—either of leading a group toward consensus or expressing an already achieved consensus—taking place by symbolic interaction within a collectivity. Furthermore, it makes use of a vocabulary of villainy—a consensual stock of images already established in the culture. (p. 72)

Villification may be institutionalized and elaborated in various ways, depending upon exigencies and historical circumstances. . . . Villification may be supported by an ideology . . . it may be hidden behind formal procedures and even an ideology that does not itself suggest the possibility of villification. But, however subtle its action or however variously it may be institutionalized, it does not lose its "grass roots" character as an expression of popular feeling. (p. 73)

As a movement, villification is a mass groping for consensus as to the nature of evil, who the villain is, what he is like, what to do about him, and how to organize toward him. (p. 73)

When "the people" are conscious of the source of turmoil (dissent), and the types of persons who compose the source (the villains), a political consciousness forms and begins to square off in terms of allegiance, a sort of "whose side are we on" evaluation. As allegiances and resources begin to polarize, social issues, positions, and events become identifiable and more clearly defined. "We assume that individuals and groups of individuals assign simplifying meanings to events, and then adjust their perceptions of detail to those comprehensive meanings" (Turner, 1969:811).

The government's inducement for support, if polarization actually comes about, is nearly complete. At this stage, with new collective interests identified, with resources amalgamating, and with legitimacy solidified in face of a threat to "all," the rallying call is the promise to save tradition, heritage, and values by dealing "effectively" with the villains.

Typically, there is a social climate favoring punishment and a general willingness to entertain scurrilous accusations, even an inclination to engage in a spontaneous villain search (Klapp, 1959:74).

At this juncture in our analysis, it seems appropriate to reflect on the neutral solidary group's shift from its former legitimacy-illegitimacy position to its present state of allegiance as a confident solidary group. Formerly, its interests were diverse and its influences were exerted accordingly. Resources available for influence were various, and specifically related to the types of pressure various groups and individuals determined to exert. Certainly individuals and groups held different opinions about when the government was acting legitimately and when it was not. In the extreme state of polarization being theoretically constructed here, most of these positions would have changed. Interests have been combined, as have influence resources. The majority opinion supports the government and defends its legitimacy to act in their interest. It is argued that this polar position has the following effects for "the people":

1. The base of critical evaluation of political activity is preempted by the demands of loyal support.
2. Government actions that would otherwise not be tolerable are accepted as legitimate and necessary for the preservation of "order."
3. Compliance to demands of the government is increased in relation to the heightened sense of union and duty.

If we assume the three "effects for the people" are realistic,[6] it is easy to picture the state's fulfillment of its promises. Having redefined the interests of the people as the control of the sources of turmoil, the state can fulfill the interests by seeking out the "villains" and curtailing their behavior. At this stage of polarization, what becomes persuasive for the one group is constraining to the other: the amount of resources that need to be committed to maintaining the new status quo are reduced by this interactive conservation.

The repression of discontent, although in the sense described is illegal or extralegal and depends on the non- or unauthorized use of power, is legitimized by the confluence of interest. This evolved legitimacy invites and hosts an *atmosphere* of repression; it allows processes of repression to develop and be active; it sanctions single acts of repression. This generalized state does not have to be one of blood and gore, nor does it have to reach actively every member of the alienated solidary group. On the contrary, any of the instruments of control and influence are available to use against the new "offender." He does not have to be physically controlled: the only requirement is to prevent him from interfering with the legitimized processes of order. Further, the penumbra of repression is such that it does not have to control predictably: indeed, its scope of intimidation is such that it is more effectively used if it is not. By selecting key figures in the "villainous" group for control, the lives of the rest of the discontented are touched symbolically. In effect, selective repression delivers notice that the established order is "on top of things" and is "prepared" and "ready."

A GOVERNMENT CONSPIRACY?

While we have defined "the people" and categorized "the villains," we have seemingly avoided defining "the government." The reasons for this reside primarily in the description of trust and legitimacy objects. "The government" is one or more or all of the "objects of trust": incumbent authorities, institutions, philosophy, and political community. The government is the total of "authorities" who have effective power in a situation. They are "the recipients or targets of influence and the agents or initiators of social control" (Gamson, 1968:36). Michael J. Brown (1969) defines the government in its repressive control function as a "control conglomerate."

The administration of control is a technical problem which, depending on its site and object, requires the bringing together of many diverse agencies that are ordinarily dissociated or mutually hostile. A conglomerate of educational, legal, social welfare, and police organizations is highly efficient. The German case demonstrates that. Even more important, it is virtually impossible to oppose control administered under the auspices of such a conglomerate since it includes the countervailing institutions ordinarily available. When this happens control is not only efficient and widespread, but also legitimate, commanding a practical, moral and ideological realm that is truly "one dimensional." (p. 33)

Brown's observation invites us to ask if the control conglomerate is "intentional," whether a government's role as repressive controller constitutes or represents a "conspiracy." Needless to say, these questions are extraordinarily complex. In beginning to face these questions, it appears that two sets of answers need to be supplied. First, does "the government" intentionally determine to "order," to follow the repressive control path rather than, or in conjunction with, that of compromise? Secondly, does a government consciously plan and act to create and maintain a redefinition of political interest, that is, to polarize the populace? Unfortunately, a definitive response cannot be made to either inquiry. This situation highlights the nature of the structural relationships involved in the political system. In the first instance, the authorities make decisions either independently *or* with a course of action in mind, that *accumulate* and have the effect of deciding what to do in the face of major discontent. It is within the state's domain of power to make and foster definitions, to decide many of the important outcomes that will be forthcoming from decisions and definitions. The "authorities" are *responsible* for the control and/or compromise course, regardless of any benevolent or malevolent intent.

Secondly, once a course of political action and response that rejects or ignores adjustment of interests has been set by the government (unless it is consciously reversed), whether there must be the "will" to polarize is a moot point. As a matter of situational definition, polarization must come about if the government is to maintain any support for its actions.

Historically, it could be demonstrated that governments have both "chanced into" repressive positions and planned to initiate repressive actions. It could be shown that governments have "unintentionally" fanned the fires of division, and again it could be shown that "authorities" have concertedly devised to polarize. The most efficient stifling of discontent is undoubtedly a product of successful planning. Yet, "unplanned" polarization and repression have essentially the same effects: the population is still divided; some individuals are still potential victims of "fate"; legitimacy and legality diverge.

OUTCOMES OF REPRESSION

Regardless of "intent," then, certain kinds of things happen and various changes are wrought in the polity. Returning to our earlier analysis, we can imagine that the type of changes that characterize a departure of legality from legitimacy somehow affect the character of a polity. The government's role is now centered around "order"—the regulation of collectivities of people for its own interest, self-preservation. (Durkheim also defines this change as repression, 1968:62-63.) Simultaneously, the original trust mandate is shaken. A segment of the people have, for all intents and purposes, been separated from the political sphere of competing interests. Authority as it was conceived has violated its dominion or extended its bounds, and power is available to cement the "new authority."

How much and how long the "new authority" is allowed to cement itself is critical to the status of the trust mandate. Table 3 conjectures possible political outcomes for democratic polities experiencing atmospheres of repression. "How much" the "new authority" is allowed to exert itself is represented in the table in terms of legitimacy; it is assumed that if a majority of the people evaluate the continuation of "new authority" as legitimate, they support its use of power as long as necessary, or until they become convinced of its illegitimacy. "How long" the "new authority" is allowed to act repressive is vaguely defined as "temporary" or "permanent." The distinction between the two temporal categories is that in the former the political community realigns itself eventually with its trust mandate, whereas in the latter the trust mandate changes and a new political system is created.

Table 3.

		Majority Evaluations	
		Legitimate	*Illegitimate*
Repressive Control	Temporary	Discontent silenced until "need" for repression ends; trust mandate compromised and restored.	Discontent popularized: "the people" reclaim authority by reform or revolution; trust mandate reaffirmed.
	Permanent	Discontent stifled: new category of oppression evolves; trust mandate changes by consent.	Discontent stifled: new category of oppression evolves; trust mandate changes by decree.

Certainly, the two "permanent" uses of repressive control represent important changes in political structure and philosophy. Essentially they indicate the possibility of repression becoming oppression. The new category of oppression includes those inveighers deemed intolerable. Their intolerable behavior would be prohibited so that manifestations of it would be subject to predictable and systematic control. The initiation of a new category of oppressed redefines formalized expectations and it redefines "the people." Correspondingly, guarantees of limits and freedoms have changed, and so have the holders of the trust. In the one case illustrated, the trust changes with the consent of the majority. Increased numbers of people are oppressed because of characteristics ascribed by the government and the people have changed their evaluation of the governmental use of authority and power and find it illegitimate. The table illustrates the conceivability of the government rejecting the evaluation and seizing authority. The new people would thus become those who govern, and the rest would be oppressed, that is, lack political rights. A small minority would be oppressing the majority.

Whether or not the temporary changes hypothesized in the table represent less important outcomes is debatable. Certainly both represent major commitments of political attitude, in terms of both legitimacy and trust. The one course indicates that the people will reclaim authority if they change their evaluation to illegitimacy. This assumes that the people can peaceably replace or remodel objects of trust in accord with their interest or that they can overpower the government to do so. If they are successful, repressive control should essentially be abolished.

The fourth alternative indicates that the majority of the people and the government can remain united in interest and action by repressing until the threat rescinds. Ironically, if the threat (as defined by the governing) is repressed, it is rescinded. In other words silencing discontent, if it is to be temporary, relies not only on repression but in the end must submit to some important outcome modification—reordering of interests—else repression cannot be let up for fear of more discontent (and this condition would signal a "permanent" change). The precarious nature of this alternative lies in the original misstatement of the source of turmoil, in the searching for villains rather than the dealing with sources of discontent.

SUMMING UP

From the foregoing analysis, it becomes more clear that political systems, by the nature of the structural relations supporting them, do have the potential cause and resources for repression. The goal of social unity anticipates a domain of repressive control, as well as behavioral and oppressive control, on the one hand, and interest serving, on the other. The theoretical presentiment of confirmed authority is its extension and abortion. The manipulation of discretionary areas and the utilization of control techniques for illegal purposes is a resource for establishing order in any polity.

How and why the repression resource can be animated has been the center of attention of this study. It should be obvious that the forces of control do not need to be exploited by the state at all times. Indeed, it is not necessary for the state to concern itself systematically with the repressive quashing of behavior until it feels its established existence is threatened and until the alternatives for order are drawn so narrowly that no other course seems feasible and/or desirable to the elite.

The implications of this analysis are ominous. How can we tell if the point described above has been reached and if a state is headed for, or is on a repressive control course? If the conjectured outcomes are tenable, it may be that we cannot "tell" until history provides us with a comparative perspective. In other words, perhaps we cannot be certain that a state course of action is repressive until we are able to observe one of the following: a tumultuous popular movement revitalizing its own claim to rule; a definitive seizure and entrenchment of power by the elite; a permanent redefinition of political intent and rule of law made by consent; or the jails and morgues filled with the politically discontented.

Such a projection is hardly palatable; it is also relatively naive in that it fails to account for the opportunity to make informed observations and interpretations of ongoing social interaction. Even though an observer may be enmeshed in the present, it is reasonable to expect that some pertinent political analysis is possible, short of "certainty." The following types of questions can be asked:

Does the state take an active and overt partisan role in defining and interpreting political events?

How is unity conceived? What is the definition of order and the conception of control that the state makes?

Are the people divided into political "camps" of supporters and discontented?

Are there recognized "villains" who are held accountable for the social turbulence?

Are contrived or expanded control "measures" tolerated as expedient and necessary?

What is the estimated congruence of legality and legitimacy?

Making the assessments that these types of questions demand is certainly far from easy. Hastening to judgment would be foolish. In order to minimize the influence of "rhetoric" and/or "interpretation," analysis and research should be undertaken as the basis for considered opinion. At the same time, abstaining from judgment would be even more foolish—both from the standpoint of science and morality.

NOTES

[1]See "The U.S. Army's Political Police," *San Francisco Chronicle,* January 27, 1970, pp. 1 and 20: "For the past four years, the United States Army has been closely watching civilian political activity within the U.S. Nearly 1000 plainclothes investigators, working out of some 300 offices from coast to coast, keep track of political protests of all kinds—from Klan rallies in North Carolina to antiwar speeches in Harvard. . . . [The Army's data bank] will not be restricted to the storage of case histories of persons arrested for (or convicted of) crimes. Rather it will specialize in files devoted exclusively to descriptions of the lawful political activity of citizens."
Also see, "H.E.W. Blacklist Bars Hundreds as Science Aides," *The New York Times,* October 9, 1969, pp. 1 and 32: "The Department of Health, Education and Welfare for years has been blacklisting hundreds of scientists, preventing them from serving on advisory panels that guide research efforts and funds. . . . Most of those excluded either had brushes with congressional investigating committees in the past or had been members of left-wing political organizations or oppose the war in Vietnam. . . . 'Security' or 'suitability' is the usual reason given by H.E.W. security people for the blacklisting. . . . The persons blacklisted include psychiatrists, psychologists, anthropologists, biochemists, physiologists, sociologists, microbiologists and social workers."

[2]*See* for example, "S.F. State Teacher 'Firings,'" *San Francisco Chronicle,* December 2, 1969, p. 3: "The Teacher's Union charged yesterday that at least 15 of its officers and members are losing their jobs at San Francisco State College because of a 'vendetta' by President S. I. Hayakawa. . . . [Union President Kelly] charges it as 'an absolute violation' of a promise against retaliation that was included in the settlement which ended the union's strike at the college this year. . . . He called it an 'attempt to get people not to join the union' and promised 'we will fight it with every legal means open to us.'"

[3]The following appeared in an article in *The Washington Star*, in 1970: "Warning! Students who want to become teachers should be forewarned not to take part in campus disruptions if they plan to teach in state schools, at least in California. . . . The warning comes from Howard Day, president of the California State Board of Education. . . . What is happening in California is this: students who have been arrested in various campus disorders are being denied teaching credentials even though they were acquitted or their cases thrown out of court. . . . In California, there is a Committee of Credentials, a branch of the State Department of Education, which screens and passes on prospective teachers. It is not bound by court action and frequently investigates an application on its own."

[4]"Agreeing" to be governed suggests that we must be speaking of an ideal type of political arrangement. For purposes of theoretical conception, we are somewhat naïvely overstepping the issues inherent in this kind of analysis. Hannah Arendt points out (1970: 98):

Consent—meaning voluntary membership must be assumed for every citizen in the community—is obviously (except in the case of naturalization) at least as open to the reproach of being a fiction as the aboriginal contract. The argument is correct legally and theoretically but not existentially. Every man is born a member of a particular community and can survive only if he is welcome and made at home within it. A kind of consent is implied in every newborn's factual situation; namely, a kind of conformity to the rules under which the great game of the world is played in the particular group to which he belongs. *We all live and survive by a kind of tacit consent, which, however, it would be difficult to call voluntary.* How can we will what is there anyhow? We might call it voluntary, though, when the child happens to be born into a community in which dissent is also a legal and defacto possibility once he has grown into a man. Dissent implies consent, and is the hallmark of free government; one who knows that he may dissent knows also that he somehow consents when he does not dissent. (Italics added)

[5]Gamson (1968:35-36) defines a solidary group in the following manner:

Solidary groups . . . are neither quasi groups nor interest groups but somewhere in between. They are collections of individuals who think in terms of the effect of political decisions on the aggregate and feel that they are in some way personally affected by what happens to the aggregate. Examples would include ethnic groups such as Jews, Negroes, Italian-Americans, and Irish-Americans; religious groups, some occupational groups, and many other categories depending on the social organization context. If one were concerned with the U.S. Congress as a system, solidary groups might include "urban congressmen," "southerners," "farm bloc congressmen" and so forth.

Solidary groups differ in their degree of cohesiveness or solidarity. More specifically, solidarity will be promoted by the following:

1. Symbolic expressions of the group as a collectivity.
2. Treatment as a group by others.
3. A common style of life, norms and values.
4. A high rate of interaction.

[6]Sociologically, there is basis to believe that these assertions are credible. Westley (1966) discusses stages of escalation of violence through legitimation. He finds that mild support for the use of violence "can be escalated into frightful extremes by the mediation of a special group given a mandate for this violence. The action becomes more severe at the same time responsibility becomes attenuated" (p. 125). This point is significant in regard to a loss of critical evaluation. Westley suggests that responsibility is attenuated by the momentum of acceptance of the exercise of delegated power.

The second assertion receives some basis for support from the findings of social psychologists. Festinger, Pepitone, and Newcomb (1962) suggest that "many of the behaviors which the individual wants to perform but which are otherwise impossible to do because of the existence, within himself, of restraints, become possible under conditions of de-individuation in a group." Singer, Brush, and Lublin (1965) confirmed this understanding of de-individuation. De-individuation suggests the possibility of positive sanction by polarized group members of each other's behavior, despite its illegal or extralegal nature.

Support for the credibility of the third point is drawn from a famous experiment by Milgram (1964). Basically, the research was designed to study the dimensions of obedience and defiance to authority in relation to administering pain (shock) to a victim. The researchers were astounded at the obedience it was possible to exact from executants:

With numbing regularity, good people were seen to knuckle under the demands of authority and perform actions that were callous and severe. Men who are in everyday life responsible and decent were seduced by the trappings of authority, by the control of their perceptions, and by the uncritical acceptance of the experimenter's definition of the situation into performing harsh acts. (p. 261)

REFERENCES

Arendt, Hannah
1970 "Reflections: Civil Disobedience." *The New Yorker,* September 12, 1970.

Brown, Michael E.
1969 "The Condemnation and Persecution of Hippies." *Trans-Action* 6:33-46.

Coser, Lewis A.
1969 "Some Social Function of Violence." *American Academy of Political and Social Science, Annals* 364:8-18.

Dahrendorf, Rolf
1958 "Toward a Theory of Social Conflict." *The Journal of Conflict Resolution* 2:170-183.

Durkheim, Emile
1958 *Professional Ethics and Civil Morals.* New York: Free Press.

Festinger, Leon, A. Pepitone, and Theodore Newcomb
1962 "Some Consequences of De-Individuation in a Group," in *Small Groups, Studies on Interaction,* ed. Hare, Borgatta and Bales. New York: Alfred A. Knopf.

Gamson, William A.
1968 *Power and Discontent.* Homewood, Illinois: The Dorsey Press.

Goffman, Erving
1961 *Asylums.* New York: Anchor Books, Doubleday.

Horowitz, Irving Louis, ed.
1964 *The New Sociology.* New York: Oxford University Press.

Klapp, Orrin E.
1959 "Notes Toward the Study of Villification as a Social Process." *Pacific Sociological Review* 2:71-76.

Levine, Robert A.
1961 "Anthropology and the Study of Conflict: An Introduction." *The Journal of Conflict Resolution* 5:3-15.

Milgram Stanley
1965 "Some Conditions of Obedience and Disobedience to Authority." In I. D. Stiner and M. Fishbein, eds., *Current Studies in Social Psychology.* New York: Holt, Rinehart and Winston, pp. 243-262.

Momboisse, Raymond M.
1970 *Blueprint of Revolution.* Springfield, Illinois: Charles C. Thomas.

Nieburg, H. L.
1970 *Political Violence: The Behavioral Process.* New York: St. Martin's Press.

Roszack, Theodore
1969 *The Making of a Counter-Culture.* New York: Doubleday.

Singer, Jerome E., Claudia A. Brush, and Shirley C. Lublin
    1965 "Some Aspects of De-individuation: Identification and Conformity." *Journal of Experimental Psychology* 1:356-378.

Skolnick, Jerome H.
    1967 *Justice Without Trial.* New York: John Wiley.
    1969 "Dialogue with Jerome Skolnick, Conducted by Gene E. Carte." *Issues in Criminology* 4:109-122.
    1969 *The Politics of Protest.* New York: Ballantine Books.

Thibaut, John W., and Harold H. Kelley
    1965 *The Social Psychology of Groups.* New York: John Wiley.

Westley, William
    1966 "The Escalation of Violence Through Legitimation." *American Academy of Political and Social Science, Annals* 364:120-126.

THE NEW RADICAL-CRIMINAL TRIALS: A STEP TOWARD A CLASS-FOR-ITSELF IN THE AMERICAN PROLETARIAT?

DAVID STERNBERG

This essay consists of three parts, all bearing on the emergence of "radical-criminal trials" in the United States in the past few years. The first section analyzes more or less abstractly the crucial distinctions between the model of the traditional criminal trial in the United States and its very recent variant, the model of the radical-criminal trial. It then attempts briefly to connect the surfacing of the radical-criminal trial with the current state of political protest in the United States. Next is presented an "anatomy" of the radical-criminal trial, in which an effort is made to extract out of the great amount of available material on major trials the basic themes of these proceedings. Even though greatly condensed, this section contains a hard core of substantive and illustrative detail essential for a roughly accurate sociological picture of the trials. The final section attempts to gauge the possible impact of these trials on the immediate future of the administration of justice in the United States.

Many (but certainly not all) of the structural circumstances of these trials are strikingly similar to the conspiracy trials of Leon Trotsky and his codefendants in St. Petersburg, 1906.[1] We know that those trials portended a vast social revolution in Russia some ten years later. Without contending that the appearance of similar trials today in the United States is an omen of general revolution, it is suggested in the final section that the radical trials may be forerunners of important gains for working-class accused persons (who constitute the vast majority of *all* accused persons) under the present bourgeois system of criminal "justice."

This is not a "value-free" sociological essay any more than are those papers that masquerade as such. The basic orientation is Marxist; the basic sympathies are with the "clients" rather than with the administrators of criminal justice.

David Sternberg, "The New Radical-Criminal Trials: A Step Toward a Class-for-Itself in the American Proletariat?" *Science and Society.* (Fall 1972) pp. 274-301. Reprinted by permission of the journal and the author.

THE TRADITIONAL CRIMINAL TRIAL

Until very recently the prevailing and largely uncontested model of criminal trials and their related pretrial hearings[2] in the United States has comprised exclusively the following six categories of active participants: the judge, and his auxiliary staff of clerks, bailiffs, and marshals; the defendant(s); the public prosecutor(s); the defense attorney(s); witnesses for the prosecution and defense; and the jury.

Not only have these groups been the exclusive legitimate actors in the criminal trial, but the patterns of interaction between and among them have been highly formalized and regularized. Thus, the judge "polices" the trial; the defense attorney speaks on behalf of his client, who does not speak out for himself; prosecutor and defense lawyer each get to question a witness in a particular style and order; witnesses answer only those questions put to them by court officials and do not "volunteer" information.

The assumption behind these trial norms is that the parties in the system and their relative power *vis-à-vis* each other will remain constant. One would expect, then, that the introduction of a new active party into the trial, or a shift in the relative power of one or more groups in this system, would force restructuring of the current prevailing model of the criminal trial.

In addition to these six active groups, a seventh *passive* group, the spectators, rounds out the contemporary picture of the United States trial. Spectators consist of varying percentages of relatives and friends of defendants, members of the press and other media, and an assortment of persons from the community who bear no particular kinship, friendship, or professional relation to the defendant, but who have variously motivated interests and curiosities about the administration of justice and its "clients." Statistically, the size of this spectator group has been small at usually routine criminal trials. In any event, the permitted presence of spectators at the trial has assured the "public" quality of criminal proceedings guaranteed the defendant by the Sixth and Fourteenth Amendments of the federal Constitution, as well as by the majority of state constitutions. For the most part, excepting certain "isolated incidents," the role of spectatorship in the past has been clear enough: passive, silent, and respectful observation of the trial/hearing process as performed by the six active groups of participants.

Criminal Trials of Radicals versus
Radical-Criminal Trials

It must be stressed that the traditional trial model briefly sketched above prevailed in essentials until nearly the end of the 1960s *even when radical defendants were involved.* That is to say, *criminal trials of political radicals,* whether they were specifically indicted for illegal political activity (e.g., the Wobblies, 1918), or whether they were accused of "conventional" crimes which at least superficially were unrelated to their political activities (e.g., Sacco and Vanzetti, 1920s), *rarely constituted radical-criminal trials.* That was so because up until the very end of the past decade dissenters, radicals, or revolutionaries, on trial under one indictment or another, generally accepted the traditional structure and process of the criminal procedure without challenging its fundamental political legitimacy.

Dwight Macdonald stresses the conventional courtroom deportment of radical defendants throughout American judicial history:

In old-style political trials, from the prerevolutionary trial in which Peter Zenger was successfully defended against His Majesty's prosecutors on a charge of publishing seditious matter, to the recent trial of Dr. Spock, et al., in Boston, both sides, in dress and behavior, accepted the conventions of the ruling establishment. . . . The defense behaved as if they shared the values and lifestyle of the Court, even when they didn't, as in the big IWW trial in 1918 under the Espionage Act. There were over a hundred defendants, the entire leadership plus the Wobblies. . . . *But although the defendants were anarchists to a man . . . bold and ingenious in antiestablishment disruption outside the courtroom . . . they behaved themselves inside it* (italics added).[3]

Nowhere, perhaps, was this continued acceptance of the old courtroom ground rules by radical defendants right into the late 1960s better illustrated than in the 1968-69 trial of Dr. Benjamin Spock for conspiracy to violate the federal draft laws. In her book, *The Trial of Dr. Spock,*[4] Jessica Mitford demonstrates that the traditional defense offered by Spock's old-style and conforming lawyers—which did in fact yield a not-guilty verdict on appeal—ironically succeeded in obscuring all the social and moral issues about U.S. involvement in Vietnam which Spock had hoped to expose in the trial. As Spock himself commented, "We sat like good little boys called into the principal's office. I'm afraid we didn't prove very much."[5] Whether the verdict was innocent or guilty, the same "good little boy" atmosphere characterized the 1960s trials of militant integrationists, draft resisters, draft-file burners,[6] criminal trespassers involved in takeovers of university buildings, and so on. In short, the militancy of the defendants almost always stopped short of the courtroom itself.[7]

Now, quite suddenly (although, as will be shown below, not unexpectedly, given the present political conditions and drastic tensions in the United States) a number of criminal trials in which radical defendants are involved have drastically challenged the kinds of "boundary-maintenance" mechanisms heretofore operating in criminal trials. The most widely publicized of these new-model trials were the Chicago Conspiracy Trial, the New York Panther 21 Trial, the New Haven Panther 14 Trial, and the Soledad Brothers and Angela Davis/Ruchell Magee trials (the last two in progress at this writing). In most of these trials the traditionally active parties have not all accepted their customary roles relative to one another, and the traditionally passive audience has assumed an active and unprecedented role in the proceedings. Consider Dwight Macdonald's evocation of the Chicago trial:

In the new-style radical courtroom tactics, either the lawyers share the alienation and often the hair style of their clients, or there are no lawyers. Also, as in the Living Theatre and other avant-garde dramatic presentations, the audience gets into the act; the spectators raise their voices, or, worse, their laughter, at crucial moments, despite all those beefy marshals. And the defendants, hitherto passive except when they had their meager moment on the witness stand—"Please answer the question, yes or no"—feel free to make critical comments on the drama when the spirit moves them.[8]

The Current State of Political Protest in the United States

Prior to a more extended discussion of changing trial styles in America, let us consider their immediate antecedents in the contemporary political setting. There is no denying that in the United States the 1960s has been a decade of unusual protest and dissent against institutions of government. In an escalatingly militant manner various alienated minority groups—particularly black people, poor people, young people, and antiwar protesters—have picketed, confronted, and challenged various departments and agencies of federal and state governments. Yet curiously, while challenges to the executive branches had become regular and frequent by the mid-1960s, the *judicial* arm of the government had remained nearly immune to direct confrontation and accounting until nearly 1970.

Throughout the 1960s people marched (or tried to march) on the White House, on national conventions of the major parties, on the Congress and sessions of state legislatures, on the Pentagon and military recruiting stations throughout the nation, but rarely, if ever, did one hear or read of a march on the Supreme Court, indeed any court.

Why were the courts relatively isolated from protest throughout the 1960s? One factor may have been the persisting image of "majesty," indeed "sacredness," that the court seems to have held for the citizenry. The fact that judges wear priestlike black robes is evidence of and sustenance for the judiciary's religious image. If the legislature and executive have been defined pretty much within the "secular" realm of society, the courts have possessed a religious aura not to be tampered with or challenged except in the most extreme of situations.

Another factor insulating the courts has been a persistent ideology that they are disassociated from and somehow "above" the political process and arena, that the judiciary is not an independent variable in the creation of law and legal policy—and thus not a proper target for those who seek a redistribution of political power in the country. That judges are often appointed (e.g., in the federal judiciary) rather than elected, in contradistinction to major legislative and executive officials, and that their terms of office are often longer than terms in the other branches of government, are sometimes given as evidence that the courts are somehow aloof and detached from the action centers of political power. Any first-year law student knows that in fact the courts "make" as much law as they "interpret," and that their "dependent" or "agent" position in the American political structure and process is largely a myth. But the point is that until very recently even vocal protest groups seem to have accepted this high-school-textbook version of the courts' role.

One important common denominator to the numerous group protests against the executive and legislative branches of government in the past decade was the idea that, in a geometrically progressive fashion, power had been removed from the hands of the vast majority of the population and consolidated in the hands of a very few "elected" officials who were generally neither respondent nor responsible to the will of the people. Of course this complaint has been echoed from the earliest days of the Republic, but it had a peculiar urgency, and was particularly well articulated by many intelligent protestors, in the multiple crises of the 1960s.

Another common denominator of the many protests, rebellions, and revolutionary movements directed at government institutions in the last decade is that in the main they have very largely failed to achieve their purposes. To take the three most prominent examples of failure of continued protest to affect government policy: the war in Vietnam continues unabated, and now has openly spread to other parts of Indochina; black people remain essentially a colonial and oppressed people within the United States; a substantial minority of the United States citizens (black and white) continue to live in a state of poverty or near-poverty with no sign of real improvement of their lot.

The specific way in which protesters have experienced failure and frustration led them to discover the relatively untouched judicial chink in the institutional armor. That is, the types of dissent activities carried out against legislative and executive institutions—e.g., liberation of neighborhoods and parks, takeover of buildings, large-scale protest meetings and marches, burning of draft records—are defined by the criminal law in terms of statutes such as criminal trespass, riot, conspiracy to riot, disturbing the peace, and destruction of government property. Protesters, then, had been moving toward an eventual direct confrontation with the courts in an oblique way when they initially challenged the other arms of government and found themselves indicted under certain criminal laws implemented in their particular cases to protect the "garrison society." Eventually it dawned upon these defendants that far from being mere "agents" of the other institutions of power, the courts themselves were another creator and center of the very status quo they were determined to change. It is at this point that the legitimacy of the judiciary is finally brought into fundamental question, and the old cry, heard earlier concerning the executive and legislative branches, that the people have been robbed of their power, is heard in a new forum of protest. That protestors would pick the *trial level* of criminal courts to mount their challenge makes sense not only in terms of their own involvement as defendants at that level, but because it is the least "majestic" and most public and accessible one in the hierarchy of the American judicial system.

That dissenter defendants would stop playing "good little boys," that their in-court challenges to the judiciary's legitimacy would tend to be highly boisterous and dramatic follows from the protesters' growing sophistication and awareness of the previously effective role of American criminal trials in keeping radicals "out of circulation" through protracted judicial proceedings, often including long-term preverdict detention. The defendants in the Chicago and Black Panther trials were determined that their revolutionary voices would not be buried in a judicial morass. To that end they performed in the courtroom in such a way that their actions would be consistent headline news.[9]

The astonishment and outrage of the judges, bailiffs, and prosecuting attorneys, when suddenly and vociferously confronted with across-the-board challenges to their authority, were predictable. The massive contempt senten-

ces handed out to all defendants and lawyers in the Chicago trial, the summary contempt sentences given by Justice John Murtagh to several spectators
at the pretrial hearings for the New York Panther 21; the gagging and shack-
ling of defendant Bobby Seale in Chicago, followed a year later (March 1970)
by Supreme Court approval of such treatment of "obstreperous" defendants
in *Illinois* v. *Allen;*[10] current research being conducted at the University of
Michigan Law School, under a Ford Foundation grant, on the viability of
various methods (plastic soundproof bubbles, separate rooms at the side of
the courtroom) to control the outbursts of defendants in court[11]—all reflect
the depth and breadth of a culture shock experienced by officers of the
criminal court. Judges and their staffs, so long accustomed to nearly absolute
deference on the part of both the general citizenry and defendants (radical
or more conventional ones), so long cloistered from real public scrutiny, so
secure in their tenure, could hardly have been expected to react in other than
a harshly repressive way when the established roles of the customary judicial
actors were drastically altered and new actors as well clamored to get on
stage and take part.

EMERGENT FEATURES OF THE RADICAL-CRIMINAL TRIAL

There already exists a massive amount of descriptive material about the
above-mentioned trials—particularly about the trial of the Chicago Eight—in
newspaper reports and articles, magazine pieces, a book-long excerpt of sections of the Chicago Eight trial transcript, and three histories of the Chicago
trial.[12] The purpose of this presentation is not to render a history of any of
these proceedings but to extract those features in the trials that appear to
be most clearly innovative and hostile to the existing model of the American criminal trial. The actual occurrences that exemplify some particular feature of radical-criminal trials will not be cited individually in the text, to
avoid excessive annotation, but each incident mentioned below is derived
from one or more published sources. These examples are intended to present
a useful and strategic new "angle" on these trials, and to provide background
for the third section of this essay, which indicates possible future implications
for the ideology and practice of criminal justice in the United States.

Role of Defendants

Perhaps the most fundamental innovation in the radical-criminal trial is
the open, incessant, and vociferous challenge made by single or multiple defendants to the very *legitimacy* of the criminal court. In fact, the resistance
of the *defendants* to the court's authority is so aggressive and *offense*-like
that it is almost paradoxical to refer seriously to the "role of the defendant"
in a sense consistent with the meaning of that term in the proceedings of a
traditional trial.

The argument that the court is illegitimate rests on the defendants'
analysis and condemnation of the existing situation in the United States.
They see themselves as political prisoners trapped by a power structure of
laws created by societal groups hostile to their interests. The court is both

an agent for these groups and institutions—most significantly, monopoly capitalism, racism, colonialism, the military-industrial complex, and incipient fascism—and also an oppressive power group in its own right. Although defendants may vary somewhat in the rank or order of their targets, all are in agreement that the criminal court's allegiances are squarely with the oppressor groups and directly hostile to the powerless classes in American society.[13] That fundamental consensus was perhaps most dramatically symbolized by the innumerable times during these trials that defendants shouted out the slogan "Power to the People."

Assuming this basic political rationale for denying legitimacy to the criminal court, what kinds of actual courtroom tactics and conduct do defendants employ in a radical-criminal trial to express their challenge and discredit the proceedings? The general procedure, implemented in many specific ways, is to flaunt the traditional rules and roles of the previously taken-for-granted norms of the courtroom social system.[14] Numerous confrontation tactics are practiced, with the aim of throwing the traditional judicial model completely out-of-whack by bewildering the entrenched courtroom personnel. Here are some of the prominent tactics, with actual examples from the major trials:

1. Defendants frequently burst out in direct verbal (and occasionally physical) attacks on judge, prosecutor, unfriendly witnesses, or the judicial process in general, shouting down their own attorneys and insisting that they be allowed to speak out for themselves about the injustice of their prosecution. During the first 12 days of the New York Panther 21 hearings, defendants interrupted the court proceedings in this manner 665 separate occasions; the nearly five-month-long Chicago trial was interrupted innumerable times. Pleas and threats by the judges directed to the defense attorneys to control their clients were largely ineffective. Threats to hold the defendants in contempt of court and send them to jail were answered with statements such as "We're *already* in jail" (Panther 21), or "I'd rather go to jail than let you get away with the lies you're telling in this courtroom" (defendant Dellinger to Judge Hoffman in Chicago).

2. Defendants rejected the legitimacy and dignity of the court by pointedly ignoring its proceedings. For example, defendants on many occasions, individually and collectively, refused to stand when Judges Murtagh (in New York) and Hoffman (in Chicago) began or terminated courtroom sessions. In some cases this led to physical altercations between defendants and marshals. During the Chicago trial defendants would frequently pay no attention to the examination of witnesses, even their own; they would appear deeply absorbed in books or newspapers instead. On several occasions certain of the Chicago defendants would casually get up and walk out on the proceedings, or fail to appear in the courtroom for a particular session.

3. Defendants mocked and parodied the ordinary legal practices and procedures of the court in a variety of ways. In Chicago, Abbie Hoffman and Jerry Rubin once appeared in court wearing black judicial robes, in obvious parody of Judge Hoffman. Sometimes surrealistic and deliberately unresponsive answers were given to "straightforward" questions, such as those of the federal attorney to Abbie Hoffman about his age, residence, name, and occupation. Or they engaged the court in ludicrous disputes and colloquies—for ex-

ample, the "Bobby Seale Birthday Cake Incident" and the "Great Bathroom Debate," both of which took place in the Chicago trial. Or defendants made legal motions for adjournment of court on bases that the bench considered "outrageous" or "unheard of." For example, during the Chicago trial the defendants moved for adjournment to celebrate the mid-October 1969 Vietnam Moratorium, and in the New York Panther hearings defendants moved for adjournment to celebrate Black Panther founder Huey Newton's birthday in mid-February 1970.

4. Defendants refused to confine their interactions with other role members in the trial system to the area of the courtroom. On a number of occasions defendants in the Chicago proceedings, their aides, and lawyers clashed in verbal and physical conflict with members of the prosecution staff in the halls outside the courtroom. On one occasion defendants Hoffman, Rubin, and Dellinger—in the company of author Norman Mailer, a defense witness—confronted Judge Hoffman in the elegant Standard Club's Men's Grill. "Hoffman, lunching with another federal judge, cast one horrified look at them, rose, and took another seat behind a huge pillar."

Throughout the four and one-half months of the Chicago trial many of the defendants, all free on bail and permitted to travel throughout the United States on weekends, gave many speeches attacking the progress of the trial and its specific personnel in detailed *ad hominem* terms. Those few defendants free on bail during the New York Panther pretrial hearings also made speeches attacking Judge Murtagh and the prosecuting attorneys.

5. Defendants attempted to restructure and reverse the roles of judge, prosecutor, and defendant, so that the judge, prosecutors, and even certain witnesses for the prosecution, would be defined as the people who should really be on trial. Bobby Seale's statement, "Judge Hoffman, it's *you* who are in contempt of the American people"; the Chicago Seven's "indictment" of Mayor Richard Daley, on the eve of his testimony at the trial, as "Chicago's leading public criminal"; the New York Panther Memorandum about Judge Murtagh stating what happened to be factually true: "We are confronted with a judge who has admitted, in fact been indicted and arrested for, ignoring police graft and corruption"—these are only rather spectacular examples of countless and everyday "condemnation of the condemners"[15] tactics practiced by defendants at the trials under review.

6. Defendants planned with and solidly supported each other in challenges to the legitimacy of the trial. Whereas multiple radical defendants in earlier American trials sat in physical proximity to one another but usually remained verbally and emotionally isolated, in the recent trials they supported each others' outbursts with verbal encouragement by shouting out slogans such as "Right On!" or even came to the physical aid of each other if the court attempted to silence one of them.

Dellinger attempted to defend Seale from the assault of federal marshals when Judge Hoffman ordered Seale to sit down. Another time, when Judge Hoffman revoked Dellinger's bail for stating a "barnyard epithet," a melee broke out among the defendants and marshals, and Rubin shouted, "You're not going to separate us! Take all of us! Take me too!"

The techniques used by defendants to illegitimate the criminal trial often indicated a "conspiratorial" element. At least two defendants, David Dellinger and Tom Hayden, have admitted that the Chicago Eight discussed delegitimating trial tactics (although with less than complete agreement among the members) before their trial began.[16] But the essential, as well as ironic, point is that the conspiracies these radical defendants engaged in were *not at all the ones for which the courts had indicted them,* namely, conspiracy to commit riot (Chicago) and conspiracy to commit arson (New York).[17] One of the hallmarks of the radical-criminal trials is that the defendants, *after* being indicted for one criminal offense or another (the specific offense itself makes little difference), "conspired" or agreed collectively to discredit the proceedings of hearings and trial. Conspiracy, in short, viewed from the perspective of the radical-criminal trial, is the *result, not the cause,* of the indictment and criminal trial.

Role of Spectators

The role of the spectators underwent at least as drastic a transformation in the radical-criminal trial as that of the defendants. If defendants changed their style of participation from abiding by the rules to constantly challenging the court's legitimacy, spectators made an equally radical leap at the end of the 1960s from a virtual abstention from overt participation in the criminal trial or hearing to wide-scale vocal and sometimes physical participation. Such uninvited intervention has lent a new and unforeseen dimension to the Sixth Amendment's provision for a "public trial."

Certainly the history of criminal trials in this country contains earlier instances in which spectators have vigorously intervened—either for or against defendants and other court personnel—and in which defendants have been obstreperous. Indeed, Roscoe Pound comments upon the often rowdy quality of the nineteenth-century American criminal trials, although he notes that this rowdiness had much diminished by the early decades of the twentieth century;[18] and evidence of occasional audience and defendant intervention can be found throughout this century, especially if the defendant was accused of a bizarre or heinous "conventional" crime or was a political radical. But the *pattern and quality* of audience participation in current radical trials is unprecedented; it may be designated *radical participation,* and thus set off from superficially or partially similar audience conduct in earlier judicial eras. The most general reason why the current intervention of court audiences is new and distinctive is that it is *conditioned by the radical performance of the defendants,* another event of very recent vintage. Keeping this relationship in mind, the following prominent features of radical trial spectator activism emerge from a reading of the court reports:

1. Whether outbursts were directed to defendants, judges, prosecutors, witnesses, other members of the audience, or to "everybody in the courtroom," the participation of the audience was very frequent and continuous, day in and day out, rather than sporadic, as were most earlier spectator interventions and disruptions. For example, in the New York Panther hearings, defendants' family members and spectator Black Panthers from the first day frequently joined the chorus of comments kept up by the defendants, repeat-

edly called out encouragement, and echoed "Black Power to the People!" when the defendants shouted out the slogan. As that hearing proceeded, young white spectators began to displace the black audience, but the harassment of the court continued unabated. Scarcely more than three weeks after the pretrial hearings had begun, Judge Murtagh suspended the hearings indefinitely, following constant interruptions by the spectators as well as by the defendants. The Chicago trial was likewise marked by incessant interventions on the part of spectators. Audience participation was also evident at the New Haven Panther hearing and trial.

2. Attempts by judges and their staffs to control or discontinue such interruptions were largely unsuccessful. To be sure, particular offenders in the audience were spotted and removed by marshals (Judge Hoffman's approach in Chicago) or summarily sentenced and imprisoned for contempt of court (Judge Murtagh's preferred technique in New York), but they were so numerous and so easily replaced that such measures could not be more than temporarily effective. Moreover, many of the audience activists, like many of the defendants, simply did not "care" about possible sanctions, and this attitude made control of the courtroom problematic on a minute-to-minute basis.

3. Most of the participating spectators shared class interests with the defendants; conversely they tended to have few ideological, economic, or communal "interests" in common with the institutionalized personnel of the court. In an earlier era, participating audiences had been at least as likely to share identification with the court's "reference groups" as with the defendant's. The Chicago trial courtroom, however, was packed for nearly five months with hippies, Yippies, and representatives of various radical and revolutionary organizations, whose interests in and attitudes about current politics and power organization were close to those of the radical defendants. The New York courtroom was populated mainly by Black Panthers and poor black people. In both courtrooms, conventional, white middle-class citizens—the kind of people who looked, dressed, and felt like the judges and prosecutors—were conspicuously absent, outside of the press corps. In general, then, defendants were inclined to perceive the audience at their trials as "the people," and to interpret interventions of the audience as "the will of the people."

4. It follows that the intervening audience in the radical trial was invariably on the side of the defendants and hostile to the institutionalized judiciary. In the progressive and interactive dialogue among and between defendants and members of the audience in the radical-criminal trial, an increasingly strengthened structure of "resonating sentiments" emerged. At the same time, the dissonance of sentiments between the court on the one hand and the defendants and the audience became magnified. Examples were the massive support the audience gave to Bobby Seale in the courtroom, time after time answering his defiant raised and clenched fist with cries of "Right On!"; the solidarity the New York Panther defendants displayed with a spectator whom Judge Murtagh ordered removed for interrupting the proceedings, one defendant saying, "If she goes out, we go out!"; the concerted outrage of the entire audience when Judge Hoffman bound and gagged Seale; the continuous open as well as sub rosa exchanges between defendants and audience

in New York and Chicago, as if the official court personnel were either absent or simply did not count. In all these instances, audience and defendants constructed a mutually supportive and subversive social reality under the very gavel and noses of the judge, prosecutors, and marshals. It was just this extra-individual build-up and persistence of shared values between defendants and audience that made it such an enveloping and formidable force for judges and even dozens of marshals to contain continually. Then too, the extensive length of the radical trials increased the resonances of shared sentiments between defendants and spectators; it reaffirmed and intensified the commitment of at least one sector of the "public"—the specialized one represented by the audience—to the defendants' cause; and it ironically perverted the state's purpose to keep some radicals "out of circulation" through drawn-out judicial proceedings.

5. The participating audience in radical-criminal trials was not *primarily* interested in (although certainly not indifferent to) the eventual "guilt" or "innocence" of the charged persons, insofar as these statutes are determined by a body which they perceive to be illegitimate. In this respect their attitudes parallel those of the defendants themselves. The primary thrust of spectator activism, then, is the radical one of discrediting the entire judicial process rather than winning a "not guilty" victory for the defendants—especially if obtaining an acquittal means "playing along" with conventional judicial assumptions of what is "right" and "just," and so on.

6. Inasmuch as the activist audience was participating along with the defendants in the construction of a radical-criminal trial, they would tend to use—within the limitations of their somewhat more peripheral position in the courtroom (both spatially and socially)—discrediting techniques similar to those discussed in detail for defendants: open defiance of officials, pointed ignoring of the proceedings, "condemning the condemners," mockery of judicial procedures. Because of their resonant relation to the defendants, spectators would often "conspire"—like the defendants—to implement these disrupting tactics.

The Proselytizing Process

Even while attempting to discredit the criminal trial in its current condition, defendants and active spectators were simultaneously trying to re-educate those groups in the trial who support the system as it is to a more radical vision of both criminal justice and American institutions. These are some of the directions taken by such conversion attempts:

1. Defendants and spectators have attempted to convert the "grassroots" personnel of the court to a radical definition of the situation. In direct confrontations, they have argued with bailiffs and marshals that their real interests lie with "the people" and the defendants, not with the judge and state prosecutor. In the Chicago trial, for example, Dellinger stated that the trial proceedings demonstrated the corruption in the political system; when Judge Hoffman ordered a federal marshal to seat him, Dellinger turned to the man and said, "You don't really think this is a fair trial, do you? You're allowed to think for yourself even though you're paid by the same

company." During the New York Panther hearings, a black woman sympathetic to the Panthers accosted a black bailiff in the hall and asked, "Whose
side are you on, brother?" When he answered, "I'm on nobody's side, sister.
I'm just trying to keep order," she snapped, "You're a pig, too."

2. When defendants took the stand to "testify" in their own behalf,
their statements were often proselytical, although both judge and prosecutor
attempted to cut off these remarks as "irrelevant." Thus, in the Chicago trial,
defendant Abbie Hoffman, over numerous objections from the prosecution,
tried to explain on the witness stand his views of youth culture, the generation gap, hippies, Yippies, guerilla theater, the exorcism of the Pentagon,
and the "politics of ecstasy." In the New York Panther hearings, defendant
Tabor employed his time on the witness stand to tell his life story in a manner that vividly brought out the oppressiveness of current American institutions toward poor people, particularly poor black people.

In the Chicago trial, defendants also tried to use many of their witnesses as proselytizers. Among these were famous, charismatic and colorful
authors, poets, singers, and civil rights leaders, who shared in a general way
the political attitudes, if not always the lifestyle, of the defendants. In every
case, however, their convertive dialogues, poems, chants, or songs, were forbidden or severely circumscribed by their prospective converts, the prosecutors
and judge, on the grounds of irrelevancy.

3. In earlier "conventional" criminal trials of radicals, the defense attorneys were rarely radicals themselves; rather they were and remained "liberals" during and after their defense of radical defendants.[19] In the recent
radical-criminal trials, however, defense attorneys tended to become (and
stay) radicalized because of the tactical strategies of the defendants and the
emergent radical structure of resonant sentiments between and among their
clients and the audience, in which the attorneys also became engulfed. Tom
Hayden penetratingly depicted the stage-by-stage painful radicalization of
the Chicago Eight's attorneys, William Kunstler and Leonard Weinglass,
through the course of the trial.[20] It was painful because, prior to the Chicago
trial, both attorneys had firmly believed in the legitimacy of the traditional
ground-rules. How far Kunstler, for example, moved from his pretrial position on this point is evidenced by his statement in court near the end of
the trial: "I am going to turn back to my seat with the realization that everything I have learned throughout my life has come to naught, that there is
no meaning in this Court, and there is no law in this Court. . . ." The ultimate rejection of the court's legitimacy by the defense attorney was supported, as were earlier more limited, more cautious ones, by the audience
shouting "Right On!"

Thus defendants in radical-criminal trials were no longer satisfied, as
earlier radical defendants in conventional trials usually had been, that their
attorneys should be legally competent; or even possess the further desidera-
tum that they believe all accused persons should be afforded a spirited defense no matter how unpopular their cause; or even possess the more committed requisite that they passionately believe in their client's "innocence"
—for all these forensic virtues operate within the assumptions and structure
of the existing judicial system, which is precisely what the defendants will

not accept. Instead, what the current defendants require, and get, at an earlier or later stage in the proceedings, are men who themselves *believe* in the defendants' political causes. They require attorneys who are themselves radical so that they will "aid and abet" the defendants in staging a radical-criminal trial. In such a staging, defense attorneys have not only identified with their clients' interests to an unprecedented extent, but in very real senses they actually became defendants themselves, as the staggeringly long contempt sentences against both Kunstler and Weinglass in Chicago demonstrated. Such heavy demands, entailing such possibly heavy punitive consequences, suggest that full-bloom radical-criminal trials cannot long persist under present conditions; the small core of "Movement" attorneys would very shortly be removed from forensic circulation by long contempt-of-court sentences.

Reaction of the Proselytized

The reaction of the institutional criminal court personnel to the radical tactics of defendants and audience constitutes the final major feature of the radical trials. Allusion has already been made to the growing dissonance of sentiments between court officials on the one hand and defendants and audience on the other as the latter groups interactively stepped up their attacks on the court's legitimacy and courtroom procedures. If the verbal prototypes for resonance between defendants and spectators have been slogans such as "Right On!" and "Power to the People," the verbal symbol best expressing the judge's dissonance with radical tactics is some variant of the expression, "Never in my many years on the bench have I ever seen . . ."—which the judge then follows with a comment on one or another innovation introduced by defendants and/or the audience, depicted above.

In all the trials under discussion the dissonance between the court and the "people" has created a "garrison" or "armed-camp" atmosphere, with the court having to protect itself not only from assaults within the courtroom, but from large protesting crowds in the surrounding corridors, streets, and plazas, who have clamored to break in and simply terminate the proceedings. In none of these trials has the court been able to maintain order without "outside" help; in none of the trials have there not been days or weeks when the trials' continued existence was problematic.

These challenges to the viability of criminal trials from the defendants, on the one hand, and the audience and citizens in the streets on the other, have urgently raised questions bearing on two related, but distinct, constitutional rights of defendants. The Sixth Amendment guarantees a criminal defendant the right to confront directly witnesses against him; and the Sixth and Fourteenth Amendments (through the "due process" clause) guarantee him the right to a "public" trial. In March 1970, the Supreme Court held unanimously that a defendant "waived" his right to confront his accusers by disorderly behavior, and could thus be gagged and bound, or even expelled and kept isolated from the courtroom while the proceedings against him continued. In the case of isolation from the courtroom, the defendant would be allowed limited and indirect confrontation with witnesses testifying against him through devices such as closed-circuit television.[21]

But this Court decision did not discuss the "public trial" guarantee to the defendant. If the defendant is isolated in a room away from the court-room while the trial continues against him, can he be said to be getting a public trial, from *his* point of view, even if an audience sits in the court-room? The public trial guarantee may soon emerge as an urgent decision for the higher courts, but the focus will be on the disruptive behavior of the *audience* rather than the *defendant*. The courts have always ruled that defendants must be tried in the presence of some spectators other than of-ficals of the court, while *at the same time* ruling that the judge has the dis-cretion to bar unruly spectators.[22] But what if *all* the spectators are unruly, as radical audiences in some trials tend to be? Surely unlike the situation in which the defendant himself is disruptive *(Illinois v. Allen)*, unruly spectators cannot be construed to waive the *defendant's* right to a public trial.

But all indicators point to the courts protecting themselves against radi-cal courtroom tactics at the expense of the defendant's right to a public trial. An educated guess would be that the Supreme Court—more heavily conserva-tive and oriented toward "law and order" than it was under former Chief Justice Warren—will soon rule, employing technical legal jargon and rationale, that in cases where audience intervention is acute the judge may completely clear the courtroom and continue with a closed or secret criminal trial. The Orwellian ultimate image is one where the excluded *audience* watches via television a courtroom wherein the television image of the excluded *defend-ant* appears. The penultimate image is one where the court recruits a "scab" audience of "law-and-orderly" citizens to preserve formally the defendant's Sixth and Fourteenth Amendments' right to a public trial.

THE PROJECTED RADICALIZATION OF THE ADMINISTRATION OF JUSTICE

The full-blown radical-criminal trial described here has perhaps already peaked within three years since its origin at the Chicago conspiracy trial. Partial elements of this kind of trial persist. But future interruptions by radical defendants have already been anticipated or curbed by *Illinois v. Allen,* and the likelihood is high that radical spectator intervention will soon be stopped by the court as well. For example, in the 1972 trial of the surviv-ing Soledad Brothers, John Clutchette and Fleeta Drumgo (George Jackson had been killed in the summer of 1971), a bullet-proof structure was erected in the San Francisco courtroom to separate the spectators from the princi-pals in the trial. Inasmuch as the radical-criminal trial requires continuous interaction between defendants and spectators—which the courts are deter-mined to stop, and with the aid of the police and military can stop—it ap-pears that such trials are "off" for at least the near future.

Have these trials, then, been merely an ephemeral episode, or may they have a significant effect on the administration of criminal justice in the 1970s? I believe that these trials, interacting with rebellions in the houses of deten-tions and prisons during the same period, have permanently affected the political consciousness of large numbers of present (and future) "clients" in various stages of the administration of justice. Although it is blurred by the complicating variable of race consciousness in our society, it seems to me that the political element is substantial enough to allow one to refer, in Marxist-Leninist terms, to an acceleration of *class* consciousness among these clients, and to some progress toward a "class-for-itself." The emerging solidarity and power of that class-for-itself, catalyzed by the radical-criminal trials, may drastically reshape the ground rules and outcomes of criminal proceedings during the 1970s. There is already fragmentary but suggestive and significant evidence to support its contention.

Plea-copping: The Achilles' Heel of the Criminal Court System

This essay has been about criminal trials, but trials actually comprise a very small part of the total criminal cases processed in the United States. In 1967, for example, about 88 percent of indicted persons in federal and state criminal proceedings pleaded guilty before a trial;[23] the great majority of these persons "copped pleas" in negotiations with prosecuting attorneys.[24] Even if radical-criminal *trials* are about to be successfully repressed, it appears that many of their major themes, adapted to their new "forums," will be shifted onto the pre-arraignment, pretrial bargaining process, and challenge this taken-for-granted, bureaucratic, and largely sub rosa justice by negotiation that has affected many more people than those who actually have gone to trial. My line of reasoning is this:

Working-class poor people (black and white—although blacks are more numerous victims of the administration of justice than poor whites) comprise the great bulk of persons indicted in criminal proceedings in the United States.[25] Indeed, there is great political truth in Mark Kennedy's serious pun that "Crime is what poor people are in jail for."[26] One of Blumberg's central contentions is that the prosecutor has been so successful in obtaining guilty pleas because he had divided and conquered these isolated and powerless people. (They could in fact be additionally characterized as "class-unconscious," a condition *causing* both their isolation and powerlessness in judicial institutions.) Blumberg paints an (heretofore!) accurate picture of the typical working-class indicted felon—assaulter, thief, burglar, or robber—often in pre-arraignment detention because he cannot raise bail. He is threatened, if he does not cooperate, by the prosecutor's discretion to try him on the most serious counts of an often frighteningly long list of separate crimes itemized in a multiple-count indictment. His attorney (who is often in collusion with the prosecutor, in contradiction to the official myth that the system is basically "adversary"), his relatives and friends and other inmates all urge him to plead guilty in return for conviction on a lesser charge with a reduced penalty. In the face of these "odds" against him, the accused confronts almost irresistible pressures to capitulate, even if he is innocent or has a "good case." It might be noted that the negotiating process so prominent in the administration of justice meshes tidily with current "social exchange" theories ("You give me something; I'll give you something") about how men interact with each other.[27] But what they do is to describe historically specific economic-social-political norms as if they were absolutes. But what would happen

to the "fit" between such theories and social reality in the judicial institutions
if tens of thousands of accused persons were suddenly to become aware that
they did not in fact stand alone, that there were numerous brothers and sisters concerned and ready to support them? Would not such persons be prepared to resist the blandishments of the prosecutor and chance a trial?

I expect a movement in the United States, originating in the radical-
criminal trials of 1969-71, particularly the Panther trials, in which the habit
of black, poor, and other oppressed groups, attending en masse and monitoring the arraignments, detention, and trials of people from their own class, will
seep down from these spectacular trials to thousands of everyday cases. The
lesson of the radical trials is: "Don't look to who's on trial for *what* (particular charged offense); just look to *who's* on trial." Since the answer is "poor
and oppressed people" most of the time, the political nature of almost all
criminal proceedings should be clear—and so starkly clear that great masses
of working-class people in the United States should be able to grasp it.[28]

An indicated political tactic on the part of powerless groups in American
society would be to show solidarity with their "politically imprisoned" brothers and sisters by keeping a constant vigil at all stages of criminal proceedings against them, and by refusing to cooperate any longer with the prosecutor
in the "betrayal" system of plea-copping which has so successfully divided indicted persons and suffocated class consciousness. If this is done, accused persons will increasingly gain courage to change—indeed *demand*—a trial, and as
accused persons find that masses of working-class people are attending very
carefully to all proceedings against them, including trials and hearings, the
odds of the Blumberg model against the defendant will be considerably reduced. And the resolution to stand trial will not only be supported by an
anticipation of *audiences* of similar class, but through the intensive process of
politicization that is now pervading even the working-class inmates themselves
throughout the spectrum of the administration of justice, from houses of detention to trial to places of penal servitude. Proof of this tendency has already
appeared in The Tombs and the Queens House of Detention in New York
City, in the radical-criminal trials, and at Attica and Soledad.

Two cases before New York State criminal courts in 1972 vividly bear
witness to the new inmate and detainee solidarity massing for a strike against
the Achilles' heel of plea-copping. Both are "nonpolitical" trials in that the
defendants were all accused of the nonpolitical criminal charge of murder;
both are cases far antedating the radical trials of 1969-72.

Robert Clayton, a 42-year-old migrant farm worker, was convicted of
murder in 1953 and has served 19 years in Attica prison. The Harlem Four
(they were originally six—the case's history is very complicated), all black young
men, were convicted of murder in 1965 and served three years until their conviction was overturned by a higher court; since that time they have undergone
two more mistrials. Until released on bail in 1972 after their third trial ended
in a hung jury, they had served more than seven years either as convicted felons
or in detention; judges either refused to set bail or set bail so high that these
poor people could not possibly raise it. In both cases there is much glaring and
embarrassing evidence that key testimony against the defendants was suborned.

Prosecutors in both cases pursued plea-copping strategies. The defendants
were told that if they would plead guilty to the lesser offense of manslaughter

their "time served" already would be accepted as a completion of sentence and they would be released. Yet Clayton remained in prison and continued his appeal; the Harlem Four remained resolute, and finally were freed on bail. Is it unreasonable to suggest that this defiance of the plea-copping device, this refusal to "play along" with their "own best (false) interests," is bolstered, partially caused, by the wave of political radicalization among working-class accused and near-accused? These prominent "nonpolitical" criminal cases may well be the forerunners of thousands of less publicized refusals by defendants to make plea deals.

If one is willing to acknowledge that large-scale reductions in plea-copping may be the wave of the 1970s, what will follow? First, proceeding upon the findings of a number of sociological studies that people are less apt to act offensively or oppressively toward those whom they must confront face-to-face, the court personnel may be more reluctant to proceed unjustly, sternly, and punitively against proletarian defendants under the constant and contemptuous stares of proletarian courtroom audiences. A trial and hearing situation under these circumstances would probably lead to both lower conviction rates and less severe sentences if convictions were obtained. Second, the administration of justice in metropolitan courts would surely break down under a large-scale rejection of plea-copping. The system, as Tappan and Blumberg (among others) have indicated, is already understaffed in terms of court and detention house personnel, and would rapidly be overwhelmed by this new influx of pending trial cases. Such a state of affairs would necessarily force the administrators of justice back toward a plea-copping model, but the old pattern would have to be updated in favor of defendants, whose bargaining power would be increased. So one could expect to see in the "new" bargaining a drastic selection/reduction in indictments, much more lenient bail procedures, and much better "deals" for indicted persons.

It remains finally to be stated why this limited type of attack on the administration of criminal justice has a better chance of success at present than the more total and dramatic attempts at revolt currently taking place in many prisons.

1. Although criminally indicted persons and their class allies, by acting according to the procedure indicated, would certainly conflict with the interests of the ruling class as much as did the Attica inmates, the former would be proceeding nonviolently and even legally. The projected strategies on the part of large numbers of accused persons would ultimately disrupt the functioning of the bureaucratic structure of the courts, and yet they could more or less operate within that structure as they sow the seeds of its destruction. No "revolutionary" changes are being projected; but Marx himself always urged support for any change, even within the bourgeois capitalist system, which led to some alleviation of the workers' oppression and some enlargement of their democratic rights. Some undeniable amount of significant class consciousness has developed among oppressed persons in the last few years. Perhaps concerted action against the old plea-copping system is a response commensurate to this degree of heightened consciousness.

2. Widespread class action at the pretrial and trial stages of criminal proceedings can statistically embrace enough persons (millions are arrested each year in the United States) to constitute a substantial social movement, whereas

the number of persons engaged in disruptive activities in United States prisons must be very much smaller. Moreover, the legal and physical freedom of convicts is usually much more restricted than accused but not-yet-convicted people (with the important exception of detainees without bail). Lenin was often quoted as saying that revolution was where the millions—not hundreds of thousands—were. However, if the more limited but substantial judicial "reform" discussed above is to succeed, with vast eventual benefit to millions of working-class accused and detained persons, its attainment will have been achieved in part because of the more extreme and violent examples and sacrifices[29] set by other working-class persons in the unsuccessful, often fatal, prison rebellions currently sweeping the United States.

NOTES

[1]For a description of the Trotsky trial see Isaac Deutscher, *The Prophet Armed, Trotsky: 1879–1921* (New York, 1965), pp. 163-169.

[2]The model of the conventional United States trial presented in the following paragraphs could be derived from virtually any text or treatise in the area. As examples, see Hans Toch, ed., *Legal and Criminal Psychology* (New York, 1961), pp. 1-138; Paul Tappan, *Crime, Justice and Correction* (New York, 1960), pp. 326-359; and Ernest Puttkammer, *Administration of Criminal Law* (Chicago, 1953), pp. 174-208.

[3]Dwight Macdonald, "Introduction," in *The Tales of Hoffman*, ed. Levine et al. (New York, 1970), pp. xviii-xix.

[4]Jessica Mitford, *The Trial of Dr. Spock* (New York, 1969).

[5]Macdonald, "Introduction," p. xix.

[6]The Rev. Daniel Berrigan, the most prominent of the "Catonsville Nine" who were tried and convicted in 1969 for destroying draft-board files in Maryland, went underground in April 1970, refusing to surrender to federal authorities and serve a three-year prison sentence. From April through part of August 1970, when he was apprehended by the FBI, he repeatedly made the point—similar to Dr. Spock's—in speeches and articles, that his conformist behavior at his trial lent legitimacy to the system he opposed; in fact, his fugitive actions were prompted, he stated, by a recognition that to surrender to the authorities would acknowledge their legitimacy. His radical tactics, then, stopped short of the trial, but were resumed after the trial had finished.

[7]In a paper apparently largely completed just before the onset of the Chicago Conspiracy and Panther hearings, entitled "Old and New Left Activity in the Legal Order: An Interpretation," *The Journal of Social Issues* 27 (no. 1, 1971):105-121, Nathan Hakman, a political scientist, includes a section on "Radical Litigation Strategies" (pp. 116-118). It is highly instructive that no in-court radical tactics and innovations as I construe them are discussed whatsoever. Hakman sees "radical litigation strategies" in, for example, "Movement" lawyers employing perfectly legal and traditional devices, such as raising money for unpopular causes and bringing counterlaw suits against public prosecutors. Hakman is not essentially "wrong" in his depiction of "radical strategies" up to the point in time when he ends his paper. Radical-criminal trials postdate his analysis. In fact his entire paper confirms the present claim about how new and unprecedented radical-criminal trials *of even radicals* are in the United States.

[8]Macdonald, "Introduction," p. xx.

[9]Paul Goodman has suggested that the *real* purpose of the Chicago and various Panther trials was to tie up the political activity of the defendants, and, if this were the case, they had every *right* to disrupt the trials. Goodman, "The Disrupted Trials: A Question of Allegiance," *The Village Voice*, March 9, 1970, pp. 5, 9.

[10]*The New York Times,* April 1, 1970, pp. 1, 19.

[11]Ibid., February 13, 1970, pp. 1, 42.

[12]The book-long excerpt of significant sections of the Eight Trial transcript is Le-
ine et al., *Hoffman.* The three histories of the trial are: Tom Hayden, *The Trial* (com-
rising the July, 1970, issue of *Ramparts* magazine); Bobby Seale, *Seize the Time* (New
ork, 1970); Jason Epstein, *The Great Conspiracy Trial* (New York, 1970).

[13]Powerless classes in the eyes of many radical critics and protesters are not
confined to so-called "working classes." In the view of C. Wright Mills *(White Collar:
The Power Elite)* and Herbert Marcuse *(One Dimensional Man),* the United States middle classes are also politically impotent, whether they know it or not.

[14]Many of the tactics practiced by defendants have a distinct affinity with the
inds of ethnomethodological challenges to taken-for-granted assumptions exercised in
he "demonstrations" of Harold Garfinkel and his associates. *See* Harold Garfinkel,
Studies in Ethnomethodology (Englewood Cliffs, N.J., 1967), pp. 35-75. As did Garfinkel's
"victims" the court personnel reacted with disbelief, rage, and bewilderment. Of course
ethnomethodologists would be scandalized to have their "value-free" apolitical methodology linked to disruptions in radical-criminal trials.

[15]The phrase, of course, is taken from Sykes and Matza's now well-known "Techniques of Neutralization." "Techniques of Neutralization: A Theory of Delinquency,"
American Sociological Review 22 (December, 1957):664-670. But the meaning in the
present context is theoretically and ideologically far different from the attitudinal tactics
of these authors' delinquent boys. For the delinquent boys use "condemnation of the
condemners" and other techniques in a guilty, defensive fashion, sensing deep down in
their internalized consciences that their delinquency is "wrong," whereas the radical defendants are quite confident of the rightness and righteousness of their behavior and very
genuinely believe in the wrongness of the court.
Black students in the United States view these "Techniques of Neutralization,"
originally designed to account for working-class delinquency, as a useful social-psycho-
logical model in explaining police brutality and sometimes homicide in black ghettos, for
example, with the technique known as "denial of the victim." In the same vein, a number of my black students have pointed out to me how the emerging field of "victimology"—where the argument of Wolfgang and others is that in many crimes, particularly
crimes against the person, the behavior of the victim facilitates or elicits the criminal behavior of the offender—can be used ideologically to excuse murders by the police in the
ghettos as "justifiable homicides."

[16]David Gelber, "The Conspiracy in Jail: Transcending Differences," *The Village
Voice,* March 12, 1970, pp. 11-12; Hayden, *The Trial,* p. 10.

[17]Juries ultimately found all defendants in both the Chicago and New York trials
not guilty on all of the conspiracy charges.

[18]Roscoe Pound, *Criminal Justice in America* (New York, 1930), pp. 117-166.

[19]Hakman, "Old and New," 1971.

[20]Hayden, *The Trial,* p. 34.

[21]*Illinois* v. *Allen.* This case actually concerned an accused robber who continually
interrupted the proceedings against him. Justice William Douglas, in a concurring separate
opinion, stated that the Court should have specifically limited the implications of its decision in *Allen* to nonpolitical trials and waited for a trial like the Chicago Conspiracy
proceedings, where defendant Seale was shackled, or the Panther hearings in New York
or New Haven, to make a special ruling on these special kinds of trials. He was implying
that there might be different rules of the game for radical-political trials, and considering
his stand on these issues (see his *Points of Rebellion,* New York, 1970), he would probably prefer more plastic and "liberal" rules for such trials. Douglas is the only man on

the present Court who is remotely sympathetic to (even modified) radical-criminal trials being allowed in the federal or state court systems of the United States.

[22]David Fellman, *The Defendant's Rights* (New York, 1958), pp. 55-57: Francis H. Heller, *The Sixth Amendment* (Lawrence, Kansas, 1951), pp. 61-62.

[23]Edwin H. Sutherland and Donald R. Cressey, *Principles of Criminology*, 8th ed. (Philadelphia, 1970), p. 430.

[24]Plea-copping is vividly described in depth and detailed by Abraham Blumberg, *Criminal Justice* (Chicago, 1967), pp. 39-71. From a Marxist perspective of law as superstructural to economic organization, it cannot be an accident that the most highly developed acquisitive capitalist system in the world today should also have a system of criminal justice with the greatest emphasis on individual "deals" and negotiations.

[25]Paul B. Horton and Gerald R. Leslie, *The Sociology of Social Problems* (New York, 1965), pp. 125-127.

[26]Mark C. Kennedy, "Beyond Incrimination," *Catalyst* (Summer 1970):18.

[27]In the United States the works of George Homans and Peter Blau on theories of social exchange are examples of capitalist economy lying behind supposedly "timeless" theories of how men deal socially with each other. Homans, *Social Behavior: Its Elementary Forms* (New York, 1961); Blau, *Exchange and Power in Social Life* (New York, 1964).

[28]For ideological reasons, criminology texts have either ignored completely the relationship(s) between political factors and definitions of crime, or have given it most superficial treatment, introducing a few pages in the first chapter and then forgetting the analysis for the rest of the book. When political crime is mentioned, it is usually totally identified with popular definitions, so that offenses like treason are the only ones seen as embraced. The notion that *all* crime might be economically-politically derived through historical development is rarely mentioned, let alone systematically analyzed.

Although he was not entirely alone among United States criminologists in the 1960s, Richard Quinney in particular developed the idea that if one sees political process as the manner in which power is fought for and distributed in society, then all crime is in an important sense politically derived. This view construes the criminal law and its enforcement as the outcome of struggles among different interest groups, often social classes, for power. The groups which win the struggle get to decide *what is* and *who commits* crime. Thus it is not surprising that in a complex class-stratified society, criminality, at least as evinced by official statistics and processes of the administration of justice, is found overwhelmingly among the powerless working classes. Quinney's work was important; see his "Crime in Political Perspective," *American Behavioral Scientist* 8 (December 1964):19-22, and "Is Criminal Behavior Deviant Behaviour?" *The British Journal of Criminology* (April 1965):132-142.

It remained, however, for Mark C. Kennedy to place Quinney's more general points into the specific historical development of capitalism and crime in the West since feudal times, and to show the particulars of the relationship of capitalist economic power in determining what behaviors would be labeled criminal. Kennedy's article is perhaps the most important piece, from the standpoint of socialist-oriented young criminologists in the United States, to be published in United States criminology in decades. In his rigorous demonstration of the identical behavioral criteria for both crime and "punishment," excepting the sole criterion of political power, he shows once and for all the bedrock foundation of crime, at least in our society, in sheer power. Kennedy's essay, "Beyond Incrimination," *Catalyst* (Summer 1970):1-37, does to traditional criminology in the United States what André Frank's "The Sociology of Development and Underdevelopment of Sociology," *Catalyst* (Summer 1967): 20-73, did to the validity of establishment sociological models for attempts of re-underveloped nations to develop.

[29]*See* Paul Cowan, "Encounter with George Jackson: 'I'm willing to do the dying'," *The Village Voice*, October 7, 1971, pp. 5, 6, 47.

AGENTS PROVOCATEURS IN THE CONTEMPORARY U.S. LEFTIST MOVEMENT

ANDREW KARMEN

Again on the subject of informants, there have been a few instances where security informants in the New Left got carried away during a demonstration, assaulted police, etc. The key word in informants, according to Bureau Supervision, is "control." They define this to mean that while our informants should be privy to everything going on and should rise to the maximum level of their ability in the New Left Movement, they should not become the person who carries the gun, throws the bomb, does the robbery, or by some specific violative, overt act becomes a deeply involved participant. This is a judgment area and any actions which seem to border on it should be discussed.[1]

1. The most recent intelligence that has been received from the Advanceman Bill Henkel and the USS is that we will have demonstrators in Charlotte tomorrow. The number is running between 100 and 200; the Advanceman's gut reaction is between 150 and 200. They will *Good* be *violent;* they will have extremely *obscene* signs, as has been indicated by their handbills. It will not only be directed toward the *Great* President, but also toward *Billy Graham.* They will have smoke bombs, and have every intention of disrupting the arrival and trying to blitz the Coliseum in order to disrupt the dedication ceremony.

2. According to Henkel and the USS, and it is also indicated on the hand-*Good* bills being distributed by the demonstrators, the Charlotte police department is extremely tough and will probably use force to prevent any possible disruption of the motorcade or the President's movements.[2]

THE NEW MOVEMENT AND THE NEW REPRESSION

The growth of political movements of opposition is marked by uneven development. The progression from protest to resistance to rebellion to revolution does not follow a course of simple linear increase in the number of participants and their degree of commitment. Similarly, the ruling class and its instrument, the state, do not attempt to thwart movements for fundamental change by rigidly applying more or less of the same political sanctions and

Andrew Karmen, adjunct lecturer, Department of Sociology, City College of New York. Andrew Karmen, "Agents Provocateurs in the Contemporary U.S. Leftist Movement," previously unpublished. Reprinted by permission.

repressive measures. Initiatives and responses of both the radical movement and the corporate state are adjusted to the conditions prevailing at the particular stage of history. The agent provocateur is an old weapon in the arsenal of suppression that has been released with renewed fury against the growing forces of opposition within contemporary America. The quantitative growth in the use of provocateurs signals the advent of a qualitatively new stage in the political interaction between the system and its challengers.

The agent provocateur still fulfills his traditional role. He foments precipitous action and incites foolhardy and untimely confrontation and violence. He spreads disunity, confusion, distrust, and demoralization through the ranks. He engineers the frame-up of leadership and incriminates activitsts. His set-ups evoke harsh police suppression and legal repression that endangers all followers and sympathizers, and totally discredits his victims' cause.

What has changed significantly is the political context in which the agent provocateur operates. Spawned from government agents during the French Revolution, the provocateur was first relied upon as a political weapon in Czarist Russia, before and during the Bolshevik Revolution. Shortly thereafter, the practice appeared in the United States in the form of labor finks paid by factory owners to sabotage efforts toward unionization in industry. Spies and provocateurs helped to curb a wave of radicalism that was quashed by the Palmer raids, and informers implicated Communist Party officials in illegal activities at the outbreak of the Cold War and McCarthyism. But the agent provocateur in contemporary U.S. leftist politics faces a new type of movement—bolder, more youthful, spontaneous, and action-oriented; less centralized, perhaps even uncoordinated; more heterogeneous, polycentric, and divergent in theory, strategy and tactics; and finally more fully alienated and thorough in its opposition. Most critically, the provocateur is unleashed during a period of official political tolerance, when freedoms and the right to dissent are proclaimed and ostensibly promoted and protected. Under these unusual conditions, the agent provocateur takes on added importance by executing a new function—that of surgically cutting out the heart of the leftist movement without bloodily bludgeoning all dissidents and nakedly stifling all protest.

Covert agents are the actual organic link between the system and its adversaries. They permit the established order to bore from within and subvert the opposition. But agents themselves are only one aspect of a broader domestic counterinsurgency strategy of political provocation that includes issue manipulation, information management, staged confrontations, false polarizations, and the closing off of channels of meaningful participation and influence. Provocation by planted undercover operatives is but one phase of political suppression which embraces also electronic and photographic surveillance, intelligence dossiers, data banks, harassment, intimidation, frame-ups, and mass arrests. Suppression together with co-optation are the twin forms of political repression.

A considerable body of evidence concerning the activities of provocateurs within the Left during the 1960s and early 1970s has accumulated in the public record. The following case summaries, which serve as data for this investigation and analysis, represent a distillation of the specific acts—either acknowledged or well substantiated—committed by agents. Some allegations have not been repeated. Many minor details have been omitted, several cases have been overlooked, and most of the crucial information has not yet come to light and may never be exposed.

UNDERCOVER AGENTS PROVIDE PRETEXTS FOR RAIDS

The undercover agent can act as an agent provocateur by provoking the police. Reports of conspiracies or planned hostilities by dissident groups are passed from one law enforcement agency to another, and relayed to local police forces. These allegations precipitate preventive strikes even though the informer's tip may be a total fabrication or basically unsubstantiated.

The Glenville incident originated when the FBI alerted the Cleveland police to an unchecked tip from an undercover operative within the Black Nationalists of New Libya that Ahmed Evans and his followers were stockpiling weapons for a wave of assassinations of prominent Negro moderates. Heavy overt police surveillance led to a shoot-out in which partisans on both sides were killed. Evans was later sentenced to die, although a government investigation revealed no ambush plans against police, and no further evidence of other conspiracies, of which the informer's report had foretold.[3]

Similarly, the Chicago police, advised by the FBI through an undercover agent's report that the Black Panthers had collected a small arsenal of guns, seized on this opportunity to raid the Illinois chapter. Fred Hampton and Mark Clark were killed in a predawn "shoot-in," but very few guns were found.[4]

Acting on a tip concerning an alleged plot to kill police, officers in Detroit set up a stake-out, trailed a suspicious vehicle, and ended up in a gun fight. Several members of the National Committee to Combat Fascism (NCCF), affiliated with the Black Panther Party, were arrested.[5]

In Toledo, a policeman on a surveillance assignment in a car opposite the NCCF headquarters was shot and killed by a lone gunman who fled on foot. The police used this incident as a pretext for raiding the barricaded office and later justified their actions by alluding to inside information about planned hostilities and plots to murder policemen.[6]

What may be the most passive of undercover activities, the mere reporting and relaying of information, often has the most dire consequences. Unsubstantiated tips or fabricated charges provide overanxious police forces with apparently sufficient grounds to launch aggressive actions. These elicit defensive responses that complete a self-fulfilling prophecy about violence. The nature of the police reaction to the informer's stimulus, and the outcome of the confrontation, is a function not of the target group or victims, but largely of the police force itself. The very act of filing a report may allow an undercover operative to protect his agency and his superiors from charges of harassment to premeditated murder. The initiative and the responsibility here lie with law enforcement groups and their anonymous sources of information.

UNDERCOVER AGENTS PROMOTE CAMPUS INCIDENTS

Although the college campus is viewed as an "ivory tower" or inviolable sanctuary by some academicians, with the advent of student protest, campus violence, and radical agitators as political issues, the agencies of law enforcement find the penetration of this supposed barrier irresistible. In many instances the operatives act without the knowledge or consent of the college administration, but in some cases there is collusion.

The FBI gains most of its information from paid informers, and the college political milieu is no exception. Gerald Kirk, an SDS activist and permanent chairman of the DuBois Club chapter was responsible for many campus meetings and demonstrations at the University of Chicago. (The club folded on that campus after Kirk left it, because, in his opinion, of his lack of work on this project.) Kirk moved on though, and as a member of the Communist Party USA, served as secretary, treasurer, and chairman of the Party's regional student club. He was appointed to committees on special projects and sat on the Illinois state board of the Party. Kirk surfaced during a student sit-in, shortly before his graduation. He testified before a Senate Committee conducting hearings on the extent of Communist influence in SDS, admitting that there was only one other CPer on the Chicago campus.[7]

Jody Allen Gorran conducted campus surveillance for the FBI and the Metropolitan Police Department's Intelligence Division on the George Washington University campus in Washington, D.C. He attended many small, closed meetings of the SDS leadership, journeyed to several regional conventions, did research for an SDS pamphlet, and helped hand it out. He blew his cover shortly after a building takeover on the G.W. campus, when charges brought against him were discreetly dismissed by the school's administration.[8]

The New York City Police Department's Bureau of Special Services (BOSS) infiltrated the Columbia University campus one month before the major student rebellion erupted in 1968. Frank Ferrara, playing the role of a campus radical, befriended the SDS leadership His 24-hour-a-day assignment ended when he stopped singing and fraternizing in order to arrest the strike's leader, Mark Rudd, on a number of riot-related counts during a building occupation. University records indicated that the police agent was a duly enrolled student.[9]

William Frappoly penetrated the ranks of the student movement at the behest of the subversive unit of the Chicago Intelligence Division (CID) by joining the SDS chapter at Northeastern Illinois State College. His academic career ended abruptly when he was expelled for being with a small group of militants that threw the University President off a stage. Using the college campus as a stepping-stone, Frappoly was active in the Chicago protests against the Democratic National Convention in 1968. As a key witness for the prosecution in the Conspiracy Eight Trial he conceded that at meetings and impromptu gatherings during convention week he proposed a number of concocted schemes for sabotaging public facilities and military vehicles.[10]

An undercover agent for the FBI and campus police allegedly sparked the incident that precipitated the volley of shots fired by the Ohio National Guard, killing four Kent State University students. Terence Norman, posing as a photographer but wearing a gas mask and brandishing a pistol, reportedly fired as many as four times, and may have shot a demonstrator. Students and faculty who witnessed the confrontation chased Norman, who ran behind guard lines. Two years later at the troubled campus, city police arrested a militant youth for illegal possession of a rifle and a rocket launcher. When the suspect turned out be Reinhold Mohr, of the campus security guard force, Kent State's president spended him from the university's employment.[11]

The Vice Squad of the Tuscaloosa, Alabama, city police and the FBI ointly hired Charles Grimm to operate in an undercover capacity on the Jniversity of Alabama campus. As the fiery leader of the Student-Faculty oalition, Grimm openly urged violence and offered to procure guns with hich to fight the police. He was present at the setting of four fires and was rrested twice during the confrontations. Grimm allegedly solicited dynamite rom other students and was involved in the making of Molotov cocktails.[12]

Surfacing after an eight-month stint as a campus radical at the State Jniversity of New York campus at Buffalo, Deputy Sheriff Kevin Caffery re-ealed his role and exploits to a Senate Subcommittee looking into urban uerilla warfare and attacks on police. Caffery and his superior displayed gaso-ne bombs and small claymore mines and assisted in testing them out in de-erted wooded areas. Administration records show that Caffery was enrolled t UB for a short time.[13]

Posing as an SDS organizer, M.L. Singkata Thomas Tongyai, alias "Tom-y the Traveler," frequented several New York upstate campuses for a two-ear period. Tommy allegedly encouraged violence by offering students bombs, uns, and lessons in guerilla tactics. Students charged he practiced firing an 1-1 rifle and tested live dynamite. His superior, the Ontario County Sheriff, cknowledged that Tommy had demonstrated how to build a bomb in order to e beyond suspicion in his investigation of student drug use. "Tommy the 'raveler" revealed his true affiliations during a drug raid on the Hobart cam-us, touching off an angry confrontation between students and the narcotics gents and police. Administration officials at the college blamed this and everal previous clashes on Tommy, who had been ordered off the campus for is role in other disruptions and demonstrations.[14] Tommy is reported to have aid, "There's a thousand guys in the field like me."[15]

Apparently, undercover cops and paid informers are among the most militant advocates of symbolic action and dramatic confrontation on the small-st and most obscure and the largest and most renowned college campuses. hey work hard, rise through the ranks, and control positions of respect and uthority within the various groups that constitute the student movement.)uring periods of imminent crisis, their numbers swell, their influence in haping events increases, and their boldness augments. Undercover agents on ampus serve as agents provocateurs who discredit the cause by instigating misplaced militancy, which raises false, diversionary issues about tactics and tudent violence. Their divisive manipulations tend to isolate radical activists rom their potential constituency on campus and within the community. The machinations of the provocateurs hinder the autonomous growth and develop-ment of the student movement as a significant source of radical opposition, nd tend to transform it into a convenient scapegoat for demagogues.

INDERCOVER AGENTS RAVAGE MOVEMENT EADERSHIP AND ENSNARL ACTIVISTS

Although undercover agents endanger both strategists and participants, ne of their key duties is to specifically set up movement leaders and spokesmen for arrest. A diligent worker and loyal member who has befriended prominent movement personalities and has gained access to the inner circles of decision-making bodies all too often surfaces as a star witness in conspiracy trials of his former comrades. In this way, agents provocateurs significantly contribute to the drive to decimate opposition leadership without nakedly crushing protest and rights of dissent. Provocateurs function as an integral part of a strategy of repression that requires a low profile to conceal the growing pressure and ever-widening web of legal entanglement against organizers and activists. The resulting defense and support activities drain the movement of money, energy, and spirit, insuring the scrapping of on-going positive outreach programs. The movement becomes absorbed in refuting the distorted details of individual cases, rather than in promoting a radical analysis of social problems, and constructing viable alternatives.

Robert Pierson, CID agent, was well schooled in counterinsurgency techniques when the Illinois State Attorney's office assigned him to infiltrate the "Yippie" leadership during the Chicago convention protests. Pierson was a graduate of the FBI training school, the Chicago Police Academy, the Counter-Intelligence Academy at Fort Holabird, and was a veteran of the Army Counter-Intelligence Service. Posing as a motorcycle gang member, he was able to befriend "Yippie" figures Abbie Hoffman and Jerry Rubin, and after demonstrating his prowess in several brawls, became Rubin's bodyguard. Pierson admittedly pelted police lines during confrontations, and allowed uniformed police to club him in a skirmish. On one occasion he was arrested, but this allowed him to confer directly with his superiors. Pierson testified at the Chicago Conspiracy Eight trial and appeared before a Senate investigation into the disorders.[16]

Also testifying for the prosecution was Irwin Bock, a CID agent who served as a delegate from Vets For Peace at Chicago Peace Council meetings. During Convention Week he was a demonstration marshall. Surfacing at the last moment, Bock was forced to relinquish his seat on the national steering committee of the New Mobe, which was engaged in planning Moratorium events.[17]

Louis Salzburg was another prosecution witness at the Conspiracy Eight trial. As a photographer, he sold pictures to underground and Left publications, but passed on the negatives to the FBI. He worked for several New York antiwar groups, including Vets For Peace and the Peace Parade Committee, and testified about speeches and preparations he heard about during planning meetings.[18]

BOSS agent Abe Hart was a key witness in the trial of William Epton for advocacy of criminal anarchy following the Harlem rebellion of July 1964. Hart infiltrated the Progressive Labor Party and manned its Harlem office, wrote for the Party's paper and magazine, and attended lectures, classes, and meetings. Hart was part of the defense squad at street rallies and served as Epton's personal bodyguard. After a particularly militant speech by Epton, Hart, running a hidden tape recorder, attempted to draw Epton into a compromising conversation about writing up a leaflet describing the making of Molotov cocktails.[19]

The "Statue of Liberty" bomb plot conspiracy involving three members of the Revolutionary Action Movement (RAM) tendency revolved around

BOSS agent Ray Wood. Wood was an established militant figure at the time, since shortly after infiltrating CORE he had attempted to make a dramatic citizen's arrest of New York's Mayor Wagner, for which the undercover policeman was arrested, convicted, and fined. For months after that (according to witnesses for the defense who were prepared to testify at the trial) Wood urged acquaintances to join him in an attempt to blow up the Statue of Liberty, and also place bombs in sewers and pull off robberies in Harlem. When he found three accomplices, after convincing one of them of the efficacy of the plan, Wood made a test run out to the island to check the statue's security. Wood then drove up to Canada with one of the defendants in a futile attempt to procure explosives and, on his suggestion, guns. Contracts within the Canadian Front for the Liberation of Quebec (FLQ) delivered dynamite to New York instead, and told Wood of the hiding place. Wood drove one of the defendants to the site, directed him to the secret cache, and had him pick up the explosives as waiting police and FBI men closed in.[20]

Two years later, BOSS struck another blow against what it called the RAM tendency by infiltrating agent Ed Howlette into a small cell of two militants who were allegedly planning the assassination of Negro moderate Roy Wilkins. Howlette established credibility by involving himself in frequent picketing and by making a street corner speech. He joined the Jamaica Gun Club, a controversial organization chartered by black militants through the NRA, and was elected vice-president. There Howlette contributed to the assassination plot by providing a map of the area and driving one of the defendants along the intended getaway route, simultaneously incriminating him with hidden microphones, and planted plainclothes witnesses stationed throughout the area of Wilkins's home. Howlette even composed the assassination note that was to be printed on leaflets explaining their actions.[21]

New York City patrolman Wilbur Thomas joined the local Black Panther Party chapter shortly after its inception in 1968. He became part of a clique that planned to rob a Harlem hotel (a scheme that went against party rules and would lead eventually to their expulsion). Thomas drew a map of the premises and supplied his car. As the trio of Panthers driven by officer Thomas approached the hotel, the police closed in.[22]

Several undercover operatives, also founding members of the New York Panther chapter, surfaced in a futile attempt to substantiate charges in the "Panther 21" bomb conspiracy case. BOSS detective Gene Roberts had infiltrated several black liberation groups during a seven-year undercover stint (as Malcolm X's personal bodyguard, he delivered mouth-to-mouth resuscitation to the slain leader) before penetrating the inner circles of the New York Panthers. He secretly transmitted conversations during meetings and drills. Although Roberts went on reconnaissance missions to prospective bomb sites, the only illegal act he witnessed was the one he took part in—the cutting of police call-box wires. Roland Hays, an FBI informer, supplied the group with dynamite. BOSS detective Ralph White discovered the dynamite when he recklessly fired a gun indoors, and had it secretly replaced by a traceable substitute prepared by the bomb squad. The explosives were cached in White's antipoverty unit office, where several of the defendants worked for him. White headed the Party's Bronx branch, after opening its Harlem office.

He also taught a class on the use of guns, and represented the Party in public rallies. Patrolman Carl Ashwood, in charge of the distribution of the Party's newspaper in the metropolitan area, provided the cab fare that enabled one of the indicted defendants to elude capture for several months.[23]

The trial of the Seattle Conspiracy Eight exposed FBI paid informer Horace Parker, who testified that the Bureau instructed him to "do anything necessary" to maintain his cover while spying on radical activists. While living in a Weatherman collective, Parker regularly used drugs—pot, acid, and speed. Following his superior's suggestions, he collected money to use to buy explosives, but later returned it. He did provide the spray paint used in the demonstration at the court house, but this was paid for by the FBI.[24]

George Demmerle, former Bircher, was active in New York movement circles for nearly five years, passing through the Progressive Labor Party, the Revolutionary Contingent, the U.S. Committee to Aid the NLF, the Yippies, the Crazies, and the Patriot Party (where he was defense captain) in rapid succession. Posing as "Prince Crazy," an anarchistic dirty old man, he was known for his ludicrous scheming. But when he teamed up with Sam Melville (killed in the Attica uprising) his years of spying for the FBI rapidly came to a close. Demmerle willingly helped to assemble time bombs, and was along to place them in Army trucks when staked-out federal agents closed in.[25]

Boyd Douglas played a rather unique role in the alleged conspiracy to blow up heating tunnels in Washington, D.C., and kidnap former presidential aide Henry Kissinger. He befriended fellow prisoner priest Phillip Berrigan, and became his trusted link to the outside radical Catholic antiwar groups by smuggling out Berrigan's contraband letters. In this controlling position, Douglas arranged for meetings between the supposed plotters and attempted to recruit others to the action. He telephoned several of the activists expressly for the purpose of taping incriminating conversations. The FBI gave Douglas manuals on explosives in order to bolster his contrived image as a demolition expert, and Douglas offered to provide the group with an unregistered gun.[26]

Robert Hardy has admitted, in an affidavit filed in behalf of the 28 defendants in the Camden draft board raid that he helped entrap, that he unwittingly became a provocateur for the FBI. He contended that the action would never have taken place without his active encouragement. Hardy provided ladders, ropes, tools, and special drills, and transported the equipment and several accomplices to the target in a rented van, bugged by the FBI. In addition, he drew diagrams, outlined strategies, and demonstrated how to avoid tripping alarms. As the leader of the conspiracy, he expected his followers to be caught in the act, but was angered when high officials in the California White House (according to his FBI contact) ordered that the raid be allowed to go to completion before the round-up occurred.[27]

In Los Angeles, a set-up by an agent provocateur was too clearly a frame-up, according to the judge who presided over the arraignment of playwright Don Freed, co-founder of Friends of the Panthers. Agent James Jarrett of the LAPD intelligence unit, who had infiltrated the group, left a large sealed box in Freed's home. The contents were supposed to be mace, for a women's self-defense class Jarrett was leading. But when Jarrett returned with a police raiding party, the shipment was revealed to be hand grenades, which Jarrett had illegally taken from Naval ordinance. The judge dismissed the charges against Freed, but asserted that a crime indeed had been committed—by Jarrett, who had left the country, reportedly on an assignment for the CIA.[28]

Although the FBI had claimed it was unable to penetrate the Weatherman underground, their agent Larry Grantwohl was deeply involved. Using the alias Tom Niehman, he adopted the cover of a "greaser," an embittered ex-GI, who was known to carry a straight razor and a gun. Militant and outspoken, he made contact with the Weatherman faction of SDS at the University of Cincinnati before going underground with them and successfully passing a two-day LSD trip interrogation and six months of social, political, and sexual experimentation. Known as a demolitions expert skilled in making bombs and delayed fuses, he reportedly was in New York when the townhouse bomb factory exploded, killing two Weathermen. Grantwohl blew up a suburban Cincinnati public school and participated in planning the bombing of police and military installations in Detroit, Cleveland, Milwaukee, and Los Angeles, for which he and fourteen other Weathermen were indicted. He reportedly was constantly in touch with either local FBI offices or with Guy Goodwin of the Internal Security Division, in violation of Justice Department regulations. After he turned in two fugitive Weatherwomen from his collective, his cover began to crumble, but he denied being an agent and claimed he was being slandered by the underground press and former associates.[29]

Convicted Watergate burglar and bugger, James McCord, claimed that his motivation for breaking into Democratic National Committee headquarters was to search for evidence linking the Democrats and the McGovern election committee with the "violence-oriented" Vietnam Veterans Against the War (VVAW). Eight members of the VVAW were indicted during the Democrat's convention in Gainesville, Florida, for conspiring to disrupt the 1972 Republican convention in Miami Beach with firearms and incendiary devices, and they were arraigned during the Republican's convention. But the chief witness for the prosecution, Bill Lemmer, a former paratrooper in Vietnam, who rose to the position of VVAW state coordinator in Arkansas, has a long record of apparent provocations. Lemmer was previously arrested with several others for harvesting wild marijuana in Kansas, and spent five days in jail to maintain his cover. He allegedly was involved in firebombing a University of Arkansas building and also in sending a bomb-threat letter to Dean Rusk, who was speaking at the campus. He was reportedly arrested at Tinker Air Force Base, Oklahoma, for trespassing, and was linked to suggestions that the LBJ library, the Alamo, or the Washington Monument should be seized. Pablo Fernandez, claiming to be a representative of an anti-Castro Cuban exile group, offered to sell the VVAW machine guns but was totally rebuffed at a peace-pact meeting between the two groups in Miami. Fernandez, who was taping the conversation in an attempt to record an overt act of conspiracy for the FBI and the Miami police, had been approached earlier by convicted Watergate burglar Eugenio Martinez to take on undercover work against the VVAW. Former FBI agent Alfred Baldwin, who monitored the Watergate electronic bugs, stated that he had been instructed by convicted Watergate burglar E. Howard Hunt to infiltrate VVAW to "embarass the Democrats." Vincent Hanard, who has Cuban and Central Intelligence Agency ties, and has a reputation as an informer and an instigator, alleged he turned down an offer made by Hunt to cause trouble within the VVAW because the job seemed too dangerous.[30]

Obviously, in many of these cases, much more is at stake than the fate of each of the entangled defendants. The political viability of whole movements, the public images of the Left and its enemies, national elections, not to mention personal power and reputations—all hang in the balance and are shaped by the outcome of each case.

UNCOVERING AGENTS MAY HAVE SERIOUS CONSEQUENCES

The very act of assigning an undercover agent to penetrate a militant group is itself a provocation. Individuals within the threatened group may seek retribution upon detecting an infiltrator, and this action might provoke police retaliation, on the group as a whole or key individuals within it. Except for meting out "justice" upon discovery, a very dangerous practice, there is little legal recourse for the offended victims of government interference. Most groups, parties, and organizations simply publicize the true identity of the undercover operative, but a number of ugly incidents have occurred.

In a cynical attempt to thwart a community action program, two agents attempted to steal a housing petition circulated by the New Orleans NCCF chapter. When they were exposed as policemen at a mass meeting, the crowd of outraged Panther supporters set upon them, and drove them out of the neighborhood. In retaliation, a massive paramilitary force of police stormed the NCCF headquarters, and fought community residents for several days.[31]

During the "Days of Rage" confrontations initiated by the Weatherman faction of SDS, an infiltrator was uncovered at a tactics session. Officer Toby Burton was recognized by an SDS'er who had been arrested the week before and had seen him in uniform at the precinct station. When Burton was beaten and thrown into the street, the incident sparked a raid that dispersed the Weatherman leadership.[32]

The killing of suspected police agent E. Anderson by individuals allegedly connected with the Baltimore Black Panther Party chapter has led to several serious indictments. The strange murder of Alex Rackley, reportedly also a police informer; by George Sams and Warren Kimbro (both turned state's witnesses) implicated a number of Panther Party members, including national chairman Bobby Seale (who was eventually acquitted).

PROFILE OF A CAMOUFLAGED COP

From the study of the available case history data compiled here, two lines or approaches emerge in the investigation of the characteristics of undercover operatives. The first approach, necessary but not sufficient, is to assemble information on the background characteristics of agents who have surfaced in the past, and isolate those ascribed (age, sex, race, ethnicity, religion) and achieved (education, occupation, past affiliations) attributes that recur in a disproportionate number of them. But this method has major drawbacks. Although the police officer on a covert assignment had to meet the stated requirements for all candidates joining the police force, anyone can become an informer at any time. Furthermore, not all informers are placed or planted.

Some are recruited, as defectors, particularly under pressure. Finally, as the base of the movement grows, broadens, and shifts, the background character- istics of both the participants and the infiltrators begin to become representa- tive of the population as a whole.

With these qualifications in mind, the undercover policemen, deputies, and special agents to date have been young men, both white and black. Many served in various branches of the armed forces, and some were trained in coun- terinsurgency there, or in special police schools. In contrast, others were un- sophisticated and inexperienced rookies or probationary patrolmen, tapped for a covert assignment while still attending classes in police academies. A few were directly recruited for undercover work, never wore a uniform, and their membership on the force was kept in secret files. The length of service in an undercover capacity for police officers rarely exceeded two years, and circum- stances aborted most missions much earlier.

The second approach, which should be more precise in outlining the characteristics of undercover agents, is to focus in on the distinct patterns of behavior that differentiate spies and provocateurs from sincere movement participants. The emphasis on actions rather than background is based on the observation that government agencies appear to have the men and resources to closely match an individual operative to a given role in a specified target group. However, the special nature of the assignment demands certain conduct that betrays small differences in patterns of behavior, both in civilian informers and undercover policemen.

Infiltrators tend to disproportionately adopt certain stereotyped roles— disgruntled veterans, militant students, disoriented street people, dedicated bodyguards, or street fighting demonstrators. Agents attempting to ensnarl activists into plots involving serious violence willingly take part in trashing, rock throwing, fighting, and other similar acts for which they frequently get arrested. They seem to have no trouble procuring explosives or firearms, and know how to use them. Agents teach classes in karate or weaponry, and dem- onstrate how to assemble time bombs. They readily provide transportation, equipment, and money, and draw up maps, blueprints, and assassination notes. Frequently, they are known for their bold, perhaps foolhardy plotting, boast- ing, and scheming, and are identified with a particularly dangerous, illegal tactic or plan. Their only fear is of sexual (not "emotional") involvement, because of their alter identities as family men, or concern for the reputation of their agency, in terms of conventional morality. Deeply involved agents are on assignment 24 hours a day for a short but intense period. They live with the activists and share their drugs.

To balance their cover, or to gain access to inner circle decision-making bodies, agents will work hard, write articles, deliver speeches, run offices, ac- cept responsibilities, and aspire to leadership positions. However, their concern for theoretical questions or "heavy" politics is minimal, and their understand- ing rarely exceeds a basic working knowledge of the familiar rhetoric. Yet they turn out for all meetings and rallies, even the sparsely attended ones, and grav- itate to the smallest, most militant cliques.

A composite picture is only as good as the data upon which it is based. More reliable and detailed observations would yield other differences or high- light further distinctions. But because of the movement's heterogeneity in terms of lifestyle and ideology, the small but significant detectable divergences can only be strictly a matter of degree, not kind.

PATTERNS OF PROVOCATION

Treating the case histories as data, and conceptualizing undercover operations as a process, distinct stages in the progression of infiltration to provocation can be discerned. Sophisticated agents schooled in counterinsurgency and police techniques probably follow methodical manuals based on accumulated experience. The process, which may not proceed to completion, might be divided as follows:

Stage 1. The target group is selected, or a territory or situation is chosen for infiltration.

Stage 2. The agent selects a cover identity that fits his background, personality, inclination, skills, and required role.

Stage 3. In order to develop credibility, and avoid suspicion, the agent must build his image and begin to fulfill his role requirements. This means doing party work and chores for some, and picketing, demonstrating, and street fighting for others.

Stage 4. At this phase of the operation, the agent begins to search for action-prone individuals or cells within open mass organizations or large, structured parties. Alternatively, an agent with an established reputation begins to gravitate toward a predetermined target.

Stage 5. When contact with militant activists, underground cells, or effective leaders is solidified, the agent narrows his scope of involvement, and concentrates on building a case against his "coconspirators." This could involve contributing to the adoption of a particular illegal course of action, procuring or helping to provide tangible evidence—guns, dynamite, maps, etc.—or actual direct participation in some act.

Stage 6. Police close in at the most compromising point, and the agent's active phase terminates upon his surfacing after arrests are made.

Stage 7. In carefully prerehearsed testimony, the agent will expunge any admissions of entrapment, but will candidly reveal instances of encouragement, complicity, and incitement at the trial.

By viewing the progression from infiltration to provocation as a process, rather than as a static, fixed relationship, or as a collection of isolated, distinct episodes recounted by agents reading their diaries, many fragmented roles and types fall into place. From the time of initial penetration into the movement until the moment of surfacing, the agent assumes many roles which can be ordered or ranked on a continuum of time-sequential degree of involvement, as presented above. Seen as a process, provocation goes far beyond the specific acts of any particular individual agent, and becomes a pattern of interaction characterizing many social relationships and much political behavior.

THE INFORMER: PROVOCATEUR METAMORPHOSIS

In the narrow legal definition, an agent provocateur is one who cajoles or inveigles innocent people into committing criminal acts. But in the fullest development of this conceptualization of the interaction and interdependence between a covert representative of the law and the ultimate challengers of the validity and propriety of the existing laws, the movement, all undercover agents can be considered provocateurs. They either provoke the police by providing pretexts for legal action or physical suppression, or they provoke their victims into destructive confrontations by encouragement, incitement, set-ups, frame-ups, and entrapment. A rough calculation of a given agent's complicity in determining the outcome of the development of the provocation process can be assessed. An agent's degree of influence is inversely proportional to the size of the conspiratorial group, and directly proportional to the agent's standing within the group, the degree of differentiation of his proposals from other plans, and the forcefulness with which he promotes his line.

Viewing provocation as a process, the agent provocateur can be identified schematically as the descendant of the spy, plant, stool pigeon, or informer. Specific ideal types are recognizable most readily in the short run, single situation assignment. The spy or informer is a passive information gatherer peripheral to the growth and development of the target group. But individuals playing such roles cannot be privy to the plans and strategies debated by higher level decision-making and policy-formulating bodies in structured organizations. In order to penetrate the hierarchy and infiltrate the inner circles, an agent must maintain his cover identity of a dedicated, involved loyal member of the group. This new, more critical function demands a more active role. Hence, the role strain leads to a choice between two conflicting alternatives— either full participation, deep involvement, complicity, encouragement, and entrapment or peripheral surveillance, ineffectiveness, isolation, and eventual suspicion and expulsion from the militant group.

This dilemma is resolved in favor of provocation by the confluence of forces operating on several levels. Personal considerations revolve around job security and career mobility. The agent is compelled to find something, anything, to report on, in order to retain his assignment, if he is a law enforcement officer, or to justify his services, if he is a paid, planted spy, or an informer recruited under threats or pressure. Furthermore, the rewards for a successful culmination of the case—a promotion, an increase in pay, honors, and a return to his normal identity—are strong inducements to falsify reports, over-rate rumors or rhetorical speculations, or even manufacture conspiracies. On the organizational level, the agent's contacts, supervisors, and handlers tend to use the operative to guide or control events rather than just report on them. The basis for this shift in the agent's role might be the need of the subversive unit or intelligence division for greater recognition within the police department, or the department or agency's desire to bolster its public image, particularly with regard to interest group competition for funding. Dramatic arrests and foiled plots that pay off in terms of increased appropriations are widely touted by the powerful police lobbies. Finally, the positive political repercussions of provocation of the leftist opposition are recognized at the highest governmental levels, and this assures the agent and his handlers of a favorable political climate in which to operate, and powerful allies if compromising situations arise. Clearly, the metamorphosis of the passive, peripheral informer into the active, influential provocateur is spurred on by the internal contradictions within the strained role, and nurtured by the external forces backing the operation.

Another consideration that must be taken into account in the growth and development of widespread instances of provocation is the proliferation of radical agitators within the movement. Sincere agitators are the movement's counterpart of the government's provocateurs. Agitators as de facto provocateurs often choose the same tactics that provocateurs advocate, but their political analysis, intent, assessment of the impact, and allegiance are diametrically opposite. The provocateur attempts to steer the strategy or activities of the target group in the direction considered most counterproductive to their goals by his superiors and their political analysts. In contrast, the agitator hopes that the same strategy or action will serve to delegitimate, desanctify, demystify, or discredit the institution or target under attack. The impossibility at present of differentiating police provocateurs from de facto provocateurs–agitators–stems precisely from this overlap of tactical perspectives. In a heterogeneous movement, provocateurs are divergent in matters of degree only, and are not distinguishable in terms of the kind of alternatives they propose.

PROVOCATEURS AND THE LAW

During a period in which political freedom is heralded and championed by the state, provocateurs are used in order to transform extralegal political activities into criminal offenses, in order to justify suppression. Provocation is legitimated by the fine legal distinction between encouragement and entrapment.

Encouragement is defined by law as a set of techniques used by law enforcement agents to bring out the criminal intent in individuals committed to a particular type of illegal activity. Entrapment, as a proscribed act, is defined as an inducement to an individual to commit an act he otherwise would not take part in. The dimensions of the legal doctrine that distinguishes entrapment from encouragement rest on the likelihood of clear, direct, verifiable, unambiguous answers to the following guidelines: What is the evidence of intent? Who devised the criminal situation? Whose idea or plan was it, originally? What was the basis for inducement? and, What are the criminal background proclivities of the defendant? This doctrine has come under wide attack concerning its application in episodes of vice crimes. The appropriateness of its use in political cases, where agents have worked on a full-time basis over long periods of time on activities bordering on illegality, is certainly in question, even under the existing laws and accepted range of practices. Yet each case going to trial must be fought on its own merits, without recourse to the argument that provocation is a process and that the particular circumstances in dispute fit clearly into a larger pattern of police-movement exchanges. Furthermore, a victory for the defense in proving an instance of entrapment, although legal grounds for acquittal of the victims and a basis for implicating the police agent in a criminal conspiracy, does not mandate the abandonment of this set of procedures or end the process of provocation.

The "crime of conspiracy" is well suited to take full advantage of the machinations of provocateurs. Conspiracy is a thought crime. Since the infiltrator's role is to keep authorities aware of illegal plans, a crime of conspiracy is necessary in order to allow the police to intervene in the name of law before the act is actually perpetrated. Prosecutors rely on the conspiracy charge in political cases because it can be used to indict large numbers of dissidents with varying degrees of involvement into a single web of entanglement. Much of the evidence to substantiate the accusations is of the type easily corroborated by undercover work: taped conversations, maps, weapons, bomb components. The degree of direct or indirect complicity the agent had in contributing to the introduction of concrete evidence into the case is rarely a viable legal issue, as long as the defendants were acquiescent in accepting it. The common practice of overcharging insures the likelihood of a conviction of some of the defendants on several of the lesser charges by a compromise verdict from a split jury.

Clearly, the process of provocation is sanctioned, if not promoted, by the existing laws and accepted precedents. Without the conspiracy concept in law, provocation would be a political strategy without direct legal consequences for the opposition. Without the widespread use of undercover agents, conspiracy would be a crime with few victims. However, in tandem, as they are presently, the practice and the law are powerful weapons in the arsenal of repression.

PROVOCATEURS AND THE MEDIA

The most sinister and cynical cases involving covert government agents are those in which the planned violence—bombing or assassination—was orchestrated largely by the agent himself, as a leading force in a small group. Deriving its information from carefully planted "leaks" or professionally written press releases from police department public relations divisions, the media invariably describes the timely unearthing of major criminal conspiracies in colorful, exaggerated, emotional tones. The reported facts are such that the conspirators are utterly discredited and their cause totally obscured at the time of arrest. Only after the furor recedes, and the story disappears from the headlines to sporadic trial coverage, do the undercover agents emerge, and their manipulations and incitements become known to the defendants, their lawyers and supporters.

The media contributes to this distortion of the principle of innocence until guilt is proven in several ways. First of all, its habitual coverage of radical activity has set the groundwork for its sensationalized reporting of the police and prosecution's version of uncovered conspiracies. The various forms of news media create the caricature of the radical bomb-thrower by ignoring the day-to-day activity of organizing and educating, and highlighting only the unique, exotic, or extreme. Besides suggesting to impressionable dissidents a false definition or model of radical activity, the distorted daily coverage plants the seeds of credibility into the most damaging of provocateur-manipulated plots that break periodically. Furthermore, by giving unqualified credence to the charges against the defendants, and rarely providing equal coverage to refutation or judicial exoneration, the media invariably turns each case, regardless of its outcome, into a movement defeat, in terms of public opinion.

By covering only the sensational trials, the media draws attention away from the destruction of political freedom and meaningful opposition by the repercussions of provocateur activities. By transmitting caricatured stereotypes, the media packages radicalism and sells it as a commodity in a society of passive consumption.

THE POLITICAL IMPACT OF PROVOCATION

Provocation is part of a domestic counterinsurgency strategy of repression and containment. The state defines ineffective means of protest and reform as legal and encourages their use by dissidents, while at the same time posing as the only other alternative serious acts of confrontation and violence with dire consequences. Provocateurs, as organic links, reinforce this false choice between restricted options for the movement in its struggle against the state.

Within the movement itself, provocateurs are extremely destructive. They tend to prevent participatory democracy and contribute to the atmosphere of fear, distrust, and animosity that permeates certain situations. They widen the gulf between groups espousing legal reformism and tendencies advocating underground activity with strict military discipline. They obstruct the growth of the movement by endangering all participants, and distort its development by interfering directly and indirectly in policy making. Their set-ups decimate movement leadership, destroy embryonic tendencies and groups, and force the adoption of a defensive posture in the face of costly court cases and unfavorable publicity.

In the face of all these negative consequences, and the movement's apparent vulnerability and helplessness, it may seem surprising that the agent provocateur is in fact the weak link in the strategy of repression, and the key to the movement's ultimate triumph. For the agent provocateur inadvertently exposes the state's own weaknesses, by deflecting the movement away from certain programs, strategies, tactics, and actions which the analysts and strategists in service to the state judge would strike at vulnerable areas, towards other less harmful issues. The use of provocateurs to control volatile political confrontations is an indication of the need of the ruling class to distort, caricature, and villify the radical challenge to their hegemony. The direct intervention of the state, through the use of provocateurs, in shaping the radical alternative, verifies the contention that the state is not neutral, or independent, but serves as an instrument of the ruling class. This interference, and the explicit mediation of the ruling class through the organs of the state, are indications of insecurity and instability, not omniscience and omnipotence.

Hence, the agent provocateur inadvertently provides a valuable service to the movement by revealing the type of programs, strategies, and tactics the movement's enemies would prefer it adopt. The provocateur bares the type of image deemed most counterproductive. The agent's manipulations disclose those aspects of social, economic, and political life where confrontations are to be avoided because they are beset by internal contradictions, while at the same time pointing out the type of scenario for a showdown that authorities would welcome.

The agent provocateur is the negation of what the effective movement activist should be. By demonstrating what should not be done, the provocateur offers some insight into the directions in which the movement should·

grow and develop. The continuing study of agents provocateurs as an abstract type, and in their concrete historical occurrences, should aid the struggle against oppression and repression, and facilitate the negation of the negation—in this instance, the building of a mass, democratic, radical social movement invulnerable to the machinations of agents provocateurs.

NOTES

[1] From a confidential FBI memo, part of the stolen Media, Pa., files, *Win Magazine*, March 1972, p. 29.

[2] From a memorandum received by H. R. Haldeman, former assistant to President Nixon, concerning demonstrations in Charlotte, North Carolina, during the 1972 presidential campaign. (The notations are Haldeman's.) Reprinted from the *New York Times*, August 2, 1973, p. 19.

[3] "Shoot-Out in Cleveland"; Staff Report, U.S. Government Commission on the Causes and Prevention of Violence (Washington, D.C.: Government Printing Office, 1969), p. 44.

[4] *New York Times*, May 16, 1970, p. 1.

[5] *New York Times*, June 30, 1970, p. 36.

[6] *New York Times*, Sept. 19, 1970, p. 12.

[7] "Investigation of SDS," Part 5, Committee on Internal Security, 91st Congress, 1st Session Hearings, pp. 1654-1705.

[8] "Investigation of SDS," Part 3-A, pp. 688-705.

[9] *New York Times*, May 23, 1968, p. 50; *New York Post*, May 22, 1968, p. 2.

[10] *Tales of Hoffmann* (New York: Bantam Books, 1970), pp. 60-61.

[11] *New York Times*, August 4, 1973, p. 55; also, *Cleveland Plain Dealer*, May 7, 1972, p. 6-A; August 5, 1973, p. 56.

[12] *Guardian*, Oct. 24, 1970, p. 4; *Daily World*, Sept. 22, 1970, p. 7; *The Militant*, Nov. 6, 1970, p. 16; *New York Post*, Oct. 10, 1970, p. 51.

[13] *Buffalo Evening News*, Oct. 9, 1970, pp. 1-13; *Washington Post*, Oct. 9, 1970, p. B-4; *Washington Evening Star*, Oct. 9, 1970, p. 4.

[14] *New York Times*, June 7, 1970, p. 62; June 19, 1970, p. 20.

[15] "Tommy the Traveler," *New York Times*, June 19, 1970, p. 20.

[16] Walker Report, *Rights in Conflict* (New York: Bantam Books, 1968), p. 224; "Disruptions of the 1968 Democratic National Convention," Commission on Un-American Activities, House of Representatives, 91st Congress, 1st Session Hearings, pp. 2391-2406.

[17] *New York Post*, Feb. 28, 1970, p. 16.

[18] *Guardian*, Sept. 29, 1969, p. 6.

[19] "Subversive Influences in Riots, Looting and Burning," Part 2, Commission on Un-American Activities, House of Representatives, 90th Congress, 2nd Session Hearings, pp. 930-949; "Operations of a Police Intelligence Unit," unpublished thesis, No. 20, by A. Bouza, John Jay College, New York library.

[20] *New York Times*, Feb. 17, 1965, p. 34; Feb. 18, 1965, p. 66; Commission on Un-American Activities, pp. 1032-1042; "*U.S.* vs. *Bowe*," *Federal Reporter*, 360 F. 2d, 1966, pp. 6-15.

21 *"People of New York* vs. *Ferguson and Harris,"* unpublished trial transcript of the testimony of agent Howlette.

22 *New York Times,* Oct. 25, 1970, p. 122.

23 *New York Times,* Nov. 17, 1970, p. 38; Feb. 5, 1971, p. 64; Feb. 17, 1971, p. 32; March 5, 1971, p. 28; March 11, 1971, p. 29; *Newsweek,* Nov. 23, 1970, p. 24.

24 *New York Times,* Dec. 6, 1971, p. 79; Dec. 8, 1971, p. 52.

25 *RAT* underground newspaper, New York, May 29, 1970, p. 6; transcript of radio interview. *New York Post,* May 23, 1970, p. 7; May 25, 1970, p. 6; *"U.S.* vs. *Melville, Demmerle, Hughey and Alpert,"* Federal Supplement No. 306, p. 128.

26 *New York Times,* Feb. 26, 1972, p. 18; *Newsweek,* Feb. 14, 1972, p. 26; *Life,* April 21, 1972, p. 54.

27 *New York Times,* March 16, 1972, p. 1; *Life,* April 21, 1972, p. 54.

28 "The CIA Comes Home," pamphlet from Justice For All, Box 3314, Beverly Hills, California, 1970.

29 *RAT,* May 8, 1970, p. 4; October 7, 1970, p. 22; also, *New York Times,* May 20, 1973, p. 56.

30 *New York Times,* August 8, 1973, p. 21; August 9, 1973, p. 24; August 11, 1973, p. 7; *Village Voice,* May 31, 1973, p. 9; *Liberation News Service,* June 13, 1973, p. 5.

31 *New York Times,* Sept. 19, 1970, p. 12; *Daily World,* Sept. 18, 1970, p. 9.

32 "Investigation of SDS," Part 7-B, p. 2475.

PART FOUR:

CORPORATE CRIME: THE DIRTY COLLAR

The criminaloid puts on the whole armor of the good. He stands having his loins girt about with religiosity and wearing the breastplate of respectability. His feet are shod with ostentatious philanthropy; his head is enclosed in the helmet of spread-eagle patriotism. Holding in his left hand the buckle of worldly success and in his right the sword of influence, he is able to withstand in the evil day and, having done all, to stand.[1]

The criminaloid that Ross is referring to is the corporate criminal of modern society. Corporate excess and crime at the top gained attention in the late nineteenth and early twentieth century; some important factors contributing to the rise of state interference with the economy and corporate dealings included (1) the movement from an agricultural to a commercial and industrial society, (2) increasing inequality in the distribution of property, and the amassing of wealth by a few, (3) a growing need to leave property in the hands of other persons, (4) the transformation of ownership of visible property into intangible powers and rights, such as corporate shares, including a system of social security in place of ownership of goods, and (5) the passage of property from private to corporate ownership.[2] The current state of this movement is highlighted by recent propaganda concerning the relationship between the activities of federal regulatory agencies and the better life we purportedly live.

"You may never meet an investigator for the United States Government but you are safer, more comfortable, and more secure because thousands of federal agents labor unceasingly in the background of American life."[3] Such information is given to reassure the citizen of his safety, but it is hardly comforting to realize that state agents are keeping surveillance on political activists and their sympathizers, and seemingly anyone in opposition to the executive branch of government. The growth and pervasiveness of social control agents for the state portends a totalitarian future based upon protection of the "good citizen."

The most important entrepreneur in criminology who sought to direct the attention of criminologists to corporate crime was Edwin H. Sutherland.

His *White Collar Crime*[4] was concerned with reforming criminology and elicited a quick response from other criminologists. A major criticism of his work dealt with the accuracy of the definition of "white-collar crime." Tappan, a lawyer-sociologist, noted that:

> Vague, omnibus concepts defining crime are a blight upon either a legal system or a system of sociology that strives to be objective. They allow judge, administrator, or—conceivably—sociologist, in an undirected, freely operating discretion, to attribute the status "criminal" to any individual or class which he conceives nefarious. This can accomplish no desirable objective either politically or sociologically.[5]

Those "mavericks" who argued for the legitimacy of white-collar crime noted that otherwise criminology would remain legalistically bound, class biased, and unable to develop accurate and inclusive theories of lawbreaking. Therefore, the question of "whose side are you on" arises.[6] It is, of course, much more comfortable and "professionally safe" to investigate "common crime" and the "common criminal" rather than "upperclass crime" and the "affluent criminal." The ramifications of such inquiry were eloquently noted by Newman:

> White-collar legislation represents the major formal controls imposed upon the occupational roles of the most powerful members of our society. Whether he likes it or not, the criminologist finds himself involved in an analysis of prestige, power, and differential privilege when he studies upperworld crime. He must be as conversant with data and theories from social stratification as he has been with studies of delinquency and crime within the setting of the urban slum. He must be able to cast his analysis not only in the framework of those who break laws, but in the context of those who make laws as well. . . . No longer is the criminologist a middle-class observer studying lower-class behavior. He now looks upward at the most powerful and prestigeful strata, and his ingenuity in research and theory will be tested, indeed![7]

Notwithstanding the "ominous" task, a number of criminologists have taken scientific pot-shots at the crimes of the upperworld. In fact, much of the white-color crime work has been generated through both respect and apprenticeship to the late Professor Sutherland. Following his theory of differential association, some of Sutherland's students—Marshall B. Clinard and Donald Cressey—and subsequent circle of friends and apprentices—Frank Hartung and his students Donald Newman and Richard Quinney—have included in their training and research definitions favorable to such inquiry.[8] Such differential association and identification is prevalent with many different approaches in various scientific disciplines. The diffusion of such favorable definitions makes white-collar crime an acceptable facet of contemporary criminological focus—nearly all texts have sections dealing with an aspect of such crimes. Furthermore, the concept has been more fully delineated and refined with subsequent investigators.

Sutherland stated that "white-collar crime may be defined approximately as a crime committed by a person of respectability and high social status in the course of his occupation."[9] He suggests in a footnote that this refers primarily to business managers and executives. More recent definitions of white-collar crime have changed the color of the collar, and I might add of the offender,[10] by including acts committed by blue-collar workers and even the poor and unemployed! According to a former chief of the fraud section, criminal division of the United States Department of Justice:

> White-collar crime is democratic. It can be committed by a bank teller or the head of his institution. The offender can be a high government official with a conflict of interest. He can be the destitute beneficiary of a poverty program who is told to hire a work group and puts fictional workers on the payroll so that he can appropriate their wages. The character of white-collar crime must be found in its modi operandi and its objectives rather than in the nature of the offenders.[11]

Thus, in the name of democracy the objectives of Sutherland's concept and work are largely discounted and the color of the collar is no longer important. While the common crime will remain disproportionately among the common folk, white-collar crime shows an affinity for all kinds of people.

Edelhertz then goes on to establish four classes of white-collar crime including (1) *personal crimes,* committed by persons operating on an individual, ad hoc basis, for personal gain in a nonbusiness context, such as income tax violation, bankruptcy, and welfare and unemployment fraud, (2) *abuses of trust,* which are crimes in the course of one's occupation which violate one's duty and loyalty, such as embezzlement, petty larceny, and false travel claims, (3) *business crimes,* crimes incidental to, and in furtherance of, business operations, but not the central purpose of operations, such as antitrust violations and fraud in advertising, and (4) *con games,* in which white-collar crimes are the central activity of business, such as medical and health frauds, land frauds, home improvement schemes, and personal improvement schemes. Although a delineation of white-collar crimes is needed, this categorization loses much in translation.[12]

Another classificatory scheme that holds to the "occupational content" of white-collar crime includes offenses committed (1) by individuals as individuals, such as a doctor, (2) by employees against the corporation in business, (3) by agents of the corporation against the general public, (4) by policy-making officials for the corporation, and (5) by merchants against consumers.[13] All of these categories present interesting areas of criminological inquiry, but our attention will be largely directed to crimes committed by corporations.[14]

In the first article, Schur lucidly points out the artificial barriers between the "good guys" and the "bad guys," and the contrast between the private and public lives of our citizenry. The "moral alchemy" that allows it to be all right to deceive the public by insisting that major institutions of higher education are primarily dedicated to teaching our youth while nearly the entire reward system is based upon specifically nonteaching tasks, such as publications, and at the same time these institutions and their leaders are "morally outraged" when General Motors falsely misleads the public in advertising, suggests the nebulous nature of fraud.[15] As Gibbons notes with regard to the increasing study of criminality among respectable citizens:

> It is likely that some major changes in criminological analysis will come about as these matters receive more attention in the future. Accumulation of evidence on the pervasive character of criminality and the interweaving

of illegal conduct into the fabric of social and economic life will compel us to abandon those comforting notions that crime is restricted to only a relatively few daring "bad guys." The study of criminality turns out to be a major task in sociological inquiry, for lawbreaking is often a central feature of the day-to-day activities of citizens everywhere in American society.[16]

Daniel Bell's suggestion that "Crime is an American Way of Life" may best be reflected in the public's acquiescence to and participation in fraudulent behavior.[17] What is seemingly shocking to Schur is the lack of public indignation. The indignation of certain segments of society has more recently been aroused through revelations by Ralph Nader, among others. Such "extremists," who are uncompromising in their claims and beliefs, are quite abhorrent to much of the public who feel very comfortable with a "public" and "private" morality that often are contradictory. In a society that strongly urges moderation in everything—like booze, sex, and food—and compromise as a way of life, the "morally righteous" entrepreneur hits a particularly vulnerable Achilles heel. The often stated adage, "Do as I say, not as I do" has in fact created nearly an entire generation who see corruption and deceit as pervasive in our society. The problem is that they took our public moral pronouncements too seriously!

To acknowledge that our major values are principal factors in the cause of our crime may be good sociology, but bad ideology for those in power. Such an assessment suggests solutions that transcend stop-and-frisk practices, preventive detention, police-community relations, community-based corrections, and so on. As role models and pace setters, those at the top weigh heavily in providing definitions favorable to law violation.[18] In order to establish "law and order" in our society, it might well be that we begin by eliminating the fraudulent excesses at the top.

Ferdinand Lundberg has provided a well-documented and incisive analysis of "crime and wealth" in his recent book.[19] Our interest and concern with the "organized underworld" has directed our attention away from the "organized upperworld." While the terms "organized crime," "mafia," and "Cosa Nostra" conjure up images of insidious, ruthless, sly, machine-gun-toting gangsters who are a major threat to our national viability, we fail to recognize that "they" merely represent the tip of the iceberg, with criminal organizations reaping the real benefits of illegal activities. Sutherland emphasized that white-collar crime is organized crime, stating that:

White collar-crimes are not only deliberate: they are also organized. Organization for crime may be either formal or informal. Formal organization for crimes of corporations is found most generally in restraint of trade, as illustrated by gentleman's agreements, pool, many practices of trade associations, patent representatives of corporations on plans regarding labor relations. Businessmen are organized formally, also, for control of legislation, selection of administrators, and restriction of appropriations for the enforcement of laws which may affect themselves.[20]

Continual revelations have further shown the criminal nature of certain organizations. For example, in the first of a series of hearings by the Senate's antitrust and monopoly subcommittee on automobile repairs in 1967, Senator

Roman Hruska of Nebraska noted that the hearings are before the wrong sub-committee. "We have a committee that deals with organized crime."[21] A two-year probe of organized crime in New York City found "widespread underworld infiltration of legitimate business in the metropolitan area," and nearly 200 "legitimate businesses" were controlled by organized crime.[22] Of course, as Lundberg noted, it may be more appropriate to say that "legitimate businesses" were increasing their control over organized crime. In fact, one might look at such interrelationships as merely corporate mergers to form a conglomerate or two! The implied power and coercive abilities of organized crime in most popular writing belies the realities of the situation according to Lundberg:

> But in these operations, the strong-arm men—agents of political parties or business groups—are the low men on the totem pole rather than the swashbuckling chiefs depicted by the newspapers. For it is they who are investigated, put on trial, pilloried in newspapers, sometimes jailed and executed, and murdered. It hardly seems a desirable way to make a living.[23]

Although Lundberg and others have noted that the mass media seem obsessed with organized crime rather than "criminal organizations," they fail to acknowledge that the mass media largely reflects the perspective of those "legitimate businesses" that must maintain respectability in the public's eye. Sutherland noted that corporate emphasis has changed from technological efficiency to "manipulation of people by advertising, salesmanship, propaganda, and lobbying. With this recent development the corporation has developed a truly Machiavellian ideology and policy."[24] The use of the media to present certain conceptions of crime, to the detriment of others, is important to maintaining the legitimacy of big business and the government. A cursory examination of criminology texts will attest to the influence such conceptions have upon their content, but some criminologists have attempted to counter such official ideology.[25] As Albert Morris observed some time ago when discussing "criminals of the upperworld":

> Unlike the criminals of the underworld, the permissive criminals of the upperworld have never been marked off and dramatized as a distinct group upon which public disapproval could be focused. They have never been rounded up by the police nor gathered together in a prison where they could be examined, cursed into some semblance of uniformity, and talked about as a special type of human being. Instead, they have been scattered among us as friends and fellow members in clubs and churches. They have contributed to organizations for the treatment of juvenile delinquents and have served in legislatures passing laws to check crime.[26]

The "normal" nature of such criminal activity is epitomized in the President's Commission Report[27] statement that white-collar crime "is often committed in the course of ordinary business activity and may not be significantly distinguishable from noncriminal business conduct." The recognition that criminal activity is part of standard operating procedures (SOP) of many businesses is highlighted in the "Great Electrical Conspiracy." Involving 45 blue-ribbon defendants and 29 corporations, it was the largest criminal case in the history of the Sherman Antitrust Act. Testimony during the trial provides insight into the "common" nature of such criminal activity. As the president of Allen-Bradley Company said: "It is the only way a business can be run. It is free enterprise." Of course the opposite sentiment is evident in the court's verdict of guilty. As Judge T. Cullen Ganey declared in sentencing the defendants, "This is a shocking indictment of a vast section of our economy, for what is really at stake here is the survival of the kind of economy under which America has grown to greatness, the free enterprise system."[28]

The assumption of a free-enterprise system is of course a myth, which might more correctly be stated in terms of degrees of freedom. Our economy is obviously freer for some than others. Free enterprise for corporations means freedom from restraints and control of government; such restrictions are looked upon as "un-American."[29] As Ross noted in his early writing:

> In criminaloid philosophy it is "un-American" to wrench patronage from the hands of spoilsmen, un-American to deal federal justice to rascals of state importance, un-American to pry into arrangements between shipper and carrier, un-American to pry the truth out of reluctant magnates.[30]

Ross also points out that their motives are pure, but their means criminal. "They want nothing more than we all want—money, power, consideration—in a word, success; but they are in a hurry and are not particular as to their means."[31] The insatiable profit motive is the raison d'être for corporations and provides the motive for such crimes. As Aristotle notes in the Politics, "Men may desire superfluities in order to enjoy pleasure unaccompanied with pain, and therefore they commit crimes. . . . The greatest crimes are caused by excesses not by necessity."[32] Thus, the high incidence of corporate crime is as easily explained as the high incidence of "normal thefts" among the poor.

Has the prosecution of the electrical companies deterred the "criminals"? Although the manifest function of the Sherman Act is to control corporate crime, the purpose appears to be more expressive and symbolic, rather than instrumental and substantive. The periodic prosecution under the act provides symbolic support for our "competitive ideology," while at the same time maintaining the conglomerate as an American way of life. The famous epitaph of Charles Wilson is pertinent, "Whatever is good for General Motors is good for America." Such an arrogant appraisal is prevalent in the attitudes of business personnel concerning investigation and control of their behavior.

Some writers have alluded to the self-interest of corporations in war, and their war crimes. In a section entitled "War Crimes," Sutherland suggests corporate war crimes include (1) violations of the special regulations in the two World Wars, (2) avoidance of war taxes, (3) restraint of trade related to war, (4) interference with war policies to maintain competitive positions, (5) violations of embargoes and neutrality, and (6) treason.[33] Congress enacted a national act in 1916 prohibiting profiteering and making it a crime, but the use of such charges is negligible. Sutherland concludes that profits are more important to large corporations than patriotism, quoting a corporate president who said, "Patriotism is a very beautiful thing but it must not be permitted to interfere with business." The rise of the garrison society[34] assures patriotism in profits for the leaders of our wartime economy. The suggestion of a wartime corporate executive appears to be a reality. Charles E. Wilson, president of General Electric, in a January 1944 address before the Army Ordinance Association proposed an alliance of military, executive branch, and large corporations in a "permanent war economy." This allegiance has created a system in which each party has a great stake in the other party's interest and success.[35]

Our attention has more recently been turned to the "war crimes" of individual soldiers,[36] but the war crimes of corporations are seldom alluded to by the media.[37] Morris also saw corporate crime to include corporations exploiting people in small unstable nations in which they do business, and government officials deliberately using untruthful, misleading, and fraudulent propaganda to stir up people to a particular course of action, such as manufacturing false evidence against a nation to induce citizens to desire to declare war against it.[38] This strikes a very contemporary note given the "revelations" of the Pentagon Papers regarding our massive involvement in Indochina.[39]

The problem of deterring corporate crime is addressed by Geis in the second article. His opening remarks suggesting an increase in upper-class criminals and a decrease in lower-class criminals would have many latent functions. It would reduce the number of state welfare families because of the incarceration of the breadwinner, prisons would benefit from increased sophistication in clientele, with more streamlined business procedures, better provision of state services, and so on. Thus, Governor Maddox's suggestion that the prisons will only improve when we get a better class of prisoners may have been prophetic. That corporate crime is lethal is pointed out in the Beech planes case. Similar charges may be appropriate relating to F111 jet crashes, automobile deaths, and mine deaths. In order to bring stiffer penalties to criminal organizations there needs to be an increased sense of moral outrage on the part of the public. This has been a theme throughout corporate crime writing from Ross to the present. However, the nature of the crime inhibits such moral indignation. Identification of both the victim and the criminal is not as clear-cut as in "normal crimes." That we are daily victimized is not usually recognized because, for example, we do not view the grocery store or department store as an accomplice, the manufacturer as a criminal, and ourselves as victims of rising costs. Sutherland noted the rational premeditation of corporate crime in (1) perpetrating crimes involving the smallest danger of detection and identification, and against which victims are least likely to fight —because consumers have been largely unorganized, diffused in harm, and lacking the information on quality of commodities, (2) selecting crimes in which proof is difficult, such as fraudulent advertising, and (3) a policy of "fixing" cases, as in the use of legislators and justice personnel.[40]

The corporate criminal receives differential treatment in the courts. Although the "adversary nature" of judicial proceedings usually weighs disproportionately upon the defense, corporations have law firms and political power superior to the prosecution. Davids notes some major differences:

> With the aid of top-quality house counsel, nationally-respected law firms, and invaluable personal contact with leading members of the federal legislature and bench, corporations can make it so difficult for the Justice Department to exact even those tokens of victory, that the Government will decide to settle the case and seek more fruitful use of its scarce legal resources elsewhere.[41]

The nature of antitrust prosecutions provides an excellent example of the double standard of justice. The Antitrust Division of the Department of Justice has concurrent jurisdiction with the Federal Trade Commission for enforcement of the four basic antitrust statutes.[42] Criminal sanctions are provided only for violations of the Sherman Act and only the Department of Justice can prosecute criminal actions. Sections 1 and 2 of the Sherman Act state that contracts and combinations in restraint of trade and acts and attempts to monopolize trade are unlawful and that persons engaged in such acts "shall be deemed guilty of a misdemeanor, and, on conviction thereunder, shall be punished by fine not exceeding $50,000, or by imprisonment not exceeding one year." Either civil or criminal actions may be filed against violators of the antitrust act. However, the President's Commission notes that criminal prosecutions are rare because of the "vagueness of the prohibition";[43] therefore, civil actions are usually filed.

The plea-bargaining carried out by the Justice Department includes the usual enticements of pleading to lesser offenses, or fewer offenses, minimizing counts of guilty pleas, allowing *nolo contendere* pleas, and reducing possible sentence and/or fine. Such practices are standard with "normal criminals" but for somewhat different reasons. Whereas the normal defendant is usually in a subordinate position financially, legally, power and prestige wise, the corporate defendant generally has more time, financial backing, political power, and prestige than the prosecution and plays a "confidence game" with the court.[44] The State gives the appearance of vindicating "justice" and the corporation has its hands slapped while essentially being allowed to continue "business as usual."

The *nolo contendere* plea is particularly important for the corporation: it is theoretically equal to a guilty plea, but defendants prefer it because they believe the judge will be easier on them, there will be less public stigma, it cannot be used against the defendant in any other action or proceeding, and the statutory presumption in favor of treble damages to the victim does not hold. Judges appear to be quite favorable to such pleas. Having the right to accept or reject them, between July 1, 1959 and July 1, 1965 *nolo* pleas were always accepted if the government didn't oppose it, and 96 percent of them were accepted when the government opposed them.[45] Therefore, the corporation appears to have this option always available. Although theoretically the *nolo* is the same as a guilty plea, the public image is less damaged with such a finding. The President's Commission notes that corporate public relations departments issue press releases after a disposition stating or giving the impression that the *nolo contendere* plea was in order to avoid delays and the expense of litigation, although subsequent court action would have vindicated them.[46]

By being allowed to plea *nolo contendere* the corporation evades treble damages which could be awarded in subsequent suits to the "victims." The defendants can deny guilt in subsequent litigation because their "guilty" plea cannot be used against them. Thus, the victims of such criminal actions are usually not benefited from the "conviction" of the defendant. The prosecution's files are locked up by such pleas and the victims are essentially impotent except to contribute to the prosecutor's case.[47] Although the State justifies such action in the name of time, money, and efficiency, the victims don't get justice.

How do we change such injustices? Geis suggests a massive propaganda campaign showing the nature, extent, and ills of corporate crime. Public information is necessary, but the extent of its merit is unknown, particularly given those who control the media. The treating of corporate criminals as criminals is necessary for deterrent purposes. The negative effects of being processed as "common criminals" are apparent in the evidence we have of its impact. The shock value of "criminals" seeing their destructive nature, such as the German pilots of World War II in Russia, suggests current analogies. What if the manufacturers of antipersonnel bombs, napalm, and defoliation chemicals saw their effects in Indochina? On the home front, auto executives would constantly visit scenes of fatalities and breathe air pollution; clothing manufacturers would be subjected to the charred remains of the victims of flammable children's wear; pharmaceutical industry executives would observe the consequences of drug addiction.

Geis notes that a listing of the "ten most wanted" corporate criminals is doubtful, but that infiltration is a possibility. Although potentially effective, it is hardly politically probable. Given the wedding of corporate elites and political elites, it is hardly likely that a political arm of the executive branch, such as the Department of Justice, will vigorously prosecute such criminals. As long as political power remains stable, "agent provocateurs" will remain among youth, political radicals, and others. The penalties for corporate crime are hardly rational in relation to the harm incurred or their deterrent effects. They must be understood in the context of political power and privilege.

It has become clear that not only are the amounts of currently authorized penalties hopelessly inadequate to punish infractions by large corporations, but that the realities of corporate life and operations today demand a basic rethinking in the areas of social control and legal responsibility.[48]

The taint of serving a criminal sentence in jail appears to be quite a potent deterrent—although one cannot legislate ethical conduct, the weight of actual jail terms appears as a promising encouragement. It should be noted, though, that no executives have been jailed since the great electrical case. The nature and extent of our criminal prosecution of criminal organizations will ultimately be decided in the political arena.

NOTES

[1] Edward Alsworth Ross, "The Criminaloid," *The Atlantic Monthly* 99 (January 1907):44-50. For an elaboration of his "criminaloid" category see his *Sin and Society,* 1907.

[2] *See* Gilbert Geis, *White-Collar Criminal* (New York: Atherton Press, 1968), pp. 1-19.

[3] Ibid., p. 10.

[4] Edwin H. Sutherland, *White Collar Crime* (New York: Holt, Rinehart, and Winston, 1961). The first edition was in 1949; he first presented the concept in his presidential address before the American Sociological Association in 1940.

[5] Paul Tappan, "Who is the Criminal?" *American Sociological Review* 96 (1957):99-100.

[6] *See* Howard S. Becker, "Whose Side are We On?" *Social Problems* 14 (Winter 1967):239-247 and Alvin W. Gouldner's rejoinder "The Sociologist as Partisan: Sociology and the Welfare State," *The American Sociologist* 3 (May 1968):103-116.

[7] Donald J. Newman, "White-Collar Crime," *Law and Contemporary Problems* 23 (Autumn 1958):735-753.

[8] *See* Geis, *White-Collar Criminal.*

[9] Sutherland, *White Collar Crime*, p. 9.

[10] Sutherland's conception of white-collar crime reflects not only the color of the collar, but of the offender, given the racist history of our society.

[11] Herbert Edelhertz, *The Nature, Impact and Prosecution of White-Collar Crime* (Washington D.C.: U.S. Government Printing Office, 1970), p. 4.

[12] Edelhertz also notes that the common elements of "white-collar crime" include the (1) intent to commit a wrongful act or to achieve a purpose inconsistent with law or public policy, (2) disguise of purpose or intent, (3) reliance by perpetrators on ignorance or carelessness of victim, (4) acquiescence by the victim in what he believes to be the nature and content of the transaction, (5) concealment of the crime by *(a)* preventing the victim from realizing he has been victimized, *(b)* relying on the fact that only a small percentage of victims will react to what has happened, and making provisions for restitution to or other handling of the disgruntled victim, or *(c)* creation of a deceptive paper, organization, or transactional facade to disguise the true nature of what has occurred.

[13] *See* Herbert A. Block and Gilbert Geis, *Man, Crime and Society* (New York: Random House, 1970), p. 308. For a discussion of "occupational crime" as a viable concept for criminological study *see* Earl R. Quinney, "The Study of White Collar Crime: Toward a Reorientation in Theory and Research," *Journal of Criminology, Criminal Law, and Police Science* 55 (1964):208-214.

[14] For an excellent analysis of the organization as a "victim" *see* Erwin O. Smigel and H. Laurence Ross, *Crimes Against Bureaucracy* (New York: Litton Educational Publishing, 1970).

[15] It was John K. Galbraith who noted that any college professor up for tenure and promotion should easily understand the corporate executive who feels for "reasons of price certainty and economic security" the rules should bend.

[16] Don C. Gibbons, *Society, Crime and Criminal Careers* (Englewood Cliffs: Prentice-Hall, 1968), pp. 342-343.

[17] *See* Daniel Bell, "Crime as an American Way of Life," *The Antioch Review* 13 (Summer 1953):131-154.

[18] Geis, *White-Collar Criminal*, notes that the prevalence of white-collar crime helps provide rationalizations for "common criminals." An example readily comes to the author's mind with regard to his work on a prison study. We had two offenders with long records working for our project on a work-release basis. During a legislative hearing inquiring into the state of prison conditions, one of the work-releasees (a robber of much repute) was accusatorily presented with the fact that he, a "common criminal," was under the

employ of the state. After attesting to the veracity of the "accusation," the gentleman responded in kind, noting that he had never been "accused" of being legally gainfully employed, and furthermore, he was not aware of the rule which states "you shouldn't mix the robbers with the thieves." The wastage, featherbedding, and fraudulent practices often evidenced in state bureaucracies confirmed his "suspicions" of "theft" in higher places.

[19] Ferdinand Lundberg, *The Rich and the Super-Rich* (New York: Bantam Books, 1969), pp. 113-154.

[20] Sutherland, *White Collar Crime,* pp. 217-233.

[21] "Car Repairs: Business or Organized Crime?" *Lincoln Journal,* October 10, 1972.

[22] "NYC Probe Shows Underworld Infiltration of Legitimate Firms," *Lincoln Journal,* October 8, 1972.

[23] Lundberg, *Super-Rich,* pp. 121-122.

[24] Sutherland, *White Collar Crime,* p. 229.

[25] Most contemporary criminology texts have a specific chapter on "organized crime," but they fail to have a chapter on "criminal organizations."

[26] Albert Morris, *Criminology* (New York: Longmans, Green, 1935), pp. 152-158.

[27] The President's Commission on Law Enforcement and Administration of Justice, *Task Force Report: Crime and Its Impact—An Assessment* (Washington D. C.: U.S. Government Printing Office, 1967), p. 106. The commission notes that "because of limited time and resources the task force has not been able to deal with 'white-collar crimes' comprehensively or in depth. Nonetheless, white-collar crime is an important part of the nation's crime problem and the task force has therefore sought in this chapter to identify and briefly discuss some of the important issues." Ibid., p. 102. The commission presents one chapter on "White Collar Crime," pp. 102-109, an entire task force report on *Organized Crime.* Of course, the emphasis of the entire inquiry upon "street crimes," "common" or "ordinary" crimes, reflects upon the nature of the offenders as much as the nature of the offenses.

[28] Ibid.

[29] Geis, *White-Collar Criminal,* notes that the law of fraud was vigorously fought in America, for as Chief Justice Stone stated, "any interference with the natural laws of greed was subversive of liberty."

[30] Ross, "Criminaloid." He presents the example of "Stars and Stripes Sam" who was a notorious looter of Philadelphia who amassed influence by making a practice of going to lodges, associations, brotherhoods, Sunday schools, and all sorts of public and private meetings, joining some, but at all making speeches patriotic and sentimental.

[31] Ross, "Criminaloid," p. 46.

[32] Quoted in Geis, *White-Collar Criminal,* p. 157.

[33] Sutherland, *White Collar Crime,* pp. 164-175.

[34] *See* Vernon K. Dibble, "The Garrison Society," *New University Thought* (Spring 1967): 106-155.

[35] Ibid.

[36] Richard A. Falk, "War Crimes and Responsibility," *Trans-Action* 7 (January 1970):33-40.

[37] For a discussion of "crimes and corporations," *see* George Wald, "Dealing with War Crimes," *Current* (August 1970):56-63.

[38] Morris, *Criminology*.

[39] Neil Sheehan, Kedrick Smith, E. W. Kenworthy and Fox Butterfield, *The Pentagon Papers* (New York: Bantam Books, 1970).

[40] Sutherland.

[41] Leo Davids, "Penology and Corporate Crime," *Journal of Criminal Law, Criminology, and Police Science* 58 (September 1967):528.

[42] *See* President's Commission, pp. 109-112.

[43] The "vagueness" of conspiracy statutes does not appear to have deterred government charges against the more generally acknowledged "subversives"—anti-war groups, draft resisters, Black Panthers, etc.

[44] Abraham Blumberg, "The Practice of Law as a Confidence Game: Organizational Co-optation of a Profession," *Law and Society Review* 1 (June 1967):15-39.

[45] President's Commission.

[46] *See* President's Commission, p. 111.

[47] *See* Edelhertz, *Impact and Prosecution*.

[48] Davids, "Penology." For a popular discussion of corporate crime and "punishment" *see* Ralph Nader and Mark Green, "Coddling the Corporations: Crime in the Suites," *The New Republic* (April 29, 1972):17-21.

A SOCIETY OF FRAUDS?

EDWIN M. SCHUR

No thinking American can doubt that fraudulent behavior is commonplace in our society. Deception and predatory economic behavior are not restricted to any particular sector of American life. On the contrary, fraud cuts across various institutional realms in such a way that we are forced to see it as a significant characteristic of our entire social system. Advertising fraud, consumer fraud, medical fraud, welfare and charity frauds, con games big and small, forgeries, embezzlements, violations of securities laws and copyright regulations—all these and more represent symptoms of an underlying systematic disorder. And, as I have pointed out, most of these substantive types of fraud themselves exist on several different levels of society, and in several different forms—with the dividing lines between legal and illegal, and within the illegal category between professional and nonprofessional, exhibiting an extremely hazy quality.

What is at least as disturbing as the widespread prevalence of fraud is the ambiguous and largely apathetic public reaction to it. The split between our public rhetoric and ideology of honesty and fair dealing, on the one hand, and our private morality of "anything goes," on the other, is evident, yet it seems to be a discrepancy about which nobody really wants to do very much. Americans have become alarmingly inured to the practice of fraud, perhaps to the extent of having concluded that it is an inevitable concomitant of their way of life, of which only the most disgruntled troublemakers would complain.

Each exposé of a particular form of institutionalized immorality is followed, after not very much time, by a return to passive acquiescence and individual willingness to "play the game." How many of us think twice about the TV-quiz show and disk-jockey payola scandals that supposedly shocked the entire country in the late 1950s? Yet the practices revealed in those inquiries represented something close to a high point in an industry's contempt for the public, and were clearly symptomatic of the far-reaching nature of attitudes favorable to fraud in our society. Noting that the "contestants" who engaged in collusive quiz-show deceptions were mostly well-educated white-collar workers and professionals, Meyer Weinberg has suggested that their behavior may have reflected their expertise in handling and managing other people.

Edwin M. Schur, "A Society of Frauds?" from *OUR CRIMINAL SO-CIETY: The Social and Legal Sources of Crime in America,* © 1969, pp. 182-190. Reprinted by permission of Prentice-Hall, Inc. Englewood Cliffs, N.J.

They did not find it difficult to enter into rigging for this, too, was nothing but a gigantic "handling" operation. Those who manipulate others make handles of themselves. Rigging was a highly profitable way of allowing one's self to be used for another's gain. The fact that it was so well paid was its cardinal justification. Was it, after all, less moral than the deliberately stalling letters a sales correspondent might write to a complaining customer? Or, less moral than a public relations adviser who helps arrange the emotions of people? Or, less moral than a professor who publishes books all but written by his graduate students?[1]

Even though some of the contestants were fairly certain that these "business" principles were wrong, all of them, Weinberg insists, had absorbed the principles and acted under their influence.

Despite tightened Federal Communications Commission control, some official recognition that much of the commercial television output is "a vast wasteland" (the famous 1961 speech by Commissioner Newton Minow), and growing interest in and (limited) support of public broadcasting schemes, we may well wonder whether the impact of these scandals on television practice was really a very potent one. Certainly the casual viewer gets the impression that, just as in the case of the electrical conspiracy, there was a rapid reversion to "business as usual." Likewise, major revelations of political corruption, of the rigging of sports events, and other similar frauds, seem to come and go over the years—for a moment giving rise to fervent exclamations of shock and dismay, but producing little meaningful change in underlying institutions and practices.

A few years ago Jessica Mitford's *The American Way of Death* appeared —a remarkable, well-documented, and biting attack on what is perhaps the apotheosis of sharp sales practice in our society, the conduct of the American funeral industry.[2] Although it achieved both critical acclaim and best-sellerdom, it is unlikely that this revealing and sensible effort appreciably influenced actual practice. Perhaps a major exception to this general tendency has been the reasonably successful effort to get the American automobile industry to institute much needed safety features in their new model cars (not exactly a reduction in "fraud," unless in the very broadest sense), which seems to have been generated largely by Ralph Nader's powerful study *Unsafe at any Speed.*[3] In this instance—and in all other instances where public concern about fraud and related practices has been translated into official action —reform occurred only after explicitly political pressure was exerted; usually this has occurred through widely publicized hearings convened by Congressional committees or regulatory agencies.

AMERICAN VALUES AND FRAUD

It would seem to be in this very broad area of fraudulent behavior, rather than in that of interpersonal violence about which the public is so greatly exercised, that underlying values of modern American life most directly promote and shape criminality. In part what may be involved here is a stratum of "subterranean values"—values that are "in conflict or in competition with other deeply held values but which are still recognized and accepted by many." Such value contradictions may sometimes reflect a clash of subcultures or interest groups, but the situation may be even more complicated than that. These contradictions "may also exist within a single individual and give rise to profound feelings of ambivalence in many areas of life. In this sense, subterranean values are akin to private as opposed to public morality. They are values that the individual holds to and believes in but that are also recognized as being not quite *comme il faut.*"[4]

As Matza and Sykes go on to point out, the search for kicks, the drive toward "big-time spending," and the emphasis on "rep" that seem significant in the causation of much delinquency and crime "have immediate counterparts in the value system of the law-abiding," as indeed does a "taste for violence." Dual cultural traditions, then, may pull the individual in opposite directions, a point Sutherland also had in mind when he noted that a modern society invariably contained both definitions favorable to the law and definitions favorable to law violation. In the area of business values especially, as I have emphasized, this kind of duality is glaringly evident. Although business transactions ostensibly are to be governed by principles of honesty, mutuality of benefit, public accountability, and even some concern for the public interest, in fact the operative values all too often support secretive and deceptive efforts to maximize self-advantage without much regard for the other parties involved or for the general good.

Of course, this undercurrent of values conducive to business crimes and related offenses is not surprising, given the extensive influence of the "business spirit" in our society. Indeed, certain of the values that help promote criminality in America are far from being subterranean in character. Thus, sociologist Donald Taft has cited the following "characteristics of American society" as having possible significance in the causation of crime: "its dynamic quality, complexity, materialism, growing impersonality, individualism, insistence upon the importance of status, restricted group loyalties, survivals of frontier traditions, race discrimination, lack of scientific orientation in the social field, tolerance of political corruption, general faith in law, disrespect for some law, and acceptance of quasi-criminal exploitation."[5] While this list is something of a hodgepodge (including some subterranean values, some more dominant ones, and also a few behaviors that are more a result of certain values than values in their own right), the first few items—dynamism, complexity, materialism, impersonality, and individualism—may be especially noteworthy. These are clearly dominant values or characteristics of American life, and they seem in some sense to have very real bearing on at least some types of criminality.

Sociologists are reluctant to accept the idea that a society's major values or dominant characteristics "cause" crime. Because of their very dominance or socially approved nature, these elements also underlie a great deal of acceptable, sometimes highly desired behavior. And in either case, to consider them as major causal factors is difficult—because of the many other factors and processes intervening "between" the values and the acts. In any case, reference to such values clearly will not enable us to predict which individuals will commit crimes and which won't, since the very same values promote both law violation and law-abidingness.

At the same time, we can hardly ignore the fact that the general quality of American life significantly shapes and colors crime problems. It is true

that the values promoting fraud are not uniquely American, nor is the institutional framework within which fraud thrives. To some extent, the impersonality, instrumentalism, and competitiveness that help to generate fraud are
intrinsic to the nature of modern urbanized society. Sociologists frequently
draw the basic distinction between the "primary relations" (intimate, spontaneous, diffuse, and guided by mutuality of ends) that tend to dominate
social interaction in small homogeneous communities, and the "secondary
relations" (segmentalized, impersonal, instrumental) that more typically characterize complex socieites. The inclination to try to "take advantage of" the
other party is, in a sense, built into the structure of social relations in our
kind of social order. Indeed, it is precisely for this reason that the so-called
formal mechanisms of social control, including law, must play such an important role in modern society.

It is also true, as I have noted, that the values that promote these kinds
of crime are not unique to capitalism. Socialist regimes have found it quite
impossible to eliminate all impulses toward accumulation of property, compe·
tition, even "profit." Nor have such regimes always found themselves able
to do away entirely with such devices as competitive advertising—even where
the competitors may be state owned and controlled. Despite these points,
it is difficult not to conclude that American society has embraced an ideology of what might be termed capitalism with a vengeance—a reverence for
the values of individualism, competition, and profit of such intensity as to
provide incentives to crime that go well beyond a level that must be considered inevitable in a modern complex society, even a basically capitalist
one.

In such a situation, in which these crime-encouraging values and characteristics are diffused throughout diverse realms of the social system, one
cannot help but be struck by the interrelatedness of numerous practices that
otherwise might be viewed as discrete items of behavior. The early French
criminologist Gabriel Tarde contended that "All the important acts of social
life are carried out under the domination of example," and stated further:
"Criminality always being . . . a phenomenon of imitative propagation . . .
the aim is to discover . . . which among these various spreadings of example
which are called instruction, religion, politics, commerce, industry, are the
ones that foster, and which the ones that impede, the expansion of crime."[6]
Although most modern social psychologists would consider "imitation" a
grossly unsophisticated concept for explaining human behavior, few would
dispute the contention that values and practices "spread" from one unit of
society to another—in fact, the attempt to spell out the complex processes
by which this may occur lies at the very heart of social psychology.

As we have seen, major explanations of crime concentrate heavily on
the significance of socialization processes and reference groups, as well as
on such factors as socioeconomic status, felt deprivation, and opportunity.
Taft has argued that "pattern setting by prestiged groups" is an important
element of the American crime situation, insisting that the level of morality
displayed by lawyers and judges, politicians, business and labor leaders, sports
celebrities, and members of other prestigious subgroups has a special influence
in shaping the "moral tone" of our society.[7] While it would not be easy to
formulate this notion in terms offering a rigorous and testable theory of crime

causation, in a more general sense it seems to have some validity. Certainly it is reasonable to think that the middle-level bank executive who embezzles has in some degree been influenced by revelations of upper-level defalcations, the professional con man by a realization that "everyone has his racket," the corporate offender by the belief that even government officials are corrupt. Surely this is what we mean when we say that "definitions favorable to law violation" exist and circulate within a society. That such definitions are so widespread makes clear why the rather glib distinction commonly drawn between "criminals" and the law-abiding is so difficult to maintain. And this existence of diffuse, almost omnipresent, crime-encouraging definitions seems also to present almost insurmountable obstacles for the would-be reformer.

CAN WE CURB SWINDLING?

It is commonly asserted, by those who feel great concern about this situation, that what is needed is a "return to morality." The emphasis usually is placed upon the reform of individuals; if each individual will only behave morally, then the entire situation will change. Without doubt, such an assertion is correct. But the problem remains: how can such modifications be effected? As some of the earlier discussion should have made clear, sociologists recognize that the motivation and behavior of man is deeply rooted in his culture and the institutional arrangements of his society. Accordingly, while it may not be a forlorn hope that at least some of the Americans now engaging in fraudulent practices might "pull themselves up by their bootstraps" and personally begin to act in a more "moral" fashion, a broadly based reduction in fraud requires a systematic program of reform that goes beyond the level of individuals.

Because that is true, and given the extent to which fraudulent behavior is deeply rooted in our present values and institutions, it is without doubt unrealistic to expect that we can eliminate it wholesale. That does not mean, however, that nothing can be done. If the American citizen really wants to, he can mount and support political and other actions that will begin to attack directly some of the institutionalized sources of fraud in our society. Presumably some of the needed reforms could be accomplished through self-regulation and internal controls on the part of particular industries and organizations. Structural change within an organization may eliminate some of the pressures and opportunities leading individuals at various levels within it to engage in certain kinds of fraudulent behavior. And of course self-imposed restraint—in competitive activities, advertising, and the like—could lead to substantial reform. It seems likely, however, that in this latter area strong government prodding, if not control, will be needed.

Sometimes it is argued that new laws will not help. Probably it is true that some fraud has been engendered by the very proliferation and complexity of our legal and regulatory provisions. Yet the failure of regulation has mainly come about through indifferent enforcement and the refusal to plug up "loopholes," rather than simply because there are too many laws. Nor is the frequent assertion that laws cannot change men's values and attitudes persuasive. Proper enforcement of laws in this area could rather quickly affect *behavior,* and studies even show that such behavioral change may later be accompanied by important changes in outlook. Furthermore, we should recognize that the area of white-collar crime and "respectable" fraud may be one of those in which the deterrent effect of criminal law is particularly strong. It is rather ironic that Americans persistently argue for stronger law enforcement aimed at offenses against which (because of the underlying pressures and situations driving people to the crime) the criminal law may have little deterrent effect, whereas here (where the offender usually has much to lose through severe sanctioning, and is often in a position to rationally assess the gains and costs of violation) little pressure for vigorous enforcement is exerted.[8]

Quite simply, a strong case can be made for clamping down on white-collar crime and related offenses. The direct cost of such crime to society is substantial, the indirect cost in terms of promoting a climate of fraud may also be great, and these are offenses that can in some considerable measure effectively be curbed by criminal law. It should similarly be possible to reduce the number of major tax "loopholes" and perhaps modify and simplify the system of deductions and exemptions in such a way as to reduce both the invitation to and opportunity for tax dodging. Perhaps one of the most central reforms would be to exert much stricter governmental control (where self-regulation proves impossible) over deceptive advertising and sales practices. We are beginning to see action of this sort, through "truth in packaging" provisions and the like, but a great deal more needs to be done. If my analysis is correct, then the content of everyday advertising must be seen to have a special significance with respect to the prevalence of fraud in modern American life. The widespread acceptance of deception and misrepresentation as a basic feature of advertising promotes on a broad scale both the inclination to perpetrate fraud and the receptiveness to fraud—and hence must be radically altered. Just how far this process can go, given the nature of our competitive economy, and precisely what forms it should take, are matters that call for a specialized knowledge I do not have. There seems little doubt, however, that substantial restriction of the most blatant forms of deception could—well within the bounds of a viable capitalism—make for a major reduction in the institutionalized encouragement to fraud.

This is the kind of suggestion that, remarkably, is all too rare in discussions of crime. To say that we should combat crime by controls on advertising may seem to "the man in the street" barely relevant to those aspects of American crime that are generating the greatest public and official attention and concern. But here we confront one major area of crime that does seem at least potentially manageable, and that may have very broad ramifications affecting the moral tenor of our legal system and our society at large. That "respectable crime" has been an object of selective inattention in American life is itself one of the major crimes of our society.

NOTES

[1]Meyer Weinberg, *TV in America: The Morality of Hard Cash* (New York: Ballantine Books, 1962), p. 222.

[2]Jessica Mitford, *The American Way of Death* (New York: Simon and Schuster, 1963).

[3]Ralph Nader, *Unsafe at any Speed* (New York: Grossman, 1965). *See also* Jeffrey O'Connell and Arthur Myers, *Safety Last* (New York: Random House, 1968).

[4]David Matza and Gresham Sykes, "Juvenile Delinquency and Subterranean Values," *American Sociological Review* 26 (October 1961):716.

[5]Donald R. Taft and Ralph W. England, Jr. *Criminology* 4th edition (New York: Macmillan, 1964), p. 275.

[6]Gabriel Tarde, *Penal Philosophy*, trans. Howell (Boston: Little, Brown, 1912), p. 362.

[7]Taft and England, *Criminology*, chap. 2.

[8]This point has recently been made by sociologist William Chambliss, "Types of Deviance and Effectiveness of Legal Sanctions," *Wisconsin Law Review* (1967):703-19.

DETERRING CORPORATE CRIME

GILBERT GEIS

STREET VS. SUITE CRIME

An active debate is underway in the United States concerning the use of imprisonment to deal with crime.[1] Enlightened opinion holds that too many persons are already incarcerated, and that we should seek to reduce prison populations. It is an understandable view. Most prisoners today come from the dispossessed segments of our society; they are the blacks and the browns who commit "street crimes" for reasons said to be closely related to the injustices they suffer. But what of white-collar criminals, and the specific subset of corporate violators? If it is assumed that imprisonment is unnecessary for many lower-class offenders, it might be argued that it is also undesirable for corporation executives. In such terms, it may appear retributive and inconsistent to maintain that a law-violating corporation vice-president spend time in jail, while advocating that those who work in his factory might well be treated more indulgently when they commit a criminal offense.

I do not, however, find it incompatible to favor both a reduction of the lower-class prison population and an increase in upper-class representation in prisons. Jail terms have a self-evident deterrent impact upon corporate officials, who belong to a social group that is exquisitely sensitive to status deprivation and censure. The white-collar offender and his business colleagues, more than the narcotic addict or the ghetto mugger, are apt to learn well the lesson intended by a prison term. In addition, there is something to be said for *noblesse oblige,* that those who have a larger share of what society offers carry a greater responsibility also.

It must be appreciated, too, that white-collar crimes constitute a more serious threat to the well-being and integrity of our society than more traditional kinds of crimes. As the President's Commission on Law Enforcement and Administration of Justice put the matter: "White-collar crime affects the whole moral climate of our society. Derelictions by corporations and their managers, who usually occupy leadership positions in their communities, establish an example which tends to erode the moral base of the law. . . ."[2]

Corporate crime kills and maims. It has been estimated, for example, that each year two hundred thousand to five hundred thousand workers are needlessly exposed to toxic agents such as radioactive materials and poisonous

Gilbert Geis, "Deterring Corporate Crime" from *Corporate Power in America* edited by Ralph Nader and Mark J. Green. Copyright © 1973 by Ralph Nader. Reprinted by permission of The Viking Press, Inc.

chemicals because of corporate failure to obey safety laws. And many of the 2.5 million temporary and 250,000 permanent worker disabilities from industrial accidents each year are the result of managerial acts that represent culpable failure to adhere to established standards.[3] Ralph Nader has accused the automobile industry of "criminal negligence" in building and selling potentially lethal cars. Nader's charges against the industry before a Congressional committee drew parallels between corporate crime and traditional crime, maintaining that acts which produce similar kinds of personal and social harm were handled in very different ways:

> If there are criminal penalties for the poor and deprived when they break the law, then there must be criminal penalties for the automobile industry when its executives knowingly violate standards designed to protect citizens from injuries and systematic fraud.[4]

Interrupted by a senator who insisted that the witness was not giving adequate credit to American industry for its many outstanding achievements, Nadar merely drove his point deeper: "Do you give credit to a burglar," he asked, "because he doesn't burglarize 99 percent of the time?"[5]

Death was also the likely result of the following corporate dereliction recounted in the *Wall Street Journal* which, if the facts are as alleged, might well be regarded as negligent manslaughter:

> Beech Aircraft Corp., the nation's second-largest maker of private aircraft, has sold thousands of planes with allegedly defective fuel systems that might be responsible for numerous crash deaths—despite warnings years in advance of the crashes that the system wasn't working reliably under certain flight conditions.
>
> Though Beech strongly denies this, it is the inescapable conclusion drawn from inspection of court suits and exhibits in cases against Beech, from internal company memoranda, from information from the Federal Aviation Agency and the National Transportation Board, and from interviews with concerned parties.[6]

After 1970, the fuel systems in the suspect planes were corrected by Beech at the request of federal authorities. Before that, the company had been found liable in at least two air crashes and had settled two other cases before they went to the jury. In one case, tried in California and now under appeal, a $21.7 million judgment was entered against Beech. Of this, $17.5 million was for punitive damages, which generally are awarded in the state only when fraud or wanton and willful disregard for the safety of others is believed to exist. At the moment, suits are pending which involve the deaths of about twenty other persons in Beech planes.[7]

Those who cannot afford a private plane are protected against being killed in a crash of a Beech aircraft, but nothing will help the urban resident from being smogged. Again Nader has pointed out the parallel between corporate offenses and other kinds of crime and the disparate manner in which the two are viewed and treated:

> The efflux from motor vehicles, plants, and incinerators of sulfur oxides, hydrocarbons, carbon monoxide, oxides of nitrogen, particulates, and many

more contaminants amounts to compulsory consumption of violence by most Americans. . . . This damage, perpetuated increasingly in direct violation of local, state, and federal law, shatters people's health and safety but still escapes inclusion in the crime statistics. "Smogging" a city or town has taken on the proportions of a massive crime wave, yet federal and state statistical compilations of crime pay attention to "muggers" and ignore "smoggers.". . .[8]

Corporate crime also imposes an enormous financial burden on society. The heavy electrical equipment price-fixing conspiracy alone involved theft from the American people of more money than was stolen in all of the country's robberies, burglaries, and larcenies during the years in which the price fixing occurred.[9] Yet, perhaps it can be alleged that corporate criminals deal death and deprivation not deliberately but, because their overriding interest is self-interest, through inadvertence, omission, and indifference. The social consciousness of the corporate offender often seems to resemble that of the small-town thief, portrayed by W. C. Fields, who was about to rob a sleeping cowboy. He changed his mind, however, when he discovered that the cowboy was wearing a revolver. "It would be dishonest," he remarked virtuously as he tiptoed away.[10] The moral is clear: since the public cannot be armed adequately to protect itself against corporate crime, those law-enforcement agencies acting on its behalf should take measures sufficient to protect it. High on the list of such measures should be an insistence upon criminal definition and criminal prosecution for acts which seriously harm, deprive, or otherwise injure the public.

The Need for Public Outrage

The first prerequisite for imposing heavier sanctions on corporate criminals involves the development of a deepening sense of moral outrage on the part of the public. A number of factors have restricted public awareness of the depth and cost of white-collar crime. That the injuries caused by most corporate violations are highly diffused, falling almost imperceptively upon each of a great number of widely scattered victims is undoubtedly the greatest barrier to arousing public concern over white-collar crime. "It is better, so the image runs," C. Wright Mills once wrote, "to take one dime from each of ten million people at the point of a corporation than $100,000 from each of ten banks at the point of a gun." Then Mills added, with wisdom: "It is also safer."[11] Pollution cripples in a slow, incremental fashion; automobile deaths are difficult to trace to any single malfunctioning of inadequately designed machinery; antitrust offenses deprive many consumers of small amounts, rather than the larger sums apt to be stolen from fewer people by the burglar. It is somehow less infuriating and less fear-producing to be victimized a little every day over a long period of time than to have it happen all at once. That many very small losses can add up to a devastating sum constitutes impressive mathematical evidence, but the situation lacks real kick in an age benumbed by fiscal jumboism.

Take, as an example, the case of the Caltec Citrus Company. The Food and Drug Administration staked out the Company's warehouse, finding sugar, vitamin C, and other substances not permitted in pure orange juice being brought into the plant. Estimates were that the adulteration practices of the

Company cost consumers one million dollars in lost value, thereby "earning" the Company an extra one million dollars in profits.[12] For the average customer, the idea of having possibly paid an extra nickel or dime for misrepresented orange juice is not the stuff from which deep outrage springs—at least not in this country at this time.

There are additional problems stemming from the class congruence between the white-collar offender and the persons who pass official judgment on him. The judge who tries and sentences the criminal corporate official was probably brought up in the same social class as the offender, and often shares the same economic views. Indeed, one Washington lawyer recently told a study group examining antitrust violations that "it is best to find the judge's friend or law partner to defend an antitrust client—which we have done."[13] Also, the prosecutor, yearning for the financial support and power base that will secure his political preferment, is not apt to risk antagonizing entrenched business interests in the community. In addition, the corporate offender usually relies upon high-priced, well-trained legal talent for his defense, men skilled in exploiting procedural advantages and in fashioning new loopholes. The fees for such endeavors are often paid by the corporation itself, under the guise that such subsidies are necessary to protect the corporate image. to sustain employee morale, and to provide an adequate defense. Finally, in the extremely unlikely event that he is sentenced to imprisonment, the corporate offender is much more apt to do time in one of the more comfortable penal institutions than in the maximum-security fortresses to which *déclassé* offenders are often sent.

White-collar criminals also benefit from two prevalent, although contradictory, community beliefs. On the one hand, neighbors of the corporate criminal often regard him as upright and steadfast; indeed, they will probably see him as solid and substantial a citizen as they themselves are. Witness, for example, the following item in the hometown newspaper of one of the convicted price fixers in the 1961 heavy electrical equipment antitrust case:

> A number of telegrams from Shenango Valley residents are being sent to a federal judge in Philadelphia, protesting his sentence of Westinghouse executive John H. Chiles, Jr. to a 30-day prison term. . . .
> The Vestry of St. John's Episcopal Church, Sharon, adopted a resolution voicing confidence in Chiles, who is a member of the church. . . .
> Residents who have sent telegrams point out Chiles was an outstanding citizen in church, civic and community affairs and believe the sentence is unfair.[14]

At the same time there is a cynicism among others about white-collar crime in general, a cynicism rooted in beliefs that the practices are so pervasive and endemic that reformative efforts are hopeless. "As news of higher immoralities breaks," Mills wrote, "people often say, 'Well, another one got caught today,' thereby implying that the cases disclosed are not odd events involving occasional characters, but symptoms of widespread conditions."[15] Wearied by expected exposé, citizens find that their well of moral indignation has long since run dry. This lack of indignation can clearly benefit the white-collar criminal. For example, the following courtroom speech, delivered by

an attorney for Salvatore Bonanno—allegedly a leading figure in the network
of organized crime—reflects public leniency toward such offenses: "It does
not speak of the sort of activity where the public screams for protection,
Your Honor," the lawyer said, his voice rising. "I think that in the vernacular
the defendant stands before you convicted of having committed a white-
collar crime and, having been convicted of a white-collar crime, Your Honor,
I most respectfully . . . suggest to the court that he should be sentenced in
conformity with people who have been convicted of white-collar crimes, and
not be sentenced on the basis of his being Salvatore Bonanno."[16]

These are some of the barriers to generating public concern; what are
the forces that need to be set in motion to surmount them?

Foremost, perhaps, is the firm assurance that justice can prevail, that
apathy can be turned into enthusiasm, dishonesty into decency. History notes
that corruption was rampant in English business and government circles until
the late 1800s, when an ethos of public honesty came to prevail, largely
through the efforts of dedicated reformers.[17] Similarly, at their origin the
British police were a rank and renegade force; today they are respected and
respectable. In fact, at least one writer believes that the decency of the English police is largely responsible for the mannerly and orderly behavior shown
by the general public.[18] Thus, change can be achieved, and such change can
have eddylike effects on other elements of social existence.

Following this alteration in the psychology of the polity, the facts of
corporate crime must then be widely exposed and explained. This process
requires investigation, analysis, pamphleteering, and continual use of mass
media outlets. It is a formidable task, but one made easier by the fact that
the ingredients for success are already present: corporate offenses are notorious and their victims—especially the young—are increasingly concerned to
cope with such depredations.[19] Also, when confronted with a problem, Americans respond by taking action to resolve the difficulty, an approach quite
different from, say, that of the Chinese. As Barbara Tuchman has noted, the
Chinese, at least in pre-Communist times, regarded passivity as their most
effective tactic on the assumption that the wrongdoer ultimately will wear
himself out.[20] The ideological basis of the American ethos was set out by
Gunnar Myrdal in his now classic analysis of racial problems in the United
States. We had to work our way out of the "dilemma" involved in the discrepancy between our articulated values and our actual behavior, Myrdal believed;[21] that resolution has proceeded, largely through the use of legal forces,
though at a painfully slow and sometimes erratic pace.

So too, perhaps, with corporate crime. Part of the public may be unduly
sympathetic, and part cynical, toward revelations of such crime, but a latent
hostility is also evident. The Joint Commission on Correctional Manpower,
for instance, found from a national survey a strong public disposition to sentence accountants who embezzle more harshly than either young burglars
or persons caught looting during a riot.[22] Similarly, a 1969 Louis Harris Poll
reported that a manufacturer of an unsafe automobile was regarded by re-
spondents as worse than a mugger (68 percent to 22 percent), and a business-
man who illegally fixed prices was considered worse than a burglar (54 percent
to 28 percent).[23]

Corporate offenses, however, do not have biblical proscription—they lack, as an early writer noted, the "brimstone smell."[24] But the havoc such offenses produce, the malevolence with which they are undertaken, and the disdain with which they are continued, are all antithetical to principles we as citizens are expected to observe. It is a long step, assuredly, and sometimes an uncertain one, from lip service to cries of outrage; but at least principled antagonism is latent, needing only to be improved in decibels and fidelity. It should not prove impossible to convince citizens of the extreme danger entailed by such violations of our social compact. "Without trust, a civilized society cannot endure," Marya Mannes has said. "When the people who are too smart to be good fool the people who are too good to be smart, the society begins to crumble."[25]

It should be noted that Americans are perfectly willing to outlaw and to prosecute vigorously various kinds of behavior on social grounds, that is, in the belief that the behaviors constitute a threat to the social fabric rather than a threat to any prospective individual victims. Thus, possession of narcotics, abortion, homosexuality, and a host of other "victimless crimes"[26] are proscribed as threats to the moral integrity of our civilization. A reading of historical records indicates without question that class bias and religious intolerance were the predominant forces which gave rise to the laws against such "immoral" behavior.[27] It is now time that the rationale offered for prosecution of victimless crimes—that they threaten the integrity of the society —be applied to where it really belongs: to the realm of corporate offenses. This rationale did not work with victimless crimes because there was no reasonable way to convince nonperpetrators, often members of the perpetrators' general social groups, that what the offenders were doing was wrong. Therefore, eventually and inevitably, the logic of the perpetrators' position moved other groups either to take on their behavior (e.g., the smoking of marijuana) or to take their side (e.g., the performance of abortions). But the rationale *can* work vis-à-vis corporate crime, given its quantifiable harm actually imposed on nonparticipating victims. Also, there is the possibility of isolating the offender from reinforcement and rationalizations for his behavior, of making him appreciate that nobody morally sanctions corporate crime; of having him understand, as the English would put it, that "these kinds of things simply are not done by decent people." It is a standard defensive maneuver for criminals to redefine criminogetic behavior into benign terms. "Businessmen develop rationalizations which conceal the fact of crime," Edwin H. Sutherland wrote in 1949 in his classic study, *White Collar Crime.* "Even when they violate the law, they do not conceive of themselves as criminals," he noted, adding that "businessmen fight whenever words that tend to break down this rationalization are used."[28]

By far the best analysis of this process—and the way to combat it—is by Mary Cameron on middle-class shoplifters caught in Chicago's Marshall Field's. Store detectives advised that Field's would continue to be robbed unless some assault on the shoplifters' self-conceptions as honorable citizens was undertaken. The methods used toward this end are described by Cameron:

Again and again store people explain to pilferers that they are under arrest as thieves, that they will, in the normal course of events, be taken in a police van to jail, held in jail until bond is raised, and tried in court before a judge and sentenced. Interrogation procedures at the store are directed specifically and consciously toward breaking down any illusion that the shoplifter may possess that his behavior is merely regarded as "naughty" or "bad". . . . It becomes increasingly clear to the pilferer that he is considered a thief and is in imminent danger of being hauled into court and publicly exhibited as such. This realization is often accompanied by dramatic changes in attitudes and by severe emotional disturbance.[29]

The most frequent question the middle-class female offenders ask is: "Will my husband have to know about this?" Men express great concern that their employers will discover what they have done. And both men and women shoplifters, following this process, cease the criminal acts that they have previously been routinely and complacently committing.[30]

The analogy to the corporate world is self-evident. As a law professor has observed, "Criminal prosecution of a corporation is rather ineffective unless one or more of the individual officers is also proceeded against."[31] A General Electric executive, for example, himself not involved in the price-fixing conspiracy, said that although he had remained silent about perceived antitrust violations, he would not have hesitated to report to his superiors any conspiracy involving thefts of company property.[32] Corporate crimes simply are not regarded in the same manner as traditional crimes, despite the harm they cause, and they will not be so regarded until the criminals who commit them are dealt with in the same manner as traditional offenders.

Harrison Salisbury tells of Leningrad women taking a captured German pilot to a devastated part of the besieged city during the Second World War, trying to force him to understand what he had been doing.[33] Persons convicted of drunken driving sometimes are made to visit the morgue so that they might appreciate the kind of death they threaten. Corporate criminals, though, remain insulated from their crimes. F. Scott Fitzgerald made the point well in *The Great Gatsby:* "They were careless people, Tom and Daisy —they smashed up things and creatures and retreated back into their money or their vast carelessness, or whatever it was that kept them together, and let other people clean up the mess they had made."[34]

How can this situation be changed? Taken together, a number of possible strategies involve widespread dissemination of the facts, incessant emphasis on the implications of such facts, and the methods by which the situation can be improved. Specific tactics might include regular publication of a statistical compilation of white-collar crime, similar to the FBI's *Uniform Crime Reports,* which now cover traditional offenses. It is well to recall that in its earliest days the FBI concentrated mostly on white-collar offenses, such as false purchases and sales of securities, bankruptcy fraud, and antitrust violations;[35] it was not until later that it assumed its "gangbuster" pose. Well publicized by the media, these FBI statistical reports form the basis for a periodic temperature-taking of the criminal fever said to grip us. Numerical and case history press releases on corporate crime would publicly highlight such incidents. It is perhaps too much to expect that there will some day be a "Ten Most Wanted" white-collar crime list, but public reporting must be stressed as a prerequisite to public understanding.

Another possibility is the infiltration of criminally suspect corporations by agents of the federal government trained for such delicate undercover work. It would be publicly beneficial to determine why and how such corporations disdain the criminal statutes they are supposed to obey. The cost would be minimal, since the infiltrators would likely be well paid by the corporation, and the financial yield from prosecutions and fines would undoubtedly more than offset any informer fees involved in the operation. To some this tactic may appear too obnoxious, productive of the very kind of social distrust that the corporate crimes themselves create. But so long as infiltration remains a viable FBI tactic to combat political and street crime, its use cannot be dismissed to combat white-collar crime. But perhaps, as an alternative, large companies should have placed in their offices a public servant who functions as an ombudsman, receiving public and employee complaints and investigating possible law violations.

There are, of course, other methods of uncovering and moving against corporate crimes, once the will to do so is effectively mobilized. Mandatory disclosure rules, rewards for information about criminal violations (in the manner that the income tax laws now operate), along with protections against retaliation for such disclosures, are among potential detection procedures. The goal remains the arousal of public interest to the point where the corporate offenses are clearly seen for what they are—frontal assaults on individuals and the society. Then, journals of news and opinion, such as *Time,* will no longer print stories dealing with the antitrust violations under the heading of "Business," but rather will place the stories where they belong, in the "Crime" section.[36] And judges and prosecutors, those weathervanes of public opinion, will find it to their own advantage and self-interest to respond to public concern by moving vigorously against the corporate criminal.

ALTERNATIVE KINDS OF SANCTIONS

Sanctions against corporate criminals, other than imprisonment, can be suggested; they are milder in nature and perhaps somewhat more in accord with the spirit of rehabilitation and deterrence than the spirit of retribution. While perhaps less effective instrumentalities for cauterizing offending sources, they at least possess the advantage of being more likely to be implemented at this time.

Corporate resources can be utilized to make corporate atonement for crimes committed. A procedure similar to that reported below for dealing in Germany with tax violators might be useful in inhibiting corporate offenses:

In Germany, . . . they have a procedure whereby a taxpayer upon whom a fraud penalty has been imposed is required to make a public confession, apparently by newspaper advertisement, of the nature of his fraud, that a penalty has been imposed, that he admits the fact, and will not do it again. This procedure is known as *"tätige reue"* [positive repentance].[37]

A former FTC Chairman has said that "the Achilles heel of the advertising profession is that you worship at the altar of the positive image."[38] The same is true of corporations; thus the value of the public confession of guilt and the public promise of reform.

There is, of course, the sanction of the heavy fine. It has been argued that the disgorgement of illegal profits by the corporation—in the nature of treble damages or other multiplicated amounts—bears primarily upon the innocent shareholders rather than upon the guilty officials. This is not very persuasive. The purchase of corporate stock is always both an investment and a gamble; the gamble is that the corporation will prosper by whatever tactics of management its chosen officers pursue. Stockholders, usually consummately ignorant about the details of corporate policy and procedure, presume that their money will be used shrewdly and profitably. They probably are not too adverse to its illegal deployment, provided that such use is not discovered or, if discovered, is not penalized too heavily. It would seem that rousing fines against offending corporations will at least lead to stockholder retaliations against lax or offending managerial personnel, and will forewarn officials in other corporations that such derelictions are to be avoided if they expect to remain in their posts. The moral to widows dependent upon a steady income will be to avoid companies with criminal records, just as they are well advised to keep their money out of the grasp of other kinds of shady entrepreneurs and enterprises. Then, perhaps, sanctions against white-collar criminality can be built into the very structure of the marketplace itself.

What of corporate offenders themselves? The convicted violator might be barred from employment in the industry for a stipulated period of time, just as union leaders are barred from holding labor positions under similar circumstances.[39] In the heavy electrical equipment antitrust cases, for instance, one convicted offender was fired from his $125,000-a-year job with General Electric, but was employed immediately upon release from jail by another company at about a $70,000 annual salary. All ex-convicts ought to be helped to achieve gainful employment, but surely nonexecutive positions can be found which would still be gainful. "Business executives in general enjoy the greatest material rewards available in the world today," it has been noted. "The six-figure salaries at the top would be called piratical in any other sphere of activity."[40] A brief retirement by corporate officials from what in other forms of work is disparagingly called the "trough" does not seem to me to be an unreasonable imposition. Why put the fox immediately back in charge of the chicken coop? I recall some years ago the going joke at the Oklahoma State Penitentiary—that Nannie Doss, a woman who had a penchant for poisoning the food of her husbands, was going to be assigned duty as a mess-hall cook and then released to take a job in a short-order cafe. It was a macabre observation, except that similar things happen all the time with corporate criminals.

There have been suggestions that the penalties for corporate crime might be tailored to the nature of the offenses. Thus, the company president who insists that he had no knowledge of the crime could, if found culpable for negligent or criminal malfeasance, be sentenced to spend some time interning in the section of his organization from whence the violation arose. The difficulties inhere, of course, in the possibility of creating a heroic martyr rather than a rehabilitated official, and in problems relating to the logistics of the situation. Yet, veterans on major league baseball teams are dispatched to Class C clubs because of inadequate performance; they then attempt to work their way back to the top. The analogy is not precise, but the idea is worth further exploration.

THE ISSUE OF DETERRENCE

The evidence gleaned from the heavy electrical equipment case in 1961 represents our best information on the subject of deterrence of corporate crime; no antitrust prosecution of this magnitude has been attempted since, and very few had been undertaken earlier. Government attorneys were then convinced (I interviewed a number of them when I was gathering information on the subject for the President's Commission on Law Enforcement in 1966) that the 1961 antitrust prosecutions had been dramatically effective in breaking up price-fixing schemes by many other corporations. By 1966, however, they felt that the lesson had almost worn off. Senate hearings, conducted after the heavy electrical equipment conspirators had come out of jail, shed further light on the subject of deterrence. One witness before the Senate Antitrust and Monopoly Subcommittee—William Ginn, a former General Electric vice-president—granted that the "taint of a jail sentence" had the effect of making people "start looking at moral values a little bit." Senator Philip Hart pushed the matter further, and drew the following remarks from the witness:

> *Hart:* This was what I was wondering about, whether, absent the introduction of this element of fear, there would have been any reexamination of the moral implications.
> *Ginn:* I wonder, Senator. That is a pretty tough one to answer.
> *Hart:* If I understand you correctly, you have already answered it. . . .
> After the fear, there came the moral reevaluation.[41]

Other witnesses who had done jail time stated with some certainty that they had learned their lesson well. "They would never get me to do it again. . . . I would starve before I would do it again," said another former General Electric executive.[42] Another man, from the same organization, was asked: "Suppose your superior tells you to resume the meetings; will they be resumed?" "No, sir," he answered with feeling. "I would leave the company rather than participate in the meetings again."[43]

These penitents were the same men who had earlier testified that price fixing was "a way of life" in their companies. They had not appreciated, they said, that what they were doing was criminal (though they never used *that* word; they always said "illegal"); and if *they* had not met with competitors, more willing and "flexible" replacements were available. They were men described by one of their attorneys in a bit of uncalculated irony as not deserving of jail sentences because they were not "cut-throat competitors," but rather persons who "devote much of their time and substance to the community."[44] The convicted felons saw themselves in similar roseate ways. The GE vice president, for instance, had written: "All of you know that next Monday, in Philadelphia, I will start serving a 30 day jail term, along with six other *businessmen* for conduct which has been *interpreted* as being in conflict with the *complex* antitrust laws (italics added)."[45] O. Henry's Gentle Grafter, speaking for himself, had put it more succinctly: "I feel as if I'd like to do something for as well as to humanity."[46]

The corporate executives were model prisoners in the Montgomery County jail. The warden praised them as the best workers he had ever had on a project devoted to reorganizing the jail's record-keeping system. Thus, to the extent that they conduct themselves more honestly within the walls than they have outside, corporate offenders might be able to introduce modern business skills into our old-fashioned penal facilities. Though they were allowed visitors two days a week, the imprisoned executives refused to have their families see them during the time, slightly less than a month, that they were jailed.[47] It was shame, of course, that made them so decide—shame, a sense of guilt, and injured pride. These are not the kinds of emotions a society ought cold-bloodedly and unthinkingly try to instill in people, criminals or not, *unless* it is found necessary to check socially destructive behavior.

What of the financial sanctions? The $437,500 fine against General Electric was equivalent to a parking fine for many citizens. That the corporations still felt the need to alibi and evade before the public, however, was noteworthy for its implication that loss of goodwill, more than loss of money or even an agent or two, might be the sanction feared most. Note, for instance, the following verbal sleight of hand by General Electric about a case that involved flagrant criminal behavior and represented, in the words of the sentencing judge, "a shocking indictment of a vast section of our economy."[48] At its first annual meeting following the sentencing of the price-fixing conspirators, General Electric dismissed suggestions that further actions might be taken to cleanse itself. The idea, advanced by a stockholder, that the Company should retrieve sums paid to the conspirators as "incentive compensation" was said to "ignore the need for careful evaluation of a large number of factors." These factors—the expense of litigation and the morale of the organization—boiled down to a concern that "the best interests of the Company are served."[49] The president of Westinghouse demanded that employees adhere to the antitrust laws *not* because failure to do so was a crime or because it damaged the public. Rather, such behavior was discouraged because "any such action is—and will be considered to be—a deliberate act of disloyalty to Westinghouse."[50]

GE president Ralph Cordiner observed in 1961: "When all is said and done, it is impossible to legislate ethical conduct. A business enterprise must finally rely on individual character to meet the challenge of ethical responsibility." But by then the president had come to understand how the public might achieve what the Company could not: "Probably the strong example of the recent antitrust cases, and their consequences, will be the most effective deterrent against future violations," he decided.[51]

So the lesson had been learned—but only partly. It was much like the mother who scolds her children about stealing by saying that their behavior upsets her and might hurt the family's reputation in the neighborhood. After several such episodes, however, and a few prison terms or similarly strong sanctions against her offspring, she might suggest that a more compelling reason for not stealing is that it is a criminal offense, and that when you get caught you are going to suffer for it. When such an attitude comes to prevail in the corporate world, we will have taken a major step toward deterring corporate crime and protecting its innocent victims.

NOTES

[1]My views on prison reform are set out in *Saturday Review*, December 11, 1971, pp. 47-8, 56.

[2]President's Commission on Law Enforcement and Administration of Justice, *Crime and Its Impact—An Assessment* (Washington, D.C.: Government Printing Office, 1967), p. 104.

[3]*New York Times,* December 27, 1971.

[4]*Los Angeles Times,* May 11, 1971.

[5]Ibid. Similarly, Nader has been quoted as saying, "If you want to talk about violence, don't talk of Black Panthers. Talk of General Motors." (Quoted in "White-Collar Crime," *Barron's,* March 30, 1970, p. 10.)

[6]G. Christian Hill and Barbara Isenberg, "Documents Indicate 4 Beech Models Had Unsafe Fuel Tanks," *Wall Street Journal,* July 30, 1971, pp. 1, 6.

[7]Ibid. *See also, Warnick* v. *Beech Aircraft Corp.,* Orange County Superior Ct., File #174046 (Calif. 1971).

[8]Ralph Nader, "Foreword," to *Vanishing Air,* by J. Esposito (1970), p. viii.

[9]Nicholas Johnson, quoted in *America, Inc.,* by Morton Mintz and Jerry S. Cohen (1971), p. 81.

[10]Brooks Atkinson, *Broadway* (1970), pp. 315-316.

[11]C. Wright Mills, *The Power Elite* (1956), p. 95.

[12]James S. Turner, *The Chemical Feast* (1970), p. 63.

[13]Mark J. Green, et al., *The Closed Enterprise System* (mimeograph, 1971), p. 319.

[14]*Sharon* (Pa.) *Herald,* February 8, 1961.

[15]Mills, *Power Elite,* pp. 343-344.

[16]Gay Talese, *Honor Thy Father* (1971), p. 479. Note also:

> Last year in Federal court in Manhattan . . . a partner in a stock brokerage firm pleaded guilty to an indictment charging him with $20 million in illegal trading with Swiss banks. He hired himself a prestigious lawyer, who described the offense in court as comparable to breaking a traffic law. Judge Irving Cooper gave the stockbroker a tongue lashing, a $30,000 fine and a suspended sentence.
> A few days later the same judge heard the case of an unemployed Negro shipping clerk who pleaded guilty to stealing a television set worth $100 from an interstate shipment in a bus terminal. Judge Cooper sentenced him to one year in jail.
> In fact, some judges don't think of white-collar criminals as criminals, legal experts say.

Glynn Mapes, "A Growing Disparity in Criminal Sentences Troubles Legal Experts," *Wall Street Journal,* September 9, 1970.

[17]Ronald Wraith and Edgar Simkins, *Corruption in Developing Countries* (1964), pp. 65-170.

[18]Geoffrey Gorer, "Modification of National Character: The Role of the Police in England," *Journal of Social Issues* (1955):24-32.

[19]"The corruption of the robber baron days was more direct. Officials made straight deals for big kickbacks and usually admitted they were wrong when caught. Now the deals are comparatively small and oblique, and all proclaim innocence at the end. The effect of this hanky-panky on the restless and critical young generation in America, however, is undoubtedly greater than the spectacular official plunder of the past." James Reston, "Washington: The Supreme Court and the Universities," *New York Times,* May 18, 1969.

[20]Barbara W. Tuchman, *Stillwell and the American Experience in China, 1911-45* (1970), chap. 11.

258   THE CRIMINOLOGIST

[21]Gunnar Myrdal, *An American Dilemma* (1944).

[22]Joint Commission on Correctional Manpower and Training, *The Public Looks at Crime and Corrections,* February 1968, pp. 11-12.

[23]"Changing Morality: The Two Americas," *Time,* June 6, 1969, p. 26.

[24]E. A. Ross, "The Criminaloid," in *White-Collar Criminal,* ed. G. Geis (1968), p. 36.

[25]Quoted in Congressional Record, Vol. 111, Part 4 (March 10, 1965), p. 4631.

[26]*See generally,* Edwin M. Schur, *Crimes Without Victims* (1965).

[27]*See e.g.,* Richard J. Bonnie and Charles H. Whitebread, II, "The Forbidden Fruit and the Tree of Knowledge: An Inquiry Into the Legal History of Marihuana Prohibition," *Virginia Law Review* 56 (1970): 971.

[28]E. H. Sutherland, *White Collar Crime* (1949), pp. 222, 225.

[29]Mary O. Cameron, *The Booster and the Snitch: Department Store Shoplifting* (1964), pp. 160-162.

[30]Ibid., p. 163.

[31]Glanville Williams, *Criminal Law—The General Part,* 2nd ed. (1961), p. 865.

[32]U.S. Senate, Committee on the Judiciary, Subcommittee on Antitrust and Monopoly, *Administered Prices,* 87th Cong., 2nd Sess., 1961, Part 28, pp. 17223-17232, 17287-17288.

[33]Harrison Salisbury, *The 900 Days: The Siege of Leningrad* (1969), p. 445.

[34]F. S. Fitzgerald, *The Great Gatsby* (1925), pp. 180-181.

[35]Max Lowenthal, *The Federal Bureau of Investigation* (1950), p. 12.

[36]*Time,* February 17, 1961, p. 84.

[37]Harold C. Wilkenfeld, "Comparative Study of Enforcement Policy in Israel, Italy, the Netherlands, the United Kingdom, and Other Countries," unpublished manuscript, Internal Revenue Service, October 7, 1965.

[38]Paul R. Dixon, quoted in *New York Times,* February 10, 1966.

[39]Joseph E. Finley, *Understanding the 1959 Labor Law* (1960), p. 24.

[40]Crossland, "Confessions of a Business Dropout," *Wall Street Journal,* December 13, 1967.

[41]U.S. Senate, *Administered Prices,* Part 27, p. 17067.

[42]Ibid., p. 16790.

[43]Ibid., p. 16694.

[44]*New York Times,* February 7, 1961.

[45]*New York Times,* February 11, 1961.

[46]William S. Porter, "The Chair of Philanthromathematics," in *The Gentle Grafter* (1908), p. 48.

[47]*New York Times,* February 25, 1961.

[48]Application of the State of California, 195 F. Supp. 39 E. D. Penn. 1961.

[49]General Electric Company, *Notice of Annual Meeting of Share Owners,* March 17, 1961, pp. 17-27.

[50]*Sharon* (Pa.) *Herald,* February 12, 1961.

[51]Ralph J. Cordiner, "Comments on the Electrical Antitrust Cases," at 9th Annual Management Conference, Graduate School, University of Chicago, March 1, 1961, p. 9.

PART FIVE:
CONTROLLING THE CONTROLLERS

The state has two major agents of social control, the military and the police. As Karmen has noted, "agents provocateurs" have been important participants in the state's attempt to eliminate internal threats to its political viability. The more "normal" routine of enforcing the voluminous amount of laws in our society falls upon the domestic soldier, that is, the police. The police are invested with the authority of the state to use the ultimate sanction for illegal behavior—death; therefore, the law enforcement official is given a great deal of real and potential power in dealing with the state's citizens.

In contemporary society the police have become increasingly bureaucratized and professionalized to cope with those who violate the law. Much of the concern for increased training and personnel has been the result of civil disorders in many cities in the 1960s. Police behavior and practices may be considered as both cause and effect of such riotous behavior—the major grievance of blacks in riot cities concerned patrol practices, harassment, brutality, and unresponsiveness.[1]

The policeman has been characterized in the ghetto as a representative of a foreign, alien colonial power which evidences economic, political, and social control over its inhabitants.[2] Given such an oppressive environment, Baldwin may be correct in his observation that the only way to police a ghetto is to be oppressive.[3] It should not be surprising to discover that the police are viewed as the front line troops in attempts to maintain order in "those areas." As Dr. Kenneth Clark noted:

This society knows . . . that if human beings are confined in ghetto compounds of our cities, and are subjected to criminally inferior education, pervasive economic and job discrimination, committed to houses unfit for human habitation, subjected to unspeakable conditions of municipal services, such as sanitation, that such human beings are not likely to be responsive to appeals to be lawful, to be respectful, to be concerned with the property of others.[4]

To understand the dynamics of contemporary issues surrounding the police, we should inquire into their origin.

In the first article, Parks shows how the history of social control in the

United States has been the history of transition from a "constabulary" to a "police society." Like the emergence of laws, the rise of the professional police force is a by-product of increasing divisiveness, inequities, and interest groups. The change from constables to a professional police force also arose because of rapid urbanization, industrialization, economic specialization, and subsequent economic inequality. The visibility of gross disparities in socioeconomic status and increasing class stratification fostered protests, rebellions, and riots. The need to maintain socioeconomic dominance by quelling such disorders was an important catalyst for the emergence of the professional police in the United States. Essentially the same reasons were the principal cause of the creation of the London police force in 1829.[5] The city was threatened by the "dangerous classes," an amorphous group of thugs, protesters, and misfits. The imagery of the "dangerous classes" provoked much fear in the minds of good citizens, and was important in discrediting opponents of the state.

Apart from controlling the dangerous classes and relieving the peaceful and propertied classes of riots, the emergence of the professional police force provided many other benefits to those in power. The ordinary, "respectable" citizen no longer had to discharge police functions, and there was less need to resort to the military for domestic social control. Furthermore, the police insulated the rich from popular violence, drawing the animosity and physical attack upon themselves. Finally, and most importantly, the establishment of an "autonomous," "apolitical" agency of law enforcement gave the appearance, if not the substance, of the separation of constitutional authority from that of social and economic dominance. This final point is one of legitimacy, and all states must maintain their legitimacy among the people if they are to avoid resorting to the use of their coercive power. It appears that with increasing inequity and stratification the degree of legitimacy given the state decreased among certain segments of society. The establishment of the professional police agent from politics helped to reaffirm the legitimacy of the laws and ultimately the state. The imagery of an impartial and apolitical law enforcement body still largely remains, notwithstanding evidence to the contrary.[6]

An important change in the conception of the law accompanied the change from constable to professional police. This was from the perspective of the enforcement agent as a respondent to complaints, to the view that such an agent should prevent crime. The change from almost entirely a "reactive" to an increasingly "proactive" agent[7] is most evident in the area of victimless crimes. In such crimes there is usually no complainant, therefore, the police must search out this crime and the criminals.[8] The significance of interests, power, and privilege vis-à-vis the law is sharply reflected in the vice laws and their selective enforcement. Many citizens may be shocked at the suggestion that laws are differentially applied to different segments of society, but there are rational reasons for such behavior.

Law enforcement agencies are bureaucratic organizations that, like other bureaucratic organizations, tend to substitute for the official goals and norms of the organization, policies and activities that maximize rewards and minimize strain for the organization.[9] This goal substitution is made possible by (1) an absence of role-occupant motivation to resist pressures toward such goal substitution, (2) the pervasiveness of discretion in the role of enforcement officials, and (3) a relative absence of effective sanctions to adhere to formal organizational norms.

Given the fact that law enforcement agencies depend upon political organizations for their resource allocation, for example, the city council, they will attempt to maximize rewards and minimize strains for the organization by formally processing those who are politically weak and powerless, and refrain from processing those who are politically powerful. Therefore, in the analysis of official crime rates, one should expect the processing of a disproportionate number of the politically weak and culturally different.[10]

The importance of cultural bias in the legal system, including enforcement agencies, should not be overlooked. Some important premises of the police value system appear to be that (1) preservation of the status quo is necessary, (2) crime is inherently bad, (3) maintenance of society is dependent upon securing the lives and property of its citizenry, and (4) public peace, order, and regularity are necessary for the survival of our society.[11] From these basic premises have come five focal concerns of the police: (1) American institutions must be respected and preserved, including its symbols, such as the flag, (2) human life, particularly American, must be respected and preserved, (3) property must be respected and preserved, (4) authority must be respected and preserved, and (5) order must be respected and preserved. Of course, such cultural bias affects the manner in which the law enforcement organization, and specific agents, respond to illegal activity.

Two alternative models of criminal law enforcement have been identified, the "crime control" model and the "due process" model.[12] Of highest priority to the crime control model is the repression of criminal activity. This requires an effort to sanction a high proportion of criminal activity, leading to more of an emphasis upon the searching out of crime, a proactive emphasis. This model assumes that of those people the police suspect of criminal activity a large proportion are guilty; therefore, the presumption is one of guilt. The due process model emphasizes the protection of the noncriminal from the power of the state. Based upon the presumption of innocence, this model provides that the state's coercive power should not be used without certain procedural safeguards being invoked. Whereas enforcement agents, courts, legislators, and the "general public" give lip service to the due process model, they largely operate under the crime control model's assumption of a suspect's guilt. This is often evident in the citizens' perception that "the police would not arrest you if you had not committed a crime, therefore, the fact of your being suspected and arrested is evidence of your guilt." The apparent correctness of this conception does not justify making the assumption, but most likely supports the contention and evidence that we are all criminals periodically. However, some of us are "more criminal" than others.

The crime control perspective is the major approach of law enforcement agencies, but the application of the two models will vary depending upon the nature of the offense and of the suspect. Given the real and potential power of the middle- and upper-class clientele, plus the cultural identification by the police, the due process model is more evident in police interactions with this group of citizenry. Thus, the demeanor of the enforcement official is an important aspect of maintaining legitimacy among those who wield power. Also, the due process model will likely prevail in those "significant cases" in which the evidence is substantial and the need for conviction great. Conversely, in those offenses of a lesser nature, such as drunkenness and petit theft, and/or committed by people who are essentially impotent politically, the crime control model is more likely to be used.

In relation to the differential application of the above mentioned models, it is significant to note that almost all of the revelations of police brutality and gross violation of individual rights have occurred in cases involving the poor, nonwhite, and culturally different.[13] The reality of police brutality (both verbal and physical) is differentially realized in different segments of the population. This is reflected in the significant differences in attitudes toward the police among different racial groups.[14] Such variations reflect differences in personal and related experiences among different segments of society. Thus, while nearly all white, middle-class citizens can attest to the "real" fact that they *have not* evidenced police brutality, many poor or nonwhite segments of society can also relate the "real" fact that they *have* experienced police brutality. Such differences follow from different socialization patterns and real experiences vis-à-vis the law and agents of the state. Thus, the suggestion that "stop and frisk," "field interrogations," "tactical squads," "no knock" provisions, and so on, should be an integral part of urban law enforcement is hardly argued with by those whose community is not inundated with such patrol practices and harassments. Needless to say, if middle-class suburbia were subjected to the surveillance and proactive techniques of the inner city there would likely be a rebellion among the citizenry. The crime and the criminal (dangerous classes) are in another part of town and, therefore, that is where the preponderance of "crime control" energies should be directed.

In recent years, a number of those from the middle class have come to the stark realization of the potential brutal and repressive nature of the state's enforcement agents. Those middle-class citizens who participated in the Civil Rights Movement activities in the 1950s and 1960s became quite familiar with the police from a "new" perspective.[15] The "Sunday school" perspective of the policeman as a friend who helps little children across the street turned to a gruesome imagery of a totalitarian monster who literally beat, antagonized, and further brutalized those attempting to assert their basic democratic rights. The manifestly oppressive nature of the state and its agents of social control is most evident during such times of social change, upheaval, and crisis.

Civil disorder and the agents of social control is the focus of the second article by Gary T. Marx. After noting that the purported causes of civil disorder are specifically related to the political persuasion of the observer, the author provides an in-depth view of such events as a social process of interaction and escalation. It is, of course, very relevant to assess such societal conceptions, because these will greatly influence the degree of legitimacy given to either the government or rioters. Since it is imperative for those in power to characterize such phenomenon largely in terms of the "dangerous classes" conception of causes, the so-called riff-raff theory of riots is held by many.[16] This approach suggests that the cause is the criminal nature of the people involved. Given legitimacy, this does not threaten the distribution of power in society. A more liberal perspective would suggest that the environment produces such problems and changes in the environment need to be made. Finally, a radical perspective suggests that the riots are a form of political protest against the debasing, oppressive colonial nature of the inhabitants' existence, and that the reason such events occur is that those in power have a stake in maintaining such inequities.[17] Such alternative perspectives of causes are particularly important since they provide varying degrees of legitimacy to those in power. Therefore, it is not unimportant to realize that the emergence of the "dangerous classes" (criminal forces) imagery is an effort to conjure up proper political support and legitimacy for the actions of those in power. Such action may be from the invoking of "martial law" to the purchase of more weaponry. As has been noted, one's location in the social structure will greatly influence one's perception of the causes of such phenomena.

The often-stated idea that the police merely reflect the dominant values and attitudes of those with power is vividly portrayed in Marx's discussion of police behavior in riots, historically. The fact that police behavior reflects dominant societal standards is apparent in their active participation and/or support of violence perpetrated by whites upon blacks. Given the context of a largely racist, manifestly oppressive society one would hardly expect agents of the law to be immune to such societal influence. In fact, it is such "recognition," through demystification of the law and the agents of the state, that aids us in better understanding the state vis-à-vis those who are perceived as actual or potential threats to its viability. Although the extent and nature of white brutality and violence against nonwhites is important to recognize, we should not forget that the coercive and oppressive power of the state has been used against other "outgroups." Historically, such targets have included Catholics, Mormons, Quakers, Wobblies, and immigrant groups.[18] More recently, such outsiders as farm labor organizers, antiwar protesters, draft resisters, and counterculture advocates have been the "yardstick" for the tolerance limits of the state.

According to Marx, agents of social control appear to be better in civil disorders the higher the level of control agency, such as the military over local police, and the more recent in history the event occurs. The events of Kent State and Jackson State would make such an interpretation difficult. The use and abuse of national guard troops and state troopers in these disorders tend to negate such a notion.

Marx points out that the law appears to be enforced with much more impartiality in recent disorders than in the past, but circumstances other than increased tolerance may be operating. Recent disorders have begun and ended in black ghettos with the destruction of black property and lives. Therefore, the police are much more willing to respond "impartially" and repress the disorders in an impartial, indiscriminate manner. In the "all-out war" strategy characterizing the 1967 Detroit riots it is difficult to see how indiscriminate shooting is better than purposeful, discriminating murder. The "we-they" psychology is still evident in the use of force.

Marx makes some excellent points regarding inappropriate control strategies. The unwillingness to negotiate in potential riot situations has often produced the anticipated consequences, a self-fulfilling prophecy. For example, the rigidity and abrasiveness of Chicago officials regarding protesters' demands helped to produce the "police riots" at the 1968 Chicago convention.[19]

A major unintended consequence of enforcement officials' indiscriminate (impartial) brutalization of participants in civil disorders and/or political protest situations is the creation of martyrs and symbolic events that galvanize oppositional support. An often noted phenomenon is the "radicalization" of those who are not involved, or only peripherally involved in the disturbance. Incidents of gross, indiscriminate brutalization[20] such as Peoples Park, Chicago Convention, Santa Barbara, Columbia, Kent State, Jackson State, Greensboro State, and Southern University provide additional substance to allegations of inhumanity and repression, and new adherents to the "outgroup."

The breakdown of police organization and their subsequent disorganization is not unrelated to the "all is fair in love and war" philosophy. By meting out their own justice via night stick, mace, and ultimately the gun, the police are providing immediate sanctions to those who dare threaten the dominant values and culture.

As Skolnick notes:

> Reports in numerous cities, including Detroit, San Francisco, New York, and Oakland, indicate that police officers have attacked or shot members of the black community, often Black Panthers, at offices, social events, and even court house halls. . . . Numerous respected commissions . . . found that the police used uncalled-for force, often indiscriminately against protesters, often regardless of whether the latter were peaceful or provocative.[21]

How can the excesses of the agents of social control be reduced? A frequent suggestion for eliminating police "deviance" is through better screening of personnel, higher pay, increasing educational standards—through professionalization. Although personality "deficiencies" have been noted by various studies, organizational demands and peer pressure appear to play a major part in determining the behavior of the role occupant.[22] Socialization into the police organization appears to be a critical variable in determining the "working personality" of the policeman and his world view.[23] The facts that police have been largely isolated from "ordinary" citizens, develop a high degree of professional solidarity, and tend toward a conservative outlook politically have provided reinforcement in the police subculture for certain kinds of deviance.

A major contemporary effort to reduce tensions between the police and certain segments of the community, such as youth and nonwhites, has been the initiation of police-community relations programs. According to the President's Task Force on Police:

> Police-community relations have two essentially different aspects. First, the substantial majority of Americans respect its police force, supports its actions, and look to it for protection. Second, a significant number of people, largely the poor or members of minority groups, fear and distrust the police. Ironically, this latter group often has the greatest need for police protection because it usually inhabits the most crime-ridden sections of our cities.[24]

It is the second segment, the poor or nonwhite, that has produced the proliferation of police-community relations programs. The riotous behavior of the 1960s in the ghettos provided the impetus for increased societal attention upon police professionalism and community relations programs.[25] In fact, the Omnibus Bill was a direct response to such crisis, providing money for increasing professionalization and armament. The implication of the twofold approach may be that if they (the minority community) can not be coped with peacefully, through community relations, the firepower exists to wage all-out war against the "enemy."[26]

Three main techniques are used by the police in their community relations program: (1) police-community relations units, (2) citizen advisory committees, and (3) special programs that bring the police into continuing contact with the community.[27] Although such programs have had varying degrees of success,[28] the ultimate success of police-community relations vis-à-vis the poor, nonwhite, and/or culturally different will be determined by the extent to which citizens' grievances are acted upon. The major grievances concern harassment and brutality; therefore, in the third article, we turn to the means by which the police can be controlled.

The major method of curbing police excesses has been court decisions regarding "exclusionary rules"—such rulings hold that evidence seized in violation of the law is inadmissible in subsequent criminal prosecution. These decisions provide further ammunition for those who suggest we are "handcuffing the police," but they touch relatively few practices of police illegality. The courts have had to enter the area of police control because of the unresponsiveness of the executive and legislative branches of government.

Civil damages may be filed under both state and federal statutes, but it is costly, timely, and difficult to prove damages given the broad interpretations of lawful behavior based upon "probable cause" and "good faith" defenses. Those who are most subject to such lawlessness are least able to deal with these contingencies. Injunctions are felt by Paulsen, et al., to be a temporary remedy for "outrageous action."

State and federal statutes include criminal sanctions for illegal police conduct, but they are rarely employed. Although there have been two federal statutes prohibiting searches in excess of warrant or without a warrant since 1921, not a single violation has appeared in state appellate courts.[29] In order to establish false arrest the defendant must have criminal intent, so the "good faith" defense is usually adequate. Since prosecutors and police are dependent upon one another, the use of the criminal law against the police is harmful to this cooperative relationship. For example, there were no criminal charges brought in the Chicago "police riot" of 1968, and no local officials were prosecuted for civil rights murders in the 1960s—in such cases the defendants were charged with depriving the victim of his civil rights! The authors note that only four cases of criminal prosecution of police—all for false imprisonment—occurred between 1940 and 1968. As they point out, the policeman must appear as a "lawless hoodlum to be prosecuted,"[30] and such official interpretations of police action are rarely made.

Internal review procedures have been largely ineffectual in sanctioning illegal police behavior. This is not hard to understand given the camaraderie, isolation, peer-pressure, and institutionalized illicit behavior discovered in numerous studies. Civilian review boards have been instituted but have largely failed to effect change because of their lack of power and resources, and organized opposition. The ombudsman may be a partial solution for effecting substantive response to citizen complaints; being independent from the police, covering all governmental agencies, and having various procedural powers makes him an attractive mechanism. As the authors note, the need for effective grievance mechanisms have emanated from a number of recent renowned commissions' reports. Now is the time to act! The ultimate solution to the cause of citizen brutalization, namely, powerlessness, necessitates a redistribution of power.

NOTES

[1] *Report of the National Advisory Commission on Civil Disorders* (New York: Bantam Books, 1968), pp. 299-322.

[2] For a discussion of the colonial perspective related to various minorities *see* Robert Blauner, "Internal Colonialism and Ghetto Revolt," *Social Problems* 16 (Spring 1969):393-408; Evertt E. Hagen, "Colonialism: The Case of the Sioux," in *On the Theory of Social Change* (Homewood, Illinois: The Dorsey Press, 1962), pp. 471-502; Joan Moore, "Colonialism: The Case of Mexican-Americans," *Social Problems* 17 (Spring 1970):463-472; and Robert Blauner, *Racial Oppression in America* (New York: Harper and Row, 1972).

[3] James Baldwin, *Nobody Knows My Name* (New York: Dell Publishing, 1962).

[4] *Report on Civil Disorders*, p. 300.

[5] Allan Silver, "The Demand for Order in Civil Disorder: A Review of Some Themes in the History of Urban Crime, Police, and Riots," in *The Police: Six Sociological Essays*, ed. David Bordua (New York: John Wiley, 1967), pp. 1-24.

[6] Jerome Skolnick, *The Politics of Protest* (New York: Ballantine Books, 1969), especially chap. 7, "The Police in Protest," pp. 241-292.

[7] Albert J. Reiss, Jr., and David J. Bordua, "Environment and Organization: A Perspective on the Police," in *The Police*, Bordua, pp. 25-55.

[8] For a discussion of "vice squad" practices *see* Jerome H. Skolnick, *Justice Without Trial* (New York: John Wiley, 1966), especially chap. 6, "The Informer System," pp. 112-138, and chap. 7, "The Narcotics Enforcement Pattern," pp. 139-163.

[9] For a discussion of these organizational contingencies *see* William J. Chambliss and Robert B. Seidman, *Law, Order, and Power* (Reading, Mass.: Addison-Wesley, 1971), pp. 261-270.

[10] For a discussion of this process in relationship to nonwhites *see* Charles E. Reasons and Jack L. Kuykendall, *Race, Crime, and Justice* (Pacific Palisades: Goodyear Publishing, 1972). It should be noted that power struggles and attempts at redistribution are continually ensuing, therefore the boundaries of those who are dominant/subordinate are also subject to change, e.g., revolution and redefinitions of crime.

[11] Daniel H. Swett, "Cultural Bias in the American Legal System," *Law and Society Review* 3 (August 1969):79-110. Some may suggest that such broad generalizations are inappropriate, particularly given the "new breed" of police officers, but most of these characteristics appear to be inherent in the role given the demands of the state to preserve itself.

[12] *See* Chambliss and Seidman, *Law, Order,* pp. 271-321.

[13] *See* Albert J. Reiss, Jr., "Police Brutality—Answers to Key Questions," *Trans-Action* (July-August 1968):10-19.

[14] The President's Commission on Law Enforcement and Administration of Justice, *Task Force Report: The Police* (Washington D.C.: U.S. Government Printing Office, 1967):146-149.

[15] For an excellent overview *see* James C. Mouledous, "Political Crime and the Negro Revolution," in *Criminal Behavior Systems: A Typology,* ed. Marshall B. Clinard and Richard Quinney (New York: Holt, Rinehart and Winston, 1967), pp. 217-231.

[16] For an excellent discussion of various perspectives, *see* Louis H. Masotti and Don R. Bowen, *Riots and Rebellion* (Beverly Hills: Sage Publications, 1968).

[17] It should be noted that whereas the Kerner Report "initially indicts" white America for the environment leading to such disorders, it subsequently places the blame on the blacks' own incapacities—housing, education, etc. The political nature of both the "problem" and the "solution" is tactfully evaded.

[18] *See* especially Gustavus Myers, *The History of Bigotry in the United States* (New York: Capricorn Books, 1960), and Ted Gurr and Hugh Graham, *The History of Violence in America* (New York: Bantam Books, 1969).

[19] Daniel Walker, *Rights in Conflict* (New York: Bantam Books, 1968).

[20] For an example *see* James A. Michener, *Kent State* (New York: Random House, 1971); I.F. Stone, *The Killings at Kent State* (New York: Vintage Books, 1970); Skolnick, *Protest;* Kerner Report; National Commission on the Causes and Prevention of Violence, *Law and Order Reconsidered* (New York: Bantam Books, 1970).

[21] *See* Skolnick, *Protest,* pp. 244-245. The entire chapter, "Police in Protest," pp. 241-292, examines the growing politicization of the police.

[22] Of course the type of "solutions" are directly related to one's assumed "causes." *See* Jack L. Kuykendall, "Police Deviance in the Enforcement Role: Situational Cooperation-Compliance-Response Hierarchy of Deviant and Non-Deviant Power Strategies," *Police* (July-August 1971):44-51.

[23] *See* Skolnick, *Justice,* pp. 42-70.

[24] President's Commission, *Police,* p. 150. For an extensive discussion see pp. 144-207.

[25] This is not to say that all, or even most, community relations programs are race-relations programs. Nonetheless, the riotous behavior of the 1960s has produced a mushrooming of police-community relation programs of a varying nature.

[26] A more skeptical view sees three major efforts for controlling the ghetto, including (1) short-term measures to pacify and contain black rebellions, (2) mid-term measures appealing to business for job training and plant investment, and (3) long-term solutions through the consolidation of public/private partnership to reclaim America's underdeveloped "native quarters." *See* Beverly Leman, "Social Control of the American Ghetto," in *The Triple Revolution,* ed. Robert Perrucci and Marc Pilisuk (Boston: Little, Brown, 1971), pp. 550-560.

[27] President's Commission, *The Police,* pp. 144-206.

[28]*See* Deborah Johnson and Robert J. Gregory, "Police-Community Relations in the United States: A Review of Recent Literature and Projects," *Journal of Criminal Law, Criminology, and Police Science* 62 (March 1971):94-103, and Gary A. Kreps and Jack M. Weller, "The Police-Community Relation Movement," *American Behavioral Scientist* 16 (January/February 1973):402-412.

[29]Chambliss and Seidman, pp. 368-394.

[30]Although those subject to "police illegality" might view the actors as "lawless hoodlums" they do not have the power to make the decision to prosecute. The state must obviously protect its protectors.

FROM CONSTABULARY TO POLICE SOCIETY: IMPLICATIONS FOR SOCIAL CONTROL

EVELYN L. PARKS

The history of social control in the United States is the history of transition from 'constabulary' to 'police society' in which the proliferation of criminal laws, enforcement officials, criminal courts, and prisons was not essentially for the protection of the 'general welfare' of society but was for the protection of the interests and lifestyles of but one segment of society—those holding positions of wealth, 'respectability', and power.

The establishment of a police society in the United States made possible a new conception of law and order in which more effective control of the population was feasible. Central to this conception were laws governing the private behavior of citizens where no self-defined victims are involved—the vice laws. Thus, the growth of the police was necessary for the growth of both law and crime.

TRANSITION FROM A CONSTABULARY TO A POLICE SOCIETY

The first official responsible for the enforcement of law and order in the New World was the constable. The law as written was oppressive—outlawing swearing, lying, sabbath breaking, and night walking—and gave to the constable almost totalitarian powers to enforce the laws.[1] However, the constable did not use his power to discover and punish deviation from the established laws. Rather, he assisted complaining citizens if and when they sought his help. This reflected the conception of law during colonial times: the written law was regarded as an ideal, rather than as prescriptions actually to be enforced.

Initially, the constableship was a collective responsibility which all able-bodied men were expected to assume. It was not a specialized occupation or an income producing job, but a service to the community. The constableship was so thankless a task, however, that as early as 1653, fines were sometimes levied against anyone refusing to serve.[2]

The constable served only during the day. At night, the towns formed a citizens' watch or nightwatch. Supposedly, each adult male took his turn, but as with the constable those who could hired substitutes. In contrast to

Evelyn L. Parks, "From Constabulary to Police Society: Implications for Social Control" *Catalyst* No. 6 (Summer 1970) pp. 76-97. Reprinted by permission of the journal.

271

our present police the concerns of the nightwatch were more closely related to the general welfare. They included looking out for fires, reporting the time, and describing the weather.

Thus, there was no *one* specialized agency responsible for social control. Not only was the power divided between the constable and the nightwatch, but initially, both were volunteer services rotated among the citizens. This lack of specialization of enforcement of law and order extended to a comparative lack of specialization in the punishment of offenders. Although prisons were constructed as early as 1637, they were almost never kept in good enough condition to prevent jailbreaks. The financial cost of jails was considered prohibitive; corporal punishments, such as whippings, were preferred.[3] Thus, there was no specialized penal system, staffed and available.

Early Police

The constabulary was not able to survive the growth of urban society and the concomitant economic specialization. Charles Reith writes that voluntary observance of the laws

can be seen to have never survived in effective form the advent of community prosperity, as this brings into being, inevitably, differences in wealth and social status, and creates, on this basis, classes and parties and factions with or without wealth and power and privileges. In the presence of these divisions, community unanimity in voluntary law observance and the maintenance of authority and order must be found.[4]

By 1800 in the larger cities the constabulary had changed from a voluntary position to a quasiprofessional one, being either appointed or elected and providing an income. Some people resisted this step, claiming that such police were threats to civil liberty, and that they performed duties each citizen should perform himself. However, in the 1840s and 1850s, the nightwatch was gradually incorporated into an increasingly professionalized police, establishing 24-hour responsibility and in other ways beginning to institute the type of law enforcement that we have today.[5]

In the 1850s, cities began to employ detectives. The earliest detectives represented an attempt to apply the conception of the constableship to urban society. That is, the duties of the detective were to assist in recovering stolen property, not to prevent crime. However, this application of the constableship to the emerging urban society proved ineffective. For one thing, to recover stolen property effectively, familiarity with criminals was a necessary qualification and quite naturally ex-criminals were often hired. For another, detectives became corrupted through taking advantage of a system known as compromises Under this system, it was legal for a thief to negotiate with the robbed owner and agree to return part of the stolen goods, if the thief could remain free. Detectives, however, would often supplement their salaries by accepting thieves' offers of a portion of the stolen goods in exchange for their immunity.[6]

Understandably, detectives were reluctant to devote their time to anything other than large-scale robbery. Murder, an amateur crime at this time, went uninvestigated. Detectives essentially served the private interests of big business at the expense of the general public.

By 1880, the detective force as such had acquired such adverse publicity that in most places they were formally abolished. Their functions and services however were incorporated into the regular police. Compromises were no longer legally acceptable.

Historical Sources of the Change from Constabulary to Police

Central to the development of the professional police is the development of economic inequality. Seldon Bacon in his study of the development of the municipal police sees the increasing economic specialization and the resulting "class stratification" as the primary cause for the development of police.[7] He argues that specialists could exploit the increasing dependence of the populace on their services. Cities responded by creating specialized offices of independent inspectors who attempted to prevent exploitation or cheating of the populace. For example, the necessity in New Amsterdam to rely on specialized suppliers of firewood led as early as 1658 to the employment of firewood inspectors. Regulation of butchers, bakers, and hack drivers showed the same consequences of the inability of the citizen to rely on his own resources in a period of increasing specialization.[8]

By the time of the emergence of the professional police, the list of regulatory or inspectorial officials had grown quite long. Bacon describes the development of "the night police, the market police, street police, animal police, liquor police, the vagabond and stranger police, vehicle police, fire police, election police, Sunday police, and so on."[9] Gradually, many of these special police or inspectors were removed from the professional police to other municipal agencies. "Only slowly did regulation for the public good and the maintenance of order become themselves specializations and the full-time career police develop."[10]

The other central element in the development of the professional police was rioting, which is closely related to economic inequality. Usually, riots are an attempt by the have-nots to seek a redress of grievances from those with power and wealth. The solid citizens, on the other hand, wanted to prevent riots, to stop the disturbances in the streets. An official history of the Buffalo Police states that in March of 1834 complaints of riot and disorder continued to pour in upon the Mayor. "Rowdies paraded the streets at night, unmolested, and taxpayers became alarmed regarding both life and property."[11] Roger Lane writes of Boston, that "The problem of mob violence . . . soon compelled the municipality to take a more significant step, to create a new class of permanent professional officers with new standards of performance."[12] David Bordua and Albert Reiss write:

> The paramilitary form of early police bureaucracy was a response not only, or even primarily, to crime per se, but to the possibility of riotous disorder. Not crime and danger but the "criminal" and "dangerous classes" as part of the urban social structure led to the formation of uniformed and military organized police. Such organizations intervened between the propertied elites and the propertyless masses who were regarded as politically dangerous as a class.[13]

Riots became so frequent that the traditional method of controlling them by use of military forces became less and less effective. Military forces were unable to arrive at the scene of trouble before rioting had already reached uncontrollable proportions. This illustrates how the military may be able temporarily to enforce laws but are ineffective for sustained law enforcement.[14] The police, not the military, represent the continued presence of the central political authority.

Furthermore, in a riot situation, the direct use of social and economic superiors as the agents of suppression increases class violence.

If the power structure armed itself and fought a riot or a rebellious people, this created more trouble and tension than the original problem. But, if one can have an independent police which fights the mob, then antagonism is directed toward police, not the power structure. A paid professional police seems to separate "constitutional" authority from social and economic dominance.[15]

These trends towards the establishment of a paramilitary police were given further impetus by the Civil War. It was the glory of the Army uniform that helped the public accept a uniformed police. Previously, the police themselves, as well as the public, had objected to uniforms as implying a police state with the men as agents of a king or ruler. A uniformed police was seen as contradictory to the ideals of the American Revolution, to a republic of free men.[16] But after 1860 the police began to carry guns, although at first unofficially. Within 20 years, however, most cities were furnishing guns along with badges.

The Professional Police and the New Concept of Law

As the cities changed from a constabulary to a professional police, so was there a change in the conception of law. Whereas the constable had only investigated crimes in which a citizen had complained, the new professional police were expected to *prevent* crime. A preventive conception of law requires that the police take the initiative and seek out those engaged in violating the law—those engaged in specific behaviors that are designated as illegal. Once an individual has been arrested for breaking a law, he is then identified, labeled, and treated as a criminal. The whole person then becomes a criminal—not just an individual who has broken a law. Since now too, professional police were responsible for maintaining public order—seen as preventing crime—they came to respond to individuals who committed unlawful acts as criminal persons—as wholly illegitimate.

Processing people through this machinery stigmatizes people—that is, publicly identifies the whole person in terms of only certain of his behavior patterns. At the same time, this often leads to acceptance by such persons of that identity. In this and other ways the transition to police society *created* the underworld. A professional police creates a professional underworld.[17]

The "yellow press" which had emerged by the middle of the nineteenth century, focused on crime and violence. This helped confirm the new definition and stigmatization of the criminal person. Reporters obtained their stories by attending police courts. Police court reportage became so popular that even the conservative press eventually came to adopt it. And the police became guides to the newly discovered underworld.[18]

The establishment of a professional police concerned with prevention increases the power of the state. Roger Lane writes:

> Before the 1830s the law in many matters was regarded as the expression of an ideal. The creation of a strong police raised the exciting possibility that the ideal might be realized, that morality could be enforced and the state made an instrument of social regeneration.[19]

With the idea of prevention, then, law loses its status as only an ideal and becomes a real prescription actually to be enforced.

Those involved in the Reform Movements of the 1830s were quick to demand the services of the new police. Although they had originally objected to hiring paid, daytime police, they soon began to welcome the police as part of the reform movement, seeing the police as "moral missionaries" eventually eliminating crime and vice.[20] As Howard Becker writes, "The final outcome of a moral crusade is a police force."[21]

During the first half of the nineteenth century, the professional police increasingly took over and expanded the duties of the constableship. This led to the police themselves becoming specialists in the maintenance of public order, which involved a transition to emphasizing the prevention of crime, and the role of law as ideal became an attempt to enforce laws as real prescriptions governing conduct. In this way the police, as an agency of the state, took over the function of social control from the members of the local community. The historical sources of the change were economic inequality and increasing riots. Thus, the police became an agency of those with wealth and power, for suppressing the attampts by the have-nots to redistribute the wealth and power.

Thus, the professional police gave the upper classes an extremely useful and powerful mechanism for maintaining the unequal distribution of wealth and power: Law, which is proclaimed to be for the general welfare, is in fact an instrument in class warfare. This is most clearly demonstrated by looking at the history of the vice laws. Social control is at its greatest when the state can declare illegal and punish acts in which all parties are willing participants.

THE VICE LAWS AS SOCIAL CONTROL: THE CASE OF ALCOHOL

The most celebrated vice problem in America is the use of alcohol. The use of alcohol dates back to early colonial times, during which nearly everybody drank: men, women, and children—it was an indispensable part of living. Drinking was usually family-centered and family-controlled, or part of community events.[22]

In early colonial times, mostly wine and beer were imbibed, with hard liquor (distilled spirits) in third place. However, hard liquor was much easier to transport as well as less subject to spoilage than wine and beer or the grains from which they were derived. As the colonies developed a market economy, this pushed the manufacturing and selling of hard liquors rather than beer and wine. The manufacturing and selling of hard liquor became an important part of the developing colonial commerce. "During the years immediately preceding the Revolution, more than 600,000 gallons were shipped abroad annually."[23]

As the manufacturing changed from wine and beer to hard liquor, so did the drinking habits of the colonists. By the end of the eighteenth century about 90 percent of the alcohol consumed in this country was in the form of hard liquor. "By 1807, it is recorded that Boston had one distillery for every 40 inhabitants—but only two breweries."[24]

Just as the drinking began to change from beer and wine to hard liquor, so also, around 1750, the context began to change from a family activity to an individual one. Men, especially young, unattached men and other "peripheral segments" of society, began to do most of the drinking.[25] Saloons and taverns, instead of the home, became the place to drink.

These changes brought about a great increase in the amount and frequency of intoxication. Spirits are more intoxicating than either wine or beer, and the context of the saloon places no restrictions on consumption. The 30 years preceding and the 50 years following the American Revolution was an era of extremely heavy drinking.[26]

The Temperance and Prohibition Movement

As the amount and frequency of drunkenness increased so did social concern about drinking. Drunkenness was often accompanied by destructive behavior. Intoxication came to be seen "as a threat to the personal well-being and property of peaceful citizens."[27] In this way, the call to moderation was an attempt to control those who were seen as a threat by the "solid" citizens. And so the Temperance Movement began in the last half of the eighteenth century.

In the 1830s the Temperance Movement altered its goal from moderation to abstinence. Why did abstinence, rather than moderation, become the symbol of respectability? Joseph R. Gusfield, who has interpreted the Temperance/Prohibition Movement in terms of its symbolic meanings and status conflicts, considers the Temperance Movement and ultimately Prohibition as a quest for honor and power. Gusfield argues that coercive reform, or the change from temperance to abstinence, became necessary with the decline of the pre-Civil War Federalist aristocracy and the rise to social and political importance of the "common man," that which is symbolized by Andrew Jackson's election to the presidency.[28]

To make the new common man respond to the moral ideals of the old order was both a way of maintaining the prestige of the old aristocracy and an attempt to control the character of the political electorate.[29]

Lyman Beecher, a leading Temperance leader, puts it more forcefully,

When the laboring classes are contaminated, the right to sufferage becomes the engine of destruction. . . . As intemperance increases, the power of taxation will come more and more into the hands of men of intemperate habits and desperate fortunes; of course, the laws will gradually become subservient to the debtor and less efficacious in protecting the rights of property.[30]

The insistence on total abstinence came just when the country's drinking habits were becoming more moderate and changing from hard liquors back again to wine and beer. In 1800, when most drinking was of hard liquor, 90 percent of the white population was from Britain. By 1840, the immigration of ethnic groups from southern, central, and eastern Europe (where drinking habits were of wine and beer) acted as a moderating influence on the drinking habits of the nation.[31] Only total abstinence, then, would be a symbol of power and respectability—moderation was not enough to indicate superiority.

The change from moderation to abstinence was reflected in the laws of Massachusetts. In 1835, a Massachusetts statute revision made single incidences of drunkenness a punishable offense. Prior to this only the habitually drunk were usually arrested. In Boston, the number of drunk arrests jumped from the few hundred annually during the 1830s to several thousand in the 1840s and 1850s. Even before the middle of the century, Theodore Parker believed that "the 'rude tuition' of courts and constables was improving the drinking habits of the Irish immigrants."[32] In 1841, the Boston Society for the Suppression of Intoxication petitioned for a doubling of the police force.[33]

Thus, the Temperance/Prohibition Movement was an effort to control the "dangerous classes," to make them conform to middle-class standards of respectability. As is so often the case, the stated goals of improving society or helping the unfortunates muted the fact that this "help" came in the form of control—the police power of the state. Not only did alcohol use come to be universally defined as a social problem, but criminal law and police enforcement was commonly seen as the solution to the problem.

The thought and research of seemingly all fields could be used to support the claims of the prohibitionists. Based on research done in the last half of the nineteenth century, scientists began to describe the negative effects alcohol has on the human body, and for the first time claimed that even moderate drinking might cause liver, kidney, and heart diseases.[34]

In 1914, psychiatrists and neurologists meeting in Chicago adopted a resolution concluding that the availability of alcoholic beverages caused a large amount of mental, moral, and physical degeneracy and urged the medical profession "to take the lead in securing prohibitory legislation."[35]

Temperance groups were even able to utilize mortality studies done by insurance companies. A study drawing on the experience of two million policy holders between 1885 and 1908, concluded that those who drank the equivalent of only two glasses of beer each day showed a mortality rate of 18 percent higher than average. Furthermore, those who drank two ounces or more of alcohol each day were found to have a mortality rate of 86 percent higher than insured lives in general.[36]

Social workers, lawyers, and judges began to claim that alcohol played an important role in crime. On the basis of a study of 13,402 convicts in 12 different states, the community leaders of one city concluded that "intemperance had been the sole cause of crime in 10 percent of the cases, the primary cause in 31 percent, and one of the causes in nearly 50 percent."[37] Alcohol was also claimed to be an important factor in prostitution and venereal disease. (One physician reported that 70 percent of all venereal infection in men under

25 was contracted while under the influence of alcohol.)[38]

In addition, Prohibitionists claimed the use of alcoholic beverages was an important factor in domestic unhappiness and broken homes. "According to a study by the U.S. Bureau of the Census, for the years 1887-1906, nearly 20 percent of all divorces were granted for reasons of intemperance."[39]

Even notable academicians argued that alcohol was one of the chief factors creating crime and that the state ought to abolish it.[40] A noted sociologist felt that instituting national prohibition would reduce crime and poverty, improve the position of women and children, benefit the home, purify politics, and elevate the status of the wage earner.[41]

The Volstead Act and Enforcement

The Prohibitionists were successful and in 1918 the Volstead Act was passed. As is well known, the attempt to enforce the Volstead Act resulted in corruption unparalleled in American history. Stories of dry agents and other governmental personnel responsible for enforcement conniving with smugglers or accepting bribes appeared in the newspapers day after day. For example, in Philadelphia, a grand jury investigation in 1928 showed that one police "inspector had $193,533.22 in his bank account, another had $102,829.45, and a third had $40,412.75. One police captain had accumulated a nest egg of $133,845.86, and nine had bank accounts ranging from $14,607.44 to $68,905.89."[4]

By the fall of 1923 in Philadelphia, things were so bad that the mayor requested President Harding to lend the city the services of Brigadier General Smedley D. Butler of the Marine Corps, a famous soldier of World War I. General Butler arrived and began a whirlwind round of raids and arrests. At first it appeared he would succeed in enforcing the Volstead Act, but then: places were found empty when raids were attempted (they had been warned); the courts would dismiss cases brought before them. General Butler stuck it out for two years before returning to the Marine Corps declaring the job had been a waste of time: "trying to enforce the law in Philadephia," he said, "was worse than any battle I was ever in."[43]

When the Volstead Act was passed, the justice department made no special preparation to handle extra violators. The result is that within a few months federal courts throughout the country were overwhelmed by the number of dry cases, and Emory R. Buckner, United States Attorney from New York, told a congressional committee in 1926 that

violators of the Volstead Act were being brought into the Federal Building in New York City at the rate of about 50,000 a year, and the United States Attorney's office was five months behind in the preliminary steps of preparing cases.[44]

The volume of lawbreakers was so tremendous that those who could pay the fines and/or bribe the officials went free. A jury trial was impossible.[45]

And so goes the story of the attempt to enforce Prohibition. It is generally thought of as such a fiasco, such an aberration of American justice that those who study it feel a need for an explanation of its existence. This need for explanation, however, usually does not extend to our other vice laws, such as drug laws, which are still seen as supporting democracy and justice for all.

THE VICE LAWS AS SOCIAL CONTROL:
THE CASE OF NARCOTIC DRUGS

The scientific condemnation of the dangers involved in the use of alcohol did not extend even to warnings about the dangers in the use of opium and its derivatives. Indeed, the use of such drugs was systematically encouraged in the nineteenth century. Opium constituted the main therapeutic agent of medical men for more than two thousand years—through the nineteenth century. A physician writes:

Even in the last half of the nineteenth century, there was little recognition of and less attention paid to overindulgence in or abuse of opium. It was a panacea for all ills. When a person became dependent upon it so that abstinence symptoms developed if a dose or two were missed, more was taken for the aches and pains and other discomforts of abstinence, just as it was taken for similar symptoms from any other cause.[46]

In 1804 a German chemist isolated morphine. In this country, morphine began to be applied hypodermically in the 1850s. At first, it was declared that administration through the skin, as opposed to through the mouth, was *not* habit forming. Although there were soon isolated warnings that the hypodermic habit was even harder to break than the oral habit, the great majority of textbooks on the practice of medicine failed to issue any warning of the dangers of the hypodermic use of morphine until 1900.[47]

In 1898 heroin was isolated. Heroin is approximately three times as powerful as morphine and morphine is more potent than opium. Opium is generally smoked while its derivatives are taken orally or with hypodermic needles.[48] At first it was also claimed that heroin was free from addiction-forming properties, possessing many of the virtues and none of the dangers of morphine and codeine. Heroin was even recommended as a treatment for those addicted to morphine and codeine. For the next few years, doctors continued to report in medical journals on the curative and therapeutic value of heroin, either omitting any reference to addiction, or assuming any addiction to be very mild and much less bothersome than morphine addiction. It was 1910 before the medical profession began to warn of the addictive dangers of heroin.[49]

Throughout the nineteenth century, if overindulgence was necessary, many preferred addiction to narcotics than alcohol. In 1889 a doctor observed:

The only grounds on which opium in lieu of alcohol can be claimed as reformatory are that it is less inimical to healthy life than alcohol, that it calms in place of exciting the baser passions, and hence is less productive of acts of violence and crime; in short, that as a whole the use of morphine in place of alcohol is but a choice of evils, and by far the lesser. . . .

I might, had I time and space, enlarge by statistics to prove the law-abiding qualities of opium-eating peoples, but of this anyone can perceive somewhat for himself, if he carefully watches and reflects on the quiet, introspective gaze of the morphine habitué and compares it with the riotous devil-may-care leer of the drunkard.[50]

During the nineteenth century it was primarily the respectable rather than the criminal classes who used the drug. It has been suggested that part of the reason the use of opium became so popular at this time was that the respectable people "crave the effect of a stimulant but will not risk their reputation for temperance by taking alcoholic beverages."[51]

Drugs could be purchased openly and cheaply from the drugstores. Not only could the narcotics themselves be bought, but many kinds of opiate-containing patent medicines were advertised. Anyone interested could buy paregoric, laudanum, tincture of opium, morphine, Womslow's Soothing Syrup, Godfrey's Cordial, McMumn's Elixir of Opium, or others.[52] "The more you drink," one tonic advertised, "the more you want." Mothers fed their babies 750,000 bottles of opium-laced syrup a year.[53]

Whereas white Americans previously had used opium in all other derivative forms, the smoking of opium was introduced by Chinese immigrants in California, and was outlawed in San Francisco in 1875.[54] This is the first time opium or any of its derivatives was outlawed in the United States. It appears that the legislation outlawing opium was an attempt to control the Chinese immigrants, to make them conform to the "American Way of Life," much as the drinking laws in Boston in the 1830s and 1840s were used to control the Irish immigrants.

The Harrison Act and Enforcement

In 1914 Congress passed the Harrison Act. While with the Volstead Act it is clear that total abstinence was the goal and intent of the law, it is unclear as to the actual intentions of Congress when the Harrison Act was passed. Some authors contend that the Harrison Act was intended only as a revenue measure, attempting to tax drugs. The desire was to regulate the use of drugs, not to impose abstinence. The careful wording of the Harrison Act which allows for medical doctors to treat or prescribe drugs for addict-patients is referred to as evidence. Whatever the original intentions of Congress, through a series of Supreme Court rulings, by 1922 the Harrison Act came to mean total abstinence for all.[55]

As with the Volstead Act, legislation of the Harrison Act was easier than enforcement. It is difficult to enforce laws preventing activities in which all parties are willing participants. This is especially true when the contraband object is very small in size. In this way, the existence of laws prohibiting crimes without victims increases the power of the police as it necessitates and legitimates a close surveillance of the population.

In order to enforce laws preventing activities in which there is no citizen-complainant, police must develop an information system and much of police energy is devoted to finding lawbreakers.[56] "The informer system has become such an intrinsic component of police work that the abilities of a professional detective have come to be defined in terms of his capacity to utilize this system."[57] Or as Westley puts it: "a detective is as good as his stool pigeon." Westley adds further that the solutions to crimes are largely the result of bargains detectives make with underworld figures.[58]

The relation of detective to informer is illustrated by the following newspaper report on the retirement of Mr. Dean J. Gavin, Detective Sergeant of the Buffalo police, after 34 years of police work, 17 of them as a member of the Narcotics Squad.

His contacts in the underworld are legion. And when he sends out a message seeking information on anything from a burglary to a narcotics delivery, the tenants in crime's jungle make certain that Dean Gavin gets the answers.

The criminals who maintain the information-gathering network for Detective Sergeant Gavin have a universal contempt for the police . . . but they respect him.[59]

Police, then, need informers to enforce the vice laws. The existence of vice laws assures the police of a sizeable group who are in need of the favors and generosity of the police, and thus are willing to serve as informers for those favors. Police can reward the cooperative informer by reduced sentences or failure to prosecute. The stiffer and more severe the penalty, the greater the amount of bargaining power or discretion in the hands of the police—the greater the penalty, the greater the power of the police.

The police-informer system rests on the ability of the police to withhold prosecution if they desire. This means the cooperation of the District Attorney and even the courts is necessary. An informer system assumes the absense of an injured party, and of a citizen complainant.

The difficulty of enforcing laws without a complainant is clearly shown in the enforcement of the narcotic laws. The addict-informer becomes the chief source of information for violation of the narcotic laws. Police attempt to arrest the big-time operator through the addict-informer. "The Bureau of Narcotics is authorized to pay the 'operating expenses' of informants whose information leads to seizure of drugs in illicit traffic."[60] Narcotic agents will supply informants with drugs, money to purchase drugs, or allow them to steal for money to purchase drugs. Thus, the law permits narcotic agents to do precisely what it forbids the doctor—supply the addicted with drugs.

Some lawyers have been disturbed at the Federal Bureau's dependence on informers. In a 1960 decision, Judge David Bazelon of the U.S. Court of Appeals for the District of Columbia Circuit criticized the Narcotic bureau:

It is notorious that the narcotics informer is often himself involved in the narcotics traffic and is often paid for his information in cash, narcotics, immunity from prosecution, or lenient punishment. . . . Under such stipulation it is to be expected that the informer will not infrequently reach for shadowy leads, or even seek to incriminate the innocent.[61]

In March 1959, in New York, a district judge acquitted a defendant who had been enticed into addiction by an informer for the Bureau of Narcotics. The judge said the defendant's participation in the crime "was a creation of the productivity of law-enforcement officers."[62]

Once an individual is labeled an addict by the police, there is no restraint on their power. Police can break into a known addict's residence. If they find narcotics in his possession or marks on his arm, they can demand that he "rat" on his source or spend 90 days in jail and face the "cold turkey" treatment. Once an individual has had "narcotic" dealings with the police, he can expect further dealings. If he should object to strong-arm methods or lack of·"due process," the police can threaten to punish him with the full force of the laws.

It appears then, that the enforcement of laws against activities in which there is no citizen complainant does not occur along legal lines. Establishing laws which proscribe such activities and establishing a police force to discover and prosecute persons who engage in such activities maximizes the possibilities of social control, in that it necessitates and legitimates a close surveillance of the population.

SELECTIVE ENFORCEMENT OF THE VICE LAWS: THE IMMUNITY OF THE POWERFUL

It has been argued that the police and the legal system serve the interests of the powerful. This has been shown previously in that the powerful are able to get their own moral values passed as laws of the land—this is part of the definition of power. Also, however, they appear to be immune from the application or enforcement of the law. This can be substantiated by looking at the mechanics of enforcement. The police tend to divide the populace into two groups—the criminal and the noncriminal—and treat each accordingly. In police academies the recruits are told: "There are two kinds of people you arrest: those who pay the fine and those who don't."[63]

William Westley asked the policemen in his study to describe the section of the general public that likes the police. Replies included:

"The law-abiding element likes the police. Well the people that are settled down are polite to policemen, but the floater—people who move around—are entirely different. They think we are after them."[64]

Westley concludes that "the better class of people," those from better residential neighborhoods and skilled workers, are treated with politeness and friendliness, because "that is the way to make them like you." In the policeman's relation to the middle class, "The commission of a crime by an individual is not enough to classify him a criminal."[65]

He sees these people [middle class] as within the law, that is, as being within the protection of the law, and as a group he has to observe the letter of the law in his treatment of them. Their power forces him to do so. No distinction is gained from the apprehension of such a person. Essentially, they do not fall into the category of potential criminals.[66]

Whereas, for people in the slums, the patrolman feels that roughness is necessary, both to make them respect the policeman and to maintain order and conformity. Patrolmen are aware that it is slum dwellers' lack of power which enables him to use roughness and ignore "due process."

Skolnick writes that the police wish that "civil liberties people" would recognize the differences that police follow in applying search and seizure laws to respectable citizens and to criminals.[67]

The immunity of those with power and wealth to having the law apply to them is so traditional that the police in one city were able to apply the normally withheld law enforcement to political officials as a measure of collective bargaining. The report of the activities of the Police Locust Club (police union) of Rochester, New York, on the front page of the local newspaper is remarkable.

The first move was to ticket cars owned by public officials for violations of the state Motor Vehicle Law.

According to the club president, Ralph Boryszewski, other steps will include:

Refusal to "comply with requests from politicians for favors for themselves and their friends."

Cracking down on after-hours spots and gambling establishments "which have been protected through the silent consent of public officials."

"These evils have existed as long as the police department has, and the public should know what's going on," Boryszewski said today. The slowdown is "really a speedup in enforcement of the law," he said. "The public won't be hurt, we're after the men who think they're above the law."[68]

A Vermont urologist was charged with failure to file an income tax return for the years 1962, 1963, and 1964. However, he entered a plea of *nolo* on the 1964 charge only. "The judge said he accepted the lesser plea solely because it might jeopardize the doctor's standing in the medical profession."[69]

Drug users who fail to fit the "dope fiend" image, that is, drug users who are from the "respectable" or upper classes, are not regarded as narcotic criminals and do not become part of the official reports. When the addict is a well-to-do professional man, such as a physician or lawyer, and is well spoken and well educated, then prosecutors, policemen, and judges alike seem to agree that "the harsh penalties of the law . . . were surely not intended for a person like this, and, by an unspoken agreement arrangements are quietly made to exempt him from such penalties."[70] The justification usually offered for not arresting addicted doctors and nurses is that they do not resort to crime to obtain drugs and are productive members of the community. "The only reason that users in the medical profession do not commit the crimes against property which other addicts do, is, of course, that drugs are available to them from medical sources."[71]

The more laws a nation passes, the greater the possible size of the criminal population. In 1912, Roscoe Pound pointed out "of one hundred thousand persons arrested in Chicago in 1912, more than one-half were held for violations of legal precepts which did not exist 25 years before."[72] Ten years ago, it was established that "the number of crimes for which one may be prosecuted has at least doubled since the turn of the century."[73]

The increase has been in misdemeanors, not felonies. Sutherland and Gehlke, studying trends from 1900 to 1930 found little increase in laws dealing with murder or robbery. "The increase came in areas where there was no general agreement: public morals, business ethics, and standards of health and safety."[74]

The prevention of felonies, and the protection of the community from acts of violence, is usually given as the *raison d'etre* of criminal law and the justification for a police system and penal sanctions. Yet, most police activity is concerned with misdemeanors, not felonies. Seldon Bacon writes

What are the crimes which hurt society so often and so intensely that the society must react to such disorder and must react in an effective way (i.e., with organization, equipment, and specialization)? The answer of the modern criminologist to this question is felonies. The case studies, however, clearly indicate that society does not react in these ways to felonies nearly as much as to misdemeanors. Indeed, the adjustment to felonious activity is a secondary if not a tertiary sphere of action. Moreover, judicial studies of the present day point to the same findings, misdemeanor cases outnumber felony cases 100 to 1. Yet the criminologists without exception have labored almost exclusively in the sphere of felonies.[75]

One writer noted that "in the three years from 1954 through 1956 arrests for drunkenness in Los Angeles constituted between 43 and 46 percent of all arrests bookings."[76] The importance of this is not in the prevalence of drunkenness as much as it is in the easy rationale afforded the police for maintaining order and conformity, for "keeping the peace."[77] Now that marijuana smoking is apparently so widespread, laws preventing its use give police an excuse to arrest anyone they see as a threat to "order."

Becker writes, "In America, only about 6 out of every 100 major crimes known to police result in jail sentences."[78] In addition, only about 20 percent of original reports find their way into criminal statistics.[79] It appears then, that the police have considerable discretion in deciding which violators to punish, or in deciding when an individual has committed a violation.

The greater the number of punitive laws, and the stiffer the penalties, the easier it is to attempt enforcement of any *one* law. Police threaten prostitutes with arrest, using the threat to get a lead on narcotic arrests; if the prostitute informs, then there is no arrest or reduced charges.[80] Liquor laws can be used to regulate or control "homosexual" bars.[81] Burglary informants as well as narcotic informants are usually addicts. Skolnick writes, "In general, burglary detectives permit informants to commit narcotic offenses, while narcotic detectives allow informants to steal."[82]

As early as 1906, Professor Ernst Freund commented upon the range of criminal legislation. "Living under free institutions we submit to public regulation and control in ways that appear inconceivable to the spirit of oriental despotism."[83]

As the laws increase in range and number, the population is criminalized, especially the population from low-economic background, minority racial groups, or nonconformists in other ways. John I. Kitsuse writes about those labeled as deviant.

For in modern society, the socially significant differentiation of deviants from the nondeviant population is increasingly contingent upon circumstances of situation, place, social and personal biography, and the bureaucratically organized activities of agencies of control.[84]

CONCLUSION

The attempt to enforce vice laws, as laws prohibiting activities in which there is no self-defined victim, is frequently referred to as the attempt to enforce "conventional morality." The implication is that other laws, like laws proscribing murder, have something like a metaphysical transcultural base. Today, however, many conventional sociologists and criminologists have come to the conclusion that *all* activities of police and criminal courts, not just those concerned with vice laws, enforce the moral order—enforce conformity—rather than enforce the law. Bordua and Reiss write, "police above all link daily life to central authority; moral consensus is extended through the police as an instrument of legitimate coercion."[85] Alan Silver sees the extension of moral consensus and the development of the professional police as aspects of the same historical development—the "police are official representatives of the moral order."[86]

This appears to be an apparent conclusion when one realizes that "nothing is a crime which the law does not so regard and punish."[87] As Durkheim suggests, yesterday's bad taste is today's criminal law.[88] Or, as Becker writes, "Deviance is not a quality of the act the person commits, but rather a consequence of the application by others of rules and sanctions to an 'offender.'"[89] F.L. Wines writes:

> Crime is not a character which attaches to an act. . . .
> It is a complex relation which the law created between itself and the lawbreaker. The law creates crime. It therefore creates the criminal, because crime cannot be said to exist apart from the criminal.[90]

As Saint Paul said, "Without the law, sin is dead."

Instituting prohibitive laws against any activity establishes the "language of punishment." The existence of "the autocratic criminal law . . . compels and accustoms men to control their fellows without their consent and against their wills. It conveys to them the idea that such must be and is inevitable."[91]

For purposes of social control, then, the effects of laws prohibiting murder and beer drinking are the same. The enforcement of both serves to maintain the unequal distribution of power and wealth.

It appears, therefore, that there are no substantive distinctions among the ideas of enforcing the moral order, enforcing conventional morality, enforcing conformity, enforcing the law, and maintaining the unequal distribution of power. Crimes are violations of those moral values that the nation-state enforces through punitive law. The morality enforced is always the morality of those in power and it is primarily enforced upon those without power. That a group's morality and value system is enforced is part of the definition of its having power. To put it thus, the unequal distribution of power and wealth is maintained in part by police enforcement of the morality and value system of those with power and wealth.

The vast number of our laws provides the means for selective enforcement, and selective enforcement means the immunity of the rich and powerful. The greater the number of laws, the easier it is to control those without power and wealth. The content of the laws is not crucial for purposes of social control. What is crucial is the power to establish the "language of punishment" (or conversely, "the language of legitimacy"), the power to institute both the enforcers of law—the police—and the violators of law—the criminals.

NOTES

[1] Carl Bridenbaugh, *Cities in the Wilderness: The First Century of Urban Life in America* (New York: A. A. Knopf, [1938] 1955), p. 64.

[2] Ibid., p. 65.

[3]Carl Bridenbaugh, *Cities in Revolt: Urban Life in America* 1743-1776 (New York: A. A. Knopf, 1955), p. 119.

[4]Charles Reith, *The Blind Eye of History: A Study of the Origins of the Present Police Era* (London: Farber and Farber, 1952), p. 210.

[5]David Bordua and Albert Reiss, Jr., "Law Enforcement," in *The Uses of Sociology* by Paul F. Lazarsfeld et al. (New York: Basic Books, 1967), p. 276.

[6]Edward Crapsey, *The Nether Side of New York* (New York: Sheldon and Co., 1872), pp. 15-16. Today, "compromises" sometimes occur in civil rather than criminal court cases, or as "out of court" settlements, available only in white-collar criminality. *See* Edwin H. Sutherland, "White Collar Criminality" in *Radical Perspectives on Social Problems*, ed. by Frank Lindenfeld (New York: Macmillan, 1968), pp. 149-159.

[7]Seldon Bacon, *The Early Development of American Municipal Police*, unpublished Ph.D. Dissertation, Yale University, 1939, vol. 1 and 2.

[8]Bacon, *Early Development*, vol. 1, cited in Bordua and Reiss, "Law Enforcement," p. 277.

[9]Ibid., pp. 279-80.

[10]Bordua and Reiss, p. 280.

[11]Mark S. Hubbell, *Our Police and Our City: A Study of the Official History of the Buffalo Police Department* (Buffalo: Bensler and Wesley, 1893), pp. 57-58.

[12]Roger Lane, *Policing the City—Boston* 1822-1885 (Cambridge: Harvard University Press, 1967), p. 26.

[13]Bordua and Reiss, p. 282.

[14]Reith, *Blind Eye*, p. 19.

[15]Alan Silver, "The Demand for Order in Civil Society: A Review of Some Themes in the History of Urban Crime, Police, and Riot," in *The Police: Six Sociological Essays*, ed. David J. Bordua (New York: Wiley, 1967), pp. 11-12.

[16]Raymond Fosdick, *American Police Systems* (New York: The Century Co., 1921), p. 70.

[17]*See* Lane, *Policing the City*, p. 54.

[18]Ibid., p. 50.

[19]Ibid., p. 222.

[20]Ibid., p. 49.

[21]Howard S. Becker, *Outsiders: Studies in the Sociology of Deviance* (Glencoe: The Free Press, 1963), p. 156.

[22]Robert Straus, "Alcohol," in *Contemporary Social Problems*, ed. Robert K. Merton and Robert A. Nisbet, 2nd ed. (New York: Harcourt, Brace, and World, 1966), p. 244.

[23]Herbert Asbury, *The Great Illusion: An Informal History of Prohibition* (Garden City, New York: Doubleday), p. 7.

[24]Straus, "Alcohol," p. 245.

[25]Asbury, *Great Illusion*, pp. 13-14; Straus, p. 246

[26]Asbury, p. 13.

[27]Straus, p. 246.

[28]Joseph R. Gusfield, *Symbolic Crusade: Status Politics and The American Temperance Movement* (Urbana: University of Illinois Press, 1966).

[29]Ibid., p. 21.

[30]Lyman Beecher, *Six Sermons on Intemperance* (New York: American Trust Society, 1843), pp. 57-58, quoted in Gusfield, ibid., p. 43.

[31]Straus, p. 249.

[32]Lane, p. 49.

[33]Ibid.

[34]J. H. Timberlake, *Prohibition and the Progressive Movement* 1900-1920 (Cambridge: Harvard University Press, 1963), p. 41.

[35]*Anti-Saloon League, Proceedings,* 1919, pp. 45-46, quoted in ibid., p. 47.

[36]Edward B. Phelps, "The Mortality from Alcohol in the United States—the Results of a Recent Investigation of the Contributory Relation with Each of the Assigned Causes of Adult Mortality," International Congress of Hygiene and Demography, *Transactions*, 1912 (6 vols., Washington, 1913), vol. 1, pp. 813-822, quoted in Timberlake, pp. 54-55.

[37]John Koren, *Economic Aspects of the Liquor Problem* (Boston, 1899), p. 30, quoted in Timberlake, p. 57.

[38]John B. Huber, "The Effects of Alcohol," *Collier's Weekly* 57 (June 3, 1916):32, quoted in Timberlake, p. 58.

[39]George Elliot Howard, "Alcohol and Crime: A Study in Social Causation," *The American Journal of Sociology* 24 (July 1918):79, quoted in Timberlake, p. 58.

[40]Howard, pp. 61-64, and 80, quoted in Timberlake, p. 60.

[41]Edward A. Ross, "Prohibition as a Sociologist Sees It," *Harper's Monthly Magazine* 142 (January 1921):188; this article was reprinted in Ross's *The Social Trend* (New York, 1922), pp. 137-160, and quoted in Timberlake, pp. 60-61.

[42]Asbury, p. 185.

[43]Ibid., p. 186.

[44]Ibid., p. 169.

[45]Ibid., pp. 169-170.

[46]Nathan E. Eddy, "The History of the Development of Narcotics," *Law and Contemporary Problems* 22 (Winter 1957):3.

[47]Charles E. Terry and Mildred Pellens, *The Opium Problem* (New York: Haddon Craftsmen, 1928), p. 72.

[48]Alfred R. Lindesmith, *Addiction and Opiates* (Chicago: Aldine, 1968 [first published 1947]), p. 208.

[49]Terry and Pellens, *Opium Problem,* pp. 78-85.

[50]J. R. Black, "Advantages for Substituting the Morphia Habit for the Incurably Alcoholic," *Cincinnati Lancet-Clinic* 22 (1889):537-541, quoted in Lindesmith, *Addiction,* pp. 211-212.

[51]Rufus King, "Narcotic Drug Laws and Enforcement Policies," *Law and Contemporary Problems* 22 (Winter 1957):113.

[52]Lindesmith, p. 210.

[53]Stanley Meisler, "Federal Narcotics Czar," *The Nation*, February 20, 1960, p. 159.

[54]Terry and Pellens, p. 73.

[55]*See* Lindesmith, p. 6, and King, "Drug Laws," p. 121.

[56]*See* Jerome Skolnick and J. Richard Woodworth, "Bureaucracy, Information and Social Control: A Study of Morals Detail," in *The Police: Six Sociological Essays*, ed. Bordua, pp. 99-136.

[57]Jerome H. Skolnick, *Justice Without Trial: Law Enforcement in Democratic Society* (New York: John Wiley), p. 238.

[58]William A. Westley, "The Police: A Sociological Study of Law, Custom, and Morality," unpublished Ph.D. Dissertation, University of Chicago, 1951, pp. 70-71.

[59]Ray Hill, "Even the Crooks He Pursues Respect Gavin," *Buffalo Evening News*, February 3, 1968, Sunday edition.

[60]Edwin M. Schur, *Crime Without Victims: Deviant Behavior and Public Policy* (Englewood Cliffs, New Jersey: Prentice Hall, 1965), p. 135.

[61]Stanley Meisler, "Federal Narcotics Czar," *The Nation*, February 20, 1960, p. 160.

[62]Ibid.

[63]Westley, "The Police," p. 95.

[64]Ibid., p. 161.

[65]Ibid., p. 166.

[66]Ibid., p. 167.

[67]Skolnick, *Justice Without Trial*, p. 147.

[68]Everson Moran, "Officials' Cars Tagged in Police 'Slowdown,'" *The Times Union*, Greater Rochester Edition, July 2, 1968, p. 1.

[69]*Rutland Daily Herald*, April 19, 1969, p. 7.

[70]Lindesmith, *The Addict and the Law*, p. 90.

[71]Ibid.

[72]Quoted in Frances A. Allen, "The Borderland of Criminal Law: Problems of 'Socializing' Justice," *The Social Service Review* 32 (June 1958):108.

[73]Ibid.

[74]Cited in Richard C. Fuller, "Morals and the Criminal Law," *Journal of Criminal Law, Criminology, and Police Science* 32 (March-April 1942):625-626.

[75]Bacon, *Early Development*, vol. 2, p. 784.

[76]Allen, "The Borderland," p. 111.

[77]Egon Bittner notes that "patrolmen do not really enforce the law, even when they do invoke it, but merely use it as a resource to solve certain pressing problems in keeping the peace." Egon Bittner, "The Police on Skid Row: A Study of Peace Keeping," *The American Sociological Review* 32 (October 1967):710.

[78]Becker, *Outsiders*, p. 171.

[79]Skolnick, *Justice Without Trial*, p. 173.

[80]Ibid., p. 125.

[81]Schur, *Crime Without Victims*, p. 81.

[82]Skolnick, p. 129.

[83]Quoted in Allen, p. 108.

[84]John I. Kitsuse, "Societal Reaction to Deviant Behavior: Problems of Theory and Method," *Social Problems* 9 (Winter 1962):256.

[85]Bordua and Reiss, p. 282.

[86]Silver, "Demand for Order," in *The Police*, ed. Bordua, p. 14.

[87]F. H. Wines, *Punishment and Reformation: An Historical Sketch of the Rise of the Penitentiary Systems* (New York: Crowell and Co., 1895), p. 13.

[88]Emile Durkheim, *The Rules of Sociological Method*, 8th ed. (Glencoe: The Free Press, 1966).

[89]Becker, p. 9.

[90]Wines, p. 24.

[91]Paul Reiwald, *Society and Its Criminals*, trans. T. E. James (London: William Heineman, 1949), p. 302.

CIVIL DISORDER AND THE AGENTS OF SOCIAL CONTROL

GARY T. MARX

Quis custodiet ipsos custodes?—Juvenal (VI.347)

The mob quails before the simple baton of the police officer, and flies before it, well knowing the moral as well as physical force, of the Nation whose will, as embodied in law, it represents.—*The Police and the Thieves,* 1856

Most of our municipalities appear to be organized solely for social service. In the presence of a mob their police officers are as helpless as their school teachers or their hospital interns.—Newspaper Report on 1919 Riot

Now, I'm not saying that the community, the people in the community of Harlem, were blameless. There was bottle-throwing, but when people throw bottles, when they throw bricks, it's the responsibility of the police to arrest, or at least restrain the culprits, the guilty parties, not indiscriminately to shoot into hotel windows and tenement houses. Not to beat people who are merely walking down the street.—James Farmer, 1964

Sure we make mistakes. You do in any war.—Police Commissioner of New York City, 1964

I don't want to hear anything you [Negro director of Human Relations Commission, counciling need to use black officers] have got to say; you're part of the problem. We know how to run a riot and we are going to handle it our way.—Deputy Chief of Police, Los Angeles, 1965

[The local police chief] rushed into his office and, grabbing the rifle ... and two boxes of ammunition, he shouted, "They've shot one of my officers. We're going to get every son-of-a-bitch down there. I'm getting goddamned tired of fooling around."—State Police Report, 1967

If you have a gun, whether it is a shoulder weapon or whether it is a hand gun, use it.—Director of Newark Police, over the police radio, 1967

To the [riot] commissioners and public alike we'd ask one question: When a law enforcement officer, faced with the extremely dangerous task of quelling what is in fact an armed rebellion, is the target of snipers' bullets, rocks, and bottles, just exactly what constitutes "undue force?" Were any of the commissioners who accuse police of using undue force on the firing line? Do they really know what they are talking about? Use of the term "undue force" is an exercise in tortured semantics that police refuse to accept. Not only is the charge without merit, it is an insult to brave men who risked their lives for the public and equally unacceptable to reasonable people. New Jersey State Patrolmen's Benevolent Association, 1968

In the final analysis [in spite of poor judgment, excessive use of firearms,

Gary T. Marx, "Civil Disorder and the Agents of Social Control" *Journal of Social Issues* (Winter 1970) pp. 19-57. Reprinted by permission of the author and the journal.

and a manifestation of vindictiveness on the part of police] the responsibility
for the loss of life and property that is the inevitable product of rioting and
mass lawlessness cannot be placed upon those whose duty it is to enforce the
law and protect the free of our society.—Report of Essex County (N.J.) Grand
Jury Investigation of Riot Deaths, 1968

    It seems . . . that it is not what you do, but how you do it and what you
call it.—John Steinbeck, 1961

The number of popular and scholarly perspectives that can be brought to bear
on the interpretation of civil disorder seems limited only by the breadth of
one's imagination and reading. Among some of the more prominent are those
that stress the increased radicalism of social movements as they evolve, the relevance of a world revolutionary struggle, the importance of an external war,
limited political access, various types of frustration, conspiracies, and agitation,
the mass media, relative deprivation and heightened aspirations, frontier traditions and a history of racial and labor violence, lower-class and criminal subcultures and youthful, Hobbesian, biological, or territorial man. Many of these
factors can be fitted into Smelser's (1962) useful value-added model of the determinants of collective behavior.

    Despite the undeniable relevance of some of these perspectives, they all
focus on factors in the predisorder situation conducive to violence. They also
tend to correspond to a particular left- or right-wing ideology. Thus conservatives tend to see disturbances as meaningless, irrational events caused by agitators activating the degenerate character of the lower classes, while liberals
are more likely to see them as spontaneous patterned protests caused by deprivation. However, there is one perspective which finds support among both the
extreme left and right, and which seeks the cause in the actual disturbance situation. This is the view which suggests that the police cause riots. (To be sure,
ideological groups differ on the particular mechanism they emphasize—the right
blaming the police for being too soft, the left blaming them for being to harsh.)

UNINTENDED CONSEQUENCES OF SOCIAL ACTION

    One of the justifications for social research is that it goes beyond our
common sense views of the world. Merton (1957) suggests that an important
task of social research is to point out the latent or unintended consequences
of human action. Thus, corrupt as early twentieth-century political machines
were, they were important in the assimilation of Irish and other immigrants;
and prostitution, whatever its moral implications, may make an important contribution to family stability. However, there are more interesting cases where
unintended consequences are the direct opposite of intended ends. Thus we
have learned that propaganda designed to reduce prejudice may actually reinforce it, that youth institutions may create juvenile delinquents who are later
made into knowledgeable and embittered criminals by the prison system, that
mental hospitals may encourage mental illness, that schools can impede learning, that welfare institutions may create dependency, and that doctors sometimes injure or even kill patients.

    In the same fashion, a review of police behavior in civil disorders of a
racial nature through the summer of 1967 suggests a number of instances where
the behavior of some social control agents seemed as much to create disorder

as to control it. After a consideration of police behavior in earlier racial disturbances, the present paper examines some of the forms and contexts in which control behavior has had these unintended consequences.

This paper does not argue that police are the main *cause* of racial disorder. Indeed, police are one of the most scapegoated and stigmatized groups in American society and many parallels may be drawn between them and ethnic minorities. Yet, as Gertrude Stein noted, the answers one gives depend on the questions one asks. There are certain questions about civil disorders that can only be answered by considering the general nature of the police-black community relationship and the interaction that occurs between these groups during a disturbance. These questions have to do with the course, pattern, intensity, and duration of the disturbance.

As Park and Blumer and later students have noted, collective behavior has an emergent character to it. It involves elements that can't very well be predicted by a static consideration of the predisturbance variables mentioned in the beginning of the paper. Civil disorder involves a social process of action and counteraction. It is here that a consideration of police behavior is relevant.

POLICE BEHAVIOR IN HISTORICAL PERSPECTIVE

As Allen Grimshaw (1963) has noted, police have been criticized for brutality and ineffectiveness in most twentieth-century racial disturbances. Any critical evaluation of recent control practices must first be put in historical perspective.

In reading about police behavior in earlier twentieth-century interracial violence, I found several reoccurring themes: (a) the police were sympathetic to (white) rioters and sometimes joined the riot themselves, (b) police often failed actively to enforce the law, and (c) when police did try to maintain law and order this often was not done in a neutral and impartial manner.

Some of the following discussion is based on reports of groups with vested interests other than (or in addition to) the dispassionate pursuit of truth. The highly charged emotional nature of civil disorder and the fact that it may cover wide areas makes research difficult. Traditional norms of police secrecy may require undue reliance on the reports of others, who are interested in overstating police misbehavior. The usual methodological strictures about this kind of historical data apply. At the same time, the very unusualness of the events leads to their receiving greater attention, making analysis somewhat easier. Social control behavior is further difficult to describe because in any one disturbance it may change markedly over time and may vary depending on the control unit in question.

Police as Rioters

Racial disorders are more likely during periods of social change—as the increased indignation of the oppressed confronts the threat to the status quo felt by the dominant group (Blumer, 1958; Shibutani & Kwan, 1965). Police represent the dominant group whose power is threatened, and tend to be recruited from those parts of the population most likely to hold negative stereotypes and to be in direct competition with blacks. It is thus not surprising that in the past police involvements in racial violence was sometimes on the side of the (white) mob rather than against it. This involvement has varied from statements of support to active participation in violence directed against nonlawbreaking Negroes.

The August 1900 New York race riot, one of the first of the twentieth century, was precipitated by a Negro killing a plainclothes policeman after the latter grabbed his woman and accused her of being a prostitute. The subsequent riot was partly led by the predominantly Irish police. In what was called a "Nigger Chase" policemen and other whites dragged blacks off streetcars and severely beat them on the street, in hotels and saloons. At the time, a white observer felt that the ambition of the police seemed to be to "club the life out of" any Negro they could find. The New York Daily Tribune printed a cartoon of a massive Tammany tiger in a police uniform swinging a club. In the background was huddled a bloodied Negro (Osofsky, 1963).

The 1906 Atlanta riot growing out of the move to disenfranchise blacks saw police arresting Negroes who had armed for self-defense and an officer shooting into a crowd of Negroes. The head of a seminary where blacks sought asylum was beaten by a police official (Franklin, 1965, p. 433).

Some of the worst instances of official rioting may be seen in the relatively well-documented East St. Louis riot of 1917, which was triggered by the killing of two policemen. In an act called "a particularly cowardly exhibition of savagery" by a congressional investigating committee, police shot into a crowd of Negroes huddled together and not offering any resistance. Some of the soldiers led groups of men and boys in attacks upon Negroes (Rudwick, 1966). Police relayed false reports of black reprisal attacks on the outskirts of the city, in order, according to the Post-Dispatch, "to scatter the soldiers so that they would not interfere with the massacre (Rudwick, 1966, p. 87)." Police also confiscated the cameras of newsmen because they had incriminating evidence. Guardsmen followed the cues of the police department. Some gave their weapons to the mob. Following the shooting of two blacks by "khaki-uniformed" men, rioters, according to a press account, "slapped their thighs and said the Illinois National Guard was all right (Rudwick, 1966, p. 48)." After indicating a number of instances of official complicity, the congressional investigating committee stated, "Instead of being guardians of the peace they [the police] become a part of the mob . . . adding to the terrifying scenes of rapine and slaughter (Grimshaw, 1963, p. 274)."

The Chicago Commission on Race Relations, while noting the unusual circumstances of the 1919 riot, felt that "certain cases of discrimination, abuse, brutality, indifference, and neglect" on the part of police were "deserving of examination." The "certain cases" included things such as a policeman approaching a Negro who lay wounded from mob attack, with the words, "Where's your gun, you black —— of a ——? You damn niggers are raising hell." Whereupon the officer then reportedly knocked the Negro unconscious and robbed him. There was also cited a case of a Negro who after asking police for protection was searched and clubbed by them and shot when he attempted to run away. (See the Chicago Commission on Race Relations, 1923, pp. 35, 38-39.)

In the 1919 Knoxville, Tennessee, disorders troops "shot up" the black section of town following an unsubstantiated rumor that Negroes had killed several whites. According to John Hope Franklin, a Negro newspaper declared,

"The indignities which colored women suffered at the hands of these soldiers would make the devil blush (Franklin, 1965, p. 475)."

In Tulsa, Oklahoma, May 31, 1921, after fighting broke out between whites and Negroes over the latter's effort to stop a lynching, local police invaded the Negro area and did much damage.

The 1943 Detroit riot was preceded by interracial violence at the Sojourner Truth Homes where police openly sided with whites and joined in fighting Negroes trying to move into public housing. During the 1943 riot, claims were made to the effect that "rather than protecting stores and preventing looting, the police drove through the troubled areas, occasionally stopping their vehicles, jumping out, and shooting whoever might be in a store. Police would then tell Negro bystanders to 'run and not look back.' On several occasions persons running were shot in the back (Grimshaw, 1963, p. 277)." It was claimed that police forced Negroes to detour onto Woodward Avenue, a street where violence against blacks was very intense.

A study of the 1943 Detroit riot reports the case of a black man shot as he fled a streetcar attacked by a mob. The man ran to a policeman and shouted, "Help me, I'm shot!" He later stated, "The officers took me to the middle of the street where they held me. I begged them not to let the rioters attack me. While they held me by both arms, nine or ten men walked out of the crowd and struck me hard blows. Men kept coming up to me and beating me, and the policemen did nothing to prevent it." This is followed a few pages later by the report of a white who stated, "A gang of Negroes suddenly seemed to assemble from nowhere at all. They dragged me from the car and were roughing me up when three policemen appeared and rescued me (Lee and Humphrey, 1943, pp. 3, 30; Shogan and Craig, 1964)."

Passive Police

More common than police rioting was police passivity. In a useful article on conditions conducive to racial disorders Dahlke stresses the relevance of weak agents of external control, police who either cannot or will not take aggressive efforts to uphold law and order (Dahlke, 1952). As with lynch violence, such a situation characterized many earlier racial disorders. Even when they desired to take action, police were usually understaffed and lacked the appropriate means to quell the disorders. Technical incapacity mixed with a nonaggressive control ideology and sympathy for the rioters often produced inaction. In the case of recent disturbances, it should be noted, the administrative confusion that has contributed to the disorders certainly has not implied approval of the violence; this article and much pre-1964 material on racial violence really deal with one-sided pogroms and biracial rioting and not with current disturbances which have more the character of colonial uprisings.

The 1904 Statesboro, Georgia, riot started when a mob entered the courtroom and overpowered the militia, whose rifles were not loaded "in tender consideration for the feelings of the mob." Two Negro prisoners were burned alive and a "wholesale terrorism" began. The leaders of the mob were not punished (Franklin, 1965, p. 433).

The congressional investigating committee studying the East St. Louis riot reports:

The testimony of every witness who was free to tell the truth agreed on condemnation of the police for failure to even half-way do their duty. They fled the scene where arson and murder were in full swing. They deserted the station house and could not be found when calls for help came from every quarter of the city. The organization broke down completely and so great was the indifference of the few policemen who remained on duty that the conclusion is inevitable that they shared the lust of the mob for Negro blood, and encouraged the rioters by their conduct (cited in Grimshaw, 1963).

Rudwick notes, "At least six or seven guardsmen stood around like 'passive spectators' during the hanging at Fourth and Broadway, and ignored pleas to save the victim's life. A few blocks away at Collinsville and Broadway a bloodied Negro sought the protection of eight guardsmen. Their mute answer was to turn bayonets on him, forcing the victim back into the arms of five assailants (Rudwick, 1966, p. 76)." There are reports of lawmen "laughingly held captive" while the mob attacked blacks.

Organization on the part of both the police and militia seemed to break down as they scattered throughout the city without officers. Fraternization with the mob was common and not conducive to efforts at restraint. Many soldiers openly stated they "didn't like Niggers and would not disturb a white man for killing them." It was reportedly a common expression among them to ask, "Have you got your nigger yet? (Grimshaw, 1963, p. 281)." The day after the riot as an ambulance came to remove part of the burned torso that a soldier was exhibiting to throngs of people with the words, "There's one nigger who will never do any more harm," a crowd of militia men "saluted . . . with shouts of merriment (Rudwick, 1966, p. 67)."

In Longview, Texas, in July 1919, police did not intervene when a group of whites with iron rods and gun butts beat a black man suspected of writing an article in the *Chicago Defender* on lynching. Nor did they try to stop the mob from burning a number of blacks' stores and homes (Waskow, 1966, p. 17).

Local authorities and police lacked the resources to control a riotous mob bent on lynching in Omaha in 1919. Some policemen surrendered their clubs and guns peacefully when the mob demanded them.

The 1919 Chicago riot was triggered by the drowning of a black swimmer who drifted across the "line" separating the "white" water from the "black" water. A white policeman refused to arrest the white thought (by Negroes) to be responsible for the death and then proceeded to arrest a Negro on a white man's complaint. Police were accused of leaving the scene of rioting on "questionable excuses." The Chief of Police and the Mayor refused to ask for troops, although the former acknowledged that his force was insufficient (Chicago Commission on Race Relations, 1923, pp. 39, 40). Outside pressure finally compelled the Mayor to ask the Governor for aid.

The following report on the 1919 Washington, D.C. riot clearly indicates something of the social process involved in the development of a collective definition conducive to violence on the part of both blacks and whites which is found in many early disorders. Blacks arm for self-defense and out of indignation while whites interpret police behavior as granting them permission to use violence against blacks with little fear of being sanctioned.

Failure of police to check the rioters promptly, and in certain cases an attitude on their part of seeming indifference, filled the mob with contempt of authority and set the stage for the demonstration the following night. In the early hours of Monday morning the attacks on Negroes were carried into sections where the black population is heavy. The whole Negro element of Washington suddenly became aware of a war on their race. . . . By Monday night the colored population held themselves to be without police protection. The mob elements among the blacks armed for war, while many of the better element of their race armed in obedience to the first law of nature. (An anonymous article in The Outlook, 1919, as quoted in Grimshaw, 1963, p. 277.)

W. E. B. Dubois charged that the Washington police intervened to stop the violence only when whites began to get the worst of it (Waskow, 1966, p. 34).

In Detroit in 1943 the NAACP took the position that, "There is overwhelming evidence that the riot could have been stopped in Detroit at its inception Sunday night had the police wanted to stop it (Lee and Humphrey, 1943, p. 73)."

Beyond police passivity in the face of attacks on Negroes, officials were criticized for delays in calling out higher levels of force and for the hesitancy to use force against whites. According to some sources the disturbance stopped only when troops appeared and a shoot-to-kill order was given wide publicity (Grimshaw, 1963, p. 283). The "inactivity" involved in the failure to call out higher levels of force is very different from that involved in failure of control agents to act once they are on the scene. Although at a more abstract level, the consequences may be much the same.

In the Cicero disturbance of 1951, the mob roughed up a black man attempting to move into an apartment, attacked the apartment, burned his furniture, and was "completely out of control." These activities were not prevented or hampered by the local police who were present. In fact, the local Chief of Police earlier had told the black man that he needed a permit to move in and threatened to arrest him if he tried to move in. The disorders continued until after the decision of the Governor of Illinois to send out National Guard troops (Grenley, 1952).

Police Partiality

In spite of well-documented instances of police involvement in rioting and police failure to take decisive action, an image of general police inaction or complicity is incorrect. In most cities efforts were make toward the control of violence. However, when police did try to maintain law and order, this was frequently not in a neutral and impartial manner. Given white control of police and a tradition of differential law enforcement, such partiality is not surprising. Partiality was often involved in the precipitating incident as well as in the police arresting on charges of rioting Negroes who were beaten by the mob or those who armed for self-defense. The pattern of stopping Negro attacks on whites was much more common than the reverse.

During the 1900 New York riot, local police courts were filled to capacity—but only with Negroes. A magistrate criticized the police and asked to see "some of the white persons who participated in the riot." His request was fulfilled when a white teenager was brought in for trying to trip a policeman (Osofsky, 1963).

In East St. Louis, "after a number of [white] rioters had been taken to jail by the soldiers under Colonel Clayton, the police deliberately turned hundreds of them loose without bond, failing to secure their names or to make any effort to identify them (Grimshaw, 1963, p. 274)."

A report on the 1919 Washington, D.C. riot notes:

Although the aggressors were white mobbists led by white men in the uniform of the United States, ten Negroes were arrested for every white man arrested (Seligmann, 1919, p. 50).

In a 1919 Phillips County, Arkansas, disturbance, according to the Negro view (later supported by affidavits of whites present at the time), whites fired from autos and then burned a church where a black tenant farmer's union was meeting. This spurred a week of violence. A few whites and many Negroes were killed. According to Waskow (1966), "hundreds of Negroes . . . were charged with murder or arrested as 'material witnesses' or for 'investigation' (pp. 121-142)." No whites were arrested at all except for one who was believed to be on the Negroes' side. Even the U.S. Army seemed less neutral here than in other disturbances. According to the *Arkansas Gazette,* the troops were anxious to get into battle with blacks in order to prevent a supposed plan to kill whites (a plan "discovered" by telling tortured Negroes what to confess to).

During the 1919 Chicago riot, twice as many Negroes as whites appeared as defendants although twice as many Negroes were injured. The State Attorney of Cook County stated:

There is no doubt that a great many police officers were grossly unfair in making arrests. They shut their eyes to offenses committed by white men while they were very vigorous in getting all the colored men they could get (Chicago Commission on Race Relations, 1923).

In a telling example, Walter White reports:

In one case a colored man who was fair enough to appear white was arrested for carrying concealed weapons, together with five white men and a number of colored men. All were taken to a police station; the light colored man and the five whites being put in one cell and the other colored men in another. In a few minutes the light colored man and the five whites were released and their ammunition given back to them with a remark, "You'll probably need this before the night is over" (White, 1919).

A criminologist expressed the belief that the police showed greater readiness to arrest blacks than whites because the officers felt they were "taking fewer chances if they 'soaked' a colored man (Chicago Commission on Race Relations, 1923, p. 35)."

After soldiers and sailors beat Mexican-Americans in the 1943 Los Angeles zoot suit riot, police who had been onlookers would move in and arrest the Mexicans for vagrancy or rioting. Military authorities were reportedly lax in not canceling leaves (*Time* magazine, June 21, 1943).

In writing about the 1943 Detroit riot, Supreme Court Justice Thurgood Marshall suggests:

The trouble reached riot proportions because the police once again enforced the law with an unequal hand. They used "persuasion" rather than firm action with white rioters, while against Negroes they used the ultimate in force: night sticks, revolvers, riot guns, submachine guns, and deer guns (Marshall, 1943).

Differential law enforcement can also frequently be seen in the different sentences received by white and black arrestees and, at another level, in the failure to punish control officials in those cases where force was misused. Grand juries and official investigating commissions have tended to label police killing of Negroes "justifiable homicide." The point of view expressed by the New York police department in its annual report about the 1900 race riot, whereby "the city was threatened with a race war between white and colored citizens . . . prompt and vigorous action on the part of the police . . . kept the situation under control," was typical of most post-riot inquiries (Osofsky, 1963). (Prominent exceptions to this tendency to whitewash disturbances were the reports of the congressional committee that investigated East St. Louis and the Chicago Commission on Race Relations.)

VARIATION IN CONTROL BEHAVIOR

In this effort to characterize control behavior in collective interracial violence prior to the 1960s, I do not mean to suggest that these themes of police rioting, inaction, and partiality were always present, nor that when they were present they applied to all actions of all policemen. Among striking examples where such a characterization does not apply are the 1919 Charleston riot between Negro and white sailors and the 1935 and 1943 Harlem riots. In Charleston, neutral police behavior may partly be understood by the fact that the rioting white sailors were outsiders not a part of the constituency of local authorites (Waskow, 1966). In Harlem only blacks were involved, so the issues of partiality and white police joining the riot are less relevant. The Harlem riots were in many ways the precursors of recent disorders (Fogelson, 1968).

Even where control behavior was the worst, heroic action on the part of some officials could be noted, as can cases of the police failing to interfere or arrest Negroes who had beaten whites. Nor should it be forgotten that often, as the Mayor of Detroit said in 1943, "The police had a tough job. A lot of them have been beaten and stoned and shot." And beyond being unprepared for their task and usually undermanned, they were the recipients of various insults about their lineage, manhood, and the nature of their maternal relationships. Under such conditions some observers might choose to emphasize their degree of restraint.

Significant variation in control behavior can often be found to be dependent on things such as region of the country, type of disturbance, nature of the issues, unit of control, and time period. Other factors being equal, conscientious impartial action to maintain law and order has been more likely where the rioting whites were not local citizens, where the disturbance was an insurrection against the local government as well as a black pogrom, where a strike or labor issue was involved, when the precipitating incident did not involve a Negro killing a police officer, and where only blacks rioted.

While conscientious impartial action is related to effectiveness, it is not synonymous with it. Among factors that seemed related to effective control are prior training, experience and planning, strong leadership from command officers and local government, the maintenance of organization and discipline within the control organization, the rapid mobilization of large numbers of personnel, and the use of Negro as well as white agents of control.

Control behavior has tended to be better the higher the level of control agency (state police, militia, and the U.S. Army) and the later one gets into the twentieth century (1900, 1919, 1943). In many cities disturbances came to an end with the appearance of outside forces and, except for the state militia in East St. Louis, relatively few criticisms of unprofessional behavior or ineffectiveness were directed against them. This was even more true of the U.S. Army than of the state forces. This is related to the fact that the army and state units often came in fresh at the end of a riot cycle. As outsiders they were uninvolved in local issues and perceived as being neutral. Their larger numbers, superior training, and military organizational structure better suited them for coping with such disorders.

However, in considering the dynamics of the riot, rather than an abstract score card of police behavior, the effect of well-publicized instances of police brutality, inaction, or partiality, no matter how unrepresentative (and they often were all too representative) was often sufficient to escalate greatly the level of rioter activity. Such misbehavior to Negroes became symbolic of past injustice and part of a generalized belief justifying self-defense and retaliatory violence, while whites interpreted it as giving them license to attack blacks.

THE 1960s: SOME CHANGES IN POLICE BEHAVIOR

In spite of the variation and qualifications noted above, in accounts of earlier disturbances the themes of police rioting, inactivity, and partiality could often be noted. Perhaps they were particularly apparent because they contrast rather markedly with police behavior in recent disturbances. We have come a long way since the 1863 New York Draft Riot where, when the president of the police board was asked about taking lawbreakers into custody he reportedly replied, "Prisoners? Don't take any. Kill! Kill! Kill! Put down the mob." Riots are now triggered when police kill or injure a Negro, rather than vice versa. Police have been much quicker to take action and this action has generally been more restrained than previously. The law has been enforced much more impartially. Particularly in the North, there are few reports of police failing to stop interracial assaults or of police firing into unarmed noncombative crowds. Considering the absolute number, size, intensity, and duration of recent disorders, there has probably been much less police rioting, less brutality, and relatively less injury inflicted upon Negroes by the police; this is all the more salient since police have been provoked to a much greater extent than earlier and have many more opportunities to use force legally against blacks than they did in previous riots.

Where police rioting has been present—as in Watts, Newark, and Detroit—this tends to be primarily in the later stages of the disturbance as police are unable to control the disorder and as they become subject to the same collective behavior phenomena as blacks (such as the breakdown of social organization, rumor, panic, innovative efforts to handle strain, etc.).

This contrasts with earlier disorders where police rioting was present from the beginning of the disturbance. That police behavior has shown considerable improvement, of course, should give no cause for rejoicing, since numerous, well-documented instances of undue and indiscriminate use of force, often deadly, can be cited.

In trying to account for these changes in police behavior, changes in the police and in the type of disorder must be considered. Police now are more professionalized and have better resources. Perhaps equally important, the task of maintaining law and order now involves suppressing blacks.

Just as the nineteenth-century emergence of a bureaucratic police force with fluid organization capable of rapid concentration greatly reduced the fear of riots, mobile units and modern communications have made it easier for the police to take rapid action. In some cases the availability of nonlethal weapons may have inhibited the use of deadly force. These factors work both ways, however. One reason a large crowd gathered so rapidly in Newark was that the beating of the cab driver involved in the initial incident was broadcast over the taxi radio system, drawing a caravan of taxis. The monitoring of police radio calls by rioters has occasionally been reported. In Newark there were reports of looters and snipers using "CBR" (Citizens' Band Radio). We can also note civil rights groups photographing activities of police as well as the reverse. In recent anti-war demonstrations some protestors could be seen wearing helmets, thickly padded jackets, gas masks, in a few cases accompanied by their own German shepherds. The pattern of neutralizing social control devices and the continual readjustment of deviants and social controllers as new technology emerges is a fascinating and unwritten story.

But beyond such technical factors is modern society's decreased tolerance for internal disorder and the ethos of the contemporary police department. The complexity and interdependence of contemporary society may have increased its vulnerability to civil disorder; at any event, its tolerance for internal violence has certainly been decreasing since 1900 (Waskow, 1966). American traditions about nongovernmental interference in private violence have tended to disappear.

Just as blacks have the misfortune of being poor when most other groups aren't, they have the misfortune of being a lower-class urban migrant group at a time when tolerance for the violence characteristically associated with such groups is less than ever. The state has increasingly come to monopolize the means of violence. To a degree that can't be very precisely measured, earlier police behavior transcended racism and must be seen in the context of police ambivalence about the control of private violence.

Citizenship rights in theory, and to an ever greater extent in practice, have been extended to all people, even the ethnically stigmatized lower classes. While this stress on the inclusion of the lower class, at least as far as blacks are concerned, can no longer be used (as many have tried to use it) to explain the presumed decline of violence in American society, it is still useful in accounting for the restraint shown them by authorities once violence breaks out. Police departments increasingly have come to stress universalistic criteria of law enforcement, as well as affective neutrality and limits on the use of force. An additional factor contributing to police restraint may be the presence of the press— in contrast to their role in earlier disturbances where the irresponsible concern of the media with Negro crime and especially rape of white women did much to raise tensions (Waskow, 1966).

To interpret these changes only in light of abstractions such as professionalization would be naïve. The police today, while in many ways different from the police in 1917, are also dealing with a very different kind of racial violence. Rather than whites attacking Negroes under the guise of an ideology of white supremacy held by the police, we find Negroes attacking stores and police under the guise of an ideology clearly not held by the latter. The task of restoring law and order today coincides with the repression of Negroes, rather than of whites as earlier. Thus, that the police have been more ready to take action is not surprising. Similarly the greater neutrality of the police (in the form of enforcing the law equally, regardless of the attributes of the lawbreaker) may partly relate to the fact that in these almost all black disturbances, few whites have been involved. Yet acknowledging such factors should not lead to a wholly cynical denial of the changes that have occurred. Police, particularly in the North, have often controlled white mobs bent on attacking civil rights demonstrators. During riots they have arrested white youths (usually on the perimeter of the disturbance area) looking for confrontations with blacks.

Given the above factors one might be led to believe that police would have been much more successful in quelling recent disorders than in the past. This is not to argue that police behavior has always been effective or humane. While the old adage told me by a veteran police official that in the past "the riot didn't start until the police arrived" may seem less true today, this is certainly not to say that the riot now stops when the police do arrive—though this has sometimes (as in the Kercheval area of Detroit in 1966 and earlier at Trumbull Park in Chicago) been the case. One observer suggests "policemen everywhere claim they know of a hundred riots squelched for every one that gets out of hand (Wills, 1968, p. 37)." For documentation on two incipient riots that didn't happen, see Wenkert, Magney, and Neel (1967), and Shellow and Roemer (1966). It is nevertheless ironic that although police are technically better prepared to control disorders and have a greater will to do so, they often have been unsuccessful. Control is more difficult now than in earlier race riots because of the greater use made of private weapons and the fact that merely separating whites from blacks and protecting black areas from white invasion is not sufficient for stopping the riot (Janowitz, 1968, p. 10). But, in addition, two important factors here are the general nature of police-black community relations and the actual behavior of police during the disturbance.

POLICE-COMMUNITY RELATIONS

In its riot analysis (inspired by what it felt were failings in the reports of the New Jersey and National Riot Commissions) the New Jersey State Patrolmen's Benevolent Association (1968) finds a "growing disrespect for law and order" to be "one of the root causes" of recent civil disorders. While much in this document could be disputed by social scientists, there is an element of truth here, although the adjective "white" might have been added to "law and order." There may be less consensus among ghetto youth on legitimacy of the police than in the past. Increasing technical proficiency and a more professional ethos are thus undercut by the decreasing respect potential rioters may hold for the police (Bouna and Schade, 1967).

Developments within the black community have meant that even the most "enlightened" police riot behavior has sometimes been ineffective. As blacks have gained in power and self-confidence through civil rights activity, and have become more politicized, the legitimacy granted police has declined. This is especially true for many of those most prone to participate in the disorders. For many of this group, police are seen as just a group of white men, meaner than most, who are furthermore responsible for the historical and current sins of their racial group. From the point of view of one youth in Watts, "The policeman used to be a man with a badge; now he's just a thug with a gun." This change in view is clearly in the eye of the beholder rather than in the behavior of the police. Though it may be true that relatively less capable people are being recruited for police work, by most criteria police are better than ever before. Ironically, indignation against the police has risen as police behavior has improved. During a five-year period in which the Chicago Police Department became increasingly professionalized, one study notes no change in police perception of how the public viewed them (Wilson, 1967).

To be sure, this negative view is held by only a minority of the black community, but it is held disproportionately by the most riot-prone group. For the general Negro community, complaints of police brutality are matched by the demand for greater police protection and indignation over the behavior of Negro lawbreakers.

The New Jersey Governor's Select Commission on Civil Disorder (1968) notes that "there was virtually a complete breakdown in the relations between police and the Negro community prior to the disorders. . . . Distrust, resentment, and bitterness were at a high level on both sides (p. 143)."

Indeed, for some blacks police come to be seen as an occupation army. Silver (1967) suggests the concomitant of this view when he notes that, for many whites in the face of black unrest, "Police forces come to be seen as they were in the time of their creation—as a convenient form of garrison force against an internal enemy (p. 22)." As the various (largely unanalyzed) organizational ties between the police and the Department of Defense become stronger, the view of the police as a counterinsurgency force takes on added significance. In reviewing police preparations for future riots, a journalist notes, "One would think the police were readying for war. Or waging it (Wills, 1968)."

Useful parallels can be drawn to the way police were often seen in other ethnically mixed societies during tense periods (such as India and Pakistan in 1948, or Cyprus or Israel more recently). Police are viewed not as neutral representatives of the state upholding a legal system but as armed representatives of their ethnic communities. At this point, whatever obedience police can command emerges primarily out of gun barrels and not out of respect for them or the law and order they are enforcing. Even here the symbolic hatred that police may inspire can inhibit the effectiveness of threats of force. In such situations using ethnically alien police to stop an ethnically inspired riot may be equivalent to attempting to put out a fire with gasoline.

In such a context control agents may not be successful even when they "refrain from entering the issues and controversies that move the crowd, remain impartial, unyielding, and fixed on the principle of maintaining law and order" —one of "an effective set of principles for troops to control a rioting mob" suggested by Smelser (1962, p. 267). This is precisely because even in being neutral the police are in one sense not being neutral. By the mere act of maintaining white (or the status quo) law and order the police have in fact entered "the issues and controversies" and on a side likely to aggravate potential rioters. As Joseph Lohman, a former police scholar and official has noted, "The police function to support and enforce the interests of the dominant political, social, and economic interests of the town (Neiderhoffer, 1967, p. 13)."

POLICE BEHAVIOR IN RECENT DISTURBANCES

As noted, earlier police inaction in riots has generally given way recently to decisive police action. Yet many disorders have escalated, not as in the past because of what police failed to do, but precisely because of what they have done. Here racial liberals and conservatives have switched in their indictments of the police. Where liberals earlier complained that police were indecisive and not tough enough, complaints of excessive use of force are now common— while conservatives suggest the opposite. In another reversal the same U.S. marshals who were looked upon favorably by liberals when they protected civil rights activities in the South, became the enemy during the march on the Pentagon. Many conservatives who expressed pleasure over the presence of the marshals in Washington were indignant when they were in the South.

I have found it useful to organize police behavior that was ineffective or seemed to have the effect of creating rather than controlling the disorders into the following three categories: (1) inappropriate control strategies, (2) lack of coordination among and within various control units, (3) the breakdown of police organization. The remainder of the paper is concerned primarily with police behavior up to the end of the summer of 1967.

Inappropriate Control Strategies

Crowd Dispersal.[1] Here I wish to consider ideas held by some control officials about disorderly crowds and the kind of police action that has flowed from such views. In the spirit of Gustav Le Bon it is sometimes assumed that crowds are uniformly like-minded, anarchic, irrational, and hell-bent on destruction. From this it may follow that all people on the street are seen as actual or potential rioters, that crowds must always be broken up, that a riot will not terminate unless it is put down, and that only a technical approach involving the use of massive force is adequate.

In all too many cases police have not gone beyond a nineteenth-century riot manual (Molineux, 1884) which stated "crushing power, exercised relentlessly and without hesitation is really the merciful, as it is necessary, course to be pursued (cited in Garson, 1969)."

Police were often responsible for the formation of the initial crowd by responding to fairly routine incidents with a large number of squad cars with loud sirens and flashing lights. In some cities, applying the traditional strategy of dispersing the crowd had unanticipated consequences and served to escalate and spread the disorders. The control problem then shifted from a crowd to guerilla-like hit and run activities more amenable (technically if not humanly, given innocent bystanders and the minor crimes) to city clearing tactics. In commenting on new riot training, a national guard officer stated, "We ran through all that crowd-control crap again. Hell, I was in Detroit two weeks and I never once saw a crowd (Wills, 1968, p. 55)."

While the formation of a crowd at the beginning seemed to be an important factor in most disturbances, it does not follow that crowds should always be dispersed, nor that when they are dispersed, force is the only means that should be used. While the crowd itself may be conducive to a lessening of inhibitions, the anger it feels may be heightened and released by precipitous police action. Here it may·be useful to distinguish a series of precipitating or initiating events.

In New Haven in 1967, for example, after some initial minor violence the crowd's mood was still tentative. A small crowd walked down the street toward police lines. As the perimeter was reached, police fired three canisters of tear gas. The crowd then ran back breaking windows and began to riot seriously.

According to a report on the 1964 Harlem riot, following the efforts of New York City's tactical patrol force to clear an intersection by swinging their clubs and yelling charge as they plowed into the crowd and broke it into smaller segments, "Hell broke loose in Harlem (Shapiro and Sullivan, 1964)." The angry but otherwise peaceful crowd then began pulling fire alarms, starting fires, and beating whites.

In Englewood, New Jersey, police efforts to force Negro bystanders into houses, whether or not they were the right house, angered and sparked violence on the part of young men. In Rockford, Illinois, the first instances of rock and bottle throwing were inspired by police efforts to clear a late-night bar crowd off the streets.

A peaceful rally protesting school practices in Philadelphia was violently broken up by the civil disobedience squad using riot plan number three. This elicited a violent response from the Negro youth. The superintendent and the president of the school board subsequently blamed the police for starting a riot (Philadelphia Inquirer, Nov. 18, 1967).

Contrary to official riot control manuals and (usually) the wishes of higher authorities, as police encounter a crowd they may break ranks, raise their night sticks above their shoulders, and hit people on the head rather than the body.

Beyond the issue of police provoking a hostile but as yet nondestructive crowd to retaliatory violence or providing a symbolic act and serving as a catalyst for the expression of the crowd's anger, the members of the crowd, once dispersed, may do more damage than the crowd itself. This may be somewhat equivalent to jumping on a burning log in efforts to put out a fire, only to see sparks and embers scatter widely. In both Milwaukee and New Haven, disorders were spread in this fashion; scattered bands of rioters presented police with a more difficult control situation than the original crowd.

An additional problem may emerge if police lack the power to clear the street or, as in Detroit, to control it once it has been cleared. In Newark after an angry crowd pelted the police station with rocks, bottles, and a few fire bombs, police made several sorties into the crowd using their clubs, and each time withdrew back to the station. Such a seesaw motion, in demonstrating police ineffectiveness and the crowd's parity with control officials, may have emboldened rioters.

Failure to Negotiate. The treatment of disorders as strictly technical problems of law and order to be solved only by force has meant that negotiations and the use of counterrioters were often ruled out. Such iron-clad rules, popular in many police circles, completely obscure the variation in types of disorder. Where the disturbance seems apolitical, unfocused, and primarily expressive and is not related to current issues or demands, and where there is no minimal organization among rioters and no one willing to take counterriot roles, there would seem to be no alternative, from the perspective of the authorities, to the graduated use of force. However, where the disturbance develops out of a very focused context involving specific issues (the demand for finding promised jobs, a particular instance of police brutality, discrimination by a business firm, disagreement over school policies, etc.), where grievances are clearly articulated and demands are present, where there seems to be some organization among rioters, and where actual or would-be spokesmen and potential counterrioters come forth, the disturbance may be stopped or dampened by entering into a dialogue, considering grievances, and using counterrioters. To resort only to force in such a situation is more likely to inflame the situation and increase the likelihood of future disorders.

The refusal to negotiate and use strategies other than a white show of force may have had disastrous consequences in Watts. The director of the Los Angeles Human Relations Commission had worked out a plan to send in 400 black plainclothes officers and several hundred antipoverty workers to make inconspicuous arrests and spread positive rumors ("the riot is over") and to withdraw white officers to the perimeter. Young gang leaders promised to use their influence to stop the riot and were led to believe that these conditions would be met.

The deputy chief of police rejected this proposal, stating among other things that he was not going to be told how to deploy his troops and that, "Negro police officers are not as competent as Caucasian officers and the only reason for sending them in would be because they have black skins and are invisible at night." To the director of the Human Relations Commission he said, "I don't want to hear anything you have got to say, you're part of the problem. *We know how to run a riot* and we are going to handle it our way." In response to the promises of gang leaders to stop the riot, he stated, "We are not going to have hoodlums telling us how to run the police department." And, "We are in the business of trying to quell a riot and we haven't got time to engage in any sociological experiments (McCone, et al., 1965, pp. 59, 61, 63, 65)." Following this refusal a full scale riot ensued.

All Blacks as Rioters. Just as it is sometimes erroneously assumed that all men at a gay bar are gay or all women standing on certain street corners at a particular time are prostitutes, so to the police any black person out on the street during a period of civil disorders may be suspect. In some cities, orders to clear an area and the panicky use of force (along with beliefs about the efficacy of getting tough) have resulted in the indiscriminate application of force to anyone with a black face, including innocent bystanders, government officials, policemen in civilian clothes, ministers, and Negro youth trying to stop the disorders.

In noting police inability to differentiate rioters from spectators, an observer of the 1964 Harlem disturbance notes, "The result was injuries to spectators and, in many cases, conversion of spectators into players (Shapiro and Sullivan, 1964, p. 57)." A factor related to failure to negotiate and the treatment of all black people on the streets as rioters involves official response to counterrioters. In many cases they were not used at all, or, once mobilized, their efforts were frustrated.

Previous role relationships have an important effect on behavior in disaster situations. While collective behavior is essentially defined by the emergence of new norms, it nevertheless occurs within a context of ongoing familial, religious, economic, political, and social relationships. In many cities the resources of the black community were effectively used in counterriot activities—quelling rumors, urging people to go home, and trying to channel indignation into less destructive protest.

During the summer of 1967 in such cities as Tampa, Florida, and Elizabeth, New Brunswick, and Plainfield, New Jersey, police were even ordered out of the disturbance area and local residents successfully patrolled the streets. The issue of whether or not police should be withdrawn is a complex one that far transcends the simplistic rhetoric of its opponents and supporters. While it was successful in the above cities, in several other cities it had the opposite effect. However, what is not really at issue is the fact that there existed a sizeable reservoir of counterriot sentiment that could have been activated in the place of, or along side of, other control activities. This counterriot sentiment was generally not counterprotest and in many cases represented considerations of strategy rather than principle. But motivation aside, failure to use counterrioters effectively may have prolonged a number of disturbances.

In Cincinnati, despite an agreement between the mayor and black leaders that the latter would be given badges and allowed to go into the riot area to help calm things, police refused to recognize the badges and arrested some of them on charges of loitering. A somewhat similar situation existed in Milwaukee. In Newark the mayor and governor gave permission to Negro volunteers to go among the people in efforts to calm the situation. Their activities were inhibited by enforcement personnel. According to the governor, they "were chased around so much by people who suspected them as participating in the riot that they had to abandon their efforts (Governor's Select Commission on Civil Disorders, 1968, p. 120)."

Beyond the general confusion in the disorders and a racially inspired (if not racist) inability to differentiate among types of Negroes, this police response was related to a view of the disorders as a technical problem to be met only by a show of force and a feeling that police competence and jurisdiction were being infringed upon. That counterrioters were often black activists, and in some cases gang youth, may have accentuated this feeling.

Official Anticipation. Thus far, the disorders considered have involved the pattern of riotous or at least disorderly Negro behavior followed and sometimes encouraged by the official response. However, there were other instances where the dynamics of the disturbance worked in the opposite direction. Here authorities (with poor intelligence reports) precipitated confrontation by anticipating violence where none was imminent and by overreacting to minor incidents that happened to occur during a major riot elsewhere.

While adequate planning and preparation are vital to effective control, they may help create a state-of-seige mentality, increase susceptibility to rumors, and exert a self-fulfilling pressure. This is particularly true when they are found with a get-tough, act-quickly philosophy. Following the Newark riot, fourteen cities in the surrounding area had some type of disorders; after Detroit, eight additional Michigan cities reported disorders. An important factor (rather than, or in addition to, psychological contagion) in the spread of violence from major urban centers to outlying communities was the expectation of a riot—and subsequent overreaction on the part of white authorities.

In New Jersey a month and a half before Newark erupted, there were reports of planned violence, and counterplans were designed. On June 5, 1967, the police chiefs of more than 75 New Jersey communities met in Jersey City to discuss the supposed plans of militant blacks to foment violence. Jersey City, Newark, and Elizabeth were reportedly given "triple A" ratings for violence over the summer. Plans to coordinate control efforts were set up and procedures for calling in the National Guard and state police gone over. Riot control training was held in a number of communities.

When Newark finally erupted, prior rumors were confirmed in the minds of many local officials in other communities and fears of anticipated violence were acted upon. In one New Jersey city, officials reacted to the rumor that Stokely Carmichael was bringing carloads of black militants into the community, although Carmichael was in London at the time. In Jersey City, 400 armed police occupied the black area several days before any disorders occurred. In Englewood, where police outnumbered participants three to one, black residents had earlier been angered by riot control exercises in which the wind had blown tear gas into surrounding Negro homes. In Elizabeth, police greatly increased patrols in the black area and residents expressed opinions such as, "The community felt it was in a concentration camp." The appearance of armed police patrols increased the likelihood of confrontation and greatly strained relations with local Negroes. Whatever an individual's feeling about civil rights, to have his neighborhood saturated with armed men in uniform in the face of minimal, sporadic, and even no disorders, often created indignation. A frequent demand was for police withdrawal or less visible show of arms. In six of seven New Jersey cities (that had disorders at the time of

Newark) chosen for study by the riot commission, removal of police from
the ghetto signalled an end to violence.

Sniping. While much sniping was attributed to control agents firing at
each other, fire-crackers, and the snapping of broken power lines, response
to the sniping that actually did exist was inadequate. Mass firing by men on
the ground at buildings, often using their private weapons, without an adequate system of accounting for ammunition spent and not under the command of a superior officer, created much havoc, killed and wounded many
innocent people, and helped escalate the violence. Such firing no doubt drew
counterfire from angry Negroes bent on retaliation or who viewed their counterfire as self-defense, in some cases creating the very sniper fire it was supposedly trying to stop. The fact that changes in policy from not shooting to
shooting looters during the Detroit riot were not announced may have increased the death toll. In a related context, if people don't hear an order
to disperse because they are too noisy, that doesn't affect the legality of
their arrest—according to guidelines put out by the San Francisco police department (1963, p. 4).

The Use of Force. In the use of force in quelling a disturbance, the
police have traditionally faced a dilemma. To underreact out of concern with
heightening tensions, because of technical incapacity, or because the seriousness of the situation is not appreciated, may permit disorders to spread rapidly
as new norms conducive to disorderly behavior emerge and as people see that
they can break rules without fear of being sanctioned. On the other hand, to
use too much force too soon may create incidents and escalate the disorders
as bystanders become involved and the already involved become ever more
indignant. In cities such as Watts, Newark, and Detroit, police departments
moved from a pattern of underreaction to overreaction, in each case inadvertently contributing to the disorders.

In Detroit a factor that came to be known as the "blue flu" may have
been relevant. Prior to the riot, in an abortive unofficial strike many officers
had called in sick. It has been suggested that some policemen in their anger
and in order to demonstrate their importance to the city went beyond the
policy of departmental restraint in underreacting during the initial disorders,
in some cases even encouraging people to loot. This police strike did not have
the tragic consequences of the 1919 Boston police strike. In fact, according
to several preriot sources, reports of crime actually went down when the police were out on strike.

There are two independent issues in the much-debated role of force in
quelling civil disorders. One has to do with the effect of threats of force on
the outbreak of disorders and the other with its effect on the course of a
disturbance once it has started.

The tensions which generate riots are not likely to be reduced by a
tough-talking mayor or police chief. Such rhetoric would seem to have little
deterrent value and may help further to polarize the atmosphere and create
fear in blacks of genocide and plans for self-defense (which are then likely
to be taken by police as proof of the need to be even tougher). However,

once disorders have begun, a get-tough policy may be more "effective." (Although the criteria of effectiveness are by no means clear; and effectiveness, if defined simply as the cessation of the disorders, may conflict radically with other cherished values of the society.)

The example of Milwaukee shows that an early display of overwhelming force can stop the disorders—though the closing of airports and highways, the presence of 4,800 national guardsmen, 800 policemen, and 200 state police after about 150 youths broke windows and looted after a dance seems rather out of proportion. Similarly, indiscriminate lethal force will temporarily scatter a crowd. A group of angry blacks protesting a segregated bowling alley in Orangeburg was broken up (in the largest single bloodletting thus far) when state police fired without warning into the unarmed group, killing three and wounding 27 others (many of whom were shot in the back).

While such force may temporarily break up the crowd (ethical considerations aside), it may create martyrs and symbolic incidents which galvanize social-movement support. Witness the cases of Lafayette and the Parisian National Guard firing on unarmed demonstrators in 1791, the Boston Massacre in 1770, the calvary's riding down peaceful demonstrators at Peterloo in 1819, the firing on unarmed petitioners at the Winter Palace in 1905, and General Dyer's massacre of Indians at Amritsar. A fruitful area of study is the sociology of martyrdom and the conditions under which repression will arouse sympathy on the part of larger audiences. Important issues here would seem to be whether the repression is directed against nonviolent or violent demonstrators and whether the protest involves a moral issue easily seen to be consistent with the basic values of the larger society.

Unfortuantely, it can't very well be said scientifically that those control practices most offensive to humane sensibilities are also those least likely to be effective, although neither can the opposite be said. Strong moral grounds clearly exist for opposing such policies, but very little is known about the likely short- and long-run consequences of different control strategies.

We can hypothetically differentiate between control practices that may have no effect on the disorders, those that cause them to escalate, and those that reduce or stop them. Empirically trying to sort these out is, however, very hard. Given the lack of sophisticated analysis with a reasonable sample, examples can be selectively chosen to show the effectiveness or ineffectiveness of almost any given strategy. In the case of the "get-tough perspective" these often are embarrassingly time-bound. Thus two cities often cited, Miami (whose police chief stated, "When the looting starts, the shooting starts") and Philadelphia ("They take your attempts to meet their demands as a sign of weakness; you have to meet them with absolute force") subsequently have experienced disorders.

There is a curious confusion in the image of man held by proponents of a get-tough policy. On the one hand, they assume that the potentially riotous individual is cold and calculating, carefully weighs the consequences of his actions, and hence will be frightened by the potentially strong sanctions. On the other hand, rioters are simultaneously thought of as completely wild and irrational people caught up in an "insensate rage."

In a related context students of criminal behavior in American society have consistently noted that harsh sanctions and capital punishment are not effective deterrents for many offenses. Some research in other countries has reported curvilinear relationships between hostile outbursts and repression (LeVine, 1959; Bwy, 1968). Student and antiwar protests are beyond the scope of this paper yet much of what has been said about police behavior during city racial disorders applies here as well. As a brief aside we can particularly note their role in aiding the success of student protests.

The state of our social engineering knowledge is admittedly limited; however, if one wanted to structure the world to be sure that university disturbances would occur, one could learn a lot by watching the unintended consequences of the behavior of university administrators. One pattern that applied to a great many disorders up to 1968 is as follows. A small number of students, often with a cause or issue that doesn't actively interest the mass of their fellows, plan or actually carry out limited peaceful protest action. The university administration tries to restrict the protest; it prevents freedom of speech and action, or it arbitrarily and without due process singles out certain activists for punishment, or it calls the police to break up a demonstration. With these administrative actions the nature of the unrest changes quantitatively and qualitatively. A basic issue now becomes free speech or police brutality or rights of due process. Latent tensions may result in additional issues such as the quality of education coming to the surface, issues which had nothing to do with the original problem or the university response. Greater unity among the protestors develops; the mass of uncommitted moderate students are drawn to their side (often in spite of initially opposing them or being indifferent to the original issue); liberal faculty and organizations in the outside community respond in like fashion. The dynamics of the situation thus involve the move from a small peaceful protest to a large disorderly and disobedient protest. (In student demonstrations abroad, use of police has often had similar consequences; in the case of France and Germany see Crozier, 1968, and Mayntz, 1968.)

In this move from limited to general protest, aged if sometimes crew-cut university administrators, confronted with a novel situation, are pulled between conservative boards of regents, trustees, and public, and the liberal academic community. They vacillate, act inconsistently and unpredictably, and may fail to grasp the essence of the situation they are confronted with; they may make undocumented (and certainly unwise) statements about the role of communists, off-campus agitators, and trouble makers; they may be unable to differentiate kinds of student demonstrators. Various deans and university officials make statements and offer interpretations that may contradict each other; agreements reached between students and authorities may be overruled or distorted by other authorities. As at Berkeley and Columbia, administrators may fail to accept the recommendations even of their own faculty or faculty-student committees set up to deal with the crisis. Students perceive university administrators as being confused, bungling, arrogant, hypocritical, and acting in bad faith; this strengthens student feelings about the legitimacy of their cause.

Finally, when authorities do act by calling in the police, police often conform to the strategy of the demonstrators, seemingly unaware that such a strategy, if not completely self-defeating, at best has no win consequences for the authority structure. There are two important issues in using police in campus disorders: first, the fact that the conflict is stopped by the naked power of the state, contrary to hallowed ideals of a liberal university; and second, the fact that insulted and provoked police sometimes lose control and use undue and indiscriminate force, thus greatly increasing the disorders. Some private schools such as Chicago, Brandeis, Roosevelt, and Reed where the police have not been called in to "solve" conflicts (partly because such schools are not under as strong external pressure from the public and government to do so) have avoided the degree of disruption and disorder, the residue of bitterness, and the concessions to students that have been present at schools such as Berkeley, Wisconsin, San Francisco State, Columbia, and Harvard where the police were called in.

Lack of Coordination Among Control Units

The historical fact that the United States did not develop a specialized national riot police as in France and Italy has probably meant prolonged disorders and greater injury and death. The constitutional delegation of the police function to states and our forty thousand separate police units means that initially each city must rely on its own inadequate resources.

In the face of major, unanticipated disorders involving a wide area and large number of people engaged in hit-and-run guerrilla-like tactics, local decentralized autonomous American police, organized primarily to fight crime, control traffic, and keep the peace, were usually ineffective. The control of such disturbances requires training and activity that are almost opposite in nature to those needed for normal police operations (Turner, 1968), and necessitates calling in other control units differing in training, organizational structure, ethos, and familiarity with the local area. Not surprisingly, difficulties often emerged as a result.

Whereas the inability to admit failure, bureaucratic entanglements, petty rivalries, and political considerations all delayed the calling out of higher levels of force, the lack of prior planning and an unclear chain of command meant further delays once other control agents finally did arrive on the scene. Local, state, and national guard units did not merge easily. Guard units, accustomed to acting in patrols, were fragmented and guardsmen were isolated from commanding officers; police, who were usually organized as one- or two-man autonomous patrol units, were to become disciplined members of military units, relying on commands from superiors and not on their own discretion. While officers from different units were together, they were often responding to separate orders. In Newark the three enforcement agencies were issued separate orders on weapons use. In commenting on the use of his men, a national guard commander in Detroit noted, "They sliced us up like balony. The police wanted bodies. They grabbed guardsmen as soon as they reached armories, before their units were made up, and sent them out—two on a firetruck, this one in a police car, that one to guard some installation." This meant that "a young man without a car or radio, without any knowledge of the city, could get stranded far away from any officer, without food or cigarettes, convinced (often rightly) that no one remembered where he was. . . . The guard simply became lost boys in the big town carrying guns (Wills, 1968)."

Technical as well as social communications problems contributed to ineffective coordination of control activities and clearly furthered the disorders. Regular radio frequencies were heavily overtaxed, and local police, state police, and the national guard operated on different frequencies. Though this had been a problem two years earlier in Watts, little had changed by the time of Detroit and Newark. In the beginning stages of the latter, state police were unable to get a clear definition of riot perimeters or where activity was heaviest. They could not obtain information about the movement of local police patrols or citizens' calls and were obliged to follow local police and fire trucks responding to calls (Governor's Select Commission, 1968). Inability to communicate was a factor in police and guardsmen firing at each other and in the belief in widespread sniping.

Poor communication within departments also had serious consequences (Cohen and Murphy, 1967; Conot, 1967). One reason the Los Angeles police department failed to employ sufficient manpower when needed was the reluctance of subordinate commanders to expose themselves to ridicule and downgrading by possible overreaction. While the Los Angeles police possessed some of the most skilled investigators in the world, trained to deal with master criminals, they could not get a true picture of what was happening in the early stages of Watts. Early on the third day of the riot, field forces knew the situation was out of control but the downtown command post was still optimistic. This is the classic problem of information flow in a bureaucracy. This highly professional department was unable to admit that a handful of what it considered hoodlums could create a major disturbance that it couldn't control.

In Plainfield, contrary actions by county and city police greatly inflamed the disorders. Plainfield had a relatively political disturbance with meetings and negotiations between blacks and city authorities alternating with violence. At one such meeting, under the auspices of community relations personnel and with city police understanding, several hundred men gathered in a county park to discuss their grievances and to choose leaders to represent them. During the meeting the violence had greatly subsided. However, this was shortlived, as the meeting was abruptly terminated by county police who said they could not meet in the park without a permit. This incensed the young men. Within an hour violence flared—that night a patrolman was killed and the destruction reached its highest point.

Further conflict among different levels of authority emerged in Plainfield between the police and local and state officials. Police felt "left out," "tired," and "poorly treated," and threatened to resign en masse (and to some observers almost mutinied) following their exclusion from negotiations which led to the release of arrested rioters, a policy of containment following the killing of a fellow officer, and the stopping by a state official of a house-to-house search for stolen carbines. The New Jersey riot inquiry felt that the circumscription of local police activities was such "as virtually to destroy the department's morale . . . [and] to limit seriously the effectiveness of the force (Governor's Select Commission, 1968, pp. 150, 153)."

In still other cases, as in Los Angeles, Boston, and New York, agreements reached by mayor's special representatives, human relations officials, and police-community relations officers who had rapport with rioters, were not honored by other policemen, creating great indignation and a sense of betrayal. In Los Angeles, the police community relations inspector was reportedly not called into the inner circle of police advisors. The chief of police was unaware that his department had been represented at an important community meeting held during the riot. A potentially ugly incident might have emerged in Detroit (May 21, 1968) when mounted police outside a building tried to drive supporters of the Poor People's March back into a building, while police on the inside were trying to drive them out. In Rockford, Illinois, in 1967, as people poured out of bars that were closing, police tried to drive them off the street that other police had already barricaded. In Birmingham in 1963, police circled several thousand blacks, on one side swinging their clubs and from the other side turning water hoses on them, catching bystanders as well as protestors—though this was no doubt all too well coordinated.

Breakdown of Police Organization: One Riot or Two?

An additional source of police ineffectiveness and abuse stems from the breakdown of organization within enforcement agencies. In most discussions of recent riots, undue emphasis has been given to the behavior of rioters. The normal concepts used to analyze collective behavior have been applied to them—emotional contagion, the spread of rumors, panic and the expression of frustration, the lessening of inhibitions, and innovative efforts to handle certain kinds of strain. Yet in several major disturbances, this perspective might equally be applied to the police. Police, lacking training and experience and often uncertain of what they were to do, sometimes became fatigued (frequently working 12 hour or more shifts with insufficient rest periods and nourishment); they were thrown off balance by the size of the disturbance and by being drawn frantically from one area to another, in some cases for false alarms seemingly coordinated with attacks and looting. As large numbers of people taunted, defied, insulted, and attacked them and they saw their fellows injured and in some cases killed, patience thinned and anger rose. Rumors about atrocities committed against them then spread.

Police may come to take violent black rhetoric and threats (which are partly related to expressive oral traditions, ritual posturing, and political infighting) too literally—as the lack of police killed by snipers and even reports that some snipers may have misfired on purpose, and the lack of attacks on known racists might imply. The belief may spread that they are in a war and all black people are their enemy. Traditional misconceptions about riotous crowds may contribute to an exaggeration of the dangers confronting them. As police control of the "turf" is effectively challenged and rioters gain control of the streets by default, the word may spread (as in Watts, Newark, and Detroit) that rioters have "beat the police." Losing face, humiliated by their temporary defeat and with their professional pride undermined, police may have a strong desire for revenge and to show their efficacy.

In a context such as the above, superior officers may lose the power to control their men. The chain of command and communication between and within enforcement agencies, often unclear to begin with, may completely break down. The most dangerous part of the disturbance is now at hand as the environment changes from a riot to a war. Some police behavior seems as much, or more, inspired by the desire for vengeance, retaliation, and "to teach the bastards a lesson" as by the desire to restore law and order.

The words of Lee and Humphrey, written shortly after the 1943 Detroit riot, are clearly relevant 26 years later: "War is to the army much what civilian outbreaks are to the police. Both offer socially acceptable outlets for the residuum of aggressiveness characteristic of each (Lee and Humphrey, 1943, p. 114)."

On the third day of the Detroit riot, an officer was overheard telling a young black on a newly stolen bicycle, "The worm is turning." And turn it did as the police took off their badges, taped over squad car numbers (this, of course, greatly reduced the number of complaints filed), and began indiscriminately and excessively using force against rioters, bystanders, and in some cases each other. The death and injury toll climbed rapidly. Some of the firing stopped only when control officials ran out of ammunition. At this time the Algiers Motel killings and "game" occurred. One of the police officers involved in this incident stated, "there was a lot of rough-housing, you know, everything just went loose [following the killing of a police officer on the third day of the riot]. The police officers weren't taking anything from anyone (Hersey, 1968, p. 134)." This would seem to be something of an understatement.

According to one high police official in secret testimony, by the fourth day of the riot "the police were out of control." There are some reports of police keeping looted goods taken from prisoners, robbing them, and of doing damage to "soul brother" stores spared by the rioters (Governor's Select Commission, 1968). Claims of brutality filed included charges of the mistreatment of women and the carving of initials on prisoners. It should be noted that such behavior occurs in spite of official riot control manuals stressing restrained use of force, and (usually) in spite of the wishes of higher authorities. Recent control manuals, while leaving something to be desired in their conceptual approach to collective behavior, stress the controlled and graduated use of force (Federal Bureau of Investigation, 1967; Mombiosse, 1967; also see Westley, 1956).

The attacking of fellow officers took two forms. It was either accidental or willful—as in the case of the beating of Negro police officers thought to be civilians because they were in plainclothes. For an example of the beating of an off-duty officer in Newark (New York Times, July 14, 1967) and the case of two black plainclothes officers beaten when the New York tactical patrol force "stampeded a crowd, . . . flailing vigorously with clubs," see Shapiro and Sullivan (1964, p. 93). A related incident not involving force occurred in Watts where a Negro plainclothesman (sent incognito to scout the Watts riot) hailed a radio car to make his report. The officer inside leaned out and asked him, "What you want, shitass jigaboo? (Wills, 1968)."

The chairman of the Newark Human Rights Commission reported that "men were being brought in, many of them handcuffed behind their backs, being carried like a sack of meal, and the fifth policeman would be hammering their face and body with a billy stick. This went on time after time. Many times you would see a man being brought into the police station without a mark on his face and when he was taken out he was brutally beaten (Governor's Select Commission, 1968, p. 118)." It has been said in jest, although there is an element of truth in it, that Newark was a classical race riot except the Italians wore blue uniforms.

Police may come to see rioters and suspected rioters, like those convicted of crimes, as having forfeited their civil rights. In Watts an officer responded to a black pedestrian who complained about being stopped on his way home from work: "Don't yell at me; you lost your rights a couple of days ago (Cohen and Murphy, 1967, p. 195)."

There often seemed to be a tendency for police behavior to become progressively worse as the disorders wore on. In Watts, Newark, and Detroit this was partly related to the entrance of higher-level control units into the disturbance. The assignment of guardsmen to accompany policemen may be seen by the latter as offering a chance to reverse earlier humiliation and gain revenge for injury and death suffered by the police. At the same time, inexperienced guardsmen, isolated from the authority of their commanding officers, may become subject to the same collective behavior phenomena as police and blacks, further adding to disorder-creating activities.

The head of the Detroit police, a former reporter, was hesitant to call out the guard, noting, "I've been on too many stories where the guard was called up. They're always shooting their own people"; and "Those poor kids were scared pissless, and they scared me (Wills, 1968, pp. 43, 44)." Calling them out was, however, a necessity to gain federal troops.

What is especially tragic is that the symbols of police legitimacy become the cloak under which much indiscriminate force is exercised upon the Negro community. It is a mistake to attribute such behavior only to the desire for revenge or to a hatred of Negroes, because part of it would seem to be equivalent to the behavior of front line soldiers who in their first combat experience kill many of their own men. That the breakdown of police organization transcends racism may also be seen in police response to student protests (such as at Columbia University) and various antiwar demonstrations.

It is important to recognize that not only was police behavior in the latter stages of several major riots brutal and probably ineffective, but that such acts were not idiosyncratic or random. They were woven into a social fabric of rumor, panic, frustration, fatigue, fear, racism, lack of training, inexperience, and the breakdown of police organization. While such a situation creates widespread fear in the Negro community and may inhibit some rioters, it can lead to (and partly results from) escalation in the level of black violence. There is an interaction process with gradual reciprocal increases in the severity of action taken on both sides. The fact that police abuses were most pronounced in Newark and Detroit, where disturbances were the most serious, does not imply a one-sided causal interpretation. Here we see the emergent character of the disorders.

Just as the belief that blacks want to kill police spreads among police so the opposite view may spread among black people. According to one account, Negro spectators in Harlem were "convinced that the policemen were the aggressors, in spite of the bricks, bottles, rubbish cans, and Molotov cocktails which flew around the intersection." According to an elderly woman, "They want to kill all of us; they want to shoot all the black people." A man agreed: "They wouldn't do all this gunslinging and clubbing on 42nd Street (Shapiro and Sullivan, 1964)."

An additional element in the misuse of official force is the view held by some policemen that they can (and indeed must) "hold court in the street," given the presumed leniency and complexity of the legal system (Reiss & Bordua, 1967). Gathering evidence that will hold in court during mass disorders and demonstrations is difficult; those arrested can often be charged with nothing more than a misdemeanor; sentencing for riot offenses tends to be lighter than for similar offenses committed in nonriot situations. The use of violence is such situations may also be related to the policemen's effort to save face and their belief that respect for their authority must be reestablished (Westley, 1953).

The breakdown of police organization and misuse of force did not happen to anywhere near the same extent in all cities that had disturbances. An important question for analysis is why in Watts, Newark, and Detroit—but not in Cincinnati or Boston? The conditions under which such police behavior appears are not well understood. There would seem to be a relationship to things such as training, the extent to which the police share social characteristics with and disagree with or are threatened and offended by the issues raised by protestors, the extent of injuries and provocation faced by police, the size and stage of the riot, the clarity of orders stressing restraint, the tightness of the command structure and whether civilian monitors and high-level government and police officials are on the scene, whether or not it is made clear to police that they will be punished for misbehavior, and whether or not police expect disturbance participants to be sufficiently punished by the legal system. That there was a breakdown of police organization in two of the most "professional" (according to the standards of the International Association of Chiefs of Police) departments in the United States, Los Angeles and Chicago, suggests that this issue goes beyond what is usually understood as police professionalism. In fact it may even be that less "professional" police departments such as Boston's have greater flexibility and a less zealous approach to potential threats to "law and order," permitting them to show greater restraint and making them more effective during a tense period.

QUIS CUSTODIET IPSOS CUSTODES?

One of the central intellectual problems for social analysis is the basis of social order. If one resolves the question of social order by relying on shared values and the internalization of standards, then this is not seen as an issue. Yet even those who answer the question of social order by stressing the importance of external force usually ignore it. In several of the major disturbances, after a period of time the tragic answer to the question of "who guards the guards" almost seemed to be "no one."

In at least one case, however, the answer to this question was higher-level authorities. In a border city whose chief of police wanted "to get every son-of-a-bitch down there; I'm getting goddamned tired of fooling around," the highly professional restraint of state police and national guard commanders seemed to prevent a police-initiated slaughter in the aftermath of minor disorders following a speech by H. Rap Brown. In the judgment of these higher-level commanders, the best control of the disorders was seen to lie in controlling the local police. The original disorders to an important extent grew out of exaggerated fears that Negroes were planning an attack on the downtown area and a state-of-seige world view among white authorities. The police chief was enraged by the wounding of a police officer which had followed instances of "white night-riding" and several shots fired by a deputy sheriff at H. Rap Brown as he walked toward the dividing line between white and black areas. The white local volunteer fire department refused to put out a fire of unknown origin at a Negro school that had been the center of controversy, resulting in several square blocks being burned down. The national guard then effectively neutralized the local police force and protected the Negro community, action which clearly contradicts the view of a monolithic, oppressive white control force. In another instance—the 1964 Harlem disturbance—James Farmer felt "the police were hysterical" and reportedly appealed to Governor Rockefeller to send the national guard to "protect the citizens of Harlem (Shapiro and Sullivan, 1964, pp. 71, 83)."

One of the manifestly unfair aspects of social organization is that those with official power are usually also those (or are intimately tied to those) who possess the power to sanction the misuse of this power. One means by which the police traditionally have been controlled is through the courts by the *exclusionary rule,* whereby illegal means used in gaining evidence or making arrests are grounds for the dismissal of a case. However, this rule only applies when convictions are sought (a factor often beyond the control of the police). In addition, many police abuses do not involve the gathering of evidence. The closeness of the police to the courts and their interdependence may inhibit the regulatory role of the former, particularly at lower levels.

Individuals can also bring costly and time consuming civil damage suits against the police, although those most likely to need redress may be least likely to have the resources necessary for a long court struggle—and establishing proof is difficult. The anonymity and confusion of a crowd situation and the tendency to remove badges make identification of offending officials unlikely. In the rare cases where police are criminally prosecuted for riot offenses, juries tend to find in their favor.

Police have also been controlled through direct political means. The rise of "good government"-inspired civil service reforms and the decline of the urban political machine makes this less likely today. Most of the now defunct Civilian Review Boards met with great police resistance, had no formal enforcement power, and could not initiate inquiries.

The means of control favored by the police is self-regulation, in a fashion analogous to specialized professions such as medicine or law. It is argued that police work is highly technical and only those who practice it are competent to judge it. Internal review mechanisms have been inadequate to say the least; there is evidence to suggest that, like the rest of us, the police can resist anything but temptation. Knowledge that they are unlikely to be subjected to postriot sanctioning may have lessened restraints on their use of violence.

In many departments there is a strong norm of secrecy surrounding police misbehavior; even when known, infractions often go unpunished.

The consequences, costs, and benefits of various means of regulating the police have not been carefully studied. It is clear from some of the data considered in this paper and from more recent events such as the Chicago Democratic Convention, the People's Park episode in Berkeley, and attacks on groups such as the Black Panthers that the control of the police is sometimes not much affected by the courts, various other checks and balances, internalized norms of fair play, nor internal police organization. The question of control and responsiveness of the police is certainly among the most pressing of domestic issues.

It has been often suggested that the most hideous crimes have been committed in the name of obedience rather than rebellion. In the Gordon Riots of 1780, demonstrators destroyed property and freed prisoners but evidently did not kill anyone, while authorities killed several hundred rioters and hanged an additional 25. In the Réveillon Riots of the French Revolution, several hundred rioters were killed, but they killed no one (Couch, 1968). Up to the end of the summer of 1967, this pattern was being repeated; police, not rioters, are responsible for most of the more than one hundred riot deaths that have occurred. To an important extent this pattern stems not from differences in will, but from the greater destructive resources of those in power, from their holding power to begin with, and from their ability to sanction. In a related context, the more than one hundred civil rights murders of recent years have been matched by almost no murders of racist whites. (Since 1968, this pattern may be changing.)

As long as racism and poverty exist American society needs relentless protest. It also needs police. It is increasingly clear that police are unduly scapegoated, stereotyped, and maligned; they are, as well, underpaid, undertrained, given contradictory tasks, and made to face directly the ugly consequences of the larger society's failure to change. It is equally clear that solutions to America's racial problems lie much more in the direction of redistributing power and income, eliminating discrimination and exploitation, than in changing the police. Nevertheless, one important factor in heeding the Kerner Commission's plea (1968) to "end the destruction and the violence, not only in the streets of the ghetto but in the lives of the people" is surely more enlightened police behavior.

NOTES

[1]Data on disorders in Plainfield, Jersey City, and Elizabeth, New Jersey; Cambridge, Maryland; Detroit, Newark, Cincinnati, Dayton, New Haven; Rockford, Illinois; and Milwaukee which are not referenced are from material in the files of the National Advisory Commission on Civil Disorders (Kerner, et al., 1968). Some of the ideas in this section have profited from discussions with and were jointly developed by Robert Shellow, Lou Goldberg, and Dave Boesel.

REFERENCES

Blumer, H.
    1958   "Race Prejudice as a Sense of Group Position." *Pacific Sociological Review*
            1:3-7.

Bouna, D., and T. Schade
    1967   "Police Riots and the Inner City and Police and Urban Unrest." Unpublished
            manuscript, Western Michigan University.

Bwy, D.
    1968   "Dimensions of Conflict in Latin America." *American Behavioral Scientist*
            2:39-50.

Chicago Commission on Race Relations
    1923   *The Negro in Chicago*. Chicago: University of Chicago Press.

Cohen, J., and W. Murphy
    1967   *Burn, Baby, Burn*. New York: Avon.

Conot, R.
    1967   *Rivers of Blood, Years of Darkness*. New York: Bantam Books.

Couch, C.
    1968   "Collective Behavior: An Examination of Stereotypes." *Social Problems*
            15:310-321.

Crozier, M.
    1968   "French Students: A Letter from Nanterre ca folie." *Public Interest*
            13:151-59.

Dahlke, A.
    1952   "Race and Minority Riots—A Study in the Typology of Violence." *Social
            Forces* 30:419-25.

Federal Bureau of Investigation
    1967   *Prevention and Control of Mobs*. Washington, D.C.

Fogelson, R.
    1968   "Violence as Protest: An Interpretation of the 1960s Riots." *Proceedings
            of the Academy of Political Science* 29:25-42.

Franklin, J. H.
    1965   *From Slavery to Freedom*. New York: Knopf.

Garson, D.
    1969   "The Politics of Collective Violence." Unpublished doctoral dissertation,
            Harvard University.

Governor's Select Commission on Civil Disorders (New Jersey)
    1968   *Report for Action*.

Grenley, W.
    1952   "Social Control in Cicero." *British Journal of Sociology* 3:322-88.

Grimshaw, A.
    1963   "Actions of Police and the Military in American Race Riots." *Phylon*
            24:271-89.

Hersey, J.
    1968   *The Algiers Motel Incident*. New York: Bantam Books.

Janowitz, M.
    1968   *Social Control of Escalated Riots*. Chicago: University of Chicago Center
            for Police Study.

Kerner, O., et al.
    1968   *Report of the National Advisory Commission on Civil Disorders*. New York:
            Bantam Books.

Lee, A. M., and N. O. Humphrey
    1943   *Race Riot*. New York: Dryden.

LeVine, R.
   1959   "Anti-European Violence in Africa: A Comparative Analysis." *Journal of Conflict Resolution* 3:420-29.

Marshall, T.
   1943   "The Gestapo in Detroit." *Crisis* 50:232-34.

Mayntz, R.
   1968   "Germany: Radicals and Reformers." *Public Interest* 13:160-72.

McCone, J. A., et al.
   1965   Governor's Commission on the Los Angeles Riots. *Volume II: Chronology.* Los Angeles.

Merton, R.
   1957   *Social Theory and Social Structure.* Glencoe, Ill.: Free Press.

Molineux, E. L.
   1884   "Riots in Cities and Their Suppression." Boston: Headquarters, First Brigade.

Momboisse, R.
   1967   *Riots, Revolts, and Insurrections.* Springfield, Ill.: Thomas.

Neiderhoffer, A.
   1967   *Behind the Shield.* New York: Doubleday.

New Jersey State Patrolmen's Benevolent Association
   1968   *A Challenge to Conscience.* Maplewood, N.Y.

Osofsky, G.
   1963   "Race Riot, 1900, A Study of Ethnic Violence." *Journal of Negro Education* 32:16-24.

Reiss, A., and D. Bordua
   1967   "Environment and Organization: A Perspective on the Police." In *The Police,* ed. D. Bordua. New York: John Wiley.

Rudwick, E.
   1966   *Race Riot at East St. Louis, July 2, 1919.* Cleveland: World.

San Francisco Police Department
   1963   "Police Control of Riots and Demonstrations." San Francisco

Seligmann, H. J.
   1919   "Race War." *New Republic* 20:48-50.

Shapiro, F. C., and J. W. Sullivan
   1964   *Race Riots.* New York: Crowell.

Shellow, R., and D. V. Roemer
   1966   "The Riot that Didn't Happen." *Social Problems* 14:221-33.

Shibutani, T., and K. H. Kwan
   1965   *Ethnic Stratification.* New York: Macmillan.

Shogan, R., and T. Craig
   1964   *The Detroit Race Riot.* Philadelphia: Chilton.

Silver, A.
   1967   "The Demand for Order in Civil Society: A Review of Some Themes in the History of Urban Crime, Police, and Riots." In *Police,* Bordua.

Smelser, N.
   1962   *Theory of Collective Behavior.* New York: Free Press.

Turner, C. C.
  1968 "Planning and Training for Civil Disorder." *The Police Chief* 35:22-28.

Waskow, A. I.
  1966 *From Race Riot to Sit-In: 1919 and the 1960s.* Garden City, N. Y.: Doubleday.

Westley, W. A.
  1953 "Violence and the Police." *American Journal of Sociology* 59:34-41.
  1956 *The Formation, Nature, and Control of Crowds.* Defense Research Board, Canada.

White, W. F.
  1919 "Chicago and Its Eight Reasons." *Crisis* 18 (Oct. 1919, no. 6).

Wills, G.
  1968 *The Second Civil War.* New York: New American Library.

Wilson, J. O.
  1967 "Police Morale, Reform and Citizen Respect: The Chicago Case." In *Police*, Bordua.

SECURING POLICE COMPLIANCE WITH CONSTITUTIONAL LIMITATIONS: THE EXCLUSIONARY RULE AND OTHER DEVICES

MONRAD G. PAULSEN, CHARLES WHITEBREAD, AND RICHARD BONNIE

The Supreme Court of the United States has evolved rules governing police conduct in making searches and arrests (now eavesdropping and wiretapping as well) from the imprecise words of the Fourth Amendment: "The right of the people to be secure in their persons, houses, papers, and effects, against unreasonable searches and seizures, shall not be violated, and no warrants shall issue, but upon probable cause, supported by oath or affirmation, and particularly describing the place to be searched, and the person or things to be seized." The Court's decisions have set constitutional limits on permissible police conduct, and in recent years these limits have become binding on state as well as federal officers.

Obviously, the content of these rules and other rules governing police conduct is likely to have a great impact on the incidence of violence in the community. If the rules permit police to use considerable force in a wide variety of situations, the level of violence rises. If the rules permit conduct which is generally considered an intolerable invasion of personal security or of privacy, we can expect outbursts of violence in protest against the sanctioned behavior. If the rules so hobble the police that convictions are extremely difficult to obtain in cases involving serious harms, the resulting anxiety and fear may themselves prove to be a breeding ground for destructive outbursts. This relationship between violence and the rules governing the police is further complicated by the fact that the methods of enforcing the rules are likely to differ in respect to their respective capacities to produce dangerous responses.

This chapter is devoted to an examination of the many ways by which police compliance might be secured. We begin with what has been historically the most controversial of the means of securing compliance—the exclusionary

Monrad G. Paulsen, Charles Whitebread, and Richard Bonnie, "Securing Police Compliance with Constitutional Limitations: The Exclusionary Rule and Other Devices" *Law and Order Reconsidered,* pp. 390-436. Report of the Task Force on Law and Law Enforcement to the National Commission on the Causes and Prevention of Violence (New York: Bantam) 1970.

rule. (The rule of exclusion obviously is also used to discourage police and other official misconduct involving other constitutional provisions, such as the Fifth Amendment's protection against being required to make self-incriminatory statements.) Thereafter we treat a wide variety of other remedies ranging from damage actions and injunctions to civilian review boards and "ombudsmen." At the conclusion we recommend a new approach to the problem of remedying police misconduct.

THE EXCLUSIONARY RULE

Until 1914 the general view of the nation's courts, state and federal, was that all material and relevant evidence should be admissible in a criminal case without regard to the manner by which it was obtained. The first important change in judicial opinion is recorded in *Weeks* v. *United States.*[1]

By a motion made prior to trial, the defendant in *Weeks* sought the return of property taken from him by police without a semblance of lawfulness. His house had been entered without a warrant and thoroughly searched in his absence. The trial court ordered the return of all the property taken save that "pertinent" to the charge against him (use of the mails for transporting lottery tickets). The Supreme Court reversed in a unanimous opinion, holding that even the material relating to the offense should have been returned. The Court based its decision on two main points:

1. The tendency of those who execute the criminal laws of the country to obtain conviction by means of unlawful seizures and enforced confessions . . . *should find no sanction* in the judgments if the courts which are charged at all times with the support of the Constitution and to which people of all conditions have a right to appeal for the maintenance of such fundamental rights,[2]

2. If letters and private documents can thus be seized and held and used in evidence against a citizen accused of an offense, the protection of the Fourth Amendment declaring his right to be secure against such searches and seizures *is of no value,* and, so far as those placed are concerned, *might well* be *stricken* from the Constitution.[3]

The first point has been echoed by Justices of impressive authority. Justice Holmes has written, "We have to choose, and for my part I think it is a less evil, that some criminal should escape than the Government should play an ignoble part."[4] Mr. Justice Brandeis put the point that the use of illegally obtained evidence, "is denied in order to maintain respect for law; in order to promote confidence in the administration of justice; in order to preserve the judicial process from contamination."[5] Judge Roger Traynor of California observed in *People* v. *Cahan,*[6] "The success of the lawless venture depends entirely on the court's lending its aid by allowing the evidence to be introduced."

The facts of *Cahan* underscore the point. The police conduct there involved two separate trespasses into a private home in order to install a microphone. The action was undertaken after permission had been received from the Los Angeles chief of police. The entire purpose of the illegal conduct was to obtain evidence for use in court. The incident was planned and approval was obtained at the highest level of police authority. It was not the case of a rookie policeman who misjudged the complicated law of search and seizure.

The spectacle of government breaking the law and employing the fruits of illegal conduct seems likely to breed disrespect for both the law and the courts. It does not seem daring to suggest that in such disrespect may lie the seeds of violent conduct.

The second point, that without the exclusionary evidence rule the constitutional guarantees of the Fourth Amendment are of "no value," has also proved persuasive in the decisive cases. In *Mapp* v. *Ohio*,[7] which extended the exclusionary evidence rule to the States, Mr. Justice Clark wrote, "[without the rule] the freedom from state invasions of privacy would be so ephemeral . . . as not to merit this Court's high regard as a freedom implicit in the concept of ordered liberty." Mr. Justice Traynor, again in *People* v. *Cahan*,[8] affirmed, "Experience has demonstrated . . . that neither administrative nor civil remedies are effective in suppressing lawless searches and seizures." At another point in that opinion, which embraced the exclusionary rule for the state of California six years before *Mapp*, Justice Traynor explained the action of the California Court: "other remedies have completely failed to secure compliance with the constitutional provisions on the part of police officers."[9]

Whether the exclusionary rule actually does effectively deter the police is a question without a firm answer. No solid research puts the question to rest. The assumption is that the police wish to convict those who commit crimes and that, if we bar the use of evidence illegally obtained, the police will conform to the rules in order to achieve that aim.

We know that the expanded application of the exclusionary rule has been accompanied by many efforts at police education. Courses in police academies, adult education programs for police sponsored by local headquarters, and courses in colleges and universities offered to police on the issues presented by the Fourth Amendment have sprung up nearly everywhere. More and more police leaders affirm the necessity for staying within the rules. More and more police departments have become interested in the formulation of guidelines for the officer on the beat who must make snap judgments. It is difficult not to credit the exclusionary rule for some of these developments.

One criticism of primary reliance on the exclusionary rule to deter police misconduct is that, despite its rationale of deterrence through deprivation of incriminating evidence, it does not deter when police act in situations where prosecution is not contemplated. If officers merely seek to harass a citizen, the exclusionary rule does not influence the officers to cease.[10]

We do see this point not as an argument against the rule, however, but rather as a reason for the creation of other remedies. The need is for supplementation, not abandonment.

Another question is: will reliance on the exclusionary rule breed police violence? If the police are "handcuffed" and are therefore unable to obtain convictions, will they impose extrajudicial punishment? Will they subject dangerous "criminals" (so identified by the police) to beatings and harassments? If so, the need is again for additional remedies—not necessarily abandonment of the rule. It is important to remember, as well, that if the police are "handcuffed" it is because of the *rules of search and seizure* and not because of the rule of exclusion. The rule of exclusion tells nothing of the rules governing the police: the exclusionary rule can operate with strict limitations on police activity as well as with limitations which permit the police a wide latitude in the choice of behavior.

However, respected authorities have recently taken the position that the exclusionary rule is not a suitable remedy in all situations. For example, Judge Henry Friendly of the U.S. Court of Appeals for the Second Circuit suggested in *United States* v. *Soyka*[11] that we ought not apply the exclusionary rule to enforce all the search and seizure rules in all kinds of cases. *Soyka* involved the admissibility of evidence taken by illegal conduct but Judge Friendly described the police behavior as an error "so minuscule and pardonable as to render the drastic sanction of the exclusion, intended primarily as a deterrent to outrageous police conduct . . . almost grotesquely inappropriate."[12] He went on to recommend a system which would apply or not apply the exclusionary rule depending on the gravity of the offense involved and the seriousness of the police misconduct.[13]

Judge Friendly's position is attractive because it suggests that a single value should not outweigh all others. The difficulty lies in the practical application of the principle. Can we articulate the suggested standard with sufficient precision so that it can be grasped by the police? Will a police officer readily know the seriousness of the offense which confronts him so he will know whether to use the "technical" or "liberal" rules of search and seizure? Can courts handily apply the proposed standards with uniformity and fairness?

The exclusionary rule not only forbids the use of evidence secured in violation of law but also of evidence derived from that originally taken. The courts may not use the "fruit of the poisonous tree."[14] Thus courts have held that fingerprints taken after an unlawful arrest are inadmissible[15] and certain statements made by an arrested person after an illegal arrest are barred from the trial.[16]

The key question is, of course, what is the "fruit" of illegal activity. Does it mean that all evidence which the police would not have "but for" the illegal conduct? If so, the sweep of the principle will be wide indeed. The Supreme Court has rejected the "but for" test and said the question is whether "the evidence to which instant objection is made has been come at by *exploitation of that illegality* or instead by means sufficiently distinguishable to be purged of the primary taint."[17]

Complaints about the broad application of the "fruit of the poisonous tree" principle, not strictly based on considerations of deterrence, have been heard from some judges. Mr. Justice White contributed a provocative discussion of the problem in his dissenting opinion *Harrison* v. *United States*[18] and in *Collins* v. *Beto*.[19] Judge Friendly argued that the judges should relate the reach of the principle to the seriousness of the police misconduct.

Also affecting the reach of the exclusionary rule is the doctrine of "harmless error," under which judgments are not to be reversed for error unless the error has prejudiced the defendant's case. The Supreme Court addressed itself to the "harmless error" question in *Chapman* v. *California*.[20] Chapman and another had been convicted upon a charge that they had robbed, kidnapped, and murdered a bartender. The California trial judge and the prosecutor had repeatedly referred to the defendant's failure to testify—a comment now forbidden by the Fifth Amendment privilege against self-incrimination.[21] Mr. Justice Black's majority opinion in *Chapman* first established that whether a federal constitutional error is harmless or not is an issue governed by federal law and that all constitutional errors are not necessarily harmful. But the Court noted that

before a federal constitutional error can be held harmless, the court must be able to declare a belief that it was harmless beyond a reasonable doubt. While appellate courts do not ordinarily have the original task of applying such a test, it is a familiar standard to all courts, and we believe its adoption will provide a more workable standard, although achieving the same result as that aimed at, in our *Fahy* case [holding that the error cannot be harmless where there is a reasonable possibility that the evidence complained of might have contributed to the conviction].[22]

Chapman's conviction was reversed. "Under these circumstances it is completely impossible to say that the state had demonstrated beyond a reasonable doubt the prosecutor's comments and the trial judge's instructions did not contribute to petitioner's convictions."[23]

On June 2, 1969, however, the Supreme Court did hold, in *Harrington* v. *California*[24] that a constitutional error in the trial of a criminal offense had been harmless, because there was "overwhelming" untainted evidence to support the conviction. The three dissenters in Harrington and some legal scholars as well, believe that the deterrent effect of the exclusionary rule will ultimately be substantially vitiated by this approach to the question of harmless error.

We believe that the exclusionary rule will and ought to endure as a primary device for securing police compliance with the law. Judge Friendly's suggestion in *Soyka*, the limitations on the "fruit of the poisonous tree" doctrine and the "harmless error" rule—each aims to escape the potentially severe implications of the rule in cases where police misconduct was not grave and where the defendant seems clearly guilty of a serious offense. The political forum echoes with the outcry that public safety is being submerged to a "literal" interpretation of constitutional limitations and that the exclusionary rule is but a sanctuary for the guilty. It is not surprising, therefore, that some judges are groping for ways to tailor the remedy to the outrageousness of the police misconduct and the gravity of the defendant's offense. We are in sympathy with this solicitude for effective law enforcement. We believe, however, the exclusionary evidence rule to be an exceedingly functional instrument for securing police compliance with the law. We should therefore be very cautious in fashioning limitations on the scope of the rule so as not to undercut its deterrent effect.

A final point about the exclusionary rule and its relation to violence: we may guess that the urge to destructive behavior is greatest when the actor is moved by a sense of frustration grounded in a feeling of injustice which he is unable to combat. The exclusionary rule, however, provides an outlet within the law for frustration stemming from the belief that the defendant has been treated unjustly by the police. By a motion to suppress, the defendant can in effect strike back at authority in the very proceeding which is aimed at convicting him. We now turn to other means, besides the exclusionary rule, of enforcing the substantive rules governing permissible police conduct.

DAMAGE REMEDIES UNDER STATE LAW

In general, a policeman is personally liable under state law for torts arising from his law enforcement activities.[25] Consideration of tort liability must proceed simultaneously on two fronts: effectiveness as a deterrent and utility as a mode of redress. In order to eliminate violent response to alleged police misconduct, our society must achieve both of these objectives. The average citizen must be confident that police misconduct is the deviant rather than the normal behavior and that he can recover for injury suffered due to police improprieties.

Substantive tort law theoretically permits recovery for some egregious acts of police misconduct. Liability for false arrest or false imprisonment may arise from a warrantless arrest lacking "probable cause." An illegal invasion of a person's home or seizure of his property constitutes a trespass to land or chattels. Because of damage limitations, however, plaintiff's victory in a suit for trespass will be only nominal unless the errant policeman has been carelessly destructive or overtly ill-willed. Where the police officer has employed an unreasonable amount of force under certain circumstances, he is liable for assault and battery. Despite the availability of these causes of action, however, the chances of adequate recovery are so slim that there is usually no inducement to sue.

The initial defect in civil recovery both as a means of redress and as a deterrent to police misconduct is the cost of suit. As the Wickersham Commission noted in 1931: "in case of persons of no influence or little or no means the legal restrictions are not likely to give an officer serious trouble."[26] Unfortunately, litigation is most costly, and consequently least attractive, in cases where redress is most needed—brutality cases in which recovery is likely to depend on the resolution of disputed factual issues necessitating a protracted trial.

If lower class litigants are to bring suit at all, their costs must be borne either by Legal Aid offices or lawyers operating on contingent fee. Yet, neither source can handle a large volume of cases and must of necessity choose only those most promising of success. Unless the state or local government bears at least part of the cost of litigation, regardless of outcome—for example, by hiring an attorney to represent indigents aggrieved by police misconduct—civil suit will be too sporadic to function adequately as either a deterrent or a means of redress.[27]

Time is a most formidable barrier to suit, especially among the poor. Because of crowded court dockets, years may pass before a case is decided. The prospect—and a limited one at that—of relief at some distant time is probably not strong enough to evoke an initial commitment, especially in light of the costs which might accrue. It should also be added that the protracted nature of litigation is also a major reason why civil suit is currently an inadequate substitute for or deterrent to violence as an outlet for citizen grievances against the police. A prospect, or even a promise, of damages two years hence is not likely to mitigate the incendiary effect of gross police misconduct which often has immediately preceded civil disorder.

Another problem is the difficulty of establishing damages even if liability is proven. As early as 1886, the Supreme Court noted that recovery of a sum sufficient to justify a police tort action is dependent on the "moral aspects of the case."[28] But the usual plaintiff lacks the "minimum elements of respectability"[29] to claim or recover for injury to reputation. Similarly, minority plaintiffs do not often recover punitive damages from predominantly middle-class juries, especially when such damages cannot be disguised as reparation for injury to reputation. Thus, since recovery is limited to actual damage for the most abused class of citizens, the Wickersham Commission conclusion, that a civil action has little deterrent value where it is most needed, is still true today.

To this point, we have endeavored to show that state civil suits are inadequate either to placate most citizens aggrieved by police misconduct or to deter police abuse. The serious questions remain whether such suits would become effective deterrents if the stated defects were cured and to what extent this result would be achieved to the detriment of legitimate law enforcement efforts.

Even if the possibility and extent of recovery were substantially increased the vindicated plaintiff would often be possessed of a meaningless judgment: police are not wealthy nor are they often bonded.[30] More important, if liability attached too readily or if there were any appreciable possibility that it would penalize honest mistakes, law enforcement would surely suffer. Complete individual liability for tortious conduct would not only discourage persons from becoming police officers but would also severely circumscribe the vigor and fearlessness with which they perform their duties.

With increasing frequency, commentators have urged that this dual defect—unredressed injury and deterrent overkill—be cured by municipal or state liability for police torts committed in the performance of their duties.[31] Except for the additional depletion of already barren state and local treasuries, the effects of governmental liability would be uniformly beneficial. It would surely facilitate redress and is a necessary condition for effective deterrence. To put it bluntly, it would slap the right wrists—namely, at the level where police policy is made. The department, under pressure from fiscal authorities, would very likely establish and enforce firmer guidelines through internal review and purge recurrent offenders.

On the other hand, it is arguable that governmental liability for police torts is not a sufficient condition for effective deterrence. Some police illegality is an inevitable concomitant of law enforcement,[32] and departmental policymakers, according to their own scheme of values, may find it prudent to violate now and pay later. Such a decision is especially likely in situations where the exclusionary rule does not apply and there is no other deterrent; that is, where prosecution is not contemplated and conviction is not the motivating factor.

In any event, a majority of states have refused to waive governmental immunity in police tort cases[33] despite repeated urgings by a multitude of legal scholars.[34] And it is unlikely that they will do so at least until the scope of liability is sufficiently limited.

Thus, the msot fruitful approach is to abandon delusions of broad deterrence and substantial redress and to concentrate on the grosser forms of abuse where the tort remedy can be useful. Actual injury caused by serious breaches of duty committed in utter disregard of proper standards of police conduct should be redressed by the courts in tort suits. The imperatives of such an approach are utilization of a good faith defense and more extensive governmental assumption of liability.

DAMAGE REMEDIES UNDER FEDERAL LAW

In addition to his state common law tort remedies, a citizen aggrieved by police misconduct may have a cause of action under 42 U.S.C. § 1983 which provides:

> Every person who, under color of any statute, ordinance, regulation, custom, or usage, of any State or Territory, subjects, or causes to be subjected, any citizen of the United States or other person within the jurisdiction thereof to the deprivation of any rights, privileges, or immunities secured by the Constitution and laws, shall be liable to the party injured in an action at law, suit in equity, or other proper proceeding for redress.

The statute in its present form is substantially unchanged from its passage in 1871 as the civil section of what is popularly known as the Ku Klux Act.[35] It is clear that this statute originally was designed to inhibit and give a remedy for the widespread abridgement of Negro rights that characterized the Reconstruction period in the South. Recently, however, the Supreme Court has read the broad statutory language to authorize civil tort suits in federal courts against state law enforcement officers,[36] and a steady stream of such cases now flows through the lower federal courts.[37]

In the landmark case, *Monroe* v. *Pape*,[38] James Monroe alleged that 13 Chicago policemen broke into his home at 5:45 A.M., routed his whole family from bed, ransacked every room in his house, detained him at the police station for 10 hours on "open charges," and finally released him without filing criminal charges against him. The Supreme Court, holding this complaint actionable under Section 1983, adopted the *Screws* and *Classic* definition of "under color of law," and noted that even action wholly contrary to state law is nevertheless action "under color of law" if the policemen are clothed with the indices of authority. Moreover, the Monroe majority held that since Section 1983 does not include the word "willfully," a complainant need neither allege nor prove a "specific intent to deprive a person of a federal right."[39] Finally, the Court reasoned that since one of the purposes of Section 1983 was to afford a federal right in federal courts, the federal remedy is supplementary to any existing state remedy and the state remedy need not be exhausted before its invocation.

The major issue that remained after the sweeping *Monroe* decision was whether some degree of bad faith or other fault in the deprivation of the citizen's constitutional rights is an element of the federal cause of action under

Section 1983. The court confronted this issue in its 1967 decision in *Pierson* v. *Ray*.[40] In that case petitioners, a group of Negro and white clergymen, were arrested for sitting-in at a segregated interstate bus terminal in Mississippi. Subsequent to their arrest and conviction, the statutory provision upon which their arrest had been based was declared unconstitutional and their cases were remanded and later dropped. In their subsequent suit for false arrest and violation of Section 1983, the Supreme Court proclaimed that the defenses of "good faith and probable cause" were available to the policemen-defendants under Section 1983 just as they were under Mississippi law of false arrest. Although the *Pierson* decision established that policemen are not strictly liable for unconstitutional activity, the scope of the defenses which it recognized is not yet clear. On the other hand, the federal defenses could be tied to state law, thereby attaching only in those states which allow a good faith defense in the subsequent invalidation context, as did Mississippi in *Pierson*. On the other hand, it would appear that the Court contemplated something broader—a federal standard of fault not tied to state law or to any particular factual context, and most observers have so assumed.

Because of the difficulty of segregating "probable cause" from the lawfulness of the conduct itself, and because "good faith" suggests a completely subjective standard, we suggest that these labels are inappropriate tools for defining the proper defense in the proper context. The purpose of a defense in a police tort suit, under state law or under Section 1983, should be to immunize conduct illegal only because of an honest mistake in judgment *or* an unforeseeable change in the law. The proper standard, and one which both state and post-*Pierson* lower federal courts in fact have been applying,[41] is whether the policeman's act was "reasonable" in light of circumstances, both legal and situational, about which he knew or should have known.

An additional question remaining after *Pierson* is the scope of police activity covered by the "rights, privileges, or immunities" clause of Section 1983. It clearly covers illegal searches or seizures and unconstitutional arrests. And there is some evidence that it also covers gross acts of police brutality, conduct which denies due process because it shocks the conscience.[42] In any event, however, Section 1983 cannot be employed to regulate the day-to-day conduct of the policeman on patrol—the seemingly trivial acts of harassment and misunderstanding which, in gross, may elicit violence against the police by ghetto residents.[43]

Nevertheless, Section 1983—like the state tort remedy—is a potentially useful device for compensating the individual citizen substantially injured by unlawful police action. To be sure, an action under Section 1983 is subject to all the intrinsic weakness of any tort remedy—limited personal assets of the police, no provision for payment of damages from municipal or state funds, the expense of maintaining the suit, the difficulty of establishing damages, the disadvantaged position of the usual plaintiff in the community, and the threat such assessments against individual policemen pose to vigorous and efficient law enforcement efforts.[44] Despite these inherent limitations, however, Section 1983's federal remedy for deprivation of constitutional rights does permit compensation of citizens whose person or property is significantly damaged due to clearly unlawful police activity.

Many commentators on Section 1983's use to control police conduct claim its application must be limited to the egregious case so that it does not hamper legitimate law enforcement by penalizing the policeman for mere error in judgment and honest misunderstanding.[45] We agree with this goal for the federal remedy as well as the state remedies, but argue that the present "probable cause and good faith" defense available to the police under *Pierson* v. *Ray* as applied in subsequent cases and as we have refined it, together with the law of damages under this section, in fact limit the scope of the remedy. Our conclusion, then, must be that, while the federal civil damages remedy cannot be a regulator of everyday police conduct, it can provide a remedy to individuals severely injured by outrageous instances of police illegality.[46] As an important and essential supplement to other devices for controlling police violence, it should be implemented at the federal level by rationalized damage rules and docket priority and at the state level by municipal assumption of liability and cost of suit.

INJUNCTION

The injunction offers the prospect of immediate relief from unconstitutional conduct and a powerful deterrent from engaging in that specific conduct. Simply as a matter of judicial equitable prerogative, such relief is easily justified. The remedies at law for this threatened or continuing deprivation of liberty are at present clearly inadequate except in a limited context, a conclusion emphatically asserted by the Supreme Court in *Mapp* v. *Ohio*[47] and reaffirmed in our discussion above. The injury may surely be irreparable, both to the plaintiff and the community.[48]

But injunctions issued against individual police officers to refrain from future violations, in addition to raising much the same substantive and practical problems noted above in connection with damages, also present an insuperable enforcement problem. The order must cover all types of illegal conduct or it cannot operate fairly; yet if an injunction issued upon proof of any illegality whatever, it would replace internal police disciplinary procedures with inflexible judicial oversight of the conduct of all police officers. Since the court's only sanction is contempt, it would be extremely heavy-handed and even more disruptive of legitimate law enforcement efforts than effective and broad damage remedies. Such a remedy represents the worst of all possible worlds.

Thus, instead of utilizing the remedial force of the injunction in a way destructive of law enforcement, a court must look to those who make the rules which the individual police officers are supposed to obey. The goal of injunctive relief should be to induce the departments to establish guidelines consistent with constitutional mandates and to use their internal disciplinary procedures to enforce these rules. Whether this goal can be achieved by equitable relief issued by either state or federal courts is the subject of this section.

The various state courts which have faced the question have left no clear statement of the law. In fact, there seem to be two separate lines of authority. Some courts have emphasized the institutional irresponsibility of injunctive interference with law enforcement activity.[49] Under this view, the plaintiff should be left to whatever civil remedies at law he has available or to his defenses in a criminal prosecution should one be brought. Other courts, perhaps a majority, have felt no institutional hesitations, but have placed heavy burdens on the plaintiff to show clearly lack of a reasonable basis for the allegedly illegal police actions and the presence of malice or bad faith.[50] Thus, even these courts have interfered only where the police are pursuing a clearly illegal course of conduct against an identifiable plaintiff or group of plaintiffs.[5]

Section 1983, discussed above, also authorizes the federal district courts to hear suits in equity against police for conduct invading constitutional rights.[52] Such suits have rarely been brought, however.[53] The United States Supreme Court approved the remedy in *Hague* v. *CIO*[54] in 1939, where it affirmed an order against a mayor, chief of police, and others enjoining them from continuing an antiunion campaign of harassing arrests, deportation of organizers, and suppression of union circulars and public meetings. Of the lower court decisions which have employed this remedy, several enjoined blatant infringements of First Amendment rights[55] and others, like *Hague* itself, enjoined schemes of conduct including attempts to enforce the law against plaintiffs but which nevertheless inhibited First Amendment rights.[56] Only two cases have involved injunctions for violations of criminal safeguards with no First Amendment overtones.

In the first, *Refoule* v. *Ellis*,[57] the police had four times detained the plaintiff without a warrant for extended periods of time, questioned him in relays, utilized force to coerce a confession, and conducted other similarly objectionable activities. The Georgia District Court issued an injunction against further warrantless detentions, questionings, beatings, and other specific illegal conduct. In *Lankford* v. *Gelston*,[58] the Fourth Circuit ordered the District Court to enjoin the Baltimore Police Department from continuing a 13-day search of ghetto residences without either warrant or consent based solely on anonymous phone tips.[59]

Refoule and *Lankford* are the only reported cases suitable for testing the validity and scope of the power of the federal courts to interfere with state and local law enforcement activities. In these cases, the courts acknowledged the principles of not interfering with administration of the criminal laws,[60] but affirmed that injunctions against such clear violations of constitutional rights could not possibly interfere with legitimate law enforcement activities.[61] And the courts were surely correct. These cases, so long as they could be brought to judicial attention, cried out for relief. Any police chief or officer continuing the illegal conduct in defiance of the court's order would have been deserving of a contempt citation.

The common elements of such egregious cases illustrate both the validity of the remedy and the limited scope of its employment: the department must be engaged in a *clearly unconstitutional course of conduct* directed against an *identifiable person or class of persons*. Such cases are most likely to involve conflicts between the police and particular organizations, such as the Black Panthers and antiwar groups, where the class is most definable and judicial reticence to interfere may be vitiated by First Amendment implications. Action filed by militant blacks[62] and antiwar groups[63] alleging systematic police harassment are now pending in the federal courts.

One recent commentator[64] has urged that the injunctive remedy be utilized not only to prohibit deliberately ordered violations of constitutional rights as in *Lankford* and *Refoule*, but also to require affirmative actions by Department superiors to prevent recurring violations which they have "passively tolerated." Although this proposal successfully identifies the crucial need in this area—the effective operation of departmental disciplinary procedures—its attempt to convert the courts into supervisors of police discipline is misguided.

Apart from a difficult problem of statutory authorization, the basic substantive defects are, first, definition and proof of violation, and, second, order-framing and sanction. On the first issue, the dispositive inquiry is whether the departmental superiors have taken adequate steps to enforce compliance with constitutional mandates. Such an evaluation would encompass policy guidelines, complaint mechanisms, and disciplinary procedures; yet judicial review of the adequacy of complaint processing and disciplinary procedures would be neither colorably judicial nor susceptible to remotely manageable standards.[65]

As to the second question—order-framing—the author proposes that the court first issue a general order directing the commissioner to correct the pattern of tolerated violations by altering his enforcement procedures in a way which achieves the desired result with a minimum adverse effect on the morale and efficiency of his department.[66] The author assumes that a good faith effort by a capable commissioner will quickly cure the ill and relieve the court of the difficult burden of making good its promise to reduce misconduct. Unfortunately, however, failures will be widespread, and the courts will sometimes have to frame a second, more specific order, itself establishing the department's disciplinary procedures,[67] and the author himself acknowledges that "such orders would seriously interfere with the Police Commissioner's management of his department and a court should make every effort to minimize the dangers inherent in such interference."[68]

In summary, although state cases are ambiguous and federal cases are sparse, it would appear that the injunction at either level is another useful fringe remedy. Where immediate relief from a clearly unconstitutional course of conduct against identifiable persons is prayed for, the injunction should issue. Otherwise the courts should not interfere directly with the enforcement of the criminal law.

CRIMINAL SANCTIONS

Although both state and federal statute books include criminal sanctions for illegal police conduct such as false arrest and trespass, they are rarely employed.[69] It is well established that in criminal prosecutions for false arrest the defendant must have criminal intent and that his good faith is a complete defense.[70] At common law no trespass to property is criminal unless it is accompanied by a breach of the peace.[71] Moreover, most states require criminal intent as an element[72] of the crime, either by statute or by judicial interpolation where the statute itself is silent.[73] Where intent is an element, the defenses of good faith[74] or color of title will lie unless there has been a breach of the peace.[75]

The dearth of case law on the subject indicates the impotency of criminal prosecution of police officers as a remedy for their misconduct. Professor

Foote, a leading authority on judicial remedies against the police, could find only four cases—all for false imprisonment—for the period 1940-55.[76] We have been unable to unearth any additional reported cases for the subsequent 13 years. No authoritative explanation has been given for the absence of prosecution for police offenses, but the reasons are not difficult to surmise. Prosecutors are probably reluctant to enforce these dormant criminal sanctions against police offenses because they anticipate, in our view correctly, a detrimental effect on law enforcement which is the goal of both departments, and because they consider the punishment too harsh.

As a supplement to state criminal remedies for police misconduct, 18 U.S.C. § 242 imposes a federal penalty on anyone who, under color of law, willfully deprives a person of his constitutional rights.[77] Because Section 242 is a criminal statute it has been narrowly construed. The Supreme Court in Screws v. U.S.,[78] upholding this statute against an attack that it was void for vagueness, interpreted the statutory requirement of willful violation to mean that the defendant must have had or been motivated by a specific intent to deprive a person of his constitutional rights.[79]

This narrow construction of the statute together with the reticence of prosecutors to bring actions against the police[80] have rendered Section 242 an impotent deterrent to police violence. Although there have been a handful of cases brought under this provision and some convictions,[81] this sanction has been applied only to the most outrageous kinds of police brutality.[82] Because the application of criminal sanctions to police misconduct is justified only when the policeman is clearly acting as a lawless hoodlum,[83] it is totally unrealistic to anticipate that this federal criminal provision will ever be transformed so as to control the conduct of the police.

Unlawful search and seizure, malicious procurement of a warrant, and excess of authority under a warrant have been punishable as misdemeanors under federal law for decades.[84] Yet the annotations following these statutory provisions dealing with illegal police activity reveal no decided cases. That these sanctions have been completely ignored for so long graphically underscores the need for remedies other than state and federal criminal statutes to deter and if necessary punish arbitrary police conduct.

As a final part of this synopsis of criminal provisions affecting the police some mention should be made of the long-standing suggestion that judges use their contempt power to discipline offending officers.[85] The contempt sanction, we have concluded, is much too harsh. Moreover, since judges are probably institutionally incapable of discovering on their own motion instances of police misconduct, this sanction would be applied only when the given facts in an adversary proceeding clearly indicate unlawful police action. Yet we already have better legal remedies for these egregious instances of police violence. Finally, since the proposed "contempt of the Constitution"[86] is an indirect criminal contempt, the accused police officer would probably have a right to a separate jury trial.[87] The prospect of a second trial militates further against stretching the contempt power to these frontiers never envisioned for it.

To this point, we have concluded that the judiciary—with some changes in substance and procedure—is the appropriate institution to deter and redress clear cases of police misconduct. The exclusionary evidence rule is a just and potent weapon to enforce constitutional mandates where a conviction is achieved. State and federal damage remedies, if rationalized and adequately facilitated, can deter and redress egregious and reckless police misconduct unattended by successful conviction. And injunctive relief may prove valuable in limited contexts where there has been an unlawful course of police conduct.

At the same time, we have also concluded that continuous administrative surveillance is better equipped than sporadic judicial oversight to cope with less extreme forms of police misconduct—conduct which is imprudent though not outrageous. Fair and speedy extrajudicial review of allegations of police harassment and other incendiary police practices could provide an essential outlet for citizen frustrations and dispel the widespread ghetto belief that police are characteristically arbitrary.

INTERNAL REVIEW

Every major police department has formal machinery for processing citizen complaints. To the extent that such machinery is fairly and effectively invoked, it can discipline misbehaving officers and deter the misconduct of other policemen. But in practice, internal review is largely distrusted by outsiders[88] for a variety of reasons.

For internal review procedures to be meaningful, complaints against the police must not only be readily accepted, but actively encouraged. Yet much criticism of police review has been directed at the hostile response of some departments to civilian complaints. In some instances, complex procedural formalities discourage filing of grievances.[89] Some departments will disregard anonymous telephone complaints and a few require sworn statements from complainants.[90] Allegations of police brutality, in particular, are often regarded as affronts to the integrity of the force which demand vigorous defense.[91] Accordingly, certain departments have in the past charged many complainants with false reports to the police as a matter of course,[92] or have agreed to drop criminal charges against the aggrieved party if he in turn abandons his complaint.[93] While most departments have abolished such practices, many potential allegations of police misconduct are apparently still withheld because of fear of retaliation.[94]

An impartial acceptance of all complaints against the police is necessary to instill confidence in a police review board. In fact, an increased volume of complaints filed with the police might often indicate that a department is winning rather than losing the trust of a community. To this end, the Police Task Force of the Crime Commission recommended that police departments accept all complaints from whatever source, process complaints even after complainants have dropped their charges, and advertise widely their search for police grievances of all types.[95] Many urban police departments have apparently adopted or already complied with these proposals.[96]

Although nearly all departments investigate all complaints, about half entrust the task exclusively to the local unit to which the accused officer was assigned.[97] The central organization usually supervises such investigations in varying degrees, but the relative autonomy of local units in gathering evidence concerning a complaint can both strain objectivity and engender further police misconduct.[98] Since investigative findings determine whether a complaint will be processed further or dismissed as groundless, a local investigating team is afforded the opportunity to clear its working comrade. Accordingly, the investigation may at times be designedly haphazard, or the complainant may be harassed into dropping his charges or a potential witness may be browbeaten into not testifying.[99] Special internal investigative units for complaints of police misconduct are common to many departments, and should be the established norm, particularly for large urban forces. Such internal special units would presumably face less conflict of interest than local units in dealing with the policeman's conduct. An outwardly more objective inquiry might reduce grounds for public suspicion of police investigation of their own misconduct.

A sizable minority of departments do not provide formal adversary hearings for allegations of even the most egregious police misconduct.[100] In such instances, the police chief or commissioner will usually determine from investigative findings whether an officer should be disciplined. In organizations where hearings are conducted before a police review board, the format varies. It has been found that almost half of departments that provide hearings hold them secretly, and one-fifth deny the complainant rights to cross-examine witnesses or bring counsel to the hearings.[101] Such secrecy and lack of procedural safeguards inevitably foster suspicion about the fairness of internal review.[102] Furthermore, the recommendations of the review boards, which usually are implemented by the police chief, are seldom disclosed to either the public or the complainant.[103] Such a practice deprives hearings of their value in promoting community relations. For a full explanation of a dismissed complaint could publicly vindicate the police officer who in fact behaved responsibly, and the news of actual disciplinary action could placate citizen indignation over police misconduct. Thus if hearings are open to the public, quasi-judicial trial procedures are followed, and review board decisions fully publicized, the popular image of the police could be profitably enhanced.[104]

A major criticism of internal review is that it seldom produces meaningful discipline of persons guilty of police misconduct.[105] Even when an officer is disciplined, the punishment is often so light as to be a token that aggravates rather than satisfies the grievant.[106] By contrast, many departments impose relatively severe penalties for violations of minor internal regulations. Thus tardiness or insubordination may warrant an automatic suspension that is more onerous than the sanction for physical abuse of a citizen.[107] The frequency of rigorous internal discipline for minor departures from departmental regulations magnifies the relative failure of police departments to discipline an officer for abusive treatment of a citizen. The inference is that internal review is more attuned to enforcing organizational disciplines than redressing citizen grievances.

Internal review is undoubtedly the quickest and most efficient method of regulating the conduct of peace officers.[108] It is perhaps axiomatic that organizational superiors are in the most favorable position to control their subordinates. Similarly, a police chief is probably best qualified to formulate the standards for police conduct. He also can utilize the best available investigative facilities plus his unique expertise in police operations to mete out appropriate disciplinary measures. A punishment decreed by an insider is likely to be accepted by both the miscreant officer and the department as a whole. On the other hand, control imposed from the outside is bound to be more sporadic and hence less effective than persistent self-discipline. Furthermore, constant second-guessing by strangers might undermine police morale and induce the kind of bureaucratic inertia that seems to plague several other governmental agencies sapped of their local autonomy.

Despite the inherent advantages of self-regulation, however, its difficulties in projecting an image of fairness with regard to complaints from the citizenry suggests that it should be supplemented by some form of external review. Whether or not internal review procedures are conducive to objective inquiry, the mechanism is seldom invoked by those minority groups which encounter the police most directly and frequently.[109] Since the police cannot redress an aggrieved citizen with money damages, the conspicuously rare punishment of policemen on the basis of outside complaints can create the popular impression that police review is a sham designed to appease rather than relieve the victims of police violence. Furthermore, this failure to win public approval deprives internal review of its efficacy as a forum for vindicating officers slandered by groundless complaints.[110]

The concept of internal review is also limited by the degree to which a departmental superior can extricate himself from the conflict of interest he faces in judging citizen complaints against the police. To be fair, he must suppress a natural feeling of loyalty toward his subordinates. On the other hand, he faces the possibility that concession to citizen demands will undermine the morale of his organization. Thus even the conscientious police commissioner may encounter difficulty in properly handling complaints. Police departments have a self-interest like any other entity, and if a police department tacitly overlooks misconduct by its patrolmen, then such a department cannot be expected to condemn itself publicly through internal review mechanisms.[111] In such a case, only an external organization can offer consistently impartial and objective review of allegations of police misconduct.

CIVILIAN REVIEW BOARDS

Dissatisfaction with both internal and judicial processing of police misconduct complaints prompted a few cities to experiment with civilian review boards. These boards, sitting independently of the police structure, adjudicated the merits of citizen grievances, either dismissing them as groundless or recommending that departmental superiors discipline the miscreant officer. Such external review was designed to project an appearance of fairness unattainable by internal mechanisms. At the same time, the civilian review boards were able to pass judgment on discourteous or harassing police practices which do not constitute judicially remediable wrongs but which nevertheless infuriate the grievant and intensify community hostility toward the police. Yet the boards did not purport to displace preexisting channels: the ultimate power to discipline remained with the police themselves, and the courts' jurisdiction over complaints was never abridged.

Civilian review boards have operated at one time or another in Philadelphia, New York City, Washington, and Rochester. The Washington board, however, could entertain only complaints referred to it by the police commissioner,[112] and the jurisdiction of the Rochester board was limited to allegations of unnecessary or excessive force.[113] Therefore, the New York and Philadelphia experiences contribute more expansively to an examination of civilian review.

The New York Civilian Complaint Review Board (CCRB), created by executive order in July 1966 and abolished by popular referendum four months later, consisted of four civilians appointed by the mayor and three policemen named by the police commissioner.[114] The CCRB was empowered to accept, investigate, and review any citizen complaints of police misconduct involving unnecessary or excessive force, abuse of authority, discourteous or insulting language, or ethnic derogation.[115] Upon receipt of a complaint, the board directed its specially assigned investigative staff of police officers to interview the complainant, the accused policeman, and any witnesses. If the investigation report revealed no serious dispute on the facts, a conciliation officer attempted to negotiate an informal settlement. If the policeman had acted properly under the circumstances, the board explained to the citizen that his grievance stemmed from a misunderstanding of the situation or of police duties. Where the officer had been mistaken or neglectful, or the injury had been minimal, the complainant was assured the misconduct had been amply considered and would not be repeated. Where both parties were at fault or where the citizen was particularly incensed, a joint confrontation of the parties was arranged which would hopefully result in mutual understanding and apologies.[116] If a complaint was conciliated or deemed unsubstantial, the accused officer was expressly notified that the complaint would not appear on his record.[117]

When the seriousness of the alleged offense or a heated dispute over the facts precluded informal conciliation, the CCRB conducted a formal hearing, at which both complainant and policeman had rights to representation by counsel and cross-examination of witnesses.[118] The board made findings of fact, upon which it either dismissed the complaint or recommended "charges" to the police commissioner. No specific disciplinary measures emerged from the CCRB, whose final rulings recommended further departmental consideration of a complaint rather than punishment.[119]

The New York CCRB elicited 440 complaints during its four-month existence, as compared to the approximate annual average of 200 received by the police-operated Complaint Review Board prior to 1966.[120] Nearly half the grievances alleged unnecessary force, but a substantial number involved discourtesy and abuse of authority.[121] Significantly, many of the complaints emerged not from the criminal context, but from police involvement in private or family disagreements.[122] That only half the complaints were filed by members of minority groups could be attributed to insufficient publicity and the CCRB's short tenure.[123] Of the 146 complaints ultimately processed by the CCRB, 109 were dismissed after investigation, 21 were conciliated, 11 were referred elsewhere, 4 culminated in recommended "charges," and 1 resulted in a reprimand from the board.[124]

The brevity of the New York experiment defies meaningful evaluation, but the Police Advisory Board (PAB) operated continually in Philadelphia from 1958 through 1967, when its normal activities were enjoined. The PAB closely resembled the CCRB, except that the Philadelphia board had no specially assigned investigative staff, held open hearings, lacked power to subpoena witnesses, and recommended specific disciplinary measures to the commissioner for valid complaints. From 1958 until mid-1966, the PAB received 571 citizen complaints, of which 42 percent alleged brutality, 22 percent harassment, 19 percent illegal entry or search, and 17 percent other misconduct.[125] During this period, the PAB recommended 18 reprimands, 23 suspensions, 2 dismissals, and 3 commendations of police officers, and 33 expungings of complainants' arrest records.[126] With few exceptions, the police department cooperated by implementing the board's proposals.[127]

The record of the PAB reveals several positive accomplishments. It evidently achieved some degree of support from the minority communities where police presence was most volatile; one-half of all complaints were filed by Negroes in a city that was three-quarters white.[128] Dispositions most frequently emerged from informal settlements.[129] This conciliation process, it is presumed, permitted grievance resolutions acceptable to both citizen and officer with a minimum of the adversary tensions normally incident to an open formal hearing. Furthermore, the complainant would often be uninterested in seeing the policeman disciplined; he may have sought only an apology or eradication of an unjustified arrest record.

The PAB also submitted an annual report to the mayor, which allowed broader expression of citizen judgment on police policies than would usually flow from the case-by-case approach. The police department followed the 1962 report's suggestion that definitive guidelines for the proper use of handcuffs be established.[130] In 1965 the PAB requested that the police rectify apparent patterns of physical mistreatment of apprehended persons in station houses and discourtesy directed at civilian inquiries.[131] The annual report thus enabled the PAB to expose the most persistent sources of citizen irritation in the interest of enabling the police both to improve their services and to enhance their public image. Finally, a prominent Philadelphian has noted he remembers no occasion prior to the board's operation in which the police department had ever disciplined an officer solely on the basis of civilian complaint.[132]

The successes of civilian review have been counterbalanced by marked failures, some of which are probably unique to the Philadelphia experience. Few complaints were filed with the PAB. The number exceeded 100 only in 1964, and the annual rate of complaints received evinces an erratic, rather than an upward trend.[133] The diminutive community response to the board was partly attributable to its lack of publicity. As a result of limited press coverage and a nonexistent publicity budget, many citizens knew nothing of the board's operation or even its existence.[134] There is also suspicion that some policemen actively discouraged complaints on infrequent occasions.[135]

In addition to being relatively ignored by the citizenry, the PAB encountered difficulties maintaining its impartial image. The board often compensated for an indigent complainant's inability to secure counsel by developing the case for him during hearings.[136] This procedure might at times have induced a policeman to suspect the board was biased against him. Positing all investigative authority over civilian complaints in the police department not only advertised the PAB's dependence on police rather than civilian judgment in the critical initial inquiries, but also produced unjustifiable delays as well. Approximately half the investigation reports were not returned to the board within 90 days of referral to the police department, and a sizable backlog of unresolved cases accumulated.[137] This lag, combined with other procedural delays, partially explains why many citizens failed to follow their initial complaints through to ultimate disposition. Finally, the PAB, having been created by mayoral fiat in 1958, was a political creature of unascertainable life and tenuous authority. Frictions with the mayor and a court challenge of its legality engendered periods of uncertainty and compromise in the board's early history,[138] and normal board operations have been suspended since mid-1967, when the Fraternal Order of Police successfully enjoined its hearings.[139]

Apart from the particularized shortcomings of the PAB in Philadelphia, its record reveals institutional deficiencies that will plague any civilian review board of the future. The PAB was subjected to the same kind of vehement police attacks that led to the abolition of the CCRB in New York City.[140] The police claimed that civilian review lowers police morale, undermines respect of lower echelon officers for their superiors, and inhibits proper police discretion by inducing fear of retaliatory action before the board.[141] The advisory nature of the PAB and its infrequent disciplinary recommendations may impeach the credibility of such allegation. But police hostility to the review board cannot be underestimated.

Probably the real issue here is that, despite their monopoly on the use of force, policemen fiercely resent being singled out among all other local governmental officials for civilian review. Implicit in the board's very existence seems to be an assumption that policemen are characteristically arbitrary or brutal and have to be watched. Since policemen apparently believe that civilian review boards symbolize society's contemptuous discrimination against them, the ill-feeling the institution provokes may not be worth the benefits it may confer. Indeed, the high controversy associated with the term "civilian review board" suggests the appellation will not be attached to any future grievance response agencies.

Another source of police antagonism may have been the adversary nature of the PAB's hearing procedures. The adversary process is not only costly and protracted, but when complainant and policeman are pitted against each other in formal opposition, hearings convey the appearance of a battleground.[142] As a consequence, the civilian review board seems in some ways to aggravate, rather than minimize, the frictions between police and community. Yet the object of external review should be improvement of existing police services, not establishment of a rival police department. To the extent that a board departs from ameliorating tensions through informal conciliation and moves toward affixing blame in formal adjudication, it fails to improve police-community relations.

To relate the defects of civilian review boards is not, however, to reject the concept of civilian review itself. Both the Kerner[143] and Crime Commissions[144] recognized the importance of independent nonjudicial review of police conduct, and yet also did not recommend that civilian review boards be established in cities where they did not already exist. Indeed, the qualified achievements of the review board seem to have flowed more from the merits of external surveillance than the mechanism that seeks to achieve it. If civilian review can be institutionalized so as to placate rather than polarize police-citizen differences, its potential may be realized. The ombudsman has been offered as just such an institution.

HE OMBUDSMAN

The Scandinavian ombudsman system has been adopted by several foreign governments in recent years, and the idea of importing it to America has received much attention.[145] The ombudsman is, most simply, an external critic of administration. In 1807, Sweden appointed the first ombudsman, who was charged with surveillance of all bureaucratic agencies. Finland adopted the institution in 1919, and by 1967 it had spread to ten other countries.[146] In the countries where he exists, the ombudsman is usually a prominent jurist, and is aided by a staff of lawyers. He is appointed by the national legislature, and in some countries has jurisdiction over municipal, as well as national administrative agencies.[147]

The ombudsman's goal is improvement of administration rather than punishment of administrators or redress of individual grievances.[148] Thus, instead of conducting formal hearings associated with adjudication, he relies primarily on his own investigations to collect information. He is authorized to receive all civilian complaints against any administrator or department. But valid complaints do not generally invoke adversary confrontations for purposes of adjudicating the propriety of past conduct by an official. Rather, individual grievances serve to alert the ombudsman to questionable administrative policies that deserve investigation. In accordance with his focus on future practices rather than past grievances, the ombudsman may even initiate investigation at his own discretion in the absence of a citizen complaint. To facilitate his inquiries, he may request explanation from an appropriate official, examine an agency's files, or call witnesses and conduct a hearing. On the basis of his findings, the ombudsman may recommend corrective measures to the agency although he cannot compel an official to do anything. In some countries, he may also prosecute a delinquent official, although this power is rarely exercised. In any case, he takes great pains to explain his conclusions to bureaucrats, complainants, and the general public. Since the ombudsman enjoys almost demi-god status in some countries, administrators are likely to heed his criticisms and citizens are not apt to be disturbed when he finds complaints groundless. Furthermore, administrators evidently feel benefitted not only by the ombudsman's rejection of warrentless accusations, but also by his suggestions of fairer and more efficient policies and procedures. At the same time, citizens can see their grievances being translated into broad policy guidelines.

Professor Gellhorn, an eminent proponent of the ombudsman ideal, has asserted its relevance to police-community relations in America. First of all, his ombudsman would avoid the tragic flaw of civilian review boards by accepting complaints about any local public servants, not just policemen.[149] Furthermore, Gellhorn contends, full processing of each citizen complaint before referral to administrative superiors for further consideration constitutes a cumbersome duplication of effort and an unjustifiable displacement of the police department as primary investigator and and arbiter of charges against its members.[150] The thrust of his argument is that meaningful improvement in police administration will emerge not from sporadic disciplinary proceedings but rather from imposing upon departmental superiors absolute accountability for the actions of their subordinates.[151] Therefore, the ombudsman should initiate his inquiries only upon charges that departmental superiors have given inadequate attention to a complaint of police misconduct. The focus of evaluation is then not the guilt of a particular policeman, but the policies and procedures by which police superiors have assessed a citizen's allegation of such guilt.[152] The ombudsman, thus relieved of the adversary adjudications that made civilian review boards so unpopular, could supposedly transcend the individual case to address himself to the broader policies of police administration

We reject Professor Gellhorn's proposal because it eliminates that conciliatory process which was the primary strength of the civilian review boards. If frustration over police practices is indeed a major cause of urban disorders,[153] and if many of the grievances which engender such frustrations can indeed be alleviated by an apology or police explanation,[154] then informal conciliation of the individual case is a necessary function of complaint channels. Because his ombudsman is in effect a court of appeals bound by the factual findings of the police department, it must be presumed that any informal accommodations Gellhorn envisions must be effected by internal processes. Yet such an arrangement presupposes a preexisting community trust of the police, the lack of which supposedly made external review desirable in the first place. When a police department is unable to project an impartial appearance, informal negotiation of a compromise between citizen and policeman must be attempted by an external agency *before* a complaint is referred to the police department for adversary adjudication. Whereas policy orientation undoubtedly offers creative possibilities for external review, the ombudsman should not divorce himself from the individual case to the degree that Professor Gellhorn recommends.

CONCLUSION AND RECOMMENDATIONS

To recapitulate for a moment, none of the remedies discussed above can successfully control the everyday conduct of the policeman on the beat—the harassment and abuse which yields no actual physical damage and results less from ill will than from poor training. The exclusionary rule can remedy denials of constitutional rights in cases which go to trial and result in convictions. Civil damage actions, state or federal, can redress egregious misconduct resulting in actual damage. Injunctive relief can halt and deter systematic misconduct directed at an identifiable person or group of persons. However, solutions for the basic problems of police-community relations cannot be imposed from the outside: as even the most pessimistic commentators have recognized, primary responsibility for everyday police discipline must rest within the police department.

Nevertheless, since internal review has been uniformly sluggish, some kind of outside pressure must be brought to bear to induce voluntary correction of illegal and otherwise abusive police conduct. Mandatory injunctions issued by federal district courts are too cumbersome for this purpose and are susceptible to complete disruption of the internal review mechanism. The civilian review boards are doomed to futility since they pit the aggrieved citizen against the police department in a formal adversary proceeding; in short, someone always wins and someone is always resentful. The ombudsman, on the other hand, shifts the focus from dispute resolution to evaluation of the department's grievance response mechanism. Yet, since the primary goals of an effective complaint mechanism are to provide an objective forum and encourage its use, individual grievances must remain in the forefront, and their dispositions must be publicized.

What is needed is a hybrid of the ombudsman and the external review agency, whose operation would have the following attributes:

1. The primary responsibility for police discipline must remain with the police department itself.
2. Nevertheless, there must be an easily accessible agency external to the police department, which processes citizen complaints in their inception rather than on appeal from the police.
3. In each case, this agency should:
   —make an independent investigation of the complaints;
   —publicly exonerate the police if the complaint is groundless;
   —in cases of misunderstanding or minor abuse, attempt to resolve the dispute through an informal conciliation meeting;
   —if efforts at conciliation should fail or if the police behavior was unacceptable, make recommendations to the department regarding discipline or ways to relieve tension;
   —keep each citizen complainant aware of the disposition of his complaint.
4. On all matters, the agency should keep the public aware of its actions and the department's response to its recommendations and should publish periodic reports and conclusions.
5. So as not to single out the police for special oversight the agency should be responsible for processing citizen complaints not only against the police but also against other basic governmental service agencies, such as those responsible for welfare and employment. (For purposes of this chapter, however, we shall focus only on the relation of such an agency to the police department.)

While we affirm that our proposed agency will possess many of the attributes of the Scandinavian "ombudsman," it nevertheless differs from it in many material respects. For purposes of simplicity, however, we will call our agency "ombudsman." Its functioning we will now describe in somewhat greater detail.

Person with claims of police misconduct shall register them directly with the ombudsman without first seeking internal police review. He and his investigative staff shall first make findings of fact. If, after such an investigation, the complaint is found to be groundless, the ombudsman shall order it dismissed. If, however, his findings indicate police impropriety, the ombudsman has two courses open to him—informal conciliation and, if that fails, recommendation to the police commissioner that disciplinary action be taken.

In the first instance, the ombudsman's most useful function is to act as a conciliation agent between the police department and the aggrieved citizen. Since many of the citizens' grievances stem from seemingly trivial incidents, the ombudsman may be able to satisfy the aggrieved citizen by bringing him together with the offending policeman. Out of such meetings might come an apology by the officer for his indiscretion and a better understanding by the citizen of the tensions of day-to-day police work.

Such conciliation procedures and favorable results may seem at first blush naïve; however, experience with ombudsmen in foreign countries indicates that conciliation is their strongest weapon in their efforts to eliminate the rough edges of modern bureaucracy.[155] The citizen will often be quite satisfied with an apology or an explanation. Thus, the cumulation of such simple meetings may do much to offset the hostility and violence which can arise when citizens feel powerless against what they perceive as thoughtless and arrogant uses of governmental power.

When a complaint is found to be meritorious and conciliation attempts have failed or are clearly unsuitable, the ombudsman shall send a recommendation to the police department that a particular officer be disciplined. The ombudsman shall make such recommendation only as the last resort in any given case. On receipt of such recommendation, the responsibility for discipline shall be with the department itself.

What if the police department decides not to act on the ombudsman's recommendation? This knotty problem really presents two separate issues— non-action in a given case and non-action in most cases (indicating a course of conduct by the department not to heed the recommendation of the ombudsman). We feel that the systematic refusal of the department to cooperate with the ombudsman can be overcome by bringing it to public light in the ombudsman's periodic reports. The force of public opinion should push a clearly defiant police department into action. Although many citizens fear undue hampering of police efforts to curb crime, few will sanction police lawlessness. Moreover, refusal to heed the recommendations of the independent ombudsman should engender indignant response even from members of the majority community who have little contact with the police.[156]

Despite our concern for refusal to act on the ombudsman's recommendation as a general course of conduct, we emphasize that the department must retain discretion in each case to decide whether there should be disciplinary action and what the punishment should be. Maintenance of police morale and efficient law enforcement require that the department make the final decision. Thus, if in individual instances the police department disagrees with the ombudsman's recommendation, the department's good faith should be accepted.

In sum, then, if the police department systematically refuses to respond to the ombudsman's recommendation with reasonable exercises of internal discipline, the ombudsman should bring this recalcitrance to public attention in his periodic reports and rely on public pressure to activate internal police machinery.

On the other hand, should the police generally follow his suggestions but occasionally refuse to act, the ombudsman should seek an explanation and accept such exercises of discretion as good faith determinations that in their opinion no action was justified.

Whatever the outcome of departmental action on the ombudsman's recommendations, his final duty in the processing of citizen complaints will be to publicize the action taken. First, he should inform the complainant directly of the action taken on his complaint. In addition, he should record both his and the department's dispositions for general information to the public. We suggest that in informing the general public he should not refer by name to the officer disciplined but merely should report that as a result of his recommendation the department fined, suspended, and so on, an officer on a given date. The purpose of informing the complainant of the outcome of the case is to give him confidence that his complaint was duly considered and acted upon. The more general record serves to keep the public aware that legitimate grievances against the police do have an effective, nonviolent outlet.

In addition to processing citizen grievances, the ombudsman should publish periodic reports. We suggest that these public reports be submitted every six months. At the very least, such reports should include statistical accounts of the number and disposition of private complaints coming to his attention. Moreover, because naked statistics are often subject to inconsistent interpretations, the ombudsman should make an assessment of the overall performance of his office and responsiveness of the police to his suggestions. We must reiterate that this assessment is the ombudsman's most potent weapon for marshalling public support and for prodding a recalcitrant police force. Together with an assessment of the ombudsman's work with the police in dealing with private complaints, the report should contain recommendations of a general nature drawn from an overview of the complaints. For example, the ombudsman might recommend that a slight change in present police practice could eliminate a substantial irritant in police-community relations.

His recommendations should extend not only to police practice guidelines but also to legislative action he deems necessary to defuse the ghettos or improve law enforcement. For instance, a very common complaint in ghetto communities is that the police do not readily respond to calls for help. If the reason is that the police force is substantially undermanned, the ombudsman could lend the authority of his voice to call for the legislative body to allocate more money for more police services. By making substantive recommendations to the legislature and suggesting guidelines for police practice to minimize citizen complaints the ombudsman's reports could be a truly effective force for vigorous yet benign law enforcement.

Finally, having described in a general way the duties of the ombudsman, we advert briefly to questions of agency structure and funding. In this regard we merely sketch our suggestions, as follows:

1. at least some of the initial funding must come from federal government because of the already great demands on municipal and state funds;
2. the agency must be locally controlled;
3. the agency must be supplied with sufficient funds to attract a first-rate investigative staff;
4. the agency must be organized to process complaints quickly and efficiently;
5. since conciliation will be its primary function, the agency must be highly visible; accordingly, we recommend that it have neighborhood offices and a publicity budget;
6. the ombudsman must be a man who can secure the cooperation of

all parties affected by his office and can muster public support for his recommendation; such men will be available only if the community is committed to the success of his project;

7. the ombudsman appointment procedure should leave him representing no particular interest group and above political pressure;
8. the ombudsman should be appointed to a single four to six year term and should be empowered to select his own staff.

A FINAL PLEA

Now, for the third time in less than three years, a Presidential Commission has recommended the creation of local citizens' grievance agencies similar to the one outlined above.[157] The President's Commission on the Causes and Prevention of Violence, for whom this chapter was originally prepared, stated in its final report, submitted to President Nixon on December 10, 1969:

> Both the President's Commission on Law Enforcement and Administration of Justice (Crime Commission) and the National Advisory Commission on Civil Disorders (Kerner Commission) recommended that local jurisdictions establish adequate mechanisms for processing citizen grievances about the conduct of public officials. That recommendation has not received the attention or the response it deserves.
>
> *To increase the responsiveness of local governments to the needs and rights of their citizens, we recommend that the federal government allocate seed money to a limited number of state and local jurisdictions demonstrating an interest in establishing citizen's grievance agencies.*[158]

It is clear that those of our nation's citizens who sit on Presidential Commissions unanimously endorse this proposal. It is our earnest hope that the nation's legislators, federal, state and local, will soon respond.

NOTES

[1]232 U.S. 383 (1914).

[2]*Id.* at 392 (italics supplied).

[3]*Id.* at 393 (italics supplied).

[4]*Olmstead* v. *United States,* 277 U.S. 438, 470 (1928). (Dissenting opinion.)

[5]*Id.* at 484. (Dissenting opinion.)

[6]44 Cal. 2d 434, 445, 282 P. 2d 905, 912 (1955).

[7]367 U.S. 643 (1961).

[8]*Supra* note 6, at 913.

[9]*Id.* at 911.

[10]Barrett, "Personal Rights, Property Rights and the Fourth Amendment," 1960 *Sup. Ct. Rev.* 46, 54-55. An example of police misconduct not reached by the exclusionary rule is the Plainfield search described in Bean, "Plainfield: A Study in Law and Violence," 6 *Am. Crim. L.Q.* 154 (1968).

[11]394 F. 2d 443 (2d Cir. 1968). (Dissenting opinion.)

[12]*Id.* at 452.

[13]*Id.*

[14]*Silverthorne Lumber Co.* v. *United States,* 251 U.S. 385 (1919).

[15]*Bynum* v. *United States,* 262 F. 2d (D.C. Cir. 1958).

[16]*Wong Sun* v. *United States,* 371 U.S. 471 (1963).

[17]*Id.* The test was formulated by Professor Maguire; *see* Maguire *Evidence of Guilt* 221 (1959).

[18]88 S. Ct. 2008 (1968). (Dissenting opinion.)

[19]348 F. 2d. 823, 835 (5th Cir. 1965). (Concurring opinion.) Judge Friendly (2d. Cir.) sat by designation in the Fifth Circuit.

[20]386 U.S. 18 (1966).

[21]*Griffin* v. *California,* 380 U.S. 609 (1965).

[22]386 U.S. at 24.

[23]Ibid., 26.

[24]89 S. Ct. 1726 (1969).

[25]Dakin, "Municipal Immunity in Police Torts," *Clev. Mar. L. Rev.* 16 (1967): 448.

[26]II National Commission on Law Observance and Enforcement, No. 8, *Report on Criminal Procedure* 19 (1931).

[27]At the very least, the civil plaintiff must bear attorney costs, and thus many actions against the police are undoubtedly precluded by the aggrieved party's lack of funds. United States Commission on Civil Rights, 1961 *Commission on Civil Rights Report: Justice,* V. 81 (1961).

[28]*Ker.* v. *Illinois,* 119 U.S. 436, 444 (1886).

[29]Foote, "Tort Remedies for Police Violations of Individual Rights," *Minn. I. Rev.* 39 (1955): 493, 500.

[30]1961 *Commission on Civil Rights Report: Justice,* 81; President's Commission on Law Enforcement and Administration of Justice (hereinafter cited as Crime Commission), *Task Force Report: The Police,* p. 199; Dakin, pp. 448-449.

[31]E.g., Foote; Fuller and Casner, "Municipal Tort Liability in Operation," *Harv. L. Rev.* 54 (1941):437; Jaffe, "Suits Against Governments and Officers Damage Actions," *Harv. L. Rev.* 77 (1963): 209; Lawyer, "Birth and Death of Government Immunity," *Clev. Mar. L. Rev.* 15 (1966): 529; Mathes S. Jones, see note 26; Tooke, "The Extension of Municipal Liability in Tort," *U. Va. L. Rev.* 19 (1932): 97.

[32]Foote, p. 515. *See* "Arrest of Wrong Person," *So. Calif. L. Rev.* 18 (1944): 162.

[33]A growing disenchantment for the doctrine has recently led some states and cities to abolish it by statute. E.g., Cal. Gov't Code § § 815.2, 825, 825.2 (1966); Minn. Stat. Ann. § 466.02 (1963); N.Y. Ct. Cl. Act. § 8 (1963); Wash. Rev. Code of Wash. Ann. § 4.920.090 (1962). Others have abolished the doctrine by judicial fiat. *Hargrove* v. *Cocoa Beach,* 96 So. 2d 130 (Fla. 1957); *Steele* v. *Anchorage,* 385 P. 2d 582 (Alas, 1963); *Stone* v. *Arizona Highways Comm.,* 93 Ariz. 384, 381 P. 2d 107 (1963); *Molitor* v. *Kaneland Community Unit Dist. No.* 302, 18 Ill. 2d 11, 163 N.E. 2d 89 (1959); *Williams* v. *Detroit,* 364 Mich. 231, 111 N.W. 2d 1 (1961); *McAndrew* v. *Mularchuk,* 33 N.J. 172, 162 A. 2d 820 (1960); *Kelso* v. *Tacoma,* 63 Wash. 2d 912, 390 P. 2d 2 (1964); *Holtyz* v. *Milwaukee,* 17 Wis. 2d 26, 115 N.W. 2d 618 (1962). A District of Columbia judge has recently ruled that the government may be sued when its policemen are accused of brutality. *Washington Post,* Jan. 7, 1969, at D1.

Five states have modified sovereign immunity where the municipality has insurance.

Idaho Code Ann. § 41-3505 (1961); Mo. Ann. Stat. § 71.185 (Supp. 1969); N.H. Rev. Stat. Ann. § 412.3 (1968); N.D. Cent. Code § 40-43-07 (1968); Ut. Stat. tit. 29, § 1403 (Supp. 1968). Illinois and Connecticut indemnify governmental employees for judgments incurred for torts committed in the course of carrying out their duties. Conn. Gen. Stat. § 7-465 (Supp. 1969); Ill. Rev. Stat., Ch. 24, § 1-4-5 (1962), §1-4-6 (Supp. 1969).

[34]See note 31.

[35]17 Stat. 13 § 1 (1871).

[36]*Pierson* v. *Ray*, 386 U.S. 547 (1967); *Monroe* v. *Pape*, 365 U.S. 167 (1961).

[37]The past 8 years have witnessed a marked increase in cases under 42 U.S.C. § 1983. The annual numbers of private civil actions filed in district courts under the Civil Rights Act are in the Annual Report[s] of the Administrative Office of the United States (Table C2):

Year	Number of Cases
1958	220
1959	247
1960	280
1961	270
1962	357
1963	424
1964	645
1965	994
1966	1,154

Not all of these cases alleged police misconduct; many were directed at other state and local officials by citizens claiming to have been unreasonably deprived of economic rights—licenses, contracts and the like.

[38]365 U.S. 167 (1961).

[39]Ibid., p. 187. Further, the Court states: "Section 1979 [now 1983] should be read against the background of tort liability that makes a man responsible for the natural consequences of his actions.

[40]386 U.S. 547 (1967).

[41]E.g., *Whirl* v. *Kern*, 407 F.2d 781 (5th Cir. 1969); *Hughes* v. *Smith*, 264 F. Supp. 767 (D.N.J. 1967). In *Whirl*, the Court held that subjective good faith could not exculpate a sheriff from § 1983 liability to a person who had been detained improperly in jail for almost nine months because of a failure to process the papers dismissing the indictment against him. The "good faith and probable cause" talisman just doesn't fit in such circumstances. In finding the requisite fault in *Whirl*, the Court simply held that this police omission was unreasonable despite the absence of bad faith.

Moreover, prior to *Pierson*, many courts applied such a standard: "One essential requirement of an action under this section is that the plaintiff show facts which indicate that the defendant, at the time he acted, knew or as a reasonable man should have known that his acts were ones which would deprive the plaintiff of his constitutional rights or might lead to that result." *Bowens* v. *Knazze*, 237 F. Supp. 826 (N.D. Ill. 1965). *See Cohen* v. *Norris*, 300 F. 2d 24 (9th Cir. 1962) (unforeseeability due to defects in a warrant may be a good defense); *Bargainer* v. *Michal*, 233 F. Supp. 270 (N.D. Ohio, 1964) (police must be protected from "honest misunderstandings of statutory authority and mere errors of judgment"); *Beauregard* v. *Winegard*, 363 F. 2d 901 (9th Cir. 1966) (where probable cause for an arrest exists, civil rights are not violated even though innocence may subsequently be established—even actual malice in undertaking an investigation will not permit recovery if that investigation produced probable cause).

[42]*Bargainer* v. *Michal*, 233 F. Supp. 270 (N.D. Ohio 1964), where the court in diction conceded the difficulty of applying § 1983 to an assault by a policeman unaccompanied by an arrest. See also, *Selico* v. *Jackson*, 201 F. Supp. 475, 478 (S.D. Cal. 1962); "[Where] . . . facts are alleged which indicate not only an illegal and unreasonable arrest and an illegal detention, but also an unprovoked physical violence exerted upon the persons of

the plaintiffs. . . . It certainly cannot seriously be urged that defendant acted as a result of error or honest misunderstanding." See *Basista* v. *Weir,* 340 F. 2d 74 (3d Cir. 1965); *Hardwick* v. *Hurley* 289 F. 2d 529 (7th Cir. 1961); *Hughes* v. *Smith,* 264 F. Supp. 767 (D.N.J. 1967); *Dodd* v. *Spokane County,* 393 F. 2d 330 (9th Cir. 1968) (assault by prison official actionable); *Jackson* v. *Martin,* 261 F. Supp. 902 (N.D. Miss. 1966) (allegation provocation shot plaintiff states a good cause of action under § 1983).

[43]*Lankford* v. *Gelston,* 364 F. 2d 197 (4th Cir. 1966). Here where police officers had, on 300 occasions over 19 days, searched third persons' homes, without search warrants and on uninvestigated and anonymous tips, for suspects, the court, in granting petitioners injunctive relief from this practice, said: "There can be little doubt that actions for money damages would not suffice to repair the injury suffered by the victims of police searches. . . . The wrongs inflicted are not readily measurable in terms of dollars and cents. Indeed the Supreme Court itself has already declared that the prospect of pecuniary redress for the harm suffered is 'worthless and futile.' Moreover, the lesson of experience is that the remote possibility of money damages serves as no deterrent to future police invasions." Ibid., p. 202.

[44]*Report of the National Advisory Commission on Civil Disorders* (Washington, D.C.: Government Printing Office, 1968), p. 159. (Hereinafter cited as *Kerner Report.*)

"Harassment" or discourtesy may not be the result of malicious or discriminatory intent of police officers. Many officers simply fail to understand the effects of their actions because of their limited knowledge of the Negro community.

In assessing the impact of police misconduct, we emphasize that the improper acts of relatively few officers may create severe tensions between the department and the entire Negro community.

[45]*See* Shapo, "Constitutional Tort: *Monroe* v. *Pape* and the Frontiers Beyond," *N.W.U.L.* Rev. 60 (1965): 277, 327-29.

[46]A sampling of the cases in which recoveries were made for police violence reveals truly outrageous conduct.

See *McArthur* v. *Pennington,* 253 F. Supp. 420 (E.D. Tenn. 1963) ($5100 total damages proper for wrongful arrest by a city policeman—$1800 out of pocket damage to plaintiff, $1600 lost wages and the rest for humiliation, mental suffering, and injury to reputation); *Brooks* v. *Moss,* 242 F. Supp. 531 (W.D.S.C. 1965) ($3500 actual damages and $500 punitive damages proper where plaintiff received a serious blow to the head and such an attack and the subsequent false criminal prosecution were clearly in violation of his constitutional rights); *Jackson* v. *Duke,* 259 F. 2d 3 (5th Cir. 1958) (award of $5000 to person who was pistol whipped, knocked down and stomped, kicked in the face, throat and stomach, falsely arrested, falsely accused of drunkenness and unlawfully jailed was not excessive).

[47]367 U.S. 643 (1961); See also *Wolf* v. *Colorado,* 338 U.S. 25, 41-44 (1949) (Murphy, J., dissenting).

[48]*Lankford* v. *Gelston,* 202; see *Pierce* v. *Society of Sisters,* 268 U.S. 510, 536 (1925).

[49]E.g., *City of Jacksonville* v. *Wilson,* 157 Fla. 838, 27 So. 2d 108, 112 (1946); *Delaney* v. *Flood,* 183 N.Y. 323, 76 N.E. 209 (1906). *See also,* Annot., 83 A.L.R. 2d 1007, 1016-17 (1962).

[50]No injunction will issue if the plaintiff fails to move that the police acted without reasonable grounds or probable cause. See *Seaboard N.Y. Corp.* v. *Wallander,* 192 Misc. 227, 80 N.Y.S. 2d 715 (Sup. Ct. 1948); *Monfrino* v. *Gutelius,* 66 Ohio App. 293, 33 N.E. 2d 1003 (1939); *Kalwin Business Men's Ass'n.* v. *McLaughlin,* 216 App. Div. 6, 214 N.Y. Supp. 507 (1926); *Joyner* v. *Hammond,* 199 Iowa 919, 200 N.W. 571 (1924). The police will also be enjoined if they acted maliciously or in bad faith. See *Hague* v. *CIO,* 307 U.S. 496 *aff'g with modifications* 191 F. 2d 774 (3d Cir. 1939); Comment, "Federal Injunctive Relief From Illegal Search", 1967 *Wash. U.L.Q.* 104, 109-110.

[51]*See,* e.g., *Upton Enterprises* v. *Strand,* 195 Cal. App. 2d 45, 15 Cal. Rptr. 486 (1961).

[52]Every person who, under color of any statute, ordinance, regulation, custom or usage ... subjects, or causes to be subjected, any citizen of the United States or other person within the jurisdiction thereof to the deprivation of any rights, privileges, or immunities ... shall be liable to the party injured in ... suit in equity, or other proper proceeding for redress. 42 U.S.C. Sec. 1983 (1964).

[53]See Note, "The Federal Injunction as a Remedy for Unconstitutional Police Conduct", *Yale L.J.* 78 (1968): 143, 146.

[54]307 U.S. 496, *Aff'g with modifications* 101 F. 2d 774 (3d Cir. 1939), *aff'g* 25 F. Supp. 127 (D.N.J. 1938).

[55]*Wolin* v. *Port of N.Y. Auth.*, 392 F. 2d 83 (2d Cir. 1968), *cert. denied* 393 U.S. 940 (1968) (enjoining the port authority from interfering with plaintiffs' distribution of antiwar leaflets at bus terminal); *Williams* v. *Wallace,* 240 F. Supp. 100 (M.D. Ala. 1965) (enjoining the governor and other officials of Alabama from interfering with proposed march by Negroes to petition the government for redress of their grievances in being deprived of the right to vote); *Local 309, United Furniture Workers* v. *Gates,* 75 F. Supp. 620 (N.D. Ind. 1948) (enjoining state police from attending union meeting held for purposes of discussion strike then in progress).

[56]*Wheeler* v. *Goodman* 6 Cr.L. 2163 (W.D.N.C. 1969) granting permanent injunction against police harassment of a privately owned hippie haven in Charlotte, North Carolina); *Houser* v. *Hill,* 278 F. Supp. 920 (M.D. Ala. 1968) (granting injunction against police found to have, *inter alia,* interfered with peaceful and lawful assemblies and failed to provide proper police protection against hostile persons intimidating these peaceful assemblies); *Cottonreader* v. *Johnson,* 252 F. Supp. 492 (M.D. Ala. 1966) (granting injunction to secure the safety and security of Negroes demonstrating against the denial of constitutional rights).

[57]74 F. Supp. 336 (N.D. Ga. 1947).

[58]364 F. 2d 197 (4th Cir. 1966).

[59]After the fatal shooting of a police officer, the Baltimore police, searching for the suspects, made over 300 searches of mostly Negro homes without warrants, proceeding on the basis of anonymous phone tips. These searches were conducted very often in an offensive manner, without the owners' consent, and without explanation by the police. The plaintiffs, Negroes, brought an action in the district court seeking a temporary restraining order and a preliminary injunction against the continuation of these tactics. No restraining order was issued, but three days later the police commissioner issued a General Order declaring that an officer must have "probable cause" to believe the suspects were inside before searching a dwelling and the searches without warrants ceased. Thereafter, the district court refused to issue a preliminary injunction because it appeared the relief was unnecessary. The illegal searches had almost completely stopped by the time the General Order was issued, and the district court was of the opinion that such searches would be prevented in the future. The Circuit Court, however, emphasized the atrocity of the police tactics, the invasion of the rights of innocent citizens and the inadequacy of any possible redress at law. They found that the General Order was inadequate as a guarantee against possible recurrences of widespread illegal searches, and therefore ordered the district court to issue the injunction.

[60]*Lankford* v. *Gelston,* pp. 201-02; *Refoule* v. *Ellis,* 74 F. Supp. at 343 (1947).

[61]Ibid.

[62]E.g., *Black People's Unity Movement* v. *Pierce,* Civil No. 848-68 (D.N.J. filed August 23, 1968); *Black Panther Party* v. *Leary,* Civil No 68-3599 (S.D.N.Y. filed September 10, 1968). It would not be surprising if current investigations into alleged police vendettas against the Black Panthers in Chicago and San Francisco culminate in civil suits under § 1983, in addition to possible criminal proceedings against the police.

[63]E.g., *Andich* v. *Daley,* Civil No. 68C. 958 (N.D. Ill., filed May 27, 1968) complaint alleged that Chicago police had in April 1968, deliberately disrupted the demonstration of antiwar protesters, a significant number of whom belonged to the Chicago Peace Council.

[64]Note, p. 147.

[65]A scheme which seems to work for one city of a particular region, size, and political atmosphere may not be appropriate for an entirely different urban climate. Such hypothetically determined judgments are best left to the legislature. Application of a successful internal review mechanism of any given police department to other departments may also be misguided, because the apparent adequacy of its complaint and disciplinary framework may be a product less of ideal procedural formalities than the quality of the people who administer them.

[66]Note, p. 149.

[67]Ibid., p. 150.

[68]Ibid.

[69]As of 1960, less than half of the states had any criminal provisions relating directly to unreasonable searches and seizures. The punitive sanctions of the 23 states attempting to control such invasions of the right of privacy are collected in *Mapp* v. *Ohio,* 367 U.S. 643, 652 note 7 (1960).

[70]*Commonwealth* v. *Cheney,* 141 Mass. 102, 6 N.E. 724 (1886) (if an officer makes an arrest and it turns out that no crime has been committed, his good faith in the performance of his official duty is a defense to a criminal prosecution, although it would not be in a civil action). See also *Commonwealth* v. *Trunk,* 311 Pa. 555, 167 A. 333 (1933); *Henderson* v. *State,* 95 Ga. App. 830, 99 S.E. 2d 270 (1957).

[71]52 *Am. Jur.* Trespass Sec. 84 (1944).

[72]*Brown* v. *Martinez,* 68 N.M. 271, 361 P. 2d 152 (1961); *Owens* v. *Town of Atkins,* 163 Ark. 82, 259 S.W. 396 (1924).

[73]*People* v. *Winig,* 7 Misc. 2d 803, 163 N.Y.S. 2d 995 (1957); *People* v. *Barton,* 18 AD 2d 612, 234 N.Y.S. 2d 263 (1962); *Barber* v. *State,* 199 Ind. 146, 155 N.E. 819 (1927).

[74]*State* v. *Faggart,* 170 N.C. 737, 87 S.E. 31 (1915).

[75]*State* v. *Turner,* 60 Conn. 222, 22 A. 542 (1891). *Whittlesey* v. *U.S.* 221 A. 2d (1966).

[76]Foote, p. 494.

[77]Whoever, under color of any law, statute, ordinance, regulation or custom, willfully subjects any inhabitant of any State, Territory, or District to the deprivation of any rights, privileges, or immunities secured or protected by the Constitution or laws of the United States, or to different punishments, pains, or penalties, on account of such inhabitant being an alien, or by reason of his color, or race, than are prescribed for the punishment of citizens, shall be fined not more than $1,000 or imprisoned not more than one year, or both. June 25, 1948, ch. 645, 62 Stat. 696. 18 U.S.C. § 242 (1964).

[78]325 U.S. 91 (1945).

[79]"But in view of our construction of the word 'willfully,' the jury should have been instructed that it was not sufficient that petitioners had a generally bad purpose. To convict it was necessary for them to find that petitioners had the purpose to deprive the petitioner of a constitutional right" p. 107.
Further: "When they act willfully in the sense in which we use the word, they act in open defiance or unreckless disregard of a constitutional requirement which has been made specific and definite."

[80]*See* Foote; *but see* Caldwell and Brodie, "Enforcement of the Criminal Civil Rights Statute, 18 U.S.C. Section 242. In Prison Brutality Cases," *Geo. L.J.* 52 (1964): 706 which suggests that since the creation of the Civil Rights Division of the Justice Department there has been more action under this statute. The cases he cites have little to do with police conduct outside the prison setting.

[81]In the area of police conduct exclusive of the prison setting there have been only 19 cases since the *Screws* decision of which 13 ended in conviction. *See* especially, *Miller* v. *United States*, 404 F. 2d 611 (5th Cir. 1968) where the court upheld the conviction of two Louisiana police officers for willful brutality and infliction of summary punishment by making their police dog bite the suspect in order to coerce a confession from him.

[82]*Williams* v. *United States*, 341 U.S. 97 (1951) (private detective holding special officers cards of city police brutally beat confessions from suspected lumber yard thieves); *Lynch* v. *United States*, 189 F. 2d 476 (5th Cir.), *cert. den.* 342 U.S. 831 (1950) (officer of laws who, having prisoner in his custody, assaulted and beat him, was found guilty under this section). See also *Apodaca* v. *United States*, 188 F. 2d 932 (10th Cir. 1951); *United States* v. *Jackson*, 235 F. 2d 925 (8th Cir. 1951); *Koehler* v. *United States*, 189 F. 2d 711 (5th Cir. 1951), *cert. den.* 342 U.S. 852, rehearing den., 342 U.S. 889.

[83]See our argument above that any looser standard would gravely and unduly hamper law enforcement efforts.

[84]68 Stat. 803, 18 U.S.C. 2236 (1948) (unlawful search and seizure); 62 Stat. 803, 18 U.S.C. 2236 (1948) (malicious procurement of a warrant); 62 Stat., 803, 18 U.S.C. 2234 (1948) (exceeding authority under a warrant).

[85]The first formulation of this proposal is in 8 Wigmore, *Evidence*, Sec. 2184 (3d ed. 1940):

The natural way to do justice here would be to enforce the healthy principle of the Fourth Amendment directly, i.e., by sending for the high-handed, over-zealous marshal who had searched without a warrant, imposing a 30-day imprisonment for his contempt of the Constitution, and then proceeding to affirm the sentence of the convicted criminal.

For a recent development of this theme, *see* Blumrosen, "Contempt of Court and Unlawful Police Action," *Rutgers L. Rev.* 11 (1957): 526.

[86]8 Wigmore, *Evidence*, Sec. 2184-85 (3d ed. 1940); and ibid., pp. 526-29.

[87]*Bloom* v. *Illinois*, 391 U.S. 194 (1968).

[88]*Field Surveys V, A National Survey of Police and Community Relations.* Prepared by the National Center on Police and Community Relations, Michigan State University, for the President's Commission on Law Enforcement and Administration of Justice, 1967, pp. 193-205.

[89]Crime Commission, *Task Force Report: The Police,* p. 195. Citizen apathy is apt not to tolerate the effort and delays incident to a complicated procedure for filing complaints. *See* Niederhoffer, "Restraint for the Police: A Recurrent Problem," *U. Conn. L. Rev.* 1 (1968): 288-296.

[90]Note, "The Administration of Complaints by Civilians Against the Police," *Harv. L. Rev.* 77 (1964):501-502.

[91]*See* Niederhoffer, "Restraint," p. 296.

[92]In Washington, D.C., in 1962 the Police Department charged 40 percent of all persons who complained of police abuse with filing a false report. By contrast, only 0.003 percent of those who reported other crimes were similarly charged. Michigan State Survey (see note 88), p. 204.

[93]Crime Commission, *Task Force Report: The Police,* p. 195.

[94]*See* J. Lohman and G. Misner, *The Police and the Community: The Dynamics of Their Relationship in a Changing Society,* II, p. 174 (1966). Governor's Select Commission on Civil Disorder, State of New Jersey, *Report for Action* 35 (1968).

[95]Crime Commission, *Task Force Report: The Police,* p. 195.

[96]Ibid.

[97]Michigan State Survey, pp. 201-202. The Harvard Study found fewer than 5 percent of responding departments relied exclusively on a special independent unit to investigate complaints. But some, such as the New York City Department, provided for review of line investigations by a specially assigned supervisor. In Los Angeles, an Internal Affairs Division had the discretion to supplement a local investigation with an independent inquiry of its own. Note, "The Administration of Complaints by Civilians Against the Police," pp. 503-05.

[98]The line investigator, whose views are likely to parallel those of his accused colleague, may not find the alleged violation particularly offensive. J. Lohman & G. Misner, II, p. 203. His disposition to vigorously investigate may also be dampened by the realization that he may be the subject of a similar investigation in the future by the defending officer. Michigan State Survey, p. 219. Finally, a sense of organizational loyalty may persuade a local investigator to whitewash the indiscretions of a compatriot in the interests of preserving the department's reputation. Niederhoffer, "Restraint," p. 296.

[99]Crime Commission, *Task Force Report: The Police,* p. 196.

[100]Note, "The Administration of Complaints by Civilians Against the Police," p. 506.

[101]Ibid., p. 507. About 40 percent of trial boards have no jurisdiction over a complaint while a civil or criminal suit is pending against either the accused officer or the complainant. That a hearing should be barred by a civil action or an unrelated criminal prosecution is inexplicable. Furthermore, 25 percent of the review boards are prohibited from hearing a complaint after a related judicial determination has exonerated the policeman or convicted the complainant. Yet the absence of legal liability seems irrelevant to the need to discipline a miscreant officer. Ibid., p. 506.

[102]Michigan State Survey, p. 223. Even when the hearings are open to the public, the complainant is rarely allowed to examine the investigation report for purposes of rebuttal. Ibid., p. 203. It has been noted that in police hearings the citizen often appears to be the one on trial, as he is barraged with irrelevant and threatening questioning, J. Lohman and G. Misner, II, p. 203.

[103]Michigan State Survey, p. 203. The complainant is typically merely assured that his grievance has been adequately handled, which leaves him feeling ignored as he suspected he would be in the first place. J. Lohman and G. Misner, II, pp. 172, 174.

[104]It would seem that the many covert incidents of internal review hurt the police more than help them. Surely all the safeguards against public exposure must lead many people to think the police's wash is dirtier than it really is.

[105]Michigan State Survey, p. 186. Prior to the establishment of a citizen Police Advisory Board, no Philadelphia officer had even been disciplined on the basis of a citizen complaint of police abuse. Coxe, "The Philadelphia Police Advisory Board," *L. in Trans. Q.* 2 (1965): 179, 185. Of 30 brutality complaints to the Inspection Officer of the Newark Police Department in 1966-67, none resulted in a policeman being charged. New Jersey Report (see note 94), p. 35.

[106]A recent study indicated that in 32 cases of proven brutality in Detroit, the punishment exceeded a written reprimand only twice. *See* Michigan State Survey, p. 186. Much criticism was directed at the leniency of a recent ruling by a police chief that an officer accused of brutality be fined $50 and ordered to attend a human relations course at the police academy. See *Washington Post,* Sept. 19, 1968, at B1, Sept. 23, 1968, at A20.

[107]In Philadelphia, "rude or offensive langage or conduct offensive to the public" invokes the same five-day suspension as "unexcused tardiness." In fact, the entire Disciplinary Code seems geared to punishing conduct the Department finds offensive to its own tastes, rather than those of the public. See J. Lohman and G. Misner, II, p. 204.

[108]For a discussion of the advantages and disadvantages of internal review, *see* Note, "The Administration of Complaints by Civilians Against the Police," p. 516.

[109]In 1966-67, fewer brutality complaints were brought to the Newark police than to other agencies, such as the Neighborhood Legal Services Project. New Jersey Report, p. 36. In addition to the citizen apathy and fear of retaliation mentioned at notes 88 and 91, above, other factors may discourage complaints by minority groups. Some persons evidently are disposed never to trust an agency against which they have a grievance. Kerner Report, p. 310. "If the black community perceives the police force as an enemy of occupation, then they are not going to take the trouble to file their complaints with the enemy." Niederhoffer, "Restraint," p. 295.

[110]"We believe that an internal review board—in which the police department itself receives and acts on complaints—regardless of its efficiency and fairness, can rarely generate the necessary community confidence, or protect the police against unfounded charges." Kerner Report, p. 162.

[111]"Perhaps the single most potent weapon against unlawful police violence is a police commander who will not tolerate it. The converse is also true: where police leaders assume a permissive attitude toward violence by their men, they are often licensing brutality." United States Commission on Civil Rights, 1961, Commission on Civil Rights Report: Justice, V, p. 82.

[112]See Report of the President's Commission on Crime in the District of Columbia (Washington, D.C.: Government Printing Office, 1966), pp. 219-23.

[113]Crime Commission, Task Force Report: The Police, p. 200.

[114]A. Black, The People and the Police 78 (1968). The author, who was Chairman of the New York Civilian Review Board, blamed the referendum results on an extensive publicity campaign against the board speared by the Fraternal Order of the Police and the fact that a "yes" vote at the polls was curiously a vote against the CCRB. Ibid., pp. 208-15.

[115]Ibid., pp. 86-87.

[116]Ibid., pp. 113-15.

[117]Ibid., p. 93.

[118]Ibid., pp. 122-26.

[119]Ibid., p. 130.

[120]Ibid., p. 94.

[121]Ibid., Appendix IV.

[122]Ibid., p. 101.

[123]Ibid., p. 100.

[124]Crime Commission, Task Force Report: The Police, p. 201.

[125]See table in J. Lohman and G. Misner, p. 236.

[126]See table, ibid., p. 245.

[127]Ibid., p. 259.

[128]Coxe, "Philadelphia Police," pp. 183-184.

[129]See table in J. Lohman and G. Misner, pp. 254-255.

[130]Ibid.

[131]Ibid., p. 255.

[132]Coxe, p. 185.

[133]See table in J. Lohman and G. Misner, p. 236.

[134]Coxe, pp. 183-184.

[135]J. Lohman and G. Misner, p. 253.

[136]Note, "The Administration of Complaints by Civilians Against the Police," p. 514.

[137]J. Lohman and G. Misner, p. 239.

[138]*See* ibid., pp. 213-15, 261-65.

[139]Judge Weinrott of the Court of Common Pleas of Philadelphia County last year reaffirmed his March 1967 ruling that since the PAB had functioned as a judicial tribunal and not as an advisory board, it was an illegal extension of the Mayor's powers. *Philadelphia Evening Bulletin,* Nov. 14, 1968, at 9.

[140]See note 114, above.

[141]J. Lohman and G. Misner, p. 262.

[142]This image probably poisoned the other incidents of review board activity as well. Police investigations for the board may have been colored by the temptation to save a fellow officer from persecution at a hearing. Similarly, many a complainant must have decided filing a grievance was not worth incurring the wrath of the police at a formal trial.

[143]*Kerner Report,* p. 162.

[144]Crime Commission, *Challenge of Crime in a Free Society,* p. 103.

[145]*See,* e.g., Walter Gellhorn, *Ombudsman and Others* (Cambridge: Harvard University Press, 1966); Gellhorn, *When Americans Complain: Governmental Grievance Procedures* (Cambridge: Harvard University Press, 1966); Donald C. Rowat, ed., *The Ombudsman, Citizen's Defender* (London: Allen and Unwin, 1965); Stanley V. Anderson, ed., *Ombudsman for American Government?* (Englewood Cliffs, N.J.: Prentice-Hall, 1968).

[146]Rowat, "The Spread of the Ombudsman Idea," in *Ombudsman for American Government?,* ibid., p. 7.

[147]*See* Bexelius, "The Ombudsman for Civil Affairs," in *The Ombudsman, Citizen's Defender,* ed. Rowat, pp. 22, 28.

[148]The following description of the ombudsman's powers is taken from Gwyn, "Transferring the Ombudsman," in *Ombudsman for American Government?,* pp. 27, 38-40.

[149]W. Gellhorn, *When Americans Complain: Governmental Grievance Procedures,* p. 192.

[150]Ibid., p. 191.

[151]Ibid., p. 193.

[152]Ibid., p. 191.

[153]*Kerner Report,* p. 284.

[154]J. Lohman and G. Misner, p. 284.

[155]Rowat; and Gellhorn, see note 145, above.

[156]See also, *Kerner Report,* p. 163.

[157]Both the Michigan State Field Survey, and the President's National Advisory Commission on Civil Disorders, pp. 162-3, made similar recommendations for strengthening police-community relations. Without reviewing in detail their conclusions, we note that our proposal differs in material respects from both.
The Michigan State study proposed an external agency which would entertain appeals from internal review, conducting independent investigations and publicizing its findings of

fact. However, filing complaints in the first instance with the police retains all of the defects of internal review—sluggishness and the appearance of bias; in this regard, by focusing on the efficacy of internal review rather than on the resolution of complaints, the study has merely embellished Gellhorn's ombudsman. Moreover, its proposed agency would not perform the conciliation function which we consider imperative.

The Kerner Commission's proposal cured these defects by empowering its external agency to process all complaints in their inception and to engage in conciliation. However, the Commission, in its sketchy recommendations, appeared to further than necessary to accomplish these goals. In the first place, it suggested the agency be authorized to institute suit in cases of unlawful police conduct. Second, it indicated that fact-finding functions should be performed in an adversary proceeding, in the presence of complainant and his counsel. Both of these suggestions, if enacted, would convey the impression that agency efforts were directed solely against the police. The first would place the ombudsman in the role of advocate rather than arbiter in situations where other means can be utilized to secure judicial relief. The second sacrifices the speed and informality we deem absolutely essential for conciliation.

[158]*Final Report of the National Commission on the Causes and Prevention of Violence* (Washington, D.C.: Government Printing Office, 1969), pp. 147, 148.

PART SIX:

CORRECTING CORRECTIONS

As the "myth of treatment" has been co-opted by correctional officials, it has ceased to grip anybody. Those closest to the offender—the correctional officers—tend to view it as a form of "brainwashing." It could be argued (and was) that if treatment didn't rehabilitate, at least it kept the lid on. And it did keep the lid on for almost two decades. Attica is a warning that it no longer can do so.[1]

Although "corrections" is the part of the criminal justice system that the public sees least of and knows least about, it is a vital facet of the whole system. The recognition that correctional institutions as constituted in the United States have been largely a colossal failure is the first step in bringing about reform; events such as Soledad, The Tombs, and Attica have further alerted our society to the need for penal reform. Such reform must be based upon knowledge of both the historical antecedents to contemporary correctional philosophies and practices and sound empirical knowledge of the social reality of institutional life. If habilitation[2] is to be the principal guiding philosophy of correctional institutions, then they should be structured to facilitate this process. As the President's Commission on Law Enforcement and the Administration of Justice recognized, pervasive changes are needed to realize the aims of habilitation in correctional institutions.[3]

Traditional correctional policies and practices have been based upon a "medical model" of deviancy, subscribing to an erroneous analogy to the physician's practice. Therefore, like a disease, an individual was to be diagnosed, prognosed, prescribed, treated, and cured of his "illness." Unfortunately, the medical model has produced a plethora of nebulous labels—psychopathic, paranoid schizophrenic—with no real measurable effect upon changing an individual's behavior. The major problem with this model has been its dependence upon the sick-well dichotomy focusing upon the individual as both cause and effect of his illness (criminality). The basic legal concept of *mens rea* is predicated on individual responsibility for one's actions, and this concept of legal culpability has been transferred to treatment models in corrections. Therefore,

357

like the leper, insane, and other "sick" people, the criminal must be isolated and treated for his illness.[4]

Contemporary criminological thought is based upon a different conception of causality and culpability. Although the individual is legally culpable for his actions, it is acknowledged that many societal factors—economic, family, peer group pressure, racism—impinge upon and effect everyone's behavior, including those who commit criminal acts and are officially labeled criminal. The circle of causality and thus treatment has broadened from the individual to the family, peer group, and community. Therefore, community-based corrections, with work-study release, furloughs, and halfway houses, have become the basis of "new" techniques of habilitation. This approach acknowledges the obvious fact that the offender, like the nonoffender, is largely a product of his family, community, and society, and that the offender will have to re-enter the community.

Community-based corrections is the trend in penology, but institutions apparently will remain in the near future and will have to "deal with" the residents. Since approximately 95 percent of those sent to correctional institutions will someday return to society, the important question is *how* will they return? Will treatment and habilitation be the paramount orientation of the institution, or will custody and oppression prevail? As citizens, we have a right to demand accountability of our institutions.[5] For our individual and collective security we should demand that our correctional system *correct.*[6] Some possible indicators would be recidivism rates, job placement rates for releasees, relationship between educational programs and market needs, and postprison inmate satisfaction.

Studies of institutional organizational structure point out the positive benefits of allowing all segments of the population, including residents, meaningful participation in institutional decision making.[7] The authoritative President's Commission on Law Enforcement and Administration of Justice[8] cites this need in order to combat feelings of alienation based on powerlessness. An important aspect of reducing mass treatment and depersonalization involves comparatively simple revisions of rules and procedures. Custody regulations should be critically assessed as to their function and effect upon the institutional atmosphere. Shared decision making could be effected through institutional councils representing all segments of the institution, namely, residents in custody, administrators, counselors, and instructors to provide direction and policy suggestions. This approach has been effectively used in Scandinavian correctional facilities.[9]

The articles in this section provide extensive elaboration upon both the state of corrections within our society and policy alternatives. In the first article, major problems are examined and some possible options are presented by the President's Commission on Violence. The priorities in corrections are sadly evident in the disproportionate amount of funding going to custody rather than treatment. Possible areas to investigate might be the monitoring of funds in local institutions to really determine priorities, for regardless of rhetorical platitudes, the distribution of funds usually speaks loudest.

Jails, an often overlooked aspect of corrections, are examined and generally indicted for their abhorrent state. An important insight into the basic nature of correctional institutions is noted in that "inherent in most prisons is an environment in which vicious and brutal degradation of inmates regularly takes place." This suggests that prisons by their very nature are inhuman and degrading, and that the dual goals of punishment and habilitation will inevitably conflict within such facilities. In fact, new beautiful facades for inmates appear to contain many of the traditional defects related to penal structures.

The title of a CBS report—"Caged Men"—aptly characterizes the conditions of prisons and jails. Likened to the ghetto, the prison is an oppressive, demeaning, dehumanizing environment which generally creates more problems than it resolves. A major problem in correcting corrections is the apathy of the public. Analogous to the "good" German in Nazi Germany, citizens are content to know that "they" (convicts) are being taken care of by the proper authorities.[10] Therefore, although the commission points out the positive benefits of jail reform, more use of probation and parole, and the betterment of habilitative services within institutions, in the end it is the public who will reap the consequences (negative or positive) of correctional policy and practices.

Professor Fox, noted penologist, provides a more recent interpretation of reform or rebellion in prisons in the second article. If our prisons are the standard for judging our civilization, we are not that removed from the "barbarism" of the past. The effects of structure and staff-inmate differences are discussed. In discussing the Soledad, San Quentin, and Attica revolts, two important facts are revealed—the significance of race and the politicization of prisoners. The history of racism in the criminal justice system has been well documented,[11] and its manifestation in corrections has been more recently revealed.[12] Whereas over one-third of those incarcerated nationally are members of racial minorities, only approximately 8 percent of correctional staff are minority members.[13] The disproportionate numbers of Chicanos, blacks, and Native Americans in correctional institutions reflects differentials in learning processes, opportunity structures, and ultimately power. This last realization has brought about increasing politicization of inmates.

Criminologists have long indicted the environment, differential opportunity structures, discrimination, unemployment, and poverty as basic causes of crime. In fact, Edwin Schur's *Our Criminal Society* eloquently argues that the "real crimes" in our society are poverty, racism, and war. It is not too difficult to see how such causal analysis has been taken as fact by inmates. This is not to suggest that criminologists are to blame for such interpretations, for they hardly are responsible for such criminogenic conditions. However, it seems to be a logical extension of a "kind of environment" assessment of cause to a political and power perspective. If the way to correct environments and conditions conducive to crime is through political change, then politicization of prisoners makes sense. In fact, this may be an important habilitative aim of community programs.[14] Such a phenomenon is not difficult to understand in the recent changes of consciousness evident among the new generation.[15]

Of particular concern to penologists is how to deal with the political criminal and the politicizing of criminals. Although our legal system does not officially recognize political crimes or criminals, they have been differentially treated in the correctional setting. There is apparently a great fear of the political criminal infecting the "common" criminal.[16] In fact, the politicization of prisoners has been increasing rapidly. The dissent and rebellion at San Quentin, The Tombs, Folsom, Soledad, and Attica has given notice to the public and correctional officials that prisoners are organizing for their collective goals.[17]

Bettina Aptheker has delineated a typology of four groupings of prisoners based upon their political views and activities or special victimization on the basis of class, racial, or national oppression.[18] She first points out that one group of prisoners is those who became effective political leaders and therefore were victims of politically inspired frame-ups. The proportion of prisoners under this category is undoubtedly small, but such cases do exist. A second group is those who have committed various acts of civil disobedience or resisted the draft; violations that were clearly political acts. These also include acts of resistance or self-defense both within and outside prisons which violate the law. Given the Civil Rights Movement, draft resistance, antiwar protests, student activism, and other militant protest in the 1960s and 1970s, this category has greatly increased. Thirdly, there are those who, because of lack of legal knowledge and political power, have been arrested and convicted of crimes that they did not commit.[19] Finally, there are the large bulk of prisoners who committed a variety of offenses who have begun to develop a political consciousness while incarcerated, such as the Soledad Brothers and Ruchell Magee, etc. How has this occurred? According to Davis (1972), the fact that there has been an increasing influx of political criminals in prisons who have organized their activities around the problems of the institution. The political receptivity of prisoners—especially black and brown—has been increased because of the heightened aggressiveness of black, Chicano, and other powerless communities, until "ordinary" criminals have been transformed into political militants. In assessing the causes of politicization she notes the changing conceptions of the causes of criminal behavior.

Prisoners—especially black, Chicanos, and Puerto Ricans—are increasingly advancing the proposition that they are political prisoners. They contend that they are political prisoners in the sense that they are largely victims of an oppressive politicoeconomic order, swiftly becoming conscious of the causes underlying their victimization.[20]

The politicization can only be understood within the context of the attempts at democratization of major social institutions. Traditionally characterized as apolitical, the university became the brunt of a rapid politicizing and conflict during the 1960s. The Civil Rights Movement, antiwar movement, poor people movement, welfare rights movement, among others, characterized the attack upon legitimacy of power distribution in our society. The law and legal institutions increasingly came under fire as they were exposed as being highly political. Attempts to democratize politics, education, and the family have spread to all social institutions. Youth, nonwhites, the poor, and other previously powerless groups are increasingly politically sensitized and since they are the prime "recruits" for correctional institutions, it will undoubtedly have ramifications for the prisons.

Therefore, as Atkins and Glick note:

One way to understand the development of political protest in prisons is to view protest activity as a political resource that is used by disadvantaged groups to gain political power and influence when more traditional sorts of political activity are unavailable or unsuccessful.[21]

The nature of prison disturbances has gone through a great deal of change during the last two decades. From the traditional prison riots demanding better living conditions to the organizing of black prisoners by the Nation of Islam has emerged the more recent revolutionary upheavals reflecting the politicization of prisoners.[22] Such disturbances may signal the end to the "myth of treatment" and to the use of prisons for solving the crime problem.[23] The emergence of "community-based corrections" as a viable alternative to the penal institution portends the demise of the penitentiary in American life. What will replace the "Walls"?

Lloyd Allen Weeks presents a prototype for community-based corrections in the final article. It is unique in many ways. First, the author is an inmate of Washington State Penitentiary and this work was the collaborative effort of many inmates. This paper was presented at a unique gathering entitled: "Institute I: A Search for the Prison of Tomorrow"[24] which took place on January 10, 1972, at the state penitentiary. Criminologists, reporters, concerned citizens, and representatives of the prison (resident, custody, administration, treatment) met to share ideas on prison reform in light of recent events—such as Attica. The introduction notes the changing character of prison populations:

> Compounding the morass of penal problems is the little known fact, at least to the taxpaying public, that approximately 700,000 of the 1.3 million incarcerated offenders consist of a revolutionary new breed of prisoners; blacks, Mexican-Americans, Indians, and an ever-present number of socially disadvantaged whites under 30 years old, who come out of subcultures which spawned this decade's protestors, radicals, and liberation movements. This articulate new breed of prisoner is politically motivated and is demanding social and humane reform at every level.[25]

This kind of exchange speaks well of the collaborative approach to correctional management and the importance of inmate impetus. The paper represents an acknowledgement of the current reform movement and is a positive statement of alternatives to traditional facilities. It is particularly of interest, since it is being proposed for repeaters and the "hard core" offenders, rather than novices.

More specificity needs to be evident in certain areas, such as criteria for selection, but this document presents a challenge to correctional leaders, public officials, criminological researchers, concerned citizens, and others. As the author notes, this is "the first 12-inch step on the journey of a thousand miles in the quest for the prison of tomorrow." However, one should not be led to believe that such "institutions" are the panacea to the problems of corrections. As Martinson acutely observed:

> The long history of prison reform is over. On the whole the prisons have played out their alloted role. They cannot be reformed and must be gradually torn down. But let us give up the comforting myth that the remaining facilities (and they will be prisons) can be changed into hospitals. Prisons will be small and humane; anything less is treason to the human spirit.[26]

It is generally recognized that the concept of community-based corrections is desirable on both treatment and financial bases. The President's Commission on Law Enforcement and Administration of Justice, and his Commission on Violence point out the valuable aspects of community involvement in habilitation; it costs approximately ten times as much to incarcerate an individual as to put him on probation or parole. Most criminologists agree that a majority of those presently incarcerated could be dealt with in the community without excessive risk.[27] The need for flexible alternatives in corrections is increasingly recognized among students and practitioners of criminology[28]—such programs as work-training release, furloughs, probation subsidy, and community-based facilities attempt to provide alternatives to better meet the realities of a truly habilitative emphasis.

One effort in the attempt to reduce the deleterious effects of correctional institutions has been to increase the number of convicted offenders placed on probation. California conducted a study in 1964 which eventuated in a probation subsidy program.[29] A major public relations program brought cooperation from various interest groups, including judges, probation staff, legislative bodies, county boards of supervision, peace officers, and civic organizations. By this conscious, planned campaign of "informing" the public, potential controversy and conflict was minimized. The major selling points were the financial savings, the inadequate nature of current probation supervision, and the need for developing experimental programs that could ultimately be funded from state dollars.

Using the principles of contingency management,[30] counties are reimbursed in proportion to the number of cases they keep in the community and out of a state institution. A minimum cost rate of any new admission was found to be $4,000; therefore, if a county reduced its rate by 10 people, it saved the state $40,000 and could receive up to this amount in state financing. Thus, the principles of behavior modification are used to influence judge's actions in order to change the flow of offenders from prisons to the community. The major effects cited by Smith have included a drop in convicted superior court defendants sent to state prison from 23.3 percent in 1965 to 9.8 percent in 1969. California Youth Authority institutions are slowly being closed, and two new institutions have remained unopened. Commitment rates from 1965-66 to 1970-71 dropped 41 percent to the California Youth Authority and 20 percent to the Department of Corrections, with an overall decrease of 31 percent. Violation rates of probationers have declined during this period. Monetarily, California has saved $185,978,820 between 1966 and 1972 through cancelled construction, closed institutions, and new institutions constructed but not opened. According to a more popular account,[31] the prison population was reduced 8 percent and recidivism has decreased from about 50 to 32 percent through this and other habilitative reforms.

Notwithstanding the positive effects of probation subsidy, some problems have been evidenced. Of particular importance is the lack of development of halfway houses for community treatment. This is a most controversial topic, for although many laud the goals of community-based corrections, when it gets down to where in the community they should be, traditional fears and stereotypes are invoked. The establishment of community-based corrections is largely dependent upon a careful, interest-specific public relations program to allay the fears and trepidations of those affected. This includes furlough,[32] work-training release, and other "innovations." Finally, the move toward community-based corrections is not based upon sound empirical studies and it will not necessarily work. As Morris and Hawkins note, penal reform is based principally upon a humanitarian ideology.

Decency, empathy, the ability to feel at least to a degree the lash on another's back, the removal occasionally of our customary blinkers to human suffering, a respect for each individual springing from religious or humanitarian beliefs—these have been the motive forces of penal reform, not any validated knowledge concerning the better prevention of crime or recidivism.[33]

Whereas this author is personally and professionally supportive of the "tear down the walls" movement, such support is based principally upon the negative aspects of these total institutions rather than the positive nature of the alternatives.[34] The "solution" to the crime problem transcends tinkering with the caboose of the criminal justice system, or with only one facet of the system. The problem is essentially a sociopolitical one, and until the great inequities of wealth, power, and privilege in our society are remedied, there will only be the appearance, rather than the substance, of substantive change.

NOTES

[1] Robert Martinson, "The Meaning of Attica," *The New Republic* (April 15, 1972):17-19.

[2] Habilitation seems more appropriate than rehabilitation in light of basic criminological research findings. Habilitation means essentially to "make suitable" or clothe, equip, or outfit—which is essentially resocialization in terms of prison inmates. Rehabilitation is to "restore a dependent, defective, or criminal to a state of physical, mental, and moral health through treatment and training." (See *Webster's New World Dictionary of the American Language*, College Edition, pp. 649, 1225. New York: The World Publishing Company, 1964.) Its moral basis is the religious concept of "falling out of grace" which fails to recognize the social and cultural plurality of our society. More specifically, the idea of restoration to a former state of well-being may be largely inappropriate for those who have evidenced a life history of differential opportunity structures and learning processes. To paraphrase a convict: "Ain't no way I want to return to a former state of my life." Furthermore, the concept of rehabilitation is too tied to religious meaning and the "medical model" of deviance to be of relevance today.

[3] President's Commission on Law Enforcement and the Administration of Justice, *The Challenge of Crime in a Free Society* (Washington, D.C.: U.S. Government Printing Office, 1967).

[4] For a discussion of the problems of this model and the interests which maintain it, *see* Charles W. Thomas, "The Correctional Institution As An Enemy of Corrections," *Federal Probation* 37 (March 1973):8-13. *See also*, Elmer H. Johnson, "A Basic Error: Dealing with Inmates as though They Were Abnormal," *Federal Probation* 35 (March 1971):39-44, and John Irwin, *The Felon* (Englewood Cliffs: Prentice-Hall, 1970), pp. 36-60.

[5] Marvin E. Wolfgang, "Making the Criminal Justice System Accountable," *Crime and Delinquency* 18 (January 1972):15-22.

[6] James A. Snowden, "A Statutory Right to Treatment for Prisoners: Society's Right of Self-Defense," *Nebraska Law Review* 50 (1971):543-566.

[7] For example, see Mayer N. Zald, "Organizational Control Structures in Five Correctional Institutions," *American Journal of Sociology* 681 (November 1962):335-345.

[8] President's Commission on Law Enforcement and Administration of Justice, *Task Force Report: Corrections* (Washington, D.C.: U.S. Government Printing Office, 1967).

[9] See Richard D. Knudten, *Crime in a Complex Society: An Introduction to Criminology* (Homewood, Illinois: The Dorsey Press, 1970); F. Lowell Bixby, "Penology in Sweden and Denmark," *American Journal of Correction* 24 (May-June 1962):18-25; Peter E. Burke, "Prison Reform in Sweden," *American Journal of Correction* 30 (May-June 1968):18-19.

[10] See Everett Hughes, "Good People and Dirty Work," *Social Problems* 10 (Summer 1964):3-11.

[11] See Charles E. Reasons and Jack L. Kuykendall, *Race, Crime and Justice* (Pacific Palisades: Goodyear Publishing, 1972); Min Sun Yee, "Death On The Yard: The Untold Killings at Soledad and San Quentin," *Ramparts* 11 (April 1973):35-40ff.

[12] George Jackson, *Soledad Brothers* (New York: Coward-McCann, 1970), and idem, *Blood In My Eye* (New York: Bantam Books, 1972).

[13] Final Report of the Joint Commission on Correctional Manpower and Training, *A Time to Act* (October 1969). The report also notes that only about 12 percent of correctional personnel are women with most of these involved in probation and parole, not institutional work.

[14] Richard Quinney, *The Social Reality of Crime* (Boston: Little, Brown, 1970).

[15] Charles Reich, *The Greening of America* (New York: Bantam Books, 1970).

[16] "There is often separation of conventional and political prisoners within the prison; if the vagueness of the law that defines political action as criminal were extended, perhaps it is feasible to define criminal behavior as political. If political behavior is criminal, as the law says, then it could be expected that old criminals may infect each other with a politics of common interest: they are all losers of society, the outsiders. If conventional and political criminals represent lawyer groups, their union could foreshadow a dangerous class struggle. All commonly punished crimes would suddenly have political implications and only the white-collar crimes, those seldom punished now, would remain as true crime." Quoted from H. Contine and D. Rainer, eds., *Prison Etiquette*, 1950, p. 51—both "convicted" pacifists during World War II. See also Virginia Engquist and Francis Coles, "Political Criminals In America: O'Hare (1923); Contine and Rainer (1950)," *Issues in Criminology* (Summer 1970):209-220. For a personal account of this, see Howard Levy and David Miller, *The Political Prisoners* (New York: The Grove Press, 1971), and Huey Newton, "My Days in Solitary," *Ramparts* (May 1973):30-34ff.

[17] For other discussions of these revolts, see Angela Y. Davis, *If They Come In the Morning* (New York: The New American Library, 1971); Herman Bodillo and Milton Haynes, *A Bill of No Rights: American Prison System* (New York: Outerbridge and Lozand, 1972); Vernon Fox, "Why Prisoners Riot," *Federal Probation* 35 (March 1971):9-14; Robert Martinson, "Collective Behavior at Attica," *Federal Probation* 36 (September 1972):3-7; *Attica: The Official Report of the New York State Special Commission on Attica* (New York: Bantam

Books, 1972); Burton M. Atkins and Henry R. Glick, *Prisons, Protest, and Politics* (Englewood Cliffs: Prentice-Hall, 1972).

[18] Bettina Aptheker, "The Social Functions of the Prisons In the United States," in *If They Come In The Morning*, ed. Angela Davis (New York: The New American Library, 1971), pp. 51-59.

[19] Criminological literature is replete with data regarding differentials in the administration of justice based upon these factors. *See*, for example, Charles E. Reasons and Jack L. Kuykendall, *Race, Crime, and Justice* (Pacific Palisades: Goodyear Publishing, 1972), and Jacobus Tenbroek, *The Law of the Poor* (San Francisco: Chandler Publishing, 1966).

[20] Angela Y. Davis, "Political Prisoners, Prisons and Black Liberation," in *If They Come*, Davis, p. 37.

[21] Atkins and Glick, *Prisons, Protest*, p. 3.

[22] For an elaborate discussion of these changes, *see* John Pallas and Bob Barber, "From Riot to Revolution," *Issues in Criminology* 7 (Fall 1972):1-19.

[23] For an excellent discussion of the rise of the penitentiary, *see* David J. Rothman, *The Discovery of the Asylum* (Boston: Little, Brown, 1971).

[24] Resident Government Council, *Institute I: A Search for the Prison of Tomorrow* (Walla Walla: Washington State Penitentiary, 1972).

[25] Washington State Penitentiary's Resident Government Council *Institute I: A Search for the Prison of Tomorrow* (Walla Walla, Washington)1972, 2.

[26] Robert Martinson, "Planning For Public Safety," *The New Republic* (April 29, 1972):21-23.

[27] *See* President's Commission on Law Enforcement and Administration of Justice, *Task Force Report: Corrections* (Washington, D.C.: U.S. Government Printing Office, 1967).

[28] "Turn 'em Loose toward a Flexible Corrections System," *Southern California Law Review* 42 (1969):682-700.

[29] Robert L. Smith, *A Quiet Revolution: Probation Subsidy* (Washington, D.C.: Department of Health, Education and Welfare, 1971). Unless otherwise cited, the following discussion of probation subsidy is based upon this work.

[30] John M. McKee, "Contingency Management in a Correctional Institution," *Educational Technology* 11 (April 1971):51-54.

[31] "How a Revolutionary Plan for Prison is Working," *U.S. News and World Report*, August 24, 1970.

[32] For a comprehensive assessment of furlough programs, *see* Robert R. Smith and Michael A. Milan, *A Survey of the Home Furlough Policies of American Correctional Agencies* (Elmore, Alabama: Rehabilitation Research Foundations, 1972).

[33] Norval Morris and Gordon Hawkins, *The Honest Politician's Guide to Crime Control* (Chicago: University of Chicago Press, 1970), p. 246.

[34] The negative functions of the prison are often cited and generally agreed upon, but there has been little discussion and attention given to the positive functions of such institutions, notwithstanding the studies of deterrence. It seems out of vogue to suggest that these places do serve "positive" functions.

PROBLEMS OF THE CORRECTIONS SYSTEM

DAVID P. STANG

They's a guy in McAlester—lifer. He studies all the time. He's secretary of the warden—writes the warden's letters and stuff like that. Well, he's one hell of a bright guy an' reads law an' stuff like that. Well, I talked to him one time about her, 'cause he reads so much stuff. An' he says it don't do no good to read books. Says he's read ever' thing about prisons, now, an' in the old times. An' he says she makes less sence to him now that she did before he starts readin. He says its a thing that started way to hell an' gone back, an' nobody seems to be able to stop her, an' nobody got sence enough to change her. He says for God's sake don't read about her because he says for one thing you'll jus' get messed up worse, an' for another you won't have no respect for the guys that work the gover'ments.[1]

The problem of acquiring an effective system of corrections is a critical part of any program to improve our institutions of criminal law enforcement. The police can and must be improved to prevent crime and apprehend a larger percentage of offenders. The courts can and must be improved to handle the criminal charges arising from a larger number of arrests and to develop a more reasoned approach to sentencing. But unless the corrections systems are also changed, the whole process may only turn out to be self-defeating.

The criminal law process is preoccupied with stopping crime and catching and convicting—as opposed to rehabilitating—criminals. Once a criminal is caught and tried and incarcerated, public interest tends to wane despite the fact that the convicted criminal is likely eventually to be released to commit further crimes. As Chief Justice Warren E. Burger recently noted, "There must be some way to make our correctional system better than the revolving door process . . . of crime, prison, and more crime."[2]

This chapter will sketch the inadequacies of our nation's prisons and jails and the sometimes shocking conditions which exist in many of them. It will also discuss some of the remedial measures which might be adopted to remove degrading conditions and to improve our prisons and jails so that they can begin to realize their stated goal of rehabilitating offenders.

Most of what we have to say is not new, the problem of corrections including sociological and treatment aspects having been presented in comprehensive detail by the Corrections Task Force of the President's Commission on

David P. Stang, "Problems of the Corrections System," *Law and Order Reconsidered,* pp. 622-651. Report of the Task Force on Law and Law Enforcement to the National Commission on the Causes and Prevention of Violence (New York: Bantam) 1970.

Law Enforcement and Administration of Justice as well as treated extensively in the report of the Violence Commission's Task Force on Individual Acts of Violence. Perhaps, however, there is also value in a briefer treatment that emphasizes, as this chapter does, our failure even to achieve minimum levels of humane treatment in some of our prisons and jails.

THE INABILITY OF CORRECTIONS TO CORRECT

We begin by noting what few persons would dispute: that because of shortages of trained personnel and suitable facilities, prisons in this country have never adequately performed their correctional function. A look back at the old times in comparison with the new times reveals that prisons are substantially unchanged insofar as they still serve as little more than cages with time locks on their doors. Before the eighteenth century, prisons were used not to punish but to detain the accused until the debtor paid his debt, the rapist was castrated, the thief's hands were cut off, or the perjurer's tongue was torn out. In 1786, the Quakers in Pennsylvania instituted incarceration as a humane alternative to hanging and torture. In an effort to have prisoners do penitence for their sins, the Quakers locked convicts in solitary cells until they died or were released. So many died or went insane that in 1825 New York's Auburn Prison introduced the practice of hard labor performed in silence. Until quite recently, American prisons relied almost entirely on the Auburn system of shaved heads, lockstep marching, and degrading toil, and locked prisoners in huge isolated pens that soothed the public's fears of escapes.[3]

In essence, prisons historically were intentionally horrible places where prisoners received their "just due." As Richard McGee so persuasively phrased it:

> The idea of retributive punishment is deeply rooted in the minds and emotions of mortal man. This attitude, and this simple atavistic impulse to punish and overpunish offenders, remains the central trunk of the administration of criminal justice throughout the world.[4]

The old stone walls have refused to crumble. Prison buildings were built most sturdily, and it has been difficult to secure their replacement. Today there are 25 prisons in the United States over 100 years old. These institutions perpetuate the old theories around which they were constructed. As an example, the Bureau of Prisons operates a federal prison in Sandstone, Minnesota, in a virtual wilderness between Minneapolis and Duluth. The institution was authorized in 1933, when northern Minnesota was a center for the activities of bootleggers. Sanford Bates, who was at that time the director of the Bureau of Prisons, decided to "put one up there where they are coming from." But by the time the prison had been built, prohibition had been repealed, and, according to the present director, "there we had an institution 16 miles from anywhere, where it gets pretty cold in the winter."[5]

No less appalling than the physical structure and condition of our nation's prisons is the number and caliber of employees on their staffs, and worse yet is the unbalanced allocation of staff personnel to offenders. Approximately 1.3 million people are under correctional authority in the United

States. Of these, only one-third are in institutions; the other two-thirds are su-
pervised in the community on probation or parole. But the ratios of staff and
costs are inverse to these proportions: only one-fifth of the money and one-
seventh of the staff are engaged with the two-thirds of the offenders who are
in the community.[6]

Of the more than 121,000 people employed in corrections in 1965, only
24,000, or 20 percent of the staff, had any connection with rehabilitation.[7]
The other 80 percent merely guarded the 426,000 incarcerated offenders. A
glance at the ratios of the 20 percent of the staff—supposedly charged with
the objective of rehabilitation—to offenders is suggestive of the reason for
their difficulties. The following statistics were compiled as a result of a special
study conducted by the Joint Commission on Correctional Manpower and
Training.[8]

Table 1.

Position	Number of inmates per staff person
Classification worker	365
Counselor	758
Psychiatrist	1,140
Psychologist	803
Physician, surgeon	986
Social worker	295
Teacher:	
Academic	104
Vocational	181
Vocational rehabilitation counselor	2,172

Clearly these figures reveal the almost impossible task facing rehabilitative personnel: their caseload is simply overwhelming.

The lopsided allocation of funds budgeted to correctional institutions
also reveals our outdated approach to the handling of prisoners. In 1965,
$435 million was expended for the operation of institutions for adult of-
fenders. According to the President's Crime Commission, "The bulk of this
. . . was spent to feed, clothe, and guard prisoners."[9] Of every dollar, 95¢ is
for custody, 5¢ is for rehabilitation.

The Corrections Task Force of the President's Crime Commission in
1967 tabulated the numbers of persons actually employed by correctional
authorities in various job categories and estimated how many additional such
personnel would be required if improvement in our nation's prisons was to
become a reality. The Corrections Task Force reported that 63,184 custodial
personnel and group supervisors were employed, but that 89,600 were needed;
2,685 caseworkers in prisons were employed, but that 10,200 were needed;
14,731 caseworkers in community-based corrections were employed, but that
44,800 were needed; 6,657 specialists such as vocational and academic
teachers, psychologists, and psychiatrists were employed, but that 20,400 were
needed. The Corrections Task Force then projected manpower requirements
for 1975 which amounted to a total of 304,000 correctional personnel, an increase of 172,837 when compared to the 121,163 actually employed in

1965.[10] These jobs presently are not being filled to within even a fraction of requirements.

These prison statistics, depressing as they are, are nowhere near so deplorable as those associated with our nation's jails, local workhouses and other facilities for detaining accused persons before and during trial and for short misdemeanor sentences. As one Crime Commission consultant put it:

> Most counties and cities persist in operating their own jails, nearly all of which are nothing more than steel cages in which people stay for periods of time up to a year. Most of the jails are custody-oriented and supervised by ill-trained, underpaid personnel. In some cases, the institution is not manned except when a police officer on duty can look in once during his eight hour shift.[11]

It is rare to find any rehabilitative program being conducted by our jails. In fact, less than 3 percent of the total staff of our nation's 3,500 jails have any rehabilitative responsibilities. Those few persons who are engaged in such programs are preposterously overloaded with case assignments. A Crime Commission study revealed these ratios between rehabilitative staff and inmates in jails and other local misdemeanant institutions:[12]

Table 2.

Position	Number	Ratio of staff to inmates
Social workers	167	1:846
Psychologists	33	1:4,282
Psychiatrists	58	1:2,436
Academic teachers	106	1:1,333
Vocational teachers	137	1:1,031
Custodial officers	14,993	1:9

Not only are our nation's prisons and jails understaffed, but the existing staffs are undertrained both before acceptance for employment and after reporting for work. With respect to custodial workers alone, the Corrections Task Force of the President's Crime Commission found that they are—

> undereducated, untrained and unversed in the goals of corrections. Unless salaries are raised, substantial improvements cannot be expected in the kind of people who can be recruited.[13]

The average prison guard is paid only between $3000-$4000 a year. Parole and probation officers, on the average, are paid as little as $5000-$6000 a year. With respect to management and other rehabilitation specialists, the Corrections Task Force asserted, their "salaries fail to attract and retain enough capable personnel and act as a ceiling on the salaries of all subordinates."[14]

One might think that intensive inservice training programs would be in existence to attempt to bridge the gap between educational requirements and actual educational attainment of correctional personnel. Surveys, however, have shown that this is not the case. The following data reflect that less than half of our correctional systems have any inservice training programs at all.[15]

Table 3.

Type of system	Systems reporting programs		Systems reporting no programs	
	Number	Percent	Number	Percent
Probation and parole systems . .	359	44	448	56
Correctional institutions	197	59	137	41
Total.	556	. . .	585	. . .

The favorite scorecard which critics use to demonstrate the results of the manifold inadequacies of the corrections system is the recidivism rate. There are no completely reliable statistics on the extent of recidivism, but it has been estimated that about 30 to 80 percent of the offenders released from correctional institutions are reimprisoned within five years, often for crimes more serious than those for which they were incarcerated originally. As the Crime Commission concluded:

For a great many offenders . . . corrections does not correct. Indeed experts are increasingly coming to feel that the conditions under which many offenders are handled, particularly in institutions, are often a positive detriment to rehabilitation.[16]

That something else may be wrong with prisons, however, other than their failure effectively to prevent recidivism, is too often overlooked by all concerned. Almost the entire emphasis of correctional critics today in on the inadequacy of the resources committed to prison systems insofar as they relate to rehabilitation: the prison buildings are not suited for rehabilitation, the staffs are not large enough nor well enough trained to accomplish rehabilitation, the allocation of funds expended by correctional institutions is not designed primarily to achieve the objective of rehabilitation. All this is true, of course—but there is another point as well. *Inherent in most prisons is an environment in which vicious and brutal degradation of inmates regularly takes place.* The existence of this environment, in and of itself, deters the realization of treatment objectives. First, the degradation of prisoners prevents the possibility of their rehabilitation, even in the rare situations where the necessary rehabilitative resources are available. Second, in situations where rehabilitative resources are unavailable, degradation tends only to further dehabilitate.

Knocking down a man is no way to build him up. And kicking a man when he is already down can never build him up. That prisons knock men down, and then often kick them besides, is amply demonstrated by the following tales of horror.

THE HORROR OF CORRECTIONS

The judges and the district attorney in Philadelphia recently showed the courage to order an investigation of the incidence of sexual assaults in local correctional institutions. The investigators from the district attorney's office and the police department concluded that sexual assaults are endemic in the Philadelphia prison system. The report estimated that during the 26-month period under investigation there were approximately 2,000 sexual assaults, involving approximately 1,500 individual victims and 3,500 individual aggressors in Philadelphia prisons. The investigators found that virtually every slightly built young man committed to jail by the courts—many of them merely to await trial—is sexually approached within hours of his admission to prison. Many young men are overwhelmed and repeatedly "raped" by gangs of inmate aggressors.[17]

One inmate described an attack as follows:

> I was laying on my bed when seven or eight inmates came to my bed, pulled the blanket off me, put it on the floor and told me to pull my pants down and lay face down on the blanket. I said, "No" and was punched in the face by one of the inmates. The inmate that punched me stated if I did not get on the floor the other inmates would gang up on me.
>
> I got on the floor and my pants and shorts were pulled off. Two inmates spread and held my legs apart while two more inmates held my hands in front of me. While I was being buggered from behind another inmate would make me suck his penis. This continued until all the inmates had attacked me and I heard one of them say it was 1:30 A.M. so let's go to bed. They put me on the bed, covered me with the blanket and one of them patted me on the behind saying good boy we will see you again tomorrow night.
>
> While I was being molested I was held by the neck and head and threatened with bodily harm if I yelled or screamed. They stated that they would beat my head on the floor if I made any outcry.[18]

This event was by no means a unique episode in the Philadelphia investigation. The district attorney of that city in testimony before the Senate Subcommittee to Investigate Juvenile Delinquency read this statement of a seventeen-year-old youth who at the time of his victimization had been charged but not tried or convicted of the offense of being a runaway:

> I was in the cell at 1801 Vine when four Negro boys started bothering me for not having underwear on. Then when we got on the Sheriff's van and started moving they told everyone that I didn't have on underwear as the van was moving they started getting close to me. One of them touched me and I told them to please stop. All of a sudden a coat was thrown over my face and when I tried to pull it off I was viciously punched in the face for around ten minutes. I fell to the floor and they kicked me all over my body including my head, and my privates. They ripped my pants from me while five or six of them held me down and took turns fucking me. My insides feel sore and my body hurts, my head hurts, and I feel sick in the stomach. Each time they stopped I tried to call for help but they put their hands over my mouth so I couldn't make a sound. While they held me, they burned my leg with a cigarette. When the van stopped at the prison, they wiped the blood from me with my shirt. They threatened my life and said they would get me in D1 if I told what happened. They said if they didn't get me in D1 they'd get me in the van again. When the door opened they pushed me to the back so they could get out first. At first, I told the guard I tripped and fell but thought I better tell the truth. I pointed out those who beat me up so bad the doctor looked at me and said I'd have to go to the hospital. They took pictures of my bruises on my body and I can just about breathe because my nose and jaw seem to be broken in many different places. I was asked by the lieutenant to write what happened and this is exactly what happened.

The Philadelphia report, shocking to anyone unfamiliar with the conditions in American prisons, is no news to professionals in the field who realize that an honest report on the county jails in numerous other parts of the country would reveal the same thing.[19]

Even before a grand jury was summoned to investigate the scandalous conditions in Chicago's Cook County Jail[20] the jail superintendent conceded publicly that deviate sex practices, the beating of inmates by other inmates, smuggling of contraband, and other vicious practices were routine in the jail. And a large portion of the men and women, boys and girls who were crowded into this institution had not yet even been convicted.[21] Interviews with 36 ex-inmates of the Cook County Jail revealed the following facts:

Eight of the 36 ex-inmates were victims of beatings, some badly, with concussion, fractures, etc.

About 75 beatings were reportedly seen by inmates.

Some inmates said that there was about one beating each day.

Four of 36 ex-inmates admitted that they were victims of sexual attacks.

About 75 sexual attacks were seen or heard.

About a dozen guards were reported as being involved in trafficking of drugs.

Reported generally: "You can get all of the 'pot' (marihuana) wanted if you have the money."

Eight incidents of burning were reported as being seen or involved in by inmates interviewed, and

Four inmates were reportedly set on fire.

Former staff and inmates reported homosexuals were shaved by staff and inmates. The use of iodine to paint heads of such inmates reportedly has been discontinued. One youth was dry shaved by two inmates reportedly, leaving many cuts on his head.[22]

One lawyer who has conducted extensive investigations of prison conditions wrote to this Commission: "The commonest denominator in all prisons is to take the dignity of the prisoner away, creating in him an abhorrence of rules of ordered society, of law enforcement, of every basic tenet of a civilized society."[23]

Not all such practices involve physical brutality among inmates. A more subtle form can be seen in the results of unnecessary solitary confinement. Dane White, aged 13, an Indian boy of Browns Valley, Minnesota, in a state of depression resulting from 41 days of isolation, hanged himself on November 17, 1968, with his belt in a county jail. A report conducted by the attorney general of Minnesota indicated that Dane White had expressed an intention to hang himself. The jail officials, however, were not sufficiently attentive to their duties to have perceived such a possibility.

Almost as depressing as solitary confinement is the opposite extreme of overcrowding. A prisoner's hostility often cannot be contained when he is thrust in a cell with so many other people that he must fight for space on the floor to sleep, let alone be accorded the simple comfort of a bed.

A recent report on the adult detention facilities in San Francisco revealed that the maximum capacity of the City Prison is 437 plus 50 females. At times during 1968 the population in that institution exceeded 600, rising once to over 900 last December. At that time only 200 mattresses were on hand, and 200-300 inmates were forced to sleep on steel springs or on the concrete floor. The recommendations of that report with respect to the City Prison suggest what life at that institution must be like:

That towels be provided to inmates who wish to shower or wash daily. At present, inmates are permitted to shower weekly. Men wishing to wash in the interim are forced to use paper towels.

That inmates be deloused and showered if they are detained in excess of 48 hours.

That inmates be provided jail clothing when detained in excess of 48 hours. This law is currently ignored.

That new inmates be given clean blankets, and that the laundering of these blankets be increased from every three months to monthly. Complaints have been received that due to the high population of City Prison, blankets are often transmitted from inmate to inmate without the benefit of fumigation or laundering.

That an adequate number of benches and tables be provided for the "dayroom" holding cell of the Women's Unit.[24]

Despite overcrowding in the San Francisco prison, authorities still feel compelled to maintain certain cells for solitary confinement, which are referred to by inmates as "the hole." On August 30, 1968, staff members of the San Francisco Committee observed inmates Richard Haudel and Clark Dunning in Isolation Cell 4, County Jail 1:

Inmate Dunning, obviously mentally ill, had been placed in this cell for "singing too loudly." Inmate Haudel was semiconscious on the floor bleeding from what appeared to be a split lip. He was incoherent, barely able to stand, and seemed to be under the influence of drugs. He had been placed in the cell following booking earlier that day and had not been seen by a physician. Inmate Dunning had been in the cell for three days and had not seen a doctor in that time. However, a previous medical report bore the evaluation "psycho."[25]

Asserting that they were not merely bleeding hearts, the Committee members cautioned that—

We do not feel that jails should be "hotels" or that prisoners should be "coddled," but we feel that punishment alone has not provided a satisfactory result. To be effective, control must be accompanied by treatment and rehabilitation so that when a prisoner is released, he is less apt to commit another crime than when he went into custody. Those of us on this Committee who have heard groans, smelled the odors, seen the hate and despair, know that this is not the case in San Francisco.[26]

City and county jails by no means have a monopoly on degradation and violent animality. The following passage, written for this Commission by a volunteer worker who for several years has seen firsthand the conditions which exist inside a youth reformatory, illustrates this failure as exhibited in one institution:

Inmates live in cell-blocks. These are relatively clean, well lighted, and reasonably well ventilated. Yet they deny the inmate the smallest degree of privacy. The net impression is that of caged people in a human zoo—including the smells of the zoo, in spite of the ventilation.

Within the formal social structure there is an extensive and powerful informal social structure created by the inmates. The staff is careful to see that members of city gangs are split up in cell-block and work assignments. Cliques are built, then, within the natural boundaries of cell-block and work assignments, and are indigenous to the prison (and, in many cases self-perpetuating; the clique will outlast the clique-members who created it). Prison cliques, like city gangs, center around natural leaders. Power struggles within and between cliques sometimes erupt in physical beatings. Much more often, however, they take the form of sexual exploitation. Homosexual relationships are very common, but they have much less to do with sexual gratification than with informal status. Homosexual rape is the ultimate prison humiliation for the victim and the ultimate achievement for the aggressor.

Aside from clique structure and interclique rivalries, the most important component of the informal social structure is race. Racial tensions are so very high that only the constantly present threat of custodial retaliation prevents the institution from being engaged in a continual race riot. The Black slogan is, of course, "Black Power." One hears it; sees it cut into school desks; finds it scrawled in library books. The Whites have no slogan, but they do have a symbol—the swastika—and since there are virtually no Jews in the institution, the hatred it stands for is directed exclusively at Negroes. White inmates have it tattooed on their bodies, carve it into desk tops, scrawl it in their books—accompanied by such epithets as "Nigger-ass bastards." Race hatreds occasionally find outlets in beatings, but again it is sexual exploitation that is the most common form of aggression.

The prison staff does what it can to contain racial aggression, but their own preconceptions are painfully obvious. They will explain that they separate the smaller inmates from the physically mature to prevent the small white boys from becoming sexual bait for the full-grown Negroes, but it does not occur to them that small Blacks may need protection from the bully whites.

Joseph R. Rowan, Executive Director of the John Howard Association of Illinois, was referring to youth reformatories when he said in testimony on March 6, 1969, before the Senate Subcommittee to Investigate Juvenile Delinquency:

If someone suggested that we treat delinquents like animals, a lot of people would raise their eyebrows. . . . In many places throughout the country they have done a better job in meeting standards for the care and treatment of animals in zoos than we have for the care of [delinquent] children.

Seldom does one hear of a zoo keeper torturing one of his animals to death. But such things have happened, and still are happening, in our nation's prisons and youth reformatories. Not long ago such an incident took place in a Louisiana state industrial school where officials beat one juvenile to death with leather straps.[27]

In a recent report on the Mississippi Delta region correctional institutions, these were the words used to describe some of the activities of the prison guards:

Archaic and brutal instruments for the maintenance of discipline and the meeting of work quotas, flogging, isolation, and a variety of "unofficial" techniques [beating with chains, blackjacks, belts, electrical tortures] were employed to an extent and for reasons which would have given pause to the least sensitive of the old plantation overseers.[28]

In the Angola Prison in Louisiana there were floggings and lengthy confinement to underground dungeons, complete absence of any rehabilitation program; unspeakable living conditions—filthy barracks, spoiled food . . . long hours of backbreaking labor in the cornfields and on the levees; armed convict guards who were rewarded for shooting "escapees"; political corruption; and an uncontrolled amount of perversion which kept men awake nights to protect themselves against sexual assault.[29]

The Tucker Farm is an Arkansas prison. A report concerning this institution was made public by Governor Winthrop Rockefeller in January 1967. A section of that report described a method of torture known to the inmates as the "Tucker telephone," consisting of:

An electric generator taken from a ring-type telephone placed in a sequence with two drywell batteries, and attached to an undressed inmate strapped to the treatment table at Tucker Hospital, by means of one electrode to a big toe and the second electrode to the penis, at which time a crank was turned sending an electric charge into the body of the inmate.

During the investigation which culminated in the above quoted report, an instrument of this description was found in a linen closet in the superintendent's home.[30]

The report also gave the following account of an incident of brutality involving an Arkansas prison superintendent and his inmate cohorts:

LL-33 stated that he and three other prisoners were planning to escape because of the treatment and not enough food. He stated they were all "slapped" around by three inmate yardmen, because they would not give them money. He stated that a line rider found out about the escape and brought them to the superintendent who whipped them with the "hide" on the buttocks with their pants down, and on the back and head. He further hit them with his fists and kicked them. The superintendent then left the building and told the riders to work them over real good. One rider got four others to help him beat them up. He stated that they came into the building with "blackjacks," wire pliers, nut crackers, and knives. He stated that they stripped all the clothes off of LL-33 and the rider stuck needles under his fingernails and toenails. They pulled his penis and testicles with wire pliers and kicked him in the groin. Two riders ground out cigarettes on his stomach and legs. One rider squeezed his knuckles with a pair of nut crackers. He stated that they worked on him all afternoon, and the next day, he was put in the field and made to go to work. He stated he was unable to work, and they put him in the hospital and would not let anyone see him until he healed up.

Such forms of prison discipline are not confined to southern prisons. In the words of an eyewitness:

One Midwestern prison I visited had concrete blocks in a dungeon to which troublesome inmates were chained naked; the dungeon was next to the prison generators and hummed and vibrated intermittently, a total body massage equivalent of the Chinese water torture. Several inmates told me that those not made docile by the chains in the dungeon were subsequently given multiple

electroshock therapy "treatments" on the upper floor of the infirmary building.[31]

In the California penal system, one prisoner

showed that during his 11-day confinement in a 6′ by 8′4″ "strip cell,"
he was not adequately protected from the wet weather; he was deprived of all
items by which he might maintain bodily cleanliness; he was forced to eat the
meager prison fare in the stench and filth caused by his own vomit and body
wastes; he could wash his hands only once every five days, and he was required
to sleep naked on a stiff canvas mat placed directly on the cold concrete floor.[32]

Recent investigations of the Dodd Committee revealed that in the state
penitentiary at Columbus, Ohio, prisoners who "talk" when ordered not to are
put naked into unlighted, solitary "strip-cells" which contain no sanitary facilities. According to the Committee staff, prisoners there are served rations only
once a day. When they need to have bowel movements, they are told to defecate
on a piece of paper then slide it under the slit near the bottom of the cell door.
The prisoners in the strip cells are issued only one single sheet of toilet tissue a
day. Prisoners can urinate only on the floor of their cell. The Dodd Committee
staff also states that no detailed records are kept at the Columbus prison which
explain the cause of death of prisoners who die while incarcerated.

The Dodd Committee staff investigations of the state penitentiary at
Richmond, Virginia, have revealed the existence of conditions similar to those
at Columbus. Prison officials at the Richmond prison told the committee staff
that the reason that one inmate remained in an unheated solitary cell for 85
days was that "he liked it there and did not want to leave."

That such uncivilized treatment of prisoners in penal institutions is not
wholly confined to state and local facilities is borne out by the following report:

Authorities at Lewisburg federal penitentiary are using the threat of homosexual rape to intimidate young Selective Service violators who protest against
what they consider oppressive prison regulations.

The prison authorities flatly deny any such policy.

But at least four draft resisters, all in their early 20s, have been threatened
since the first of the year with assignment to "the jungle"—two of the penitentiary's dormitories where known homosexual attackers are quartered.

Three of these COs were actually assigned to "the jungle"; one was sexually assaulted by at least three different inmates March 19 and had to be taken to
the Lewisburg prison hospital.

The situation has become so serious that the prison's psychiatrist, Dr.
Wolfram Reiger, and its chief psychologist, Dr. Karl Elnig, indicated at a recent
staff meeting that they would bring the matter to the attention of higher authorities in Washington if this policy is not abandoned.[33]

Other documented acts of official mistreatment of prisoners by correctional personnel have included the forcing of prisoners to lie naked on concrete
cell block floors at temperatures of 40°;[34] necessitating prolonged exposure of
prisoners to primitive plumbing encrusted with filth;[35] the arbitrary withholding
of food, indiscriminate clubbings by guards, and repeated use of tear gas.[36]

The experience of offenders while they are in prison is obviously important and often decisive to their future conduct after they are released. Instead of

reducing the incidence of violence in American society, however, our prisons often actually contribute to it. They can sometimes amount, as has been said, to "vocational training in hate, violence, selfishness, abnormal sex relations, and criminal techniques."[37] The administrator of a state correctional system has likened the prison to the ghetto as a crime-generating environment:

It is my feeling that correctional institutions generally have contributed to violence in exactly the same way that ghettos have made their contribution; through all of the demeaning characteristics of the ghetto or the institution. The correctional institution takes people who particularly need a sense of self-pride, self-respect, and self-dignity; and instead of providing opportunity for growth of these personal characteristics it regiments, represses, and demeans the individual in countless ways.[38]

CRUEL PUNISHMENT AND THE FAILURE OF THE COURTS

Before we can begin to talk meaningfully about "rehabilitation," we must be sure that psychological counseling and recreation programs represent something more than a half-hour breather from subjection to an overwhelming atmosphere of degradation and dehumanization. Even if one does not agree that a substantially greater share of public moneys should be spent on prison rehabilitation programs, still one cannot argue that conditions of the kind that we have discussed in the previous section should not be swiftly and vigorously eliminated. Yet they persist today, and they persist in the face of these plain, clear words of the Eighth Amendment to our Constitution:

Excessive bail shall not be required, nor excessive fines imposed, *nor cruel and unusual punishments inflicted.*

The Eighth Amendment has been interpreted by the Supreme Court to mean "that punishments of torture . . . and all others in the same line of unnecessary cruelty, are forbidden."[39] The basic principle underlying that Amendment is, in the words of Chief Justice Warren, "nothing less than the dignity of man."[40] It is designed, he further commented, as a "basic prohibition against inhuman treatment."[41] One legal scholar, interpreting the Chief Justice's remarks in the Trop case, stated the principle in these terms:

Even the most loathsome criminal, justly convicted of a heinous offense by due process of law, has a moral claim upon the society which has condemned him: his humanity must be respected even while he is being punished. The State must not deny what is undeniable: that this man, though condemned, is still inalienably a man. To fail to treat him as a human being is to commit a new crime and to cause the shadow of guilt to fall on those who punish as well as on him who is punished.[42]

Our courts have from time to time *stated* the principle of humane prison treatment—but they have not, by and large, effectively *applied* it.

Due process, it would seem, is another right that prisoners are entitled to enjoy. During the past two decades the U.S. Supreme Court, by virtue of the due process clause, has championed the rights of hundreds of thousands of persons, many of whom, ironically, are now in prison. The Court has vigorously applied the fundamental fairness concept of the due process clause to preconviction procedures.

Through the due process clause, the privilege against self-incrimination, protection against illegal search and seizure, the right to a speedy trial, the right to compulsory process, the right of confrontation and cross-examination . . . right to counsel, and the right to a jury trial, all have been made applicable to the states.[43]

It is unfortunate that the Supreme Court, after having leaned over backwards to ensure due process to so many hundreds of thousands of criminal defendants, seems like most everyone else to have failed at "thinking about what comes next." Perhaps, however, the Court may yet intervene in the interest of correctional reform by means of the due process clause. Mr. Justice Douglas once commented that "due process, to use the vernacular, is the wild card that can be put to such use as the judges choose."[44] One leading legal scholar in the field of correctional law recently noted, perhaps prophetically:

Thus far, the judges have not often played their wild card in encounters with the correctional process. These encounters are increasing, and with the "wild card" available, it is important that the courts understand what values are sought to be protected by due process norms, to estimate if current procedures achieve these values, and, if not, how best to correct and remodel them.[45]

Judge Sobeloff, U.S. Court of Appeals of the Fourth Circuit, in an opinion[46] condemning the laxity of Virginia prison officials in granting wholesale discretion to untrained lower-rank personnel in the administration of disciplinary cell blocks, observed that the courts are not called upon and have no desire to lay down detailed codes for the conduct of penal institutions. But he stressed that courts have the duty to act when men are unlawfully exposed to the capricious imposition of added punishments.

Surely the courts also had no desire to formulate codes of conduct for the police and prosecutors. But they have been vigorously doing so with their Fourth, Fifth, and Sixth Amendment decisions for the past 20 years, much to the chagrin of some police and some prosecutors. The time is long overdue for a parallel development in the area of corrections, where a virtually uncontrolled discretion continues to exist, and there are signs that this development has begun.

Parents of an incarcerated youth who was beaten to death by prison personnel were awarded damages by a Louisiana court.[47] The Supreme Court has construed the Federal Tort Claims Act to be applicable to federal prisoners, and a number of such suits have been successfully brought by prisoners with awards ranging from $750 to $110,000.[48] The Civil Rights Act has been used by state prisoners with increasing results. Mandamus, injunctive relief, declaratory judgments, and even contempt for violation of the order of the court "to keep and hold safely" the prisoner are tools increasingly available to lawyers to use in solving old but yet uncorrected problems. In such developments as these, some commentators see, at last, the "demise of judicial abstention" in the prison field.[49]

Fred Cohen has summarized the challenge to the courts in these words:

The basic hurdle is the concept of a prisoner as a nonperson and the jailer as an absolute monarch. The legal strategy to surmount this hurdle is to adopt rules and procedures that permit manageable diversity, thereby maximizing the prisoner's freedom, dignity, and responsibility. More particularly, the law must respond to the substantive and procedural claims that prisoners may have, as a consequence of their conviction and confinement, claims relating to the maintenance of contact with institutions and individuals in the open community and claims relating to conditions with the institutions.[50]

This challenge must be met by the law—by the courts and by the bar—if our prisons are to stop being, as they too often now are, training camps for every kind of human viciousness.

ALTERNATIVES TO INCARCERATION

If our correctional facilities routinely fail to correct the inmate and sometimes actually degrade him, then it is obviously wise policy to avoid incarcerating offenders to the extent that the safety of society permits. There are several stages in the criminal justice system of which alternatives to incarceration present themselves.

Prevention of needless incarceration of arrestees is the goal of two projects sponsored by the Vera Institute of Justice. The Manhattan Summons Project since mid-1967 has been in effect in every police precinct in New York City. The purpose of the project is to avoid, when possible, incarceration following the arrest of suspects prior to trial. The operation of the summons procedure is relatively simple. After arrival at the stationhouse the arrestee is informed of the opportunity of being interviewed to determine if issuance of a summons may be substituted for the arrest process. If the defendant consents, he is interviewed by the arresting officer to ascertain his roots in the community. Various criteria are used to determine the adequacy of the defendant's roots. Upon verification of these roots, the defendant is issued a summons and released.

During the first year of citywide operation of this project, 21,426 defendants potentially eligible for a summons were brought before desk officers. Of these, 14,232, or approximately 66 percent, were issued summons. The remainder of cases which were not summonsed were divided between the 2,367 defendants who failed to qualify and the 4,827 who refused to be interviewed. As of June 30, 1968, of those persons required to appear in court for arraignment, only 638 failed to appear. This represents a "jump" rate of only 4.5 percent.

The second Vera program is the Manhattan Court Employment Project, which has been funded by the U.S. Department of Labor. Its purpose is to screen, counsel, and place in jobs or job training defendants from the Manhattan Criminal Courts. The underlying assumption of this project is that a person with a job that he likes, which offers him some future advancement, is less likely to risk his economic state in the community through criminal activity than one who is not so employed.

At the time of arrest, a person is in need of and usually receptive to many kinds of help. He may require temporary welfare assistance, medical attention, counseling for himself and his family, vocational advisory service, skill training, remedial education—and a job. All these needs can be met by one or more public and private agencies currently operating in New York and most other cities. Rather than duplicate any existing services, the Project marshalls the diverse services required by a participant, making them readily available and assisting him to get the maximum benefit from them.

By early April 1969, the Manhattan Court Employment Project had been in operation 14 months, with a total of 594 participants up to that date. The project works with defendants for an average of 4½ months each and has recommended dismissal of charges for 36 percent, with almost all recommendations being accepted by the court. Both the court and the district attorney have shown increasing confidence in the project, as made clear by their willingness to allow defendants charged with more serious crimes to participate. In its early months, the project took only defendants charged with misdemeanors and few with more than minimal prior records, whereas 40 of the 100 most recently accepted participants were felons, and an equal number had prior criminal records.

Another opportunity to avoid incarceration arises at the sentencing stage in the criminal justice process, when the judge (or other sentencing authority) decides whether to imprison the convicted offender or to place him on probation. A number of difficulties are associated with this decision. First is the judge's need for a good presentence investigation on the offender. But the National Survey of Corrections showed in 1965 that presentence investigations were available only in approximately 61 percent of the cases of juveniles who were placed on probation or sent to juvenile institutions; among adult felony offenders the proportion was 66 percent; while for misdemeanants sentenced to jails or placed on probation, presentence investigations were available in less than 20 percent of the cases. Moreover, the investigations which are made often do not contain adequate information. In too many cases, judges are asked to make the critical decisions between prison or probation blindfolded.

Furthermore, the effective use of probation for supervising offenders in the community instead of incarcerating them is severely limited by lack of facilities. Only 31 states have probation services for juveniles available in every county. In one state, only two counties have juvenile probation services. A child placed on probation in the other counties is assumed to be adjusting satisfactorily until he is brought back to court on a new charge. Probation services for misdemeanants also are rare. Consequently, those offenders who are most likely to benefit from supervision in the community frequently must be sent to institutions (or allowed to remain in the community with no supervision).

Even where probation services are available, intensive treatment of offenders in the community requires a high ratio of staff to offenders (although not so high as the ratio required in institutions). However, the Crime Commission found that the present caseloads of probation officers prevent them from performing their functions effectively. Instead of the current 14,700 probation and parole officers employed in the country, 44,800 are needed if screening services are to be provided and if caseloads are to be reduced to an average of 35 per officer.[51]

Experiments have shown that with improvements in personnel probation can be used successfully for far more offenders than currently are sentenced to community supervision. In Saginaw County, Michigan, a demonstration project increased the number and qualifications of members of the probation staff. At the same time, the court began to use probation much more liberally. The result of the experiment was that the rate of violations of the conditions of probation was reduced by almost one-half.[52] In California, a Community Treatment Project established by the Youth Authority has been experimenting with intensive treatment in the community for youths sentenced by the courts to institutions. The success rate of project participants has been significantly higher than that of their counterparts sent to institutions.[53]

Even with greatly increased ratios of staff to offenders, community treatment is much less expensive than incarceration. In 1965, it cost an average of $3,600 a year to keep a youth in a training school. It cost less than one-tenth of that amount to keep him on probation. Even allowing for the substantial improvements required to make community programs more effective, they are less costly than incarceration. Thus, in an effort to reduce the costs of supporting inmates in state prisons, the California Legislature authorized the payment of subsidies to the counties for each offender placed on probation instead of being sent to a state institution. Between July 1966, when the Probation Subsidy Program went into effect, and July 1968, the state saved approximately $10.5 million in the first 2 years of the program's operation.[54]

Finally, parole represents another alternative to incarceration—in this case, an alternative to *further* incarceration. But again we are confronted with the inadequacies of personnel and facilities. For example, the Crime Commission's Report encouraged the establishment of residential community centers to which offenders could be referred after their release from correctional institutions, the purpose of such centers being to enable residents to adjust gradually to their families, their jobs, and their responsibilities as citizens. Nonetheless, the number of people actually served by such centers is *de minimis*. In New York City, for example, 40 people are housed in a Federal Community Treatment Center, and 16 others are at a local youth center. Aside from some narcotics centers, there are no other halfway house facilities in the city. Yet facilities of this kind and new approaches to supervision seem mandatory if parole is to work. Simply adding parole officers will not improve parole services. Some of the most disappointing experiments in this regard were carried out in California several years ago.[55] Caseloads were cut substantially but research indicated that little change in parole revocation rates resulted. Having more time to do the same thing does not result in improvement.

Quite different results occurred in another experiment which tailored the treatment program to the individual offenders. Youths were then assigned to caseloads in which a parole officer was responsible for no more than 10 to 12 offenders.[56] After 5 years of study, it was found that those treated in differential treatment caseloads of small size had a revocation rate of 28 percent. A comparable randomly assigned group who went through a standard institutional program followed by supervision in the community in conventional undifferentiated caseloads had a revocation rate of 52 percent.

An important part of this program, besides the employment of a classification system and small caseloads, was the use of a program center which served as a recreational and counseling facility and sometimes as a place for short-termed detention for some offenders in danger of serious violations of their parole. The use of centers of this kind, in which offenders generally live at home while receiving treatment during the day, has been shown to have considerable promise in several studies.[57] Their chief program component has been group counseling of a highly confronting nature. Used in conjunction with a well-designed parole program, these alternatives to incarceration seem to be appropriate vehicles for the treatment of many violence-prone offenders because of their accessibility to the community under controlled conditions.

In considering parole, it is worth bearing in mind that the alternative of continued incarceration usually means eventual release with no supervision of any kind. Statistics from the Federal Bureau of Prisons indicate that about 35 percent of the persons released from prison annually are released with no supervision at all. Among misdemeanants over 92 percent of all inmates released from jails are simply turned loose at the expiration of their sentence with no assistance or control in the community.[58] Data are not available on the kinds of offenders released by parole rather than by outright discharge. Most correctional administrators contend, however, that those offenders who are most likely to fail have a lower probability of being paroled and thus are most likely to be released with no supervision at all.

REHABILITATION PROGRAMS IN INSTITUTIONS

If adequate funds were to be made available to the corrections systems, it would become possible to implement the many current recommendations for programs designed to rehabilitate incarcerated offenders. Public safety will always demand the isolation of substantial numbers of violent offenders, and there is no reason other than lack of national will why rehabilitation and incarceration must continue to be two mutually exclusive goals. Without in any way attempting to treat the question of rehabilitation in detail, I do wish to point out a few examples of the kinds of programs that the corrections system could have if the nation wanted it that way.

Educational and vocational training for prisoners was one of the areas of corrections examined by the Crime Commission, and it is an area that is usually considered important in connection with the rehabilitation of the antisocial violent offender who is identified with a delinquent subculture. The Crime Commission had the following recommendations:

> Correctional institutions should upgrade educational and vocational training programs, extending them to all inmates who can profit from them. They should experiment with special techniques such as programed instruction.
>
> States should, with federal support, establish immediate programs to recruit and train academic and vocational instructors to work in correctional institutions.
>
> States should work together and with the federal government to institute modern correctional industries programs aimed at rehabilitation of offenders through instilling good work habits and methods. State and federal laws restricting the sale of prison-made products should be modified or repealed.[59]

Under an adequate vocational training program for our correctional institutions, the offender would be permitted a reasonable degree of freedom to demonstrate his abilities and choose the vocational area in which he is most interested. A uniform job placement test would also be administered to all offenders concerning whom vocational training is judged to be one important mode of individualized treatment. Once interest and ability are ascertained, the offender ideally would be transferred to an institution specializing in the teaching of that particular skill. The training process would make every effort to stimulate real working conditions, including the payment of reasonable wages. Of course, out of these wages, the inmate should be required to pay for room and board in the institution and whatever other services or products he feels a need for, including medical and psychiatric treatment.

Major state and federal prisons would coordinate their vocational training efforts so that each institution specialized in teaching one specific skill. For the small number of institutions which presently teach a skill for which there exists an economic demand, the costs of maintaining modern equipment usually preclude effective training in other vocational skills. Thus, even if an offender is assigned to an institution where a useful and challenging vocation is effectively being taught, he currently must learn that skill whether or not he has interest and ability to do so.

A National Prisoner Savings and Loan Association would be chartered and a compulsory inmate savings program would be instituted in which at least a proportion of all earnings would be set aside to help meet postrelease expenses.[60]

As a logical extension of the coordinated vocational traning program, there is no reason why the specialized skills being taught at several of the institutions could not be academic ones. A specified number of major institutions could develop educational centers for the teaching of grade school, high school, and college level subjects. To be effective, such academic training programs would (1) carefully select only those who can benefit more from concentrated academic, as opposed to vocational, education (although learning in one area is not necessarily incompatible with learning in the other); and (2) require each selected participant to study over a period of minimum duration which has as its goal the attainment of a specified academic objective (e.g., a grade school or high school equivalent education, the equivalent of one year in junior college, etc.).

The vocational-educational system would offer some imaginative new programs of the kind that are currently being experimented with. One such program is that of Harold Cohen and his associates who in 1965 initiated a pilot program of "educational therapy" at the National Training School for Boys.[61] The program is built on the theory of reinforcement and consists essentially of providing a facilitative environment and rewards meaningful to the inmate for learning tasks beginning at his level of capability. Conditions existing in the economic reality of society, including associated rewards and frustrations, were incorporated in the prison setting.

In practice, the program provides boys in the training schools with an opportunity to acquire points—each point being worth one cent—by completing programed lessons in academic subjects, presented by teaching machines, and by passing examinations on these materials. The money thus acquired may be used to buy meals more desirable than standard institutional fare, recreational privileges and opportunities, soda, snacks, cigarettes, and other things of value. Peer reinforcement is encouraged and achieved by bringing an exceptional performance to the attention of other inmates; achievement is also visible to fellow inmates in the "standard of living" that an inmate is able to afford by virtue of points he has earned.

Conventional classroom procedures are absent since classroom experiences have been unrewarding for most of the inmates—approximately 90 percent of whom were school dropouts before being committed to the training school. Each student proceeds at his own pace, but the motivation generated by the prospect of an immediate and valued payoff keeps the pace typically rapid. An inmate reports to the teacher only after he has mastered a lesson; hence, he can be reinforced not only in points but also in social response. Cohen comments:

> We might state then, using emotional terms, that he gains a sense of pride and dignity both with his own performance which came about out of being correct (above 90 percent level of performance), and being able to show this success to another human being. Correctness starts to pay off in points, new skills, and successful relationships with people. . . . When a student moves further into the curriculum, we replace the machine with the human being as the main giver of reinforcement. This schedule of a direct human relationship between the student and the teacher is brought about not by a prescribed one-half hour meeting set in advance—but by a program need, sequenced and placed by the student's own learning behavior.[62]

The total program is thus geared to demonstrating that the investment of effort in learning pays off in ways that can be immediately and directly appreciated. The basic concept of the program is thus not punitive—although an inmate may be "deprived" relative to other inmates if he makes no effort—and it is not the approach of casework—although an inmate may "buy" various services, including counseling, if he has acquired sufficient resources through his own efforts to do so and if that is the way he chooses to spend his points. The foundation of the program is thus the substitution of a meaningful reward system for the conventional reward system that has failed to reach these youths or to which they have failed to respond.

This program has not been in operation long enough to have yet generated data on the postrelease performance of the boys who have participated. The effects on inmates in the institution are, however, definitely encouraging. Academic achievement among youths commonly regarded as impossible or difficult to teach has been markedly improved. Furthermore, students have made progress in "social and attitudinal behaviors" as well as academically.

> These newly acquired educational skills act as a program which reinstates in the young deviant the promise that he can be "normal." "Normal" in this case means that he can be successful in an area where he formerly was unsuccessful and, furthermore, that this success will provide him with the ticket to reenter the mainstream of the American adolescent world—the public school system and the choice of opportunities follow.[63]

CONCLUSION

The President's Crime Commission concluded its treatment of corrections by observing that "the ineffectiveness of the present system is not really a subject of controversy." The report of the Violence Commission's Task Force on Individual Acts of Violence also bears this out, as do the many excellent reports published by the Joint Commission on Correctional Manpower and Training. The existence of inhumane conditions in many of our prisons and jails is perhaps more controversial, but to the extent that such conditions exist, the need for national action is even clearer. Men of goodwill may dispute the amount and kinds of investments which we should be making in the rehabilitation of offenders, but none can defend our failure to respect the Eighth Amendment's prohibition of cruel punishment of offenders.

In testimony before this Commission, Myrl E. Alexander, Director of the Federal Bureau of Prisons, urged that we underscore the need for implementation of the Crime Commission's recommendations for improving the correctional system. He referred to the Crime Commission's call to the federal government to assume a far larger share of the responsibility for providing the impetus and direction to needed changes, and he estimated we could profitably quintuple within 5 years the $1 billion now being spent on corrections at the federal, state, county, and municipal levels. In the jails, workhouses, penitentiaries, and reformatories of this country we receive, control, and release an estimated 3 million persons annually: our national investment is woefully inadequate to the task of protecting society against further crimes by these offenders.

NOTES

[1] John Steinbeck, *Grapes of Wrath.*

[2] Speech before the American Bar Association's Annual Convention in Dallas, Texas, Aug. 11, 1969.

[3] *See* President's Commission on Law Enforcement and Administration of Justice (hereinafter cited as the Crime Commission), *The Challenge of Crime in a Free Society* (Washington, D.C.: Government Printing Office, 1967), p. 162; Richard A. McGee, "What's Past is Prologue," *Annals* 381:1.

[4] McGee, ibid., p. 3.

[5] Testimony of Myrl Alexander before the Violence Commission, Oct. 30, 1968.

[6] Crime Commission, *Task Force Report: Corrections,* p. 1.

[7] Crime Commission, *The Challenge of Crime in a Free Society,* p. 162.

[8] Joint Commission on Correctional Manpower and Training *Second Annual Report,* 1967-68 (Washington, D.C.: 1968), pp. 2-3.

[9] Crime Commission, *Task Force Report: Corrections,* p. 5.

[10] Ibid., p. 96-99.

[11] Ibid., p. 75.

[12] Ibid.

[13] Ibid., p. 95.

[14]Ibid.

[15]Herman Piven and Abraham Alcabes, "Education, Training and Manpower in Correction and Law Enforcement," Source Book II, in Service Training, U.S. Dept. of Health, Education, and Welfare, (1966) pp. 3, 139.

[16]Crime Commission, *The Challenge of Crime in a Free Society*, p. 159.

[17]Allen J. Davis, *Report on Sexual Assaults in the Philadelphia Prison System and Sheriff's Vans* (Philadelphia, 1968), p. 3.

[18]Ibid., p. 1.

[19]Bruce Jackson, "Our Prisons Are Criminal," *New York Times Magazine*, Sept. 22, 1968, p. 62.

[20]*See*Bill Davidson, "The Worst I've Seen," *Saturday Evening Post*, July 13, 1968, pp. 17-22.

[21]Ibid.

[22]App. D. to the testimony of Joseph R. Rowan Before the Senate Subcommittee to Investigate Juvenile Delinquency, Mar. 6, 1969.

[23]Letter from Philip J. Hirschkop to Commission on Violence, Aug. 22, 1968.

[24]The Advisory Committee for Adult Detention Facilities for the City and County of San Francisco, *Annual Report* (1969), pp. 3-5.

[25]Ibid., p. 25.

[26]Ibid., p. 2.

[27]*Lewis v. State*, 176 So. 2d 718, 729-730 (La. App. 1965).

[28]Southern Regional Council, *Special Report—The Delta Prisons: Punishment For Profit* (Atlanta: Southern Regional Council, 1968), p. 3.

[29]Ibid., pp. 5-6.

[30]Ibid., p. 17.

[31]Bruce Jackson, "Our Prisons Are Criminal," *New York Times Magazine*, Sept. 22, 1968, p. 57.

[32]Fred Cohen, *The Legal Challenge To Corrections: Implications for Manpower and Training* (Washington, D.C.: Joint Commission on Correctional Manpower and Training, 1969), p. 73.

[33]"Discipline by 'Rape' at U.S. Prison," *National Catholic Reporter*, Apr. 23, 1969, p. 6.

[34]*Roberts v. Peppersack*, 256 F. Supp. 415, 419 (D. Md. 1966).

[35]*Wright v. McMann*, 387 F. 2d 519, 521 (2d Cir. 1967).

[36]*Landman v. Petyon*, 370 F. 2d 135, 137-138 (4th Cir. 1966). Our recitation of prison violence could be lengthened. For more examples of documented cases, *see* Hirschkop and Milleman, "The Unconstitutionality of Prison Life," *55 U. Va. L. Rev.* 795 (1969).

[37]California Youth and Adult Corrections Agency, *The Organization of State Correctional Services and the Control and Treatment of Crime and Delinquency* (1967) p. 152.

[38]Letter from Paul W. Keve, Commissioner of Corrections, State of Minnesota, to the President's Commission on the Causes and Prevention of Violence, Oct. 9, 1968. *See also* John P. Conrad, "Violence in Prison," *Annals* 364:113 (Mar. 1966), for an evaluation of the working restraints preventing violence in American prisons. The incidence of violence is

represented as relatively low in consideration of the potential of a "violent culture" such as to be found in the prison environment.

[39]*Wilkerson* v. *Utah,* 99 U.S. 130, 135-136 (1878).

[40]*Trop* v. *Dulles,* 356 U.S. 86, 100 (1958).

[41]Ibid.

[42]Note, "Revival of the Eighth Amendment: Development of Cruel Punishment Doctrine by the Supreme Court," *Stan. L. Rev.* 16:966-1000 (1964).

[43]Cohen, *Legal Challenge,* p. 12.

[44]William O. Douglas, "The Bill of Rights Is Not Enough," *N.Y.U.L. Rev.* 38:207, 219 (1963).

[45]Cohen, *Legal Challenge.*

[46]*Landman* v. *Peyton,* see note 36.

[47]*Lewis* v. *State,* see note 27.

[48]Cohen, p. 74.

[49]Hirschkop and Milleman, "Unconstitutionality," p. 813.

[50]Cohen, p. 74.

[51]Crime Commission, *Task Force Report: Corrections,* p. 97.

[52]Paul W. Keve, *Imaginative Programming in Probation and Parole* (Minneapolis, Minn., 1967), p. 55.

[53]Goldfarb, Problems in the Administration of Justice in California (Report to the California Legislature, Feb. 1, 1969), p. 45.

[54]California Department of Youth Authority, *Probation Subsidy Program,* unpublished report, Aug. 1968.

[55]"Special Intensive Parole Unit, 15-Man Caseload Study," California Department of Corrections, Division of Adult Parole, Sacramento, Calif. (Nov. 1956), and "Special Intensive Parole Unit 30-Man Caseload Study," California Dept. of Corrections, Division of Adult Parole, Sacramento, Calif. (Dec. 1958).

[56]*See* Marguerite Q. Warren et al., "Community Treatment Project, 5th Progress Report," California Youth Authority, Sacramento, Calif. (Aug. 1966).

[57]For a full discussion of such projects, *see* Lamar T. Empey, "Alternatives to Incarceration" (Washington, D.C.: Department of Health, Education, and Welfare, Office of Juvenile Delinquency, 1967).

[58]U.S. Department of Justice, Federal Bureau of Prisons, "Prisoners in State and Federal Institutions for Adult Felons, 1966," *National Prisoner Statistics* (Washington, D.C.: Government Printing Office, Aug. 1968), p. 29.

[59]Crime Commission, *Task Force Report: Corrections,* pp. 53-55.

[60]See the more detailed recommendations in chap. 13, "The Correctional Response," in the report of this Commission's Task Force on Crimes of Violence.

[61]Harold Cohen, "Educational Therapy: the Design of Learning Environment," *Research in Psychotherapy* 3:21-53 (1968).

[62]Ibid.

[63]Ibid., p. 29.

PRISONS: REFORM OR REBELLION?

VERNON FOX

Prisons have been in existence for approximately two centuries. The first prisons were in Ghent, Belgium and in Simsbury, Connecticut in 1773. They were substitutes for the banishment and transportation "beyond the seas" or to Siberia which had been the practice of countries in eliminating serious criminals for two centuries before. Prior to that, serious offenders were either executed by a variety of methods, banished, or enslaved, generally to the victim or his family.

The modern penitentiary movement was an American contribution to corrections begun in 1790 by the Quakers in Philadelphia at the Walnut Street Jail. In 1815, a different type of prison system at Auburn in which harsh discipline, silence, congregate work during the day, and solitary confinement at night were the primary components. The Boston Disciplinary Society under the leadership of Reverend Louis Dwight adopted the Pennsylvania System. Serious controversy continued for many years in the early nineteenth century between proponents of the Auburn System and proponents of the Pennsylvania System led by Reverend Dwight. European observers reported the more humane to be the Pennsylvania System, and Europe, together with other parts of the world, including Latin America, adopted it. In America, however, the more economical Auburn System became popular. Consequently, American prisons began historically with a tradition of security and harsh discipline.

All societies tended to treat their offenders and nonproductive people with less favor than the self-supporting, law-abiding citizen. Consequently, all societies have refused to provide the criminal or the welfare recipient with more than the least of its self-supporting and law-abiding citizens. Known as the "doctrine of least eligibilities" or, sometimes, the "doctrine of less eligibility," it has resulted in prisoners receiving the minimum living standards that society could afford commensurate with its humanitarian values. The result is a place of deprivation, both in terms of basic needs and culture. It is for this reason that many writers have indicated that the prison can be used to judge the advance of a society. Certainly, the prison conditions can be used as a base line or a point of departure by which the society it serves can be measured. Probably it was best said by Winston Churchill to the House of Commons in 1910 when he said, "The mood and temper of the public with regard to the treatment of crime and criminals is one of the most unfailing tests of the civilization of any country."[1]

Vernon Fox, "Prisons: Reform or Rebellion?" Prepared especially for this volume.

PROBLEMS IN PRISON

Problems begin in the streets and then find their way into the prisons and the universities. The same problems that have occurred in prison have occurred outside, the difference being that the prison is a closely confined and generally deprived environment. The result is that small things seem to be more important in prison than outside.

Major prisons have been built frequently in rural areas away from urban centers. This provides problems in staffing the institutions. Most competent professional persons want to be in close association with professional colleagues and near universities and cultural centers. Consequently, it is unusual that competent psychiatrists, medical staff, psychologists, social workers, and other professional personnel can be attracted to live near and work in these "boondock" prisons. In addition, the low-salaried custodial staff must be hired from the surrounding area. The correctional officers and other supporting staff frequently come from the rural areas where the prisons have been built. On the other hand, the majority of the inmates come from urban areas. The average age of the staff is frequently in the early 40s while the average age of prisoners is generally in the high 20s. Even with the limited academic preparation of many prisoners, many of them compare favorably with the low-salaried personnel hired from the rural areas. In a few places where new officers and other personnel have been given the same tests as those given the inmates, the favorable showing by the inmates has discouraged the continued use of the same tests for new personnel. Problems arise in daily interaction when prisoners compare favorably with their keepers.

Whether these problems should be as significant as many inmates view them can be debated. The primary difference between prisoners and their keepers that is unfavorable to the prisoners is in the area of emotional maturity and ability to get along with authority. All the prisoners have been arrested and convicted of major crimes, while a custodial officer or other staff of the prison have generally never been convicted of a major crime. Prison populations have included physicians, lawyers, professors, educators, and other professional persons. On the other hand, there are many people who cannot read or write who have never been in jail. Consequently, the difference in sophistication may not be intrinsically to the point. Nevertheless, the inmates see this problem of differential capability in a manner disparaging to the prison staff and, therefore, the effectiveness of the prison program is diminished.

The same civil rights issues, religious issues, and other social issues appear in prison as appear in the city. The prison reflects the society it serves.

SOLEDAD, SAN QUENTIN, AND PRISONER REACTION

As late as the 1950s, prison administrators were relatively immune from major policy influences by inmates. There was right to counsel, loosely interpreted, some freedom of religion, though limited to orthodox practices, and the beginning freedom of inmates to send uncensored letters to certain specified government officials. The first major shift in this pattern was when the U.S. District Court declared in 1962 that the Black Muslims at the District of

Columbia Youth Center at Lorton, Virginia, did constitute a religion and should be allowed to practice within the institution, a decision that altered several administrative routines, including diet. This decision came soon after the American Correctional Association had passed a resolution that the Black Muslims were not a legitimate religion and, in fact, constituted a threat to the safety and security of the institutions. Through the 1960s, the shift from administrative power to some recognition of "inmate power" began to accelerate until today when prisoners' unions exist.

The Soledad incident in January 1970 is symbolic of this threat to administrative power and has become a cause célèbre among black militants, white radicals, and some liberals. On January 13, 1970, a white guard opened fire on a group of prisoners brawling in the special yard at Soledad's maximum security disciplinary unit after the inmates ignored his warning. Four shots left three black inmates dead and a white inmate wounded. The brawl was surmised by prison officials to have been racial. On January 14, a group of 13 black prisoners at the adjustment center began a hunger strike, demanding federal investigation of the shooting. The following day, a Monterey County grand jury found the deaths of the three blacks "justifiable homicide," whereupon a white guard was killed at Soledad by being thrown over a third gallery railing onto a concrete floor in the cell-block. Three black men, subsequently known as the "Soledad Brothers," were charged eight days later with the murder—George Jackson, John Clutchette, and Fleeta Drumgo. They had also become close to Angela Davis, a friend of George Jackson. They were subsequently transferred to San Quentin.

Jackson's prison letters were published in 1970 under the title, *Soledad Brothers.*[2] It was an articulate and powerful revolutionary manifesto. Most of the letters were to his parents, who neither understood nor agreed with him when he cursed them bitterly for training him to be a slave. One review says that "Jackson makes Eldridge Cleaver look like a song-and-dance man on the Ed Sullivan show."[3] Another review said,

If one wants more black revolutionary rhetoric, these letters should satisfy him. It is possible, however, that we've had enough of this sort of thing.[4]

Some of the statements were, "This is one nigger who is positively displeased," "I'll never forgive," "War without terms," and, to Angela Davis, "They have created in me one irate, resentful nigger."

On August 7, 1970, when an inmate, James D. McLain, was on trial for stabbing a white guard at San Quentin in 1969, Jackson's younger brother, Jonathan P. Jackson, entered the Marin County Courtroom at San Rafael, California, about seven miles north of San Francisco, near San Quentin. Jackson entered the courtroom, uncovered his carbine, tossed a pistol to McLain, and shouted for everyone to line up. McLain telephoned the sheriff's office and said, "Call off your dogs, pigs, or we'll kill everyone in this room!" Using Judge Haley as a hostage with pistol pressed against his neck, McLain ordered the deputies to drop their weapons, which they did. The gunmen went about 300 yards to a waiting rented van and 100 deputies, policemen, and prison guards converged on the van, beginning a shoot-out that killed three people, including Jonathan Jackson and the judge. Ruchell Magee, accused with Angela

Davis of conspiracy to smuggle the guns into the courthouse, was accused of killing Judge Haley. The trial in this case was transferred to San Quentin, as of August 23, but Judge Joseph Wilson transferred it back to Marin County on October 3. On August 25, nearly a thousand inmates at San Quentin staged a strike protesting the trial inside the walls, but they were forced back into their cells by tear gas. The trial of the Soledad Brothers was transferred to San Diego on September 18. After a 14-week trial, Angela Davis was acquitted on June 5, 1972. While there was adverse reaction in some quarters, including national commentators, Miss Davis said that the jury was composed of "the people."

On August 24, several hundred demonstrators marched outside the prison walls demanding the freedom of all political prisoners and the Soledad Brothers. At the same time, about 800 inmates inside the prison demanded the appointment of black and Mexican-American wardens, the closing of the maximum security disciplinary units at Soledad and San Quentin, and the dissolving of the California Adult Authority. They also demanded that all forms of capital punishment and mass genocide be abolished and that death-row prisoners be given political asylum in countries under the flags of Africa, Asia, Russia, North Korea, and other points where the American revolutionaries have established the free world solidarity pact. Simultaneously, about 500 youthful demonstrators, mostly white radicals, paraded in front of the Federal Building in San Francisco demanding that the three blacks be freed and that all political prisoners should be freed. Specifically, they demanded that seven Mexican-American youths accused of killing a white policeman be set free and that Black Panther inmates should be regarded as political prisoners and be treated in accordance with the Geneva Agreements with respect to prisoners of war.

A UPI story dated December 14 said that, "Another guard was stabbed today at racially tense Soledad Prison where two guards and five inmates were killed earlier this year."[5] By this time, correctional officers or "guards" in California and elsewhere throughout the country had become apprehensive of constant danger in the prisons, were looking for defensive measures, and some had found other jobs.

On the afternoon of August 21, 1971, three guards and three inmates were killed at San Quentin in the maximum security disciplinary unit where 20 most difficult prisoners were held. George Jackson had just received a visit from Stephen Bingham, a 29-year-old lawyer. A gun had been smuggled into the maximum security disciplinary unit, probably in Jackson's long Afro hair. Jackson produced the gun after the visit when a skin search was attempted, announcing, "This is it!" whereupon Sgt. Jere Graham was shot at the base of the skull and his throat was cut with a razor. Jackson was shot and killed as he ran for the gate in an effort to break out of the maximum security disciplinary unit. In his cell were found two dead guards, two dead prisoners, and a wounded guard—all white and all with their throats slashed. One guard and Sgt. Graham had also been shot. Two other white prisoners lived through the ordeal by remaining silent in their cells with their doors closed.

Mrs. Georgia Jackson, mother of George Jackson, insisted that the prison break was fabrication, that "they" had been trying to "set him up" for ten-

and-a-half years and "they" finally did it. Many blacks in and out of prison have called Jackson's death an "execution." Among many blacks, the right or wrong of the shooting is not the issue, but the conditions of prisons and the atmosphere of the killing has become more important. They consider that too many blacks are being held in prison in comparison with the number of crimes they commit. The explanation must be racist and political. Another interpretation was put forward in May 1972, when each of the widows of the three dead guards filed suits demanding $23,000,000 in damages for herself and her children, stating that Warden Louis S. Nelson of San Quentin knew that George Jackson and probably other inmates were planning to escape.

It becomes obvious from this sequence of events that California's prisons were seething. Racial and ethnic feeling was intense, particularly among blacks and Mexican-Americans. Other incidents elsewhere indicate that this expression in California prisons was only a manifestation of a generalized feeling and movement throughout the country. Some of the same feeling has been expressed elsewhere on university campuses, in the streets, in political campaigns, in prisons and, more particularly, in the interpretations of what happened at Attica.

THE REBELLION AT ATTICA

The mood of the prisons throughout the country in 1971 where the majority of prisoners are from the black, Mexican, or Puerto Rican minorities, was almost revolutionary. George Jackson said it well in *Soledad Brothers:*

There are still some blacks here who consider themselves criminal—but not many . . . believe me, my friend, study and think, you will find no class or category more aware, more embittered, desperate or dedicated to the ultimate remedy—revolution. The most dedicated, the best of our kind—you'll find in the Folsoms, San Quentins, and Soledads.[6]

They were at Attica. New York's prison population is more than 70 percent black or Puerto Rican, mostly younger men from urban areas. New York's prison staff is predominantly white, three-fourths 34 years of age and older, and predominantly from the rural areas around the prisons. Guards at Attica insisted that they never beat any prisoners with their nightsticks, but many of them referred to it openly as their "nigger stick."[7]

At the Men's House of Detention in Manhattan, frequently known as "The Tombs," there were about two thousand men, awaiting trial in a facility constructed for less than a thousand. They were there because they could not afford bail. On August 8, 1970, 30 black prisoners captured 2 white prisoners as hostages and demanded the return of a black prisoner who had been removed from the floor for striking a guard. The hostages were released when the inmate was returned to his cell. On August 10, five white guards were taken hostage and held for eight hours. A manifesto was written by the inmates listing mistreatment of black and Puerto Rican prisoners. On October 1, prisoners took the Long Island Branch of the Queens House of Detention, taking seven hostages and demanding an interview with city officials. The

Brooklyn House of Detention was taken the following day. These disturbances were quelled with gas and nightsticks after futile efforts to negotiate. In the state system, there were strikes at Attica and Napanoch almost simultaneous with the problems in the city system. In early November, 1970, black inmates at Auburn demanded a day's vacation on Black Solidarity Day and 45 hostages were taken. The situation ended peacefully, however. In December 1970, Russell Oswald, a progressive corrections administrator, took over as Commissioner of Corrections, replacing a "lock-em-up" commissioner from the "old school." On May 12, 1971, the prisoners at Attica mailed a "manifesto" to Oswald that contained 30 demands, followed on July 2 by a letter signed by five inmates containing 27 demands, with the prisoners signing the letter designated as a negotiating committee. On August 22, the prisoners at Attica marched to the mess hall for breakfast, walking as usual through the serving lines, but picked up nothing and walked to their seats and sat down looking straight ahead and not making a sound. Each was wearing a black armband or black shoelaces around their arms, or had black cloth pinned on them. On August 29, New York State Senator Samuel Greenberg released a report that the prisons lacked medical and other treatment programs. On August 30, about 300 men from A-block reported to the infirmary on sick call. Oswald flew to the prison on September 1, talked with Warden Mancusi and others, and made a tape recording that was played to the inmates on September 4 outlining his plans, progress, and problems. His presentation came through to the inmates as upper-middle-class; that would have been effective in the legislature, but the inmates heard, "money is scarce," "these things take time," and the inmates saw that all that was being offered were promises.

On Wednesday afternoon, September 8, guards at Attica claimed that white inmate Ray Lamorie and black inmate Leroy Dewer were fighting after a touch football game, but the inmates say that Lamorie was demonstrating the lineman's tactics for Dewer. Inmates milled in the yard, preventing an arrest, but the inmates were picked up that night after they were locked in their cells. A black inmate, Herbert X. Blyden, who had signed the July manifesto at The Tombs and was an inmate leader, wrote a letter on September 8 to State Senator John R. Dunne, commenting on the effects of Oswald's presentation to the inmates and warned of danger, but the letter did not arrive until September 13. Meanwhile, word had circulated that the black inmate taken into custody had been beaten and "the word," nigger, had been used.

The riot started spontaneously about 9:00 A.M. on September 9 at the second breakfast feeding, when cell 17 in A-block where an inmate had been "keep-locked" awaiting discipline was opened by a passing inmate. Some confusion among officers and administration about how to react left the inmates committed to disobedience and violence. The riot exploded. The inmates went to Times Square in the center of the prison where tunnels from blocks A, B, C, and D converge. A young guard, William Quinn, was on duty at Times Square, ran to the roof, was caught, beaten, and thrown to the ground. Officer Quinn was subsequently taken to safety by two inmate leaders, including "Brother Herb" Blyden, was hospitalized in Rochester, but died at 4:30 P.M. on Saturday, September 11. The inmates picked up 38 hostages, guards or civilian employees. They secured the D-block yard and held it. Oswald arrived at the prison at 2:00 P.M., followed a few minutes later by Professor of Law Herman Schwartz, of the University of Buffalo, who had been associated for a long time with the ACLU's Prisoner Rights Project, and Arthur Eve, a black Democratic state assemblyman from Buffalo. Both were respected by the inmates. Schwartz and Eve were first to meet with them. The inmates wanted to interview Oswald before television cameras and in the presence of newsmen. Against the advice of others around him, Oswald went into D-yard with Schwartz about 4:00 P.M. Negotiations went on during the evening and on Friday, September 10. On Friday, one of the inmates threatened Oswald with taking him, too, but the other inmates shouted him down. During his next statement, however, Oswald left the yard and did not return.

During the first night, 38 inmates gave their mattresses to the hostages. On Friday, white inmates Barry Schwartz and Kenneth Hess were taken by the other inmates to join Michael Privatera as "guilty" of such things as trying to smuggle a guard's billfold out to his family. Privatera had hit other prisoners with a nightstick and had "menaced" the hostages. Sometime between Friday and Monday, they were "executed" by slashing their throats.[8]

A Committee of Observers was formed to negotiate with the prisoners that included the range of viewpoints from William Kuntzler, the Black Panthers, and the Puerto Rican Young Lords, to a "moderate" legislator, to two conservative state assemblymen from upstate New York. There were 17 in the group, finally, with Bobby Seale of the Black Panthers excluded from the prison, while the Black Muslims did not join the group. On Friday, the inmates presented 5 ideological demands and 14 "Practical Proposals." Through negotiation, these were restated by the Committee of Observers with inmate help as 28 demands, which Commissioner Oswald signed on Saturday and sent to the inmates in D-block. The inmate vote turned down the agreement. Brother Richard Clarke ripped the agreement in half. The points had referred to basic needs for health, legal assistance, political activity, and grievance procedures. Some of the difficulty was the fact that the inmates were not organized and the viewpoints of the Committee were so disparate that any agreement would be difficult.

By Sunday, September 12, there was obvious hatred built up among the guards and the citizens outside the prison against the Committee of Observers and the rebellious inmates. The State had obviously decided to quit negotiating and to apply force. Similarly, the corrections officials became hostile. As divergent as the viewpoints of the Committee were, they all agreed to send a message to Governor Rockefeller and to the news media based on the fact that the Committee "is now convinced a massacre of prisoners and guards may take place in this institution." They asked Governor Rockefeller to meet with the Committee, which he did not do. The Committee did succeed in postponing the attack until Monday, but they were held in the steward's room under guard and with a dead telephone, cut off when the Committee tried to convey the message to the news media. The Committee was convinced that they, too, would be shot during the attack if it could have been "covered." As the Observers left the yard for the last time on Sunday, Brother Richard Clarke hugged and kissed each member goodby and asked them,

Tell my wife and children that I am ready to die. I cannot live any longer as a caged beast. I know they are going to kill us. Tell them we are doing this so, in the event my children or grandchildren should slip along the way, they will not have to live like dogs. Tell them it is better to die like a man than to live like a dog.[9]

On Monday, Commissioner Oswald came in about 7:30 A.M. to indicate that he would give the prisoners a one-hour ultimatum, which he did at 7:46. The attack began at 9:43 after helicopters had dropped CS gas, which stings the eyes and skin and gives a sensation of suffocation. State police fired into the group of helpless prisoners, killing 30 prisoners and 9 hostages. The action lasted about 15 minutes. Subsequent brutality by officers beating inmates, making them "run the gauntlet," name-calling, and other forms of maltreatment merely underscore the intensity of the hatred in this situation.

Two top assistants to Oswald reported that the attack was necessary because prisoners had been seen slashing the throats of the hostages. Further, Officer Michael Smith was seen being emasculated and his sex organs pushed into his mouth—"Mau Mau style." One of the administrators gave details, including the blood-soaked location in the yard where the slashings occurred. The medical examiner, Dr. John F. Edlund of Monroe County, said that all hostages had died of gunshot, rather than slashed throats, and Officer Michael Smith came out of the situation completely unhurt. State assemblymen on the Committee of Observers have said they believe that the "monstrous lie" must have been calculated as a rationale for the attack and New York officials had not counted on an uncooperative medical examiner. "When the wrong medical examiner got hold of the bodies, did his job, and released his findings, the authorities were stunned."[10] They used several approaches to "correct" the findings of the medical examiner, including bringing in two famous pathologists to check the findings, but they agreed with Dr. Edlund in every particular.

The situation at Attica indicates the hatred and intense feeling that occurs between prisoners and their keepers without any common base for communication. While some have said that there is a "new breed of prisoners," other professionals have said that "it is the old breed of prison guards and administrators—who have to modernize their thinking."[11]

PUBLIC REACTION TO ATTICA

Public reaction to prison problems and their handling is central to the question of prison reform because they, as the body politic, determine the directions these public institutions and programs may take. The issue as to whether rebellion continues or reform occurs to alleviate some obvious problems will be decided politically. Public and political reaction to prison riots and, therefore, to prison reform is generally mixed. Many man-on-the-street opinions prefer a show of force and giving rebellious prisoners no quarter. On the other hand, there were many examples of enlightened leadership expressing shock and concern at the "massacre" at Attica. The Executive Board of the New York Society of Clinical Psychologists formally expressed their shock and concern in a letter to Governor Nelson Rockefeller dated September 14,

1971. A newsman reported that "unfortunately, the public is divided on which direction to turn," referring to the possibilities of prison reform as a result of the Attica situation.[12]

Emotional behavior is translated into public policy as well as intellectual behavior with the balance shifting from legislature to legislature, from time to time, and from political leader to political leader. There are many punitive people distributed throughout "the public," which is why applicants for police and other "people-controlling" positions are carefully screened. Punitive attitudes and authoritarian personality patterns permeate society, appearing with greater frequency in occupations demanding exactness and clear-cut decisions and less frequently in the social and behavioral sciences. Studies of these authoritarian personalities indicate that they manifest feelings and prejudices, become vindictive easily, and are power oriented.[13] Significant personality differences have been found between 107 potential jurors divided into groups who could and who could not render a guilty verdict carrying the death penalty.[14] Many other studies of dogmatism,[15] moral judgment,[16] and authoritarian personality[17] are available and they all relate to the handling of violence by prison inmates and the issue of prison reform.

The day after the Attica crisis, Representative Murphy of New York called for prison reform in the United States Congress, followed by many senators and representatives. Representative Rangel of New York, a black, called conditions "immoral." The majority of congressional statements attacked penal conditions and inadequate correctional services, while a few were more critical of the specific way the Attica situation itself was handled. A House Select Committee on Crime was established under the chairmanship of Representative Claude Pepper (D-Florida) to inquire into prison conditions in the United States and determine how the United States government could be of assistance. The tenor of this committee was critical.[18]

Reaction to the manner in which the riot at Attica was handled varied widely. The newspapers in the large metropolitan areas were rather consistently critical, though President Nixon and Vice President Agnew both supported Governor Rockefeller's decision to use State Police firepower. *The New York Times* said editorially that the agreement between Governor Rockefeller's office and the union of state prison guards makes a mockery of prison reform and repeated the statement of the New York State Senate Committee on Crime and Correction that "any penal system which falls short of affording to its prison inmates the fundamental dignities to which all human beings are entitled demeans our society and threatens its future safety."[19] On the following page, Governor Ronald Reagan of California wrote that we cannot accept the idea that the law can be broken with impunity by those who shout political slogans.[20] Counterbalancing the large-city critical editorial opinion, the newspapers from the smaller cities and rural areas tended to be supportive of the way the Attica situation was handled. The middle-sized cities tended to present a better balance of both viewpoints.

Many editorials were duplicated in various papers throughout the country. Sample opinions supporting the use of state police firepower at Attica were as follows:

The stupidity of the liberals who are beating their breasts in publications and on TV screens all over the United States, calling the tragedy at Attica an indication of wrongdoing on the part of 'society' and bleeding constantly for 'penal reform' is as dangerous as it is stupid. (*Vermont Sunday News,* St. Albans, Vermont, September 26, 1971)

The 'bleeding hearts' among us will cry out again for prison reform. They will bemoan the loss of life and condemn prison officials for their actions. But we had better become aware of a serious crisis that confronts this nation. In our society today, there are those persons who preach violence as a means of social change. They are dangerous and will kill for the sake of killing. That is the lesson from Attica that comes through loud and clear. (*Martinsburg Journal,* Martinsburg, West Virginia, September 21, 1971)

Nobody will ever know how many lives were saved by the resolute refusal of Governor Rockefeller to grant amnesty for crimes within Attica's walls. . . . Let those who deplore the outcome recognize that armed rebellion is never put down by platitudes or distant judgments by those not faced with the grave decisions that have to be made. (*Ashbury Park Press,* Ashbury Park, New Jersey, September 15, 1971)

One of the principles guiding the actions of New York officials was that the hostage principle must not be allowed to work. (*Times-News Record,* Leighton, Pennsylvania, September 16, 1971)

It was a decision based on the fundamental concept that law must prevail over violence and anarchy. (*New Jersey Herald,* Newton, New Jersey, September 15, 1971)

Those who advocate or applaud change through violence when real change is possible and is occurring through peaceful means are not championing human justice or dignity, but just the opposite—injustice and the greatest indignity of all, death, usually of the innocent—this is the lesson of Attica. It is a lesson that should be carefully studied by the inmates of all prisons in the country. (*Sun Gazette,* Williamsport, Pennsylvania, September 20, 1971; *Burlington Times,* Willingboro, New Jersey, September 22, 1971; and *Evening Sun,* Hanover, Pennsylvania, September 20, 1971)

This rescue attempt, which saved the lives of at least 29 of the hostages, is now being called a 'massacre' by this nation's largest news-gathering agency. The use of 'massacre' in this connection constitutes the infliction of the AP's subjective, editorial opinion upon the news. (*Lynchburg News,* Lynchburg, Virginia, September 18, 1971)

Some of the opinions critical of the way the situation at Attica was handled were as follows:

We condemn the intransigent decision to risk the use of state troopers at Attica. When the scales of justice are weighing law and order against life, itself, the threat of a time limit must not jeopardize the delicate balance. (*Sun-Reporter,* San Francisco, California, September 18, 1971, in agreement with an editorial in the *San Francisco Examiner,* on September 14, 1971)

The memory of the slaughter of Attica will linger with the nation for a long time. . . . The deaths of the hostages was a horrible price to pay for regaining control of the prison. (*States-Item,* New Orleans, Louisiana, September 18, 1971, in agreement with a similar editorial in the *Washington Post,* Washington, D.C.)

'We're humans and want to be treated like humans' was a remark made by one of the Attica State prisoners during a television broadcast. . . . Man's inhumanity to man is the greatest problem, whether in, or outside, the prisons. (*Delray Beach News Journal,* Delray Beach, Florida, September 23, 1971)

Special sympathy and admiration are due Commissioner Oswald. A humanitarian, a reformer of prisons, he was forced by extremists into an action that will haunt him unfairly and unjustly. (*The Times,* Roanoke, Virginia, September 17, 1971)

Stubborn refusal of Americans to come to grips with the problem of how to deal with society's misfits. An enlightened and progressive top state penal officer cannot go it alone in the face of noncaring and custodial vindictiveness at lower echelons. (*Daily Dispatch,* New Kensington, Pennsylvania, September 20, 1971)

So the incredible happened. Even at the calculated sacrifice of some of the prison guards being held as helpless hostages, national guardsmen and state troopers were ordered to attack. (*Light,* San Antonio, Texas, September 15, 1971; *News-American,* Baltimore, Maryland, September 16, 1971)

There is reason to think it would have been wiser to continue mediation efforts and outwait the rebels. (*Daily Herald,* Tyrone, Pennsylvania, September 20, 1971, in agreement with a similar editorial in the *Covington Virginian,* Covington, Virginia)

The massive number of editorials and columns regarding Attica can not be repeated here, but the above excerpts provide over a half-dozen examples of each of the polarized positions taken on the handling of the Attica riot. Repeating, there was a tendency for the large, metropolitan papers to be critical of New York officials, the smaller cities and rural areas supported the use of force and suggested that it should have been used earlier, while editorials from the middlesized cities tended to provide a better balance of opinion.

The international press was uniformly critical of the way Attica was handled, with the Soviet news agency, Tass, being quite vehement. A sampling of other foreign papers was as follows;

Something is terribly wrong in America. (two-column subheadline in *Sun Herald,* Sydney, New South Wales, Australia, September 19, 1971)

The idea that blacks are prisoners in a white man's world was espoused by the late Malcolm X, and this view is widely held among black convicts. Black prisoner's crime may or may not have been a political action against the state, but the state's action against him is always political. Black militancy and prison violence were linked long before Attica. (*Athens Daily Post,* Athens, Greece, September 24, 1971)

He (Governor Rockefeller) campaigned in 1968 on the slogan, "Mit Gott und Brüderlichkeit (God and Brotherhood)." Then, after Attica, he made the statement that he had justly acted and buried the casualities. ("Die Schüssebefehl von Attica," *Stern,* Hamburg, Germany, September, 1971, NR 40, pp. 31-40)

Nothing more powerful than the idea that they are being repressed by a racist society. 'These are not hostages, they are human beings,' said a prisoner, 'and we want to be treated like human beings, too.' (*South China Morning Post,* Hong Kong, September 18, 1971)

The majority of prison troubles in the United States is among Negroes and Puerto Ricans. (*L'Union,* Reims, France, September 16, 1971)

Police said, 'If they resisted, they were shot. We had a job to do.' [critical] (*South China Morning Post,* Hong Kong, September 15, 1971)

The majority of criminals are white, but the majority of prisoners are black. Something is wrong is America. ("Scandale des Bagnes Americains: Pourquoi Attica?" *Voix Ouviere,* Geneve, Switzerland, September 25, 1971)

Conditions in American prisons are bad and they are racist. ("Rifiutano il Cibo i Presunti Capi Della Rivolta nel Carcere di Attica," *La Norve Sardegna,* Sassari, Sardinia, Italy, September 21, 1971)

In Britain, they prefer batons—but the U.S. likes bullets. (*Morning Herald,* Newcastle, New South Wales, Australia, September 18, 1971)

In an age of violence, Attica stands out for stark, shuddering horror. (*Sun Herald,* Sydney, New South Wales, Australia, September 19, 1971)

Racist oppression was developed in the USA, shown by the massacre at Attica. (*L'Echo du Centre,* Limoges, France, September 18, 1971)

People are human—no need for Attica. (*Japan Times,* Tokyo, Japan, September 17, 1971)

Rockefeller may face murder charges. (*E.L. Dailey Dispatch,* Zambia, Central Africa, September 22, 1971)

A prison should not force its guards into brutal repression nor drive its inmates to the point of desperation. (*The Gisborne Herald,* Gisborne, Aukland Province, New Zealand, September 20, 1971)

[Critical of] racist policies in American justice, including Angela Davis. (*Utrechts Nieusblad,* Utrecht, The Netherlands, September 17, 1971; and *De Volkskrant,* Amsterdam, The Netherlands, September 25, 1971)

In summary, domestic editorial reaction to the way Attica was handled was divided. The international press was uniformly critical of America, viewing the handling of the Attica situation as symptomatic of a general social pathology. This view was consistent from the Scandinavian countries to Africa, England to Japan, and in Latin America. It is such reaction, both domestic and foreign, that presses democratic governments to pay attention to the philosophical determinants in society.

REFORM BY COURT ORDER

When neither the administration nor the legislature has acted in the area of prison reform, the courts have acted. A landmark case that concerned broadly the field of corrections was the *Morris v. Travisano* case in Rhode Island[21] in 1970, when the federal court declared in favor of the inmate that conditions in the Adult Correctional Institution at Cranston, Rhode Island, constituted "cruel and unusual punishment" in violation of the Eighth Amendment and placed the prison under jurisdiction of the federal court for 18 months to give state authorities time to correct the situation. In January 1970 Federal Judge J. S. Henley had given Superintendent J. Bruton of Tucker State Prison Farm in Arkansas a one-year suspended sentence for cruelty to prisoners, the sentence having been suspended to prevent Bruton's death were he to be confined in the prison system, himself.[22] Subsequently, Judge Henley had declared the conditions in the prison system to be unconstitutional and gave the State of Arkansas until April 1 to improve them or he would close Tucker and Cummins.[23]

Another important case enjoined the Virginia prisons from some of their disciplinary practices.[24] Bread and water diets were declared unconstitutional. The use of chains, handcuffs, tape, or tear gas, except in emergency, were banned. No inmate can be kept nude or restrained for longer than it takes to bring a doctor. No inmate can be placed in a solitary cell with another inmate except in emergency. Minimum due process standards were to be implemented immediately. Access to counsel through confidential mail and interviews were upheld and were not to be abridged. In this vein, disciplinary procedures at San Quentin were also found by a different federal court to be short of the due process requirements.[25] There are several other court decisions that are important, but all can not be listed here. A few examples are the *Nolan* v. *Fitzpatrick* case that protects the access to the news media by the inmates.[26] Further, regulations banning all inmate assistance in the preparation of writs of habeas corpus and other legal work for other inmates are unconstitutional.[27] Inmates can be protected against informal reprisals for rebellion on the part of the state and correctional officials and staff.[28] It becomes obvious that the courts will act in the direction of prison reform if the administration and legislatures do not.

EFFECTS OF REFORM

The way to make a bomb is to build a strong perimeter, generate pressure inside, and attach a detonator. Conversely, the way *not* to make a bomb is *not* to develop a strong perimeter, *not* to generate pressure inside, and to eliminate the detonator. The strong perimeter and pressure inside are inherent in the large, maximum security prison. The detonator is generally a relatively insignificant event like a conflict between an officer and an inmate in the yard. Modern prison reform must be in the direction of eliminating or providing a safety valve for the strong perimeter, reducing the pressure inside, and ameliorating incidents that might trigger riot. The current trend toward closing large institutions, toward more medium- and minimum-security institutions, more work release and furloughs, has effectively reduced the strong outside perimeter or has provided the safety valve. Smaller institutions with more personal contact between inmates and staff will reduce the pressure generated inside. Community-based corrections programs eliminate both these predisposing causes of riot completely. Finally, upgrading the correctional officer by selective recruiting and by education and training will reduce, through better understanding of human behavior, the incidents that trigger riots.

Simultaneously, all these moves are based on sound developmental principles. The modern prison was a substitute for the banishment of 200 years ago and the strong security of it was designed to achieve that substitute. This runs counter to the modern philosophy of corrections which purports to correct the offender and return him to society as a self-respecting, wage-earning citizen. Banishing or removing the offender from society to teach him to live in it seems to be self-defeating. On the contrary, the emphasis on community-based correction, work-release, furloughs, and other methods of maintaining contacts of the offender seem to be less traumatic in their reduced "social surgery" than the maximum security prison. Removing a person from society to teach him to live in it is like keeping a child away from a violin long enough to make him a good musician! The beneficial consequences and the economy involved by fewer people having to live on welfare and fewer people having to be custodially maintained, combined with the beneficial effects of constructively supported contacts with the community, make these reforms valuable to society.

The trend toward more community involvement in corrections has been under way since the early 1950s, when riots called public attention again to the prison problem. The trend has been definitely toward community involvement, it has accelerated in the last three or four years, the literature has supported it, and there is evidence that it will continue.

The effects of community involvement in corrections appear to be positive. The PICO project in California, the Saginaw project in Michigan, the experiments in small probation caseloads in Los Angeles, and other evaluations of community-based corrections have been optimistic. Probation already is the most successful phase of the correctional process. More offenders successfully complete probation and do not repeat offenses than do those who have been in prison or on parole. Removing the offender from his community only as a last resort, and then not in complete exile or banishment, is sound in terms of personality development and economical in terms of administration. It appears obvious that the correctional reforms already underway are valuable, will continue, and will have a positive effect.

CONCLUSIONS

Whether American prisons will experience reform or continue in rebellion remains at issue. Authoritarian people with intense feelings and anti-offender attitudes view prison reform as "giving in" to convicts and "coddling" prisoners. They will tend to keep things as they are or provide stronger security, which will foster further rebellion. On the other hand, people in the social and behavioral sciences tend to place greater emphasis on developmental principles and support prison reform in the directions of community involvement, smaller institutions, and more competent staff. Society is the only loser if a prison system fails to rehabilitate its inmates. After Attica, many have begun to ponder the social consequences of a poor penal system, regardless of the viewpoint.[29]

A letter from the widow of a murdered man seems to be appropriate here.

Sirs:

I am the widow of a man who was murdered one year ago, and I can satisfy the wondering about how I feel in regard to privileges and humane treatment for prisoners.

To punish, to dehumanize, to emasculate, to wreak other popular forms of civilized vengeance upon those convicted of crimes does not lessen by a single degree my pain and loneliness, nor does it ease one problem in my life. The caging and animalistic treatment prisoners receive in most prisons only assure me that our children will continue to live in a world filled with violence and hate, a world in which they, too, might someday be murdered. A person who is not possessed of human dignity, self-respect and self-love cannot react to society except with hatred, selfishness, and brutality. For God's sake—and ours—let us get on with the task of prison reform.

Mary L. Ehrlichmann

Minneapolis, Minnesota[30]

Cost-benefit analysis is the accountant's way of assessing the relationship between expenditures and productivity. The productivity of American prisons today contribute heavily to the crime rate at a time when sufficient knowledge of human behavior is available to reduce it significantly. Whether the resources can be afforded to implement this knowledge into practice in American prisons is not really the issue. A single mile of interstate highway, a single bombing mission in Vietnam, or 24 feet to the moon would provide resources to improve significantly any prison system in the land.

NOTES

[1] Harry Elmer Barnes and Negley K. Teeters, *New Horizons in Criminology,* 3rd ed. (Englewood Cliffs, New Jersey: Prentice-Hall, 1959), p. 50, quoting from Evelyn Ruggles-Brise, *The English Prison System* (London: Macmillan, 1910).

[2] George Jackson, *Soledad Brothers: The Prison Letters of George Jackson* (New York: Coward-McCann, 1970).

[3] *New York Times Book Reviews,* November 22, 1970, p. 10.

[4] *America* 123 (December 19, 1970):550.

[5] *New York Times,* December 15, 1970.

[6] George Jackson, *Soledad Brothers,* p. 31.

[7] Herman Badillo and Milton Haynes, *A Bill of No Rights: American Prison System* (New York: Outerbridge and Lazard, 1972), pp. 25-26.

[8] Ibid., p. 49.

[9] Ibid., p. 89.

[10] Ibid., p. 100.

[11] E. Preston Sharp and W. Donald Pointer, "Prison Officials are Frustrated by Neglect and Public Apathy," *The Americana Annual— 1972, Yearbook of the Encyclopedia Americana* (1972), p. 44.

[12] Arthur Hoppe, "Prison Reform is in the Wind," *The Baltimore Evening Sun,* October 5, 1971.

[13] *See* T. W. Adorno, Else Frenkel-Brunsick, Daniel J. Levinson, and R. Nevitt Sanford, in collaboration with Betty Aron, Marcia Hertz Levinson, and William Morrow, *The Authoritarian Personality* (New York: Harper, 1950).

[14] Robert E. Thayer, "Attitude and Personality Differences Between Potential Jurors Who Could Return a Death Verdict and Those Who Could Not," Proceedings of the Annual

Convention of the American Psychological Association, 1970, Washington, D.C., pp. 445-446.

[15]Stanley Stark and Yerachmiel Kugel, "Toward an Anthropology of Dogmatism: Maladjustment, Modernization, and Martin Luther King," *Psychological Reports* 27 (August 1970, no. 1):291-309.

[16]Russell Eisenmen, "Teaching About the Authoritarian Personality: Effects on Moral Judgement," *Psychological Review* 20 (Winter 1970, no. 1):33-40.

[17]Gary Schwendiman, Knud S. Larson, and Stephen C. Cope, "Authoritarian Traits as Predictors of Candidate Preference in 1968 United States Presidential Election," *Psychological Reports* 27 (October 1970, no. 2):629-630.

[18]See *American Prisons in Turmoil (Part I): Hearings before the Select Committee on Crime, November 29- December 3, 1971,* House of Representatives, 92nd Congress, Washington, D.C., February 1972.

[19]"Mockery of Prison Reform," editorial in *The New York Times,* Thursday, October 7, 1971, p. 46.

[20]Ibid., p. 47.

[21]*Morris* v. *Travisano,* Civil Action 4192, United States District Court for District of Rhode Island, 1970.

[22]*New York Times,* January 19, 1970, page 37, column 2.

[23]*New York Times,* February 19, 1970, page 32, column 3.

[24]*Landman* v. *Royster,* No. 170-69, United States District Court, Eastern District of Virginia, Alexandria, 1971.

[25]*Clutchette* v. *Procunier,* No. C-70, 2497 AJZ, United States District Court, Northern District of California, opinion rendered June 21, 1971.

[26]*Nolan* v. *Fitzpatrick,* Nos. 71-1156 and 71-1166, United States Court of Appeals, 1st Circuit, Boston, opinion rendered November 4, 1971.

[27]*Johnson* v. *Avery,* 393 U.S. 483, 1969 (Tennessee case). Also *Novak* v. *Beto,* No. 31116 United States Court of Appeals, 5th Circuit, New Orleans (Texas case), opinion rendered December 9, 1971.

[28]*Inmates of the Attica Correctional Facility et al.* v. *Nelson Rockefeller et al.,* Nos. 284, 334, Docket Nos. 71-1931, 71-1994, United States Court of Appeals, 2nd Circuit, opinion rendered December 1, 1971.

[29]John R. Dunne, "An Eyewitness Report on Five Terrible Days at Attica," *The American Annual–1972: Yearbook of the Encyclopedia Americana* (1972), p. 48.

[30]Taken from the *Bulletin,* Delaware Council on Crime and Justice, Inc., Wilmington, Delaware, October, 1971, p. 1.

THE PRISON OF TOMORROW

LLOYD ALLEN WEEKS

INTRODUCTION

Few informed people would challenge the statement that "Corrections has made tremendous strides in the field of penal development within the past decade."

This period can be considered as the most progressive era in the nation's penal history. The changes that are occurring within the penal system are reflective of the public's growing involvement in institutional programs and the state legislatures' progressive legislation concerning penal facilities and programs.

Hopefully, the next shift will be to exchange the isolated, repressive Auburn model prison for the Community-Based Corrections Center. This is a departure from the philosophy of corrections that was centered on protecting society from the criminal by isolating him. Further penal corrections will insure society's safety by rehabilitating and treating a large number of offenders in small community-based institutions.

There, individual treatment can become a reality. Since the number of offenders would be reduced to one hundred, these smaller institutions could be oriented to pinpoint problems and work out programs that the sheer size of the existing prisons makes infeasible. It would also allow the offender to be self-supporting whenever possible since he could be on work-release to the community in which the prison is located. These regional institutions would ideally be located in strategic metropolitan areas where professional and community resources could also be utilized to rehabilitate the offender.

One of the difficulties in making the Community-Based Corrections Centers a reality is that there has been almost a total absence of research for this new concept in corrections. Some halfway house programs are now in operation but the idea of an offender serving a portion of his sentence under treatment methodology has not been realized. These halfway houses, like the Work-Training Release Programs, have suffered from a lack of adequate facilities and funds to implement them.

The prime purpose of this report is to propose an innovative model and methodology for the Community-Based Corrections Center. The project outlined in this analysis is a pilot venture which, if successful and validated for correctional soundness and effectiveness, can be expanded into a state network of community-based centers.

These centers would each house one hundred men, reducing the present population of adult institutions and hopefully also reducing recidivism and

Lloyd A. Weeks, "The Prison of Tomorrow" Previously unpublished paper.

costly long-term imprisonment. It is a bold approach to the problem of corrections, one that is relevant in light of the pressing needs of the nation's penal problems.

But these ideas may be successful in attaining the overall goal of corrections, one that the present system all too often fails to achieve. These centers will aid in the successful reintegration of the offender into the community as a productive and self-supporting citizen.

DEVELOPMENT OF A PROTOTYPE: PROBLEMS AND PRIORITIES

The primary question confronting correctional planners today is not whether offenders should be treated in a community but how treatment there could be facilitated safely, economically, and successfully. Clearly, those dangerous offenders who would threaten society should be incarcerated until they can safely be released.

Traditional prisons have the dual drawbacks of being cut off physically from communities as well as perpetuating conditions within the walls that foster a further retreat from society. However, the community-based corrections system would eliminate these shortcomings.

Traditionally, correctional facilities have been located in rural areas that are remote from the communities in which the offender was apprehended, tried, and sentenced, or from the community in which he lived. National figures indicate that in 98 percent of the cases, correctional facilities are the most isolated part of the criminal justice system. Therefore, the first consideration in planning a model correctional facility is to choose a suitable location.

Within the thick walls and multilocked doors of the archaic prison structures has been another isolation, but in a more critical sense. There have been no uniform policies and statutes to govern what to do with, to, or for the offender. The offender is seldom governed by any but the most broadly written policies and statutes, ones that are rarely scrutinized by either the courts or public officials. No longer can the isolated Auburn system be used or misused by both the criminal justice system and the public as a rug under which over half a million offenders may be conveniently swept and be relegated to obscurity.

By realistically innovating the location as well as the traditional model of the correctional institution, offenders will no longer be cut off from valuable and essential professional and community services which can be prime ingredients in resocializing the offender. Much of the congestion and undesirable effects of institutionalization, from jail to prison, are the result of failing to provide an alternative treatment program for offenders who pose no threat to society.

Within the walls of many correctional facilities are offenders who should travel no further along the full course from arrest to charge than placement in a Community-Based Corrections Center. This consideration is absolutely necessary for society's protection and the offender's own welfare. It is also against the philosophy of corrections and unprofitable from all standpoints to place any but the most dangerous offenders in traditional facilities.

However, devising and instituting alternative ways of treating and housing offenders is a long and complicated process. It must begin with the public's understanding of the nature and limitations of the present correctional apparatus in dealing with the majority of offenders. The public must be made aware of its role and responsibility in resocializing offenders.

In order to inform the public, a massive public awareness program will be needed before the actual implementation of the Community-Based Corrections Center. The concept of the community-based center should be communicated by a public relations team. This team should be composed of both offenders and correctional staff, as well as representatives of state government who can lend support to the implementation of the proposals of the resident team.

In the past, innovations in penal reform or changes in correctional models have largely been achieved through political expediency by bureaucrats or by grant recipients initiating a halfway house that was patterned after the religious or alcoholic recovery unit. However, the idea of the Community-Based Corrections Center is not a piecemeal offering; it is not an incorporation of another state's programs and correctional models. It is an attempt to confront the public and officials with methods of alleviating the present system's shortcomings. The officials of the entire criminal justice system must stop operating entirely by tradition and be receptive to innovations that can reduce recidivism and replace the repeater with the responsible citizen.

The self-government experiment, one of the recent innovations in the correctional system, has already proven to be a valuable source from which knowledgeable and articulate resident speakers can be drawn. These men are highly adept at addressing the problems and priorities of correctional reform. If these men are accompanied by a knowledgeable staff who will compliment their insights and proposals, perhaps the public will take a greater interest in the ideas and arguments for instituting Community-Based Corrections Centers.

THE PROTOTYPE MODEL
Physical Structure

The traditional Auburn model institution tends to isolate offenders from society, both physically and psychologically, by cutting them off from schools, jobs, friends, families, and other supportive influences. The goals of reintegration can be furthered more effectively be working with offenders in the community rather than by long-term incarceration in fortress-like buildings. While such institutions may serve the functions of punishment and retribution, their artificial environment undermines self-reliance and self-control and makes the reintegration of offenders into society more difficult.

Studies have revealed that regardless of the type and quality of correctional institutions or related halfway facilities—whether they are huge maximum security prisons or open forestry camps devoid of guards and fences, whether they are oppressive and brutal or offer a variety of rehabilitative programs—there remains an inherent sameness about places where people are kept against their will. It is disturbing to note that nowhere in the volumes of research on correctional facilities has there ever emerged a plan that departs from the traditional custody unit or halfway facility.

Therefore, the pilot project outlined here is of immediate value since it incorporates the changes that are essential in achieving the ultimate goals of Community-Based Corrections Centers of the future.

Location

The prototype model should be built and located as closely as possible to the urban center of a large metropolitan area, but situated away from areas of high crime frequencies and prevalent criminal elements. By locating the model near population centers, close relations could be maintained with schools, employers, and universities. By its central location, the unit would provide an excellent setting for research and experimentation and could serve as a proving ground for needed innovations. Not only would the pilot project be accessible to universities and other research centers, but its size and flexibility would foster a climate that is friendly to inquiry.

Features

Architecturally, the model will resemble as nearly as possible a normal residential setting on a scale and design similar to a motel or apartment house. While it probably would have several high-security units for short-term detention, it would approximate a homelike structure. The units will be built to house one hundred offenders as well as having facilities for at least two live-in members of the correctional staff and their families.

The model proposes that each offender have his own unique room and that he be allowed to have a key to the door of his room. This privilege will be on the honor system. In addition the facility will have a homey dining room instead of the traditional cafeteria.

In addition to these living quarters, the facility will also have classrooms with sliding dividers similar to motel convention rooms. There will also be recreational facilities, day rooms, a boutique shop, a library, as well as a barber shop and a laundry. A full basement will feature hobby-craft rooms and space where self-supporting industries could be developed such as leathercraft or woodwork.

Functions and Methodology

In the past, all states have implemented diverse programs and pre-judicial procedures for handling juveniles and first offenders in an effort to stem the rate of recidivism. The merits of such programs have already received much attention and have been scientifically documented and validated. However, in seeking effective alternatives for the "repeater," who makes up the hard core of the nation's crime problem, several shortcomings of our present corrections system should be noted.

1. Recidivism is rising and constitutes a major problem within the correctional framework.
2. Present policies and programs largely exclude recidivists in favor of the younger and lesser offender when choosing inmates for available treatment and rehabilitative services.

3. There is a near absence of community resocialization or treatment programs geared primarily toward this high ratio of repeaters.
4. There is a need for a specialized system of treatment within a community-based setting to direct effective treatment toward the potential or actual recidivist.

The prime goal of the proposed prototype will be to effectively treat selected offenders comprised largely of the potential or actual recidivist. These men will participate in a work- or training-release program during the day and will be returned to control at night. Treatment programs will be aimed at long-term offenders and help them become adjusted to society gradually rather than being paroled directly from maximum-security institutions without adequate treatment and resocialization.

The public and correctional officials often overlook the fact that between 60 and 80 percent of today's prison population is comprised of repeaters. Therefore, 80 percent of the initial one hundred offenders selected to populate the prototype model should be chosen from the ranks of the potential or actual recidivist. There are three reasons why such a radical departure from usual selection processes would be advantageous.

First, repeaters seldom pose a threat to society since the majority are serving sentences for crimes of theft that involve no victims other than themselves. Second, rehabilitation is hardly possible for them under the current crowded conditions within prisons. And last, repeaters could be self-supporting in a community-based center at a substantial saving to the state budget. At the same time the repeater would have a greater opportunity for successful rehabilitation through the services that are not available within the present framework. The Community-Based Corrections Center could be the key to ending the repeater's cyclical existence.

New Approaches to Treatment

The overwhelming inadequacies and shortcomings within the correctional framework will not yield to simple solutions. Overcoming institutional shortcomings will require a wide variety of remedies including improved methods of selecting both the offender-participants and the staff for the community-based center and allocating funds for its financing. Other important considerations are the revamping of the existing policies and procedures and the adopting of more effective internal and external controls.

Styles of Management

The salient feature of the treatment program that will be implemented in the prototype model will be the concept of self-government. This collaborative approach to management will incorporate a staff composed of selected residents and correctional personnel. This group will work together toward rehabilitative goals and encourage the residents toward greater acceptance of responsibility in the reintegration process.

In the traditional institutional system, even with new treatment approaches, a collaborative relationship of this type would be hampered by unnecessary conflicts generated by the repressive atmosphere that is inherent to the institution. Prison communities tend to foster tension between offenders and staff. Even under ideal conditions, these tensions can erupt into anger toward—and yet complete dependence on—institutional authorities.

The collaborative approach to self-government and resident government council's sharing responsibility will serve to reverse this common pattern. Within the prototype model, for example, the correctional staff's counseling resources would be utilized to a greater extent, both informally with individual residents and also in organized group discussions. Likewise, utilizing peer-group influence, the resident staff would serve as counselor-aids, thereby performing valid administrative and rehabilitative functions in the greater part of the program.

This collaborative management will be further enhanced if the staff is augmented by persons from the community with whom the residents can interact and identify. Such organizations as M-2 Job Therapy may be involved actively in the task of reintegrating the offenders into the mainstream of the community. This will involve recruiting outsiders who can help the residents develop motivation for needed vocational, avocational, and other self-improvement goals. Volunteers and subprofessionals could be utilized fully in the community-based prototype.

Involvement of the offenders in treatment and management functions is one of the most outstanding aspects of the collaborative concept. In the majority of resident activities, the offender will serve in responsible roles after being carefully selected by a newly devised method (discussed later) and by a board or committee composed of correctional staff and resident representatives.

As the relationship between staff and residents eases, there will also be a reduction in "convict politician's" power and much of the traditional distance between staff and residents will dissolve when collaborative functions are instituted. The experiment of self-government at Washington State Penitentiary at Walla Walla has already established the precedent in the value of utilizing residents in specific areas such as resident government councilmen, counselor-aids, and in assigning residents to job, work, and living units as well as in decisions involving disciplinary and administrative functions.

In the Community-Based Corrections Center, the resident council shall be comprised of at least 10 of the total 100 members. Each member will represent nine peers; peer-pressure will be fully utilized in these ten-man units in conjunction with the influence of staff and other supportive influences. The process for selecting the peer-group leaders must be carefully adhered to and check systems must be devised to prevent unstable residents from entering into peer-group leadership. These checks would also prevent a resident-dominated program as under the past "con-boss" situations.

The resident staff, like probation and parole officers, will also be active in arranging for participation by residents in community activities as well as guiding and counseling the residents. Each resident who is not involved in regular work or a training program will be assigned full duties in maintenance or administrative work and will be considered as a work-release participant and be paid accordingly. Each resident will also be charged comparative room and board prices with the exception of men who are idle because of a lack of available work or training or those who are incapacitated. All others will be expected to assume full duties in the maintenance and operation of the unit as compensation for their care and treatment. Each resident will be fully self-supportive at all times.

ADMINISTRATIVE STRUCTURE AND METHOD OF SELECTION: RESIDENT AND STAFF

At all times and in all phases of its operation, the prototype model will be under the direction of Corrections. Administrative supervision will be maintained by the superintendent, who will serve as the project coordinator and leading member of the selection board that will screen all candidates for participation in the experimental project as well as the staff. The Resident Government will have a dual position on the selection board.

In the past, candidates for such programs as New Careers and other aid programs, were selected in a random and haphazard fashion with a large number not performing to expectation. This was caused, in part, by a failure to bring the superintendent's approval and the Resident Government's knowledge of the candidate into focus. In the model under discussion, and in future development of this idea, the state penitentiary would serve as the hub or base of operations in selecting the residents for community-based corrections.

Method of Selection

The first one hundred residents will be selected in the following manner: the superintendent will choose ten residents from both maximum and minimum security who will initiate the advance program and will serve as the first Resident Government staff at the new unit. He shall designate a public relations team (comprised of as many as he deems appropriate) and a member of the correctional or administrative staff who will accompany the residents on an extensive speaking tour in the metropolitan area.

There, the team will initiate the advance public information that is needed to acquaint people with the forthcoming project. This team will also make initial contacts with officials and public organizations who will be supportive in developing the prototype. This advance team would require a ten-day leave that should be free from unnecessary restrictions. Therefore, the residents should be released on furloughs under existing policies. The staff or correctional officer should be maintained as regular-duty service but lodging and other expenses for travel should be paid for by the project.

Following the completion of plans to begin construction on the model unit, the advance team would again need travel authority in order to contact unions and building contractors who would be involved in construction. Attempts would be made to arrange for at least 20 residents to be hired as apprentices or on-the-job trainees. At this point (contingent upon acceptance by union and contractors to hire residents on a work-training release basis) the superintendent and the RGC would screen the entire penitentiary population and present the most ideally suited 20 residents.

These men will be the vanguard for the ultimate one hundred residents who will comprise the initial resident force at the prototype unit. Arrangements for room and board for the 20 workers and the 10 members of the RGC team can be made in accordance with presently established work-and-training release facilities. Another alternative would be to house the men in any approved facility until the prototype was ready for occupancy.

At the completion of the prototype's construction, the RGC and the superintendent shall again screen the population and select the remaining 70 residents to complete the control group for the experimental unit. These men would be transferred as quickly as living facilities were readied in the new unit.

Criterion for Selection

Resident staff will be selected on the basis of the resident's initiative and demonstrated ability to function in a responsible manner. Additional criteria may be incorporated by the RGC, the superintendent, or the Secretary of Social and Health Services. However, as much as possible, a dual partnership in the selection of prospective residents for the new unit will be exercised.

It is essential to utilize the resident staff's knowledge in evaluating the candidates since they may possess information that is unknown to the authorities and would diminish the candidate's eligibility for the program. Therefore, the greatest utilization of the RGC must be made in the initial selection and the ultimate administration of the program.

Selection of the correctional staff, with some exceptions, must be on a similar basis. It is recognized that the parole officer who will serve the unit will be assigned by that department while other personnel may be appointed by state correctional officials. Yet, if at all feasible, the RGC concurrance with the staff selected shall be given the greatest consideration.

The project administrator, selected in a like manner, must be a person qualified in either penology, the social sciences (involving past experience with offenders), or the human relations field (where he has served in a truly rehabilitative role). He should possess at least a master's degree in one of the above-mentioned fields and, if possible, have some teaching background in a correctional institution.

The correctional staff should not exceed three, two living in or near the prototype unit. One member of the staff and one member of the RGC should be mobile for public relations purposes and for weekly contact with the penitentiary. These men should be allowed to travel and spend a period of time every month at each of the institutions in order to maintain continuity and a confidential rapport with the total population.

Method of Treatment and Supportive Services

The method of treatment and rehabilitation must be based on known and proven principles with ample latitude for innovation. The project administrator shall be responsible for developing the treatment program in conjunction with the head of the Department of Corrections, and with involvement of the resident staff. Particular stress will be placed on experimentations by the School of Social Work and related social services of the university and community organizations.

One significant form of treatment will be small-group encounters with constant stress on social and therapeutic counseling of the individual. Each resident will be involved in group and individual treatment programs. At all times, the prototype population will be a self-governing, self-actualizing body geared toward total responsibility and economic self-sufficiency for the resident and his family. The question of resident-family living arrangements must be decided after full evaluation of the initial experimental model by its first administrative body. However, a small number of units may be built for possible family occupancy by the resident working staff.

Funding and Operational Costs

An initial grant of $1 million is needed to build the prototype and to conduct the experiment on a three-year, longitudinal basis. During this time, the model will become self-supporting and will not need funding beyond the first year. After sufficient validation has been obtained to substantiate the value of community-based corrections, the remainder of the initial grant will go toward establishment of two other centers.

The source of the grant may be from the Law and Justice Planning Commission, LEAA, the Office of Economic Opportunity, or any other legal resource. The ultimate goals call for five such community centers to be in operation within three years after validation of the experimental model. Major emphasis will be on first reducing the population at the state penitentiary, then on the reformatory.

CONCLUSIONS

The impetus for community-based corrections has evolved through many years of costly failure in centralized and large institutions. The model and methodology proposed here is correctionally sound, has the utmost degree of safety built in for community security, is economically superior to the present high-cost institutions, and will be more effective in achieving the ultimate goals of Corrections.

Built into the long-range development of the new Corrections will be a procedure whereby substantial numbers, of those who on the basis of facts known to police, judges, and parole authorities, can be dealt with via community-based corrections. It would serve as an alternative to the formal machinery of justice where correctional staff might invoke short-term detention, overnight or for a few days, as a sanction or discipline to head off an offender from prospective trouble. It could also house minor rules violators on parole and nondangerous offenders with short sentences (one to three years).

Mainly, however, the prototype unit and later models will serve as a prerelease center to ease the transition of long-term recidivists into community life. It is also an alternative to the present-day failing of isolated institutions. The prototype unit, upon validation, will serve as the base for a network of separate group units and residential centers to be used for some offenders as a final step before complete release.

In the fully developed model of the new Corrections, the resident population will be fully utilized for their value as "offenders as a source of manpower." Community service work, juvenile prevention work, and New Careers

ay be possible areas of potential use of the offender. The prototype will be
n ideal proving ground for developing this concept and for performing ex-
erimentation in treatment and resocialization programs.

The proposed model may not be the perfect plan, but nevertheless it
ould help to shift the trend of national corrections from temporary and
ostly banishment of offenders to a carefully devised combination of control
nd individualized treatment in an atmosphere where true rehabilitation can
ake place.

It is not a panacea for crime reduction or even the ultimate answer to
orrectional treatment, but it will open doors of experimentation and inquiry
rom which the ultimate relief in recidivism will come. The Community-
ased Corrections Center will hasten the day when the majority of offenders
ill be released to a productive, growth-oriented, community-integrated, and
w-abiding manner of living.

Success in any endeavor is the progressive realization of predetermined,
ersonal, and worthwhile goals. As the knowledgeable reader will note, the
leas that have been outlined are comprised of goals that were fashioned by
any progressive and humane thinkers. Success is a journey, not a destination.
his presentation is the first 12-inch step on the journey of a thousand miles
1 the quest for the prison of tomorrow.